Constitutional Crossroads

Law and Society Series
W. Wesley Pue, Founding Editor

We pay tribute to the late Wes Pue, under whose broad vision, extraordinary leadership, and unwavering commitment to sociolegal studies our Law and Society Series was established and rose to prominence.

The Law and Society Series explores law as a socially embedded phenomenon. It is premised on the understanding that the conventional division of law from society creates false dichotomies in thinking, scholarship, educational practice, and social life. Books in the series treat law and society as mutually constitutive and seek to bridge scholarship emerging from interdisciplinary engagement of law with disciplines such as politics, social theory, history, political economy, and gender studies.

Recent books in the series:

For a complete list of the titles in the series, see the UBC Press website, www.ubcpress.ca.

Constitutional Crossroads
Reflections on Charter Rights, Reconciliation, and Change

Edited by Kate Puddister and Emmett Macfarlane

UBCPress · Vancouver · Toronto

31 30 29 28 27 26 25 24 23 22   5 4 3 2 1

Printed in Canada on FSC-certified ancient-forest-free paper (100% post-consumer recycled) that is processed chlorine- and acid-free.

Library and Archives Canada Cataloguing in Publication

Title: Constitutional crossroads : reflections on Charter rights, reconciliation, and change / edited by Kate Puddister and Emmett Macfarlane.
Names: Puddister, Kate, editor. | Macfarlane, Emmett, editor.
Series: Law and society series (Vancouver, B.C.)
Description: Series statement: Law and society | Includes bibliographical references and index.
Identifiers: Canadiana (print) 20220265585 | Canadiana (ebook) 2022026564X | ISBN 9780774867917 (hardcover) | ISBN 9780774867931 (PDF) | ISBN 9780774867948 (EPUB)
Subjects: LCSH: Canada. Canadian Charter of Rights and Freedoms. | LCSH: Canada. Constitution Act, 1982. | LCSH: Constitutional history—Canada. | LCSH: Civil rights—Canada. | LCSH: Law—Political aspects—Canada. | LCSH: Indigenous peoples—Civil rights—Canada.
Classification: LCC KE4381.5 .C673 2022 | LCC KF4483.C519 C673 2022 kfmod | DDC 342.7108/5—dc23

Canadä

UBC Press gratefully acknowledges the financial support for our publishing program of the Government of Canada (through the Canada Book Fund), the Canada Council for the Arts, and the British Columbia Arts Council.

This book has been published with the help of a grant from the Canadian Federation for the Humanities and Social Sciences, through the Awards to Scholarly Publications Program, using funds provided by the Social Sciences and Humanities Research Council of Canada.

Printed and bound in Canada by Friesens
Set in Helvetica Condensed and Minion by Apex CoVantage, LLC
Copy editor: Lesley Erickson
Proofreader: Judith Earnshaw
Cover designer: Martyn Schmoll

UBC Press
The University of British Columbia
2029 West Mall
Vancouver, BC V6T 1Z2
www.ubcpress.ca

To junior scholars and graduate students studying law and politics in Canada;

the future of a thriving field

Contents

Acknowledgments

Constitutional Crossroads is a collaborative effort under the banner of the Courts and Politics Research Group (CPRG). Founded and administered by this book's editors, CPRG is a community of political scientists that study law and politics in Southern Ontario. It currently has over twenty members at ten universities. This book is the third of such collaborations.

We would like to thank the contributors to this volume for their excellent work and for their commitment to bringing a substantial volume together quickly.

We are grateful to Randy Schmidt and the editorial team at UBC Press for guiding the book through the editorial process. Both Kate and Emmett have worked with Randy previously and it was a pleasure to do so again. Many thanks to Katrina Petrik for her support as production editor. Our thanks as well to the anonymous reviewers for their helpful comments and suggestions.

We would also like to thank our colleagues at the University of Guelph and the University of Waterloo for their continued support. A special word of thanks to Brendan Dell who provided valuable organizational assistance during the conference that led to this book.

Kate would like to thank her family, in particular her parents, Mike and Marie, for their constant support (another book and still no maps ...). Thanks to Kevin, Yvette, Madeline, and André for being a welcome distraction from work. Most of all, Kate thanks her husband Graham. His unwavering support, love, and confidence in her make it all possible.

Emmett would like to thank his parents, Don and Eileen, and his sister, Aingeal, for their continued support and encouragement. As always, his wife, Anna, and daughter, Thea, are the keys to his success.

Constitutional Crossroads

Introduction

Complex Legacies: The Promise, Challenges, and Impact of the *Constitution Act, 1982*

Emmett Macfarlane and Kate Puddister

THE ENTRENCHMENT OF Canada's *Constitution Act, 1982*,[1] containing the *Charter of Rights and Freedoms,* Aboriginal and treaty rights, and a new amending formula, signified many things to many people.

For some, it embodied the idea of patriation, a unique term for an exceptional situation: an otherwise independent country, unable to achieve major formal constitutional change without the legislative assistance of a foreign parliament, wresting domestic control of its constitutional future. On this score, 1982 represents, finally, the realization of a fully sovereign Canada.[2]

For others, it is synonymous with failure, a lost opportunity to bridge core societal cleavages and address inherent tensions in competing constitutional visions, from the dualist perspectives of a linguistic and cultural minority represented largely (though not exclusively) by Quebec to an intense regionalism in what had evolved into one of the most decentralized federations in the world. For all that was gained, attempts to address perceived inequities in Canadian federalism or to enact reform of central institutions proved unworkable. The aftermath was another decade of megaconstitutional politics, and more failure, all leading to the near breakup of the country and putting a powerful cultural chill on future efforts at formal constitutional change.[3]

For many, the 1982 achievement was a triumph in both substantive and symbolic terms, bestowing upon Canada a newly realized shared conception of nationality in the form of a rights document, soon to be enforced with ample zeal by an empowered judiciary. On the twin "political purposes" of the Charter – national unity and the protection of rights and freedoms – much might be said, but the Charter's enduring popularity in all parts of the country arguably speaks to its success on this front.[4]

For Indigenous peoples in Canada, it may be most accurate to say that 1982 represented a complex mix of hope and skepticism. Section 35's Aboriginal and treaty rights reflected the hard-fought battle for inclusion and recognition of the rights embodied in the treaties between the Crown and many of the pre-existing societies inhabiting the continent prior to European contact. These rights were recognized long ago in one of the founding elements of the Canadian Constitution, the Royal Proclamation of 1763, but their formal entrenchment in the 1982 act opened a potential path to more robust judicial enforcement and a fundamental reorientation in the state-Indigenous relationship. Yet the wording of section 35, both limited by reference to the "existing" rights of Aboriginal people and open-ended in its lack of specificity, raised many questions.[5] The subsequent jurisprudence has been subject to important criticism.[6]

Now, four decades later, it is time to assess and analyze the legacy of the *Constitution Act, 1982*. As is evident from the contributions to this volume, the 1982 constitutional package raises questions relating to a host of fundamental issues: sovereignty and the legitimacy of various institutions in exercising authority, including the Crown and the courts; Canadian identity and pluralism within a multinational, multicultural, and diverse country struggling with historical and ongoing systems of oppression; the scope and limits of rights; competing constitutional visions and the place of Quebec within them; the relationship between the state and Indigenous peoples, particularly in a new era of reconciliation and the limits of consultation and accommodation within that context; and constitutional amendment, including the status of central institutions such as the Crown, the Supreme Court, and the Senate, the place of cities in our constitutional fabric, and the nature and method of constitutional change. Four decades after 1982, Canada is at a constitutional crossroads. Questions remain, and existing and emerging challenges must be confronted in light of how these issues, and more, have evolved.

With a focus on the themes of rights, reconciliation, and constitutional change, and offering insights into institutional relationships, public policy, and the state of the fields of law and politics, this book brings together an unprecedented assembly of established and rising stars in political science and law to analyze different aspects of Canada's constitution in the twenty-first century. Contributors participated in a three-day conference organized by the Courts and Politics Research Group. Founded in 2016 by Emmett Macfarlane and Kate Puddister, this group is a collection of Canadian scholars who study courts, constitutions, and the law from a political science perspective. We are pleased to note that this volume contains a mix of senior and junior scholars of the field, ensuring a wide-ranging set of diverse perspectives and insights brought to bear on the volume's core themes.

Eschewing purely historical or descriptive essays, the volume presents forward-looking, argumentative, and analytically reflective contributions. The goals of the collection are to provide a unique and robust account of the 1982 constitutional reform after forty years and to reflect on and analyze empirical and normative scholarship that has shaped our understanding of the Constitution.

Institutional Relationships

The Charter ushered in a structural transition of Canada's system of government from one of parliamentary sovereignty to one of constitutional, if not
judicial, supremacy. Debates over the Charter have spanned a host of issues,
including normative contestation over the role of courts and the way in which
judicial review of rights ushered in social change.[7] Concerns about judicial
power or activism – and what segments of society were being privileged under
the Charter – traversed both sides of the ideological divide.[8] Progressive critics
cited early cases limiting labour rights, narrowing the scope of equality, or
granting benefits to corporations, while conservative critics pointed to social
changes wrought by Charter litigation in areas such as same-sex equality and
abortion or the courts' significant expansion of rights for the criminally accused.

These normative debates also highlighted the discretionary and political
nature of judicial decision making, perceived interpretative abuses against the
text or purpose of specific provisions, and broader dissatisfaction with the
legalization or judicialization of politics. They also mapped on to institutional
analyses of the relationships at stake under the Charter, including significant
attention devoted to the concept of a dialogue between courts and legislatures
about the policies at stake. This aspect of the literature ultimately did little to
move either the defenders of judicial power or the critics, as the debate over the
empirical and conceptual usefulness of the concept remains unsettled (and has
possibly exhausted its utility).[9] In a comparative perspective, Canada also came
to exemplify a middle ground between parliamentary sovereignty and judicial
supremacy or a "weak form" model of judicial review under the Charter, a debate
that itself became mired somewhat in the question of whether Canada truly
meets the conditions for this model or whether, in practice, it is a traditional
strong form system.[10]

What did emerge from these debates was an increasingly rich empirical,
theoretical, or nuanced account of the institutional dynamics under the Charter,
from Janet Hiebert and Jim Kelly's works on the legislative and executive
branches to Kent Roach's call for recognizing the complexity of some of the
interinstitutional dynamics at play to Dennis Baker's work on coordinate constitutionalism.[11] This has been bolstered by new analyses of the executive-court
relationship by scholars such as Matthew Hennigar that provide fresh insights
into what motivates government decisions and better inform our understanding
of the institutional dynamics at stake.[12] One example of this might be events
analyzed by Hiebert that reveal the limited seriousness with which the federal
Cabinet considers bureaucratic assessments of Charter compatibility of legislation, something that might temper advocates of a more assertive legislative or
executive approach to the Charter or in responding to judicial decisions.[13]

Another example of this relationship concerns the use of references, or advisory opinions, which arguably allow governments to preserve political capital by strategically shunting controversial decisions to the courts. Recent books by Kate Puddister and Carissima Mathen shine new light on this process.[14] Many aspects of the institutional relationships under the Charter remain ripe for study, including the work of parliamentary committees in scrutinizing bills and the approach of different governments to rights issues.

The study of judicial decision making itself has made important advances in the last fifteen years. Dave Snow and Mark Harding describe the scholarly literature as becoming "less normative, more explicitly comparative, and committed to methodological rigor."[15] One area exemplifying this turn is studies of the Supreme Court analyzing judicial behaviour and the various factors informing judicial outcomes.[16] This work builds on earlier empirical analyses, especially by Peter McCormick, who is notable for his extensive investigation of judicial decision making by way of descriptive statistics.[17] Given the extensive legal scholarship on the growing body of jurisprudence under the Charter, it may be time to revisit some of the earlier normative debates. The last four decades have produced a wealth of scholarship and a profoundly better understanding of the work of the courts, the competing and complementary institutional roles at stake, and the scope and limits of rights. It is time to reflect on what we know, where we are, and where we are going.

Writing almost forty years ago, Peter Russell opined that the Charter would fundamentally change many aspects of Canadian politics, serving to "judicialize politics and politicize the judiciary."[18] In the opening chapter of this volume, Mark Harding revisits some of Russell's predictions from the early days of the Charter to assess how Canadian politics has changed in the Charter era through an examination of changes to the Supreme Court of Canada appointment process, the authoritative nature of judicial decisions, and the use (or disuse) of the notwithstanding clause. Harding concludes that as a student of Canadian federalism, parliamentary governance, and legal culture, Russell made many predictions about the political consequences of the Charter that have come to fruition; however, the manner in which governments have chosen to strategically embrace the judicialization of politics for political gain shows an impact of the Charter he did not fully anticipate.

In Chapter 2, Emmett Macfarlane revisits judicial activism, a concept firmly entrenched in the normative and empirical debates over judicial review of the Charter. Judicial activism is a heavily contested and amorphous concept, and political scientists and legal scholars have disagreed over its definition and application as an empirical measure of court behaviour. Contra those who advocate abandoning the concept, Macfarlane argues that a nuanced account of judicial activism can help frame key features of judicial decision making and calls for its application in light of advances made in recent years in understanding how courts operate.

When the *Constitution Act, 1982* was adopted, many feared that it (and particularly the *Charter of Rights and Freedoms*) would serve to centralize Canadian federalism, limiting the diversity and powers of the provinces. In Chapter 3, Gerald Baier provides a critical reflection on the legacy of the centralization thesis and argues that the Charter has not been the centralizing force some predicted. Baier suggests that any decline in provincial autonomy post-1982 has resulted from the provincial governments' failure to assert provincial difference and identity and from a tendency to favour the politics of intergovernmental relations as a means to navigate Canadian federalism.

In Chapter 4, Mark Tushnet examines the Charter's international influence. Tushnet raises a puzzle: the Charter's origins and unique design largely emanate from its domestic context and the complexity and challenges of Canadian plurinational diversity, yet its influence appears significant elsewhere. Tushnet's examination of section 33's notwithstanding clause (not adopted wholesale elsewhere but influential in balancing a middle ground between political and judicial constitutionalism) and structured proportionality through section 1's *Oakes* test suggests Canada provides "proof of concept" for the viability of certain constitutional features in other jurisdictions.

In Chapter 5, Andrew McDougall explores the success of the Charter as a national symbol, pointing especially to its widespread and enduring popularity, and he contrasts this popularity with the scholarly literature's focus on questions of legitimacy. McDougall highlights the rich and largely untapped potential of analyzing the Charter as a political document and an entrenched part of Canadian culture and national identity, aspects scholars have not properly reconciled in their focus on institutional debates.

The relationship between the public and the Charter is examined further by Erin Crandall, Andrea Lawlor, and Kate Puddister in Chapter 6. Using media reports on the Charter as a proxy for public conversation, the authors assess the nature of "Charter talk" through an empirical analysis of over twenty-five hundred news articles on the Charter over forty years. They find that early Charter coverage was driven by a court-focused narrative until the early 2000s, when the government became the key actor in Charter narratives, a change that reflected partisan and electoral politics. While the media consistently covered legal rights and fundamental freedoms, coverage of equality rights and the notwithstanding clause was more sporadic, driven by specific Charter cases or intergovernmental conflicts.

How the media frames coverage of the Charter's notwithstanding clause receives sustained focus by Dave Snow and Eleni Nicolaides in Chapter 7. Their analysis reveals the important effects of negative or positive assessments of the policy at stake and the ideological orientation of media outlets in the framing of the use (or the threat of use) of the notwithstanding clause. The study has significant implications for understanding how section 33 is conceptualized and understood by the public.

These chapters lend themselves to rich considerations for future research, including study of the internal dynamics of decision making that implicate Charter rights within specific institutions and branches of government and how particular institutional configurations – including federalism, parliamentary sovereignty, executive power, national identity, media coverage, and public opinion – shape public policy and the rights of Canadians.

Charter Rights

Critical engagement with specific sections of the Charter, specific rights, and specific policy issues is another fundamental area of scrutiny. Beyond the Charter's impact on institutional relationships, judicial power, national attitudes, or other influences, its substantive impact on rights and public policy has been an important area of study.[19] The evolution of the Supreme Court's jurisprudence relating to freedom of association,[20] freedom of expression,[21] or equality rights[22] demonstrates the oscillating forms of disagreement and politics at the heart of constitutional interpretation. The court's decisions have affected entire policy landscapes in areas from abortion to criminal justice.[23] The chapters in this section engage a broad range of Charter rights, and although not every section of the Charter receives focused attention,[24] the contributions to this section provide a thorough and substantial assessment of key components of the 1982 act and cover a broad terrain of topics and questions.

In Chapter 8, Tamara Small highlights an important tension in election law – lawmakers who create rules governing elections are also subject to those rules, thus creating the opportunity for election law to be created in partisan self-interest. In a review of section 3 jurisprudence, Small assesses how the Supreme Court of Canada renders decisions that limit partisan self-interest in election law. While partisan self-interest is certainly present in Canadian election law, Small concludes that the court rarely reviews the actions of political actors and its capacity to provide oversight for partisan self-interest has been quite limited. This is an important finding given ongoing and future debates over various aspects of electoral regulation, including those implicating electoral boundaries and the reapportionment of seats in Parliament and controversies over the regulation of third-party advertising in provinces such as Ontario. With potential legislation designed to address misinformation, disinformation, and "false news" that might implicate the integrity of elections, this area of public policy can also have significant implications for free expression.

The impact of Charter litigation on public policy is perhaps most apparent in section 7 cases. Over the past forty years, the Supreme Court has given the principles of fundamental justice found in section 7 an expansive interpretation, far beyond what had been envisaged by the Charter's framers.[25] In Chapters 9 and 10, Matthew Hennigar and Brenda Cossman reflect on the impact of the court's interpretation of section 7 and consider how this section will shape future areas of litigation and policy debates. Hennigar evaluates some of the significant jurisprudential developments in the interpretation of section 7 and considers a variety of future directions for application, including positive socioeconomic rights (like a right to housing), access to medical procedures, and the ongoing litigation surrounding sex work. The political and jurisprudential regulation of sex work and sex workers is examined further in Cossman's contribution. Cossman argues that despite the perception that governance of sex work has become more liberalized, the regulation of sex work has ultimately been structured by abjection and disgust, which serve to perpetuate the exclusion of sex workers from social life.

Analysis of section 7 continues in Chapter 11, in Eleni Nicolaides's examination of medical assistance in dying policy and litigation post-*Carter*.[26] Moving away from a court-centred analysis, Nicolaides addresses the federal government's creation and subsequent reform of assisted dying policy, notable for its attempt to embrace a coordinate approach to constitutional interpretation and the balancing of rights. Nicolaides's analysis sheds light on the important role of government decision making in constitutional interpretation, contributing to our understanding of the relationship between the courts and Parliament.

While section 7 jurisprudence has embroiled governments and courts in fundamental and moralistic debates about the limits of government power, the impact of the Charter is perhaps most evident in the criminal justice system. Indeed, most Charter litigation arises in criminal proceedings, where courts are routinely asked to assess the limits of police powers, the admission of evidence, and the pretrial and trial rights of the criminally accused.[27] Although the Charter has had a profound impact on police powers and processes, it has provided little relief for those who are disproportionally targeted by police power, and much work remains in addressing the various insidious impacts of systemic discrimination in the Canadian criminal justice system.

In Chapter 12, Kent Roach examines the impact of the Charter on police powers and the RCMP in an analysis that explores the intersection of policing and race and the fundamental problems of systemic discrimination in the

Canadian criminal justice system. Through a review of the Supreme Court's jurisprudence regarding interrogation, search and seizure, and the court's attempts to regulate police misconduct, Roach demonstrates that the executive and legislature overwhelmingly rely on the courts to regulate and limit police powers. Because courts are limited to reviewing police conduct in individual cases, judicial decisions are constrained in their scope and capacity to effect changes in policing on a broad and systemic level. Considering the role of the RCMP as an agent of colonialism, evidence of gender-based violence within the ranks of the force, and increasing public scrutiny of how police interact with different communities (in particular Black and Indigenous communities), Roach argues that the legitimacy of the RCMP and policing in general are at a crossroads in Canada.[28] Roach's work highlights the need for scholars of law and politics to devote sustained attention to the study of policing.

Section 15 equality rights have been referred to as "the Charter's most conceptually difficult provision" by the Supreme Court of Canada, which also noted that equality itself is "an elusive concept."[29] Over the past four decades, the court's approach to section 15 and the wider impact of the right to equality have received much criticism for being restricted and ineffective for equity-seeking groups.[30] In Chapter 13, Joshua Sealy-Harrington assesses the Supreme Court's equality jurisprudence in *Andrews*[31] and *Fraser*,[32] illustrating the court's marginal engagement with racial discrimination claims for Black and Indigenous peoples. Sealy-Harrington makes it clear that the Charter has done little to address systemic and anti-Black and anti-Indigenous racism even though race is a protected ground under section 15. Building on Justice Abella's reasoning in *Fraser*, Sealy-Harrington calls on racial justice advocates to direct the Charter's substantive equality framework towards advancing both systemic and positive equality claims aimed at remedying the discrimination and structural conditions of Black and Indigenous peoples.

Kerri Froc continues the analysis of equality jurisprudence under section 15 in Chapter 14. In her analysis of women's sex-discrimination cases at the Supreme Court of Canada, Froc finds that women's claims have only been marginally more successful compared to men's, with a success rate of 28 percent compared to 26 percent, respectively. Froc argues that women's claims are focused on challenging laws that adversely impact women as a result of gendered conduct, rather than strictly biological sex, an approach that is often incompatible with the court's focus on a biological-based understanding of sex discrimination. To move towards achieving sex equality, Froc asserts that section 15 jurisprudence must recognize discrimination that results from both biological sex and how gender is practised in Canadian society.

In Chapter 15, James Kelly examines the legacy and policy impact of Quebec's Bill 101 (Charter of the French Language) and the Supreme Court's decisions in *Ford* and *Devine*.[33] Kelly finds that although the Quebec government modified its approach to promoting the French language in 1993 in a manner that appeared to comply with the court's decisions in *Ford* and *Devine*, the public face of commercial expression in Quebec remains overwhelmingly French. Kelly's analysis highlights the important role of private actors (such as commercial businesses) as agents of policy implementation.

Although specific constitutional rights protecting language were enshrined in sections 16 to 23 of the Charter, language rights in Canada have a long history. Because of this legacy, language protections in Canada have been rather piecemeal in nature. In Chapter 16, Stéphanie Chouinard examines the nature of language protection and the various Charter-based disputes that have occurred throughout the Charter's history. Looking to the future, Chouinard maps directions for language rights, including the extension of language protections beyond what is explicitly stated in the Charter, to the expansion of the *Indigenous Languages Act*. She cautions that Charter-protected language rights may be insufficient to respond to the evolving demands of official-language communities in years to come.

Along with codifying a series of rights, the Charter also includes remedial measures in section 24. Section 24(2) empowers courts to exclude evidence gathered by law enforcement in a manner that violated Charter rights. It has profoundly changed police practice and criminal trials in Canada. In Chapter 17, Lori Hausegger, Danielle McNabb, and Troy Riddell examine the impact of the 2009 *Grant* ruling, a Supreme Court case that modified the exclusion test for evidence.[34] The authors find that, post-*Grant*, evidence is slightly less likely to be excluded and extralegal factors such as political ideology only play a limited role in shaping judicial decisions regarding the exclusion of evidence. Perhaps their most interesting finding is significant variation in the exclusion of evidence across provincial courts of appeal, suggesting that Canada's penultimate appellate courts merit further attention from scholars.

Reconciliation

The entrenchment of Aboriginal and treaty rights under section 35 came with significant uncertainty given it was largely left to the courts to identify the content and scope of those rights. Jurisprudential developments, including the recognition of a duty to consult and accommodate, have had a systemic and profound impact on decision-making processes at all levels of government and across virtually every ministry and policy area. And yet the duty to consult has not lived up to the promise of fully protecting the rights at stake, as it has arguably failed to empower Indigenous communities and to fulfill the requirements of either the historical or modern treaties or the right to self-government.

Scholarship on section 35 has examined jurisprudential and policy developments in relation to the state's obligations to uphold Aboriginal and treaty rights. Criticism of the courts includes their penchant for originalist and therefore narrow interpretations, freezing Indigenous rights in time, in stark contrast to the liberal and "living" interpretation granted to Charter rights.[35] Kiera Ladner and Michael McCrossan, on the occasion of the twenty-fifth anniversary of the *Constitution Act, 1982,* wrote that the courts "abandoned the path set before them in favour of sustaining Canada's colonial legacy."[36]

Intervening political events, including the Idle No More movement and the Truth and Reconciliation Commission, have placed a heightened emphasis on reconciliation and the development of a nation-to-nation approach to the Crown-Indigenous relationship. Scholars have only begun to analyze the role of the courts and section 35 in relation to these developments.[37] A similar body of work is developing on the implementation of the United Nations Declaration on the Rights of Indigenous Peoples (UNDRIP) in Canada.[38] Many of these analyses identify the deficiencies of section 35 as a central impediment to progress. In the case of UNDRIP, Shiri Pasternak notes that "[b]oth the federal and provincial governments have stated that UNDRIP legislation will be interpreted in line with section 35 of the Constitution. This means that domestic legal precedents will be paramount over international principles. While this may protect Aboriginal and treaty rights in some cases, it also may narrow the realm of possibility from what is being imagined through UNDRIP."[39]

A considerable literature has developed around the duty to consult and accommodate under section 35 since its articulation in the 2004 *Haida Nation* case.[40] This research includes primarily legal assessments on jurisprudential issues or questions of sovereignty[41] and studies examining the policy process and policy impact of the principle.[42] The challenges of the duty to consult framework – and the *Constitution Act*'s role in affecting political, policy, or legal principles such as reconciliation, treaty federalism, the nation-to-nation relationship, and UNDRIP – are generational in nature. As Canada struggles to fulfill its responsibilities in a renewed era of reconciliation, the fortieth anniversary of section 35 provides an opportunity to critically assess the state-Indigenous relationship under the Constitution.

In Chapter 18, Peter Russell explores the central challenge of how Indigenous constitutional traditions, as well as Indigenous peoples' self-government and inherent sovereignty, might operate in a context where we are beginning to recognize the coexistence of more than one constitutional order. Implicit in this analysis is the fundamental question of the extent to which Indigenous peoples live, or will live, within or outside the Constitution of Canada. Russell explores the progress made since 1982 on this front and the increasing acknowledgment that sovereignty over Canada will be shared between federal, provincial, and Indigenous orders of government.

In Chapter 19, Jeremy Patzer and Kiera Ladner examine the courts' record under section 35's Aboriginal and treaty rights and section 25 of the Charter. They find that while section 35 has brought protection for those rights, courts and governments have sought to limit the scope and purpose of what was entrenched to "manage" rather than transform the constitutional vision. In their analysis, the failure to fully acknowledge Indigenous peoples' sovereignty and their legal and constitutional orders equates to ignoring what was embedded in 1982. Given the greater attention paid to reconciliation in political discourse and the stated policy objectives of Canadian governments, Patzer and Ladner's conclusion serves as an important launching pad for future scholarship on what a more transformational policy agenda might look like and, more significantly, how it might be implemented.

In Chapter 20, Rebecca Major and Cynthia Stirbys analyze section 35 from the perspective of the Crown's quest for "certainty" regarding its obligations and the state-Indigenous relationship. The failure to add specificity to section 35 in subsequent constitutional conferences, in their view, puts power in the hands of Indigenous peoples. Even though the courts perpetuate colonialism, the progress that has been made to expand rights and title to land means Indigenous peoples are capturing control over certainty even as the Canadian state seeks to dominate. In this sense, section 35 is part of a toolkit used by Indigenous peoples to reclaim their own authority over Indigenous lands and resources.

In Chapter 21, Minh Do examines longer-term governance arrangements regarding the management of land and resources in the face of the famed duty to consult and accommodate. Do notes that the duty to consult is subject to criticism as an inadequate framework for protecting rights and argues that policy theories examining horizontal governance arrangements may be a useful lens through which to explore Indigenous-Crown partnerships in strategic land-use planning, while upholding the state's constitutional obligations under the duty to consult and accommodate doctrine.

In Chapter 22, Samuel LaSelva interrogates the legacy of Alan Cairns's work on the relationship between the state and Indigenous peoples. At once critical of the assimilationist perspectives that dominated so much of Canada's state policy and cautious about the nation-to-nation conception articulated in the Royal Commission on Aboriginal Peoples, Cairns's nuanced and penetrating scholarship is intensely controversial. By forcing us to think more specifically about how Indigenous and non-Indigenous peoples can live together, and not simply next to each other, LaSelva notes that Cairns raised challenging and uncomfortable questions for which he did not have all the answers and on which important opportunities for future scholarship remain.

Constitutional Change

The patriation of the Constitution and the establishment of a homegrown amending formula arguably marked the final cementing of Canadian sovereignty and established the parameters for future constitutional change. Patriation also had an acute impact on Canada's constitutional culture, as subsequent events exacerbated national unity tensions and debates over the place of Quebec in Canada's federal system. The perception that Quebec never "signed on" to the 1982 constitutional compromise has blighted discussions of formal constitutional amendment ever since. The implications for Canadian constitutional change, arguably resulting in a formal constitutional stasis and a focus on informal reform, has had considerable consequences for the evolution of the Constitution and the politics surrounding reform. It also has implications for understanding Canada's constitutional identity. It is time to reflect on these various issues.

In Chapter 23, Richard Albert provides an analysis of the way the constitutional amending formula has been changed, not through formal modifications to its text but by judicial decisions, new legislated rules at the federal and provincial levels, and political culture around constitutional reform. The disjuncture between the requirements of the constitutional text and the reality of amendment in practice leaves Canada virtually unable to achieve formal constitutional change, a development that threatens, in Albert's view, the democratic rule of law values of predictability, transparency, and accountability.

In Chapter 24, Félix Mathieu and Dave Guénette examine the constitutional changes of 1982 from the perspective of Quebec and the rejection of a constitutional dualism that many in Quebec view as fundamental to the original founding compact. In elaborating on this perspective, the authors advance an understanding of Quebec's long-standing refusal to accept the 1982 act to the extent it represented a rupture of Quebec's sociopolitical myth and the legitimacy with which it conceives of the constitutional order.

In Chapter 25, Philippe Lagassé critically analyzes the evolution of the Crown and key jurisprudential developments in characterizing the meaning of "the Queen." These interpretations, in Lagassé's view, expose a constitutional abeyance with considerable consequences for how we conceive of a Canadian Crown distinct from the Crown of the United Kingdom. In Lagassé's view, the Supreme Court has delayed an inevitable debate about how Canada identifies or selects its monarch, who is the personification of the Canadian state and sovereign authority.

In Chapter 26, Ran Hirschl explores the Constitution's deficiencies as it relates to cities and municipalities, which, by virtue of their lack of constitutional status, remain entirely dependent on provincial legislation for their powers and revenue. The rigidity of the 1982 amending formula makes formal changes to this status quo unlikely, but the political reality has long outgrown its 1867 entrenchment. This, Hirschl argues, encourages stagnation and places great pressures on municipalities to deliver core services, live up to the values of the Charter, and manage front-line responsibilities pertaining to social integration and multicultural accommodation. Hirschl suggests several potential tools – including city charters, electoral reform, and bolstered cooperative federalism – to strengthen the place of local government in Canada's constitutional arrangements.

Each of these chapters is replete with nuanced accounts of the challenges presented by constitutional change in Canada, challenges that remain, or are increasingly becoming, critically urgent. Together, the contributors make clear that more research is needed.

Canada stands at a constitutional crossroads. The chapters that follow bring together a diverse and exceptionally talented group of scholars from the fields of law and politics to contemplate, interrogate, and engage in analytical reflection on the *Constitution Act, 1982* on its fortieth anniversary. The contributions to this volume provide an unparalleled and thorough account of the Constitution and its impact after forty years, with a focus on the themes of rights, reconciliation, and constitutional change, offering rich insight that will undoubtedly inform public and scholarly conversations about the Constitution in years to come.

Notes

1 *Constitution Act, 1982*, being Schedule B to the *Canada Act 1982* (UK), 1982, c 11.
2 Peter H. Russell, *Constitutional Odyssey: Can Canadians Become a Sovereign People?*, 3rd ed. (Toronto: University of Toronto Press, 2004).
3 Keith Banting and Richard Simeon, eds., *And No One Cheered: Federalism, Democracy and the Constitution Act* (Toronto: Methuen, 1983).
4 Peter H. Russell, "The Political Purposes of the Canadian Charter of Rights and Freedoms," *Canadian Bar Review* 61 (1983): 30–54.
5 Brian Slattery, "The Hidden Constitution: Aboriginal Rights in Canada," *American Journal of Comparative Law* 32, 2 (1984): 361–91.
6 John Borrows, "Challenging Historical Frameworks: Aboriginal Rights, the Trickster, and Originalism," *Canadian Historical Review* 98, 1 (2017): 114–35.
7 F.L. Morton and Rainer Knopff, *The Charter Revolution and the Court Party* (Peterborough: Broadview Press, 2000); Miriam Smith, "Ghosts of the Judicial Committee of the Privy Council: Group Politics and Charter Litigation in Canadian Political Science," *Canadian Journal of Political Science* 35, 1 (2002): 3–29.

8   Allan C. Hutchinson, *Waiting for CORAF: A Critique of Law and Rights* (Toronto: University of Toronto Press, 1995); Morton and Knopff, *The Charter Revolution and the Court Party;* Christopher P. Manfredi, *Judicial Power and the Charter: Canada and the Paradox of Liberal Constitutionalism,* 2nd ed. (Oxford: Oxford University Press, 2001); Andrew Petter, *The Politics of the Charter: The Illusive Promise of Constitutional Rights* (Toronto: University of Toronto Press, 2010).

9   Peter W. Hogg and Allison A. Bushell, "The Charter Dialogue between Courts and Legislatures (or Perhaps the Charter of Rights Isn't Such a Bad Thing After All)," *Osgoode Hall Law Journal* 35, 1 (1997): 75–124; Christopher P. Manfredi and James B. Kelly, "Six Degrees of Dialogue: A Response to Hogg and Bushell," *Osgoode Hall Law Journal* 37, 3 (1999): 513–27; Peter W. Hogg, Allison A. Bushell Thornton, and Wade K. Wright, "Charter Dialogue Revisited: Or 'Much Ado about Metaphors,'" *Osgoode Hall Law Journal* 45, 1 (2007): 1–65; Carissima Mathen, "Dialogue Theory, Judicial Review, and Judicial Supremacy: A Comment on Charter Dialogue Revisited," *Osgoode Hall Law Journal* 45, 1 (2007): 125–46; Emmett Macfarlane, "Dialogue or Compliance? Measuring Legislatures' Policy Responses to Court Rulings on Rights," *International Political Science Review* 34, 1 (2012): 39–56; Emmett Macfarlane, "Conceptual Precision and Parliamentary Systems of Rights: Disambiguating 'Dialogue,'" *Review of Constitutional Studies* 17, 2 (2012): 73–100; Aileen Kavanagh, "The Lure and the Limits of Dialogue," *University of Toronto Law Journal* 66, 1 (2015): 83–120.

10 Janet L. Hiebert, "Parliamentary Bills of Rights: An Alternative Model?," *Modern Law Review* 69, 1 (2006): 7–28; Mark Tushnet, *Weak Courts, Strong Rights: Judicial Review and Social Welfare Rights in Comparative Constitutional Law* (Princeton: Princeton University Press, 2008); Stephen Gardbaum, *The New Commonwealth Model of Constitutionalism: Theory and Practice* (Cambridge: Cambridge University Press, 2013).

11 Janet L. Hiebert, *Charter Conflicts: What Is Parliament's Role?* (Montreal/Kingston: McGill-Queen's University Press, 2002); James B. Kelly, *Governing with the Charter: Legislative and Judicial Activism and Framers' Intent* (Vancouver: UBC Press, 2005); Kent Roach, *The Supreme Court on Trial: Judicial Activism or Democratic Dialogue?*, rev. ed. (Toronto: Irwin Law, 2016).

12 Matthew A. Hennigar, "Exploring Complex Judicial-Executive Interaction: Federal Government Concessions in Charter of Rights Cases," *Canadian Journal of Political Science* 43, 4 (2010): 821–42; Matthew A. Hennigar, "Why Does the Federal Government Appeal to the Supreme Court of Canada in Charter of Rights Cases? A Strategic Explanation," *Law and Society Review* 41, 1 (2007): 225–50; Matthew A. Hennigar, "*Reference re Same-Sex Marriage:* Making Sense of the Government's Litigation Strategy," in *Contested Constitutionalism,* ed. James Kelly and Christopher Manfredi (Vancouver: UBC Press, 2009), 209–30; Christopher Manfredi, "Conservatives, the Supreme Court of Canada, and the Constitution: Judicial Government Relations, 2006–2015," *Osgoode Hall Law Journal* 52, 3 (2015): 951–83; Matthew A. Hennigar, "Unreasonable Disagreement? Judicial-Executive Exchanges about Charter Reasonableness in the Harper Era," *Osgoode Hall Law Journal* 54, 4 (2017): 1245–73; Emmett Macfarlane, "'You Can't Always Get What You Want': Regime Politics, the Supreme Court of Canada, and the Harper Government," *Canadian Journal of Political Science* 51, 1 (2018): 1–21.

13 Janet L. Hiebert, "The Charter, Policy, and Political Judgment," in *Policy Change, Courts, and the Canadian Constitution,* ed. Emmett Macfarlane (Toronto: University of Toronto Press, 2018), 81–102.

14 Kate Puddister, *Seeking the Court's Advice: The Politics of the Canadian Reference Power* (Vancouver: UBC Press, 2019); Carissima Mathen, *Courts without Cases: The Law and Politics of Advisory Opinions* (Oxford: Hart Publishing, 2019).

15 Dave Snow and Mark S. Harding, "From Normative Debates to Comparative Methodology: The Three Waves of Post-Charter Supreme Court Scholarship in Canada," *American Review of Canadian Studies* 45, 4 (2015): 451–66.

16 C.L. Ostberg and Matthew E. Wetstein, *Attitudinal Decision Making in the Supreme Court of Canada* (Vancouver: UBC Press, 2007); Donald R. Songer, *The Transformation of the Supreme Court of Canada: An Empirical Examination* (Toronto: University of Toronto Press, 2008); Donald R. Songer, Susan W. Johnson, C.L. Ostberg, and Matthew E. Wetstein, *Law, Ideology, and Collegiality: Judicial Behaviour in the Supreme Court of Canada* (Montreal/Kingston: McGill-Queen's University Press, 2012); Emmett Macfarlane, *Governing from the Bench: The Supreme Court of Canada and the Judicial Role* (Vancouver: UBC Press, 2013).

17 For example, see Peter McCormick, *Supreme at Last: The Evolution of the Supreme Court of Canada* (Toronto: Lorimer, 2000). See also Ian Greene, Carl Baar, Peter McCormick, George Szablowski, and Martin Thomas, *Final Appeal: Decision-Making in Canadian Courts of Appeal* (Toronto: Lorimer, 1998).

18 Russell, "The Political Purposes of the Canadian Charter of Rights and Freedoms," 51.

19 Emmett Macfarlane, ed., *Policy Change, Courts, and the Canadian Constitution* (Toronto: University of Toronto Press, 2018).

20 Brian Langille, "The Freedom of Association Mess: How We Got in It and How We Can Get Out of It," *McGill Law Journal* 54, 1 (2009): 177–212; Brian Langille and Benjamin Oliphant, "The Legal Structure of Freedom of Association," *Queen's Law Journal* 40 (2014): 249–300; David J. Doorey, "Back to the Future of Canadian Labour Law," *Industrial Relations* 75, 2 (2020): 195–208.

21 Emmett Macfarlane, ed., *Dilemmas of Free Expression* (Toronto: University of Toronto Press, 2022).

22 Margot Young, "Social Justice and the Charter: Comparison and Choice," *Osgoode Hall Law Journal* 50 (2013): 669–98; Jennifer Koshan and Jonnette Watson Hamilton, "The Continual Reinvention of Section 15 of the Charter," *UNB Law Journal* 64 (2013): 19–53; Jonnette Watson Hamilton and Jennifer Koshan, "Adverse Impact: The Supreme Court's Approach to Adverse Effects Discrimination under Section 15 of the Charter," *Review of Constitutional Studies* 19, 2 (2015): 191–236; Jena McGill and Daphne Gilbert, "Of Promise and Peril: The Court and Equality Rights," *Supreme Court Law Review* 78 (2017): 235–57; Kerri A. Froc, "A Prayer for Original Meaning: A History of Section 15 and What It Should Mean for Equality," *National Journal of Constitutional Law* 38 (2018): 35–88; Emmett Macfarlane, "Positive Rights and Section 15 of the Charter: Addressing a Dilemma," *National Journal of Constitutional Law* 38, 1 (2018): 147–68; Fay Faraday, "One Step Forward, Two Steps Back? Substantive Equality, Systemic Discrimination and Pay Equity at the Supreme Court of Canada" *Supreme Court Law Review* 2, 94 (2020): 301–34.

23 Rachael Johnstone, *After Morgentaler: The Politics of Abortion in Canada* (Vancouver: UBC Press, 2017); James B. Kelly and Kate Puddister, "Criminal Justice Policy during the Harper Era: Private Member's Bills, Penal Populism, and the *Criminal Code of Canada*," *Canadian Journal of Law and Society* 32, 3 (2017): 391–416.

24 Reflection on and assessment of the reasonable limits clause, freedom of association, conscience and religion, and multiculturalism all warrant further attention by scholars, while we are pleased to note that freedom of expression receives sustained focus in a new volume; see Macfarlane, *Dilemmas of Free Expression*.

25 Peter Hogg, "The Brilliant Career of Section 7 of the Charter," *Supreme Court Law Review* 58 (2012): 195–210.

26 *Carter v Canada (Attorney General)*, [2015] 1 SCR 331.

27   Kelly, *Governing with the Charter.*

28   Jane Gerster, "The Dark Side of the RCMP," *The Walrus,* October 20, 2021, https://thewalrus.ca/can-the-rcmp-be-saved/; Michel Bastarache, *Broken Dreams, Broken Lives: The Devastating Effects of Sexual Harassment on Women in the RCMP* (Ottawa: Government of Canada, 2021).

29   Jennifer Koshan and Jonnette Watson Hamilton, "The Continual Reinvention of Section 15 of the Charter," *UNB Law Journal* 64 (2013): 19–53, quoting *Andrews v Law Society of British Columbia,* [1989] 1 SCR 143 [*Andrews v Law Society of British Columbia*], and *Law v Canada (Minister of Employment and Immigration),* [1999] 1 SCR 497.

30   *Ibid.* See also Bruce Ryder and Taufiq Hashmani, "Managing Charter Equality Rights: The Supreme Court of Canada's Disposition of Leave to Appeal Applications in Section 15 Cases, 1989–2010," *Supreme Court Law Review* 51 (2010): 505–52.

31   *Andrews v Law Society of British Columbia.*

32   *Fraser v Canada (Attorney General),* 2020 SCC 28.

33   *Ford v Quebec (Attorney General),* [1988] 2 SCR 712; *Devine v Quebec (Attorney General),* [1988] 2 SCR 790.

34   *R v Grant,* [2009] 2 SCR 353.

35   John Borrows, "Frozen Rights in Canada: Constitutional Interpretation and the Trickster," *American Indian Law Review* 22, 1 (1997): 37–64; Borrows, "Challenging Historical Frameworks."

36   Kiera L. Ladner and Michael McCrossan, "The Road Not Taken: Aboriginal Rights after the Re-imagining of the Canadian Constitutional Order," in *Contested Constitutionalism: Reflections on the Canadian Charter of Rights and Freedoms,* ed. James B. Kelly and Christopher P. Manfredi (Vancouver: UBC Press, 2009), 264.

37   Alexander Hudson, "Next Steps for the Idle No More Movement: A Public Law Perspective," *Aboriginal Policy Studies* 3, 1–2 (2014): 149–63; Kim Stanton, "Reconciling Reconciliation: Differing Conceptions of the Supreme Court of Canada and the Canadian Truth and Reconciliation Commission," *Journal of Law and Social Policy* 26 (2017): 21–42; Pamela McCurry, "Section 35 Legal Framework: Implications for Evaluation," *Canadian Journal of Program Evaluation* 34, 3 (2020): 400–12.

38   Sara Mainville, "Hunting Down a Lasting Relationship with Canada: Will UNDRIP Help?," *Osgoode Hall Law Journal* 57, 1 (2021): 98–126; Andrew M. Robinson, "Governments Must Not Wait on Courts to Implement UNDRIP Rights concerning Indigenous Sacred Sites: Lessons from Canada and *Ktunaxa Nation v. British Columbia*," *International Journal of Human Rights* 24, 10 (2020): 1642–65.

39   Shiri Pasternak, "B.C. Might Want to Align with UNDRIP, but Does UNDRIP Align with B.C.?," in *The UN Declaration on the Rights of Indigenous Peoples in Canada: Lessons from B.C.,* ed. Hayden King (Toronto: Yellowhead Institute, 2020), 18. See also Sherry Pictou, "Mi'kmaq and the Recognition and Implementation of Rights Framework," Yellowhead Institute Brief, June 5, 2018, https://yellowheadinstitute.org/2018/06/05/mikmaq-rights-framework/.

40   *Haida Nation v British Columbia (Minister of Forests),* [2004] 3 SCR 511, 2004 SCC 73.

41   Dwight G. Newman, *Revisiting the Duty to Consult Aboriginal Peoples* (Saskatoon: Purich, 2014); Robert Hamilton and Joshua Nichols, "The Tin Ear of the Court: *Ktunaxa Nation* and the Foundation of the Duty to Consult," *Alberta Law Review* 56, 3 (2019): 729–60; Richard Stacey, "Honour in Sovereignty: Can Crown Consultation with Indigenous Peoples Erase Canada's Sovereignty Deficit?," *University of Toronto Law Journal* 68, 3 (2018): 405–39; Jeremy Webber, "We Are Still in the Age of Encounter: Section 35 and a Canada beyond Sovereignty," in *From Recognition to Reconciliation: Essays on the Constitutional Entrenchment of Aboriginal and Treaty Rights,* ed. Patrick Macklem

and Douglas Sanderson (Toronto: University of Toronto Press, 2016), 63–99; Lorne Sossin, "The Duty to Consult and Accommodate: Procedural Justice as Aboriginal Rights," *Canadian Journal of Administrative Law and Practice* 23, 1 (2010): 93–113.

42 Minh Do, "Throughput Legitimacy and the Duty to Consult: The Limits of the Law to Produce Quality Interactions in British Columbia's EA Process," *Canadian Journal of Political Science* 53, 3 (2020): 577–95; Michael McCrossan, "Contrasting Visions of Indigenous Rights, Recognition, and Territory: Assessing Crown Policy in the Context of Reconciliation and Historic Obligations," in *Policy Change, Courts, and the Canadian Constitution,* ed. Emmett Macfarlane (Toronto: University of Toronto Press, 2018), 356–77; Martin Papillon and André Juneau, *Canada: The State of the Federation 2013: Aboriginal Multilevel Governance,* Institute of Intergovernmental Relations (Montreal/Kingston: McGill-Queen's University Press, 2015); Rachel Ariss, Clara MacCallum Fraser, and Diba Nazneen Somani, "Crown Policies on the Duty to Consult and Accommodate: Towards Reconciliation?," *McGill Journal of Sustainable Development Law* 13, 1 (2017): 1–58.

Part 1
Institutional Relationships

1

The Political Purposes of the Charter
Four Decades Later

Mark S. Harding

THE CHARTER'S SIGNIFICANCE is often viewed in revolutionary terms.[1] Peter H. Russell was one of the first scholars to anticipate how significantly the Charter would reorient the character of Canadian politics. In "The Political Purposes of the Canadian Charter of Rights and Freedoms,"[2] Russell critiqued the sponsors of the Charter by predicting the actual effects of a new constitutional rights document on the country. Russell foresaw that, rather than simply fostering national unity or providing enhanced rights protection, the Charter's most far-reaching consequence would be its tendency to "judicialize politics and politicize the judiciary."[3] In addition to anticipating the growth of judicial power in Canada, what is most remarkable was Russell's foresight concerning numerous and often subtle institutional externalities the Charter would have on other aspects of Canada's political ecosystem.

It is not this chapter's goal to provide a running tally of Russell's predictions; Russell himself revisited some of these at the time of previous Charter anniversaries.[4] Instead, this chapter aims to serve two purposes. First, it uses Russell's early predictions as a way to reflect on how the Charter has changed Canadian politics and highlights its effect on subsequent scholarship. The principal areas I revisit concern centralization, the selection of Supreme Court judges, the authoritative nature of judicial decisions, and the notwithstanding clause. In my discussion, I also highlight areas where Russell's predictions were half right. These include his expectations that the Canadian judiciary would be ideologically balanced, that policy issues would be systematically reviewed from a rights perspective, and that governments would benefit politically in certain ways from the judicialization of politics. Second, this chapter seeks to contextualize how Russell's appreciation of Canada's specific constitutional culture – with its unique combination of federalism and parliamentary democracy – aided him in anticipating the significant and subtle impacts of a new constitutional bill of rights. Nearly forty years after its publication, Russell's article remains so foundational precisely because he understood the unfolding logic of many of the institutional changes the Charter would bring to Canada's political system.

Russell and the Canadian Constitution

It is often observed that Canada's governing structure rests on two fundamental institutional pillars: federalism and responsible government.[5] The Constitution's division of powers and Westminster-style legislatures produce an underlying institutional logic that explains much of how Canadian politics function. Since 1982, some observers have wrestled with whether the addition of the Charter is a third institutional pillar in its own right, with Jeremy Clarke arguing that "[f]ar from simply grafting a new pillar onto the constitutional structure, the Charter effected a profound transformation of the existing ones."[6]

Throughout his career, Russell has taken Canada's institutional logic seriously, considering judicial review and Canada's rule-of-law tradition as potent factors that interact with its federal and parliamentary pillars.[7] Russell's work is grounded in an approach that combines aspects of what some call traditional political science and old institutionalism, which emphasize the formal structures of government and broader regime types.[8] Russell's 1983 article, like much of his writing, is descriptive and normative. Its "central theoretical interest" was "to probe the peculiar nature of judicial power," and his specific question of consideration was, "What is the proper role of the judiciary in the liberal democratic state?"[9]

When considering what effect the Charter would have on Canada, Russell first and foremost situated Canada as a liberal democratic regime. He noted how many countries lacking charters of rights at that time (Canada, Australia, New Zealand, and the United Kingdom) were still liberal democracies and that the absence of a rights document does not preclude the protection of core rights in liberal democracies.[10] Russell believed these core rights – "political freedom, toleration, due process of the law and social equality" – were not at any serious risk so long as Canada maintained its status as a liberal democratic regime. While Russell was well aware the Charter would have significant implications for Canada's institutional ecosystem, he predicted its controversies would primarily regard who prescribes the limits on what he called our "secondary rights."[11] Russell anticipated not only prominent secondary rights issues, such as police powers and abortion rights, but also more obscure matters such as compulsory retirement and discrimination in employment practices.[12] Beyond rights, Russell also thought one of the Charter's most significant reverberations in Canada's institutional environment would be its effect on federal-provincial relations.

Centralization

Strengthening national unity was a central goal of the Charter's architects. Russell noted how Quebec's demands for more autonomy had to be "countered by proposals designed to have a unifying effect on Canada,"[13] and that both Prime Ministers Pearson and Trudeau had advocated proposals that would produce institutional unification to suppress decentralizing demands. Pierre Trudeau in particular claimed the Charter would help articulate the country's common values and symbolically foster a view of Canada as a bilingual and multinational nation.[14]

Russell highlighted how several specific Charter provisions spoke to Trudeau's desire to strengthen the federal government against the centrifugal forces of separatism and provincialism. For instance, Russell viewed the mobility rights in section 6 and the linguistic rights in sections 16–23 as designed to counteract the "balkanization" of provincial standards. Beyond these specific provisions, however, Russell thought the real way in which the Charter would act as a nationalizing instrument would be through judicial review: "It is primarily through judicial decisions interpreting the Charter – applying its general terms to particular laws and government activities – that the Charter will come to play an important part in the on-going political life of Canada."[15] The sponsors of the Charter had stressed that it would not diminish provincial powers, but Russell was unpersuaded. "These disavowals of any centralizing implications of the Charter," Russell wrote, represent an "anachronistic view of the judicial process that the policy making role of the judiciary, above all in interpreting the broad language of a constitutional Bill of Rights, could be denied."[16]

Russell did not believe Canadian politics would become less polarized under the Charter; instead, the nature of political conflicts would shift from those that divided regions to those that divided neighbours. Because the Charter gives a constitutional dimension to issues such as pay equity and abortion, "[j]udicial decisions on the Charter will be unifying in that the very debates and controversies they produce will be national."[17] The Supreme Court's decisions would unify Canadians in the sense that they would be less distracted by regional ressentiments and more prone to disagree about "rights talk" at the national level.[18] This process – whereby the Supreme Court would act as a national policy-making body, "a kind of national Senate reviewing the reasonableness of provincial laws and policies" – would be the primary mechanism of unification under the Charter.[19]

This prediction originated the centralization thesis, that the Supreme Court's enforcement of new national Charter standards would homogenize provincial diversity in various areas of public policy (see Baier, Chapter 3 in this volume). This issue was a prominent concern in the early years of scholarship following the Charter,[20] and it is still debated now.[21] F.L. Morton was one of the most vocal scholars raising the issue of Charter centralization. For Morton, the Charter gave the federal government the upper hand over the provinces (especially Quebec) by enabling it to indirectly sponsor litigation challenging language laws and other provincial policies.[22] Morton argued that the Charter gave specific interest groups – linguistic organizations chief among them – the ability to have their policy preferences transferred from the legislative venue, where they are numerically weak, to a more sympathetic venue in the form of the Supreme Court in Ottawa. More recently, Morton has made a similar claim about the "centralist bias" in the federal Court Challenges Program, which typically involves "the *federal* government funding rights-advocacy groups to challenge *provincial* policies."[23]

Some scholars (including Russell) raised doubts that the Supreme Court had been as centralizing as Morton and others feared.[24] Morton criticized these rejoinders for being overly legalistic, too focused on wins and losses, and willing to dismiss exceptions to the rule.[25] Because language policy was so central to the Parti Québécois's *raison d'être,* for example, Morton argued it is too simplistic to view the judicial evisceration of Bill 101 as just another provincial law being invalidated. Yet James Kelly's subsequent study of judicial outputs found that centralization was not as significant as critics such as Morton had suggested.[26] Instead of homogenizing provincial policies in the name of Charter compliance, the Supreme Court, Kelly found, was often sensitive to provincial diversity through a process of federalization. These findings were reinforced by Jeremy Clarke's study showing the Supreme Court has been sympathetic to the provinces in Charter cases when their policies were defended on the grounds of federalism.[27]

Collectively, the research of Morton, Kelly, Clarke, and others – all of which builds on Russell's centralization thesis – provides knowledge about the complex ways the Supreme Court has interpreted the division of powers alongside the Charter, spurring a debate that continues in this very volume. As Douglas Brown, Herman Bakvis, and Gerald Baier note, "[T]here is controversy about the proper way to measure the effects of the Charter on legislative diversity. Numbers alone don't always tell the whole story."[28] It would be incorrect to say the court's interpretation of the Charter has had *no* homogenizing effects, particularly given the evidence of discreet policy fields such as language rights.[29] However, that effect has not been as totalistic as some skeptics predicted.

The Politics of Judicial Selection

A different form of centralization looms over the post-Charter politics of judicial selection. Canada has American-style federalism, a British-inspired unified judicial structure, and an executive-dominated parliamentary system. Because decisions over judicial personnel are the purview of the executive, Russell foresaw that if the Supreme Court began invalidating provincial laws with greater frequency under the Charter, this would mean the "federal government's monopoly over the power to appoint judges, not only to the Supreme Court of

Canada but to all of the higher provincial courts, will be increasingly questioned."[30]

As Russell predicted, the decade following the adoption of the Charter provided a burst of enthusiasm for provincial input into the selection processes of federal judicial appointments. Both the Meech Lake and Charlottetown Accords would have given provincial input into Supreme Court appointments.[31] Quebec's Meech Lake demand, whereby its provincial government would select its three seats on the Supreme Court, was especially controversial. Critics such as Pierre Trudeau worried it would allow provincial governments to mould the political orientation of the court's decision making in a decentralist direction, thereby weakening the federal government and subverting the potential for an expansive interpretation of the Charter.[32] While Meech and Charlottetown ultimately failed to meet the necessary thresholds for approval, some lesser changes to federal judicial appointments were made. In 1988, the Mulroney government implemented reforms allowing some input from provincial legal elites to the selection process to section 96 (provincial) and section 101 (federal) courts, though these changes did not pertain to Supreme Court appointments.[33] Although this certainly constitutes increased provincial input in federal judicial selections, it amounts to a consolation prize compared to the demand to handpick judges on the Supreme Court.

Formal demands for provincial oversight over Supreme Court appointments diminished after the Charlottetown Accord. However, scholars and politicians maintained an interest in providing some parliamentary input into appointments.[34] Paul Martin's efforts to address Canada's "democratic deficit" included the first measure of legislative oversight of Supreme Court appointments, which included some provincial participation, albeit from legal elites rather than provincial governments.[35] Stephen Harper expanded on the modest Martin reforms by adding a legislative question-and-answer session with the prospective Supreme Court appointee, although the process still did not remove prime ministerial discretion over appointments. Justin Trudeau then modified the Harper process by maintaining the oral hearing and expanding the scope and mandate of the advisory committee for Supreme Court appointments. Overall, the various changes to judicial appointments at the federal level have mostly involved strengthening or diluting the influence of legal elites and government appointees on advisory committees, without increasing direct provincial influence in selection.[36]

Although provinces have not gained the substantive oversight they desired in the early days of the Charter, Russell's attention to the effect of the federal nature of our governing structure on the Supreme Court remains germane. Three episodes warrant attention in this regard. First, the Harper government's failed appointment of Marc Nadon showed provincial governments can indirectly play a role in Supreme Court appointments. In 2014, a Toronto lawyer filed an action concerning the constitutionality of the government's decision to appoint Nadon, a Quebec-based judge on the Federal Court of Appeal, to fill one of the three seats set aside for Quebec judges.

The Quebec government also wanted legal clarity over the eligibility criteria, on the basis that Quebec jurists should sit to defend and articulate Quebec's unique social values and legal traditions. After the Harper government submitted these issues to the Supreme Court in a reference, a six-to-one decision ultimately found that the appointment was unconstitutional, and Nadon's appointment was revoked.[37]

The controversy over the Nadon appointment reveals the interesting ways that a government's ideological preferences for its appointees interact with the constraints of federalism when making an appointment to the Supreme Court. Ideologically, given the dearth of small-c conservative judges in Canada, Harper sought to appoint individuals who would be reliably deferential to the elected branches of government.[38] Justice Nadon, who had a quiet reputation for both judicial deference and an affinity to conservativism, was seen as a suitable candidate.[39] The fact that the Harper government's shortlist to fill the Quebec vacancy on the Supreme Court was drawn almost entirely from members of the federal courts rather than Quebec's superior courts rankled both Quebec's and Canada's legal elite, as "Federal Court judges had a reputation in some legal circles for being too deferential to government."[40] Yet the opposition to Nadon's appointment also reflected considerations pertaining to federalism. Nadon's appointment was suspicious from the point of view of many in the Quebec legal community and the government of Quebec, which preferred Supreme Court appointees who could act as a check on federal overreach. By preventing the federal government from appointing a federal court judge from Quebec to the Supreme Court, the outcome of the reference thus satisfied decentralizers worried about an overbearing federal judiciary. Moreover, as Thomas Bateman notes, the Supreme Court's opinion constitutionalizing provisions of the *Supreme Court Act* and expanding the scope of amendment procedures in Part V of the *Constitution Act, 1982* also confirmed Russell's famous prediction that the Charter would judicialize politics and politicize the judiciary. The "rigid amending formulae" and the constitutionalization of "so many aspects of Canadian politics" significantly reduced Harper's ability to both "rebalance" the Canadian federation and ideologically reshape the Supreme Court despite a decade in power.[41]

The second episode demonstrating the continued persistence of federalism in judicial selection took place in 2016, when Justin Trudeau's government briefly considered abandoning the long-standing practice of regional allocation of Supreme Court seats. After Justice Thomas Cromwell announced his impending retirement, the government considered appointing an Indigenous judge to sit on the court for the first time, even if it meant not appointing an Atlantic Canadian. Following blowback from opposition MPs and even the threat of a constitutional challenge by Newfoundland and Labrador's law society, the Trudeau government backed down, eventually appointing Malcolm Rowe, a non-Indigenous judge from the Court of Appeal of Newfoundland and Labrador.

The third episode related to the Trudeau government's ongoing insistence on appointing bilingual jurists to the Supreme Court. In 2021, the government announced its intention to formally legislate bilingualism after years of making it a nonlegislated requirement.[42] This proposal, which some consider an unconstitutional amendment to the composition of the Supreme Court, is sure to continue these tensions over region, language, and merit, particularly as some argue it will reduce the pool of qualified western Canadian and Indigenous judges.[43] If recent history is any guide, this issue will likely be headed to the Supreme Court for consideration. The fact that the Supreme Court so often gets the authoritative "final say" – even on issues concerning its own composition – speaks to yet another issue Russell anticipated nearly four decades ago.

The Authoritative Nature of Judicial Decisions

Perhaps the most prominent scholarly post-Charter debate concerns the proper relationship between courts and legislatures. Russell's 1983 article anticipated that the courts, and the Supreme Court in particular, would be the final arbiter of Charter disputes: "[T]he judicial branch will be the most important forum for the systematic application of Charter standards ... Judicial opinions will be authoritative on the specific meanings given to the Charter's general principles" (see Macfarlane, Chapter 2 in this volume).[44] Relatedly, Russell wondered whether the Supreme Court's privileged interpretative position, coupled with increasing legalism, could stifle public debate about controversial matters, about which citizens can disagree, that ought to be in the traditional domain of politics.[45]

Interestingly, although there is strong evidence that the last forty years have vindicated these predictions, Russell himself has since downplayed their significance. In 2009, he acknowledged he had been among the first people to raise concerns about judicial activism but distanced himself from critics of judicial power, whom he felt exaggerated the nature of the threat.[46] He likewise argued that the Charter had not led to a broader "clos[ing] off [of] political debate and discussion," pointing to issues such as abortion, labour relations, and same-sex marriage.[47] While Russell is correct that it is not completely verboten to address these issues in public, there is evidence that Supreme Court Charter decisions on these issues have constrained both legislative disagreement and public discourse, evidence for the latter coming in Emmett Macfarlane's research on the Canadian variant of "rights talk."[48] In terms of the policy issues Russell himself mentions, abortion is rarely discussed without reference to the *Morgentaler* ruling, which struck down criminal prohibitions but left room for some federal restrictions.[49] Likewise, in a few short decades, labour rights transitioned from being legislatively defined to judicially supervised as a direct result of the Charter.[50] Following the court's opinion in the *Same-Sex Marriage Reference,* many, including legal scholars, acted as if the court had addressed the constitutionality of the traditional definition of marriage, even as the court refused to answer the question.[51] One could add the ongoing controversy surrounding the federal government's new assisted-dying law, the discourse surrounding which is dominated by the question "Will the courts accept it?" rather than "Is this good policy?" (see Nicolaides, Chapter 11 in this volume).[52]

While the Charter has not rendered debate on any policy issue truly off-limits, Charter-based judicial decisions do more than simply shape the contours of debate. Symbolically and informally, the court's pronouncements on the Charter are typically treated by the public, the media, and legislators as the final word. While Russell in 2009 was more optimistic about the discourse on judicialized policy issues than he had been in 1983, the "danger" he warned about – that "questions of social and political justice will be transformed into technical legal questions and the great bulk of the citizenry who are not judges and lawyers will abdicate their responsibility for working out reasonable and mutually acceptable resolutions of the issues which divide them" – does seem to have become a reality.[53] Equally telling in this regard is the history and practice of the notwithstanding clause.

The Notwithstanding Clause

One reason Russell was not overly concerned over the "false spectre" of judicial activism was his long-standing defence of the Charter's section 33 notwithstanding clause, which allows Parliament and provincial legislatures to pass laws that operate notwithstanding certain Charter provisions.[54] For Russell, section 33 is an important nod to Canada's political tradition of parliamentary democracy, one of the central pillars animating our governing structure.[55] However, the notwithstanding clause has not been able to withstand the pull of the authoritative nature of judicial decisions. Russell predicted that "[b]ecause of the adverse political consequences that a government would usually risk in using [the notwithstanding clause], I very much doubt that it will be frequently used."[56]

Four decades on, Russell's prediction is mostly accurate, especially considering its nonuse at the federal level. The clause has been used mostly by Quebec, though it has experienced a significant revival at the subnational level in the last few years. Six provincial bills have invoked the clause since 2017, and four have passed. While Tsvi Kahana has shown that the clause was used more than many experts had noticed, it is still rare.[57] Eleni Nicolaides and Dave Snow found the clause has been used only twenty times as of 2020 (excluding re-enactments), the vast majority in Quebec before 2001.[58]

Indeed, until recently, many scholars assumed that the clause had become a dead letter. In 2001, Christopher Manfredi lamented that the clause appeared to be considered a poisoned chalice.[59] Howard Lesson likewise thought the clause would go the way of disallowance and reservation – formally available but effectively unavailable.[60] Richard Albert argued as recently as 2018 that it risks falling into desuetude, at least at the federal level.[61] The infrequent use of the notwithstanding clause is often thought to have been caused by the Quebec government's use of section 33 in response to *Quebec v Ford,* which led many outside of Quebec to view it as toxic.[62] Even scholars who prefer robust legislative responses to judicial rulings view the clause as a largely ineffective vehicle for interinstitutional disagreement.[63] Given the restoration of the clause by several different provincial legislatures, it might be time to reconsider not if the clause can be used but whether some uses are more defensible than others.[64]

Even in light of recent events, Russell's prediction that the use of the notwithstanding clause would be rare and controversial has largely been borne out. However, his most lasting contribution pertaining to the clause has been as one of its most ardent defenders. Russell believes the notwithstanding clause has great democratic value for our constitutional system by allowing elected governments a constitutional mechanism to provide principled disagreement with the courts over rights-based issues.[65] His later work has pointed to specific cases – such as the *Provincial Judges Reference* on judicial salaries and *RJR-Macdonald* on tobacco advertising – that represent precisely the kind of judicial overreach section 33 was supposed to alleviate.[66] Russell's enthusiastic defence of the notwithstanding clause, coupled with his prophetic 1983 prediction about its minimal use, complements his other prediction about the authoritative nature of judicial decisions as the final arbiter for Charter issues – even when many believe the judiciary has erred, as Russell did with the *Judges Reference* and *RJR-Macdonald.*

Discussion and Conclusion

Writing four years after the publication of "The Political Purposes of the Charter," Russell remarked that while the judiciary had been considered to be largely apolitical over the early part of his career, this was no longer the case: "[O]ur political and legal cultures have changed – *somewhat* ... [and] the Charter of Rights and Freedoms has no doubt been a catalyst for this change."[67] The addition of "somewhat" was classic Russell – always measured, never an alarmist when addressing the Charter's impact. What motivated Russell's 1983 essay was a desire to question reductive messaging about the Charter's effects by its chief sponsors – that it would promote national unity and enhance rights protection without adverse effects. Russell knew that Canadian politics was undergirded by long traditions of federalism, Westminster-style legislatures, and a legal culture that already took judicial review and constitutionalism seriously. He recognized that adding a charter of rights would create new tensions among Canada's institutional pillars, some intended, others not.

Russell saw that our integrated and unified judicial structure would make the Supreme Court the principal venue to litigate both national and provincial policies for consistency with a newly agreed-upon set of constitutional values. In so doing, he launched what we now call the "centralization thesis." Subsequent scholarship has demonstrated that the impact of centralization was not as significant as some feared but that there has been some homogenization in areas such as language, abortion, and labour rights. Russell also recognized a corollary of increased centralization, namely, that provincial governments would demand some oversight over federal judicial selection procedures. While requests for constitutional amendments recognizing a provincial role in Supreme Court appointments have diminished since the era of megaconstitutional politics, provincial governments and their legal communities still care deeply about the federal monopoly on the selection of these judges, as the Nadon affair and Justin Trudeau's Supreme Court appointments attest. In recent years, the monopoly of the federal executive has been questioned as well, as the Harper and Trudeau governments adjusted the process for reviewing Supreme Court judges, albeit while maintaining the prime minister's ultimate selection authority.

Russell knew that our pre-1982 acclimatization to judicial review in federalism disputes meant the Supreme Court's pronouncement on Charter issues would be treated authoritatively. He also recognized, as dialogue theorists would subsequently argue, that these authoritative judicial decisions could nevertheless leave substantial room for governments to respond; that while "legal results shape the constitutional capacity of government ... they do not determine how that capacity is used."[68] And while Russell later distanced himself from the harshest critics of judicial power in Canada, his early concern about the transformation of questions of justice to technical legal questions is one that remains relevant today, particularly as fears that bureaucratic "Charter proofing" might take precedence over making good policy during the legislative process. The authoritative role of the judiciary is even more manifest in the last of

Russell's predictions detailed above – the rarity of invocations of the section 33 notwithstanding clause – even as proponents (Russell included!) have made the persuasive case that Canada is better off for having included the clause in the constitutional compromise of 1982.

A short essay like this cannot capture the many other predictions Russell made in 1983. Some, such as his expectation of "periods of both judicial conservatism and judicial liberalism," did not come to fruition.[69] As it turns out, Canadian judges have been less ideologically divided than their American counterparts.[70] Relatedly, Russell predicted it "unlikely that the ideological profile of the judiciary will differ dramatically from that of the countries' dominant political elite."[71] The accuracy of this assertion depends on how one defines Canada's elite, as shown by the Harper Conservatives' interaction with the judiciary. Despite appointing a majority of Supreme Court justices, Harper was unable to appoint reliably deferential ones and presided over a streak of high-profile judicial losses concerning prostitution, safe injection sites, and criminal-justice policy. Macfarlane argues that Harper was unable to pierce the previous bipartisan consensus (or "Charter regime") whose orthodoxy was dominant in the Canadian legal establishment.[72] Perhaps Russell's assumption about elites was half-right. He was incorrect in his belief that Canada's Supreme Court would mirror the American one, where elite ideological diversity is reflected in the judiciary. Yet there is a strong argument to be made that Canada's more ideologically homogenous Supreme Court reflects a "dominant political elite" (and especially legal elite) that could not be broken by a decade of governance critical of the Charter regime. As Bateman writes, Nadon's revoked appointment reflects one battle in a larger challenge by the Harper government to an "ideological consensus that has defined post-Charter Canada," one that some "have long associated ... with the central Canadian law schools of 'Official Canada,' the 'Laurentian consensus,' or the 'Court Party.'"[73] If we consider the Harper Conservatives outsiders to this ideological consensus, Russell's prediction looks accurate indeed.

Russell also expected there would develop "a more systematic review of public policies in terms of the rights and freedoms included in the Charter."[74] This systematic review has occurred, though it has produced yet another unintended consequence of the Charter: the strengthening of the Ministry of Justice, rather than Parliament's Justice Committee, at the expense of other government departments.[75] Finally, Russell's prediction that "the process of judicial review will normally be 'turned on,' so to speak, by individuals and groups, not by governments," certainly presaged the influential role of interest groups in Charter litigation.[76] However, he perhaps understated how governments would use courts for their own ends. Governments have legal expertise as "repeat players," the budgets to play the long game, the power to decide if and when to appeal rulings, and the ability to make strategic use of the reference power.[77] Governments' privileged access and ability to manipulate the judicialization of politics for political benefit has been as much a feature of the last forty years of Charter politics as any other.

In assessing Russell's 1983 predictions about how the Charter would change the way Canada is governed, I have tried to highlight how many novel developments in the post-Charter scholarship reflected his concerns. Because of his familiarity with Canada, the United States, and liberal democratic politics more generally, Russell was unconvinced that the Charter's effects would be limited to mollifying national unity while strengthening rights protection. He knew that the Charter would not lead to a more united country merely by being a "fancy document that hangs on the school-room wall, that is recited in citizenship classes and eulogized in after-dinner speeches."[78] Instead, Russell recognized that adding an entrenched-rights document would have far-reaching political implications beyond the statements made by architects of the Charter, including Pierre Trudeau. His argument flowed from his understanding of how Canada's unique political-institutional environment – combining federalism, parliamentarism, and a robust rule-of-law tradition – would be affected by this new constitutional document.

It is worth remembering the title of Russell's famous article to ask: What are the "political purposes of the Charter"? And were those purposes achieved? Here, it is necessary to return to the Charter's chief architect: Pierre Trudeau. Some scholars refer to Trudeau's statesmanship as Machiavellian.[79] This might sound jarring to those who only associate Machiavelli with political deception or ruthlessness. But Machiavelli also said the most admirable princes were the ones who founded new constitutions that persist long after their demise, and in this sense, the label seems appropriate.[80] Trudeau's 1982 reforms did not end constitutional politics but, over time, the horizons of constitutional conflict have diminished as the rigid constitutional amendment formulae have prevented any major change to the core of his pan-Canadian vision.[81] True, the *Constitution Act, 1982* did not eradicate the nationalist and separatist visions of the Parti Québécois; it is still constitutionally permissible to preserve the French language and even pursue separation. However, the Supreme Court's jurisprudence in the intervening years has preserved the rights of Quebec's anglophone minority while raising the political and legal barriers to exit.[82] In this sense, the purposes of the Charter Russell identified – national unity and rights protection – have, in fact, been strengthened, though in ways Trudeau himself did not anticipate.

Irrespective of whether the political purposes of the Charter have been achieved, much of the post-Charter debate in political science can be traced to

Russell's central insight in 1983: that the Charter would, first and foremost, "judicialize politics and politicize the judiciary." His article has informed debates over activism, interinstitutional dialogue, judicial appointments, the notwithstanding clause, and so much more. Of course, Russell's contributions to Canadian constitutional thought go well beyond that: one of the ironies of Russell's work is that despite being a pioneer of Charter scholarship, he is also one of the first scholars who began to lament the fetishizing of the Charter at the expense of other pressing constitutional matters.[83] His subsequent scholarship has stressed the danger of eroding civic knowledge about parliamentarianism, the lack of concern over the rise of executive dominance, and the incomplete inclusion of Indigenous peoples within the Canadian constitutional order.[84] It is a testament to Russell's breadth that the importance of these topics has since risen. Yet it is also a testament to the depth of Russell's political thought that his prescient assessment of the political purposes of the Charter remains so crucial to understanding Canadian politics today. What will the coming decades of Charter politics bring? I cannot claim to possess Russell's foresight when it comes to predictions, but I offer a few developments worth keeping an eye on. First, the growth and impact of more heterodox legal organizations, such as the Runnymede Society and the Canadian Constitution Foundation, suggests there is an appetite within the Canadian legal community for more debate and litigation in matters concerning rights and constitutionalism. I doubt these efforts will translate into the high degrees of influence associated with the Federalist Society in the American context, but these organizations' activities in and outside courtrooms will be instrumental in bringing additional diversity to Canada's judicialized politics.[85]

The second area of development concerns whether the province of Quebec's renewed use of the notwithstanding clause is just a blip or the beginning of the new normal of constitutional brinksmanship by Quebec. The premiership of François Legault has shown electoral viability through a new approach to soft nationalism. Several commentators have noted the novel and broadly popular way Legault's Coalition Avenir Québec (CAQ) pursues cultural conservatism built around nationalism without pursuing separation, a selective approach to immigration, and a willingness to use section 33 to insulate its policies on religious expression and language rights from Charter challenges.[86] Federal politicians keen on courting Quebec voters to form a government in Ottawa have been reticent in condemning the CAQ government too harshly, particularly with respect to Bill 21, a law invoking section 33 to restrict the use of religious symbols (see Kelly, Chapter 15 in this volume). Russell might remind us that our Constitution produces a tension between the need for consistency for rights protection and our desire to respect federal diversity. Our leaders will need to choose which aspect of the Constitution deserves greater veneration.

As we move into the fifth decade of a post-Charter Canada, we must remember what Russell taught us: while the Charter represents a significant shift in the way Canada is governed, it needs to be appreciated alongside the other pillars of our institutional ecosystem. At root, our rule-of-law tradition and federal character mitigated through parliamentary democratic institutions continue to be as or more important than our Charter of Rights.

Notes

I would like to thank Jeremy Ernest for his research assistance on this project. Thanks also to Dave Snow, the volume's editors, and the anonymous reviewers for their feedback on this chapter. Lastly, I want to thank Peter Russell for continuing to inspire and influence students of the Canadian Constitution.

1   F.L. Morton and Rainer Knopff, *The Charter Revolution and the Court Party* (Peterborough: Broadview Press, 2000); Peter McCormick, *The End of the Charter Revolution: Looking Back from the New Normal* (Toronto: University of Toronto Press, 2014).

2   Peter H. Russell, "The Political Purposes of the Canadian Charter of Rights and Freedoms," *Canadian Bar Review* 61, 1 (1983): 30–54.

3   *Ibid*, 51.

4   Peter H. Russell, "The Political Purposes of the Charter: Have They Been Fulfilled? An Agnostic's Report Card," in *Protecting Rights and Freedoms: Essays on the Charter's Place in Canada's Political, Legal, and Intellectual Life*, ed. Philip Bryden, Steven Davis, and John Russell (Toronto: University of Toronto Press, 1994), 33–44; Peter H. Russell, "The Charter and Canadian Democracy," in *Contested Constitutionalism: Reflections on the Charter of Rights and Freedoms*, ed. James B. Kelly and Christopher P. Manfredi (Vancouver: UBC Press, 2009), 287–306.

5   Alan Cairns, *Disruptions: Constitutional Struggles from the Charter to Meech Lake*, ed. Douglas E. Williams (Toronto: McClelland and Stewart, 1991), 97; Patrick Malcolmson, Richard Myers, Gerald Baier, and Thomas M.J. Bateman, *The Canadian Regime: An Introduction to Parliamentary Government in Canada*, 6th ed. (Toronto: University of Toronto Press, 2016), xii.

6   Jeremy Clarke, "Beyond the Democratic Dialogue, and towards a Federalist One: Provincial Arguments and Supreme Court Responses in Charter Litigation," *Canadian Journal of Political Science* 39, 2 (2006): 294.

7   Peter H. Russell, *The Judiciary in Canada: The Third Branch of Government* (Toronto: McGraw-Hill, 1987), 47; Peter H. Russell, "The Supreme Court and Federal-Provincial Relations: The Political Use of Legal Resources," *Canadian Public Policy* 11, 2 (1985): 162.

8   James Ceaser, *Liberal Democracy and Political Science* (Baltimore, MD: Johns Hopkins University Press, 1990), ch. 3; B. Guy Peters, *Institutional Theory in Political Science: The "New Institutionalism"* (New York: Continuum, 2005), 6–10.

9   Russell, *The Judiciary in Canada*, xiii. Russell appears to have undergone an evolution in his thinking on this broad question. Early in his career, he was skeptical of the benefits of a judicially enforced rights document, and he preferred democratic means for deciding civil liberties: see Peter H. Russell, "A Democratic Approach to Civil Liberties," *University*

of Toronto Law Journal 19, 2 (1969): 109–31. In contrast, his recent work is more sympathetic to rights-based constitutionalism, particularly with respect to the legal victories won by Indigenous peoples: see Peter H. Russell, *Canada's Odyssey: A Country Based on Incomplete Conquests* (Toronto: University of Toronto Press, 2017), 390, 434–38.

10 Russell, "Political Purposes of the Charter," 46.

11 *Ibid*, 44.

12 *Ibid*, 41; *McKinney v University of Guelph*, [1990] 3 SCR 229; *Vriend v Alberta*, [1998] 1 SCR 493.

13 Russell, "Political Purposes of the Charter," 32.

14 *Ibid*, 33, 36.

15 *Ibid*, 40.

16 *Ibid*, 42.

17 *Ibid*, 41.

18 Emmett Macfarlane, "Terms of Entitlement: Is There a Distinctly Canadian 'Rights Talk'?," *Canadian Journal of Political Science* 41, 2 (2008): 303–28.

19 Russell, "Political Purposes of the Charter," 42.

20 Dave Snow and Mark S. Harding, "From Normative Debates to Comparative Methodology: The Three Waves of Post-Charter Supreme Court Scholarship in Canada," *American Review of Canadian Studies* 45, 4 (2015): 453.

21 Douglas Brown, Herman Bakvis, and Gerald Baier, *Contested Federalism: Certainty and Ambiguity in the Canadian Federation* (Don Mills, ON: Oxford University Press, 2019), 78–79.

22 F.L. Morton, "The Effect of the Charter of Rights on Canadian Federalism," *Publius: The Journal of Federalism* 25, 3 (1995): 173–88.

23 F.L. Morton and Dave Snow, "Interest Groups and Access to Judicial Power," in *Law, Politics, and Judicial Process in Canada*, ed. F.L. Morton and Dave Snow, 4th ed. (Calgary: University of Calgary Press, 2018), 252 (emphasis in original).

24 Russell, "An Agnostic's Report Card," 37–38; Rainer Knopff and F.L. Morton, "Nation Building and the Charter," in *Constitutionalism Citizenship and Society in Canada*, ed. Alan Cairns and Cynthia Williams (Toronto: University of Toronto Press, 1985), 133–82; Alan Cairns, *The Charter versus Federalism: The Dilemmas of Constitutional Reform* (Montreal/Kingston: McGill-Queen's University Press, 1992).

25 Morton, "The Effect of the Charter of Rights," 174–77.

26 James B. Kelly, "Reconciling Rights and Federalism during Review of the Charter of Rights and Freedoms: The Supreme Court of Canada and the Centralization Thesis, 1982–1999," *Canadian Journal of Political Science* 34, 2 (2001): 321–55.

27 Clarke, "Beyond the Democratic Dialogue," 305.

28 Brown, Bakvis, and Baier, *Contested Federalism*, 78–79.

29 Troy Q. Riddell, "Explaining the Impact of Legal Mobilization and Judicial Decisions: Official Minority Language Education Rights outside Quebec," in *Contested Constitutionalism: Reflections on the Charter of Rights and Freedoms*, ed. James B. Kelly and Christopher P. Manfredi (Vancouver: UBC Press, 2009), 187–208; Stéphanie Chouinard, "Section 23 of the Charter and Official-Language Minority Instruction in Canada: The Judiciary's Impact and Limits in Education Policymaking," in *Policy Change, Courts, and the Canadian Constitution*, ed. Emmett Macfarlane (Toronto: University of Toronto Press, 2018), 230–49.

30 Russell, "Political Purposes of the Charter," 42–43.

31 Peter H. Russell, "The Supreme Court Proposals in the Meech Lake Accord," *Canadian Public Policy* 14 (1988): 93–99. Once Quebec's demands were "provincialized" and essentially extended to the other provinces, the federal government would have been

expected to consult lists of candidates to fill vacancies on the Supreme Court sent from the provincial governments.

32 Morton, "The Effect of the Charter of Rights," 184.

33 In terms of provincial representation, these committees included the chief justice of the province under consideration, the provincial attorney general, and members from the provincial law society and Canadian Bar Association.

34 Peter H. Russell and Kate Malleson, *Appointing Judges in an Age of Judicial Power: Critical Perspectives from around the World* (Toronto: University of Toronto Press, 2006); Peter H. Russell, "Reform's Judicial Agenda," *IRPP Policy Options* 20, 3 (1999): 12–14.

35 The Martin government struck a committee consisting of MPs, members of the law society from the province under consideration, a former judge, and two individuals selected by the minister of justice from the province.

36 For a detailed account, see Morton and Snow, *Law, Politics and the Judicial Process*, 117–37.

37 *Reference re Supreme Court Act, ss 5 and 6,* [2014] 1 SCR 433.

38 Emmett Macfarlane, "Much Ado about Little," *Policy Options,* October 15, 2015, https://policyoptions.irpp.org/fr/magazines/october-2015/stephen-harper-and-the-judiciary/much-ado-about-little.

39 Sean Fine, "Doctrine Is 'Everything' for Marc Nadon, the Outspoken Conservative Justice Rejected by Canada's Supreme Court," *Globe and Mail,* October 2, 2019, https://www.theglobeandmail.com/canada/article-marc-nadon-supreme-court-canada-runnymede-society.

40 Carissima Mathen and Michael Plaxton, *The Tenth Justice: Judicial Appointments, Marc Nadon, and the Supreme Court Act Reference* (Vancouver: UBC Press, 2020), 133.

41 Thomas M.J. Bateman, "The Other Shoe to Drop: Marc Nadon and Judicial Appointment Politics in Post-Charter Canada," *Journal of Parliamentary and Political Law* 9, 1 (2015): 187.

42 Government of Canada, "English and French: Towards a Substantive Equality of Official Languages in Canada," February 19, 2021, https://www.canada.ca/en/canadian-heritage/corporate/publications/general-publications/equality-official-languages.html.

43 Gerard Kennedy, "The Trudeau Liberals Go around Attorney General Again, This Time over Bilingualism," *National Post,* February 24, 2021, https://nationalpost.com/opinion/gerard-kennedy-trudeau-liberals-go-around-attorney-general-again-this-time-over-bilingualism.

44 Russell, "Political Purposes of the Charter," 47.

45 *Ibid,* 52.

46 Russell identified four reasons he was not overly concerned with the Charter's impacts: (1) the notwithstanding clause provides a backstop, (2) the Charter is popular with Canadians, (3) police forces rather than legislatures are more affected because of the Charter's new legal guarantees, and (4) the judiciary is balanced in its interpretation of the Charter. See Russell, "The Charter and Canadian Democracy," 294–96.

47 *Ibid,* 288.

48 Macfarlane, "Terms of Entitlement."

49 *R v Morgentaler,* [1988] 1 SCR 30.

50 Mark S. Harding and Rainer Knopff, "Constitutionalizing Everything: The Role of 'Charter Values,'" *Review of Constitutional Studies* 18, 2 (2013): 141–60.

51 *Reference re Same-Sex Marriage,* [2004] 3 SCR 698; Matthew Hennigar, "*Reference re Same-Sex Marriage:* Making Sense of the Government's Litigation Strategy," in *Contested Constitutionalism: Reflections on the Charter of Rights and Freedoms,* ed. James B. Kelly and Christopher P. Manfredi (Vancouver: UBC Press, 2009), 209–30; Kate Puddister,

"A Question They Can't Refuse? The Canadian Reference Power and Refusing to Answer Reference Questions," *Canadian Political Science Review* 13, 1 (2020): 34–53.

52 Colby Cosh, "What's the Point of Parliament If Judges Overrule Laws Using Personal Guesswork?," *National Post*, February 4, 2021, https://nationalpost.com/opinion/colby-cosh-whats-the-point-of-parliament-if-judges-overrule-laws-using-personal-guesswork.

53 Russell, "Political Purposes of the Charter," 52.

54 Russell, "The Charter and Canadian Democracy," 294.

55 Peter H. Russell, "The Notwithstanding Clause: The Charter's Homage to Parliamentary Democracy," *Policy Options*, February 2007, http://irpp.org/wp-content/uploads/assets/po/the-charter-25/russell.pdf.

56 Russell, "Political Purposes of the Charter," 41.

57 Tsvi Kahana, "The Notwithstanding Mechanism and Public Discussion: Lessons from the Ignored Practice of Section 33 of the Charter," *Canadian Public Administration* 44, 3 (2001): 255–91.

58 Eleni Nicolaides and Dave Snow, "A Paper Tiger No More? The Media Portrayal of the Notwithstanding Clause in Saskatchewan and Ontario," *Canadian Journal of Political Science* 54, 1 (2021): 63. This figure includes Quebec's omnibus use of the clause as a single use and excludes instances where a bill never received royal assent. However, this figure does not include the Ontario government's 2021 use of the notwithstanding clause in response to a lower court decision restricting campaign finance rules. It also does not include the Quebec government's 2022 use of s 33 as part of strengthening its language laws in Bill 96.

59 Christopher P. Manfredi, *Judicial Power and the Charter: Canada and the Paradox of Liberal Constitutionalism*, 2nd ed. (Oxford: Oxford University, 2001).

60 Howard Leeson, "Section 33, the Notwithstanding Clause: A Paper Tiger?," *IRPP Choices* 6 (2000): 1–24.

61 Richard Albert, "The Desuetude of the Notwithstanding Clause," in *Policy Change, Courts, and the Canadian Constitution*, ed. Emmett Macfarlane (Toronto: University of Toronto Press, 2018), 146–65.

62 *Ford v Quebec (AG)*, [1988] 2 SCR 721; Dave Snow, "Notwithstanding the Override: Path Dependence, Section 33, and the Charter," *Innovations: A Journal of Politics* 8, 1 (2009): 1–15.

63 Dennis Baker, *Not Quite Supreme: The Courts and Coordinate Constitutional Interpretation* (Montreal/Kingston: McGill-Queen's University Press, 2010), 116; Rainer Knopff, Rhonda Evans, Dennis Baker, and Dave Snow, "Dialogue: Clarified and Reconsidered," *Osgoode Hall Law Journal* 54, 2 (2017): 625–26.

64 Mark Mancini and Geoffrey Sigalet, "What Constitutes a Legitimate Use of the Notwithstanding Clause?," *Policy Options*, January 20, 2020, https://policyoptions.irpp.org/magazines/january-2020/what-constitutes-the-legitimate-use-of-the-notwithstanding-clause/.

65 Peter H. Russell, "Standing Up for Notwithstanding," *Alberta Law Review* 29, 2 (1991): 293–309; Russell, "The Notwithstanding Clause."

66 *Reference re Remuneration of Judges of the Provincial Court (PEI)*, [1997] 3 SCR 3; *RJR-MacDonald Inc v Canada (AG)*, [1995] 3 SCR 199.

67 Russell, *The Judiciary in Canada*, xiii (emphasis added).

68 Peter W. Hogg, Allison A. Thornton, and W.K Wright, "Charter Dialogue Revisited: Or 'Much Ado about Metaphors,'" *Osgoode Hall Law Journal* 45, 1 (2007): 1–65; Russell, "The Supreme Court and Federal-Provincial Relations," 162.

69 Russell, "Political Purposes of the Charter," 49.

70 Some scholars have shown that the Canadian Supreme Court judges' voting behaviour is ideological but also more nuanced than in the American context. See Cynthia L. Ostberg

and Matthew E. Wetstein, *Attitudinal Decision Making in the Supreme Court of Canada* (Vancouver: UBC Press, 2007), 4, 7, 14, 209.

71 Russell, "Political Purposes of the Charter," 49.

72 Emmett Macfarlane, "'You Can't Always Get What You Want': Regime Politics, the Supreme Court of Canada, and the Harper Government," *Canadian Journal of Political Science* 51, 1 (2018): 1–21.

73 Bateman, "Other Shoe to Drop," 186.

74 Russell, "Political Purposes of the Charter," 46.

75 Janet Hiebert, *Charter Conflicts: What Is Parliament's Role?* (Montreal/Kingston: McGill-Queen's University Press, 2002), 9, 16–17; James B. Kelly, *Governing with the Charter: Legislative and Judicial Activism and Framers' Intent* (Vancouver: UBC Press, 2005).

76 Russell, "Political Purposes of the Charter," 47; Morton and Knopff, *The Charter Revolution and the Court Party*; Gregory Hein, "Interest Group Litigation and Canadian Democracy," in *Judicial Power and Canadian Democracy*, ed. Paul Howe and Peter H. Russell (Montreal/Kingston: McGill-Queen's University Press, 2001), 214–54; Christopher P. Manfredi, *Feminist Activism in the Supreme Court: Legal Mobilization and the Women's Legal Education and Action Fund* (Vancouver: UBC Press, 2004).

77 Troy Q. Riddell and F.L. Morton, "Government Use of Strategic Litigation: The Alberta Exported Gas Tax Reference," *American Review of Canadian Studies* 34, 3 (2004): 485–509; Hennigar, "*Reference re Same-Sex Marriage*"; Vuk Radmilovic, "Governmental Interventions and Judicial Decision Making: The Supreme Court of Canada in the Age of the Charter," *Canadian Journal of Political Science* 46, 2 (2013): 323–44; Kate Puddister, *Seeking the Court's Advice: The Politics of the Canadian Reference Power* (Vancouver: UBC Press, 2019).

78 Russell, "Political Purposes of the Charter," 36.

79 Bateman, "Other Shoe to Drop," 187; Guy Laforest, *Trudeau and the End of a Canadian Dream* (Montreal/Kingston: McGill-Queen's University Press, 1995).

80 Niccolò Machiavelli, *The Prince*, 2nd ed., trans. Harvey C. Mansfield (Chicago: University of Chicago Press, 1998), ch. 6, 24–25: "But once they have overcome them and they begin to be held in veneration, having eliminated those who had envied them for their quality, they remain powerful, secure [and] honored."

81 For a description of the amendments since 1982, see Emmett Macfarlane, "Introduction – Striking a Balance: The Players and Procedures of Canada's Constitutional Amending Formula," in *Constitutional Amendment in Canada*, ed. Emmett Macfarlane (Toronto: University of Toronto Press, 2016), 9.

82 James B. Kelly, "The Charter of the French Language and the Supreme Court: Assessing Whether Constitutional Design Can Influence Policy Outcomes," in *Policy Change, Courts, and the Canadian Constitution*, ed. Emmett Macfarlane (Toronto: University of Toronto Press, 2018), 250–68; *Reference re Secession of Quebec*, [1998] 2 SCR 217.

83 Russell, "An Agnostic's Report Card," 42.

84 Peter H. Russell, *Two Cheers for Minority Government: The Evolution of Canadian Parliamentary Democracy* (Toronto: Emond, 2008); Russell, "The Charter and Canadian Democracy," 297–98; Russell, *Canada's Odyssey*.

85 Steven Teles, *The Rise of the Conservative Legal Movement: The Battle for Control of the Law* (Princeton, NJ: Princeton University Press, 2008).

86 Sean Speer, "What François Legault's Popularity Says about Quebec Conservativism," *National Post*, April 5, 2021, https://nationalpost.com/opinion/sean-speer-what-francois -legaults-popularity-says-about-quebec-conservatism; Ben Woodfinden, "Québec and the Conservative Party," *The Dominion*, August 25, 2020, https://thedominion.substack. com/p/qubec-and-the-conservative-party.

2
Revisiting Judicial Activism

Emmett Macfarlane

THE ENTRENCHMENT OF the *Charter of Rights and Freedoms* in 1982 sparked a new, intensified focus on judicial power and the role of courts. Many of these debates were framed by judicial activism. Judicial activism is one of the most frequently employed concepts in the study of courts and constitutionalism. It is also one of the most regularly derided, widely described as elusive if not substantively vacuous, a veritable Rorschach test for how the person applying it happens to view the broader enterprise of judicial review, a particular judicial decision, or even a specific judge. It is used in both descriptive (empirical) and value-laden (normative) contexts.

In North America alone, the term "judicial activism" appears each year in hundreds of journal articles and hundreds more media stories and op-eds.[1] It has entered the scholarly ether in application to countries such as India, Israel, South Korea, and Ireland.[2] Many invoke it without defining it. Judicial activism stands as an important concept precisely because if it did not exist, we would need to come up with a term to describe courts or judicial behaviour reflecting the zealous exercise of power or decisions that exceed the appropriate boundaries of the judicial role. The first of these reflects the most popular empirical definition of judicial activism, the latter the normative dimensions. Both, I argue, are ultimately crucial to any meaningful application of the concept.

It is tempting to survey the cacophony of different uses and definitions proffered in the vast law and politics literatures and conclude from this complexity, as some have, that we should simply abandon the concept. I argue that this would be a mistake.

Scholars conceptualizing judicial activism have become stuck on the unfortunate desire to develop a measure or definition that will definitively identify the full universe of activist cases and distinguish them from those that are not. This is an exercise in futility. Judicial activism is an empirical phenomenon, but it can only be assessed in relation to the normative expectations we hold about the proper role of courts. This is where the concept's utility becomes clear: it forces us to think about the various factors that inform the appropriate boundaries of judicial review and the political nature of judicial decision making. We should abandon the notion that it is possible to conceptualize judicial activism in a way that prevents all disagreement over specific cases.

Yet it is not enough to simply call on people employing the concept to be specific about their own definition and leave it at that. Some uses of the term are unproductive or unhelpful, often because we are already armed with more precise, distinct concepts for the ascribed behaviour or because they offer understandings so vague as to be unmeasurable or entirely subjective. In what follows, I appraise the many different conceptions of judicial activism invoked in the academic literature. I then briefly review some of the key measurement and normative debates. I conclude with an examination of the ways judicial activism has manifested in the Canadian context since the entrenchment of the *Constitution Act, 1982*. I argue it is most apt to consider judicial activism as measured against the role-normative conceptions we have of the judiciary. This means assessing judicial activism in light of the courts' willingness to exercise judicial review and the nature of those uses in relation to the boundaries of the courts' role and the extent to which political discretion animates specific decisions.

Conceptualizing Judicial Activism

A survey of the literature identifies at least twenty-seven distinct understandings of judicial activism:

- developing or changing legal principles (i.e., "making law")[3]
- exercising judicial review to effect or block policy change by the elected branches (often juxtaposed against restraint or deference)[4]
- results-oriented policy change or the imposition of judicial policy preferences based on the judges' ideological beliefs[5]
- liberal decisions[6]
- *illegitimate* court-driven change beyond the proper role of courts or a violation of the separation of powers[7]
- changes in precedent or doctrine[8]
- decisions contrary to the constitutional text or intent of the framers[9]
- changes to the substance of a law rather than the preservation of democratic political processes[10]
- remedial activism or the degree of policy prescriptiveness[11]
- a desirable activity reflected in enforcing the Constitution, or the belief that judges are well suited to settling important constitutional questions[12]
- "threshold activism," such as liberalizing rules related to standing, justiciability, or entertaining purely political questions[13]
- the use of activist rhetoric, including bold proclamations[14]
- extensive or unnecessary use of obiter[15]
- the use of comparative or international sources in judicial decisions[16]

- scope; that is, maximalist versus minimalist decision making[17]
- difficult decisions made on the basis of absent, incomplete, or complex rules[18]
- decisions that spark a negative legislative reaction, such as legislation to undo or override the decision[19]
- decisions that spark a negative administrative reaction, such as noncompliance[20]
- decisions sparking a negative judicial reaction, such as subsequent decisions to overturn[21]
- decisions that spark a negative public reaction[22]
- pronouncing on values as opposed to the law[23]
- an abdication of responsibility (the idea that deference is also "activist")[24]
- the failure of judges to recuse themselves when appropriate[25]
- illogical or flawed reasoning (judicial error)[26]
- an "empty political epithet" (instances where the concept is employed when someone simply does not like the outcome)[27]
- the use of rights as trumps (insensitivity to limits on rights or other social interests)[28]
- a court is divided rather than unanimous.[29]

Some of these conceptualizations should be dismissed as either unhelpful or distinct from judicial activism because they are better classified by other terminology. For example, a judge's questionable refusal to recuse is better understood as an ethical issue rather than as an act of activism per se.

Many of the other definitions offered may not be "activist" at all, depending on the circumstances. Judges changing legal principles is arguably a natural part of the role of courts, especially in the common law tradition. The same thing should be said about judges struggling with difficult or complex cases; in fact, it is arguably the "hard cases" that necessitate the existence of final appellate courts. The substance versus process distinction is also unhelpful in the context of constitutions that have substantive rights clauses, as the Canadian Charter does. Whether a decision is unanimous or rendered by a narrow majority tells us nothing about its substance or impact. And it is unclear why judicial citation of comparative sources is necessarily activist.

Overturning precedent may or may not be activist; indeed, perhaps it was the original precedent that was unduly activist.[30] The use of lofty rhetoric or extensive obiter could be done in the name of restraint or the court not exceeding its proper role.[31] The presence of these factors cannot *on their own* be evidence of activism; only a contextual assessment of each case can inform us, as I explore below.

Similarly, flawed, illogical, or erroneous decisions are not necessarily activist. As Craig Green writes, "[A]djudicative flaws are too diverse and idiosyncratic to merit a generalized heading like 'activism' ... Some mistakes result from judicial incompetence, for example, and it is clear that incompetents are only sometimes activists."[32] Nor can decisions be assessed solely on whether one finds an outcome desirable, which is distinct from a question of activism. Judicial activism thus necessarily involves the *nature* of the decision making rather than the normative desirability of the outcome.

Nor should deference, or the "abdication" of the judicial role, be conflated with activism. Although the dominant "activism versus restraint" understanding may be simplistic, it has the virtue of recognizing that the activism concept is fundamentally situated in the context of unelected judges employing the power to invalidate the actions of the democratic branches of government.

Nor should our identification of activist decisions rely too heavily on the reactions of other actors. It is certainly true that public opinion may serve as a diffuse constraint on judicial discretion. Judges are keenly aware that the legitimacy of the courts relies on public acceptance, and so a court that released a *Brown v Board of Education*-style decision every week would see its status dwindle abruptly.[33] But public opinion about a specific decision tells us little about the legal or even democratic propriety of that decision, especially in the rights context where there is some expectation that defending minority and unpopular interests is, in principle, an accepted component of the courts' role.

Similarly, legislative or administrative resistance to a decision tells us little about the appropriateness of a given judicial decision. Moreover, in many instances, the legislature may not be able to respond at all, and a decision that exceeds the appropriate bounds of judicial reasoning "deserves criticism as 'activist' even though it retains full operative force."[34] On the other hand, some commentators point to the much-vaunted notion of Charter "dialogue" to suggest that a debate over activism has less utility for Canada.[35] This is a well-worn debate, and I have written elsewhere that the evidence suggests that dialogue is much less common than its proponents suggest and that even when legislatures successfully respond to judicial decisions in a manner that departs from their strict policy prescriptions, those subsequent efforts are often struck down.[36] Lower court judgments invalidating recent legislative responses in the context of medical aid in dying and sex work laws only provide further evidence that courts tend to retain the final word (perhaps it is dialogue that should be discarded as an unhelpful concept).[37]

Other factors may facilitate judicial activism but should not be mistaken for activism itself. For example, the breadth of a decision, one of maximalist rather than minimalist scope, may exacerbate the impact of an activist decision to the extent it applies to a broader array of contexts than it otherwise would. Scope might thus be an important factor in our normative judgment of a court's activity. Similarly, threshold activism that expands the rules of standing or justiciability may broaden the issues upon which a court can have an impact, but depending on the legitimacy of those doctrinal changes, they may or may not be activist in and of themselves. Remedial activism – the exercise of specific policy pronouncements or discretion over the imposition of remedies – may also enhance the activist nature of a decision, but in some contexts, it might be framed as restraint. The Supreme Court's use of suspended declarations of invalidity, for example, is purportedly used to give legislatures more time to develop policy responses to Charter decisions.[38]

One popular conception of judicial activism relates to interpretive fidelity, or decisions that allegedly deviate from the constitutional text or framer's intent. A focus on this factor risks replicating debates over preferred theories of interpretation, which makes identifying activism exceedingly difficult. Judicial creativity must indeed have limits, and there are cases where an assessment of activism must account for decisions that seem to violate widely accepted standards of interpretation. One such example, which I discuss below, is instances of "judicial amendment" of the Constitution, when judges make decisions that depart so significantly from ordinary constitutional interpretation that they effectively add to, remove from, or alter existing constitutional provisions when recourse to the constitutional amending formula should have been required. These instances, however, are relatively rare, and scholars should be cautious about muddling interpretive disagreements into debates about activism.

We are left with a handful of definitions, which happen to be the most frequently cited in the extant literature. The first, advanced most often by political scientists, equates judicial activism with the exercise of judicial review powers, especially decisions that invalidate statutes or block government policies. Canadian studies have employed this definition, drawing often on Peter Russell's description of activism as "the willingness of courts to impose constitutional limits on government action."[39] These studies have found that government losses account for approximately one-third of Charter cases decided by the Supreme Court.[40] The second is the notion that judicial activism is primarily about "results-oriented" reasoning and that judges impose their personal policy preferences – usually presented as a contest between ideological liberals and conservatives – when they engage in judicial review. The third and final definition is that judicial activism is embodied by decisions in which a court has somehow gone beyond the boundaries of its proper role.

Debating the Core of Judicial Activism

Deriving government loss rates in cases where courts exercise judicial review is a popular measure of judicial activism at least in part because it is easily quantifiable. Yet the basic figures tell us little about the nature of the laws or policies at stake or the reasonableness of the court's decisions. Without added contextual detail, it is difficult to assess whether a one-third government loss rate reflects a relatively restrained or a relatively activist court. The question becomes, relative to what?

The problem is apparent when one turns to how the results of such studies are interpreted. One pair of legal scholars arrive at a 37.6 percent government loss rate in Charter cases before the Supreme Court and conclude their analysis by noting that the "question should no longer be merely whether judicial activism is good, but also whether judicial activism is real."[41] It is a mystifying conclusion given that the figure, to many ears, sounds like quite a lot of judicial activity!

Perhaps the simple quantitative measure at least provides a sense of whether the court is more or less active over time. Yet even that depends on the nature of the cases coming before it – perhaps some governments pass riskier policies. There is also the problem that simple counts do not tell us much about the importance of certain cases. Scholars conducting these studies also acknowledge that judicial reasons are more important than outcomes.[42] Others note that most of the court's activity under the Charter has been in relation to executive action such as scrutinizing police powers, something that is plainly less of an affront to democratic principles than invalidating statutes passed by the legislative branch.[43] Moreover, most of the time the court does invalidate legislation, it does so in relation to laws that may or may not be supported by the current governing coalition (and, in many cases, to laws that were passed prior to the entrenchment of the Charter itself).[44]

Defenders of the courts, who rightly see the charge of judicial activism as often implying impropriety or at least judicial overreach, point out that it is a myth that judges can simply avoid deciding Charter cases.[45] Others assert that the real activism lies in a conservative desire for deference.[46] The judges themselves have reminded us that they did not volunteer so much as had the responsibility of judicial review of rights thrust upon them.[47] This latter point is quite true but also beside the point. The issue is not whether courts exercise power, but how they exercise it.

The most significant issue with simple quantitative measures is that they strip the concept of judicial activism of its normative significance. Outside of political science, "judicial activism" is most commonly employed to refer to the political or "undue" nature of certain decisions. If the social science literature refuses to engage with the term as it is most commonly invoked, its exercises in measurement ultimately have little meaningful utility. As Caprice Roberts writes, "[A]llegations of judicial activism are inescapably normative because they presuppose claims about how judges should behave. In the end, efforts to quantify judicial activism either draw on insufficiently acknowledged and contestable evaluative judgments or lose all connection to the phenomenon they purport to analyze."[48] Political scientists employing a quantitative measure defend it as "preferable to one that requires qualitative judgments between 'due' and 'undue' judicial incursions into public policy"[49] but the same authors admit that the "real disputes in the literature are about whether the Supreme Court has been *too* active and/or exercises its activism outside the parameters of its constitutional authority."[50]

It seems clear that qualitative judgment is unavoidable in the context of conceptualizing judicial activism. We thus need an added element to our understanding of judicial activism. Could it be ideologically driven or results-oriented reasoning? The first response to this conception from defenders of the judiciary is to deny that such a thing happens. Former chief justice Beverley McLachlin writes that the "spectre of agenda-driven judging is, to the best of my knowledge, just that – a spectre. If established, it would be a terrible thing and could not be tolerated. But it is not established."[51] Such denials ring hollow in the face of the empirical turn in the study of judicial behaviour in Canada in the last fifteen years.[52] There is considerable evidence demonstrating the impact of ideology on judging, especially in the context of constitutional law.[53] It is certainly true that courts tend to be passive recipients of litigation and, thus, do not enjoy full discretion to set a particular policy agenda and pursue it. But we are also well past stubborn resistance to legal realism in Canada. Most legal scholars and even judges acknowledge that judges' innate sense of justice or policy beliefs cannot be completely separated from their work. Some judges publicly embrace the idea. Recently retired justice Rosalie Abella tells us that the Supreme Court is properly understood as "the final adjudicator of which contested values in a society should triumph."[54]

It is now commonplace among legal commentators to recognize specific judges as "conservative" in criminal law cases or "liberal" in equality-rights cases. Indeed, this helps illuminate why there are both left-wing and right-wing critics of judicial activism. Defenders of judicial review point out an alleged irony that left-wing critics are concerned about decisions that favour corporations or the wealthy while conservative critics lament the influence of a progressive elite on social issues.[55] Yet it is no irony if both sides can point to different cases where such political preferences are at play.

Kent Roach argues, correctly in my view, that it is a myth to portray judicial discretion as virtually unlimited, as the most vociferous critics wielding the concept of judicial activism do. In *Governing from the Bench,* I note that most claims about judicial activism made during the first few decades of the Charter were made without a sufficient understanding of how the Supreme Court operates. My analysis of the court, drawn from interviews with not only judges but also their law clerks and an analysis of cases and other sources, concludes that, first, as critics of the court's role under the Charter contend, the court's decision making is fundamentally political, not only because it is enmeshed in substantive policy issues but also because the justices have substantial discretion in settling the issues that come before them. Second, and on the other side, decision making on the court is distinct in form and substance because the justices are bound by a host of procedural and legal rules and by a set of role-related norms and conventions that constrain and shape the extent to which their decisions are merely representations of their personal policy preferences."[56]

It is therefore not enough to simply refer to "political" decisions by the courts as "activist": the political elements of such decisions are inescapable, especially in the context of judicial review of broadly worded rights provisions. The key question for the results-oriented conception of judicial activism is, At what point does the discretion enjoyed by judges permit personal ideologies to override distinct aspects of the judicial role? We thus need to turn to a role-centric account of judicial activism that identifies when a court is guilty of overreach or of substituting its own policy preferences for those of representative institutions.

A Role-Based Understanding of Judicial Activism

What does a role-centric understanding of judicial activism entail? In some instances, it may be possible to apply relatively objective benchmarks for assessing when the judiciary exceeds its proper role. One such benchmark might include decisions that amount to judicial amendment of the Constitution. Elsewhere, I have defined judicial amendment as "a judicial decision that effectively adds to, removes from, or modifies the constitution in a manner that is inconsistent with, or not plausibly contemplated by, the text in its original or modern meaning, the intent or purposes of the relevant provisions, and the expectations of the broader political community as to what the constitution contains."[57] The key benchmark indicating a court has exceeded the proper boundaries of judicial review in cases of judicial amendment is the effective usurpation of amending authority from those actors designated in the amending formula.

One example of judicial amendment is the Supreme Court's creation of a duty to negotiate in *Reference re Secession of Quebec.*[58] Neither the text nor the purpose of the amending formula – which is a comprehensive code for amendments to the Constitution – contemplates such a duty, and in creating it, the court exceeded the scope of issues before it in the reference itself, which concerned the constitutionality of a unilateral declaration of secession by a province. It thus stands as an example of judicial activism in the sense of the court exceeding its proper authority.

The court can also exceed the proper boundaries of judicial review even when it does not amend the Constitution per se but adopts an overly expansionist or extratextual interpretation of the Charter to prescribe specific policy change. In the 1997 judicial salaries reference, the court imposed a process involving independent commissions for legislative determinations of judicial salaries.[59] The dissenting opinion by Justice Gérard La Forest correctly expresses deep concern with how the majority relied in part on the preamble to the *Constitution Act, 1867,* to apply the unwritten principle of judicial independence and also ignored the relatively narrow context under which section 11(d) of the Charter applies. Adding to this, La Forest notes, "I am all the more troubled since the question involves the proper relationship between the political branches of government and the judicial branch, an issue on which judges can hardly be seen to be indifferent, especially as it concerns their own remuneration."[60]

Even the courts' fiercest defenders acknowledge that these cases reflect judicial activism, although they defend the decisions themselves because the court has "left room" for political actors or for Parliament to fill in the details on the obligations imposed.[61] This underscores that identifying activism is distinct from how we might judge certain outcomes.

Another example of courts exceeding their proper role is when they intrude on matters that are best left resolved by other decision makers. One such area would be the recognition or application of constitutional conventions[62] (Adam Dodek describes the distinction between recognition and enforcement as "artificial and untenable").[63] The "bold statescraft, questionable jurisprudence" of the *Patriation Reference* that helped get us the *Constitution Act, 1982* is the pre-eminent marker of the "constitutional dangers" of judicial recognition of conventions.[64] In that reference, the court's majority recognized a convention requiring a "substantial degree of provincial consent" before major amendments to the Constitution could proceed. Peter Hogg accuses the court of "acting outside its legal function and attempting to facilitate a political outcome. Indeed, the only justification for even considering the convention question would be to influence the political outcome."[65] Dodek warns that there "already have been and there will continue to be attempts to use this aspect of the *Patriation Reference* to manipulate the courts into influencing a particular political outcome."[66]

A failed legal challenge asserting that federal fixed-date election legislation created a binding convention preventing prime ministers from calling snap elections is perhaps the most notable recent example of an attempt to get courts to enforce conventions and was, fortunately, rebuffed.[67] Yet reasons for concern persist, including the Supreme Court of the United Kingdom's recent decision limiting the power of royal prerogative to prorogue Parliament.[68] The justiciability of a request for prorogation is highly questionable, and given that Canada has had its own contemporary controversies around prorogations, the temptation for judicial interference will be real. Whatever the propriety of judicial involvement in this area, such a decision would be undeniably activist. The governor general is the appropriate person to determine whether a particular request should be heeded. Moreover, politics is the appropriate venue for the resolution of any controversies surrounding prorogation, as Canada's experience in the 2008 prorogation affair ably demonstrated.[69]

The examples thus far might suggest that truly activist decisions are generally rare. Yet activism is not limited to intrusions on readily identifiable benchmarks such as the constitutional amending authority or political matters of convention and prerogative. Some of the boundaries surrounding judicial review are hinted at in the lengthy list of definitions of activism described in the preceding sections. I have argued that courts overturning precedent, engaging in lofty rhetoric, or developing law in a manner that does not flow directly from the constitutional text are not *necessarily* instances of activism. None of those indicators should be employed as a simplistic proxy for the concept. Yet a contextual analysis of cases that incorporate a variety of these factors, especially in relation to decisions that flow inexorably from judicial policy preferences, present a strong case for judicial activism in its most fundamental sense.

A good example of activism in this contextualist understanding includes the court's modern freedom of association decisions recognizing a right to collective bargaining[70] and the right to strike[71] under the Charter, in which the court ultimately turned full circle on earlier jurisprudence finding those rights were not encompassed by section 2(d).[72] In assessing the activist nature of these decisions, several factors listed above are present, including the overturning of precedent, bold rhetoric, and a textual provision at stake whose plain reading is not suggestive of an economic right to withhold labour.

In overturning the court's own precedent on whether section 2(d) protected a right to bargain collectively, the majority in the 2007 *Health Services* case argued that the earlier court failed to recognize the importance of labour relations history in Canada, that it placed undue emphasis on judicial restraint or "push[ed] deference too far," that it conceived of freedom of association as an individual right rather than recognizing its collective qualities, that it failed to recognize that collective bargaining could be distinguished from the goals or objects of an association, and that its overall approach to free association was "decontextualized."[73] On none of these points does the majority identify a fundamental change in evidence about labour relations or in the law itself, in stark contrast to other cases where the court has overturned precedent.[74]

The court's core reasons for overturning the decision on a right to collective bargaining amount to an assertion that the previous court was simply too restrained and read freedom of association too narrowly. The new interpretation is less about a change in facts, evidence, or the law so much as a change in the personnel on the court and their conception of a just interpretation of section 2(d). The relevance of the justices' personal policy preferences is underscored by Justice Abella's majority judgment finding a right to strike in 2015, which boldly proclaimed that "[c]learly the arc bends increasingly towards workplace justice" and that it "seems to me to be the time to give this conclusion constitutional benediction."[75]

This is not to say the court's original findings on these matters were somehow politically neutral or the "correct" conclusions. It is fair to suggest that the court in 1987 adopted a conservative view on the scope of 2(d). Yet in overturning the precedent on the right to strike, the contemporary court majority offers little but a political essay grounding an economic right to withhold labour in the broadly worded provision on free association. The dissenting justices warn their colleagues that they are "wrong to intrude into the policy development role of elected legislators by constitutionalizing the right to strike."[76] The court majorities in these contemporary cases exercise a wide degree of political discretion to displace the policies established by elected legislatures, and the language of Abella's reasons reinforces the role that policy preferences play.

This conclusion risks inviting the challenge that many of these factors – political discretion especially – are present in virtually all Supreme Court cases under the Charter. Yet some cases, including those that result in the court blocking the decisions of state actors or even striking down legislation, are more textually grounded, remain firmly rooted in established precedent, or have a more complete, less contestable evidentiary basis. Take, for example, *Trociuk v British Columbia*, finding that provincial legislation permitting the arbitrary exclusion of fathers from being identified on their children's birth registration information constitutes an unjustifiable infringement of equality rights.[77] The legislation plainly discriminated on the basis of sex and included no recourse for fathers who could be excluded without good reason, or any reason at all. The legislation was not crafted with any care to proportionality (nonetheless, for an analysis of the court's poor reasoning and focus on biology and insensitivity to gendered relations in this case, see Froc, Chapter 14 in this volume).

Another example would be the court's finding of an unreasonable limit on religious freedom in the 2006 *Multani* case.[78] The court's decision concerned a school board's governing council's refusal to accept a reasonable accommodation to permit a Sikh student to wear his kirpan, a ceremonial dagger, to school. Although the decision was purportedly on the basis of school safety, the court accepted the strong evidence that the accommodations at issue helped to ensure student safety – indeed, that the risks were "very low" – and that an absolute prohibition failed to minimally impair the student's religious freedom. It is difficult to characterize these cases as especially activist in demeanour, even though they involve the court invalidating legislation or policies set by state actors.

Assessments of activism need to account for the laws and policies subject to judicial review. Nonetheless, it is perhaps best to view judicial activism as lying on a spectrum rather than as a simple dichotomy between decisions that are activist and those that are not. Take, for example, *PHS Community Services Society,* where the court determined that the federal minister of health's refusal to extend an exemption for InSite, Vancouver's supervised injection facility, violated its clients' section 7 right to life, liberty, and security of the person.[79] The decision prevented the federal government from shutting down the facility and to some extent could be read as granting an indirect positive right of access to a service to those suffering from addiction in Vancouver.[80] The case could thus be viewed as a novel, even bold, application of the Charter. Yet the decision was firmly grounded in compelling evidence about the effectiveness of the facility and the harms associated with forcing its closure. It was also a minimalist decision in that the court explicitly limited its holding to the minister's specific decision in the context of InSite (rather than mandating supervised consumption sites beyond InSite or interfering with the legislative provisions establishing ministerial exemptions). It was arguably an activist decision but one with precise reasoning and narrow scope, making it far less activist than it might otherwise have been.

Many cases arguably fall into this category, making it difficult to definitively count or measure rates of judicial activism. If that were all the term "judicial activism" was useful for, it might be worth dropping it from our vocabulary. Instead, I would endorse the view of Tom Campbell, who argues that judicial activism "is a term of political criticism and all terms of political criticism are fluid and contested. If we were to give up our political vocabulary on the grounds of indeterminacy, there would be preciously little political discourse left."[81]

Conclusion

My analysis makes a case for identifying the fundamental core of judicial activism and eschewing the quest for a simple, countable measure. Activism is not the function of a light switch. Instances where the courts exercise judicial review can be counted. Yet this simple measure deprives the concept of judicial activism of its normative relevance. What matters in debates about judicial activism is *how* judicial power is exercised, especially as measured against a meaningful conception of the judicial role.

I argue against conflating a host of factors with judicial activism in favour of recognizing either their distinctive nature or using them as contextual information for analyzing judicial decision making. The result is an approach that makes judicial activism readily identifiable in some contexts and contestable in others. The contestability of judicial activism should not be regarded as some sort of fatal flaw. A debate over whether certain decisions are activist should be welcome precisely because commentators disagree about the proper role of courts. What judicial activism does is help us think about the different aspects of the judicial role and how to understand the boundaries of judicial review and the relationship between branches of government. Judicial activism is best understood as both an empirical and normative assessment of the use of judicial power and a fitting object of study for political scientists and legal scholars.

Some of the courts' more prominent defenders recognize the existence of activism but point to positive public opinion about the Charter, the presence of the notwithstanding clause, and the fact that most of the judicial assertion of power has been directed to executive action, and especially police powers, as reasons to not join in league with the most vocal critics of the judicial role.[62] This underscores that the presence of judicial activism should not always be equated with accusations of illegitimacy or impropriety.

A key criticism of my approach might be that it would simply devolve into a debate dominated by subjectivity, to which there are two responses. First, such debates would involve no more subjectivity than those involving the interpretation of the quantitative measures described above. As noted, some scholars conclude that a 37 percent activism "measure" implies activism may not even exist. This is no less subjective a conclusion than a qualitative assessment of individual cases. Second, we need to be attentive to the normative elements we incorporate into an analysis of judicial activism. It will not do to focus on whether a particular outcome is desirable. Nor is it particularly useful to debate interpretative approaches. Instead, assessments of whether a court has engaged in activist behaviour, be it by exceeding the proper limits of its role or by allowing politics to dictate the outcome of a decision, must rely on identifiable features of a given decision. Is there concrete evidence to support a particular outcome, or have justices substituted their personal preferences? Has the court reached a conclusion only by abandoning long-held doctrine? If the court has overruled precedent, does it ably justify doing so? These questions may still require interpretive judgment and will inevitably result in disagreement in some cases, but they do not boil down to mere questions of personal taste such as whether one likes an outcome or not.

A more fruitful path for future scholarly attention is to leverage judicial activism as a frame for analyzing judicial power. My analysis suggests myriad ways that activism can manifest, and there are likely more. The study of judicial behaviour in Canada has grown increasingly sophisticated in the last two decades, and this empirical turn offers many opportunities to connect fresh empirical insights to the more normative debates of the 1980s and 1990s.

The courts continue to wield significant policy-making and political power. The nature of judicial decision making is complex, as are the interinstitutional relationships at stake. We should not be surprised to find that a central concept in analyzing these issues is also complicated or even messy. Rather than abandoning it, it is time to start engaging with that complexity in a more forthright and nuanced manner.

Notes

1 Keenan D. Kmiec, "The Origin and Current Meanings of Judicial Activism," *California Law Review* 92, 5 (2004): 1442. A search in Factiva, a global news database, finds 2,010 results for the last five years in North American outlets.
2 See Brice Dickson, ed., *Judicial Activism in Common Law Supreme Courts* (Oxford: Oxford University Press, 2007); Gavin Healy, "Judicial Activism in the New Constitutional Court of Korea," *Columbia Journal of Asian Law* 14, 1 (2000): 213–34.
3 Ronald Dworkin, *Taking Rights Seriously* (Cambridge, MA: Harvard University Press, 1977), 137.
4 Alpheus Thomas Mason, "Judicial Activism: Old and New," *Virginia Law Review* 55, 3 (1969): 387; Kmiec, "The Origin and Current Meanings," 1464; Caprice L. Roberts, "In Search of Judicial Activism: Dangers in Quantifying the Qualitative," *Tennessee Law Review* 74, 4 (2007): 574–75; F.L. Morton and Rainer Knopff, *The Charter Revolution and the Court Party* (Peterborough, ON: Broadview Press, 2000), 15; Sujit Choudhry and Claire E. Hunter, "Measuring Judicial Activism on the Supreme Court of Canada: A Comment on *Newfoundland (Treasury Board v NAPE)*," *McGill Law Journal* 48 (2003): 532; Rory Leishman, *Against Judicial Activism: The Decline of Freedom and Democracy in Canada* (Montreal/Kingston: McGill-Queen's University Press, 2006), 195; C.L. Ostberg and Matthew E. Wetstein, *Attitudinal Decision Making in the Supreme Court of Canada* (Vancouver: UBC Press, 2007), 77–79; Troy Riddell, "Measuring Activism and Restraint: An Alternative Perspective on the Supreme Court of Canada's Exclusion of Evidence Decisions under Section 24(2) of the Charter," *Canadian Journal of Criminology and Criminal Justice* 58 (2016): 101.
5 Mason, "Judicial Activism," 397; Arthur Schlesinger Jr., "The Supreme Court: 1947," *Fortune*, January 1947, 201; Kmiec, "Origin and Current Meanings," 1476; Tom Campbell, "Judicial Activism: Justice or Treason?," *Otago Law Review* 10, 3 (2003): 312; Vanessa Iyer, "The Supreme Court of India," in *Judicial Activism in Common Law Supreme Courts*, ed. Brice Dickson (Oxford: Oxford University Press, 2007), 166–67; Roberts, "In Search of Judicial Activism," 574–75; Frank B. Cross and Stefanie A. Lindquist, "The Scientific Study of Judicial Activism," *Minnesota Law Review* 91, 6 (2007): 1754; Daved Muttart,

The Empirical Gap in Jurisprudence: A Comprehensive Study of the Supreme Court of Canada (Toronto: University of Toronto Press, 2007), 146–47; Ostberg and Wetstein, *Attitudinal Decision Making,* 77–79.

6 Bradley C. Canon, "Defining the Dimensions of Judicial Activism," *Judicature* 66, 5 (1983): 237.

7 *Ibid,* 239; Michael J. Perry, "Judicial Activism," *Harvard Journal of Law and Public Policy* 7, 1 (1984): 70–71; Bruce Harris, "Judicial Activism and New Zealand's Appellate Courts," in *Judicial Activism in Common Law Supreme Courts,* ed. Brice Dickson (Oxford: Oxford University Press, 2007), 301; Roberts, "In Search of Judicial Activism," 574–75; Cross and Lindquist, "Scientific Study of Judicial Activism," 1754; Craig Green, "An Intellectual History of Judicial Activism," *Emory Law Journal* (2009): 1199.

8 Roberts, "In Search of Judicial Activism," 574–75; Canon, "Defining the Dimensions," 239; Margit Cohn and Mordechai Kremnitzer, "Judicial Activism: A Multidimensional Model," *Canadian Journal of Law and Jurisprudence* 18, 2 (2005): 353.

9 Harris, "Judicial Activism and New Zealand's Appellate Courts," 284; Roberts, "In Search of Judicial Activism," 574–75; Canon, "Defining the Dimensions," 239; Perry, "Judicial Activism," 69; Kmiec, "Origin and Current Meanings," 1476.

10 Canon, "Defining the Dimensions," 239; Cohn and Kremnitzer, "Judicial Activism," 353.

11 Canon, "Defining the Dimensions," 239; Kmiec, "Origin and Current Meanings," 1471; Roberts, "In Search of Judicial Activism," 587.

12 Kmiec, "Origin and Current Meanings," 1451.

13 Cohn and Kremnitzer, "Judicial Activism," 353; Muttart, *Empirical Gap in Jurisprudence,* 145–46.

14 Cohn and Kremnitzer, "Judicial Activism," 353; Melanie Janelle Murchison and Richard Jochelson, "Canadian Exclusion of Evidence under Section 24(2) of the Charter: An Empirical Model of Judicial Discourse," *Canadian Journal of Criminology and Criminal Justice* 57 (2015): 115–58.

15 Cohn and Kremnitzer, "Judicial Activism," 353; Murchison and Jochelson, "Canadian Exclusion of Evidence."

16 Roberts, "In Search of Judicial Activism," 574–75; Cohn and Kremnitzer, "Judicial Activism," 353.

17 Roberts, "In Search of Judicial Activisim," 591; Margaret L. Moses, "Beyond Judicial Activism: When the Supreme Court Is No Longer a Court," *University of Pennsylvania Journal of Constitutional Law* 14, 1 (2011): 161–214; Cohn and Kremnitzer, "Judicial Activism," 353.

18 Cohn and Kremnitzer, "Judicial Activism," 353.

19 *Ibid.*

20 *Ibid.*

21 *Ibid.*

22 *Ibid.*

23 *Ibid.*

24 Roberts, "In Search of Judicial Activism," 581; Cohn and Kremnitzer, "Judicial Activism," 353; Lorraine Eisenstat Weinrib, "The Activist Constitution," *Policy Options,* April 1999, 28.

25 Roberts, "In Search of Judicial Activism," 588–89.

26 Green, "Intellectual History of Judicial Activism," 1201.

27 Roberts, "In Search of Judicial Activism," 595; Muttart, *Empirical Gap in Jurisprudence,* 14; Peter H. Russell, "The Charter and Canadian Democracy," in *Contested Constitutionalism: Reflections on the Canadian Charter of Rights and Freedoms,* ed. James B. Kelly and Christopher P. Manfredi (Vancouver: UBC Press, 2009), 295.

28 Kent Roach, *The Supreme Court on Trial: Judicial Activism or Democratic Dialogue,* 2nd ed. (Toronto: Irwin Law, 2016), 121.

29 Cohn and Kremnitzer, "Judicial Activism," 353; Murchison and Jochelson, "Canadian Exclusion of Evidence."

30 Cross and Lindquist, "Scientific Study of Judicial Activism," 1764–65.

31 Riddell, "Measuring Activism and Restraint," 92.

32 Green, "Intellectual History of Judicial Activism," 1217–18.

33 *Brown v Board of Education,* 347 US 483 (1954); Emmett Macfarlane, *Governing from the Bench: The Supreme Court of Canada and the Judicial Role* (Vancouver: UBC Press, 2013), 172–76.

34 Green, "Intellectual History of Judicial Activism," 1224.

35 Kent Roach, "The Myths of Judicial Activism," *Supreme Court Law Review* 14 (2001): 297–326.

36 Emmett Macfarlane, "Dialogue or Compliance? Measuring Legislatures' Policy Responses to Court Rulings on Rights," *International Political Science Review* 34 (2013): 50–51.

37 *Truchon c Procureur general du Canada,* 2019 QCCS 3792; *R v Anwar,* 2020 ONCJ 103.

38 Emmett Macfarlane, "Dialogue, Remedies, and Positive Rights: *Carter v Canada* as Microcosm for Past and Future Issues under the Charter of Rights and Freedoms," *Ottawa Law Review* 49, 1 (2017): 107–29.

39 Peter H. Russell, Rainer Knopff, and F.L. Morton, eds., *Federalism and the Charter: Leading Constitutional Decisions* (Ottawa: Carleton University Press, 1989), 19.

40 F.L. Morton, Peter H. Russell, and Troy Riddell, "The Canadian Charter of Rights and Freedoms: A Descriptive Analysis of the First Decade, 1982–1992," *National Journal of Constitutional Law* 5 (1995): 1; Choudhry and Hunter, "Measuring Judicial Activism," 557; Christopher P. Manfredi and James B. Kelly, "Misrepresenting the Supreme Court's Record? A Comment on Sujit Choudhry and Claire E. Hunter 'Measuring Judicial Activism on the Supreme Court of Canada,'" *McGill Law Journal* 49 (2004): 741–64.

41 Choudhry and Hunter, "Measuring Judicial Activism," 557.

42 *Ibid,* 536.

43 Russell, "Charter and Canadian Democracy," 290–94.

44 Emmett Macfarlane, "'You Can't Always Get What You Want': Regime Politics, the Supreme Court of Canada, and the Harper Government," *Canadian Journal of Political Science* 51, 1 (2018): 1–21.

45 Roach, "The Myths of Judicial Activism," 298–99.

46 Weinrib, "Activist Constitution," 28.

47 Bertha Wilson, "We Didn't Volunteer," in *Judicial Power and Canadian Democracy,* ed. Paul Howe and Peter H. Russell (Montreal/Kingston: McGill-Queen's University Press, 2001), 73–79.

48 Roberts, "In Search of Judicial Activism," 570.

49 Manfredi and Kelly, "Misrepresenting the Supreme Court's Record?," 745.

50 *Ibid,* 746.

51 Beverley McLachlin, "Courts, Legislatures and Executives in the Post-Charter Era," in *Judicial Power and Canadian Democracy,* ed. Paul Howe and Peter H. Russell (Montreal/Kingston: McGill-Queen's University Press, 2001), 70.

52 Dave Snow and Mark S. Harding, "From Normative Debates to Comparative Methodology: The Three Waves of Post-Charter Supreme Court Scholarship in Canada," *American Review of Canadian Studies* 45, 4 (2015): 451–66.

53 Ostberg and Wetstein, *Attitudinal Decision Making;* Macfarlane, *Governing from the Bench.*

54 Rosalie Abella, "An Attack on the Independence of a Court Anywhere Is an Attack on All Courts," *Globe and Mail*, October 26, 2018, https://www.theglobeandmail.com/amp/opinion/article-rosalie-abella-an-attack-on-the-independence-of-a-court-anywhere-is/.

55 Roach, "The Myths of Judicial Activism," 310.

56 Macfarlane, *Governing from the Bench*, 188.

57 Emmett Macfarlane, "Judicial Amendment of the Constitution," *International Journal of Constitutional Law* 19, 5 (2021): 1894–1924.

58 *Reference re Secession of Quebec*, [1998] 2 SCR 217.

59 *Reference re Remuneration of Judges of the Provincial Court (P.E.I.)*, [1997] 3 SCR 3.

60 *Ibid*, para 302.

61 Roach, *The Supreme Court on Trial*, 157–59.

62 Emmett Macfarlane, "The Place of Constitutional Conventions in the Constitutional Architecture, and in the Courts," *Canadian Journal of Political Science* 55, 2 (2022): 322–41, doi:10.1017/S0008423922000051.

63 Adam Dodek, "Courting Constitutional Danger: Constitutional Conventions and the Legacy of the *Patriation Reference*," *Supreme Court Law Review* 54 (2011): 127.

64 Peter Russell, "Bold Statescraft, Questionable Jurisprudence," in *And No One Cheered: Federalism, Democracy and the Constitution Act*, ed. Keith Banting and Richard Simeon (Toronto: Methuen, 1983), 210; *Re: Resolution to amend the Constitution*, [1981] 1 SCR 753; Dodek, "Courting Constitutional Danger."

65 Peter W. Hogg, "Comments on Legislation and Judicial Decisions," *Canadian Bar Review* 60 (1982): 314.

66 Dodek, "Courting Constitutional Danger," 120.

67 *Concacher v Canada (Prime Minister)*, [2009] FCJ No 1136, 2009 FC 920 (FC).

68 *R (on the application of Miller) v The Prime Minister*, [2019] UKSC 41 (September 24, 2019).

69 Emmett Macfarlane, "Prorogation, Politics and the Courts: A Canadian Perspective," Judicial Power Project, October 4, 2019, http://judicialpowerproject.org.uk/emmett-macfarlane-prorogation-politics-and-the-courts-a-canadian-perspective/.

70 *Health Services and Support – Facilities Subsector Bargaining Assn v British Columbia*, [2007] 2 SCR 391, 2007 SCC 27 [*Health Services*].

71 *Saskatchewan Federation of Labour v Saskatchewan*, 2015 SCC 4, [2015] 1 SCR 245 [*Saskatchewan Federation of Labour*].

72 *Reference Re Public Service Employee Relations Act (Alta.)*, [1987] 1 SCR 313.

73 *Health Services*, paras 24–30.

74 *Carter v Canada (Attorney General)*, 2015 SCC 5, [2015] 1 SCR 331.

75 *Saskatchewan Federation of Labour*, para 1, para 4.

76 *Ibid*, para 105.

77 *Trociuk v British Columbia (Attorney General)*, [2003] 1 SCR 835, 2003 SCC 43.

78 *Multani v Commission scolaire Marguerite-Bourgeoys*, [2006] 1 SCR 256, 2006 SCC 6.

79 *Canada (Attorney General) v PHS Community Services Society*, 2011 SCC 44, [2011] 3 SCR 134.

80 Emmett Macfarlane, "Positive Rights and Section 15 of the Charter: Addressing a Dilemma," *National Journal of Constitutional Law* 38, 1 (2018): 147–68.

81 Campbell, "Judicial Activism – Justice or Treason?," 311.

82 Russell, "The Charter and Canadian Democracy," 290–94.

3

Revisiting the Charter Centralization Thesis

Gerald Baier

CANADIAN CONSTITUTIONALISM, FOR so many years following Confederation, was so singularly focused on federalism that scholars could be forgiven for approaching the dramatic constitutional changes of 1982 primarily through the lens of how it would affect the federal system. Rather than solely pondering the constitutional and cultural shift to come from entrenching a bill of rights, they often asked, What does this mean for federalism? The intergovernmental conflict and negotiation that produced the 1982 compromise brought into high relief rival constitutional worlds clashing with the adoption of a pan-Canadian bill of rights and a legislatively decentralized federation, so, in hindsight, this should be no surprise. The immediate aftermath of the adoption of the 1982 constitution was also marked by contesting visions of the federation. This conflict was most clearly felt in the dynamics of unsuccessful constitutional change that followed in the wake of the Meech Lake and Charlottetown Accords. Both fights paired off what Alan Cairns taught us to label a government's (federal) constitution and a citizens' (rights) constitution.[1] Again, it was natural to speculate about the consequences of the Charter for Canadian federalism.

One way to assess the consequences of 1982 for Canadian federalism is to point out that the Charter was not the most consequential part of the document for the federal system. Of more significance to federalism was the amending formula and the near assurance (then not entirely comprehended) that mega-constitutional change would forever fail. Other chapters in this volume cover this development and its consequences for the future of Canadian federalism and constitutionalism. My focus is the Charter and its impact on the federal institutional and cultural character of the country post-1982, but it pays to remember that Charter centralization (if it exists) might be balanced by other factors. Federalism observers expected the Charter to inevitably lead to the centralization it intended. I argue that the Charter has not had as strong a centralizing effect as predicted. There has been some universalizing of protections and culture since the inception of the Charter but nothing overwhelming. I further argue that if the post-1982 era has seen a decline in provincial autonomy, the Charter and the courts may not be to blame.

Federalism was certainly intended to be disrupted by the adoption of the Charter. Pierre Trudeau's aim was as much to foil the nationalist claims of Quebec and the less obviously justified but equally strong provincial loyalties of western Canada as it was to advocate for a universalist liberal set of rights protections. The governments most motivated by their provincial particularisms were the ones most institutionally obstinate about opposing the Charter project. The compromises of Charter drafting nodded towards these objections by specifically empowering governments to be able to limit the scope of rights in section 1 and to be able to override rights protections for some of the enumerated categories via section 33. An evaluation of Charter centralization can (and will) start with an evaluation of the effectiveness of these built-in safeguards. My account is not an empirical examination or scorecard of which governments have won and which have lost in the game of Charter litigation. That work has been ably done by others at various points in the last forty years.[2] The verdict has been that centralization has not been particularly strong. Instead, my purpose is to inquire as to why centralization has been so tepid and, perhaps more tellingly, why provincial autonomy (with rare exceptions) has been so timidly asserted in the post-1982 era.

The Thesis

The potential for Charter centralization was first recognized by its collective authors, a goodly portion of whom sought to limit the document's potential to do just that. While the federal government's Charter architects went all-in on the unifying and universal character of a constitutional bill of rights, provincial participants in the constitutional renewal process were either more skeptical or openly hostile to the notion or promotion of a pan-Canadian identity and the constitutional entrenchment of such a vision. The well-known history of compromise that marked the birth of the *Constitution Act, 1982* revealed ample tension between provincial governments seeking to protect both the structural power of provinces as constitutional actors (most forcefully achieved in the new amending formulae) and provincial legislative autonomy after patriation.

The Charter, almost by definition, sought to undermine the rational instinct of the provinces to protect their legislative autonomy. The introduction of a uniform set of rights to be defined and enforced by central (judicial) institutions was bound to be a threat to provincial majorities or, at the very least, majoritarian institutions such as legislatures. The national popularity of a bill of rights did little to dampen the determination of the provinces to hold onto what they had been given by the original Constitution and to be wary about enhancing the ability of the courts to hold provincial legislation up to new pan-Canadian constitutional standards. The popularity of a charter did, however, mean that the premiers were obliged to work with the proposal however odious they may have found it.

Trudeau's determination was an equal match to that of his provincial antag-
onists. The Charter's origins are certainly part of a broader liberal transformation
in the wake of the Second World War, but the appeal of the Charter to Trudeau
was its ability to contest the more illiberal appeals to belonging being made by
the provinces – most notably Quebec but also provinces in western Canada. As
Samuel LaSelva summarizes, "the political purpose of the Charter sprang from
Trudeau's desire to save Canada from the particularisms that threatened to
destroy it."[3] Those particularisms were rooted in linguistic and cultural differences and reflected indirectly in the differing legislative priorities of provincial
governments. The negative consequences of those legislative choices often
amounted to infringement of the kind of rights that would be protected by the
Charter. Certainly, the more egregious examples of those kinds of approaches
under the Duplessis regime in Quebec were part of Trudeau's motivation. The
entrenched legislative jurisdiction of the provinces in Canada's 1867 constitution
ensured the provinces of that autonomy without written universal liberal protections to interfere. Many would argue that this was, at least in part, the purpose
of federalism to begin with. Federalism is not entirely about subunit autonomy;
all varieties of the model come with more tension than that. Union, if not outright centralization, is always a goal. As LaSelva states the truism, "[A] federal
state strives for unity, yet constitutionalizes division."[4]

In the aftermath of the 1981 negotiations and the subsequent adoption of the
Constitution Act, 1982, observers predicted that the changes would reverse some
of the decentralizing trends of Canadian federalism, with the judiciary in the
vanguard. Charter protections would provide the ammunition for "Charter
Canadians" to challenge the policy prescriptions of the provinces, particularly
as they encroached on individual or group rights in the Charter, including
minority languages inside and outside of Quebec and more dispersed, cross-
cutting communities, including those of race, gender, and age protected in the
equality provisions of section 15. In anticipation of such a change, the provinces
advocated the inclusion of a notwithstanding clause, granting their legislatures
(and the federal Parliament) the right to counter findings of unconstitutionality
in pursuit of these kinds of broader collective goals.

As Janet Hiebert has pointed out, even those less skeptical about the value of
the notwithstanding clause – such as Howard Leeson, then-adviser to the Saskatchewan premier, Alan Blakeney – credit the notwithstanding clause's existence to political manoeuvring, exhaustion, and forced compromise rather than
logical consistency with the goals of either side of the constitutional negotiation.[5]
If centralization via the Charter was a fear for the holdout provinces, the notwithstanding clause appears to have been the safety blanket that could encourage
provinces to adopt it anyway.

In contrast, Lorraine Weinrib describes the adoption of the Charter as the transformation of Canada from a legislative to a constitutional state.[6] The legislative state is ever sensitive to public opinion and popular majorities or, at the very least, parliamentary pluralities. What Dicey called the ever-wakeful popular sovereign, which he of course contrasted with the "slumbering sovereign" of written constitutions, which seek to enshrine immortal principles. The Charter did not overcome federalism's particularisms so much as limit any legislature's ability to infringe on rights. For Weinrib, the treatment of historical religious minorities (particularly non-Christians) by the federal Parliament is as emblematic of the problems of a pre-Charter world as any provincial example (including provincial legislation that targets Christian and non-Christian religious minorities). The intent to move to a more "constitutional" state where parliamentary sovereignty is constrained by constitutional text and by the subsequent judicial enforcement of rights is as much a constraint on the ambitions and exercise of the federal Parliament as on the provincial legislatures, the presumed focus of Pierre Trudeau's reformist zeal.

Weinrib may overemphasize the transformation that accompanied the Charter, and a brief critique of her thesis helps to demonstrate the appropriate frame to evaluate the Charter's effect on federalism. While the 1867 constitution included many elements redolent of a legislative rather than constitutional state (the preamble comes to mind), it also embraced constitutionalism through its federal elements. While founders such as John A. Macdonald may have hoped the federal system would be self-regulating, or at the very least supervised by the federal Parliament through the extraordinary powers of reservation and disallowance, political considerations quickly drove the system to a more "constitutional" footing and the enlistment of the judiciary to patrol federal-provincial boundaries.[7] The mere existence of federalism, particularly a division of powers with enumerated roles for the federal and provincial legislatures, ensured that constitutionalism would trump parliamentarism in Canada almost from the start. The compromise of the Judicial Committee of the Privy Council as a colonial legislative body that acted like a judicial institution and the eventual increased legitimacy of the Supreme Court of Canada in a more explicitly judicial role paved the way for a more complete constitutionalism with the adoption of the Charter.

Nevertheless, many critics of the Charter at its adoption and since have focused on the Charter's potential for mischief towards provincial legislative and governmental autonomy. It is perhaps unclear if they are uncomfortable more with the procedural empowerment of the judiciary in Charter affairs or the privileging of pan-Canadian standards over the preferences of provincial legislatures. Despite majoritarian claims, the combination of political-party and electoral systems usually means that legislative majorities are only reflective of a plurality of preferences within the provinces anyway. In the critics' reading, the Charter conflicts with the logic of federalism and the history of Canadian constitutionalism. Contrary to Weinrib's view, provinces, like the federal government, have always been limited in their jurisdictional reach. In that regard, they have never enjoyed parliamentary sovereignty the way their Westminster prototype has. However, within those legislative spheres, prior to the Charter, the provinces worked with only self-imposed limitations, say in the form of provincial human rights statutes or other legislatively imposed restrictions (which could be removed at the behest of future parliamentary majorities).

Centralization and Design

Was the Charter really so centralizing by design? Institutionally, it would seem that the uniquely Canadian elements of the Charter (what Kent Roach calls its "modern" features) and the mode of engagement that they set up between courts and legislatures were intended to potentially overcome those centralization concerns.[8] This is not a new observation. Much weight in this interpretation of the Charter is put on section 33, the notwithstanding clause. That provision was intended as a parliamentary escape clause for those provinces who choose to use it. That certainly appears to be the accepted wisdom of critics of section 33, who often point to the "discomfort" or "hesitation" of the provinces to fully accept a rights instrument like the Charter as a restriction on their parliamentary sovereignty. Those who fought most fiercely for the notwithstanding clause sold it as a kind of insurance, albeit limited, against restraints on the full exercise of legislative powers. So at least part of the design of the Charter was to defy the obvious effort at centralization if provinces were willing to actively assert their desire to override certain rights.

There are sensible democratic arguments to be made for both sections 1 and 33 as features of a more mature approach to rights recognition and a more conscious balancing of mutual or coordinate roles in rights interpretation and recognition for both legislatures and courts.[9] However, section 33 is almost invariably seen in the light of hesitation or unease with the very notion of rights protection. Provincial exercises of the override have not helped with that reputation (see Snow and Nicolaides, Chapter 7 in this volume). The blanket use of the override by the Quebec legislature to protest the adoption of the *Constitution Act, 1982* and then the override of rights related to Bill 101 and the *Ford* decision were emblematic of the purposes to which the override could be put. Section 33 was either invoked as an overall protest of the intent of the Charter or to specifically uphold majority-language legislation in a province.

Roach characterizes the Charter as "modern" for incorporating the experiential lesson of an older, more overly literal view of the scope of a bill of rights. In more literal settings, like the United States, the job of defining the scope of rights has fallen to courts given that constitutionally enumerated rights cannot be protected in the extreme form that their simplicity may imply. All legislation, by a reasonable definition, is in violation of one or another open-ended right. Constitutional regimes depend on some authoritative interpreter – usually a high court – to settle borderline issues where some limitation of rights is necessary to pursue a broader public purpose, or where legislation is necessary to prevent the harm that might come from too zealous an enjoyment of rights. Constitutions are obliged to be a little parsimonious about the scope of rights, either to ensure textual brevity or to mask compromise and uncertainty or even ambiguity about what is being protected.[10] Recognizing this requirement and dividing some of the power for the interpretation of the scope of rights and the ability to justify limits is more mature or modern. Section 1 is the subtle version of the ability of governments and legislatures to define limits on the scope of rights. An override is a blunter instrument and is hampered somewhat by its inelegant design. Reputationally, section 33 suffers from the impression (and its origins) that it was included in the Constitution to allow legislative majorities, federal or provincial, to circumvent individual protections in pursuit of the collective goals that the nominally majoritarian legislature wants to pursue.

I linger on this point only to recognize that the anticipated primary remedy for the presumed centralization of the Charter has largely been discredited in public opinion. Roach and others have advocated for its renaissance to promote more explicit "balancing" of institutional roles in the definition and protection of rights, but there has been little enthusiasm for such ideas in the public. Recent concern about Quebec's religious symbols law, much like the language laws before it, has reignited some of this controversy, including what might be the appropriate response to the province's use of the notwithstanding clause.[11] If section 33 has not been completely delegitimized, it has a negative enough reputation that there are routine, if ill-informed, calls to either amend it out of the Constitution or to find some other remedy to limit its use.[12]

What does this suggest about the centralist intent of the Charter? The centralization thesis, I would argue, relies on a presumption that section 33's weak public legitimacy will prevent provinces from actualizing the compromise attendant at the Charter's birth. That cannot be an institutional given. As unsavoury as many might find it, section 33 remains a strong counter to the pull of Charter uniformity. In order for centralization to defy the institutional roadblocks put in its way, section 33 must be cast as logically or fundamentally incompatible with the ethos of the Canadian constitution or wholly cast out of the constitutional order. Proponents of the former view have been relatively successful. The latter goal may prove impossible, and so section 33 remains an impediment to the full realization of Charter centralization.

Section 1 and the general ability of legislatures to apply limits may be subjected to a similar inquiry. The evolution of jurisprudence and legislative practice in the Charter era has made governments slightly more conscious of the need to provide pre-emptive justification for potential rights violations as part of the legislative drafting process. So-called Charter proofing suggests that governments self-censor their legislation based on prior judicial determinations of what is and is not permissible. With a uniform set of guarantees operative at the federal level, Charter proofing would seem to be a kind of self-policing norm of centralization.

But Charter proofing is both more and less than simply editing legislation for presumed Charter compliance. Charter proofing may also be about giving legislation the appropriate armour to weather judicial scrutiny. Section 1 justifications, which centre on the concept of reasonable limits found in free and democratic societies, can include rationalizations that draw on the permissibility of federalism diversity. Should the law be challenged, ensuring that the legislative record indicates attempts to preserve such values may strongly signal the government's intent to courts engaged in section 1 analysis. Articulating such justifications through the drafting and legislative process is far superior to post hoc rationalizations formulated by government lawyers seeking to defend challenged laws in court. The democratic benefits of such an approach go beyond more dialogic Charter analysis. A stronger legislative record requires governments, provincial and federal, to take the legislative process seriously enough to at least articulate justifications for potential limits and to defend those justifications against official opposition.[13]

This kind of analysis conforms with Kelly's finding that the Supreme Court in the first half of the Charter era was willing to entertain justifications for limits based on the reasonable variations in needs and perspectives that provinces might articulate in their defence. This case was further strengthened by the Supreme Court's endorsement of federalism as a fundamental constitutional principle in the *Reference re Secession of Quebec*. The court explicitly noted that the Constitution "recognizes the diversity of the component parts of Confederation, and the autonomy of provincial governments to develop their societies within their respective spheres of jurisdiction."[14] As a small empirical measure of that case's impact, at the time of writing, the CanLII database found nearly four hundred judicial citations to the reference. Many of these citations are in support of the notion that Canada is founded on democracy and the rule of law, but many also cite the court's determination that federalism be taken into account when interpreting portions of the Constitution outside the division of powers. Again, the structure of the Charter, through section 1, offers a counterweight to the rhetorical, universalist potential of a rights instrument.

Centralization by Silence

Where the centralization doomsayers may have been more correct has been in the broader sociocultural impact of the Charter. It is easy to acknowledge that there has been some on-the-ground experience of centralization via invalidation of provincial laws. The logic of a bill of rights in a federal system still suggests that universalist liberal values are going to conflict with the more particularistic preferences of provincial communities, especially if those provincial communities have dynamic characteristics of language, race, or religious heritage that may have consequences for minorities outside of those demographics.

An illustrative example would be the struggle for same-sex marriage equality, which was complicated further by a division of legislative authority regarding the solemnization and definition of marriages between the provinces and the federal government.[15] To the degree that the provinces had control over the subject, there was invariably going to be some variation in acceptance or approaches to the recognition of same-sex partnerships, whether marriages or some other legal category. The existing federal jurisdiction (including a reluctant effort to normalize the practice across the country) and the "centralizing" power of the Supreme Court did what the centralizers said the Charter would do. While the power to define marriage was always the federal Parliament's, the solemnization did allow for some variation in recognition among the provinces. These complications were cleaned up by the court's ruling in *Reference re Same-Sex Marriage* that the federal Parliament had the appropriate authority to define marriage and that its proposed definition, which would be inclusive of marriage between any two persons, was consistent with the Charter's standard of equality.[16] The result was perhaps not much more centralizing than if the Charter did not exist, as the jurisdiction already belonged to the federal Parliament. To the extent that provincial variation in solemnization and recognition of marriage was made uniform, the example could be said to be one of centralization, but the desire for similar kinds of standards is reflected in the division of powers and the inherent centralization of provisions such as the Criminal Code. Those compromises were reflective of the baseline compromises of federalism that predated the Charter and reflect the character of the federal bargain in Canada, past and future.

The culprit in many Charter critics' minds is the Supreme Court. Supreme Court justices are certainly central government actors with abundant incentives and institutional encouragements to think like central government actors. But that alone is not proof that they are centralizers by nature. They have never been reliable central government partisans, or provincial government partisans for that matter. The informal and imperfect regional representation formula assures that not all provinces will even have personnel on the court. But presumptions about federally appointed judges being sympathetic to the federal government or more inclined to accept federal government arguments do not bear out in practice. If anything, the Supreme Court seems to contort itself not to do the opposite but to strike a balance wherever it can. It certainly is a balancer in the division of powers, and it carries that sensitivity towards federalism into its Charter work.[17]

The Charter was never expected to be a secret centralizing force. Its goals and process were transparent and predictable. However, whatever centralization it has created has been much more subtly achieved than the centralization thesis presumes. There has not been an undue number of invalidations of provincial legislation. The Supreme Court, despite taking on a more prominent role in the public affairs of the country and reinforcing deference and prestige towards its justices, has not proven itself an overtly politicized institution. The court, armed with the Charter, has never been prepared to go to battle with federalism for the aggrandizement of pan-Canadian political institutions and perspectives. But perhaps proponents of the centralization thesis never expected anything too overt. Instead, the logic of liberal constitutionalism would just erode provincial particularisms slowly and surely until one day there was nothing left of federal diversity. A sort of centralization by neglect. That kind of centralization may be stealthy and silent, but it may be more the product of provincial reluctance to assert community difference or diversity than the imposition of uniform standards on provincial communities. Provincial governments might be reading public opinion and acknowledging relatively widespread support for the virtues of the Charter when choosing to be so reserved, but perhaps there are other reasons.

A likely one is lack of engagement with the idea of unique provincial constitutional cultures that could be reflected in a more explicit vision that challenges Charter protections from a nominally more democratic position. Peter Russell's seminal text on the contemporary history of the Canadian constitution begins with the realization that Canadians had not "constituted themselves a sovereign people."[18] That task has been complicated today by the competing sovereignty claims of Indigenous peoples and by the near unworkability of the mechanisms for the assertion of sovereignty embodied in the Constitution's amending formula. We can add to that the puzzling unwillingness of the provinces to constitute themselves as proper sovereigns. Federalism would seem to give the provinces every opportunity to articulate themselves, but it hasn't happened. It is not a practice that Canadians are familiar with at the federal level, so maybe it is difficult to do at the provincial level too. The notable exception is Quebec. The saga of Quebec's place in Canada almost always revolves around questions of sovereignty and who should have it for the people and lands of Quebec. Perhaps it is the exception that proves the rule. Even so, assertions of Quebec's provincial identity and distinctiveness from the rest of Canada through constitutional means are relatively limited.

If there is centralization because of the Charter, then the provinces are as much to blame as any other provision or institution. The provinces have not opted for constitutional self-expression for reasons we can only speculate on. The provinces have rarely declared sufficient opposition to Charter rights in the pursuit of different collective goals. This could be for one of two reasons.

First, asserting provincial difference via provincial constitutions may be counterproductive. As F.L. Morton notes, provincial constitutions are subject to the Canadian Charter, and the mere adoption of a provincial constitution could invite Charter-based scrutiny of provincial assertions.[19] Casting policy differences as matters of provincial or community values without an accompanying grant of sovereign immunity for provincial constitutions would mean that, like all other provincial statutes, such an exercise would be subject to both Charter review and the constitutional jurisdiction of the Supreme Court. Quebec's recent efforts to revive nationalist aspirations and to use the forums available to the provinces risk this kind of backlash. Federally appointed judges will eventually decide if the legislative assertions of national identity made through language laws or laws related to the display of religious symbols are constitutional. This is the centralization thesis with high stakes. What will it provoke? Acceptance of pan-Canadian standards or a Quebec backlash to a constitution it never signed and can't amend? Indeed, the long game of sovereigntists has always been to prove that the Canadian federation is not capable of accommodating Quebec's identity. If the Supreme Court of Canada finds Bill 21 incompatible with the Charter, we'll certainly have a test case for whether such assertions of provincial identity are worth the effort. The eventual resolution of legal challenges to the law should keep the fortieth anniversary year of the new Constitution an interesting one.

Second, the provinces may be happy with the less than grand ways they get to assert identity, namely, through the rawer politics of intergovernmental relations and, at their peak, the constitutional amending process. Other chapters in this volume survey the challenges of constitutional amendment in the period since patriation. One thing is certain about the process. The provinces exercise considerable power to shape proposals and changes in constitutional direction. Even the day-to-day of intergovernmental relations provides provincial governments with abundant opportunities to act and feel empowered. This is another truism of Canadian federalism. Governments drive diversity in the federation but often in directions that appeal to governments more than to the provincial communities they serve. As an illustrative example, the amount of intergovernmental struggle over labour market policy over the last twenty years is by no measure commensurate with the public's interest or awareness. What is clear in the post-1982 world is that a modicum of centralization may have been achieved in terms of liberal constitutional norms regarding things such as equality or democratic rights, but provincial governments will happily trade those losses of policy discretion for increased power over social, health, and economic policy at the provincial level, especially if they can win generous federal financial support through one stream of fiscal federalism or another.

What the federal system seems less good at since 1982 is having a productive dialogue between provincial and federal communities. Governments are satisfied with the scraps of amending authority and the ever-present opportunity to engage in intergovernmental wrangling and less interested in trying to define and represent provincial communities in their legislative approaches. With the exception of Quebec, there may be nothing terribly substantive to distinguish the provinces, in the way that proponents of the centralization thesis feared. Maybe there is "no there, there" in terms of substantive provincial differences that need expression in provincial legislation but might run into trouble with the Charter. Federal diversity may simply be overplayed for strategic advantage or standing in the forums where the provinces have proven resilient advocates of decentralization, to the point that Canada is now seen as one of the more decentralized federations in the world.

Revisiting Charter Centralization

After close to forty years in Charterland, have the worries of the Charter centralists come to pass? Has the Charter been any more of a constraint on provincial autonomy than the rest of the Constitution? The evidence collected by others suggests that the centralizing effects of the Charter have not been overwhelming. Provincial governments lose in court, but so does the federal government, and the Supreme Court is receptive to the notion that federalism is a defining characteristic of the Canadian state and worthy of recognition in the analysis of permissible limits on Charter rights. Centralization, however, is not exclusively about win or loss rates in court. There has been an acceptance of the pan-Canadian values articulated by the Charter that has resulted in less assertiveness by provincial governments in their efforts to define provincial communities. What might be more empirically true is that in the Charter era, we have not witnessed as much expression of provincial variability or identity as one might expect from a diverse federation. Diversity comes in many forms in a federation. And, as W.S. Livingston sees it, the role of a federal constitution is to acknowledge and accommodate territorially occurring differences in the form of instrumentalities that allow for their expression.[20] Canadian scholars have long debated the organic nature of those diversities and have included the possibility of government amplification of difference as a feature of federal diversity.[21]

The existence of such a beast as a provincial constitution, as section 45 of the *Constitution Act, 1982* explicitly recognizes, means that there is an opportunity for more formal expression of provincial difference if the centralist tides of the Charter threaten to overwhelm provincial identities. Provincial governments – and, moreover, provincial communities – have been reluctant to seize that opportunity. In the early years of this century, several provinces seemed prepared to redefine their democracy in important ways through reform to their electoral systems. Proposals in British Columbia, Quebec, New Brunswick, and Prince Edward Island would have made changes of constitutional consequence through alterations to the electoral system. None of them met with the approval of a provincial majority.

In retrospect, worries over Charter centralization are both justified and misleading. One reason for this paradox may be the distinctive lack of provincial constitutional character in Canada. To the degree that the Charter has repressed its development, the goal of centralization has been achieved. However, there are occasional exceptions to the rule that suggest that Charter centralization has not been as complete as its proponents would have liked. Overall, the character of Canadian federalism that the Charter was intended to alter has not changed much. Canadian federalism is still decentralized and regionalism and provincialism are still strong. The Charter has become the cultural, and to some degree legal, touchstone that it was intended to be without deflating provincial identities, which were not well enshrined to begin with. Admittedly, this is a matter of interpretation or perception, but I think a case can be made that centralization has not been the Charter's primary impact.

Ultimately, the Charter is emblematic of tensions inherent in federalism generally and to which Canada is no stranger. The contention that a liberal bill of rights is fundamentally incompatible with a federal system may be in error. Half of the federalism equation is some set of values or aspirations that unite or hold it together even while other strong forces pull it apart. Unity without unification means that some autonomy is going to be permitted to constitutional subunits, but the existence of an umbrella community at the federal level also entitles individuals to an identity and protections that defy the intentions and preferences of provincial communities.

Notes

1 Alan Cairns, *Charter versus Federalism: The Dilemmas of Constitutional Reform* (Montreal/Kingston: McGill-Queen's University Press, 1992).

2 James Kelly, "Reconciling Rights and Federalism during Review of the Charter of Rights and Freedoms: The Supreme Court of Canada and the Centralization Thesis, 1982 to 1999," *Canadian Journal of Political Science* 34, 2 (2001): 321–55.

3 Samuel LaSelva, *The Moral Foundations of Canadian Federalism: Paradoxes, Achievements, and Tragedies of Nationhood* (Montreal/Kingston: McGill-Queen's University Press, 1996), 82.

4 *Ibid*, 82.

5 Janet Hiebert, "Notwithstanding the Charter: Does Section 33 Accommodate Federalism?," in *Canada: The State of the Federation 2017. Canada at 150: Federalism and Democratic Renewal*, ed. Elizabeth Goodyear Grant and Kyle Hanniman, Institute of Intergovernmental Relations (Montreal/Kingston: McGill-Queen's University Press, 2019), 59–84.

6 Lorraine Eisenstat Weinrib, "Canada's Constitutional Revolution: From Legislative to Constitutional State," *Israel Law Review* 33, 1 (1999): 13–50. doi:10.1017/S0021223700015880.

7 Jennifer Smith, "The Origins of Judicial Review in Canada," *Canadian Journal of Political Science* 16, 1 (1983): 115–34.

8 Kent Roach, *The Supreme Court on Trial: Judicial Activism or Democratic Dialogue* (Toronto: Irwin Law, 2001).

9 For example, see Dennis Baker, *Not Quite Supreme: The Courts and Coordinate Constitutional Interpretation* (Montreal/Kingston: McGill-Queen's University Press, 2010); Janet Hiebert, *Charter Conflicts: What Is Parliament's Role?* (Montreal/Kingston: McGill-Queen's University Press, 2000).

10 David Thomas, *Whistling Past the Graveyard: Constitutional Abeyances, Quebec, and the Future of Canada* (Toronto: Oxford University Press, 1997).

11 Grégoire Webber, Eric Mendelsohn, and Robert Leckey, "The Faulty Received Wisdom around the Notwithstanding Clause," *Policy Options*, May 10, 2019; Robert Leckey, "Advocacy Notwithstanding the Notwithstanding Clause," *Constitutional Forum* 28, 4 (2019): 1–8.

12 Erna Paris, "Quebec Is Effectively an Illiberal Democracy: Opinion," *Globe and Mail*, May 17, 2021, A11.

13 Janet Hiebert, *Limiting Rights: The Dilemma of Judicial Review* (Montreal/Kingston: McGill-Queen's University Press, 1996).

14 *Reference re Secession of Quebec*, [1998] 2 SCR 217, 251.

15 See Linda White, "Federalism and Equality Rights Implementation in Canada," *Publius* 44, 1 (2014): 157–82; Miriam Smith, "Federalism, Courts, and LGBTQ Policy in Canada," in *Handbook of Gender, Diversity and Federalism*, ed. Cheryl Collier, Joan Grace, and Jill Vickers (Surrey, UK: Edward Elgar, 2020), 107–19.

16 *Reference re Same-Sex Marriage*, [2004] 3 SCR 698.

17 Gerald Baier, *Courts and Federalism: Judicial Doctrine in the United States, Australia and Canada* (Vancouver: UBC Press, 2006).

18 Peter H. Russell, *Constitutional Odyssey: Can Canadians Become a Sovereign People?* 3rd ed. (Toronto: University of Toronto Press, 2004).

19 F.L. Morton, "Provincial Constitutions in Canada" (paper presented at the "Conference on Federalism and Sub-national Constitutions: Design and Reform," Bellagio, Italy,

March 22–26, 2004), http://statecon.camden.rutgers.edu/sites/statecon/files/subpapers/morton.pdf.

20 W.S. Livingston, *Federalism and Constitutional Change* (London: Oxford University Press, 1956).

21 Alan Cairns, "The Governments and Societies of Canadian Federalism," *Canadian Journal of Political Science* 10, 4 (1977): 695–726.

4

Autochthony and Influence
The Charter's Place in Transnational Constitutional Discourse

Mark Tushnet

THIS ESSAY JUXTAPOSES two facts to create a modest paradox, which it then attempts to resolve. The first fact is that the Charter appears to have had a significant impact on constitutional discourse around the world.[1] The essay focuses on the influence of section 33, the notwithstanding clause, and the *Oakes* test for applying the doctrine of structured proportionality to constitutional review. The second fact is that the Charter, including section 33 specifically and the *Oakes* test inferentially, was the product of a process aimed at resolving a persistent *domestic* constitutional problem different from those faced in nations where the Charter has been influential. The paradox is that a process and documents that were Canadian to the core have been influential outside of Canada.

The proposed resolution is two-fold. First, the politics underlying the Charter process required that provincial governments almost unanimously endorse the Charter. Section 33 was an inducement to such agreement for several provincial governments. Second, the substantive solution the Charter proposed was a concept of plurinationalism that incorporated a commitment to reasonable accommodations among what were presented in the Charter as the nation's plurinational subcomponents.[2] That commitment was embodied in the general limitations clause of section 1, which in turn became the foundation for the *Oakes* test. In a sense, then, the aspects of the Charter that influenced transnational constitutional discourse were byproducts of solutions to entirely domestic problems.[3] Yet, once made available to the world community, those aspects could be detached from the domestic circumstances that gave rise to them.

The Charter exemplifies the fact that constitutional developments are often autochthonous, tightly connected to domestic circumstances, and yet sometimes some such developments appear to influence constitutional developments elsewhere. Constitutionalists in "target" jurisdictions could dismiss developments in the "origin" jurisdiction as irrelevant because they were the result of solutions to domestic problems different from those in the target jurisdictions.[4] Sometimes that indeed happens, but sometimes it doesn't. My suggestion is that constitutionalists in the target jurisdiction see that the developments of interest, designed to solve a specific problem in the nation of origin, might also solve a different problem that they face.[5] I've come to think of this thusly: constitutionalists in the target jurisdiction see the developments in the nation of origin as something like a "proof of concept." That is, they say that whatever initial skepticism one might have about what they propose, the example of the nation of origin shows that their proposal *might* work.[6]

The Charter's Origins and Plurinationalism

My discussion locates the Charter's origins in quite general conditions of the Canadian constitutional order in the middle of the twentieth century.[7] I concede at the outset that my argument is interpretive and speculative. It focuses on selected aspects of the Charter story and views them through what might be a lens that reveals little to other observers. I hope that at least the speculation provokes reflection and gives skeptics the opportunity to develop counterarguments in a productive dialogue.

Constitution-drafting exercises provide the opportunity for a polity and its political leaders to conceptualize their nation.[8] The basic condition facing Canada in the 1970s was uncertainty about whether Canada would remain one country. Quebec separatism was a persistent component of national politics, recurrently flaring up into a constitutional crisis.[9] Pierre Trudeau believed (correctly, in my view) that Canada couldn't progress along most dimensions of interest – economic, social, and others – until the "problem" of Quebec was resolved.[10] As Trudeau saw the issue, one important component of the problem was the way the issue was posed, as a two-sided conflict between anglophone and francophone communities within Canada. Trudeau believed that the solution lay in reconceptualizing "Canada" as a plurinational state.[11] Doing so would displace provincial identities by placing a new national one on top of them. And it would allow francophones to find themselves comfortably within a plurinational Canada (rather than as displaced French women and men) without threatening anglophone understandings of *their* place in the nation.[12]

With reconceptualization as the predicate for dealing with the issue of Quebec's position within a unified Canada, the next step was clear: engage in a drafting exercise. That exercise was constrained by politics. It had to be national and deliberative rather than imposed from the outside – a true patriation rather than a mere amendment to the *BNA Act* formally done in London. And it had to gain support throughout the nation, and in particular from political leaders in every province – or in enough provinces to make the claim that the exercise was a truly national one credible.[13]

Canada's plurinationalism would be manifested in the new *Charter of Rights and Freedoms*. Several provisions recognized the rights of linguistic minorities (see Chouinard, Chapter 16 this volume). Doing that and no more, though, would have left Canada binational rather than plurinational. Treating Canada as a binational state wouldn't have solved the "problem" of Quebec because it would emphasize francophones' permanent minority status (and anglophones' numerical dominance, of course). Plurinationalism opened the possibility of fracturing the anglophone majority into different "nations of ultimate origin," so to speak: Canadians of Chinese heritage, for example, wouldn't "merely" be anglophones. Section 27 expressly recognized Canada's "multicultural heritage." That was straightforward and plurinational, but section 27 was only an interpretive guide. A guide to what? Interpreting the Charter's substantive rights provisions.

Political considerations precluded large-scale (in the event, any) changes in the structures of Canadian governance. For example, plurinationalism couldn't be acknowledged by giving First Nations or Canada's nascent world cities a place within the structure of governance. Identifying protected rights had to be the vehicle for achieving plurinationalism. Of course, by the early 1980s, any constitution-drafting exercise would inevitably focus on constitutional rights. By then, there was a standard checklist of rights. That left relatively little room for making the list a vehicle for asserting a distinctive national identity.[14]

Section 1's general limitations clause captures the unavoidable reality that constitutional rights are never unlimited in a formulation that implicitly describes Canada as a "free and democratic society." That isn't distinctive, of course, but the fact that limitations must be "demonstrably justified" and that the clause is a general one rather than tailored to specific individual rights does express an understanding of Canada as a society guided by reason not only in the protection of rights but also in their assertion. It can be taken as a rejection of what has since been described as "rights inflation."[15] The general limitations clause expresses Canada's national character as reasonable and accommodative (including the accommodation of the many components of a plurinational Canada).[16] What Etienne Mureinik famously called a culture of justification was expressed in the general limitations clause.[17]

Section 33 has been described as a "unique innovation in constitutional design" associated with the list of rights.[18] It was included in the Charter to satisfy concerns among some politicians that – again in modern circumstances – the guaranteed rights would have to be fully enforceable in the courts in a manner inconsistent with the tradition of parliamentary sovereignty. A successful reconceptualization of Canada as plurinational required that the constitution-drafting exercise succeed, which meant that these political-conceptual objections had to be overcome. In this sense, section 33 was a key element in the reconceptualization of Canada's national identity – albeit a byproduct of the political context within which the drafting exercise occurred.

Before concluding, I note that the patriation project may well have had other motivations or effects beyond the creation of a plurinational constitutional identity. It's been suggested, for example, that a national charter of rights, each right presumptively attractive to almost everyone, might centralize national identity and nationalize political debate. These effects aren't inconsistent with the account I've sketched and, indeed, nationalization of pretty much anything would support the argument that the project was aimed at creating a new national identity – though not that that identity would be plurinational.

To summarize: two important elements of the Charter – the general limitations clause (and the proportionality test it generated) and section 33 – resulted mainly though not, of course, exclusively from the effort to solve the "problem" of Quebec by reconceptualizing Canada as plurinational rather than binational. In that sense, the clause and section exhibit some of the characteristics of an autochthonous constitution – one rooted in distinctive national conditions.[19] Yet the Charter and the associated jurisprudence seem to have had a significant influence on constitutional developments elsewhere. The remainder of this essay examines this (perhaps minor) puzzle.

How Can an Autochthonous Constitution Influence Other Constitutions? Section 33

As I've noted, Sujit Choudhry includes section 33 in his account of the migration of constitutional ideas. Strikingly, though, the section 33 mechanism – a time-limited majoritarian override of judicial constitutional interpretations – has not been widely adopted, or even tweaked and then adopted.[20] In what sense, then, was section 33 a constitutional idea that travelled abroad?[21]

Despite an unpromising beginning, within a decade of the Charter's adoption, section 33 had been identified *outside* of Canada as suggesting a new weak form of constitutional review.[22] That occurred against a long historical and geographical background. By the middle of the twentieth century, two "models" of constitutional enforcement were widely available. In political constitutionalism, constitutions are to be enforced by legislators and executives subject to control by voters.[23] In judicial (originally mislabeled "legal") constitutionalism, constitutions are enforceable by the courts. Importantly, within judicial constitutionalism, courts are to interpret the constitution de novo: judges are to base their interpretations on their own inquiry into the Constitution's meaning. They can give legislative and executive interpretations whatever weight the judges believed those interpretations were due, whether those interpretations were explicit in the available legal materials such as legislative debates and legal briefs or implied from the simple fact of enactment. Sometimes, though, courts can and (when the model is implemented) do conclude that the legislative and executive interpretations are due no weight at all.[24]

Political and judicial constitutionalism are stark alternatives: either the legislature and executive have the final word, or the courts do.[25] Specifically, constitutions do not have and (the thought appears to have been) cannot have constitutional – institutional – guarantees of judicial deference to constitutional judgments made by political actors responsible to the people. True, legal scholars have identified a principle of judicial restraint that judges *could* adopt, but they haven't developed institutional mechanisms for ensuring that judges *would* do so.[26]

Section 33 offered an institutional approach that combined, but of course modified, both political and judicial constitutionalism. Courts could continue to interpret the Constitution de novo but subsequently deliberated legislative and executive interpretations could displace judicial interpretations.[27] Section 33 showed that constitutional review was a continuum, with political and judicial constitutionalism at the endpoints and many possible institutional mechanisms in between. Choudhry's formulation, that constitutional ideas migrate, is exactly right: the *idea* of a continuum, brought out by devising an institutional mechanism between the end points, migrated even if the specific mechanism didn't.

The way India's experience with constitutional amendment was and is now understood in the field of comparative constitutional law and in the practice of constitutional design illustrates section 33's influence (in the sense I've described). Constitution designers understood that constitutional amendments can override judicial interpretations of the Constitution. For example, the Eleventh Amendment to the US Constitution did just that. Designers did not see constitutional amendments as modifying judicial constitutionalism, though, because they imagined that amending the Constitution would be difficult. In the terms of today's theory of constitutional design, the original constitution is an exercise of the people's constituent power, and amendments are an exercise of their delegated constituent power. The latter is thought to be possible only if the amendment rule is significantly different from the rule used to adopt ordinary legislation. What if the amendment rule is relatively lax?

India's constitution has such an amendment rule. Simplifying a bit: amendments require approval by a majority of both houses (rather than by a majority of a quorum) and by two-thirds of those present and voting. There need not be any subsequent action, such as ratification in a referendum. The very first amendment overrode a Supreme Court decision invalidating a sedition conviction and prospectively overrode the possibility that pending litigation would invalidate important land-law reforms. Scholars could have seen the amendment rule as a mechanism for combining judicial and political constitutionalism. But, as far as I know, they didn't. Why not?

A constitutional amendment differs from section 33 in that it modifies a constitutional provision permanently rather than suspending the provision's operation for five years. So, for example, India's First Amendment took the sedition law off the books, whereas a section 33 override would have made it inapplicable for five years (unless the override were renewed). Once we see constitutional amendments as potentially overriding court decisions, though, the possibility of a "sunsetted" constitutional amendment should come to mind relatively quickly. Indeed, the debate over adopting the initial constitutional amendment could point out that, if experience proved the amendment ill-advised, it would be relatively easy to delete the amendment from the Constitution through a subsequent amendment.

Further, India's amendment rule, though *relatively* easy, isn't all that easy. If I've done my calculations right, a government supported by a highly disciplined party with 76 percent of the seats in Parliament can ram through an amendment. And, notably, that described India in its first years and some later ones. Without a dominant party of that sort, perhaps, even an easy amendment rule doesn't place the Constitution in an intermediate place in the continuum between political and judicial constitutionalism.

Treating India as a special case, though, probably doesn't fully account for the sense that section 33 really did introduce a new constitutional idea. The reason is that systems with easy amendment rules can fall somewhere within the continuum with respect to overrides that have significant cross-party support.[28]

Section 33 changed the conceptual framework of constitutional review from one with two options to one with a continuum of options. That having occurred, constitutional theorists and designers could play around with other institutional mechanisms between the poles: the "new Commonwealth model" with declarations of incompatibility,[29] invigorated parliamentary scrutiny of proposed legislation for constitutionality,[30] and, someday, perhaps constitutional provisions expressly empowering courts to interpret the Constitution but not entirely de novo. Section 33 shows that a decidedly autochthonous constitutional provision, the product of unique local circumstances, can indeed be influential elsewhere – even when the provision itself is not directly incorporated into any other constitution.

How Can an Autochthonous Constitution Influence Other Constitutions? Proportionality in Canada

Constitutional review is a normative practice performed in varying institutional settings. Here, I offer the outlines of an argument for the proposition that Canada's version of structured proportionality – the *Oakes* test – has been influential because of its location in a legal culture of accommodation, which, as I've already argued, was instantiated in the Charter's plurinationalism.[31]

The *Oakes* test has been widely cited because it is a particularly perspicuous statement of what structured proportionality requires, but that, I argue, is not the most interesting way in which Canadian proportionality doctrine has been influential. A forewarning: readers may understandably conclude that the argument is a very long jurisprudential wind-up that delivers a rather small pitch about Canadian influence.

I start with the normative practice. A decision maker (judge) with the power to authoritatively determine (with finality) the constitutionality of all legislation would decide about each statute whether, in her all-things-considered view, it was constitutional.[32] She can concretize that judgment in two equivalent doctrinal formulations: unstructured balancing or structured proportionality.[33] The best defence of structured proportionality is that it communicates what the judge believes to be the relevant considerations more effectively than does unstructured balancing. Communicates to whom? To an attentive audience – lawyers in the first instance, the citizenry more broadly. The audience thus plays an important part in the defence of structured proportionality.

What of the institutional setting? As is well-known, the United States is the locus of unease with proportionality doctrine and the source of more categorical, hard-edged, rule-like constitutional doctrine. Although some have suggested that the very idea of "rights" is better captured in categorical rules than in all-things-considered judgments (hereafter ATC judgments),[34] in my view, the better argument for the US approach is institutional – second-order rather than first-order.[35]

Return to our judge who wants constitutional law to reflect her ATC judgments. Restated, she wants the sets of statutes upheld as constitutional and struck down as unconstitutional to match her ATC judgments as closely as possible. She can guarantee that outcome where she can make such judgments about all statutes. That, in turn, can occur when she is the only judge on the premises – that is, where constitutional review is concentrated and the judge has jurisdiction over challenges to every statute, including the possibility of taking up constitutional questions sua sponte.[36]

What happens when constitutional review is dispersed to judges whose decisions are subject to review by our judge? Nothing changes if she is able to review every decision by lower-court judges. No matter what the formal doctrine is, she will be able to determine constitutionality by making her best ATC judgment.

The story is different, though, if the reviewing court lacks the institutional capacity to review all lower-court decisions. Take the simplest example – doctrine that expressly tells judges that they should determine constitutionality by making ATC judgments. Our judge knows that some, perhaps many, lower-court judges will come to different ATC judgments than she would. Sometimes that will occur because they bring different considerations to bear or give the same considerations a different weight than she would. I think of these judges as "individualist," confident about their ability to arrive at good ATC judgments. Alternatively, as I've sometimes put it, the lower-court judges would arrive at a different result because they are not as legally adept as she is. And, importantly, our judge also knows that she won't be able to review all the decisions where lower-court judges differ from her ATC judgments.

In these circumstances, the judge has to go through something like the following internal dialogue: "I know that I can produce the best set of outcomes by making ATC judgments. If I tell lower-court judges to make ATC judgments, the set of outcomes will fall short of that. Is there some way I can reduce the gap by giving those judges different instructions?" Note that I've now introduced a second audience for constitutional doctrine – lower-court judges who are supposed to follow the doctrine the high court lays out.

And here's where categorical rules come in. Such rules eliminate from the judge's view some considerations that our judge knows will sometimes be relevant to *her* ATC judgment. If lower-court judges give those considerations the "wrong" weight (from our judge's point of view), eliminating them from the lower-court judges' consideration – that is, telling those judges to follow the categorical rule might produce a set of outcomes closer to the set the judge would generate from her own ATC judgments. Here's our judge's internal dialogue. "True, this lower-court decision, following my categorical rule, ignores what I believe to be a relevant consideration. It turns out, though, that if *I* made an ATC judgment, I'd reach the result that the lower court did, and if *that judge* took that consideration into account, he'd reach a result different from the one the rule produced – and I might not be able to review that decision. So, overall, the categorical rule produces a set of outcomes closer to my ATC judgments than would a doctrine telling lower court judges to balance (or do proportionality review, which is equivalent in this regard)."

There's a further wrinkle. Suppose our judge gets jurisdiction over a lower-court decision that reached a "mistaken" (from her ATC perspective) result. She can correct the result and bring the set of outcomes closer to her preferred set not by adopting proportionality but by creating a categorical exception to the initial categorical rule.[37] Followed often enough, this project will generate a quite complicated rule set – good from our judge's point of view, because the set of outcomes is better, but perhaps not so good when we think of the rule set as a complicated bunch of instructions to lower-court judges. Here's where what I earlier called legal adeptness comes in. Our judge might say to herself: "I know that I can navigate through the complicated rule set to get all and only the results that match my ATC judgments. Lower-court judges, thankfully, are not so adept. Often enough, they'll find themselves 'blocked,' unable to figure out how to fit their mistaken ATC judgments into the set of rules. And when they're blocked, they'll follow a subset of the rules that – aha! – produces the result I'd reach through an ATC judgment."[38]

All this is very complicated, of course, and isn't a defence of any specific set of categorical rules.[39] What it brings out, though, is the fact that audiences matter. Structured proportionality is better than unstructured balancing in communicating to the attentive audience. That characteristic, though, doesn't show that proportionality is better than categorical rules – because resolving *that* question requires thinking about communicating and guiding the audience of lower-court judges. Under some circumstances, systems with dispersed judicial review will perform worse using proportionality than using categorical rules.

And here's where the Canadian example matters. Proportionality appears to work reasonably well in Canada, which does have a system of dispersed review. What might account for that outcome? I suggest that it results from what I think of as an "accommodating" legal culture within Canada.[40] Lower-court judges aren't the individualists I described; the things they think relevant to an ATC judgment and the weights they give those things aren't dramatically different from those of Supreme Court judges. And Supreme Court judges don't think of themselves as dramatically more adept than their lower-court colleagues.

And, finally, as suggested at the outset, Canada provides a proof of concept that proportionality can work well in systems with dispersed constitutional review. The "proof" rests on the existence of a culture of accommodation. And the Charter's commitment to plurinationalism both instantiates and supports that culture. Elsewhere, such a culture might be supported by other features of the nation's constitutional identity. But I suspect, in the absence of such a culture – for example, where a legal culture of individualistic judicial judgment prevails – proportionality might not be, in David Beatty's famous phrase, "the ultimate rule of law."[41] In some sense, then, Canada can provide us with both a form of positive influence (proportionality review can work well in some systems of dispersed review) and a form of negative influence ("when the legal culture is of the right sort"). My personal view is that the positive influence has been reasonably large but the negative influence too small.

Conclusion

The Charter's plurinationalism was a solution to an intensely local problem. Two of its distinctive features were byproducts of the need to embed that solution in a constitutional document. Section 33 resolved a political conflict that stood in the way of making the Charter a statement about Canadian national identity. Almost any constitution-making exercise in the late twen-tieth century would have generated something like a proportionality doctrine, and Canada's formulation, though particularly felicitous, wasn't unique either. What mattered was that Canada had a system of dispersed constitutional review, a potentially inhospitable system for proportionality doctrines that achieve the goals judges seek from them. Plurinationalism allowed propor-tionality to work in such a system because it supported a perhaps pre-existing accommodative legal culture.

I have framed my comments by referring to the Charter's "influence" around the world. Notably, though, section 33 itself hasn't travelled well, and I believe the verdict isn't yet in on the success of proportionality doctrine on other systems with dispersed constitutional review. In my view, though, the project of creating a plurinational Canadian constitutional identity has been a success – notwithstanding, so to speak, that that identity wasn't consolidated immediately after 1982 (or, indeed, perhaps for several decades) and that many in Quebec's political elite still don't accept the solution (see Mathieu and Guénette, Chapter 24 in this volume). Compared with the fate of other separatist movements in major democracies – in Catalonia and Scotland, for example, with Ireland's unification being the flip side of separatism – the current state of Quebec sep-aratism seems to me to indicate that, at least for now, the Charter project, as I've described it, has been successful. And, in terms of constitutional longevity, forty years is nothing to shake a stick at.

Return, though, to the title of Choudhry's collection and focus not on its first noun but its last: "The Migration of Constitutional *Ideas.*" The Charter's influ-ence lies in Canada's demonstration that political and judicial constitutionalism sit at the ends of a continuum of institutional possibilities and in its demonstra-tion that a legal culture's character – accommodative or individualistic – can matter for the structure of constitutional doctrine.

Notes

1 I believe that most informed observers would find this obvious. For a modest bit of "empirical" support, I note that in his book on proportionality, Aharon Barak, a leading scholar of comparative constitutional law and former president of the Supreme Court of Israel, cites the Constitution of South Africa most often, followed by the Canadian Charter, then by Israel's Basic Law: Human Dignity, and Germany's Basic Law. He cites *Oakes* ten times, followed by eight and seven citations to Israeli decisions of which he was the author. Aharon Barak, *Proportionality: Constitutional Rights and Their Limita-tions* (Cambridge: Cambridge University Press, 2012), vii (Table of Constitutions), xxiv, xix, xxvi (Table of Cases).
2 A note on terminology: I use "plurinational" rather than "multicultural" because, in my view, the constitutional project involves populations described in nationalistic terms (associated with geography, in particular) rather than cultural ones. But I also don't

think that much turns on this terminological choice. If readers find it easier to understand the project as a multicultural one, they should feel comfortable in doing so.

3 I draw the term "byproduct" from Jon Elster, *Sour Grapes: Studies in the Subversion of Rationality* (Cambridge: Cambridge University Press, 1983).

4 I use the word "target" as a shorthand to identify a jurisdiction where constitutionalists think about the relevance of developments elsewhere, without intending to convey the meaning that constitutionalists in the nation of origin intend to export their ideas to a specific jurisdiction or, indeed, anywhere.

5 In the Canadian examples I examine here, the apparent influence flowed from something developed as an intermediate step in the overall solution to the Canadian problem. I don't know whether that's an example of a broader phenomenon.

6 Seen in this light, this essay is a contribution to the literature on what Sujit Choudhry notably describes as the migration of constitutional ideas: *The Migration of Constitutional Ideas* (Cambridge: Cambridge University Press, 2006).

7 My presentation, particularly in its references to Pierre Trudeau's understandings and conceptualizations, should be taken as a "rational reconstruction" of the events and ideas. I don't know whether Trudeau thought the things I attribute to him, or whether he did so in the rationalized order I present them, but I believe that the reconstruction makes sense of what he did.

8 This proposition is associated with Kelsenian and Schmittian constitutional theory.

9 One metaphor is that Quebec separatism was a persistent low-grade fever that occasionally reached an acute stage but never quite disappeared.

10 I use scare quotes to signal that, in my view, the political/sovereign status of Quebec is no more an objective problem than is, say, that of Puerto Rico or South Sudan or, indeed, the Maritime provinces.

11 I use the somewhat anachronistic term "plurinational" deliberately, as against the more common "binational" and "multicultural." On the difficulties of "binational," see the next paragraph. "Multiculturalism," though almost as good a term as "plurinationalism," doesn't capture the distinctive importance of nations of origin to the creation of a Canadian identity (for example, that there can be a LGBTQ+ culture or a Mennonite culture). I note that I am agnostic on the question of whether Trudeau consciously understood plurinationalism to be the solution he was proposing, though I suspect that such an understanding was at least latent in his constitutional thinking.

12 My sense is that a key move was to situate First Nations firmly within the plurinational understanding but that the cosmopolitanism of Vancouver and Toronto rapidly became part of the plurinational understanding. I find support for this in James Tully's influential work *Strange Multiplicity: Constitutionalism in an Age of Diversity* (Cambridge: Cambridge University Press, 1995), which places Canada's experience with First Nations at the heart of the analysis.

13 Note here that the US Constitution was drafted in a context where existing law seemingly required the states' unanimous consent but, as proposed, claimed that it would have a binding effect when nine of the existing thirteen states agreed to it.

14 Section 7's phrasing – "life, liberty, and security of the person" – may be an example of both the ability to make the list of rights distinctive (as an obvious and intended rejection of the US formulation "life, liberty, and property") and of the limits of that ability. Note, for example, that the drafters of the Constitution of India made the same choice decades earlier.

15 For a discussion, see Kai Moller, "Proportionality and Rights Inflation," in *Proportionality and the Rule of Law: Rights, Justification, Reasoning,* ed. Grant Huscroft, Bradley W. Miller, and Grégoire Webber (Cambridge: Cambridge University Press, 2014), 155–72.

As the relevant doctrine has developed, assertions of rights infringements have, indeed, escalated even as findings of rights violations have not (in some views). I personally find the distinction between infringements and violations analytically helpful but understand the argument that nonlawyers might too often see a determination that a right has been infringed as inconsistent with the conclusion that the right hasn't been violated.

16 I'm reasonably confident that Canadian scholars, not necessarily legal ones, have made this point already, but I am not familiar enough with the relevant literature to be able to point to examples.

17 Etienne Mureinik, "A Bridge to Where? Introducing the Bill of Rights," *South African Journal on Human Rights* 10, 1 (1994): 31–48.

18 Choudhry, *The Migration of Constitutional Ideas*. I discuss the claim of uniqueness below.

19 In this case, the national conditions blended political circumstances – the "problem" of Quebec and the need to gain widespread agreement on the Charter – with a cultural one, the preexisting understanding of Canada as binational. I suspect that all autochthonous constitutions, which might mean all constitutions, similarly blend political and cultural considerations, though in varying proportions.

20 In my view, there's no significant difference between an override adopted after a judicial decision and the insertion of a preemptive override in legislation likely to be challenged on constitutional grounds, at least where the legislation at issue is important and constitutional views are unlikely to change. In both, the legislature expressly takes the position that its constitutional interpretation is the correct one, and the preemptive override saves resources that would be wasted on litigation and, where necessary, parliamentary mobilization after a court decision. (This is a modification of my published views from several decades ago, in Mark Tushnet, "Policy Distortion and Democratic Debilitation: Comparative Illumination of the Countermajoritarian Difficulty," *Michigan Law Review* 94, 2 (1995): 245–301.)

21 Adopting an "override" mechanism has been proposed in quite a few venues, including Israel, but rarely adopted. One recent Israeli Basic Law includes an override clause, but attempts to incorporate a generally applicable one have foundered.

22 See Tushnet, "Policy Distortion and Democratic Debilitation." I write "within a decade" because I had started working on the ideas in the article several years earlier. (I should add that s 33's unpromising beginning in its use by Quebec might have turned into an unpromising history – and yet the influence I attribute to s 33 remains.)

23 Political constitutionalism allows courts to interpret, and perhaps distort, legislation in a constitution-respecting way, but they can't disapply a statute if they conclude that, as interpreted, it is inconsistent with the Constitution.

24 It oversimplifies the account only a bit to say that the courts would give the legislative and executive interpretations the weight they rationally deserved but did not give any weight (or only a quite modest amount of weight) to the mere fact that legislatures and executives acted with a warrant from the people.

25 Subject to the possibility of constitutional amendment, a matter I examine below.

26 For reasons that I don't fully understand (and that haven't been adequately explored in the literature of which I'm aware), the solution adopted in the Nordic constitutional tradition – constitutionality is assessed by reasonably robust and not entirely politicized institutions within the legislature and executive branches while language in the Constitution itself confines judicial invalidation to cases where the constitutional violation is "evident" – did not travel outside that region. (The reasons probably include parochialism among academics outside the region, the region's isolation from the main currents of constitutional theorizing, and the relative inaccessibility of Nordic languages to speakers of languages that have been the common currency of constitutional scholarship.)

27   As others have observed, the overall institutional arrangement that includes s 33 should probably be understood to require that judges offer de novo interpretations that give legislative and executive judgments on constitutional questions only the weight they rationally deserve. On this view, which I think is probably correct, Canada's institutional design strongly counsels against a principle of judicial restraint. At least that's so if the institutional design were implemented as seemingly planned. That, though, doesn't seem to have occurred, and so ideas about judicial restraint should probably still be among those that judges use to interpret the Charter.

28   My current favoured example of this is India's Ninety-Ninth Amendment, creating a judicial appointments commission, passed by a nearly unanimous – and cross-party – vote in the lower house. (The Supreme Court held it to be inconsistent with the structural requirement of judicial independence and invalidated it.)

29   Stephen Gardbaum, *The New Commonwealth Model of Constitutionalism: Theory and Practice* (Cambridge: Cambridge University Press, 2012).

30   Janet Hiebert and James B. Kelly, *Parliamentary Bills of Rights: The New Zealand and United Kingdom Experiences* (Cambridge: Cambridge University Press, 2015).

31   The full-scale argument would take more words than are available in this essay, and its main points would be elaborated in more detail and qualified in many ways. For a more detailed version of some, but only some, of the argument, see Mark Tushnet, "Three Essays on Proportionality Doctrine," Harvard Public Law Working Paper No. 16–43, https://papers.ssrn.com/sol3/papers.cfm?abstract_id=2818860.

32   I believe that this simply asserts that, in contexts where they can be made, all-things-considered normative judgments are required by minimum rationality requirements. I note, as well, that this exposition doesn't deal with complications associated with the fact that the courts with which we are usually concerned (apex courts) are collegial bodies.

33   That is, both doctrinal formulations allow the judge to identify and rest judgment upon every consideration relevant to her all-things-considered judgment.

34   See, for example, Grégoire Webber, *The Negotiable Constitution: On the Limitation of Rights* (Cambridge: Cambridge University Press, 2009).

35   Considered purely on the level of the normative practice, the second-order argument resembles the argument for rule utilitarianism versus act utilitarianism. For myself, I am persuaded by the argument that rule utilitarianism can always be reduced to act utilitarianism by specifying a sufficiently complex set of rules – and that the counter to *that* argument is fundamentally institutional. For the reduction argument, see David Lyons, *Forms and Limits of Utilitarianism* (Oxford: Clarendon Press, 1965). (I note that thinking about the rule-versus-act utilitarianism discussion has influenced my analysis of proportionality versus categorical constitutional doctrine.)

36   Here, the image should be of the suo moto practice in the Supreme Courts of India and Pakistan.

37   As noted above, this is the technique by which rule utilitarianism is reduced to act utilitarianism (as I understand Lyons's argument).

38   I draw the term "blocked" from Duncan Kennedy, *A Critique of Adjudication: Fin de siècle* (Cambridge, MA: Harvard University Press, 1998) (describing "impacted" legal fields), although he doesn't focus on how blocking is related to legal adeptness.

39   I find confirmation of my argument in an article by the late Stephen Reinhardt, an extremely adept judge who explained that he always worked his way through the rules the US Supreme Court gave him to reach the result that matched his ATC judgment, only to find himself regularly reversed by a Supreme Court majority that simply wanted to reach a different ATC judgment: Stephen R. Reinhardt, "The Demise of Habeas Corpus and the Rise of Qualified Immunity: The Court's Ever-Increasing Limitations on the

Development and Enforcement of Constitutional Rights and Some Particularly Unfortunate Consequences," *Michigan Law Review* 113 (2015): 1219–54.

40 Another relevant factor is probably the relatively low caseload of the Canadian Supreme Court, which allows its members to review many, perhaps nearly all, lower-court judgments, reaching results that one or a few justices believe erroneous from their ATC point of view.

41 For me, the fact that the United States doesn't have such a culture means we should be cautious in endorsing the pro-proportionality views of Vicki C. Jackson and Jamal Greene.

5

It Works in Practice, but Does It Work in Theory?
Accepting the *Canadian Charter of Rights and Freedoms* as a National Symbol

Andrew McDougall

IF FORTY YEARS of the Charter have taught us anything, it is that Canadians love it. It is one of the most unifying, identifiable symbols in the country, a symbol with broad and deep national recognition and solid and durable support. Canadians' views of the Charter, and the rights that it guarantees, have been built on four decades of experience. Given that the median age in the country is around forty years old, about half of the population has never known Canada without the Charter. It remains broadly depoliticized given its origins in the patriation crisis. There are no calls for its repeal, in Quebec or elsewhere. There are no major suggestions for constitutional reform of the Charter. Nor are there significant calls for reform of the judiciary or how judges are selected, however necessary reforms may have been in the past and present. Unlike in the United States, where judges are often household names, Canadians are not well versed with the backgrounds of those who sit on the courts, suggesting they see little need to track the partisanship of the bench. As recent elections have shown, there is no interest among politicians to gain any kind of partisan advantage by "politicizing the courts."

And yet those involved in the study of the Charter have never seemed to fully reconcile themselves to these facts. Debates on the Charter often focus on whether there is a legitimacy crisis in Canada's judiciary or the process of judicial review. This question arguably reached its peak between 2000 and 2010, during the fight between the so-called Calgary School and the dialogue theorists, a fight that has thankfully receded over the past decade. While there is now wide acceptance that the Charter is legitimate beyond question, scholarship has failed to adequately address or theorize its wild popularity. The question is relevant because it informs many of the debates that surround the Charter and its role in Canadian society.

I argue that the literature on the Charter needs to move away from the subtext that the Charter generates a legitimacy crisis for the Canadian judiciary and rights interpretation and towards a political understanding of the document as an entrenched part of Canadian culture and national identity. Essentially, scholars have recognized but never reconciled themselves to this fact. Early debates on the legitimacy of judicial review, the notwithstanding clause, and judicial selection were necessary and will always be with us, of course. They were also perfectly understandable, given Canada's experience with the Bill of Rights and the desire to advance rights in Canada onto a more concrete footing. Today, however, in light of the Charter's acceptance by Canadians, scholars can consider new questions with the benefit of distance from the Charter's entrenchment. While the atomizing implications of the Charter for concepts of citizenship and democracy have been widely discussed in academia, ordinary Canadians are unbothered by their new status as "Charter Canadians." Reconciling ourselves to the place of the Charter in the minds of Canadians will open new avenues for research and debates about the role and the importance of the Charter over its next forty years.

The Charter as a National Symbol

The popularity of the Charter is simply beyond question, but more importantly, it has become a unifying part of our identity. When Statistics Canada ran a poll in 2015 on what Canadians identified as their top national symbol, it was the Charter; at 93 percent, it carried the day. The Royal Canadian Mounted Police, hockey, the national anthem, and even the Canadian flag were less popular.[1] That level of support may have grown over time. In 2007, for example, SES Research found that support for the Charter was more popular among younger people, but it was overwhelmingly popular. The same poll undercut fears people had about the Charter and the role it plays in Canada. Canadians did not think the Charter was making Canada more like the United States, a fear raised in the run-up to its adoption, for example. The much-debated notwithstanding clause ranked low as a fear among Canadians. Interestingly, less than half of respondents had ever heard of it.[2]

As is always the case with the Charter, the question remains as to whether it has been tainted in Quebec, given the conditions under which it was adopted. It does not appear so. On the thirtieth anniversary of the Charter's entrenchment, Crop conducted a poll on Quebecers' views on patriation and the Charter. The poll found that 88 percent of Quebecers thought the Charter was a good or very good thing, leaving a sense that patriation did no lasting damage to the Constitution in the eyes of ordinary people. Interestingly, 80 percent of people thought that patriation itself was a good or very good thing, in light of the fact that the Constitution, up to that time, had been British.[3] While it is true that Quebec symbolically did not sign the Constitution in 1982, survey results like this challenge the narrative, dominant among Canada's elites, that Quebec is politically estranged from the Charter and the broader constitutional order.

Nor do judges get a rough ride from Canadians for the activism of their rulings or for acting antidemocratically. While there has been a lot of focus and attention on whether the Charter has been delegitimized in the eyes of the public by the opaque process of appointing judges, again one can look for and fail to find evidence. In 2015, Angus Reid found that the Supreme Court of Canada was more popular among Canadians than the US Supreme Court was among Americans, 75 percent to 64 percent, respectively.[4] This has been supported by more rigorous academic research. In a study of Canadian attitudes towards the legitimacy of the court, Erin Crandall and Andrea Lawlor found little to suggest that the public had any issue with the decisions of the court or that the decisions they were making were hurting its image in the eyes of Canadians.[5] One wonders what Justice Wagner was worried about when he decided that the court needed to relocate physically to Winnipeg to get at a "democratic deficit" in 2019.[6] Furthermore, the influence that the Charter has been gaining internationally has been the subject of academic commentary.[7]

Polls, of course, can be misleading and highly variable; they are always prone to selection bias. But it is worth observing that if it is indeed true that Canadians dislike the Charter, feel that judges have too much power, or that the Constitution needs reform, no major political party is prepared to endorse or run on such a program. Although there has been considerable tinkering with the selection of Supreme Court judges at the federal level over the past two decades, there is little to suggest that the pressure to do so has come from outside, rather than inside, the political and legal system. The inconsistent staying power of some of these changes and their low visibility also suggests that it is the product of "inside baseball" rather than pressure from the electorate to do something about widely perceived problems. While growing the diversity of the bench is a clear, needed, and laudable goal, the debates around how to do it have not sparked a loss of confidence in the court. It certainly has not struggled with an optics problem similar to that in the United States over both partisanship and diversity concerns.

A Very Canadian Document

The Charter was introduced to be a unifying national symbol. But the framers could only take it so far after the document was entrenched and the courts took over. Without any question, part of the explanation for why the Charter is so secure among Canadians can be traced to the attention that the court has paid to the specificities of the Canadian case.

The Charter got off to a tough start, adopted as it was against the backdrop of a national unity crisis and a severely isolated Quebec. Indeed, in the aftermath of 1982, Quebec symbolically immunized all of its laws with the notwithstanding clause. But the court moved quickly to secure the place of the Charter there and to otherwise ensure that the Charter reflected Canadian realities. This happened within the first decade, perhaps most importantly when the court confronted Quebec's language laws in Bill 101 in *Ford v Quebec (A.G.)*.[8] The Charter was adopted against the background of a country deeply divided along language lines and during a long simmering national unity crisis. The legal terrain around the court was very tenuous; the court could easily have blown the project up through aggressive readings of the *Charter of the French Language*. The court's compromise – that English could be reduced in size to one-third the size of French but not extinguished entirely on commercial signage – was a canny step. The Government of Quebec, in Liberal hands when the decision came down, found the compromise acceptable, and there was no need to immunize Quebec's law against Charter scrutiny with the notwithstanding clause. The court signalled that the French language in Quebec had nothing to fear from the Charter.

The sensitivity of the language question was a theme in early cases, and the protections grew as the years went on. The issue of language was central in *Re Manitoba Language Rights*, which invalidated the untranslated laws of Manitoba while endorsing the use of the suspended declaration of invalidity.[9] The ruling effectively secured the rights of the minority francophones while acknowledging that Manitoba had, for better or worse, long since anglicized. The court also pushed in a substantive direction on minority language education rights in *Mahe v Alberta*, guaranteeing institutional autonomy to parents over the schools.[10] This reached the high-water mark in *Doucet-Boudreau v Nova Scotia (Minister of Education)*, where the court found an unreasonable delay in the building of a francophone school in Nova Scotia and supported lower-court rulings that would oversee its construction at speed.[11] But the court also managed to reconcile the rights of anglophones and francophones inside Quebec with a skilful reading of section 23 to find a balance between the need to preserve French and not unnecessarily limiting English in the province. There were early stumbles when it came to guaranteeing substantive linguistic equality in state institutions, such as the courts. But the situation improved dramatically with the arrival of Justice Bastarache in cases such *R v Beaulac*, where the court pointed out that it was the duty of the country to actively promote both official languages.[12] Altogether, effective division-of-power cases, recognition of the specificity of Quebec's culture, and a robust language jurisprudence helped resolve the question of Quebec in Canada. The major cases surrounding national unity effectively ended with *Reference re Secession of Quebec*, but by 1998, it was clear that Quebec had nothing to fear in the Charter.[13]

Interpreting the Charter effectively against the backdrop of megaconstitutional politics was probably the most important factor ensuring that the

Charter would be accepted by the general public in all parts of the country. But the court also took Canadian approaches in other areas. The *Morgentaler* cases led to a sustainable situation around the status of abortion from a constitutional and political perspective. The court also demonstrated tremendous skill in *Reference re Same-Sex Marriage*, where it declined to rule definitively on the unconstitutionality of the existing definition of marriage while legislation expanding it to same-sex couples was before Parliament.[14] Politically charged at the time, the court signalled that it would never get too far ahead of public opinion. Other cases centred on social issues have been more muddled, perhaps because Canadians are themselves more evenly divided. The case of *Rodriguez v British Columbia (Attorney General)*, upholding the prohibition on medically assisted death, only to be reversed in *Carter v Canada (Attorney General)*, is a good example.[15] The court struggled equally with the morality and ethics of the sex trade in *Canada (Attorney General) v Bedford*.[16] But one can also make the argument that in both cases the court was in line with evolving public opinion.

The court's large and liberal interpretation of rights against the backdrop of multiculturalism did much to secure its place in a diversifying Canada. One example of this is the endorsement of hate-speech laws in *R v Keegstra*, which was in marked contrast to the American approach.[17] When qualified with cases such as *R v Zundel*, the court presented a balance on a polarizing topic that received a lot of attention at the time but has not returned as a political debate.[18] The court has also been fearless in diverging from American practice in many areas in cases that have been widely studied and lauded. The contrast between *Harper v Canada (Attorney General)* and *Citizens United v Federal Election Commission* is a textbook example of the Canadian court protecting democracy differently than do the Americans.[19] While deciding how much money third parties should be able to spend in elections may be a matter of debate, the muted public reaction to *Harper*'s finding that spending limits were constitutional (and the multiparty acceptance of that case, including the respondent, Stephen Harper himself) stands in contrast to the deeply divisive debates surrounding *Citizens United* that still play in the United States. The court has also taken a profoundly different tack on the question of partisan gerrymandering, which is unpopular in Canada and the United States. But in the United States, the Supreme Court has shown a much more relaxed approach than in Canada (see, for example, *Gill v Whitford* for a discussion of the court's ambiguity on the subject).[20] By contrast, the Supreme Court of Canada's findings in *Reference re Prov Electoral Boundaries (Sask.)*, in which it adopted the "effective representation" standard for drawing boundaries, are a clearer statement about how to draw boundaries to account for community.[21] While not addressing partisan redistricting per se, the ruling suggests there would be little room for it. That judges rather than elected officials contribute to keeping politics out of the drawing of electoral boundaries likely raises the stature of judges in Canadian politics. Finally, cases such as *Shelby County v Holder,* which voided federal preclearance provisions in the *Voting Rights Act* of 1965, leave many with the sense that the American Supreme Court is unprepared to defend all citizens equally.[22] The ambiguity on gerrymandering, the acceptance of unlimited money in politics, and the racial tensions that still exist in elections have arguably assisted the post–Donald Trump assault on election integrity and trust, as well as giving a sense that the political system is broken and in the pocket of the wealthy. This is in marked contrast to the Canadian approach.

The SCC has also signalled in a number of noteworthy cases the importance it places on diversity. In cases such as *Multani v Commission scolaire Marguerite-Bourgeoys,* the lengths it would go to ensure religious freedom were eyebrow-raising.[23] But here, too, the court has signalled that the jurisprudence would be firmly rooted in the Canadian experience. While it would do much to defend religious freedom and equality, there were clear limits. Denominational schools in Ontario remain not just on solid footing in the Charter, in section 29, but with the full endorsement of the court. In *Reference re Bill 30, An Act to Amend the Education Act (Ont.),* and *Adler v Ontario,* the court made it clear that these institutions were part of Canada's heritage.[24] Although the court had little room to manoeuvre in light of the text, the language it used made it clear it saw the schools as part of the historical compromise that had created Canada in the first place and that their objectives should be fully embraced.

In reference to Indigenous peoples, the court has faced the task of developing jurisprudence in a context that is perhaps just as sensitive as what it had to face with Quebec. However, whereas the Charter was interpreted to include and assure Quebec of the safety of its cultural and linguistic rights, in the realm of Indigenous politics, the court took the opposite approach: keep the Charter out of it. This approach relies on the decision of the framers to keep Indigenous rights outside of it, in section 35, supplemented with a nonderogation clause for Indigenous rights in section 25. But the court's skilful embrace of the concept of *sui generis* rights in the Indigenous realm has kept the jurisprudence largely on a separate track and confined to section 35. That section has developed into a mini Charter, bringing flexibility to the concept of "existing" rights and determining through it how a right can be established, managed, and ultimately infringed. In comparison, the section 25 nonderogation clause of the Charter has not developed in any significant way, suggesting little conflict between Charter and Indigenous rights. This has isolated the Charter from major issues in Indigenous constitutional interpretation. That Charter and Indigenous rights should so rarely conflict is understandable, but it was not foreordained. When major legal and political controversies explode over the rights and guarantees of Indigenous peoples in Canada, as they very often do, the Charter is invariably sidelined in the discussion. This has insulated it from what is likely the most significant political and constitutional cleavage in Canada today.

Looking over the last several decades, one struggles to point to a truly polarizing case of the court analogous to *Bush v Gore, Roe v Wade,* or *Citizens United v FEC.*[25] The closest would almost certainly have to be the *Morgentaler* trilogy, although the politics of abortion are still far less toxic than in the United States. There have been unpopular decisions in the criminal law context, to be sure, that provoked a strong parliamentary response.[26] But no case carries the ongoing political weight with the public like some of the American precedents cited above, leaving the Charter a wildly popular political symbol nearly everywhere.

Literature on the Charter: The Theory versus Lived Experience

The early literature on the Charter centred on debates that could be found in other countries with similarly entrenched constitutions. This made sense. Since Canada had never had an entrenched bill of rights, research into the legitimacy of judicial review, judicial selection, the notwithstanding clause, and the relationship of the Supreme Court to Parliament was urgent and desperately needed. Among the biggest fears was that the Charter would be an Americanizing instrument that would undercut Canadian practice and tradition. There is little doubt that this fear reflected broader Canadian sensitivity regarding the United States, the decline of the British Empire, and what an independent Canada would look like. The refusal to implement the Bill of Rights into the *Constitution Act, 1867* had arisen out of a concern, at least partially, for preserving the Diceyan version of parliamentary supremacy.[27] The rejection of the American approach extended beyond Canadian academics; it had support in the judiciary and at the Supreme Court.[28] Of course, the early writing was often concerned with how the Canadian Charter measured up against the US equivalent, as well as how it was different from the Bill of Rights.[29] Early commentators such as Peter Hogg focused on the notwithstanding clause, noting the likely unpopularity of the section. Perhaps setting the tone, Hogg signalled his interest in the clause and the value that he saw in it.[30] But there was little doubt in people's minds that the Charter was going to be a far more consequential document than the Bill of Rights that preceded it, a sentiment captured by Peter Russell's assessment that the Charter marked the judicialization of politics and the politicization of the judiciary.[31] Russell was plugged into the fact that the document was supposed to be, and would likely be, a unifying symbol for the country, a theme he remained committed to during the 1980s.[32] There was concern that patriation would fatally undermine the Charter in Quebec, but there was never much animosity towards the Charter, then or since.[33]

By the end of the first decade, the major themes that would shape writing about the Charter had emerged. By 1990, the importance of the Charter to Canada's legal development was accepted, and the debate focused on its impact and the judiciary's embrace of the Charter over the Bill of Rights.[34] Confronted with a Supreme Court unafraid of nullifying laws inconsistent with the Charter, scholars began to take a more thorough look at the legitimacy of judicial review and the issues that it might cause for democracy. In this, scholars moved in tandem with the court, which was itself interested in the question in early cases such as *Law Society of Upper Canada v Skapinker; Hunter et al v Southam Inc.; Re BC Motor Vehicle Act;* and *R v Big M Drug Mart Ltd,* where the court signalled that it was open to the American approach of judicial review notwithstanding some possible objections.[35] It elucidated the robust approach it would take to interpreting the Charter, which meant moving away from the tradition of legal formalism that had been the norm for much of Canada's constitutional history.[36]

The concern with judicial review was clear.[37] In the first ten years, the assessment was generally that it had only a modest impact on laws.[38] The popularity of the Charter was certainly coming into view, giving rise to the concept of "Charter Canadians" and the document's role as a symbol.[39] But even here the split was beginning to emerge over the question of how it had shaped the politics of the country and whether some groups were perhaps doing better than they would have previously. There was also a sense that there was something questionable about support for the Charter and the willingness of Canadians to give themselves over to the courts. Naturally, there was work done on how the Charter affected public policy and how fear of litigation might shape the way it is developed.[40] These themes remained the same, as the Charter approached its twentieth anniversary. The middle years were dominated by a concern to rescue the Charter from the fears of the countermajoritarian difficulty, the sense that judicial invalidation of popularly passed laws was in some way illegitimate. There was always an assumption, usually held by the right, that the Charter remained an alien presence in the Constitution. The slow-moving nature of judicial interpretation meant that this sense was never dispelled. There was also a continuing examination of the notwithstanding clause as a novel mechanism even though it was becoming ever more apparent that it was almost never used and the public had no interest in it.

It was during this time that "Court Party" adherents squared off against dialogue theorists, usually against the backdrop of the same-sex marriage debate. The former group, led by Ted Morton and Rainer Knopff, published *The Charter Revolution and the Court Party*, a benchmark statement for those worried about the Charter's impact on Canadian democracy.[41] Published in 2000, the book made a nuanced and convincing argument that the Charter had fundamentally reshaped Canadian democracy. Morton and Knopff argued that the Charter had privileged the legal profession and the judiciary in a way that allowed them to reshape Canada along lines important to them rather than what might have passed through ordinary parliamentary action. Equity-seeking groups – including gays and lesbians, women, and Indigenous peoples – were the primary beneficiaries of this change. But those with a unifying vision of citizenship – "social engineers" bent on reshaping society, postmaterialists pursuing abstract causes, and civil libertarians – benefitted. This Court Party, defined by its elitism, effectively left the concerns of ordinary people behind.[42] What differentiated them was the power that rights bestowed on them, at the expense of more universally accessible levers of democratic citizenship expressed through Parliament and other forms of popular action. This attack on the Charter spawned a decade of discussion. Nearly everything that followed was aimed at rescuing the Charter from these charges. Notable here was Kent Roach's *The Supreme Court on Trial*, which closely examined the debate around judicial activism to find that the concerns were overblown and that the real issue might be excessive judicial deference.[43] More open to the need for parliamentary action in defining rights was Janet Hiebert, who argued Parliament should continue to play an important role in defining rights and showed how courts have been very receptive at times to parliamentary participation in rights discourses.[44]

But by far the most important contribution to the debate over the last twenty years has been dialogue theory, which first appeared in Canada in 1997.[45] It built on American antecedents, but it has never been as important in the United States as in Canada.[46] Still, the idea has travelled broadly outside of Canada.[47] Dialogue theory broadly holds that the branches of government are not fundamentally in tension. Instead, dialogue theorists argue that there is no conflict at all; the Supreme Court and Parliament are in dialogue. Coming to this conclusion required a couple of mental moves – the idea that each institution was responsive to the other, a unique understanding of what counted as a dialogue, and acceptance that a dialogue framework was appropriate for the courts. Dialogue theory was hugely influential, sparking a long line of literature on what counted as a dialogue[48] and the impact and measurability of any dialogue in the courts and legislatures.[49] In fact, the number of publications on it began to spur something of a backlash; by 2010, there were those arguing that this line of argument had tapped out.[50]

A similar story played out regarding the notwithstanding clause. The clause's antecedents resided in both the Bill of Rights and a number of provincial human rights codes. But even at the time it was adopted, many doubted the public would warm to it, and it was controversial among the drafters. Academic interest in it was instant and could be polarizing.[51] The literature has since evolved substantially.[52] Scholars tied into dialogue theory to get around the problem of courts acting without democratic checks.[53] But the problem that haunted the notwithstanding clause was that there was little, if any, public appetite to use it. It has only been used around twenty times and often in the most quotidian, humdrum situations that left one wondering why it had been employed.[54] Somewhat perversely, this lack of use itself became a puzzle of intense interest.[55] But what was clear was that the public was thoroughly disengaged.

Giving the Charter Its Due: Understanding Success

The past ten years have seen some decline in these traditional themes. A more empirical turn has been taken when it comes to how the courts operate, and there is a growing literature on the "policy impact" of the courts. Still, judicial selection, the notwithstanding clause, dialogue theory, and judicial review remain central concerns. It is not that these topics should receive no attention, but other themes deserve attention. These include other sections of the Constitution that have seen important developments in a number of areas, such as a blossoming Indigenous rights scholarship, the strategic legitimacy of the court as an actor in a democracy, and the role of religion in public life. But when it comes to the Charter, the literature has never fully moved away from the gnawing concern that the Charter is beset by a problem of legitimacy.

What would some of this work look like? I suggest three areas where embracing the implications of the Charter's success would lead to interesting work. First, an important, unexplored political question is why the Charter has succeeded with the public when it might very well have failed. Here, two questions hang over the Charter. The first is connected to its popularity with the Quebec people. The fact that they endorsed it so strongly after patriation has never been fully accounted for. More accurately, it has never been fully admitted. This may reflect a taboo over calling the constitutional question closed, but the time is ripe to better understand how a document born at the time that it was and that experienced such a difficult first decade came out so unscathed in the end. The Bill of Rights was probably doomed from the start, simply because it was only a federal statute. But not necessarily so. A related question would be to better understand why it has never been viewed as an American import. Canadians have always been skittish about culture and the differences that separate them from their US neighbours. As noted, Peter Russell correctly guessed early on that the Charter would turn into a symbol. But it was not inevitable that the introduction of American-style constitutionalism would be embraced by the public. Furthermore, the Charter has never menaced Canadian culture; instead, it has become intertwined with it to the extent that it is now seen as a distinguishing part of it. The process through which that happened is important to understand.

Second, what is it in the Charter that Canadians find so compelling? It could be that they are attracted to the procedural guarantees in the legal-rights section. In theory, they may associate them with similar rights in the US constitution and be familiar with them through popular media. It is true that many of these rights in the criminal process, such as section 8, arrived with the Charter, and that may have been part of the attraction for the public.[56] The one section that we do have public opinion data on, the notwithstanding clause, suggests only tepid interest, at best (see Snow and Nicolaides, Chapter 7 in this volume). Perhaps it's that Canadians associate it with multiculturalism, as provided in section 27. Perhaps the equality guarantee alone is enough to solidify its value in the eyes of the public. There may be a vague appreciation that the right to vote and other democratic values are contained in the Charter. Certainly, for some in minority language communities, the provisions pertaining to official languages might be part of the picture. The problem is we don't know. What is it (or what sections) are Canadians most interested in, and why?

Of course, it may not just be what is in it but what was left out. As discussed, we have little understanding of the political importance of separating Charter and Indigenous rights. The study of Indigenous rights has grown enormously in the last fifteen years, a signal achievement in the scholarship of rights in Canada and illustrative of the growing importance that Indigenous conceptions of rights and power are having in the national debate. But while separation of the Indigenous discussion from the Charter discussion has historically been seen as wise (given the liberal conception of rights in the Charter, which is not always transferable to Indigenous conceptions of rights), scholars of the Charter would do well to better understand the implications of the separation. Does the lack of content here insulate the Charter from what is the most important constitutional debate facing Canada today? Does the lack of a firm footing for Indigenous rights in the Charter affect the way that the public perceives Indigenous rights? What is the role of the Charter in the ongoing process of reconciliation, if any? None of these questions has yet gained much attention.

Finally, embracing that the Charter "works" can allow for it to be studied as a case of judicial success. For those interested in the courts, a good use of time would be to get a better accounting of how the Supreme Court gained legitimacy all on its own. Here, the ball is already rolling, and there are a number of articles that help put together an answer.[57] But while this work looks at the court in relation to the Constitution in general, how the court has defended its position so effectively through Charter-specific guarantees is worth examining. It is again something of a marvel that Canadians do not hear about particularly odious or controversial cases when they are in an election; neither party has an appetite to publicize the judiciary. There has been promising work done, in particular by Mark Tushnet, demonstrating that the unique Canadian approach to the Charter has gained wide influence in other places around the world.[58]

Scholars would be wise to pick up on these themes and continue to elucidate them further. We could learn a lot about Canadian culture and identity, offer material for a comparative perspective on why some bills of rights succeed, and provide better insight into what the rights priorities of Canadians actually are. This work would certainly be of interest to scholars of the European Court of Justice, the expulsion of which was so important for supporters of Brexit, or scholars of the Spanish judiciary, whose rulings on Catalonia's autonomy in Spain have had the opposite effect as what came out of the *Secession Reference*. How the rights dialogue has unfurled with so little public opposition in Canada, contrary to the opinion of Morton and Knopf, is a mystery that would be of international interest. But the first step is admitting we don't have a problem.

Conclusion

Although debates about the legitimacy of judicial review, the relationship of the Supreme Court with Parliament, and the changes that the Charter ushered in for citizenship were necessary and valid in the early years, they have been thoroughly studied. While work should continue on these themes, new areas of research will present themselves when there is more acceptance of the secure place the Charter has in Canadian public opinion and the trust Canadians put in the judiciary.

Turning forty can be a difficult moment in the life of an individual, but in the case of the Charter, it has never been more successful or secure. It has been grounded in a thoroughly Canadian rights jurisprudence by a court that holds unusual skill in sensing mainstream public opinion. The reputation of the document has only grown over time, leaving some of the early fears about the role it would play in Canada looking outmoded and misguided. Getting over hesitancy to accept the Charter would encourage the growth of already emerging strains of scholarship, which would, in turn, help us better understand rights dialogue in Canada and the major political debates that exist in the country today.

Notes

1 Greg Quinn, "Survey Finds We Like the Charter of Rights More Than Hockey," *Calgary Herald*, October 1, 2015, https://calgaryherald.com/news/national/canadians-like -hockey-they-love-the-constitutional-bill-of-rights.

2 Nik Nanos, "Charter Values Don't Equal Canadian Values: Strong Support for Same-Sex and Property Rights," *Policy Options*, February 1, 2007, https://policyoptions.irpp.org/ magazines/the-charter-25/charter-values-dont-equal-canadian-values-strong-support -for-same-sex-and-property-rights/.

3 Canadian Press, "Quebecers Back Constitution and Federalism in New Poll," *Huff-Post Canada*, October 12, 2011, accessed March 3, 2021, https://www.huffingtonpost. ca/2011/10/12/30-years-later-vast-majority-support-constitution-charter-of-rights-and -freedoms-poll_n_1007121.html.

4 Angus Reid Institute, "Canadians Have a More Favourable View of Their Supreme Court Than Americans Have of Their Own," *Angus Reid Institute* (blog), August 17, 2015, https://angusreid.org/supreme-court/.

5 Erin Crandall and Andrea Lawlor, "Measuring Attitudes towards the Supreme Court of Canada" (paper presented at the Canadian Political Science Association Annual Conference, Vancouver, June 5, 2019).

6 Richard Wagner, "Meet the Judges: Get to Know Your Supreme Court – Remarks by the Right Honourable Richard Wagner, P.C., Chief Justice of Canada," Supreme Court of Canada, September 25, 2019, https://www.scc-csc.ca/judges-juges/spe-dis/rw-2019-09 -25-2-eng.aspx.

7 Mark Tushnet, "The Charter's Influence around the World," *Osgoode Hall Law Journal* 50, 3 (2013): 527–46. The point has been noted for some time now. For a popular overview of how the Charter stacks up internationally against the US Constitution, see Adam Liptak, "U.S. Court Is Now Guiding Fewer Nations," *New York Times*, September 17, 2008, https://www.nytimes.com/2008/09/18/us/18legal.html.

8 *Ford v Quebec (AG)*, [1988] 2 SCR 712.

9 *Re Manitoba Language Rights*, [1985] 1 SCR 721; on suspended declarations, see Brian Bird, "The Judicial Notwithstanding Clause: Suspended Declarations of Invalidity," *Manitoba Law Journal* 42, 1 (2019): 23–49.

10 *Mahe v Alberta*, [1990] 1 SCR 342.

11 *Doucet-Boudreau v Nova Scotia (Minister of Education)*, [2003] 3 SCR 3.

12 *R v Beaulac*, [1999] 1 SCR 768.

13 *Reference re Secession of Quebec*, [1998] 2 SCR 217.

14 *Reference re Same-Sex Marriage*, [2004] 3 SCR 698, 2004 SCC 79.

15 *Rodriguez v British Columbia (Attorney General)*, [1993] 3 SCR 519; *Carter v Canada (Attorney General)*, 2015 SCC 5.

16 *Canada (Attorney General) v Bedford*, 2013 SCC 72.

17 *R v Keegstra*, [1990] 3 SCR 697.

18 *R v Zundel*, [1992] 2 SCR 731.

19 *Harper v Canada (Attorney General)*, [2004] 1 SCR 827, 2004 SCC 33; *Citizens United v Federal Election Commission*, 558 US 310 (2010).

20 *Gill v Whitford*, 585 US (2018), 8–12.

21 *Reference re Prov Electoral Boundaries (Sask.)*, [1991] 2 SCR 158.

22 *Shelby County v Holder*, 570 US 529 (2013).

23 *Multani v Commission scolaire Marguerite-Bourgeoys*, [2006] 1 SCR 256, 2006 SCC 6.

24 *Reference re Bill 30, An Act to Amend the Education Act (Ont.)*, [1987] 1 SCR 1148; *Adler v Ontario*, [1996] 3 SCR 609.

25 *Bush v Gore*, 531 US 98 (2000), *Roe v Wade*, 410 US 113 (1973), or *Citizens United v FEC*.

26 See, for example, Kent Roach, "Twenty Years of the Charter and Criminal Justice: A Dialogue between a Charter Optimist, a Charter Realist and a Charter Sceptic," *Supreme Court Law Review* 9, 2 (2003): 39–64.

27 Walter S. Tarnopolsky, "The Historical and Constitutional Context of the Proposed Canadian Charter of Rights and Freedoms," *Law and Contemporary Problems* 44, 3 (1981): 175, https://doi.org/10.2307/1191216.

28 *Ibid*, 181.

29 Walter S. Tarnopolsky, "The New Canadian Charter of Rights and Freedoms as Compared and Contrasted with the American Bill of Rights," *Human Rights Quarterly* 5, 3 (1983): 227–74, https://doi.org/10.2307/762024.

30 Peter W. Hogg, "Canada's New Charter of Rights," *American Journal of Comparative Law* 32, 2 (1984): 298, https://doi.org/10.2307/840470.

31 Peter H. Russell, "The Political Purposes of the Canadian Charter of Rights and Freedoms," *Canadian Bar Review* 61, 1 (1983): 51–52; Hogg, "Canada's New Charter of Rights," 305.

32 Russell, "Political Purposes of the Canadian Charter," 36–37; Peter H. Russell, "Constitutional Reform of the Judicial Branch: Symbolic vs. Operational Considerations," *Canadian Journal of Political Science* 17, 2 (1984): 227–52.

33 Anthony G. Careless and Donald W. Stevenson, "Canada: Constitutional Reform as a Policy-Making Instrument," *Publius* 12, 3 (1982): 98, https://doi.org/10.2307/3329790.

34 E.R. Alexander, "The Supreme Court of Canada and the Canadian Charter of Rights and Freedoms," *University of Toronto Law Journal* 40, 1 (1990): 1, https://doi.org/10.2307/825895.

35 *Law Society of Upper Canada v Skapinker*, [1984] 1 SCR 357, *Hunter et al v Southam Inc.*, [1984] 2 SCR 145, *Re BC Motor Vehicle Act*, [1985] 2 SCR 486, and *R v Big M Drug Mart Ltd*, [1985] 1 SCR 295; Alexander, "Supreme Court of Canada," 1–3.

36 See, for example, Patrick J. Monahan, "At Doctrine's Twilight: The Structure of Canadian Federalism," *University of Toronto Law Journal* 34, 1 (1984): 47–99, https://doi.org/10.2307/825449.

37 Alexander, "Supreme Court of Canada," 39; F.L. Morton, "The Effect of the Charter of Rights on Canadian Federalism," *Publius* 25, 3 (1995): 181, https://doi.org/10.2307/3330693.

38 Morton, "Effect of the Charter of Rights," 175–77; see also F.L. Morton, Peter H. Russell, and Troy Riddell, "The Canadian Charter of Rights and Freedoms: A Descriptive Analysis of the First Decade, 1982–1992," *National Journal of Constitutional Law* 5, 1 (1994): 1–60; Janet Hiebert, "The Charter and Federalism: Revisiting the Nation-Building Thesis," in *Canada: The State of the Federation 1994*, ed. Douglas Brown and Janet Hiebert (Kingston: Queen's University, Institute of Intergovernmental Relations, 1994), 153–78.

39 Alan Cairns, *Charter versus Federalism: The Dilemmas of Constitutional Reform* (Montreal/Kingston: McGill-Queen's University Press, 1992); Peter H. Russell, "The Political Purposes of the Charter: Have They Been Fulfilled?" (paper presented at the meeting of the British Columbia Civil Liberties Association, "Conference on the Charter: Ten Years After," Vancouver, May 15, 1992); Morton, "Effect of the Charter of Rights," 177n32.

40 See, for example, Patrick Monahan and Marie Finkelstein, "Introduction: The Charter of Rights and Public Policy," in *The Impact of the Charter on the Public Policy Process*, ed. Patrick Monahan and Marie Finkelstein (Toronto: York University Centre for Public Law and Litigation, 1993), 1–48.

41 F.L. Morton and Rainer Knopff, *The Charter Revolution and the Court Party* (Peterborough, ON: Broadview Press, 2000).

42 *Ibid*, 80.

43 Kent Roach, *The Supreme Court on Trial: Judicial Activism or Democratic Dialogue* (Toronto: Irwin Law, 2001).

44 See Janet Hiebert, *Limiting Rights: The Dilemma of Judicial Review* (Montreal/Kingston: McGill-Queen's University Press, 1996); Janet Hiebert, *Charter Conflicts: What Is Parliament's Role?* (Montreal/Kingston: McGill-Queen's University Press, 2002).

45 Peter W. Hogg and Allison A. Bushell, "The Charter Dialogue between Courts and Legislatures (or Perhaps the Charter of Rights Isn't Such a Bad Thing After All)," *Osgoode Hall Law Journal* 35, 1 (1997): 75–124; Peter W. Hogg, Allison Bushell Thornton, and Wade Wright, "Charter Dialogue Revisited: Or 'Much Ado about Metaphors,'" *Osgoode Hall Law Journal* 45, 1 (2007): 1–65; Peter W. Hogg and Ravi Amarnath, "Understanding Dialogue Theory," in *The Oxford Handbook of the Canadian Constitution*, ed. Peter Oliver, Patrick Macklem, and Nathalie Des Rosiers (Toronto: Oxford University Press, 2017), https://doi.org/10.1093/law/9780190664817.003.0049.

46 See Alexander M. Bickel, *The Least Dangerous Branch: The Supreme Court at the Bar of Politics*, 2nd ed. (New Haven: Yale University Press, 1986).

47 For an excellent introduction to the contemporary scholarship, see Geoffrey Sigalet, Grégoire Webber, and Rosalind Dixon, "Introduction," in *Constitutional Dialogue: Rights, Democracy, Institutions*, ed. Rosalind Dixon, Geoffrey Sigalet, and Grégoire Webber, vol. 21, Cambridge Studies in Constitutional Law (New York: Cambridge University Press, 2019), 1–32, and related materials.

48 Christopher P. Manfredi and James B. Kelly, "Six Degrees of Dialogue: A Response to Hogg and Bushell," *Osgoode Hall Law Journal* 37, 3 (1999): 513–27.

49 Emmett Macfarlane, "Dialogue or Compliance? Measuring Legislatures' Policy Responses to Court Rulings on Rights," *International Political Science Review* 34, 1 (2013): 39–56, https://doi.org/10.1177/0192512111432565; Roach, *Supreme Court on Trial*; Hiebert, *Charter Conflicts*; Robert J. Sharpe and Kent Roach, *The Charter of Rights and Freedoms*, 5th ed. (Toronto: Irwin Law, 2013), 40–43.

50 Andrew Petter, "Taking Dialogue Theory Much Too Seriously (or Perhaps Charter Dialogue Isn't Such a Good Thing After All)," *Osgoode Hall Law Journal* 45, 1 (2007): 147–67.

51 Hogg, "Canada's New Charter of Rights," 298; John D. Whyte, "On Not Standing for Notwithstanding," *Alberta Law Review* 28, 2 (1990): 347; Peter H. Russell, "Standing Up for Notwithstanding," *Alberta Law Review* 29, 2 (1991): 293–309, https://doi.org/10.29173/alr1563.

52 For a great overview of the literature, see Dwight Newman, "Canada's Notwithstanding Clause, Dialogue, and Constitutional Identities," in *Constitutional Dialogue: Rights, Democracy, Institutions*, ed. Rosalind Dixon, Geoffrey Sigalet, and Grégoire Webber, vol. 21, Cambridge Studies in Constitutional Law (New York: Cambridge University Press, 2019), https://doi.org/10.1017/9781108277938.

53 Russell, "Standing Up for Notwithstanding."

54 Tsvi Kahana, "Understanding the Notwithstanding Mechanism," *University of Toronto Law Journal* 52, 2 (2002): 221–74, https://doi.org/10.2307/825966.

55 Russell, "Standing Up for Notwithstanding"; Tsvi Kahana, "The Notwithstanding Mechanism and Public Discussion: Lessons from the Ignored Practice of Section 33 of the Charter," *Canadian Public Administration* 44, 3 (2001): 255–91, https://doi.org/10.1111/j.1754-7121.2001.tb00891.x; David Snow, "Notwithstanding the Override: Path Dependence, Section 33, and the Charter," *Innovations* 8 (September 2008): 1–15; Janet Hiebert, "The Notwithstanding Clause," in *The Oxford Handbook of the Canadian Constitution*, ed. Peter Oliver, Patrick Macklem, and Nathalie Des Rosiers (Toronto: Oxford University Press, 2017), https://doi.org/10.1093/law/9780190664817.003.0033.

56 Roach, "Twenty Years of the Charter and Criminal Justice," 43.
57 See, for example, Vuk Radmilovic, "Strategic Legitimacy Cultivation at the Supreme Court of Canada: Quebec Secession Reference and Beyond," *Canadian Journal of Political Science* 43, 4 (2010): 843–69; Robert Schertzer, *The Judicial Role in a Diverse Federation: Lessons from the Supreme Court of Canada* (Toronto: University of Toronto Press, 2016).
58 Tushnet, "The Charter's Influence around the World."

6

Charter Talk

How Canadian Media Cover Rights and Politics

Erin Crandall, Andrea Lawlor, and Kate Puddister

WRITING IN 1992, Alan Cairns noted, "The constitutional conversation precipitated by the Charter is not confined to courtrooms and does not require a law degree of its participants."[1] In his foundational book, *The Charter versus Federalism*, Cairns went on to argue that, unlike the *Constitution Act, 1867*, which is primarily centred on the legal jurisdictions and powers of governments ("the government's constitution"), the *Constitution Act, 1982*, and especially the Charter, is the "people's constitution," because it empowers individuals with specific constitutional rights, ultimately providing a constitutional identity. Despite this populist description, it is still not entirely clear where the "people" fit within the day-to-day operations of the Charter. Most Canadians do not attend court proceedings or other forums such as Parliament where the Charter is interpreted and applied, and only a tiny portion of Canadians will ever engage in Charter litigation. Instead, the public relies on the media as an intermediary to connect with government institutions, including courts. In practice, the bulk of the public's Charter conversation ("Charter talk") happens in news coverage of the Charter and constitutional litigation.

In this chapter, we take up Cairns's notion that the Charter is not confined to courtrooms or legislatures and consider the public conversation about the Charter in Canadian media over the past forty years. Our analysis relies on media reporting on the Charter as a proxy for public conversation for a few reasons. Media are the primary source of information for the public regarding the Charter, and news coverage of judicial decisions and political debates regarding the Charter shape public knowledge and opinion.[2] News coverage is essential for the promotion and protection of the open court principle (that courts are open physically and metaphorically), and the media serve as an important intermediary in providing the public access to justice.[3] Media coverage of the Charter in general and judicial decisions interpreting the Charter in particular play a vital role in ensuring the legitimacy and transparency of the legal system as a whole. Indeed, legal and political actors must rely on the media to convey information about the law and legal concepts to the public, as most members of the public will not access judicial decisions first-hand. Media coverage also plays an important and influential role in shaping how other political actors and institutions respond to and engage with the Charter and legal decisions made about the Charter.[4] Unlike narrower institutional and parliamentary records, such as *Hansard,* committee-meeting transcripts, and the judicial process itself, media permit conversation among actors, creating a public dialogue that is open and less constrained by institutional norms. Thus, the media are an important venue for dialogue about the Charter outside of courtrooms, serving as a forum for public debate regarding the Charter by citizens, legal actors, and political elites alike.

To examine the public conversation surrounding the *Charter of Rights and Freedoms,* we focus on two factors. First, who are the primary actors associated with these conversations, and what proportion of the narrative do they account for? Does news coverage focus more on the actions of courts or the government and has this shifted over time? Second, what areas of the Charter make up the main foci of Charter coverage? In addressing these questions, we are concerned with both Charter inputs (sections of the Charter that drive discussion and disputes) and Charter outputs (judicial decisions and Charter cases).

We analyzed 2,560 articles from the *Globe and Mail* and the *National Post* that reference the Charter from 1982 to 2020, thus offering a broad assessment of how the media covers the court system and the Charter, with attention to changes over time. Our findings centre on three areas: (1) which actors dominate the conversation about the Charter, (2) which aspects of the Charter are most frequently discussed and debated in the news media, and (3) which cases have had the greatest presence in the national conversation about the Charter. We find that coverage of the Charter was driven by a court-focused narrative until the early 2000s, after which government became a more prominent actor in Charter narratives. Second, we see evidence of a sustained narrative on legal rights and fundamental freedoms, while other sections – namely, equality rights and the notwithstanding clause – are marked by punctuations of interest around key cases or intergovernmental conflicts. Finally, we find little by way of a consistent and sustained case-based narrative, though a few cases, including *Morgentaler* (1988), *Khadr* (2008), and *Vriend* (1998) appear to have some resilience, as they are referred to beyond their initial period of discussion.[5]

The Existing Literature: Media, Courts, and the Charter

While we may hypothesize that media coverage of the Charter has changed over the four decades of its existence, there is no existing research well-equipped to guide our expectations. Research on media coverage of Canadian courts and the Charter is most often focused on a single Supreme Court case, a series of cases focused on a single topic, or a particular aspect of the Charter like the notwithstanding clause. Florian Sauvageau, David Schneiderman, and David Taras provide the most comprehensive analysis to date by examining media coverage of the Supreme Court of Canada over a one-year period.[6] They highlight the unique relationship between the media and courts – that the court must rely on the media to communicate its decisions to the public and to help foster legitimacy for its work. However, the court, its work, and the Supreme Court justices themselves do not lend themselves to easy news coverage, as the justices do not routinely engage with the media, and the decisions rendered by the court are often complex and abstract.[7] Emmett Macfarlane's examination of rights talk in Canadian media provides another assessment of media coverage of the Charter in a general sense.[8] Through an examination of news coverage of salient Charter rights cases over a five-year period, Macfarlane finds that news coverage of rights tends to be simplistic, which raises concerns regarding citizens' understanding of the complex nature of rights and their limits, ultimately impacting the quality of political debate and the development of public policy.

Other assessments of the relationship between the media and the courts focus on a single issue, such as use of the notwithstanding clause (see Snow and Nicolaides, Chapter 7 in this volume) or a single case or area of jurisprudence. For example, Lydia Miljan's analysis of media coverage of *Saskatchewan v Whatcott*, a case concerning hate speech, finds that journalists relied on legal framing in their coverage.[9] Erin Crandall, Kate Puddister, and Mark Daku study media coverage of the Supreme Court of Canada's medically assisted dying decisions by comparing coverage of *Rodriguez* (1993) and *Carter* (2015) to assess if news coverage of the court has changed over time.[10] In comparing the coverage of decisions that occurred over twenty years apart, the authors find little change in media coverage, regardless of substantive differences in how the court has approached the issue of assisted dying, moving from prohibition to decriminalization, with increased reliance on social science evidence by the court. Other work at the intersection of the Charter and media includes Eleni Nicolaides and Dave Snow's examination of media coverage of political debates on the use of the notwithstanding clause in Ontario and Saskatchewan.[11] The authors assess the accuracy and tone of media coverage of the notwithstanding clause, finding that although coverage was generally accurate, the clause was frequently portrayed negatively and that coverage reflected the ideological orientation of the news outlet. Importantly, much of the existing literature on media coverage of Canadian courts is largely qualitative in nature and relies on manual content analysis, with the exception of Crandall, Puddister and Daku, who employ automated dictionary-based content analysis using Lexicoder.[12] This leaves ample room for analyses that engage in larger-scale evaluations of trends over time and can shed light on how media narratives have changed (or not) since the Charter's inception.

In the forty years since the adoption of the 1982 constitution, the media landscape in Canada has changed in fundamental ways. The rise of digital communications has forced legacy media to offer hybrid (print and digital) formats while competing with digital-only content creators such as Buzzfeed for readers, link clicks, and advertising revenue. Access to digital technology has created new opportunities for journalists reporting on courts, including electronic access to court documents and, depending on the court, the ability to live blog/Tweet and access online streaming of proceedings.[13] The digital age has also brought considerable challenges, especially financial ones for legacy media.[14] As a result, there are fewer Canadian journalists assigned to cover Canadian courts and politics, and those who do are not likely to have a specialization in law. The digital age has also brought change to Canadian courts, though it has been far less transformative. While most courts operate a Twitter feed and the Supreme Court routinely live-streams its proceedings, in general, Canadian courts have taken a conservative approach to integrating digital technology into the courtroom and have not changed the nature of engagement with the media in any significant respect.[15] Thus, while our focus on the *Globe and Mail* and *National Post* in this chapter allows for a consistent measure of media coverage over time, we also acknowledge that the media landscape over this same time period has changed, and this may have implications for both content and readership.

Method and Data

To analyze media coverage of the Charter, we gathered all articles from the *Globe and Mail* and *National Post* from April 1, 1982, to December 31, 2020, that included the term "Charter of Rights and Freedoms" in the headline or lede paragraph.[16] This produced a total of 2,560 articles, with an average of 65 articles per year. We inductively scanned the text corpus using computer-assisted automated text retrieval tools for all phrases (two to five words) and words of substantive import that appeared in the corpus over twenty-five times.[17] From there, we manually separated these terms into categories associated with the dimensions we were interested in capturing: (1) people/institutions associated with Charter commentary, (2) the prominence of discourse pertaining to specific Charter rights and freedoms, and (3) the prominence of key Charter cases. A summary of categories and terms is available in Table 6.1.[18] We coded these using an automated process, capturing each mention of a term in any sentence. Accordingly, depending on its contents, each sentence could be coded with multiple terms. Once all articles were coded, we exported the frequencies of each code by article for analysis.

Table 6.1

Categories and example terms

People and institutions	
Courts	Lower court, superior court, provincial court, Supreme Court, Court of Appeal (appeal court), all the names of the chief justices
Government	Federal government, provincial government, the Crown, the political parties, prime minister, premier, attorney general, minister of justice (justice minister), the names of the attorneys general, the names of the prime ministers
Experts	Lawyer (counsel for), law society, Bar Association, law professor (professor of law),
Law enforcement	Police, RCMP, OPP, Sûreté du Québec, law enforcement

Charter of Rights and Freedoms	
Limits	Section 1, reasonable limits, *Oakes* test
Fundamental freedoms	Section 2, freedom of conscience, religion, thought, expression, peaceful assembly, association, speech
Democratic rights	Section 3, right to vote, democratic rights
Legal rights	Section 7, life, liberty, security of the person, unreasonable search or seizure, arbitrarily detained or imprisoned, arrest or detention, unreasonable delay, cruel and unusual treatment
Equality rights	Section 15, discrimination, gender equality, same-sex marriage (and variants)
Notwithstanding clause	Section 33, notwithstanding clause

Prominent cases	
Cases	*Hunter v Southam* (1984), *Big M* (1985), *Oakes* (1986), *Morgentaler* (1988), *Andrews* (1989), *Irwin Toy* (1989), *Askov* (1990), *McKinney* (1990), *Sparrow* (1990), *Keegstra* (1990), *Stinchcombe* (1991), *Rodriguez* (1993), *Dagenais* (1994), *Vriend* (1998), *Law v Canada* (1999), *Little Sisters Books* (2000), *Doucet-Boudreau* (2003), *Figueroa* (2003), *Same-Sex Marriage* (2004), *Chaoulli* (2005), *Bedford* (2013), *Carter* (2015), *Jordan* (2016)

Note: For the category "People and institutions," a review of the most active nongovernment intervenors at the Supreme Court was also performed. See Lori Hausegger, Matthew Hennigar, and Troy Riddell, *Canadian Courts: Law, Politics, and Process*, 2nd ed. (Oxford University Press, 2015). However, all of these legal groups received fewer than twenty-five mentions each.

The use of computer-assisted automated text retrieval made it feasible for us to examine a large body of news stories that spanned several decades. The use of this broader kind of categorical analysis, as opposed to manual content analysis, did come with some trade-offs worth acknowledging. While manual content analyses offer the precision of reading each word of an article in the context in which it was written, they limit the number of texts that can be evaluated in a restricted time period. Manual approaches are also not immune from inaccuracies. Manual content analyses rely on multiple coders coding the same texts to ensure validity. Yet manual approaches are often noted to show some degree of inconsistency between coders. Thus, even with manual approaches, random and systematic errors will enter the coding process. Automated methods may introduce systematic error, but given the outsourcing of the coding process to software, random error is not introduced. Nevertheless, we mitigated some of the weaknesses associated with automated coding operations by conducting a manual validation of the codes in 10 percent of the articles. We also used QDA Miner's keyword-in-context feature to ensure that terms and case names were being appropriately coded. Where inconsistencies or inaccuracies were found, we established exclusion rules or introduced stop words (e.g., "court" but not "courting"); we refined and updated the coding accordingly. Similarly, we considered the limitations of our sources. While analyzing coverage from the *Globe and Mail* and *National Post* should provide a representative picture of national English media coverage of the Charter, these newspapers do not capture regional and local variation in coverage. Considering that partisan identification is a significant factor for explaining public attitudes towards the Charter,[19] with Conservatives tending to be less supportive and Liberals more supportive, and that party strength is regionally distributed in Canada, it seems reasonable to anticipate differences in media coverage of the Charter at the local level.[20] Future research that looks at differences between regional media coverage, therefore, would be valuable.

Findings

Because this was the first longitudinal study of media coverage of the Charter, our analysis was largely exploratory. Accordingly, we did not test formal hypotheses but did have some general expectations. The Charter's considerable public popularity and high visibility have been fairly consistent over time. We therefore did not anticipate any trends that would suggest a significant drop in media coverage of the Charter. That said, changes in government, high-profile and politically salient court cases, and public debate and use of the notwithstanding clause made it reasonable to expect punctuations in media coverage over time. We therefore anticipated that the primary actors associated with Charter conversations and the proportion of the narrative they account for in the media would fluctuate. Likewise, we anticipated observing variance over time in the sections of the Charter that made up the foci of media coverage. Altogether, by looking at both outputs (judicial decisions and Charter cases) and inputs (sections of the Charter driving discussion and disputes), our analysis provides important insights into the public conversation about the Charter, or "Charter talk."

In our analysis, we consider four categories of actors: judicial actors (e.g., the Supreme Court, lower courts, judges, the chief justices), government actors (e.g., prime ministers, ministers, party leaders), legal experts (e.g., lawyers providing case commentary, law and political science professors), and law enforcement (e.g., police, including federal and provincial police forces such as the RCMP and Ontario Provincial Police, and other law-enforcement agencies such as the Canada Border Security Agency) (see Table 6.1 for examples and the codebook – available from the authors – for a full listing). We operationalize the content of the Charter by its respective sections (though we only consider sections 1–15 and 33 because of their prominence in academic and media discourse).

We found that legal experts and government actors appear in news stories with nearly equal frequency (45 percent versus 44 percent), and law enforcement follows closely in frequency of mentions (39 percent), suggesting that criminal justice has been a major focus of Charter media coverage.[21] Interestingly, courts were the least likely to be mentioned (33 percent). This may be a surprising finding to some given how closely intertwined the Charter and courts are commonly viewed. It is worth noting, however, that in comparison to the other categories that can easily have multiple actors appear in a single news story (e.g., attorney general, federal government, provincial government), it is more likely that the specific court hearing a Charter case will be referenced. The frequency of mentions of Charter sections is also informative. Legal rights, which capture coverage of section 7 of the Charter (life, liberty, and security of the person), are the most frequently mentioned (in 21 percent of stories), again suggesting that Charter coverage is often focused on criminal justice. Fundamental freedoms, which captures section 2 (freedom of expression, assembly, etc.), also received considerable media mentions (17 percent), while mentions of equality rights (section 15) and democratic rights (section 3) were referenced less frequently. Mentions of the reasonable limits clause (section 1) and the notwithstanding clause (section 33) appeared with near equal frequency, but only in a relatively small number of Charter news stories.

In Figure 6.1, we examine more closely the number of mentions of institutional actors and track the trend over time. When put into conversation with our

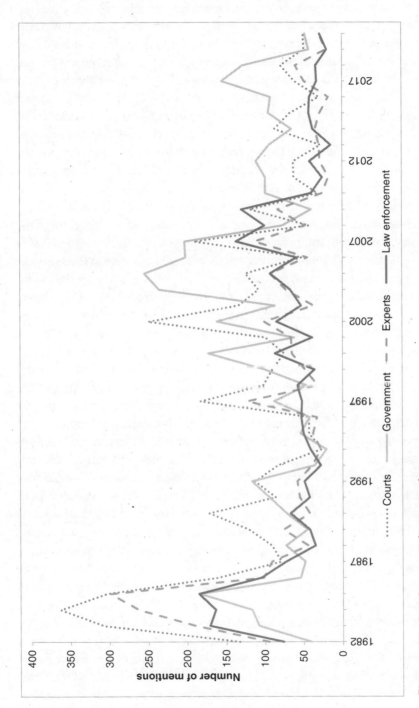

Figure 6.1 Number of mentions of institutional actors

earlier observations, which look at the percentage of news story mentions, an interesting story emerges. For the courts, the highest number of mentions comes in the early years of the Charter, a time when the Supreme Court was deciding groundbreaking cases that set out the foundations of Charter jurisprudence. These early years of Charter coverage were also a time that saw a higher proportion of federal and provincial statutes being overturned on Charter grounds.[22] The dominance of the courts in these early years of Charter media coverage, therefore, is arguably not surprising. This is contrasted with media mentions of government, which are comparatively low in the early Charter years, but surpass the courts beginning in the early 2000s. By comparison, legal experts and law enforcement receive far fewer mentions. Whereas government and legal experts were included at the same rate, proportionately, in stories, the actual number of mentions shows that governments were at the centre of the discourse, with legal experts providing only supplementary commentary. This is congruent with what one may expect about media coverage. While government or court action "drives" the story by providing the venues in which Charter issues play out, legal experts are called upon to comment on these developments, though they, themselves, rarely play a generative role in this narrative.

Altogether, Figure 6.1 indicates that Charter talk is primarily undertaken by the branches of government. The change in coverage between the courts and government over time is therefore particularly interesting. Whereas the courts appear to be the dominant actor in media coverage in the early years of the Charter, since 2004, this position has switched to government. The pivotal marker appears to be from 2004 to 2006, when media mentions of government significantly surpass mentions of the courts. This period featured two federal elections in as many years where federal party leaders Paul Martin (Liberal) and Stephen Harper (Conservative) repeatedly debated Parliament's proper role in legislating rights and the use of the notwithstanding clause. A central focus of this debate was same-sex marriage, which the Supreme Court had issued a reference opinion on in 2004 (see Figure 6.2 for a corresponding analysis).[23] The court decision and ensuing legislation that removed legal barriers to same-sex marriage were used to contrast the leaders' approaches to Charter rights, with Harper promising a free vote on the issue in the House of Commons and Martin claiming "Harper's views on same-sex marriage would hamper the Conservative Leader's ability to govern."[24] In similar fashion, Martin attempted to introduce the use of the notwithstanding clause as a wedge issue to distinguish the two leaders, pushing Harper to state whether, as prime minister, he would use the notwithstanding clause to reintroduce a definition of marriage that limited the union to one man and one woman.[25] Notably, this Charter talk happened within, rather than between, branches of government.

While this specific Charter debate receded with the resignation of Martin as Liberal Party leader in 2006, government has remained the most mentioned institutional actor in Charter media coverage. Interestingly, in more recent years, it is not the federal government driving these mentions, but provinces that have enacted or have considered enacting the notwithstanding clause. Whereas for the majority of its existence the notwithstanding clause, which permits a provincial legislature or the federal Parliament to declare that a law shall operate notwithstanding certain provisions of the Charter, was seen as so politically controversial as to be effectively unusable, it has recently experienced a comeback, with several provinces either proposing or enacting the clause.[26] This is further borne out in the data, which show that correlations between mentions of court actors and section 33 of the Charter have a weak but significant association ($p < .001$), whereas correlations between government actors and section 33 show a moderate and significant correlation ($p < .001$). This suggests there is a stronger narrative throughout this time period about government use of the clause compared with the courts' jurisprudence in this area.

In his media analysis of seven Supreme Court Charter cases, Macfarlane finds that the notwithstanding clause was referred to in one-quarter of all articles, suggesting substantial media saturation.[27] Figure 6.2 provides a longitudinal look at Charter media coverage and shows how attention to the notwithstanding clause has ebbed and flowed significantly over the forty years of the Charter. The first dramatic spike in media mentions of the notwithstanding clause was in 1989, in the midst of the countrywide debate on the Meech Lake Accord and a year after the Supreme Court's decisions in *Ford* and *Morgentaler*, which both prompted interest in section 33.[28] The *Morgentaler* decision, which ruled that the criminalization of abortion was unconstitutional and violated a woman's right to security of the person under the Charter, was politically divisive and, as Figure 6.4 shows, it received the most media coverage of all Supreme Court Charter cases. This media attention carried over to Parliament's unsuccessful efforts to legislate on abortion in response to the ruling, with some advocating for the use of the notwithstanding clause in order to recriminalize abortion.[29] The greatest amount of media attention came in 2005 in response to the Charter debate that occurred between Martin and Harper. A final sizeable spike in mentions of the notwithstanding clause occurred in 2018–19 and was attributable to provincial efforts to use the notwithstanding clause, specifically in Saskatchewan in relation to separate school boards and in Ontario in relation to the restructuring of Toronto's city council. Notably, even though the federal government has never enacted the notwithstanding clause, it was federal debates around its use that received the most national media attention, perhaps indicating a difference in focus between national and regional media coverage of the Charter.

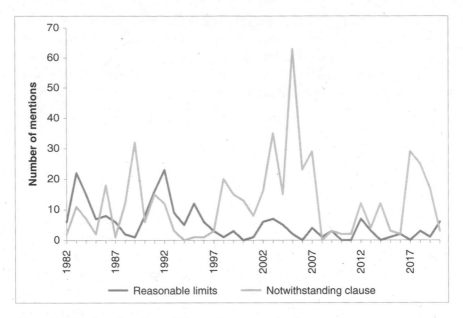

Figure 6.2 Number of mentions of Charter "government" sections

Figure 6.2 also presents media coverage of section 1, the Charter's reasonable limits clause. The reasonable limits clause, which sets out that all Charter rights are subject "only to such reasonable limits prescribed by law as can be demonstrably justified in a free and democratic society," is a defining feature of all Charter jurisprudence and a critical piece of any rights dialogue that may (or may not) take place between the legislatures and the courts.[30] Its coverage in the media is therefore essential to the public's understanding of the Charter. In his study, Macfarlane finds that coverage of Charter decisions in the early 2000s did little to explain the Supreme Court's reasonable limits analysis, suggesting "that Canadians, as consumers of news, are only rarely exposed to the notion that the Charter explicitly mandates a consideration of the limits or boundaries of its guarantees."[31] Our data show that media coverage of the reasonable limits clause has actually decreased over time, indicating that concerns over the public's lack of understanding of the Charter may be more warranted today than twenty years ago.

Figure 6.3 examines the weight given to each section of the Charter in media coverage. With the exception of democratic rights, we found considerable attention to Charter rights in the early years of the Charter. This media saturation dropped off considerably by the late 1980s, arguably supporting Peter McCormick's view of the end of the "Charter revolution" (at least when it comes to media coverage) that "this is no longer the high drama of the early days, and the

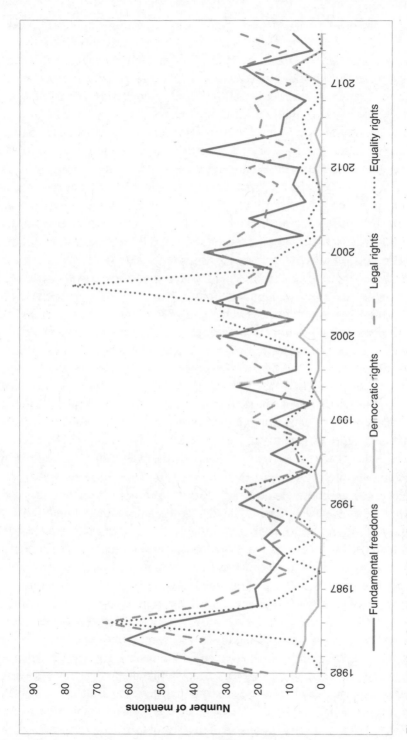

Figure 6.3 Number of mentions of Charter "rights" sections

surprises are small, few and far between."[32] The decreasing number of Charter cases heard by the Supreme Court year to year may also have been a contributing factor.[33] Fundamental freedoms and legal rights featured regularly throughout the time period under investigation. Coverage of section 2 saw some increases in coverage at the outset of the Charter's implementation and again in 2007 and 2013 in response to challenges to religious freedoms in Quebec while the government considered various forms of secularization of the public sphere. By contrast, coverage of section 7 appeared to be case-driven. Spikes in coverage in 2002, 2007, and 2008 were consistent with the Supreme Court's jurisprudence in *Gosselin* and *Khadr*.[34] A considerable portion of coverage is centred on section 15 equality rights, with notable increases in coverage in 1985, the year that section 15 came into effect, and in 2005, corresponding with the Harper-Martin rights debate on same-sex marriage. By contrast, there was little discussion of section 3, democratic rights, though there were small increases in coverage in 1991 and 2018. The former was in response to a reference decision on Saskatchewan's Electoral Boundary Commission.[35] The latter was a reflection of the Ontario provincial premier's attempt to use the notwithstanding clause to restructure Toronto's city council (see Small, Chapter 8 in this volume).[36]

Finally, Figure 6.4 looks at the most prominent Charter cases as measured by media mentions. It is worth considering how media coverage of Charter cases, as a proxy for public importance, may differ from assessments of the legal importance of Charter cases. "Legal importance" is a necessarily messy measure, but an effort to rate the most important Supreme Court decisions by legal experts on the twenty-fifth anniversary of the Charter is a helpful guide.[37] Of the group of cases decided between 1982 and 2007, nine of the twelve appear in Figure 6.4, suggesting that there is some degree of correlation between media coverage and the perceived legal importance of Charter cases. The *Morgentaler* (1988) decision received the most media mentions of all Charter cases, though *Khadr* (2008), which dealt with extraterritorial application of the Charter, and *Vriend* (1998), which dealt with discrimination based on sexual orientation, also received considerable attention.[38] Counting aggregate citations of a case is a fairly loose measure of impact, but when accompanied by a measure of how often the case was mentioned in the years subsequent to the Supreme Court's ruling, a slightly more nuanced understanding of perceived public importance is possible. While the cases that garnered the most mentions were continuously referenced in the years following the release of the associated judgment, there is also a separate set of cases that were mentioned (proportionately) more in the years following their decision and steadily so. Cases such as *Sparrow* (1990, Indigenous rights), *Rodriguez* (1993, medical assistance in dying), *Dagenais* (1994, publication bans), and *Carter* (2015, medical assistance in dying) were revisited in the media with

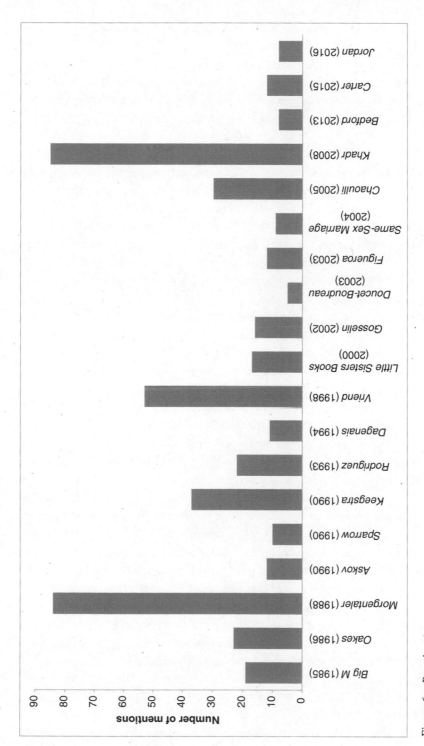

Figure 6.4 Prominent cases

some frequency in the years following their release, likely because of their continuing importance to salient public policy issues such as resource-distribution policy, election advertising, and health.[39] This suggests that while coverage of cases is largely based on the salience of a case at the time the decision is released, the continued mention of a case reflects a relationship to public policy change and highly politicized issues or events.

Discussion and Conclusion

The *Charter of Rights and Freedoms* and the protections afforded within it have become a part of Canadian identity over the past forty years (see McDougall, Chapter 5 in this volume).[40] Canadians certainly rely on the rights outlined in the Charter in their daily lives, even if general knowledge of the depth and application of those laws remains relatively low. This information gap is not without its consequences. Canadians have strong opinions about the Charter, and the actors who enforce it, but what is less clear is the volume and type of information upon which they base these evaluations. For example, Canadians overwhelmingly support the courts having the "final say" over the government in Charter conflicts.[41] Yet we have little idea of whether that is because trust for the judiciary is stronger than that for elected officials or whether it may have something to do with what Canadians have learned about the Charter through public discourse.[42] Likewise, recent research suggests that Canadians' support of the courts is becoming increasingly politicized, with Conservatives in particular being less likely to support the courts, though we do not know what role the media play in informing this support.[43] The findings presented here cannot answer these larger questions but do provide insight into how media coverage may be informing the views of Canadian citizens regarding the Charter and its relationship to the courts and politics. Our media analysis uses an inductive approach to get a sense of the general state of Charter talk, so our findings are necessarily disparate. Nonetheless, when taken together, they form a picture of Charter media coverage driven by an elite government/court narrative often focused on criminal justice and politically divisive social issues and punctuated by moments of high media coverage of certain Charter provisions, particularly the notwithstanding clause.

As an entry point for our analysis, the introduction referenced Cairns's notion that the Charter is not confined to courtrooms or legislatures. What we found, in fact, is that while Charter talk is not exclusively confined to courtrooms and legislatures, they are certainly the major focus of media coverage. Media coverage of the Charter, in other words, is elite-driven. This is especially apparent when looking at coverage of the notwithstanding clause, where political debate and legislative action produced large spikes in media mentions. The debate between federal party leaders Martin and Harper in 2004–06 also proved a pivotal moment for media coverage of government and the notwithstanding clause. Since the 2000s, media mentions of the government have outpaced those of the courts, which may suggest that political frames have been more dominant in the later years of Charter coverage.

Our results also indicate a clear focus on criminal justice and the Charter, with coverage of legal rights (section 7) and cases such as *Morgentaler* and *Khadr* featuring prominently. Considering that the majority of Charter litigation arises in routine criminal proceedings, where courts are asked to interpret the constitutionality of provisions of the *Criminal Code*, the scope of police powers, the rights of the criminally accused, and various trial procedures, this finding is not surprising.[44] Moreover, criminal law often intersects with important and politically salient questions of morality and social policy, like medically assisted dying and abortion. Recall that *Morgentaler*, along with *Khadr*, dominated our measure of case mentions in the media. The issue of abortion and the *Morgentaler* case has taken up a notable space in Canadian political discourse and public policy that has endured long after the 1988 decision. Abortion is far from being a settled issue for some; Paul Saurette and Kelly Gordon note that as of 2013, there were at least forty-three private member's bills concerning abortion put before Parliament and that national antiabortion rallies drew ten thousand to fifteen thousand attendees.[45] Additionally, Dr. Henry Morgentaler, the litigant at the centre of the case, remained a prominent figure in abortion politics in Canada, participating in public debates and litigation surrounding abortion rights until his death in 2013. *Khadr* also featured prominently in our case analysis, and the legacy of this case has lasted long after the 2008 Supreme Court decision regarding the infringement of Omar Khadr's section 7 rights by the Canadian government's failure to turn over evidence. Along with various protracted legal battles, Khadr received extensive media coverage stemming from his imprisonment in the Guantanamo Bay military base, his status as a child soldier, and the Harper Conservative government's refusal to repatriate Khadr to Canada. While Khadr successfully sued the Canadian government for his mistreatment and illegal imprisonment, his legal battles and attempts to return to Canada were undoubtedly politicized by the Harper government.[46] These kinds of highly politicized and publicly divisive cases are more likely to be covered by the media.[47] Consequently, while these cases may not necessarily be representative of Charter cases and jurisprudence as a whole, the public may nonetheless be more likely to associate them with the Charter given their comparatively high media coverage.

If the Charter is part of the "people's constitution," then understanding the media's coverage of the Charter is one of the ways we can better understand how people are represented in and informed about constitutional debate, making it an area of Charter research deserving of further attention. This chapter shows that national media coverage of the Charter has changed over the four decades of its existence. A number of novel findings are offered here, but this chapter also points to areas for future research, including possible differences in media coverage between national and local media sources. Given how essential public support is to the institutional legitimacy of the courts, research that investigates the effects of media coverage of the courts and decision making on public support would also be worthwhile.

Notes

1　Alan C. Cairns, *Charter versus Federalism: The Dilemmas of Constitutional Reform* (Montreal/Kingston: McGill-Queen's University Press, 1992), 4.

2　Erin Crandall, Kate Puddister, and Mark Daku, "Covering the Court: News Media Framing of Physician-Assisted Dying from *Rodriguez* to *Carter*," in *What's Trending in Canadian Politics? Understanding Transformations in Power, Media, and the Public Sphere,* ed. Mireille Lalancette, Vincent Raynauld, and Erin Crandall (Vancouver: UBC Press, 2019), 237–56; Lori Hausegger, Matthew Hennigar, and Troy Riddell, *Canadian Courts: Law, Politics, and Process,* 2nd ed. (Don Mills, ON: Oxford University Press, 2015), 130; Florian Sauvageau, David Schneiderman, and David Taras, *Last Word: Media Coverage of the Supreme Court of Canada* (Vancouver: UBC Press, 2011).

3　Kate Puddister and Tamara A. Small, "Navigating the Principle of Open Court in the Digital Age: The More Things Change, the More They Stay the Same," *Canadian Public Administration* 62, 2 (2019): 207.

4　Crandall, Puddister, and Daku, "Covering the Court," 237–38.

5　*R v Morgentaler,* [1988] 1 SCR 30 [*Morgentaler*]; *Canada (Justice) v Khadr,* [2008] 2 SCR 125, 2008 SCC 28 [*Khadr*]; *Vriend v Alberta,* [1998] 1 SCR 493 [*Vriend*].

6　Sauvageau, Schneiderman, and Taras, *Last Word*.

7　*Ibid,* 8–10. However, current Supreme Court Chief Justice Richard Wagner appears to have made an effort to engage more regularly with media.

8　Emmett Macfarlane, "Terms of Entitlement: Is There a Distinctly Canadian 'Rights Talk'?," *Canadian Journal of Political Science* 41, 2 (2008): 303–28.

9　*Saskatchewan (Human Rights Commission) v Whatcott,* [2013] 1 SCR 467; Lydia Miljan, "Supreme Court Coverage in Canada: A Case Study of Media Coverage of the *Whatcott* Decision," *Oñati Socio-Legal Series* 4, 4 (2014): 709–24.

10　*Rodriguez v British Columbia (Attorney General),* [1993] 3 SCR 519 [*Rodriguez*]; *Carter v Canada (Attorney General),* [2015] 1 SCR 331 [*Carter*]; Crandall, Puddister, and Daku, "Covering the Court."

11　Eleni Nicolaides and Dave Snow, "A Paper Tiger No More? The Media Portrayal of the Notwithstanding Clause in Saskatchewan and Ontario," *Canadian Journal of Political Science* 54, 1 (2021): 60–74.

12　Crandall, Puddister, and Daku, "Covering the Court."

13　Puddister and Small, "Navigating the Principle of Open Court"; Tamara A. Small and Kate Puddister, "Play-by-Play Justice: Tweeting Criminal Trials in the Digital Age," *Canadian Journal of Law and Society* 35, 1 (2020): 1–22.

14　Dwayne Winseck, "Media and Internet Concentration in Canada, 1984–2018: Digital Media and Internet Industries in Canada," Canadian Media Concentration Research

Project, Carleton University, 2019, https://www.cmcrp.org/media-and-internet-concentration-in-canada-1984-2018/.

15 Andrew J.A. Mattan, Kate Puddister, and Tamara A. Small, "Tweet Justice: The Canadian Court's Use of Social Media," *American Review of Canadian Studies* 50, 2 (2020): 229–44; Puddister and Small, "Navigating the Principle of Open Court." It is worth noting that during the early phases of the COVID-19 pandemic, many courts transitioned proceedings online.

16 Note that we purposefully excluded the period leading up to the Charter, as we are not aiming to capture the discourse that went into the Charter's successful passage through Parliament.

17 We consider a word or phrase to be of substantive import if it makes reference to legal analysis, the judiciary, or government actors or activities.

18 The full codebook is available from the authors.

19 Angus Reid Institute, "Canadians Have a More Favourable View of Their Supreme Court Than Americans Have of Their Own," 2015; Joseph F. Fletcher and Paul Howe, "Public Opinion and the Courts," *Choices* 6, 3 (2000); Elizabeth Goodyear-Grant, J. Scott Matthews, and Janet Hiebert, "The Courts/Parliament Trade-Off: Canadian Attitudes on Judicial Influence in Public Policy," *Commonwealth and Comparative Politics* 51, 3 (2013): 377–97.

20 Crandall, Puddister, and Daku, "Covering the Court," found some evidence of regional differences in media coverage in their analysis of Supreme Court cases on medically assisted dying. See also Nicolaides and Snow, "A Paper Tiger No More?"

21 For more on criminal justice and the Charter, see James B. Kelly and Kate Puddister, "Criminal Justice Policy during the Harper Era: Private Member's Bills, Penal Populism, and the Criminal Code of Canada," *Canadian Journal of Law and Society* 32, 3 (2017): 391–415.

22 Christopher Manfredi, "Conservatives, the Supreme Court of Canada, and the Constitution: Judicial-Government Relations, 2006–2015," *Osgoode Hall Law Journal* 52, 3 (2016): 951–84.

23 *Reference re Same-Sex Marriage*, [2004] 3 SCR 698, 2004 SCC 79. For more on the politics of the reference power, see Kate Puddister, *Seeking the Court's Advice: The Politics of the Canadian Reference Power* (Vancouver: UBC Press, 2019).

24 Jane Taber, "Personal Jabs Signal Shift in Campaign Tone: Negative Strategy Appears to Have Begun Earlier Than Political Observers Expected," *Globe and Mail*, December 19, 2005.

25 See, for example, "No Cause to Remove the Override Clause," *Globe and Mail*, January 11, 2006.

26 Nicolaides and Snow, "A Paper Tiger No More?"; Grégoire Webber, Eric Mendelsohn, and Robert Leckey, "The Faulty Received Wisdom around the Notwithstanding Clause," *Policy Options*, May 10, 2019, https://policyoptions.irpp.org/magazines/may-2019/faulty-wisdom-notwithstanding-clause/.

27 Macfarlane, "Terms of Entitlement."

28 *Ford v Quebec (AG)*, [1988] 2 SCR 712; *Morgentaler*.

29 Rachael Johnstone, *After Morgentaler: The Politics of Abortion in Canada* (Vancouver: UBC Press, 2017).

30 Peter M. Hogg, Allison A. Bushell Thornton, and Wade K. Wright, "Charter Dialogue Revisited: Or 'Much Ado about Metaphors,'" *Osgoode Hall Law Journal* 45, 1 (2007): 1–65; Emmett Macfarlane, "Dialogue or Compliance? Measuring Legislatures' Policy Responses to Court Rulings on Rights," *International Political Science Review* 34, 1 (2013): 39–56; Christopher P. Manfredi and James B. Kelly, "Six Degrees of Dialogue: A Response to Hogg and Bushell," *Osgoode Hall Law Journal* 37, 3 (1999): 513–27.

31   Macfarlane, "Terms of Entitlement," 311.

32   Peter J. McCormick, *The End of the Charter Revolution: Looking Back from the New Normal* (Toronto: University of Toronto Press, 2015), xix.

33   *Ibid,* 172–77.

34   *Gosselin v Quebec (AG),* [2002] 4 SCR 429, 2002 SCC 84; *Khadr.*

35   *Reference re Prov Electoral Boundaries (Sask.),* [1991] 2 SCR 158.

36   At the core of the debate was whether the appropriate Charter protection to the alleged infringing law fell under s 2 or 3 and, consequently, whether the s 33 override could apply. See Jamie Cameron and Bailey Fox, "Toronto's 2018 Municipal Election, Rights of Democratic Participation, and Section 2(B) of the Charter," *Constitutional Forum* 30, 1 (2021): 1–18.

37   The Court.ca, "Top 10 Charter Cases: As Revealed at the Symposium on the 25th Anniversary of the Charter, a Tribute to Chief Justice Roy Mcmurtry," April 12, 2007, http://www.thecourt.ca/top-10-charter-cases-as-revealed-at-the-symposium-on -the-25th-anniversary-of-the-charter-a-tribute-to-chief-justice-roy-mcmurtry/.

38   *Khadr; Vriend.* Note that references to the *Khadr* (2008) case are frequently made in coverage of the *Khadr* (2010) case. It also received additional attention in 2017 upon the federal government's financial settlement with Omar Khadr.

39   *R v Sparrow,* [1990] 1 SCR 1075; *Rodriguez; Dagenais v Canadian Broadcasting Corp,* [1994] 3 SCR 835; *Carter.*

40   For a discussion of Canadian constitutional identities, see Eric M. Adams, "Canadian Constitutional Identities," *Dalhousie Law Journal* 38, 2 (2015): 311–43.

41   This is in response to the Canada Election Study question "If a law conflicts with the *Charter of Rights,* who should have the final say – the courts or the government?" In 2008, 81 percent of respondents said "the courts"; in 2011, 71 percent said "the courts"; and in 2015, 77 percent said "the courts." See also, Goodyear-Grant, Matthews, and Hiebert, "The Courts/Parliament Trade-Off."

42   Erin Crandall and Andrea Lawlor, "Public Support for Canadian Courts: Understanding the Roles of Institutional Trust and Partisanship," *Canadian Journal of Law and Society* 37, 1 (2022): 91–112.

43   *Ibid.*

44   James B. Kelly, *Governing with the Charter: Legislative and Judicial Activism and Framers' Intent* (Vancouver: UBC Press, 2005). Kelly notes that between 1982 and 2003, nearly two-thirds of all Supreme Court Charter decisions involved legal rights.

45   Paul Saurette and Kelly Gordon, "Arguing Abortion: The New Anti-abortion Discourse in Canada," *Canadian Journal of Political Science* 46, 1 (2013): 158.

46   Ian Greene, "Who's to Blame for the Khadr Payout? Stephen Harper, Mostly," iPolitics, July 11, 2017, https://ipolitics.ca/2017/07/11/whos-to-blame-for-the-khadr-payout-stephen -harper-mostly/.

47   Todd A. Collins and Christopher A. Cooper, "Case Salience and Media Coverage of Supreme Court Decisions: Toward a New Measure," *Political Research Quarterly* 65, 2 (2012): 396–407.

7

Notwithstanding the Media
Section 33 of the Charter after *Toronto v Ontario*

Dave Snow and Eleni Nicolaides

THE NOTWITHSTANDING CLAUSE has made a prominent return to provincial politics in Canada. It has been included in six bills in four different provincial legislatures since 2017, four of which have passed into law. After a brief review of the clause's history, we examine the content and politics of those six bills. We then draw from an original dataset of 275 Canadian media articles published about arguably the most contentious recent invocation: Ontario's 2018 *Efficient Local Government Act*, which included the clause to cut the size of Toronto City Council during the municipal election in response to an Ontario Superior Court of Justice decision that had deemed the timing of the cut unconstitutional.[1]

In particular, we focus on how these media articles framed the notwithstanding clause and how that framing was associated with positive or negative assessments of the government's policy and the judicial decision that preceded the legislation. We find that the notwithstanding clause, the government's policy, and the judicial decision that preceded the use of the clause were all subject to far more negative than positive framing and that the relatively few media articles authored by academics broadly followed these trends. We also show that nega tive assessments of the notwithstanding clause were strongly associated with negative assessments of government policy. Moreover, the ideological orientation of the news outlet had a strong effect on the author's framing of the clause, with the vast majority of positive assessments of the use of the clause appearing in the conservative *Toronto Sun* or *National Post*. We conclude with a discussion of this evidence in light of public opinion data on Charter disputes involving courts and legislatures and a discussion of what the evidence about section 33's popularity can tell us about the future of the clause itself.

The Notwithstanding Clause
The origins of the notwithstanding clause include its precursor in section 2 of the 1960 Canadian Bill of Rights, which permitted "an Act of the Parliament of Canada" to "expressly declare ... that it shall operate notwithstanding the Canadian Bill of Rights."[2] The idea of a notwithstanding clause had been discussed among First Ministers for years leading up to the Charter's adoption and was an important part of the compromise necessary to get western Canadian premiers to accept the Charter.[3] As Dwight Newman recounts, progressive

Saskatchewan premier Allan Blakeney and conservative Alberta premier Peter Lougheed were strong advocates for the clause's inclusion in the Charter, believing that it would allow legislatures to protect rights excluded from the constitutional text (e.g., to health care) and to disagree with judicial interpretations of rights.[4]

Section 33(1) of the Charter allows the federal Parliament or provincial legislatures to declare that an act or provision of an act will operate notwithstanding certain provisions in the Charter. These Charter provisions include sections 2 (freedoms of conscience/religion, thought/expression, peaceful assembly, and association), 7 (rights to life, liberty, and security of the person), 8–14 (legal rights concerning seizure, detention, criminal proceedings, and punishment), and 15 (equality rights). Explicit references to Parliament, provincial legislatures, and a legislative or parliamentary act indicate that the clause is a legislative tool requiring scrutiny associated with a legislative bill. Section 33(2) ensures that while the declaration is in effect, the relevant act or provision "shall have such operation as it would have but for the provision of this Charter referred to in the declaration." Section 33(3) states that a declaration including the clause "shall cease to have effect five years after it comes into force," which ensures that, absent repeal, an election will occur during that period. Section 33(4) allows Parliament or legislatures to re-enact a declaration once it ceases to have an effect.

The Notwithstanding Clause, 1982–2017

Before the recent uses of the clause between 2017 and 2022, provincial legislatures had used it eighteen times: fifteen in Quebec, and once each in Alberta, Saskatchewan, and Yukon. In 2001, Tsvi Kahana identified seventeen of these uses in his important empirical work on the many unnoticed invocations of section 33; we subsequently identified the eighteenth use in Quebec's 2005 legislation regarding religious instruction in public schools.[5] In addition to its initial "omnibus" use of the clause in every bill from 1982 to 1985 to protest the passage of the *Constitution Act, 1982*, Quebec's National Assembly used the clause for various policies pertaining to pensions, education, and agriculture. Quebec's most controversial use was its sign law following the Supreme Court's decision in *Ford*, which had held that requiring French-only outdoor commercial signs unjustifiably infringed freedom of expression under the Charter.[6] This use occurred amid nationalist political protests against the Supreme Court ruling and was subject to a backlash in the rest of Canada that undermined support for the Meech Lake Accord and Quebec's distinct-society clause therein.[7]

Alberta invoked the clause in Bill 202, the *Marriage Amendment Act*, which sought to maintain the heterosexual definition of marriage in response to the

Supreme Court's equality rights jurisprudence on same-sex relationships.[8] Because the Supreme Court ultimately ruled that the definition of marriage was federal jurisdiction, this law was effectively unconstitutional for violating the federal division of powers.[9] Saskatchewan invoked section 33 in a back-to-work law after the Saskatchewan Court of Appeal had ruled that a similar back-to-work law violated freedom of association under the Charter; however, after the Supreme Court of Canada subsequently ruled in 1987 that section 2(d) of the Charter did not protect the right to strike, the use of the clause became unnecessary.[10] Finally, Yukon invoked section 33 in its *Land Planning and Development Act* to protect against possible equality-rights violations concerning nominations to its land-planning board by the Council of Yukon First Nations.[11] It was enacted but not brought into force.[12]

The federal Parliament has never used the clause, although many prime ministers considered it. Liberal Prime Minister Pierre Trudeau made a commitment in private writing to a Catholic archbishop to use the clause to prevent Canada's abortion law from being struck down.[13] Conservative leader Stephen Harper, while in opposition, said he would use "all necessary steps" to protect the heterosexual definition of marriage.[14] Neither leader ultimately introduced legislation containing the clause as prime minister. During the 2006 election campaign, Prime Minister Paul Martin promised that, if re-elected, his government would remove the federal Parliament's ability to use the notwithstanding clause from the Charter.[15] However, Martin's Liberals were defeated in the election, and the federal ability to use the clause remains.

The Notwithstanding Clause, 2017–22

In recent years, four provincial legislatures have introduced six pieces of legislation invoking section 33, though only four of those laws passed. The first of these was Saskatchewan's response to the decision of the Court of Queen's Bench for Saskatchewan in *Good Spirit*, which held that the provincial government's funding of non-Catholic students to attend a Catholic school infringed sections 2(a) and 15(1) of the Charter.[16] In 2017, Saskatchewan invoked section 33 in Bill No. 89, *An Act to amend The Education Act, 1995*. The bill, which received royal assent in 2018, sought to maintain funding for non-Catholic students to attend Catholic separate schools. Because the Court of Queen's Bench decision was overturned by the Court of Appeal in 2020, the law has not yet come into force.[17] In 2018, after the Ontario Superior Court of Justice held that the Ontario government's reduction of the number of wards from forty-seven to twenty-five during the Toronto municipal election violated the Charter, the Ford government introduced identical legislation, this time invoking the notwithstanding clause.[18] Ultimately, the legislation was removed from the order paper after a stay of the trial judge's ruling by the Ontario Court of Appeal (discussed below).[19]

In 2019, Quebec passed Bill 21, *An Act respecting the laicity of the State,* which prevents workers in government departments, municipalities, law enforcement, the judiciary, public transit, school boards, and health care from wearing religious symbols.[20] That same year, New Brunswick introduced Bill 11, *An Act Respecting Proof of Immunization.* Bill 11 would have required children to have proof of immunization from certain diseases to attend public schools and early learning and childcare centres, and would have permitted only medical (as opposed to religious or conscientious) exemptions. The bill was ultimately defeated in a free vote even after the clause was removed in committee.[21] In 2021, Quebec introduced Bill 96, a sweeping piece of legislation that would, among other things, amend the Canadian constitution to declare that Quebecers form a "nation" and that French is the only official language of Quebec. Bill 96 also invokes the notwithstanding clause, as the bill contains several sections that strengthen French-language provisions originally contained in Quebec's controversial 1977 *Charter of the French Language.* In 2022, Bill 96 passed through Quebec's National Assembly and received royal assent. The latest introduction of the notwithstanding clause was Ontario's 2021 *Protecting Elections and Defending Democracy Act* (Bill 307), which reintroduced restrictions on third-party election spending that had been struck down by the Ontario Superior Court of Justice. Bill 307 received royal assent on June 14, 2021. As Ontario's 2018 bill invoking the notwithstanding clause did not ultimately pass, this marked the first time an Ontario law invoking the notwithstanding clause received royal assent. In total, four provincial laws invoking the notwithstanding clause have passed between 2018 and 2022.

A nascent scholarly literature has developed in response to recent provincial invocations of section 33. Drawing from the Saskatchewan experience, legal scholar Dwight Newman argues that section 33 is a beneficial tool for legislatures to offer coordinate constitutional interpretations of rights, correct judicial error, and maintain a role for legislatures in rights protection.[22] He suggests that Saskatchewan's use to maintain separate school funding and school choice exemplifies this, as Saskatchewan's bill responds to practical policy concerns that would have arisen from implementing the judicial decision.[23] Considering the recent use by Saskatchewan as a positive example, Meaghan Campbell likewise writes that the United Kingdom should adopt a clause that would formally require the government to justify deviations from the *Human Rights Act.*[24]

In a recent broad-ranging study, Janet Hiebert distinguishes between "federalist" and "democratic" uses of section 33. Democratic uses protect legislation due to ideological or political disagreements with court jurisprudence, whereas federalist uses protect provincial autonomy, culture, competency, or legitimacy.

Hiebert found a relatively even split among nineteen uses of the clause, with eleven federalist and eight democratic; nine of the eleven federalist uses were by Quebec, including 2019's Bill 21, which sought to pursue cultural objectives.[25] Hiebert argues that Saskatchewan's 2018 use also constituted a "federalist" use of the clause given that religious education is a policy with varied provincial approaches.[26] Echoing Hiebert's findings, Guillaume Rousseau and François Côté's survey of the literature demonstrates that Quebec's francophone scholars largely view section 33 as a tool to maintain Quebec's parliamentary sovereignty, autonomy, and culture.[27]

Several legal scholars have expressed concern that recent invocations of the clause reflect a growing populism. Richard Mailey believes the "new populism" could undermine the political understanding of section 33 as a tool to be used only in exceptional circumstances.[28] Leonid Sirota contends that recent invocations normalize the clause and lead to exploitation by "unscrupulous populists."[29] Robert Leckey argues that uses by Ontario and Quebec demonstrate a "majoritarian willingness to override [rights] without justification."[30] In this vein, Leckey recommends challenging these new laws using Charter provisions to which the clause does not apply; this argument is echoed by legal scholar Kerri Froc, who advocates a constitutional challenge against Quebec's Bill 21 using section 28 of the Charter, which guarantees rights equally to the sexes.[31] Others have suggested that recent invocations should lead to a change in the way judges evaluate the clause. Grégoire Webber, Eric Mendelsohn, and Robert Leckey argue that, even when laws invoke the notwithstanding clause, judges should review those laws and, if necessary, declare that they violate the Charter even if they cannot provide remedial declarations declaring the laws of no force or effect.[32] Sirota goes one step further, suggesting courts can still offer a remedy for any violation of claimants' rights that do not otherwise affect the statute's operation.[33] Maxime St-Hilaire and Xavier Foccroulle Ménard reject this interpretation, suggesting that the textual arguments do not align with the purposive nature of Canadian judicial review, the Supreme Court's interpretation in *Ford*, or the framers' intent.[34]

This brief survey of the recent section 33 scholarship demonstrates that, while there is division surrounding the clause and its operation, many scholars remain critical of the clause both in the abstract and in its specific application. Is this criticism shared by the Canadian media? To determine that, we explored the response to Ontario's recent experience with the notwithstanding clause.

Ontario and Section 33: The *Efficient Local Government Act*

Ontario's first proposed use of section 33 was in response to the ruling in the Ontario Superior Court of Justice in *City of Toronto et al v Ontario (Attorney General)*.[35] At issue in the case was the constitutionality of the Ford government's move to reduce the size of Toronto City Council from forty-seven to twenty-five wards during a municipal election through Bill 5, the *Better Local Government Act*. In his ruling, Justice Belobaba found that the timing of Bill 5 – in the middle of the election campaign – unjustifiably infringed candidates' right to freedom of expression under section 2(b) of the Charter. He also held that the increase in the number of constituents per ward infringed voters' freedom of expression, because voting is an expressive activity that encompasses the right to effective representation.[36] After he found the infringements were not saved as a reasonable limit under section 1 of the Charter, Justice Belobaba struck down the impugned provisions and ordered that the election proceed with forty-seven wards.[37]

On the same day of the ruling, Ontario premier Doug Ford announced that his government would appeal the ruling and introduce a bill in the legislature to re-enact the ward changes by invoking the notwithstanding clause. Ford stated: "I believe this decision is deeply concerning and wrong and the result is unacceptable to the people of Ontario," and "If you want to make new laws in Ontario – or in Canada – you first must seek a mandate from the people."[38] Most controversially, Ford justified the decision to use the clause by saying (of Justice Belobaba), "I was elected. He was appointed."[39] The Ford government introduced Bill 31, the *Efficient Local Government Act*, at first reading on September 12, 2018, including a notwithstanding declaration covering all the Charter sections (2 and 7–15) to which section 33 applies.

On September 19, the Court of Appeal for Ontario granted a stay of the ruling, finding a strong likelihood that Justice Belobaba had erred in his interpretation and allowing the election to go forward with twenty-five wards.[40] The government, which had previously noted that it would not proceed with the use of section 33 if it were granted a stay, withdrew Bill 31 from the order paper, and the election was held with twenty-five wards.[41] In a later decision based on a full hearing of the case on its merits, a three-to-two majority of the Court of Appeal upheld Bill 5's constitutionality.[42] In October 2021, the Supreme Court narrowly upheld the Court of Appeal ruling in a five-to-four decision.[43]

Data, Methods, and Results

To assess how Ontario's legislation containing the notwithstanding clause was discussed in the media, we draw from an original dataset of 275 articles mentioning the notwithstanding clause in eight online news sources: Canada's two main national newspapers (*Globe and Mail* and *National Post*), four online national news websites (CBC News, CTV News, Global News, and *Maclean's*), and Ontario's two highest-circulating newspapers (*Toronto Star* and *Toronto Sun*). To create the dataset, we searched for articles that mentioned the notwithstanding clause between September 10 and September 26, 2018, which covers the period from Justice Belobaba's decision to one week after the Ontario Court of Appeal issued its ruling to stay the decision. The articles were coded by two coders using qualitative content analysis.[44]

Of the 275 articles that mentioned the notwithstanding clause, nearly three-quarters (74.5 percent) were written by authors employed by the news outlet; 10.5 percent were written by guest authors, 9.8 percent had an organization as author (such as "Star Staff" or "Canadian Press"), and 5.1 percent were unsigned editorials. The articles were fairly evenly distributed between the Toronto-area outlets (42.9 percent), the two national newspapers (30.5 percent), and the other national news outlets (26.5 percent). We distinguished between two categories of articles: "hard news" stories ($n = 167$, 60.7 percent of all articles) and "opinion" pieces ($n = 108$, 39.3 percent). As Table 7.1 shows, most opinion articles (90.7 percent) came from four sources: the Toronto-area newspapers (*Toronto Star* and *Toronto Sun*) and the national newspapers (*Globe and Mail* and *National Post*).

To determine precisely how much coverage the clause received, we organized the articles by their main topic. While there was considerable overlap among topics – for example, both Emmett Macfarlane's article (coded as the "Ontario Superior Court decision") and Philip Slayton's article on the topic of judicial activism (coded as "other") discussed the clause in detail – coders were asked to identify a single "main topic" for each article.[45] Fully 48 percent ($n = 132$) of the stories in the dataset were on the topic of the notwithstanding clause (either in the abstract or on Ontario's specific proposed use). By contrast, 24 percent of articles ($n = 66$) were on the policy issue of cutting Toronto City Council;

Table 7.1

Breakdown of news outlets

News outlet	All articles (%)	Opinion articles (%)
Toronto Star	28.0	28.7
Toronto Sun	14.9	23.1
Globe and Mail	12.7	19.4
National Post	17.8	19.4
Maclean's	3.6	7.4
CBC News	10.2	1.9
CTV News	10.5	0.0
Global News	2.2	0.0
	$n = 275$	$n = 108$

13.1 percent ($n = 36$) focused on the court cases (10 for the Ontario Superior Court case and 6 on the Court of Appeal's decision to stay the ruling); and 14.9 percent ($n = 41$) had a topic coded as "other." Of the 108 opinion articles, 42.6 percent ($n = 46$) were on the main topic of the notwithstanding clause.

Our analysis here focuses primarily on how authors portrayed three issues: the notwithstanding clause, the government's policy, and the Ontario Superior Court decision that preceded the legislation. We draw from the political science literature regarding "tone" in media analysis.[46] Four factors were taken into consideration when measuring tone. First, we measured the author's tone; our assessment did not consider whether quoted sources were positive or negative towards the notwithstanding clause. Second, we measured the author's tone towards the notwithstanding clause independently of the author's tone towards the policy of reducing the size of Toronto City Council or the judicial decision itself. Third, because authors often do not write their own headlines, our analysis of tone did not include headlines. Finally, coders erred on the side of neutrality, so an author's tone needed to be clearly negative or positive to be coded as such. Because hard news articles were overwhelmingly neutral in tone towards the policy (166/167, 99.4 percent) and the notwithstanding clause (165/167, 98.5 percent), we focus below on the tone in the 108 opinion articles, which include 94 op-eds and 14 unsigned editorials.

The coders first assessed the authors' tone towards the policy of reducing the size of Toronto City Council itself. An example of a positive assessment comes from the late *National Post* columnist Christie Blatchford, who "agreed with [Premier] Ford that [Toronto City Council] is an insanely ineffective body ... and that shrinking it might well help."[47] An example of a negative assessment was law professor Alice Wooley's criticism in the *Globe and Mail* that the legislation made changes to city council "without presenting any evidence to show that the changes are necessary and desirable ... in the middle of an election campaign, with no opportunity for candidates or the city government to adapt to what is being required."[48] In the 108 opinion articles, the author's tone was three times more likely to be negative (55.6 percent of opinion articles) than positive (17.6 percent) towards the policy.

For the purposes of our analysis, we divided the eight news outlets into three ideological categories: progressive (*Toronto Star*), conservative (*National Post* and *Toronto Sun*), and centrist (the remaining five sources). As Table 7.2 shows, we found that a newspaper's ideological orientation was strongly associated with the author's tone towards the policy in opinion articles, particularly for the conservative outlets: 39.1 percent of the articles published in the conservative outlets were positive towards the government's policy, compared with only a single article (3.2 percent) in the progressive *Star* and no articles in the centrist

Table 7.2

Tone towards city council cuts (opinion articles)

	Progressive (%)	Centrist (%)	Conservative (%)	All outlets (%) (N)
Positive	3.2	0.0	39.1	17.6 (19)
Neutral	25.8	29.0	26.1	26.9 (29)
Negative	71.0	71.0	34.8	55.6 (60)
	n = 31	n = 31	n = 46	**n = 108**

tau-b = -0.364, $p < .001$

outlets. Indeed, the two conservative outlets accounted for 94.7 percent (18/19) of all articles with a positive tone towards the Ontario government's policy.

Coders also assessed the "primary reason" for an author's positive or negative tone towards the Ford government's policy. Among authors who viewed the government's policy negatively, the most common reason (46.7 percent, $n = 28$) was that the government should have not made the change in the middle of an election period. The next two most common reasons were that the change to city council undermined democracy (15 percent, $n = 9$) or that it reflected Premier Ford's personal vendetta against Toronto City Council (13.3 percent, $n = 8$). Of the nineteen authors who were positive towards the government's policy, the most common reasons were that Toronto would be better off with fewer city councillors (36.8 percent, $n = 7$) or that the court had been wrong to intervene in the first place (36.8 percent, $n = 7$).

Coders also measured how authors portrayed the notwithstanding clause independent of how they portrayed the Ontario government's policy decision. An example of a positive portrayal was political scientist Emmett Macfarlane's claim in *Maclean's* that the clause was "included in the Charter precisely to provide a safeguard against judicial overreach, and to allow institutions to have measures against each other."[49] An example of negative portrayal was *Globe and Mail* columnist Marcus Gee's description of the clause as a "dubious instrument" and the "nuclear option."[50] As Table 7.3 shows, we found similar trends for the notwithstanding clause as with the policy itself: negative portrayals (40.7 percent) were more than twice as common as positive portrayals (18.5 percent) of the clause. The author's tone towards the notwithstanding clause was also strongly associated with the ideology of the news outlet. Authors of opinion articles in the conservative *Toronto Sun* and *National Post* were twice as likely to characterize the notwithstanding clause positively (30.4 percent) as negatively (15.2 percent), while the centrist sources (9.7 percent positive, 51.6 percent

Table 7.3

Tone towards notwithstanding clause (opinion articles)

	Progressive (%)	Centrist (%)	Conservative (%)	All outlets (%) (*N*)
Positive	9.7	9.7	30.4	18.5 (20)
Neutral	22.6	38.7	54.3	40.7 (44)
Negative	67.7	51.6	15.2	40.7 (44)
	n = 31	*n* = 31	*n* = 46	*n* = 108

tau-b = -0.406, *p* < .001

Table 7.4

Policy tone and notwithstanding clause tone (opinion articles)

	Policy positive (%)	Policy neutral (%)	Policy negative (%)	All opinion articles (%)
Clause positive	42.1	17.2	11.7	18.5
Clause neutral	57.9	58.6	26.7	40.7
Clause negative	0.0	24.1	61.7	40.7
	n = 19	*n* = 29	*n* = 60	*n* = 108

tau-b = 0.444, *p* < .001

negative) and the progressive *Toronto Star* (9.7 percent positive, 67.7 percent negative) were far more likely to portray the clause negatively than positively. Among the forty-six opinion articles whose main topic was the notwithstanding clause, the proportion of positive articles was slightly higher, though negative portrayals still outweighed positive ones: 30.4 percent of those articles were positive, 23.9 percent were neutral, and 45.7 percent were negative towards the clause.

Measuring the two tones independently also allowed us to test whether negative portrayals of the notwithstanding clause were associated with negative portrayals of the policy issue itself. As Table 7.4 shows, in opinion pieces, there was a strong – though by no means perfect – relationship between an author's tone towards the policy of cutting city council and their tone towards the notwithstanding clause. Of the nineteen authors who had a favourable view of the government's decision to reduce the size of Toronto's city council, none viewed the notwithstanding clause negatively. By contrast, among the sixty authors who viewed the city council cuts negatively, only 11.7 percent were positive towards the notwithstanding clause, compared with 61.7 percent who were negative about the clause.

We also measured authors' portrayal of Justice Belobaba's Ontario Superior Court of Justice decision that precipitated the bill invoking the notwithstanding clause. Coders first determined whether the author of each article "assess[ed] the quality of the judicial decision" (which excluded articles that did not mention the decision or merely mentioned it in passing) and subsequently determined whether the author's assessment of the decision was positive, neutral, or negative. In total, thirty-six articles assessed Justice Belobaba's decision, and the vast majority were negative: 4 (11.1 percent) were positive, 2 (5.6 percent) were neutral, and thirty (83.3 percent) were negative.

The four positive assessments of Justice Belobaba's decision included *Star* columnists Martin Regg Cohn's and Edward Keenan's descriptions of the decision as "devastating" and containing "successful arguments," the *Toronto Star* editorial board's depiction of the decision as "a pithy, persuasive ruling," and *Toronto Sun* columnist Jim Warren's claim that the decision "reflects what everyone with common sense agrees."[51] Examples of negative assessments include lawyer Phillip Slayton calling the decision "legally dubious and likely to be overturned on appeal" and *Toronto Sun* columnist Andre Marin referring to it as a "legal abomination."[52] Many commentators mentioned Justice Belobaba's nonjudicial language – especially his colloquial use of "Crickets" to signify nonanswers from the province – and all three scholars who assessed the decision noted his conflation of Charter jurisprudence related to freedom of expression and the right to vote.[53]

Three variables were strongly associated with how Belobaba's opinion was assessed: the ideological orientation of the news outlet, the author's tone towards the government's policy, and the author's tone towards the notwithstanding clause. In terms of news outlets, the key factor was whether the article was published in the *Toronto Star*. The *Star*, a left-leaning newspaper committed to social justice through its Atkinson principles, has been strongly critical of the Progressive Conservatives under Premier Ford; as shown above, its authors were generally critical of the Ford government's legislation limiting the size of city council.[54] Table 7.5 shows a striking difference between the *Star*, which published three of the four articles with a positive depiction of Justice Belobaba's decision, and all other outlets. Indeed, 60 percent (3/5) of *Toronto Star* articles assessing Belobaba's decision were positive, and 40 percent were negative. In all other venues combined, there was only one positive assessment (3.2 percent) out of thirty-one articles – from Jim Warren, a Liberal strategist and columnist at the *Toronto Sun* – compared with twenty-eight negative assessments (90.3 percent). The conservative papers contained most of the assessments overall

Table 7.5

Assessment of the Ontario Superior Court of Justice decision

	Progressive (*Toronto Star*) (%)	Centrist (*Globe and Mail*, CBC, *Maclean's*)[a] (%)	Conservative (*National Post* and *Toronto Sun*) (%)	All outlets (%)
Positive	60.0	0.0	4.2	11.1
Neutral	0.0	14.3	4.2	5.6
Negative	40.0	85.7	91.7	83.3
	n = 5	*n* = 7	*n* = 24	***n* = 36**

[a] No assessments of the decision were made in CTV News or Global News.

and most of the negative ones (22/24, 91.7 percent), though authors in the conservative papers were only slightly more likely than centrist ones (91.7 percent versus 87.5 percent) to view the Belobaba decision negatively. The media response to Justice Belobaba's decision indicates that, although the courts remain popular in the abstract, those authoring opinion pieces in major news outlets are willing to be critical of judicial decision making, even on Charter issues.

Table 7.6 shows that an author's assessment of Justice Belobaba's decision was negatively associated with that author's tone towards the policy of cutting city council. Of the thirty-six authors who assessed Belobaba's decision, all nineteen who were positive or neutral towards the city council cuts were critical of the judicial decision. By contrast, all six authors who assessed Justice Belobaba's decision positively (four) or neutrally (two) had a negative assessment of the Ford government's policy. Table 7.6 shows a similar trend for the notwithstanding clause, with positive assessments of the clause associated with negative assessments of Justice Belobaba's decision.

We also examined the extent to which scholars authored news articles. Only a small proportion of the articles in the dataset – 10/275, or 3.6 percent – were authored by academics. Of those ten articles, seven were written by law professors and three by political scientists. Seven had the notwithstanding clause as their main topic, compared with one on the policy issue (cutting city council), one on the Ontario Superior Court of Justice court case, and one "other." While it is difficult to extrapolate too much from only ten articles, some comparisons with the broader set of opinion articles in the dataset are nevertheless interesting. First, none of the ten articles written by professors were positive in tone towards the Ford government's policy of cutting city council; three were neutral, and seven were negative. With respect to the notwithstanding clause, two authors

Table 7.6

Tone towards policy/clause and judicial assessment

	Positive (%)	Neutral (%)	Negative (%)	Total (%)
	Tone towards policy[a]			
Judicial positive	0.0	0.0	23.5	11.1
Judicial neutral	0.0	0.0	11.8	5.6
Judicial negative	100.0	100.0	64.7	83.3
	n = 12	*n* = 7	*n* = 17	***n* = 36**
	Tone towards notwithstanding clause[b]			
Judicial positive	0.0	7.1	30.0	11.1
Judicial neutral	0.0	7.1	10.0	5.6
Judicial negative	100.0	85.7	60.0	83.3
	n = 12	*n* = 14	*n* = 10	***n* = 36**

[a] tau-b = −0.412, $p < .05$
[b] tau-b = −0.388, $p < .05$

were positive, four were neutral, and four were negative. Only three scholars assessed Justice Belobaba's decision, but all three assessed it negatively. Broadly speaking, the trends from the broader dataset of opinion articles – critical of the policy, the notwithstanding clause, and Justice Belobaba's decision – were true for scholars as well.

Finally, it is worth noting the extent to which the overall negative tone towards the cuts to city council and the notwithstanding clause reflected public opinion. Contemporaneous polling from IPSOS found 58 percent of Ontarians (and 57 percent of Canadians) opposed to the Ford government's legislation invoking the clause, compared with 42 percent of Ontarians (and 43 percent of Canadians) who supported it. Opposition was even more pronounced when respondents were specifically asked about the courts: 67 percent of Ontarians (and 68 percent of Canadians) agreed with the statement "What Premier Ford is doing is fundamentally undemocratic. Once a court has ruled against a law they have passed they should obey what the court has said."[55] This is consistent with previous public opinion research that showed support for courts over legislatures in times of conflict over Charter rights. Polling from Angus Reid in 2015 found that, while the Supreme Court was more popular than courts in general (61 percent of respondents expressed either "quite a lot" or "a great deal" of confidence in the Supreme Court, compared with 51 percent for courts generally), both were more popular than other institutions, including Parliament (28 percent).[56] Ontario's public opinion data from 2018 shows that public opinion remains unfavourable towards governments and legislatures in Charter conflicts with the judiciary, even when the judicial decision itself has been subject to negative media coverage.

Discussion and Conclusion

Of the six provincial bills that have invoked the notwithstanding clause since 2017, Ontario's 2018 bill was arguably the most contentious. Even though it ultimately did not pass through the legislature, Bill 31 led to significant media coverage; 275 articles mentioned the clause over a seventeen-day period across the eight news outlets we surveyed.

Ontario's experience can tell us much about the place of the notwithstanding clause on the eve of the Charter's fortieth anniversary. Most notably, the notwithstanding clause remains unpopular both in the media (as shown by our dataset) and with the broader public (as shown by polling). This is not to say that the clause has no defenders, nor that the clause should never be used because of its unpopularity. In the aggregate, however, the Ontario experience demonstrates that public and media opinion continues to favour the courts over legislatures in conflicts over Charter rights, even in the face of unpopular judicial decisions.[57]

Our analysis also demonstrates that media coverage of the notwithstanding clause is shaped by ideology and partisan politics. While the clause was portrayed negatively in the aggregate, criticism varied depending on the ideological orientation of the news outlet and was strongly associated with an author's view of the cuts to city council itself. Authors at the progressive *Toronto Star* were more likely to be negative about the clause (and positive about the judicial decision to which it was responding), whereas authors at the conservative *National Post* and *Toronto Sun* were more positive about the notwithstanding clause and the government's policy of cutting the size of city council. This demonstrates that support for the notwithstanding clause cannot be divorced from the political context in which it is invoked. It is also worth noting that the clause's mini resurgence from 2017 to 2022 took place solely in provinces governed by conservative parties – the Saskatchewan Party, the Coalition Avenir Québec, and the Progressive Conservatives in Ontario and New Brunswick. Even when the policies (such as mandatory vaccinations in New Brunswick, funding for religious schools in Saskatchewan, and limiting third-party pre-election spending in Ontario) are not those traditionally associated with conservative parties, it is nevertheless true that only right-of-centre parties have introduced legislation invoking the clause in recent years.

At this point, it is too early to tell whether this portends a "normalization" or a populist revival of the clause among conservative parties, as some scholars have predicted.[58] On the one hand, the clause's mini resurgence continues: Quebec's Bill 96 and Ontario's Bill 307, both introduced in 2021, show that the clause is no longer the dead letter it once was. On the other hand, if the clause remains as unpopular among the English-speaking media and the Canadian public as our research suggests, its political popularity could weaken, especially outside of Quebec. Previous polling data from 2007 had shown that fewer than half of Canadians were aware of the existence of the notwithstanding clause.[59] Based on the considerable media attention given to Ontario's Bill 31 (and probably Quebec's Bill 21 and Bill 96), it is likely that more Canadians are now familiar with the clause. Yet our analysis suggests that the newfound familiarity is unlikely to have increased its popularity, given the overall negative media coverage and polling data. Indeed, the raw majoritarianism of Premier Ford's rationale for invoking the clause to cut the size of city council in the middle of a 2018 municipal election – "I was elected. He was appointed" – has done little to instill the image of the clause as an instrument to engage in reasonable disagreement with the judiciary about reasonable limits on Charter rights. True, this did not stop Doug Ford's government from introducing legislation invoking the clause again in 2021 – legislation that, unlike the *Efficient Local Government Act,* ultimately passed. However, if the Canadian public finds that familiarity with the clause breeds contempt, its continued invocation in legislation is by no means guaranteed.[60]

Whether the notwithstanding clause's newfound political popularity becomes a long-term trend or a temporary blip, we are not yet convinced that the clause's comeback has had a major impact on rights protection in Canada. After all, governments and legislatures frequently violate Charter rights, with or without the notwithstanding clause. As one commentator noted, passing an otherwise identical bill without the notwithstanding clause, as several opposition MPs proposed in New Brunswick, simply gives the impression that "infringing individual rights is fine so long as you don't admit to it."[61] Defenders of section 33, of course, note that invoking the notwithstanding clause does not always constitute a *prima facie* rights infringement; that the clause was included in the Charter to allow legislatures to disagree with judicial interpretations of rights; and that the judicial decisions in Saskatchewan and Ontario to which the clause was proposed as a response were themselves questionable applications of Charter jurisprudence.[62] Such normative defences of the clause have been made since before the Charter's creation, and recent interest from provincial governments provides an excellent opportunity to continue such debates. However, the empirical evidence from Ontario's recent foray into the politics of section 33 does not suggest the clause's popularity has improved. It thus remains an open question whether Ontario's *Efficient Local Government Act* has contributed to a full-scale revival of the notwithstanding clause or, paradoxically, hindered its long-term popularity.

Notes

The authors would like to thank Ana-Maria Nizharadze for her valuable research assistance, and Edward Koning and Brendan Dell for their support with methodological considerations.

1 *City of Toronto et al v Ontario (Attorney General)*, [2018] ONSC 5151 [*City of Toronto et al v Ontario*].

2 Dwight Newman, "Canada's Notwithstanding Clause, Dialogue, and Constitutional Identities," in *Constitutional Dialogue: Rights, Democracy, Institutions*, ed. Geoffrey Sigalet, Grégoire Webber, and Rosalind Dixon (Cambridge: Cambridge University Press), 214. See also Adam Dodek, "Canada as a Constitutional Exporter: The Rise of the 'Canadian Model' of Constitutionalism," *Supreme Court Law Review* 36 (2007): 9.

3 Newman, "Canada's Notwithstanding Clause," 214.

4 *Ibid*, 219.

5 Tsvi Kahana, "The Notwithstanding Mechanism and Public Discussion: Lessons from the Ignored Practice of Section 33 of the Charter," *Canadian Public Administration* 44, 3 (2001): 255–91. For a description of Kahana's work and Quebec's 2005 law, see Eleni Nicolaides and Dave Snow, "A Paper Tiger No More? The Media Portrayal of the Notwithstanding Clause in Saskatchewan and Ontario," *Canadian Journal of Political Science* 54, 1 (2021): 60–74. Like Kahana, our count excludes re-enactments and counts Quebec's omnibus use as a single use.

6 *Ford v Quebec (Attorney General)*, [1988] 2 SCR 712.

7 Janet L. Hiebert, "Notwithstanding the Charter: Does Section 33 Accommodate Federalism?," in *Canada at 150: Federalism and Democratic Renewal*, ed. Elizabeth Goodyear Grant and Kyle Hanniman (Montreal/Kingston: McGill-Queen's University Press, 2019), 72–74.

8 *Ibid*, 74.

9 Alberta also included the notwithstanding clause in Bill 26, *The Institutional Confinement and Sexual Sterilization Compensation Act*, but withdrew the bill amid public outcry over the attempt to limit compensation for victims of government-forced sterilization. Kahana, "The Notwithstanding Mechanism," 267–68.

10 *Ibid*, 269. See *Reference Re Public Service Employee Relations Act (Alta.)*, [1987] 1 SCR 313.

11 Kahana, "The Notwithstanding Mechanism," 265.

12 *Ibid*, 258.

13 *Ibid*; Newman, "Canada's Notwithstanding Clause," 211.

14 Christopher P. Manfredi, "Same-Sex Marriage and the Notwithstanding Clause," *Policy Options*, October 2003, 21–24.

15 "Liberal Platform Doesn't Include Notwithstanding Clause Ban," CBC News, January 11, 2006, https://www.cbc.ca/news/canada/liberal-platform-doesn-t-include-notwithstanding-clause-ban-1.585843.

16 *Good Spirit School Division No 2014 v Christ the Teacher Roman Catholic Separate School Division No 212*, [2017] SKQB 109.

17 *Saskatchewan v Good Spirit School Division No 204*, 2020 SKCA 34.

18 *City of Toronto et al v Ontario.*
19 *Toronto (City) v Ontario (Attorney General),* [2018] ONCA 761 [*Toronto (City) v Ontario*].
20 Jonathan Montpetit, "As Fight over Quebec's Religious Symbols Law Shifts to Courts, Legal Experts Debate Best Way to Challenge It," CBC News, July 8, 2019, https://www.cbc.ca/news/canada/montreal/as-fight-over-quebec-s-religious-symbols-law-shifts-to-courts-legal-experts-debate-best-way-to-challenge-it-1.5204112.
21 Jacques Poitras, "MLAs Vote to Drop Notwithstanding Clause from Mandatory Vaccination Bill," CBC News, June 16, 2020, https://www.cbc.ca/news/canada/new-brunswick/mandatory-vaccination-bill-11-notwithstanding-clause-1.5614659.
22 *Ibid.* Also see Peter Russell, "The Notwithstanding Clause: The Charter's Homage to Parliamentary Democracy," *Policy Options,* February 2007, http://irpp.org/wp-content/uploads/assets/po/the-charter-25/russell.pdf.
23 Newman, "Canada's Notwithstanding Clause."
24 Meghan Campbell, "Reigniting the Dialogue: The Latest Use of the Notwithstanding Clause in Canada," *Public Law* 1 (January 2018): 1–10.
25 *Ibid,* 75–76.
26 Hiebert, "Notwithstanding the Charter," 75.
27 Guillaume Rousseau and François Côté, "A Distinctive Quebec Theory and Practice of the Notwithstanding Clause: When Collective Interests Outweigh Individual Rights," *Revue générale de droit* 47, 2 (2017): 343–431.
28 Richard Mailey, "The Notwithstanding Clause and the New Populism," *Constitutional Forum* 28, 4 (2019): 14.
29 Leonid Sirota, "The Notwithstanding Clause's Toxic Legacy," *Policy Options,* May 2017, https://policyoptions.irpp.org/magazines/may-2017/the-notwithstanding-clauses-toxic-legacy/.
30 Robert Leckey, "Advocacy Notwithstanding the Notwithstanding Clause," *Constitutional Forum* 28, 4 (2019): 1–6.
31 Kerri A. Froc, "Shouting into the Constitutional Void: Section 28 and Bill 21," *Constitutional Forum* 28, 4 (2019): 19–22. As of writing, challenges on this basis are ongoing in Quebec courts.
32 Grégoire Webber, Eric Mendelsohn, and Robert Leckey, "The Faulty Received Wisdom around the Notwithstanding Clause," *Policy Options,* May 10, 2019, https://policyoptions.irpp.org/magazines/may-2019/faulty-wisdom-notwithstanding-clause/; see also Grégoire Webber, "Notwithstanding Rights, Review, or Remedy? On the Notwithstanding Clause and the Operation of Legislation," *University of Toronto Law Journal* 71, 4 (2020): 510–38, https://doi.org/10.3138/utlj-2020-0066.
33 Leonid Sirota, "Concurring Opinion," May 23, 2019, https://doubleaspect.blog/2019/05/23/concurring-opinion/.
34 Maxime St-Hilaire and Xavier Foccroulle Ménard, "Nothing to Declare: A Response to Grégoire Webber, Eric Mendelsohn, Robert Leckey, and Léonid Sirota on the Effects of the Notwithstanding Clause," *Constitutional Forum* 29, 1 (2020): 43. The authors also reject Sirota's argument that s 33 does not apply to the Charter's remedial provisions from "Concurring Opinion."
35 *City of Toronto et al v Ontario.*
36 *Ibid,* paras 27–60.
37 *Ibid,* paras 8–11.
38 Ontario, "News Release: Doug Ford Announces Action to Uphold the Better Local Government Act," September 10, 2018, https://news.ontario.ca/opo/en/2018/09/doug-ford-announces-action-to-uphold-the-better-local-government-act.html.

39 Ryan Flanagan and Daniel Otis, "Ford Says He'll Use Notwithstanding Clause in Attempt to Force Cuts to Toronto Council," CTV News, September 10, 2018, https://www. ctvnews.ca/canada/ford-says-he-ll-use-notwithstanding-clause-in-attempt-to-force -cuts-to-toronto-council-1.4086779.

40 *Toronto (City) v Ontario (Attorney General).*

41 Jeff Gray, "Ford Government Will Not Exploit Override Clause If Stay Is Granted, Provincial Lawyer Says," *Globe and Mail,* September 18, 2018, https://www.theglobeandmail. com/canada/toronto/article-ontario-government-to-hold-off-on-notwithstanding -clause-if-it-wins/.

42 *Toronto (City) v Ontario (Attorney General).*

43 *Toronto (City) v Ontario (Attorney General),* 2021 SCC 34.

44 Coders answered twenty-four questions per article. Both coders initially coded thirty sample articles; intercoder reliability ranged from 93 to 100 percent for each question that was retained. The full dataset also contains news articles from the *Saskatoon Star-Phoenix* and the *Regina Leader-Post.* Articles from those two outlets were included in a previous article comparing Saskatchewan and Ontario but are excluded from our analysis here, which focuses solely on Ontario and national media. For a longer description of the methodology, the codebook, and other descriptive statistics, see Nicolaides and Snow, "Paper Tiger No More?"

45 Emmett Macfarlane, "Doug Ford's Law to Slash Toronto Council Is Unfair: But the Court Shouldn't Have Spiked It," *Maclean's,* September 10, 2018, https://www.macleans. ca/opinion/doug-fords-law-to-slash-toronto-council-is-unfair-but-it-should-not-be -struck-down/; Philip Slayton, "Judicial Activism Protects Us from the Tyranny of the Majority," *Globe and Mail,* September 14, 2018, https://www.theglobeandmail.com/ opinion/article-judicial-activism-protects-us-from-the-tyranny-of-the-majority/.

46 Stuart N. Soroka, Antonia Maioni, and Blake Andrew, *2006 Federal Election Newspaper Content Analysis* (Montreal: Observatory on Media and Public Policy, McGill University, 2006); Dave Snow, "The Social Construction of Naturopathic Medicine in Canadian Newspapers," *Policy Studies* (2019): 1–21, https://doi.org/10.1080/01442872.2019.1704234.

47 Christie Blatchford, "Doug Ford Has a Point: He Was Elected; the Judge Was Not," *National Post,* September 11, 2018, https://nationalpost.com/opinion/christie-blatchford -doug-ford-has-a-point-he-was-elected-the-judge-was-not.

48 Alice Woolley, "Where Is Ford's Respect for Municipal Government: The Heart of the Rule of Law?," *Globe and Mail,* September 19, 2018, https://www.theglobeandmail.com/ opinion/article-where-is-fords-respect-for-municipal-government-the-heart-of-the/.

49 Macfarlane, "Doug Ford's Law."

50 Marcus Gee, "Doug Ford Is Challenging the Rule of Law Itself," *Globe and Mail,* September 10, 2018, https://www.theglobeandmail.com/canada/toronto/article-doug -ford-is-challenging-the-rule-of-law-itself/.

51 Martin Regg Cohn, "The New Doug Ford Reverts to His Old Self," *Toronto Star,* September 10, 2018, https://www.thestar.com/opinion/star-columnists/2018/09/10/the-new -doug-ford-reverts-to-his-old-self.html; Edward Keenan, "Doug Ford Unleashes the Politics of Maximum Chaos," *Toronto Star,* September 10, 2018, https://www. thestar.com/opinion/star-columnists/2018/09/10/doug-ford-unleashes-the-politics -of-maximum-chaos.html; Star Editorial Board, "Doug Ford Is Trampling on the Rights of All Ontarians," *Toronto Star,* September 10, 2018, https://www.thestar.com/ opinion/editorials/2018/09/10/doug-ford-is-trampling-on-the-rights-of-all-ontarians. html; Jim Warren, "Doug Ford Is Wasting His Energy on This Council Fight," *Toronto Sun,* September 15, 2018, https://torontosun.com/opinion/columnists/warren-doug -ford-is-wasting-his-energy-on-this-council-fight.

52 Slayton, "Judicial Activism"; Andre Marin, "Court of Appeal Rights Justice Belobaba's Wrong," *Toronto Sun,* September 19, 2018, https://torontosun.com/news/provincial/marin-court-of-appeal-rights-justice-belobabas-wrong.

53 Ted Morton, "Provinces Demanded 'Notwithstanding' Powers for Good Reason: They Should Use Them," *National Post,* September 14, 2018, https://nationalpost.com/opinion/ted-morton-provinces-demanded-notwithstanding-powers-for-good-reason-they-should-use-them; Carissima Mathen, "Doug Ford's Powers Are Not Limitless: Thanks to a System He Neither Understands Nor Values," *Globe and Mail,* September 10, 2018, https://www.theglobeandmail.com/opinion/article-doug-fords-powers-are-not-limitless-thanks-to-a-system-he-neither/; Macfarlane, "Doug Ford's Law."

54 Toronto Star, "Atkinson Principles," https://www.thestar.com/about/atkinson.html.

55 Darrell Bricker, "Majority of Torontonians (54%), Ontarians (58%) and Canadians (57%) Oppose Doug Ford's Use of Notwithstanding Clause to Reduce the Size of Toronto City Council," Ipsos, September 20, 2018, https://www.ipsos.com/en-ca/news-polls/majority-torontonians-oppose-ford-notwithstanding-clause-city-council.

56 Angus Reid, "Canadians Have a More Favourable View of Their Supreme Court Than Americans Have of Their Own," August 16, 2015, http://angusreid.org/supreme-court/. Previous scholarship found that Canadians preferred courts to legislatures by more than a two-to-one margin and that this ratio was stable during surveys conducted in 1987, 1999, and 2006. See Elizabeth Goodyear-Grant, J. Scott Matthews, and Janet Hiebert, "The Courts/Parliament Trade-Off: Canadian Attitudes on Judicial Influence in Public Policy," *Commonwealth and Comparative Politics* 51, 3 (2013): 385.

57 Further research is required to determine the extent to which this reflects diffuse support for courts more generally or specific support for individual judicial decisions. The polling data above, coupled with the unpopularity of Justice Belobaba's decision in the media, suggests that opposition to the notwithstanding clause reflects diffuse support for courts. For a discussion of diffuse versus specific support, see Lori Hausegger and Troy Riddell, "The Changing Nature of Public Support for the Supreme Court of Canada," *Canadian Journal of Political Science* 37, 1 (2004): 23–50.

58 Sirota, "Toxic Legacy"; Mailey, "New Populism."

59 Nik Nanos, "Charter Values Don't Equal Canadian Values: Strong Support for Same-Sex and Property Rights," *Policy Options* 28, 2 (2007): 50–55; Emmett Macfarlane, "Terms of Entitlement: Is There a Distinctly Canadian 'Rights Talk'?" *Canadian Journal of Political Science* 41, 2 (2008): 312.

60 Indeed, even governments that propose using the clause seem wary of its use. As of this writing, Saskatchewan's 2018 law has not yet come into force, as it was not required after the Court of Queen's Bench decision was overturned by the Court of Appeal. In 2018, the Ontario government chose to remove Bill 31 from the order paper after the Court of Appeal issued its stay, rejecting the opportunity to pass the law in anticipation of higher-court decisions. Finally, the clause was removed from New Brunswick's bill at committee after many, including the premier, voiced their concerns about its inclusion. See Poitras, "MLAs Vote to Drop"; Silas Brown, "Inclusion of Notwithstanding Clause Endangering New Brunswick Mandatory Vaccination Bill," Global News, November 27, 2019, https://globalnews.ca/news/6225053/notwithstanding-clause-new-brunswick-vaccination-bill/.

61 Colby Cosh, "Where Infringing Individual Rights Is Fine So Long as You Don't Admit to It?," *National Post,* December 5, 2019, https://nationalpost.com/opinion/new-brunswick-where-infringing-individual-rights-is-fine-so-long-as-you-dont-admit-to-it.

62 Morton, "Provinces Demanded Notwithstanding"; Newman, "Canada's Notwithstanding Clause," 214.

Part 2
Charter Rights

8

Policing Partisan Self-Interest?
The Charter and Election Law in Canada

Tamara A. Small

ELECTIONS ARE CONSIDERED by many as the cornerstones of democracy. The rules of the electoral game or election law matter profoundly. Election law regulates matters such as who can participate in elections, how campaigns are conducted, and how votes are counted. Until 1982, statutory law, not constitutional law, generally governed the functioning of elections in Canada. This meant that election law was rarely subjected to judicial review.[1] The *Constitution Act, 1867* had little to say about elections. The only substantive mention is in section 41, which notes that provincial electoral laws would continue to govern federal elections until Parliament established its own legislation. This meant that most elections held in Canada's first fifty years were run using provincial laws that varied from province to province. The *Dominion Elections Act* finally established federal control of election law in 1920. The *Constitution Act, 1982* is, therefore, a turning point in the story of elections in Canada, with the entrenchment of democratic rights in the *Canadian Charter of Rights and Freedoms*. These rights enabled the judicial review of federal and provincial election law in Canada for the first time.

There is an interesting tension in election law, in that those who make it are also subject to it. Indeed, some aspects of election law, especially the rules governing campaigning and regulation of political parties and candidates, are particularly relevant. Some argue that governing parties craft election law to give themselves an advantage at the ballot box – that is, partisan self-interest shapes election law. This has led some, such as American legal scholar John Hart Ely, to suggest that courts should "police" election law because elected officials simply cannot look beyond their vested interests. The "ins," he writes, "have a way of wanting to make sure the outs stay out."[2] In the spirit of reflecting on the impact of the Charter in elections, this essay explores this notion of policing partisan self-interest. It advances the argument that the Supreme Court of Canada has not been a venue for judicial oversight of self-interested election law. While partisan self-interest is certainly real, more often than not, cases at the highest court rarely review the actions of political actors. The chapter concludes by considering the merits of the policing self-interest debate within the academic literature.

The Role of Courts in Election Law

As other chapters in this book attest, there has long been a concern about the proper reach of the Supreme Court of Canada. One of these is related to the issue of political questions – that is, are there questions that the judiciary should decline to address because they are not proper questions for adjudication and should be left for resolution by other institutions of government?[3] The issue of political questions is particularly relevant to election law as a good portion of election law governs the activities of political actors. In the literature, there is a debate about the extent to which there should be judicial involvement in the electoral process. There are a couple of arguments against it. First, in their analysis of section 3 and electoral boundaries, Rainer Knopff and F.L. Morton argue against the participation of unelected judges in election law. Decisions about representation should be left to citizens or their representatives: "When it is performed by unelected, unaccountable judges in the absence of any clear constitutional rule the implication is that the legislatures themselves are unfit to make this choice."[4] Second, within the Canadian context, it has also been suggested that politicians have been cleaning up faulty electoral rules on their own for decades; therefore, there is no reason for judges to be involved.[5] The franchise provides a good example. The early franchise was extremely restrictive. At Confederation, the act of voting was a privilege conferred on affluent men; unpropertied men, women, racial and religious minorities, and Indigenous people were excluded. However, around the turn of the twentieth century, restrictions began to fall, and Indigenous people finally received the unconditional franchise in 1960. Well before the Charter, many significant democratic reforms occurred in the areas of the franchise, electoral boundaries, and electoral administration. John C. Courtney concludes his democratic audit of Canadian elections by claiming, "At the federal, provincial, and territorial levels the Canadian electoral regimes of the early twenty-first century are in almost all respects vastly different from those of the nineteenth century."[6] This side of the debate can be best summed up by the oft-cited words of US Supreme Court justice Felix Frankfurter: "It is hostile to a democratic system to involve the judiciary in the politics of the people ... Courts ought not to enter this political thicket."[7]

However, others are less convinced that election laws are political questions in which judges should defer to elected politicians.[8] The argument here is that election law *requires* judicial oversight because politicians cannot be trusted to make effective election law because of their partisan self-interest – that is, the government in power will rig the system to (1) benefit itself and (2) make it more difficult for its opponents, to the point of trying to exclude some of them from the electoral process.

According to electoral reform scholar Dennis Pilon, "It should surprise no one that parties approach the question of institutional design from a perspective of how it will affect them electorally."[9] Throughout Canada's history, governing parties, regardless of their political stripe, have been accused of making self-interested election law. It is worth highlighting a couple of current and historical examples. Consider the recent attempt to change the voting system by Justin Trudeau's Liberal government. Despite claims that the 2015 election would be the last federal election to use the first-past-the-post voting system, it still exists. I suggest elsewhere that the Liberals thwarted their own voting reform process once it became clear that there was little support for their preferred voting system.[10] The Conservatives have also been accused of this. In 2014, the Stephen Harper Conservatives introduced the *Fair Elections Act,* which had several aspects that could be interpreted as working in favour of the Conservatives. For instance, the act made a number of changes to the office of the chief electoral officer (CEO) that seemed to weaken the office. These changes, however, must be seen in the light of a decade-long conflict between the Conservatives and the former chief electoral officer.[11]

Other particularly egregious historical examples are the *Wartime Elections Act* and the *Military Voters Act,* passed in 1917 by Prime Minister Robert Borden. As a bundle, the two laws systematically enfranchised some voters while disenfranchising others to increase the number of electors favourable to the Conservative's war effort. Some women got the vote in 1917, women who had a close connection to the war effort, including nurses who had served and female family members of men that had served. On the other hand, conscientious objectors and naturalized British subjects who were from an enemy country lost their right to vote.[12] The history of elections in Canada could be interpreted as demonstrating that politicians can fix their mistakes. Others are not so sure; rather, they see the history of election law as evidence that parties engage in biased rule making. Therefore, "courts should treat electoral laws with a certain amount of scepticism."[13]

This analysis does not wade into this debate too deeply. Rather, it seeks to assess if there is any evidence of this self-interest policing by the courts in Canada. As the examples provided show, there is good reason to believe that governing parties do engage in partisan self-interest. The entrenchment of democratic rights, discussed next, would allow the courts the opportunity to engage in judicial oversight of this sort of behaviour, if they were so inclined.

Section 3: The Right to Vote and More
The democratic rights of Canadians were entrenched in sections 3–5 of the Charter in 1982. Unlike other sections of the Charter, there were no comparable democratic rights in the 1960 Bill of Rights. Section 3 states that "every citizen

of Canada has the right to vote in an election of members of the House of Commons or of a legislative assembly and to be qualified for membership therein." Section 4 states that unless there are extraordinary circumstances, like a national emergency, no government can stay in office for more than five years, while section 5 states that the legislatures in Canada must sit at least once every year.

It is section 3 that is of relevance to the functioning of elections in Canada. Compared to other sections, section 3 is powerful in the sense that it does not contain any internal limitations, and it cannot be overridden by section 33, the notwithstanding clause.[14] Moreover, it is one of the few Charter rights reserved for Canadian citizens.[15] The courts have ruled that section 3 is limited to federal and provincial elections only and does not apply to referendums, municipal elections, or First Nations band council elections.[16] Democratic rights generated "little excitement" for the framers of the 1982 constitution.[17] The inclusion of section 3 was merely declaratory – that is, it entrenched well-accepted rights that most Canadians already enjoyed.[18] That said, Elections Canada's *A History of the Vote in Canada* describes the Charter as "one of the most significant influences on electoral law in the postwar years."[19]

On the face of it, section 3 seems to be limited to (1) the right to vote and (2) candidacy rights. However, as Justice Iacobucci notes in *Figueroa v Canada*, "*Charter* analysis requires courts to look beyond the words of the section. In the words of McLachlin C.J.B.C.S.C. (as she then was), '[m]ore is intended [in the right to vote] than the bare right to place a ballot in a box.'"[20] Consequently, court decisions have extended the meaning of section 3 to be much more inclusive of the electoral system, extending to electoral boundaries, campaign financing, and the regulation of political actors. In explaining how the courts have interpreted electoral rights in Canada, Yasmin Dawood uses the term "bundle of rights."[21] She argues that the court has recognized four rights in section 3:

1 the right to effective representation
2 the right to meaningful participation
3 the right to equal participation
4 the right to a free and informed vote.

These four rights have been articulated by the Supreme Court of Canada in *Reference re Provincial Electoral Boundaries (Saskatchewan); Figueroa;* and *Libman v Quebec*, respectively. The first two rights are described by the court as the central objectives of section 3. The final two rights come from the interconnection between section 3 and the freedom of expression right in section 2(b).

This relationship between section 2(b) and section 3 has been termed the egalitarian model.[22] The egalitarian model of elections has been articulated by the Supreme Court of Canada in *Libman* and *Harper v Canada*. Under this model, free speech must be balanced by fairness; this model is premised on the notion that individuals should have an equal opportunity to participate in the electoral process. Some scholars suggest that the egalitarian model is a central narrative of Supreme Court decisions, that this notion of fairness pervades much of their jurisprudence.[23] However, Christopher Bredt and Markus Kremer disagree; they argue that inconsistency best describes electoral jurisprudence in Canada and that it is difficult to predict how the court will interpret section 3.[24] Nevertheless, this broader interpretation of section 3 potentially provides the court with a greater opportunity to police the self-interest of political parties in making election law.

Policing Partisan Self-Interest?

Compared to other sections of the Charter, such as fundamental freedoms or equality rights, the Supreme Court has not adjudicated a lot of section 3 cases. Table 8.1 presents the eleven cases where the Supreme Court has adjudicated provincial and federal election law since 1982.[25] The first case, the *Saskatchewan Reference* (1991), made it to the highest court almost ten years after the entrenchment of democratic rights.

Table 8.1

Federal and provincial election law cases at the Supreme Court

Case	Section	Issue	Partisan	Ruling
Reference re Prov Electoral Boundaries (Sask.), [1991] 2 SCR 158	3	Electoral boundaries	Yes	Upheld
Sauvé v Canada (Attorney General), [1993] 2 SCR 438	3	Voting rights of prisoners	No	Struck down
Haig v Canada (Chief Electoral Officer), [1993] 2 SCR 995	3	Voting rights in a referendum	No	Upheld
Harvey v New Brunswick (Attorney General), [1996] 2 SCR 876	3	Candidacy prohibition after electoral violation	No	Upheld
Libman v Quebec (Attorney General), [1997] 3 SCR 569	2(b)	Regulation of third parties advertising	Yes	Struck down
Thomson Newspapers Co v Canada (Attorney General), [1998] 1 SCR 877	2(b)	Blackout of opinion polls in newspapers	No	Struck down

Table 8.1

(Continued)

Case	Section	Issue	Partisan	Ruling
Harper v Canada (Attorney General), [2000] 2 SCR 764	2(b)	Regulation of third parties advertising	Yes	Upheld
Sauvé v Canada (Chief Electoral Officer), [2002] 3 SCR 519, 2002 SCC 68	3	Voting rights of prisoners	No	Struck down
Figueroa v Canada (Attorney General), [2003] 1 SCR 912, 2003 SCC 37	3	Registration of political parties	Yes	Struck down
R v Bryan, [2007] 1 SCR 527, 2007 SCC 12	2(b)	Premature transmission of election results	No	Upheld
Frank v Canada (Attorney General), 2019 SCC 1, [2019] 1 SCR 3	3	Voting rights of Canadians living abroad	No	Struck down

As is evident, a wide range of electoral issues has been contested. This section advances the argument that the Supreme Court of Canada has not been a venue for judicial oversight of partisan self-interest in election law. Before doing so, it is essential to explain what is meant by "partisan self-interest." This is complicated by the fact that none of the authors discussed earlier who raised the alarm of partisan self-interest seemed to have defined or operationalized the concept. Even though partisan self-interest is such a problem that it requires specific judicial oversight, the nature of the problem is conceptually murky.

Recall that partisan self-interest in election law was earlier defined as a law designed to provide an advantage to its maker at the ballot box – that is, intended law would (1) benefit them and (2) make it more difficult for their opponents. However, with this definition, we are left with a measurement problem. How does one measure intent on the part of political actors? It is not as if we can use the statements of elected officials as evidence. It would be counterintuitive to expect that elected officials would make public statements about the "real" purpose of the law being based in their own self-interest. At best, we can assess for *perceived* partisan self-interest. That is, an argument can be made using objective facts as to whether the law in question can be seen to be benefitting its maker while limiting opportunities for the maker's opponents. Two final points of clarification on this definition: first, saying an election provision can be perceived as self-interested is not a normative statement about the provision itself, or that self-interest is the primary or guiding motivation of elected officials when creating these provisions. Indeed, there may be valid reasons for such laws. This analysis does not make assessments about the rightness or wrongness of partisan self-interest. Second, it is not being suggested that the Supreme Court is purposely engaging in judicial oversight of partisan self-interest. Rather, the analysis simply shows whether the resulting decision had the effect of limiting the perceived self-interest.

Rather than dealing with the cases from oldest to newest, they are divided into two categories: cases where no perceived partisan self-interest is evident and cases where one exists. As Table 8.1 shows, seven of the eleven election law cases contained no opportunity for the Supreme Court to engage in this form of judicial oversight because, as will be demonstrated, it was difficult to locate any sort of perceived partisan self-interest.

Cases with No Perceived Partisan Self-Interest

Sauvé and *Sauvé #2*
These two cases are dealt with together as they deal with the same topic: the prohibition of prisoner voting. In *Sauvé* (1993), the Supreme Court upheld the lower court's decision, stating that a total prohibition against inmate voting in the *Canada Elections Act* (CEA) was too broad. That same year, Jean Chrétien's Liberal government amended the CEA to remove the voting exclusion for prisoners serving less than two years. In *Sauvé #2* (2002), the Supreme Court overturned the decision of the Federal Court of Appeal on voting disqualifications for inmates serving more than two years. The Supreme Court's rulings on prisoner voting are two of the more controversial cases in Canadian electoral law.[26]

While these cases are significant in many ways, it is difficult to see how the prohibition serves a perceived partisan self-interest for any elected official or that one party has benefitted over the others based on the provision. The prohibition against inmate voting in Canada was established in 1898. Thus, it has been supported tacitly and explicitly by (Progressive) Conservative and Liberal politicians for more than a hundred years. Indeed, after *Sauvé #2*, neither the Liberals under Chrétien nor the Conservatives under Harper, both of whom made significant changes to election law during their tenure, amended the language of the CEA to remove the voting disqualification for inmates serving two years or more.[27] This even though Elections Canada was making it possible for prisoners to vote since the ruling through the use of mobile polls.[28]

Haig v Canada

As mentioned earlier, section 3 does not apply to provincial or federal referendums. This was determined in the case *Haig v Canada* (1993). In 1992, Graham Haig found himself in an administrative quagmire regarding the rules governing referendums on the Charlottetown Accord. Haig had moved provinces during the campaign; he was ineligible to vote in Quebec because he did not meet the six-month residency requirement, nor was he eligible to vote in Ontario because he no longer resided there. The Supreme Court upheld both the Quebec and federal referendum laws in 1993. The ruling distinguished that whereas elections are binding on governments and citizens, a referendum is "basically a consultative process, a device for the gathering of opinions."[29] According to the Supreme Court, neither section 3 nor 2(b) applied to a referendum. Even if it were possible to suggest there was perceived partisan self-interest on the part of federal and Quebec politicians (in the latter case, it is entirely possible, as the sovereigntist Parti Québécois established the referendum rules), it would be irrelevant to this analysis. If a referendum is a "creation of legislation," as the court ruled, then the government of the day has the capacity to set the rules of participation without judicial oversight.

Harvey v New Brunswick

Harvey v New Brunswick (1996) is one of a few provincial election law cases heard by the Supreme Court over the past forty years. In question was a provision of the New Brunswick *Elections Act* that stated that any person convicted of a corrupt or illegal election act would be disqualified for five years from being elected to or sitting in the Legislative Assembly. Fred Harvey won a seat in the 1991 provincial election and was later convicted under the *Elections Act*. He lost his seat and was banned from running for five years. He challenged the provision under section 3, that every Canadian citizen is qualified for membership in federal and provincial legislatures. In 1996, the Supreme Court upheld the New Brunswick law, ruling that the impugned section enhanced "the integrity of the electoral process," a pressing and substantial concern.[30] Additionally, the five-year disqualification was considered a minimal and proportional impairment of section 3. New Brunswick's disqualification for corrupt electoral practices is even older than the prisoner-voting prohibitions. As Andrew Heard notes, the provision at issue in *Harvey* dates from 1791.[31] The provision was tacitly supported by governments of both political stripes for all of New Brunswick's history as a province. Even if the rule hurts one party or another in the short term, it is difficult to see how it benefits one party over another in the long term, especially if, after five years, the individual can run again as a candidate. It is difficult to see how any perceived partisan self-interest exists in this case.

Thomson Newspapers Co v Canada

Thomson Newspapers Co v Canada (1998) is a section 2(b) case. At issue was the 1993 ban or "blackout" on the publication of opinion polls in the final seventy-two hours of a federal election. These changes were introduced by the Chrétien Liberals. While the provision did not specify newspapers or television broadcasters, given the media landscape in the 1990s, this law generally focused on their activities. Critics of the law, including Thomson and Southam newspapers, argued the provision was not a justifiable violation of sections 2(b) and 3 of the Charter. The government argued that the seventy-two-hour ban on opinion polls was a justifiable infringement of freedom of expression. The main rationale was to ensure that the opinion polls did not unduly influence voters. The Supreme Court disagreed, striking down the provision as a violation of freedom of expression.

On the face of it, this provision might seem to fit into partisan self-interest – that a government, regardless of political stripe, would want to avoid the publishing of polls in the final days of an election campaign if it were doing poorly. However, several scholars show that the nonpartisan bodies are an important part of this discussion. For instance, Nicholas Devlin notes that there were calls for restrictions on polling and publication as early as 1966 by the Barbeau Committee on Election Expenses.[32] This was also taken up by the Royal Commission on Electoral Reform and Party Financing, better known as the Lortie Commission.[33] A significant number of briefs submitted to the Lortie Commission advocated some regulation of polling during campaigns.[34] The Lortie Commission's final report was the basis for several amendments to the CEA by the Chrétien Liberals, including the regulation of opinion polls. The evidence seems to suggest that nonpartisan advice rather than self-interest was at play in the regulation of opinion polls in 1993.

R v Bryan

R v Bryan (2007) is another section 2(b) case. In 2000, Paul Bryan was prosecuted for posting election results from Atlantic Canada on his website prior to the polls closing in the West. The CEA prohibited the premature transmission of election results from Eastern Canada before the polls closed in the rest of the country. Bryan challenged the constitutionality of the provision, arguing it was an unjustified infringement on his freedom of expression. In 2007, the Supreme Court disagreed, ruling it was a justifiable limit on free speech. As seen above, the ban on premature transmission of election results has existed in Canada for a very long time. Created for radio, the ban had been in place since 1938, which meant it had been tacitly supported by Liberal and (Progressive) Conservative governments for years.[35] Moreover, in its ruling, the Supreme Court relied on discussions of the ban from the Lortie Commission; the majority cited the final report, noting that "Canadians feel very strongly about premature release of election results."[36] It is difficult to see this provision as anything more than administrative.

Frank v Canada

Frank v Canada (2019) shares a number of similarities with *Sauvé* and *Sauvé #2* as it deals with a prohibition on voting. A section 3 Charter challenge was raised by two Canadians unable to vote in the 2011 election because of a restriction in the CEA on voting by citizens who had been living abroad for more than five years. The Supreme Court struck down the provision in 2019. This was unsurprising because of the "progressive enfranchisement narrative" that exists in Canadian electoral jurisprudence.[37] Canada has one of the widest franchises in the world; many restrictions that exist in other countries, such as prisoner or felon disenfranchisement, have been struck down because of section 3.[38]

The prohibition became part of Canadian law with the aforementioned overhaul of election law in 1993.[39] However, this particular provision also had a long history. With the exception of Canadian Forces personnel, residence of some term has been a requirement to vote since Confederation in both provincial and federal law.[40] In addition to this history, it is difficult to see how one party would benefit over another based on this prohibition.

Taken together, these seven election law cases provide partial evidence supporting my argument. The Supreme Court cannot be a venue for judicial oversight of partisan self-interest if it does not hear cases that even allow it to do so. Most of the cases above deal with administrative issues surrounding the function of an election rather than issues during the campaign itself. The next section explores cases where an argument can be made for perceived self-interest. However, like this section, it will be shown that these four cases do little to advance the notion that Supreme Court decisions have resulted in the policing of partisan self-interest.

Cases with a Perceived Partisan Self-Interest

Reference re Prov Electoral Boundaries (Sask)

The *Saskatchewan Reference* (1991) was the first section 3 election law case to reach the Supreme Court. As the name implies, it deals with the process of redrawing electoral boundaries. The redistribution process is inherently political. For almost a hundred years, the redrawing of boundaries was left in the hands of politicians provincially and federally. In practice, this meant governments, of all political stripes, engaged in "partisan and blatantly self-serving" gerrymandering that sought to maximize their support while minimizing support for the Opposition.[41] In 1955, Manitoba became the first province to replace the government-dominated partisan redrawing of electoral boundaries with an independent process; all other governments eventually followed suit. While the process had become less partisan, the rules guiding redistribution remained in the hands of elected politicians.

The *Saskatchewan Reference* decided the constitutional validity of constituency maps prepared under the Saskatchewan government's *Representation Act, 1989*. Rainer Knopff and F.L. Morton highlight that the appearance of partisan motivation is important in the history of this case. Even though an independent boundary commission drew the new boundaries, the rules allowed the commission to draw them in a way that seemed to benefit the governing Progressive Conservative Party (see Hirschl, Chapter 26 in this volume): "The imbalance between urban and rule representation created the widespread impression that the Tory government was using reform to consolidate its electoral power base in rural Saskatchewan."[42] This led to the creation of two interest groups in opposition to the new boundaries, both of which launched Charter challenges. The Progressive Conservative government suggested that partisan motivations were at the heart of their opposition; both were "widely perceived as having tacit support" for the provincial NDP.[43] Faced with a Charter challenge, the government referred the act to the Saskatchewan Court of Appeal, and it eventually went to the Supreme Court. For the first time in this analysis, we find a law, the *Representation Act, 1989*, that fits into our definition of a perceived self-interest law.

Interestingly, the first election law that went to the Supreme Court was not a straightforward section 3 case. As discussed, the language in the Charter is silent on most aspects of electoral activity. Thus, the *Saskatchewan Reference* helped to flesh out what section 3 truly meant. The Supreme Court upheld impugned provisions in the Saskatchewan law. The decision held that the right to vote guaranteed by the Charter was "not equality of voting power per se but the right to 'effective representation.'"[44] This interpretation is crucial for determining whether the court policed self-interest in this case. The answer is no. Seeing the right to vote as more than voter parity means that unelected officials still maintain significant discretion in the creation of electoral boundaries. John Courtney considered the effects of the *Saskatchewan Reference* on redistribution rules across the country and concluded that "if it served a government's purpose it was invoked; if it did not, it was not."[45] This implies that election laws across the country post–*Saskatchewan Reference* could still be considered self-interested.

Figueroa v Canada

The Supreme Court was essentially asked to determine what a political party was in Canadian election law in *Figueroa* (2003). Even though Canada is a party-centred democracy, where parties are crucial to electoral and legislative activities, parties have been considered voluntary associations – and, therefore, outside of statutory law – for much of Canadian history. It was not until 1970 that federal political parties were formally recognized by statute. The 1970 legislation stipulated that for a political party to qualify for registration and associated benefits, it had to run candidates in at least fifty electoral districts. Benefits of registration include the following: party name on the ballot, ability to issue official income-tax receipts for donations, access to free and paid prime broadcasting time, and the ability to qualify for a refund of 50 percent of election expenses.[46] Following the 1993 federal election, the Communist Party of Canada (the third oldest continuous political party in Canadian history) lost its party status for failing to nominate at least fifty candidates. In addition to losing access to the aforementioned benefits, the party was forced to liquidate assets, pay debts, and remit an outstanding balance to Elections Canada. The Communist Party leader, Miguel Figueroa, challenged the fifty-candidate threshold as a violation of section 3.

Given the benefits of registration, the threshold of what constitutes a party is an important question, one that certainly fits into our conceptualization of perceived partisan self-interest. A high threshold will serve to limit the ability of small political entities to be considered statutory parties and participate in elections. When Heather MacIvor reviewed the history of the 1970 legislation, she noted that the Liberals and Progressive Conservatives wanted a higher threshold; however, the smaller parliamentary parties "castigated the government for discriminating against smaller parties and trying to prevent the emergence of new parties."[47] From a self-interest perspective, older and more established parties benefit from a high threshold by making it harder for smaller parties to remain and newer ones to be established.

The Supreme Court struck down the fifty candidate threshold in 2003. The court determined there was no reason to believe that a political party running fewer than fifty candidates could not act as "both a vehicle and outlet for the meaningful participation of individual citizens in the electoral process."[48] In striking down this law, the court did not focus on political parties per se but rather parties as vehicles for citizen participation. That is, the fifty-candidate threshold interferes with the capacity of certain citizens to participate in elections.[49] As mentioned, *Figueroa* is a fundamental case in Canadian politics because it is one of the cases that help to broaden the meaning of section 3 beyond the right to vote. However, from a self-interest perspective, the implication of the ruling is that major and established parties cannot use election law to keep those who want to challenge their supremacy out of the political process. In 2004, the Liberal government amended the CEA, removing the threshold by defining a political party as an organization "one of whose fundamental purposes is to participate in public affairs by endorsing one or more of , its members as candidates and supporting their election."[50] This is the first and only case in this analysis in which the argument regarding judicial oversight can be made.

Libman v Québec and *Harper v Canada*

Both *Libman v Québec* (1997) and *Harper v Canada* (2000) deal with the expenditures of entities that are not political parties or candidates in elections. Federally and in some provinces, these entities are better known as third parties. A third party is a person or group other than a candidate, political party, or an electoral district association; this includes individuals, businesses, unions, and interest groups. Third parties participate in elections through advertising. Federally, attempts at third-party regulation began in 1974. The entrenchment of section 3 led to a legislation-litigation back and forth for many years. The regulation of third-party advertising is one of the most legally contested election policies in Canada.[51]

Third-party regulation certainly meets the definition of perceived partisan self interest.[52] Banning third parties outright (which the federal government attempted in 1983) or placing limits on their ability to spend money on advertising before and during an election campaign restricts the participation of third parties. Third parties can cause headaches for political parties and candidates, as some regularly and specifically target parties, leaders, and candidates in their ads or raise issues that parties would rather avoid (e.g., abortion).[53] As Lisa Young and Joanna Everitt note, while political parties are important players in elections, "there is no reason to give them a monopoly over such debates during the election period."[54] To be sure, political parties and candidates do face limits on their spending before and during campaigns. However, the limits on third parties are often comparatively slight. Opponents of third-party regulation pointedly refer to these restrictions as a "gag law."[55]

Libman is a case involving provisions in Quebec's *Referendum Act*, which limited third-party spending in the 1995 referendum. In *Harper*, Stephen Harper, who was then president of the National Citizens Coalition, launched a challenge to new spending limits in the 2000 CEA. Both cases are freedom of expression cases. That is, the limit on third-party advertising is seen as a limit of the ability of third parties to speak. In both cases, the Supreme Court upheld the provisions, suggesting that the limits on third-party spending were justifiable under the Charter because they were a means of promoting equality of participation. Harper thus ended a thirty-year-old odyssey regarding third-party spending.[56] With the laws restricting third-party advertising being upheld, there is little evidence that *Libman* and *Harper* provided any judicial oversight into the actions of elected officials. Overall, of the four cases discussed in this section, only one could be interpreted as limiting the partisan self-interest of political actors. Even when presented with the opportunity, there is little that would allow us to see the court as a venue for this sort of judicial oversight.

The Conceptual Murkiness of Partisan Self-Interest

This analysis is situated in the debate found in the legal and political science literature about whether election law is an appropriate venue for the courts. Many argue that it is because of the propensity for elected officials to create laws that perpetuate their own power. The question guiding this analysis is, to what extent can Supreme Court decisions be seen as policing self-interest? For if they did, elected officials might alter their behaviours. The result would be better and fairer election law. However, in reviewing forty years of electoral jurisprudence, this idea of policing self-interest does not seem particularly relevant in the Canadian context.[57] In part, this is because of the types of cases the Supreme Court has adjudicated. Only four of the eleven cases examined – *Thomson, Libman, Figueroa,* and *Harper* – are cases about what happens *during* a campaign rather than administrative rules pertaining to the election. The latter type of cases do not provide much opportunity for policing, even if the court was inclined to do so. To be sure, this is only part of the story. Several cases have been heard in lower courts that may be relevant to understanding partisan self-interest. For instance, *Reform Party of Canada et al v Canada* was heard at the Alberta Court of Appeal in 1995. It considered the allocation of broadcasting time according to seats in the House of Commons.[58] Further research on lower-court decisions could alter the conclusion of this analysis.

Perhaps a more significant contribution here is the discussion of the conceptual murkiness of partisan self-interest. As has been pointed out, many scholars have raised partisan self-interest as a legitimate concern worthy of special attention by the judiciary. Even scholars that are not normatively committed to the concept raise it as a credible concern for political science and law to consider. While there is little doubt that governing parties engage in partisan electoral calculation in making election law (and probably other laws as well), how one gauges this is unclear. While the approach used here may be reasonable for academic analysis, how the courts would assess it is difficult to imagine. Those who make the argument for judicial oversight or policing of election law need to do better in explaining not only why courts should engage in oversight but *how* they might do it. Perhaps it is not a question of whether judges should enter the political thicket of election law, but more about whether the thicket is too dense to enter in the first place.

Notes

1 Heather MacIvor, *Canadian Politics and Government in the Charter Era* (Don Mills, ON: Oxford University Press, 2013).
2 John Hart Ely, *Democracy and Distrust: A Theory of Judicial Review* (Cambridge, MA: Harvard University Press, 1980), 106.
3 Geoffrey Cowper and Lorne Sossin, "Does Canada Need a Political Questions Doctrine?," *Supreme Court Law Review* 16 (2002): 343.
4 Rainer Knopff and F.L. Morton, *Charter Politics* (Scarborough, ON: Nelson Canada, 1992).
5 MacIvor, *Canadian Politics.*
6 John C. Courtney, *Elections* (Vancouver: UBC Press, 2004), 160.
7 *Colegrove v Green,* 328 US 549 (1946), para 7 and 9.
8 Yasmin Dawood, "Democracy and the Right to Vote: Rethinking Democratic Rights under the Charter," *Osgoode Hall Law Journal* 51 (2013): 251; Michael Pal, "Three Narratives about Canadian Election Law," *Election Law Journal: Rules, Politics, and Policy* 16, 2 (2017): 255–62.
9 Dennis Pilon, *The Politics of Voting: Reforming Canada's Electoral System* (Toronto: Emond Montgomery, 2007), 166.
10 Tamara A. Small, "Promises, Promises: Assessing the Liberal's Electoral Reform Agenda," *Canadian Studies* 89 (2020): 41–64.
11 Pal, "Three Narratives."
12 Elections Canada, *A History of the Vote in Canada,* 3rd ed. (Ottawa: Chief Electoral Officer of Canada, 2021), https://www.elections.ca/res/his/WEB_EC%2091135%20History%20of%20the%20Vote_Third%20edition_EN.pdf.
13 Yasmin Dawood, "Democratic Rights," in *The Oxford Handbook of the Canadian Constitution,* ed. Peter Oliver, Patrick Macklem, and Nathalie Des Rosiers (Toronto: Oxford University Press, 2017), 733.
14 Heather MacIvor, "Judicial Review and Electoral Democracy: The Contested Status of Political Parties under the Charter," *Windsor Yearbook of Access to Justice* 21 (2002): 479–518; MacIvor, *Canadian Politics.* Also see *Sauvé v Canada (Chief Electoral Officer),* [2002] 3 SCR 519, 2002 SCC 68.
15 Department of Justice, "Section 3 – Democratic Rights," Charterpedia, https://www.justice.gc.ca/eng/csj-sjc/rfc-dlc/ccrf-ccdl/check/art3.html.
16 Dawood, "Democratic Rights"; Department of Justice, "Section 3."
17 James R. Robertson and Sebastian Spano, *Electoral Rights: Charter of Rights and Freedoms* (Ottawa: Library of Parliament, Research Branch, 1999).
18 MacIvor, *Canadian Politics.*
19 Elections Canada, *A History of the Vote in Canada,* 126.
20 *Figueroa v Canada (Attorney General),* [2003] 1 SCR 912, 2003 SCC 37, para 19 [*Figueroa*].
21 Dawood, "Democracy and the Right to Vote."
22 MacIvor, *Canadian Politics.*
23 Colin Feasby, "Constitutional Questions about Canada's New Political Finance Regime," *Osgoode Hall Law Journal* 45 (2007): 513; Pal, "Three Narratives."

24 Christopher D. Bredt and Markus F. Kremer, "Section 3 of the Charter: Democratic Rights at the Supreme Court of Canada," *National Journal of Constitutional Law* 17 (2004): 19.

25 It is worth noting that this list excludes *Opitz v Wrzesnewskyj*, which was heard by the Supreme Court in 2012. Electoral-outcome cases are adjudicated according to provisions in the *Canada Elections Act* rather than the Charter. This chapter also excludes cases on other aspects of democratic rights.

26 Christopher P. Manfredi, "The Day the Dialogue Died: A Comment on *Sauvé v Canada*," *Osgoode Hall Law Journal* 45, 1 (2007): 105–24; Pal, "Three Narratives."

27 Elections Canada, *A History of the Vote in Canada*.

28 Kathleen Harris, "Locked Up, but Not Left Out: More than 22,000 Inmates Eligible to Vote," CBC News, August 25, 2015, https://www.cbc.ca/news/politics/canada-election -2015-prisoners-voting-1.3202010.

29 *Haig v Canada (Chief Electoral Officer)*, [1993] 2 SCR 995, para 5.

30 *Harvey v New Brunswick (Attorney General)*, [1996] 2 SCR 876, para 38.

31 Andrew Heard, "The Expulsion and Disqualification of Legislators: Parliamentary Privilege and the Charter of Rights," *Dalhousie Law Journal* 18, 2 (1995): 380–407.

32 Nicholas E. Devlin, "Opinion Polls and the Protection of Political Speech: A Comment on *Thomson Newspapers Co v Canada (Attorney General)*," *Ottawa Law Review* 28, 2 (1997): 411–32.

33 Established by the Progressive Conservative government of Brian Mulroney in 1989, the Lortie Commission was mandated to inquire and report on the appropriate principles, processes, and rules that should govern federal elections.

34 Colin C.J. Feasby, "Public Opinion Poll Restrictions, Elections, and the Charter," *University of Toronto Faculty of Law Review* 55, 2 (1997): 241–68.

35 Tamara A. Small, "Digital Third Parties: Understanding the Technological Challenge to Canada's Third Party Advertising Regime," *Canadian Public Administration* 61, 2 (2018): 266–83.

36 *R v Bryan*, [2007] 1 SCR 527, 2007 SCC 12, para 36.

37 Pal, "Three Narratives."

38 See André Blais, Louis Massicotte, and Antoine Yoshinaka, "Deciding Who Has the Right to Vote: A Comparative Analysis of Election Laws," *Electoral Studies* 20, 1 (2001): 41–62.

39 Fraser Duncan, "Residency and the Right to Vote under Section 3 of the Charter: A Frank Exchange of Views," *Saskatchewan Law Review* 83, 2 (2020): 169–202.

40 *Frank v Canada (Attorney General)*, 2019 SCC 1, [2019] 1 SCR 3, para 85.

41 Courtney, *Elections*, 47.

42 Knopff and Morton, *Charter Politics*, 337.

43 *Ibid.*

44 *Reference re Prov Electoral Boundaries (Sask.)*, [1991] 2 SCR 158, 160.

45 John C. Courtney, *Commissioned Ridings: Designing Canada's Electoral Districts* (Montreal/Kingston: McGill-Queen's University Press, 2001), 203.

46 Elections Canada, "Registration of Federal Political Parties," October 2020, https://www. elections.ca/content.aspx?section=pol&dir=pol/bck&document=index&lang=e.

47 Heather MacIvor, "The Charter of Rights and Party Politics: The Impact of the Supreme Court Ruling in *Figueroa v Canada (Attorney General)*," *Choices* 10, 4 (2004): 6.

48 *Figueroa*, para 39.

49 *Ibid*, para 38.

50 *Canada Elections Act*, SC 2000, c 9.

51 Erin Crandall and Andrea Lawlor, "Third Party Policy and Electoral Participation after *Harper v Canada:* A Triumph of Egalitarianism," in *Policy Change, Courts, and the Canadian Constitution,* ed. Emmett Macfarlane (Toronto: University of Toronto Press, 2018), 210–30.

52 Full discourse: the contested provisions in both *Figueroa* and *Harper* were endorsed by the Lortie Commission.

53 "Working Families Coalition Targets Patrick Brown in New Attack Ad," CBC News, October 24, 2017, https://www.cbc.ca/news/canada/toronto/ontario-election-patrick -brown-working-families-tv-ad-1.4367266.

54 Lisa Young and Joanna Everitt, *Advocacy Groups* (Vancouver: UBC Press, 2004), 122.

55 Herman Bakvis and Jennifer Smith, "Third-Party Advertising and Electoral Democracy: The Political Theory of the Alberta Court of Appeal in *Somerville v Canada (Attorney General)* [1996]," *Canadian Public Policy* 23, 2 (1997): 164–78, https://doi. org/10.2307/3551483.

56 For good overviews of these cases, see Christopher P. Manfredi and Mark Rush, *Judging Democracy* (Peterborough, ON: Broadview Press, 2008), and Colin Feasby, "Continuing Questions in Canadian Political Finance Law: Third Parties and Small Political Parties," *Alberta Law Review* 47 (2009): 993–1016.

57 This is not to suggest the concept is not relevant in other political contexts, such as the United States, where John Hart Ely developed the concept.

58 *Reform Party of Canada et al v Canada (Attorney General),* (1993) 145 AR 272 (CA).

9

The Most Important Charter Right?
The Rise and Future of Section 7

Matthew Hennigar

PETER HOGG OBSERVED on the thirtieth anniversary of the Charter that section 7's right to life, liberty, and security of the person had enjoyed a "brilliant career," rising from humble origins (and low expectations) to become a crucial check on what Hamish Stewart terms the state's "failures of instrumental rationality."[1] Just after that anniversary, the Supreme Court of Canada (SCC) further refined the meaning – and expanded the potential impact – of section 7 in the landmark case *Bedford v Canada,* about sex work, and used this framework in its 2015 *Carter* decision legalizing medical assistance in dying (MAiD).[2] These developments appear to reinforce Stewart's conclusion that section 7 "has proved to be one of the most fertile, even protean sections of the Charter," and that "perhaps more than any other section of the Charter, section 7 has increased the law-making power of the courts and particularly of the Supreme Court of Canada."[3] However, subsequent judicial decisions – particularly in *Safarzadeh-Markhali,* concerning how courts should determine the purpose of legislation – raise questions about the future of judicial activism using section 7 and whether lower courts will follow the Supreme Court's lead.[4] The legislative responses to these landmark rulings, which do not simply comply with the court, also suggest the need for a more nuanced assessment.

After briefly outlining the structure and scope of section 7, this chapter analyzes the *Bedford* and *Carter* decisions, their implications, and the legislative responses. Along the way, I note where the courts have been asked to push the boundaries of section 7 and judges have largely declined, such as positive social welfare rights and "economic liberty." Finally, based on the existing literature and comparative lessons from abroad, I close by considering a host of issues that promise to engage section 7 squarely in the coming years, including revisiting sex work, MAiD, private medical insurance, and the self-induced intoxication defence in criminal trials; government responses to pandemics; positive rights to abortion, safe-injection sites, and shelter; and environmental rights. Notwithstanding those jurisprudential developments that may temper the impact of section 7, it is likely to retain its central place in rights-based litigation strategies on an incredibly broad range of issues.

The Structure of Section 7

Judicial review of public policy under the Charter requires that a claimant be able to articulate their claim as a *legal* right that exists within that document. The Charter's rights are often quite narrow in focus and exclude the property rights and "due process of law" that drive many cases in the United States.[5] This narrows the basis for rights claiming in Canada and underlines the importance of section 7: life, liberty, and security of the person cover a great deal. Also, unlike some parts of the Charter that apply only to Canadian citizens, section 7 applies to "everyone" physically present in Canada[6] and, potentially, individuals abroad affected by the actions of Canadian state officials.[7] Section 7 does not, however, protect "corporations and other artificial entities incapable of enjoying life, liberty or security of the person."[8] To date, lower courts have also excluded animals,[9] though some scholars argue for "quasi-person" status or some form of citizenship that could fall under section 7's protections.[10]

Section 7 actually contains three distinct rights – to life, to liberty, and to the security of the person – and a claimant need only show that one of the three has been infringed. This fact alone significantly expands section 7's potential scope, which is extraordinarily broad. The right to "life" means that state action may not deprive someone of their life, but both the meaning of "life" and the threshold for causation – that is, how high does the *risk* of death have to be to trigger a violation? – are unclear from the text. After evading such issues for many years in abortion cases,[11] the SCC ruled in *Chaoulli* that when extended wait times for elective surgeries increase the risk of death, they violate the right to life.[12] The right to liberty means, at minimum, a presumption against physical restraint by the state but is also engaged by state compulsion such as extradition, involuntary medical treatment, or the collection of DNA in the criminal justice process. Before 2015, the SCC showed only muted support for the broader idea that liberty requires "a degree of autonomy in making decisions of fundamental personal importance" without state interference.[13] "Security of the person" has been interpreted to mean freedom from harm by the state, including both physical harm and "serious state-imposed psychological stress,"[14] when making "profoundly intimate and personal choices."[15]

Section 7's protections thus touch on some of the most profound interests of individuals in a liberal democracy and cover an enormous range of potential policies and regulatory contexts. Stewart observes that section 7 may also provide "residual" protections not clearly enumerated in the rest of the Charter's "Legal Rights" section (sections 8–14).[16] Despite this extraordinary scope, the text of section 7 conspicuously excludes two types of rights that would have significantly expanded its reach: positive economic rights (such as to social programs or the necessities of life)[17] and property rights. Efforts to persuade the SCC that section 7 implicitly contains positive economic rights have been notoriously unsuccessful to date, most squarely in *Gosselin v Québec*,[18] but the majority explicitly left the door open "that a positive obligation to sustain life, liberty, or security of the person may be made out in special circumstances."[19] Concerns about property-rights-based challenges to business regulations and key social programs such as medicare, as occurred during the *Lochner* era in the United States, led the drafters of the Charter to exclude such rights.[20] The courts have respected this decision by the framers and rebuffed claims of "economic liberty" that would have "admit[ted] property by the back door when it was shut out of the front."[21]

The SCC did not similarly defer to section 7's authors concerning its internal limit, that the rights to life, liberty, and security of the person can be deprived if governments respect "the principles of fundamental justice" in doing so. It is well documented that federal and provincial officials opted for this phrase, rather than "except by due process of law," in an effort to restrict the impact of judicial review.[22] However, as has been widely observed, the SCC quickly rejected a restrictive approach to "fundamental justice" and ushered in the potential for both substantive and procedural review of legislation and regulations.[23] This has massively expanded the capacity for judicial review under section 7.

The actual principles of fundamental justice are not specified in the Charter and have been developed by judges incrementally over time. By 1993, the SCC had settled on a more structured approach to determining the principles,[24] and writing on the thirtieth anniversary of the Charter in 2012, Hamish Stewart identified over two dozen principles that had been accepted by the court. He noted that the most important ones required that legislation be "rational."[25] In particular, violations of the rights in section 7 must not be overbroad, arbitrary, or grossly disproportionate. These principles played a crucial role in the leading section 7 cases of the last decade, but as we'll see, the court's approach to the right's internal limit underwent a significant shift as well.

Recent Developments in Section 7 Jurisprudence

Canada v Bedford

Jurisprudentially speaking, *Canada v Bedford* (2013) is probably the most important section 7 case of the last decade. The case saw the SCC revisit Canada's prostitution laws, which were upheld against a different section 7 challenge in the 1990 *Prostitution Reference*.[26] The exchange of money for sex was itself legal, but nearly everything about the sex trade, including solicitation, "bawdy-houses" (brothels, or just using one's own home), and "living on the avails of prostitution," was illegal under the Criminal Code. The consequence was to effectively force sex workers onto the streets and prohibit them from employing staff such as security, drivers, or administrative assistants. The SCC accepted the argument in *Bedford* that this web of hypocritical laws made sex work more dangerous and so violated the workers' security of the person in a way incompatible with the principles of fundamental justice, namely, by being overbroad and grossly disproportionate to Parliament's goal of discouraging "public nuisances" and the exploitation of prostitutes by pimps. For similar reasons, the laws were unreasonable under section 1 of the Charter and struck down.

Parliament's response in 2014 was to make the purchasing of sex illegal with prosecution aimed at buyers,[27] effectively removing the central problem in *Bedford* that the laws made an otherwise legal activity unsafe. The law now makes it clear that Parliament considers the sex trade inherently exploitative and unsafe and also ostensibly allows sex workers to operate with greater safety (but see discussion below and Cossman, Chapter 10 in this volume). *Bedford* clearly had (arguably unintended) policy consequences for prostitution policy, but the case's greater impact lay in how it shaped the court's approach to section 7's principles of fundamental justice in two key ways.

The first is the court's shift towards an individualistic analysis, whereby any violation of the principles of fundamental justice can be established by showing that effect "on a *single* person, without regard for empirical evidence as to how well the law achieved its purposes."[28] In other words, a law that infringes the right to life, liberty, and security of the person in a way that is overbroad, grossly disproportionate, or arbitrary for even one person is enough to render the law unconstitutional. Moreover, that "single person" could just be a "reasonably hypothetical" scenario.[29] This has two main implications: it is much easier for a judge to find a section 7 infringement; and concerns about the impact and effectiveness of laws at the societal level are left to section 1, along with a weighing of collective benefits against the costs to rights-holders. The latter creates the possibility – widely seen as impossible before *Bedford* – that a law that violates section 7 could be upheld as a reasonable limit under section 1.[30] The Ontario Court of Appeal did so in *R v Michaud*,[31] but the SCC has not to date – despite the fact that it could have addressed this novel finding by accepting Michaud's application for leave to appeal yet, surprisingly, declined.[32]

The second important jurisprudential development in *Bedford* is the clarification and apparent elevation of three principles: that laws should avoid over-breadth, gross disproportionality, and arbitrariness. Prior to *Bedford*, the court had defined these concepts somewhat inconsistently, sometimes suggesting they were all just aspects of overbreadth,[33] and had generally been reluctant to invoke them to strike down laws.[34] Here, the court attempted to clarify that each is a distinct principle of fundamental justice, defining each as: "arbitrariness (where there is *no connection* between the effect and the object of the law), overbreadth (where the law goes too far and interferes with *some* conduct that bears no connection to its objective), and gross disproportionality (where the effect of the law is grossly disproportionate to the state's objective)."[35] The justices cited Hamish Stewart's observation that all three stem from "failures of instrumental rationality," where the law is "inadequately connected to its objective or in some sense goes too far in seeking to attain it."[36] While other principles of justice previously "found" by the courts continue to exist, the SCC and many lower courts have relied almost exclusively on overbreadth and arbitrariness to strike down laws under section 7 since *Bedford*.[37] (Gross disproportionality was largely rendered redundant in *Nur* and *Lloyd* – successful challenges to mandatory minimum-sentencing provisions, where the court indicated that it should be claimed under section 12's right against cruel and unusual punishment or treatment, despite the fact that the modes of analysis in sections 7 and 12 are not identical.)[38] In *R v Chan,* an Ontario Crown attorney even went so far as to suggest that the court *must* measure laws impugned under section 7 against the three principles in *Bedford,* a claim the trial judge rebuffed.[39] Nonetheless, it is clear that the principles highlighted in *Bedford* have come to occupy a central place in section 7 jurisprudence, as the SCC itself noted in *Carter*.[40]

Although it is surely good that the principles of fundamental justice require laws to be logical and carefully tailored to achieve their purpose, some have criticized the court's heavy emphasis on individual impact and instrumental rationality. They observe that virtually any law that engages in "line drawing" or is based on aggregate risk assessment will be overbroad for somebody.[41] Another concern is that a focus on instrumental, or "means-ends," rationality may lead courts to accept laws that are substantively unjust; that is, the court finds the legislative purpose clearly articulated and the means chosen effective but does not consider whether that purpose is objectionable.[42] This would effectively represent a retreat to procedural review. On a similar note, some worry that courts will cease recognizing new, more substantive principles of fundamental justice that reflect changing societal values.[43] As of this writing, the SCC has embraced only one new principle since 2011 – that lawyers have a "duty of commitment to the client's cause"[44] – and refused to endorse "proportionality in sentencing."[45] Perhaps the most important issue, however, concerns how courts determine legislative purpose. Because instrumental-rationality analysis under section 7 involves comparing the law's purpose and effect on an individual, identifying the former is crucial. *Bedford* raised serious concerns about how judges interpret – or, more accurately, construct – legislative purpose.

Previous cases had established that purpose construction was not "purely historical" nor what Crown attorneys said it was. In *Bedford,* the SCC largely ignored or overtly misstated Parliament's objectives and substituted its own, which it then found to have been pursued in an overbroad and grossly disproportionate manner.[46] As many have observed, purpose construction is easy for judges to manipulate to reach their desired policy outcome, especially – as it was at the time of *Bedford* – when "there is no clear methodology for identifying the purpose of laws or policies against which its means are to be tested."[47]

The court's ruling in *R v Safarzadeh-Markhali* in 2016, building on *R v Moriarity* and *R v Appulonappa* the year before, appears to respond to this criticism, by laying out for the first time a rigorous methodology for legislative purpose construction.[48] This approach includes characterizations of purpose that are "precise and succinct," are of intermediate generality, accept government objectives at face value, and acknowledge that multiple objectives can exist and require judicial harmonization. Methodologically, judges are instructed to prioritize, in order, statements of purpose in the legislation itself; legislative text, context, and overall scheme; and legislative history and other "extrinsic evidence" such as ministerial speeches, parliamentary debates, and committee hearings.[49]

There are several implications of this new approach. The first and most important is that it could significantly constrain judicial flexibility over purpose construction or, at the very least, make that process much more transparent. Similarly, by prioritizing the legislative text and any embedded statements of purpose, it suggests that courts should show greater deference to the legislature in this process. There is still, however, considerable room for judicial interpretation via the "harmonization" of multiple purposes, the reconciliation of conflicting evidence, and adjudging the appropriate level of generalization in legislative purpose. *Chaoulli* provides a good example of the last of these. In finding the law restricting private medical insurance arbitrary, the majority characterized Quebec's objective as "providing effective health care under the public health system," while the dissenting justices took a more nuanced view: "to provide high quality health care, at a reasonable cost, for as many people as possible in a manner that is consistent with principles of efficiency, equity and fiscal responsibility."[50] It remains to be seen if the new construction rules will prevent this sort of disagreement, and the *Chaoulli* example raises a concern about favouring "precise and succinct" characterizations that lack sufficient nuance. As Marcus Moore notes, it is also unclear whether academic sources, government reports, and social context are "extrinsic evidence";[51] if so, then these may provide even more diverse perspectives that give judges greater interpretive discretion. Finally, the jurisprudential impact of *Safarzadeh-Markhali* on purpose construction ultimately depends on whether the lower courts and the SCC, especially as the latter experiences personnel turnover, will consistently follow these rules. As noted in the last section, lower courts largely have not so far.

Carter v Canada

Carter (2015) is probably the Supreme Court's highest-profile section 7 decision in the last decade and is notable for several reasons. I will address these only briefly, given Eleni Nicolaides's extensive and insightful discussion of this case in her contribution to this volume (Chapter 11). First, *Carter* concerns the sensitive topic of MAiD/assisted suicide, a procedure that, while polarizing, has high levels of support across Canada and especially in Quebec. Second, it was a "second-look"[52] case that overturned the Supreme Court's problematic and sharply divided (five to four) 1993 ruling in *Rodriguez* that the ban on MAiD did not violate section 7, even for terminally ill individuals experiencing great suffering who physically cannot take their own lives. Third, the court ruled unanimously in *Carter* that the Criminal Code's ban on MAiD infringed all three of section 7's rights, making it a rare example of a successful right to life claim (for "forcing some individuals to take their own lives prematurely")[53] and the first time a majority of the court endorsed a liberty-as-personal autonomy claim – in this case, "the right to make decisions concerning ... bodily integrity and medical care."[54] Fourth, *Carter* is noteworthy for blurring the distinction between negative and positive rights and raising the possibility that section 7 may guarantee the latter.[55] Although largely framed as a negative rights decision, with rights violations caused by state interference with end-of-life decisions, the court's logic implies that if provinces fail to create the infrastructure for MAiD – a requirement of positive state action – they will be in violation of section 7. Finally, the case had a major policy impact by directly spurring Parliament to legalize MAiD,[56] although the new law, by requiring death to be "reasonably foreseeable" and excluding mental illness, did not fully comply with the court's eligibility guidelines. The legislative sequel was also notable for Parliament's – and especially the Senate's – extensive engagement with what section 7 requires and the open invocation of Parliament's authority to interpret the Charter ("coordinate construction").[57] Some have also averred that the court's decision to (repeatedly) suspend its remedy of invalidating the impugned provisions facilitated Ottawa's noncompliance.[58] Parliament's ability to respond "creatively" to a Supreme Court ruling proved short-lived, however, as the 2019 *Truchon* decision – citing *Markhali* on purpose construction – declared the "reasonably foreseeable death" requirement unconstitutional under sections 7 and 15 of the Charter.[59] On March 17, 2021, *An Act to amend the Criminal Code (medical assistance in dying)*[60] removed that requirement and opened MAiD to those suffering from mental illness by 2023.

I have tried to sketch out some of the most important jurisprudential developments, broadly speaking, regarding section 7 since the thirtieth anniversary of the Charter. In doing so, I have surely overlooked consequential cases in some areas, such as immigration[61] and extradition.[62] Nonetheless, the preceding review permits us to consider in the next section – without prognosticating on the outcome – several areas where section 7 is likely to be implicated in the future, including in some upcoming cases from the lower courts.

Future Directions?

"Second Look" Cases: Sex Work and Self-Induced Intoxication

The constitutional issues surrounding sex work are far from resolved,[63] and at least one lower court has declared key sections of the 2014 law that prohibit "influencing" others into prostitution unconstitutionally arbitrary, overbroad, and grossly disproportionate, for criminalizing "noncoercive, non-exploitative relationship[s] which might simply enhance the health and safety of the potential sex worker."[64] Another trial court upheld the law,[65] albeit in the different context of underage sex workers. In April 2021, an Ontario Superior Court judge struck down several parts of the 2014 regime as overbroad and grossly disproportionate in making sex work unnecessarily more dangerous in nonexploitative situations,[66] though this decision was reversed by the Ontario Court of Appeal in February 2022.[67] Another legal challenge was launched in March 2021 by the Canadian Alliance for Sex Work Law Reform.[68]

Another section 7 issue that has returned to the courts is whether "automatism" from self-induced extreme intoxication can be a defence in cases of violent offences, including sexual assault. The Supreme Court's 1994 *Daviault* ruling found that section 7 required that the accused be able to raise this defence, but Parliament's legislative response in section 33.1 of the Criminal Code reversed this.[69] Since then, lower courts have disagreed about whether section 33.1 violates section 7 and, if so, is a reasonable limit.[70] In June 2020, the Ontario Court of Appeal – the only appeal court to have ruled on the issue – struck down the provision,[71] and the SCC has granted leave to appeal and as of this writing has heard oral arguments. Notably, none of the lower courts in the recent sex work and "automatism" cases explicitly employed the rigorous *Markhali* approach to purpose construction, and in the 2021 *R v NS* case, the trial judge put more weight on expert witness testimony than Parliament's and the minister's rationales for amending prostitution laws. The Ontario Court of Appeal's reversal in *R v NS* rejected that approach as inconsistent with *Markhali*.

Access to Medical Procedures

While not technically a "second look" case, *Cambie Surgeries* is, like *Chaoulli*, a section 7 challenge to provincial laws that prohibit private medical insurance for surgical procedures covered by the public insurance system (medicare), or doctors in the public system from extrabilling patients.[72] The BC surgeons claim that it violates patients' rights to life, liberty (in the "autonomy" sense endorsed in *Carter*), and security of the person to prevent them "from accessing private medically necessary healthcare, including private surgeries, when they are unable to access timely care in the public system."[73] Justice Steeves of the BC Supreme Court dismissed the claim in a thorough and voluminous ruling. He did find that the public system's wait times for elective surgeries infringed security of the person but – contrary to *Chaoulli* – not the right to life, for lack of evidence.[74] Using the *Bedford* approach to the principles of fundamental justice and citing *Markhali* on purpose construction, Justice Steeves found that the infringement was not arbitrary, overbroad, or grossly disproportionate and would be saved by section 1 in any case. The BC Court of Appeal agreed in June 2021 to hear the plaintiffs' appeal, and it seems likely that the case will eventually make its way to the SCC.[75]

Notwithstanding the recent legislation enhancing access to MAiD, it is likely that there will be further demands to improve access for those suffering from degenerative cognitive impairments, such as Alzheimer's disease and other dementias, who fear that by the time they reach the point of wanting MAiD, they will no longer be considered mentally competent under the law. This is likely to create the same issue flagged as a violation of the right to life in *Carter*, that the law forces some to end their lives prematurely. Lack of access to MAiD for this group is likely to generate further section 7 claims, specifically for advance directives. Notably, the Senate voted to add advance directives to the 2021 MAiD law, but the House of Commons rejected it.[76]

While there has been relatively little litigation regarding abortion since the late 1980s, that may not remain the case. Formal decriminalization in 2019 has presumably fully rendered abortion a medical procedure under provincial jurisdiction, and the Supreme Court's 1993 *Morgentaler* ruling implies that any provincial attempt to effectively ban or severely restrict abortion will be considered *ultra vires* for trespassing into the federal criminal law power.[77] To the extent that physicians consider an abortion medically necessary in a physical, psychological, or emotional sense, the logic of *Carter* suggests that provinces must also make abortions reasonably accessible. There are, however, large geographic areas of Canada with little to no access,[78] which might give rise to future section 7 claims.

On a similar note, in light of Canada's "other" recent (and ongoing) epidemic – the opioid crisis and record numbers of fentanyl-related overdoses – we might see a section 7 claim that governments must provide safe-injection sites.[79] This would go beyond the 2011 ruling in *PHS Community Services Society* ["Insite"] that the federal minister of justice had to continue granting an existing safe-injection facility an exemption from antidrug laws when the evidence proved the site saved lives and improved public health.[80]

Positive Socioeconomic Rights

The prospect of a successful claim in court that section 7 includes positive socioeconomic rights admittedly appears slim. Homelessness and poverty as section 7 issues have attracted a great deal of supportive commentary from high-profile commentators, however, such as Bruce Porter, Martha Jackman, Margot Young, and (now Justice) Lorne Sossin.[81] As they note, courts have routinely invoked *Gosselin* but without seriously engaging with its caveat that positive rights *could* be found under section 7 or reconciling *Gosselin* with those cases, like Insite and *Carter,* where the state implicitly has been found to have "positive obligations." Moreover, distinctions between "negative" and "positive" rights are often illusory, resting on a narrow conception of "state action" that includes, for example, a ban on MAiD but not a conscious government decision to slash funding to homeless shelters, affordable-living projects, and social-assistance programs. While Emmett Macfarlane is right to argue that "incorporating entirely new rights into the [Charter] absent the required constitutional amending process is a major jurisprudential leap,"[82] one could argue that what are being requested in cases like these are not "new rights" so much as applying existing rights to a more fulsome understanding of state action.

The most important case to address homelessness as a section 7 issue is *Tanudjaja,* in which the plaintiffs challenged a broad range of state funding cuts and policy inaction, rather than any specific laws.[83] A majority of the Ontario Court of Appeal dismissed the case in 2017 as nonjusticiable issues of "pure policy," without considering the claimants' arguments on the merits. The SCC refused leave to appeal, as it has in other positive rights cases,[84] which may signal that the court is keeping its options open in this area.

Government Responses to Contagions and Pandemics

Outbreaks and especially full-blown pandemics such as COVID-19 can generate section 7 claims in several ways. First, section 7 is squarely implicated in concerns that sweeping emergency powers invoked by governments during threats of contagion may infringe on civil liberties.[85] Examples of this are rights-based objections to quarantine periods, business lockdowns, travel bans, mandatory vaccination, or vaccine "passports."[86] One such case was launched in July 2020 by the antivaccination group Vaccine Choice Canada and another, remarkably, by several Ontario police officers who oppose lockdowns.[87] Second, section 7 applies where people housed or incarcerated by the state are unnecessarily exposed to infection due to mismanagement or deliberate administrative decisions: government-run long-term care homes and prisoners (including those awaiting trial or refugee determination hearings) immediately spring to mind. The John Howard Society and several prisoners in British Columbia, for example, launched a constitutional challenge to extended prisoner isolation and service reductions during COVID-19.[88] Third, pandemics engage the potential for positive rights-based claims like those discussed above, particularly by vulnerable groups such as the homeless or those made unemployed by government lockdowns. The second and third scenarios may entail claims based on government "inaction" or, more accurately, a conscious decision not to act – for example, to *not* hire extra staff, segregate residents, pay for personal protective equipment, and so forth.[89] It is not clear why such decisions do not engage the rights to life and security of the person, particularly if sound evidence existed at the time that different decisions would have prevented illness and saved lives. A fourth scenario involving section 7 and pandemics emerged from the shocking "Freedom Convoy" protests in 2022 against the government's public health measures, which included a month-long occupation of the nation's capital and shorter blockades of border crossings into the United States. These events prompted Parliament's unprecedented invocation of the *Emergency Measures Act*, albeit for only one week, to provide authorities with greater powers to seize vehicles and freeze bank accounts linked to the protests. The Canadian Civil Liberties Association has criticized this response as an excessive intrusion on Charter rights, including section 7, and sued the federal government.[90]

Environmental Rights

There is a tremendous wealth of literature regarding existing and potential recognition of environmental rights via section 7, including rights to clean drinking water, protection against pollution, and government action on climate change.[91] Lynda Collins notes that there are two distinct approaches to environmental rights claims: the first focuses on environmental deprivations of existing human rights, such as the right to life or security of the person; the second, and more daunting in Canada, on "the creation of an independent human right to a healthy environment."[92] The former entails an "ecologically literate reading" of the Charter that recognizes environmental quality as a necessary precondition to the enjoyment of its rights.[93] Courts in India and South Africa have endorsed such claims, finding a right to clean water and air under the right to life, and it is not hard to imagine similar arguments by Indigenous nations suffering from chronically contaminated drinking water. Several young climate-change activists recently sued the federal government over its support of the fossil fuel industry, claiming it violated their section 7 rights, but the Federal Court summarily dismissed the case for lacking a "reasonable cause of action or prospect of success."[94] A similar case is now before the Ontario courts but with a more specific challenge to the Ford government's elimination of the province's "cap and trade" system for carbon emissions.[95] As with cases about medicare and homelessness, environmental rights claims are often hampered by high evidentiary burdens and judicial concerns about justiciability. However, justiciability should pose less of a barrier to environmental claims, as "governments at all levels in Canada have thoroughly and vigorously occupied the field through comprehensive environmental Acts and agencies"[96] that constitute state action under the Charter. These actions include state-operated facilities that pollute; government licences or permits that allow industries to pollute; and government failure to enforce environmental legislation.[97] Similarly, many individuals have standing to make environmental challenges.[98] It therefore seems likely that Canada will witness more section 7 claims to environmental justice in the coming years.

Conclusion

In the last forty years, section 7 has been implicated in a remarkable range of policy areas, including criminal justice, drugs, immigration, national security, medicare, abortion, assisted suicide, prostitution, social assistance, and climate change. Given the broad purchase of "life, liberty, and security of the person," the section's requirement of instrumental rationality comes very close to representing a right to proportionate, evidence-based policy making. No other Charter right can lay claim to such sweeping scope. However, as the preceding discussion reveals, many attempts to claim section 7 fail, and under *Bedford*'s individualistic approach to the principles of fundamental justice, it is increasingly probable that laws that run afoul of section 7 will be nevertheless upheld under section 1 due to their collective benefit. The court's attempt in *Markhali* to rein in judicial discretion when constructing the purpose of laws may also lead to greater deference to legislatures, although the lower-court evidence to date on that is mixed. Thus, while section 7 seems to provide fertile ground for future claims like those surveyed above, it very much remains to be seen whether the judicial activism witnessed in the last decade in cases such as *Bedford* and *Carter* represents the future or a high-water mark from which the courts will retreat.

Notes

My thanks to Sorayyah Chityal for her research assistance with part of this chapter; any errors remain my own.

1 Peter W. Hogg, "The Brilliant Career of Section 7 of the Charter," *Supreme Court Law Review: Osgoode's Annual Constitutional Cases Conference* 58 (2012): 195–210; Hamish Stewart, *Fundamental Justice: Section 7 of the Canadian Charter of Rights and Freedoms* (Toronto: Irwin Law, 2012), 151.

2 *Canada (Attorney General) v Bedford*, 2013 SCC 72 [*Bedford*]; *Carter v Canada (Attorney General)*, 2015 SCC 5 [*Carter*].

3 Hamish Stewart, *Fundamental Justice: Section 7 of the Canadian Charter of Rights and Freedoms*, 2nd ed. (Toronto: Irwin Law, 2019), 371, 372.

4 *R v Safarzadeh-Markhali*, 2016 SCC 14 [*Safarzadeh-Markhali*].

5 Hogg, "Brilliant Career of Section 7," 195.

6 Including refugees (*Singh v Minister of Employment and Immigration*, [1985] 1 SCR 177) and foreign nationals fleeing justice elsewhere (*Kindler v Canada (Minister of Justice)*, [1991] 2 SCR 779; *Reference Re Ng Extradition (Can.)*, [1991] 2 SCR 858).

7 Stewart, *Fundamental Justice*, 2nd ed., 66. See *R v Hape*, 2007 SCC 26; *Canada (Prime Minister) v Khadr*, 2010 SCC 3.

8 *Irwin Toy v Quebec (Attorney General)*, [1989] 1 SCR 927.

9 *R v Krajnc*, 2017 ONCJ 281.

10 For example, Sue Donaldson and Will Kymlicka, *Zoopolis: A Political Theory of Animal Rights* (Oxford: Oxford University Press, 2013); Angela Fernandez, "Not Quite Property, Not Quite Persons: A 'Quasi' Approach for Nonhuman Animals," *Canadian Journal of Comparative and Contemporary Law* 5, 1 (2019): 155–232; Maneesha Deckha, *Animals as Legal Beings: Contesting Anthropocentric Legal Orders* (Toronto: University of Toronto Press, 2020).

11 *Borowski v Canada (Attorney General)*, [1989] 1 SCR 342; *Tremblay v Daigle*, [1989] 2 SCR 530.

12 *Chaoulli v Quebec (Attorney General)*, 2005 SCC 35.

13 *R v Morgentaler*, [1988] 1 SCR 30 [*Morgentaler*], per Wilson J, 166. See also the slim majority in *Blencoe v British Columbia (Human Rights Commission)*, 2000 SCC 44 [*Blencoe*], but the case did not actually involve a claim of that nature. The court rejected such a claim in *R v Malmo-Levine*, [2003] 3 SCR 571; *R v Caine*, 2003 SCC 74, regarding the recreational use of marijuana.

14 *Morgentaler*, 32, per Dickson CJ and Lamer J.

15 *Blencoe*, para 86.

16 Stewart, *Fundamental Justice*, 2nd ed., 5.

17 The attempt to add such "social rights" to the Constitution failed along with the rest of the Charlottetown Accord in the 1992 referendum.

18 *Gosselin v Québec (Attorney General)*, 2002 SCC 84. The claim was that s 7 guaranteed adequate living standards from state assistance.

19 *Ibid*, para 83.

20 Barry L. Strayer, "The Evolution of the Charter," in *Patriation and Its Consequences: Constitution Making in Canada*, ed. Lois Harder and Steve Patten (Vancouver: UBC Press, 2015), 84.

21 Hogg, "Brilliant Career of Section 7," 196.

22 Anne Bayefsky, *Canada's Constitutional Act 1982 and Amendments: A Documentary History*, 2 vols. (Toronto: McGraw-Hill, 1989); Strayer, "Evolution of the Charter," 84–85.

23 *Re BC Motor Vehicle Act*, [1985] 2 SCR 486.

24 *Rodriguez v British Columbia (Attorney General)*, [1993] 3 SCR 519. See also the court's adoption of a formal three-part test in *Canadian Foundation for Children, Youth and the Law v Canada (Attorney General)*, 2004 SCC 4.

25 Stewart, *Fundamental Justice*, 1st ed., chs. 4–5. See also Alana Klein, "The Arbitrariness in 'Arbitrariness' (and Overbreadth and Gross Disproportionality): Principle and Democracy in Section 7 of the Charter," *Supreme Court Law Review* 63 (2013): 377–402; Hogg, "Brilliant Career of Section 7."

26 *Reference re ss 193 and 195.1(1)(c) of the Criminal Code (Man)*, [1990] 1 SCR 1123.

27 *Protection of Communities and Exploited Persons Act*, SC 2014, c 25.

28 Hamish Stewart, "*Bedford* and the Structure of Section 7," *McGill Law Journal* 60, 3 (2015): 585.

29 *R v Heywood*, [1994] 3 SCR 761.

30 Stewart, "*Bedford* and the Structure of Section 7."

31 *R v Michaud*, 2015 ONCA 585 [*Michaud*]. The law in question requires speed limiters of 105 kilometres per hour on commercial trucks, and the accused's was set to 109.4. Because drivers sometimes – but rarely – need to go faster than 105 to avoid accidents, the law infringed the driver's security of the person and was arbitrary in such cases. The Ontario Court of Appeal found that the overall benefit of the law, however, justified those rare s 7 violations. See Lilliane Cadieux-Shaw, "A Reluctant Justification: *R v Michaud* Uses *Bedford* Approach to Justify Section 7 Infringement," TheCourt.ca, September 23, 2015, www.thecourt.ca/a-reluctant-justification-r-v michaud-uses-bedford-approach-to-justify-section-7-infringement/.

32 Matthew Hennigar, "Unreasonable Disagreement? Judicial-Executive Exchanges about Charter Reasonableness in the Harper Era," *Osgoode Hall Law Journal* 54, 4 (2017): 1252.

33 Stewart, "*Bedford* and the Structure of Section 7," 577.

34 Andrew Menchynski and Jill R. Prsooor, "A Withering Instrumentality. The Negative Implications of *R. v. Safarzadeh-Markhali* and other Recent Section 7 Jurisprudence," *Supreme Court Law Review* 81 (2019): 75–96.

35 *Bedford* (emphasis in original).

36 *Ibid*, para 107, citing Stewart, *Fundamental Justice*, 1st ed., 151.

37 Menchynski and Presser, "A Withering Instrumentality," 80.

38 *R v Nur [R v Charles]*, 2015 SCC 15; *R v Lloyd*, 2016 SCC 13; Stewart, *Fundamental Justice*, 2nd ed., 186–87. The approach to s 12 compares sentences under existing law, while s 7 analysis, as discussed below, compares the purpose of the law to its effect on constitutionally protected interests.

39 *R v Chan*, 2018 ONSC 3849. The accused relied on other, older principles of fundamental justice.

40 *Carter*, para 72.

41 Hogg, "Brilliant Career of Section 7"; Klein, "The Arbitrariness in 'Arbitrariness'"; *Michaud*, paras 99, 148–50; Stewart, *Fundamental Justice*, 2nd ed.

42 For example, by being "substantively unfair" or unjustly targeting and punishing "the politically and socially powerless": Menchynski and Presser, "A Withering Instrumentality," 88. See also Hart Schwartz, "Circularity, Tautology, and Gamesmanship: 'Purpose' Based Proportionality-Correspondence Analysis in Sections 15 and 7 of the Charter," *National Journal of Constitutional Law* 35 (2015): 105–29.

43 Menchynski and Presser, "A Withering Instrumentality"; Klein, "The Arbitrariness in 'Arbitrariness.'"

44 *Canada (Attorney General) v Federation of Law Societies*, 2015 SCC 7.

45 *Safarzadeh-Markhali*.

46 Hennigar, "Unreasonable Disagreement?," 1266–67. This study found that in over one-third of cases involving federal criminal laws, the SCC only upheld Parliament's objective in s 1 analysis after rejecting the attorney general of Canada's characterization of it before the court. In those cases, the court reframed the law's objective but then found that the means used to achieve it were irrational, overbroad, or disproportionate under s 7.

47 Klein, "The Arbitrariness in 'Arbitrariness,'" 384.

48 *R v Moriarity*, 2015 SCC 55; *R v Appulonappa*, 2015 SCC 59.

49 Marcus Moore, "*R. v. Safarzadeh-Markhali*: Elements and Implications of the Supreme Court's New Rigorous Approach to Construction of Statutory Purpose," *Supreme Court Law Review*, 2nd ser, 77 (2017): 223–53.

50 *Chaoulli*, paras 135, 236.

51 Moore, "*R. v. Safarzadeh-Markhali*," 235.

52 Peter W. Hogg, Allison A. Bushell Thornton, and Wade K. Wright, "Charter Dialogue Revisited: Or 'Much Ado about Metaphors,'" *Osgoode Hall Law Journal* 45, 1 (2007): 1–65.

53 *Carter*, para 57.

54 *Ibid*, para 66.

55 Emmett Macfarlane, "Dialogue, Remedies, and Positive Rights: *Carter v Canada* as a Microcosm for Past and Future Issues under the Charter of Rights and Freedoms," *Ottawa Law Review* 49, 1 (2017): 121.

56 *Act to amend the Criminal Code and to make related amendments to other Acts (medical assistance in dying)*, SC 2016, c 3.

57 Eleni Nicolaides and Matthew Hennigar, "*Carter* Conflicts: The Supreme Court of Canada's Impact on Medical Assistance in Dying Policy," in *Policy Change, Courts, and the Canadian Constitution*, ed. Emmett Macfarlane (Toronto: University of Toronto Press, 2018), 313–35.

58 Macfarlane, "Dialogue, Remedies, and Positive Rights"; Dave Snow and Kate Puddister, "Closing a Door but Opening a Policy Window: Legislating Assisted Dying in Canada," in *ibid*, 40–60.

59 *Truchon c Procureur général du Canada*, 2019 QCCS 3792.

60 SC 2021, c 2.

61 For example, *Appulonappa*, 2015, and *B010 v Canada (Citizenship and Immigration)*, 2015 SCC 58, which held, respectively, that refugee claimants cannot be prosecuted or denied on the basis of "assisting human smuggling" when that assistance was providing humanitarian aid to fellow passengers. See also *Canada (Citizenship and Immigration) v Harkat*, 2014 SCC 37, upholding Canada's revised security-certificate regime.

62 *India v Badesha*, 2017 SCC 44, holding that extradition is permitted even when there are serious doubts about the reliability of assurances against the use of torture upon return.

63 See, for example, Angela Campbell, "Sex Work's Governance: Stuff and Nuisance," *Feminist Legal Studies* 23, 1 (2015): 27–45; Hamish Stewart, "The Constitutionality of the New Sex Work Law," *Alberta Law Review* 54, 1 (2016): 69–88.

64 *R v Anwar*, 2020 ONCJ 103.

65 *R v Boodhoo and others*, 2018 ONSC 7205.

66 *R v NS*, 2021 ONSC 1628.

67 *R v NS*, 2022 ONCA 160.

68 Canadian Alliance for Sex Work Law Reform, "News!!! Sex Worker Human Rights Groups Launch Constitutional Challenge," March 30, 2021, http://sexworklawreform.com/sex-worker-human-rights-groups-launch-constitutional-challenge/.

69 *R v Daviault*, [1994] 3 SCR 63.

70 *R v McCaw*, 2018 ONSC 3464, paras 30–47. See also Dennis Baker and Rainer Knopff, "*Daviault* Dialogue: The Strange Journey of Canada's Intoxication Defence," *Review of Constitutional Studies* 19, 1 (2014): 35–58.

71 *R v Sullivan*, 2020 ONCA 333.

72 *Cambie Surgeries Corporation v British Columbia (Attorney General)*, 2020 BCSC 1310.

73 *Ibid*, para 4.

74 Notably, a s 7 challenge to Alberta's restrictions on private medical insurance in *Allen v Alberta*, 2015 ABCA 277 was also rejected for lacking a sufficient evidentiary basis; the Supreme Court refused leave to appeal.

75 For a thorough examination of legal challenges to medicare, see Colleen M. Flood and Bryan Thomas, eds., *Is Two-Tier Health Care the Future?* (Ottawa: University of Ottawa Press, 2020).

76 Jacques Gallant, "Canada Has a New Law on Medical Assistance in Dying: Here's What It Means," *Toronto Star*, March 17, 2021.

77 *An Act to amend the Criminal Code, the Youth Criminal Justice Act and other Acts and to make consequential amendments to other Acts*, SC 2019, c 25 [Bill C-75]; *R v Morgentaler*, [1993] 3 SCR 463.

78 Rachael Johnstone, "Canadian Abortion Policy and the Limitations of Litigation," in *Policy Change, Courts, and the Canadian Constitution*, ed. Emmett Macfarlane (Toronto: University of Toronto Press, 2018), 336–55.

79 Brynn Leger, "Freeze on Overdose Prevention Sites Engages Charter Rights," Rabble. ca, August 30, 2018, https://rabble.ca/columnists/2018/08/freeze-overdose-prevention -sites-engages-charter-rights.

80 *PHS Community Services Society v Canada (Attorney General)*, [2011] 3 SCR 134.

81 Martha Jackman and Bruce Porter, "Rights-Based Strategies to Address Homelessness and Poverty in Canada," in *Advancing Social Rights*, ed. Martha Jackman and Bruce Porter (Toronto: Irwin Law, 2014), 65–106; Margot Young, "*Charter* Eviction: Litigating Out of House and Home," *Journal of Law and Social Policy* 24 (2015): 46–67; Vasuda Sinha, Lorne Sossin, and Jenna Meguid, "Charter Litigation, Social and Economic Rights and Civil Procedure," *Journal of Law and Social Policy* 26 (2017): 43–67; Martha Jackman, "One Step Forward and Two Steps Back: Poverty, the *Charter* and the Legacy of *Gosselin*," *National Journal of Constitutional Law* 39 (2019): 85–121.

82 Emmett Macfarlane, "The Dilemma of Positive Rights: Access to Health Care and the *Canadian Charter of Rights and Freedoms*," *Journal of Canadian Studies* 48, 3 (2014): 58.

83 *Tanudjaja v Canada (Attorney General)*, 2014 ONCA 852.

84 See Jackman, "One Step Forward," 113–15.

85 Janet E. Mosher, "Accessing Justice amid Threats of Contagion," *Osgoode Hall Law Journal* 51 (2014): 919–55; Colleen M. Flood, Vanessa MacDonnell, Jane Philpott, Sophie Thériault, and Sridhar Venkatapuram, eds., *Vulnerable: The Law, Policy and Ethics of COVID-19* (Ottawa: University of Ottawa Press, 2020); Colleen M. Flood, Vanessa MacDonnell, Bryan Thomas, and Kumanan Wilson, *Reconciling Civil Liberties and Public Health in the Response to COVID-19* (Ottawa: Royal Society of Canada, 2020); Marie-Eve Couture-Ménard, Kathleen Hammond, Lara Khoury, and Alana Klein, "Answering in Emergency: The Law and Accountability in Canada's Pandemic Response," *UNB Law Journal* 71 (2021): 1–46; Amy Goudge, "Balancing Legality and Legitimacy in Canada's COVID-19 Response," *National Journal of Constitutional Law* 41 (2021): 153–83.

86 Emmett Macfarlane, "Public Policy and Constitutional Rights in Times of Crisis," *Canadian Journal of Political Science* 53 (2020): 299–303.

87 Colin Butler, "Details Emerge of Vaccine Choice Canada Lawsuit over Coronavirus Response," CBC News, August 13, 2020, https://www.cbc.ca/news/health/coronavirus -charter-challenge-1.5680988; Colin Butler, "Group of Ontario Police Officers Launches Charter Challenge of Pandemic Restrictions," CBC News, May 4, 2021, https://www.cbc. ca/news/canada/london/police-oath-pandemic-legal-challenge-1.6012099.

88 "B.C. Inmates File Constitutional Challenge over COVID-19 Restrictions," CBC News, March 7, 2021, https://www.cbc.ca/news/canada/british-columbia/b-c-inmates-file -constitutional-challenge-over-covid-19-restrictions-1.5940082.

89 Some provinces, such as British Columbia and Ontario, commissioned investigations into their early pandemic responses for long-term care; rights-based challenges may result from such findings, which were damning in Ontario's case.

90 CCLA, "CCLA Will Fight Invocation of *Emergency Measures Act* in Court," February 17, 2022, https://ccla.org/press-release/ccla-will-fight-invocation-of-emergencies-act-in- court-2/.

91 For example: Lynda M. Collins, "An Ecologically Literate Reading of the Canadian Charter of Rights and Freedoms," *Windsor Review of Legal and Social Issues* 26 (2009): 7–48; Nathalie J. Chalifour, "Environmental Justice and the Charter: Do Environmental Injustices Infringe Sections 7 and 15 of the Charter?," *Journal of Environmental Law and Practice* 28 (2015): 89–124; Lynda M. Collins, "Safe-Guarding the *Longue Durée*: Environmental Rights in the Canadian Constitution," *Supreme Court Law Review* 2nd ser, 71 (2015): 520; Dustin W. Klaudt, "Can Canada's 'Living Tree' Constitution and Lessons from Foreign Climate Litigation Seed Climate Justice and Remedy Climate Change?," *Journal of Environmental Law and Practice* 31 (2018): 185–242; Nathalie J. Chalifour and Jessica Earle, "Feeling the Heat: Climate Litigation under the Canadian Charter's Right to Life, Liberty, and Security of the Person," *Vermont Law Review* 42 (2018): 690–770.

92 Collins, "Safe-Guarding the *Longue Durée*," 520.

93 Collins, "An Ecologically Literate Reading."

94 *La Rose et al v Canada,* 2020 FC 1008.

95 Morgan Sharp, "Virtual Day in Court for Youth Climate Activists Ends without Verdict," *National Observer,* July 13, 2020.

96 Collins, "An Ecologically Literate Reading," 32–33.

97 Collins, "Safe-Guarding the *Longue Durée*," 525.

98 Chalifour and Earle, "Feeling the Heat," 718.

10
Sex Work, Abjection, and the Constitution

Brenda Cossman

How, IF AT all, have forty years of the *Charter of Rights and Freedoms* changed the regulation of sex and sexuality? I am interested in the constitutional law of sex, the area of law where constitutional rights and/or values have been brought to bear on the regulation of sex and sexuality more generally. While some scholars have suggested a shift in judicial approaches to sex, from a morality-based to a harms-based approach, I remain less sanguine about the legacy.[1] In this chapter, I focus on the regulation of sex work. The Supreme Court considered the constitutionality of Canada's criminal laws regulating sex work in the *Prostitution Reference* in 1990 and two decades later, in *Canada v Bedford*. Building on the scholarship around affective governance, I argue that, despite doctrinal changes and an apparent liberalization of judicial attitudes, the constitutional law of sex work remains infused with abjection, disgust, and the expulsion of sex workers from social life. The constitutional governance of sex work continues to be haunted by a double-edged sword of abjection, which constitutes sex workers as both tragic victims and sexual deviants, with the spectre of both unbridled desire and sexual danger threatening the social order.

Affective Governance and the Double-Edged Sword of Abjection

Scholars of affective governance have explored the roles that emotion and affect play in contemporary regimes of governing.[2] Many explore the role of affect in the neoliberal shift to self-governance, how subjects come to regulate themselves through affect and emotion. Others consider the ways that emotions are deployed in governing subjects. Recently, feminist scholars have examined the role that affective governance plays in regulating sex work.[3] Affect and emotion, they argue, have been crucial in constituting sex workers as "others."[4] Birgit Sauer, for example, explores the ways in which disgust and shame mobilize in the affective strategies of abolitionist movements that lobby governments to criminalize prostitution and punish clients.[5] Eilís Ward has examined affect's role in regulating prostitution reform in Ireland in terms of the psychic discomfort towards "errant female sexuality."[6] The fear of contagion sticks onto the bodies of sex workers and requires their expulsion from the social order. It is part of a process of cultural abjection, wherein sex workers are constituted as abject and must therefore be cast out or, in Ward's terms, "killed off."

Building on Ward's work, I argue that abjection is central to the affective governance of sex work in Canada. The concept of abjection is associated with the work of Julia Kristeva, who describes it as a psychic process of casting out that which threatens the boundaries of the self. The abject is "neither object nor subject, but an entity that was radically excluded from our moral symbolic order"; it is that which "disturbs identity, system, order. What does not respect borders, positions, rules. The in-between, the ambiguous, the composite ... what highlights the fragility of the law."[7] The abject constitutes the terms by which the subject defines what is "I" and what is "not I"; the "not I" that threatens must be cast out. Abjection is a process that operates through disgust. As Sara Ahmed observes, "abjection is bound up with the insecurity of the not; it seeks to secure 'the not' through the response of being disgusted."[8]

While Kristeva's psychoanalytic focus explores the individual psychic processes of abjection, other scholars have deployed a more social and political account of abjection. Imogen Tyler argues that such a conceptualization of abjection describes the "violent exclusionary forces ... forces that strip people of their human dignity and reproduce them as dehumanized waste, the dregs and refuse of social life."[9] Judith Butler considers the ways in which regulatory norms of "bodily formation produce a domain of abjected bodies," bodies that do not qualify as "fully human." For Butler, these bodies serve as the "constitutive outside," "delegitimized bodies that fail to count as bodies."[10] While Butler speaks of the sex and gender norms that produce abjected bodies, such as homosexual, aged, and diseased bodies, the prostitute body has been similarly abjected. It is a body that has been repeatedly cast out, as threatening the moral and social order, with the affects of disgust and shame sticking to the abjected body.

Ward has considered abjection's role in the affective governance of sex workers in the Irish law-reform campaign. While sex workers presented themselves as subjects seeking recognition, the Irish state repudiated their claim, "recognis[ing] only that which was tolerable viz the tragic, abject victim of sexual violence, needing rescue and rehabilitation."[11] While this was a vision consistent with the feminist abolitionist campaigners, Ward notes that the Irish state also relied on an older affective narrative of abjection around women's sexuality in general and sex workers in particular. She notes how earlier Irish campaigns presented the prostitute "as a vulnerable, helpless creature and yet at the same time a sexually active woman who could corrupt the social and moral order and ... blackmail respectable men."[12] Ward argues that a similar script circulated in the recent campaign, in which "the person selling sex was an abject, helpless figure, doubly victimised by her past and her current activities, in need of protection. Yet, she was also inherently untrustworthy."[13]

Caitlin Janzen and colleagues have explored a similar process in Canadian media representations of violence against street sex workers.[14] They argue that media representations triggered the process of cultural abjection, constructing the sex worker as an abject other: "[T]he street sex worker exists as not quite; not quite a victim, not quite an agent, not quite a woman, and often not quite a person."[15] They explore how these media representations constitute street sex workers in and through images of defilement as a threat to civilized society. The casting out of the bodies of these sex workers is part of a constant "redrawing of boundaries between 'Me' and 'Not Me,'" particularly in relation to accepted and intolerable displays of female sexuality.[16] They identify a similar duality in the way in which abjection operates, that is, in a way "so that the bodies of women who engage in street sex work can simultaneously be regarded as absolutely vulnerable and dangerously threatening."[17]

Abjection operates on two levels: a tragic victim of violence and an aberrant female sexuality. This duality and its contradictory visions of prostitution correspond to what I refer to as the double-edged sword of abjection. Prostitution and, more significantly, prostitutes have been abjectified in and through two archetypes: the helpless victim and the sexual deviant. The first is a vulnerable, tragic figure whose victimization deprives her of subject status; she cannot speak for herself. The second is the sexually active and thereby deviant woman whose visibility threatens to corrupt the social and moral order. She, too, defies subject status; she is too dangerous, too corrupt, too untrustworthy to be given a voice. The abject cannot speak; or, rather, the abject cannot be heard. It is a double-edged abjection that haunts the legal regulation of prostitution.

In the sections that follow, I explore the ways in which this double-edged sword of abjection underlies the Supreme Court's decisions on the constitutionality of Canada's sex work laws, which have twice been considered by the court, first in the *Prostitution Reference* (1990) and again in *R v Bedford* (2013).[18] It is a tale of two solitudes, officially reconciled by the court by distinguishing the nature of the constitutional challenges. However, the differences between these cases also represent the two polarities of abjection. A close reading of the Supreme Court's decisions on sex work reveals how sex workers have been constituted through this double-edged sword of abjection, which deploys its affect of disgust, thereby setting the discursive terrain for the casting off of sex workers in the subsequent criminal reform. In the *Prostitution Reference,* the sex worker does not speak; she is described only as the sexually deviant public nuisance from which society must be protected. In *Bedford,* a different sex worker arrives, one that is abjected through her victimized status. It is in and through this double-edged sword of abjection that the Supreme Court has constituted the sex worker as an entity that does not belong and cannot belong.

Despite striking down the law in *Bedford*, the Supreme Court set the discursive frame for the subsequent affective governance of prostitution in the *Protection of Communities and Exploited Persons Act.*

The *Prostitution Reference:* Nuisance as Abjection

In the *Prostitution Reference*, the majority of the Supreme Court upheld the constitutionality of the bawdy-house (then section 193) and communicating-for-the-purposes-of-prostitution provisions (then section 195.1(1)) of the Criminal Code. Chief Justice Dickson, writing for the majority, with a concurring opinion by Justice Lamer, held that although the section 7 liberty interest was engaged because of the possibility of imprisonment, neither provision violated the principles of fundamental justice. Similarly, although the communication provisions violated the freedom of expression rights under section 2(b), the prohibition was a reasonable limit within the meaning of section 1. The court's reasoning on the section 7 challenge was relatively narrow, and none of the opinions engaged with the nature of prostitution itself.[19] The discussion on the freedom of expression challenge to the communication provisions, however, was much broader in nature and is therefore the focus of the following analysis.

Dickson CJ's opinion focused overwhelmingly on prostitution as a public nuisance. The communication provision was, in his view, "meant to address solicitation in public places and, to that end, seeks to eradicate the various forms of social nuisance arising from the public display of the sale of sex ... [T]he legislation is aimed at taking solicitation for the purposes of prostitution off the streets and out of public view." In his view, the nuisance associated with street prostitution was significant, and therefore "the eradication of the nuisance-related problems caused by street solicitation is a pressing and substantial concern."[20]

Lamer J's opinion framed the objective of the communication provisions more broadly. He agreed that one of the objectives of the law was to prevent the nuisance of street prostitution, which he framed as including "impediments to pedestrian and vehicular traffic, as well as the general confusion and congestion that is accompanied by an increase in related criminal activity such as possession and trafficking of drugs, violence and pimping."[21] However, Lamer J was of the view that this was not the only objective. The communication provisions were also intended to address the harm of street prostitution to women. Quoting with approval from the Ontario Advisory Council on the Status of Women that "[p]rostitution is a symptom of the victimization and subordination of women and of their economic disadvantage," Lamer J shifted the problem of prostitution from public nuisance to the surrounding community towards the harm of prostitution as degrading to women and a harm to prostitutes themselves. He highlighted the risks of street prostitution for adolescents in particular, who are lured into prostitution by pimps who initially befriend them but come to control them through relationships of dependency, drug addiction, and physical violence. However, Lamer J remained equally concerned about the exposure of prostitution to both adolescents and the public more generally. In his view, the communication provisions aimed to minimize both "the exposure to potential entrants into the trade" and the broader "public exposure of prostitution ... restricting the blight that is associated with public solicitation for the purposes of prostitution." While Lamer J expanded the idea of harm to include the dehumanizing, exploiting effects of prostitution on women, his interpretation still hinged on the harm of looking.[22]

In her dissenting opinion, Wilson J framed the objective of the communication provision somewhere in between Dickson J and Lamer J. For her, the objective was broader than the nuisance of obstructed streets and sidewalks but narrower than preventing young women from entering into prostitution. She stated that although she did not disagree that prostitution was degrading to women, it was not the objective of the provision. Rather, Wilson concluded that the objective of the communication provision was to prevent the "social nuisance" of street prostitution, which included its secondary effects: "the harassment of women, street congestion, noise, decreased property values, adverse effects on businesses, increased incidents of violence, and the impact of street soliciting on children who cannot avoid seeing what goes on."[23] For Wilson J, the harm of street prostitution was not the harm to prostitutes themselves but the harm of public exposure to the surrounding community. In her view, "The legislature clearly believes that public sensitivities are offended by the sight of prostitutes negotiating openly for the sale of their bodies and customers negotiating perhaps somewhat less openly for their purchase." It is the "social nuisance arising from the public display of the sale of sex ... the high visibility of these activities is offensive and has harmful effects on those compelled to witness it, especially children." For Wilson J, too, then, the harm was the harm of looking, of watching. Ultimately, Wilson J reached a different conclusion on the constitutionality of the impugned communication law. While the social nuisance was a pressing and substantive objective, the violation of expressive freedom was not, in her view, proportional, particularly given that prostitution itself was not criminalized.

Close inspection reveals an underlying concurrence across their differences of opinion. Prostitution – and hence the prostitute herself – is an excess that needs to be removed from public view. Lamer J's and Wilson J's opinions deploy imagery that animates disgust and danger. While Lamer J comes closest to the later discursive and governance shift to the prostitute as victim, he too remained concerned with the "blight" of prostitution itself. "Blight" – a thing that spoils or damages, decay, destruction – is a word frequently deployed in relation to prostitution. Its meaning conjures an image of street prostitution as that which damages, as decay in its own right, and the prostitute as that (not even who) which must be hidden from public view; she must be cast out. Across the three opinions, there was an unstated agreement that seeing prostitution is itself a harm, but the precise harm was never articulated. The justices refer to the blight and the offensiveness of public display. Blight, as spoilage and decay, just like offensiveness, is an unstated appeal to disgust. Prostitution's harm is one of disgust, a performance of abjection that has to be removed from public view.

Throughout the *Prostitution Reference*, sex workers themselves have no subjectivity. Prostitution is nowhere considered from the perspective of the prostitute herself. The overarching argument is not that prostitution is danger-ous to prostitutes; it is that prostitutes themselves are dangerous to the social order. They are, at best, the object of regulation, but they are to be regulated as abject, as that which must be expelled. While Lamer J's opinion gestured towards the later discourse of harm to women, he stopped short of recognizing the subjectivity of prostitutes themselves; the abjection at work here is one of sexual deviance that must be removed from view, lest it corrupt the social and moral order.

Bedford: Harm as Abjection

More than twenty years later, the prostitution-related offences were challenged once again in *R v Bedford*. Terry Jean Bedford, Valerie Scott, and Amy Lebovitch challenged the constitutionality of the bawdy-house provision (section 210), the living-on-the-avails provision (section 212(j)), and the communication-for-the-purposes-of-prostitution provision (section 213(c)), which prohibited communicating in public for the purposes of prostitution. In contrast to the *Prostitution Reference,* the Supreme Court held that each of the laws was unconstitutional. Each was found to violate section 7 of the Charter, particularly the right to security of the person. The court held that each law made prostitution more dangerous and thereby violated the security of the person of sex workers.

The court in *Bedford* first needed to distinguish the *Prostitution Reference*. In the court's view, the earlier decision was based on the liberty interest of section 7 and in relation to section 195, section 2(b), of the Charter. Those issues were, for the court, settled. However, the earlier decision did not consider the con-stitutionality of the provisions from the perspective of the security-of-the-person interest in section 7. The court could therefore revisit the constitutionality from a perspective that was not, in fact, settled law. However, the liberty–versus–security-of-the-person analysis may be the least significant difference between the two judgments. In *Bedford*, the court adopted an entirely different vision of prostitution, one that abjectifies but does so in an entirely different way. Prostitution is depicted exclusively in the discourse of danger and victimization.[24] The decision is a parade of the horrors that sex workers face, largely at the hands of clients.

In the court's view, the impugned provisions take a dangerous activity and make it more dangerous: "The prohibitions at issue do not merely impose conditions on how prostitutes operate. They go a critical step further by imposing *dangerous* conditions on prostitution; they prevent people engaged in a risky – but legal – activity from taking steps to protect themselves from the risks."[25] The court emphasized how each provision prohibited sex workers from taking precautions that could reduce their risk. The bawdy-house law prohibited in-calls and prevented prostitutes from "setting up indoor safeguards like receptionists, assistants, bodyguards and audio room monitoring, which would reduce risks."[26] The living-off-the-avails provision similarly prohibited prostitutes from reducing risk by preventing them from "[h]iring drivers, receptionists, and bodyguards," each of which could increase their safety. Similarly, the communication provision took a dangerous activity and made it worse. Communicating with potential clients "allows prostitutes to screen prospective clients for intoxication or propensity to violence, which can reduce the risks they face." However, the law prevented sex workers from being able to screen clients by prohibiting the very communication "that would allow street prostitutes to increase their safety," including screening and setting terms for the use of condoms or safe houses.

The federal and Ontario governments tried to argue that there was not a sufficient causal connection between the laws and the risks to sex workers, since "prostitutes choose to engage in an inherently risky activity." The court rejected the argument, and, in so doing, downplayed the agency and consent of sex workers:

[W]hile some prostitutes may fit the description of persons who freely choose (or at one time chose) to engage in the risky economic activity of prostitution, many prostitutes have no meaningful choice but to do so. Ms. Bedford herself stated that she initially prostituted herself "to make enough money to at least feed myself" ... As the application judge found, street prostitutes, with some exceptions, are a particularly marginalized population. Whether because of financial desperation, drug addictions, mental illness, or compulsion from pimps, they often have little choice but to sell their bodies for money.[27]

While the court did not reject the possibility of agency outright, it minimized it, holding that while prostitutes "may retain some minimal power of choice ... these are not people who can be said to be truly 'choosing' a risky line of business."[28] In rejecting the government argument, the court observed that "[t]he causal question is whether the impugned laws make this lawful activity more dangerous." In the court's view, the fact that violence may occur at the hands of "pimps and johns" was immaterial: "The impugned laws deprive people engaged in a risky, but legal, activity of the means to protect themselves against those risks. The violence of a john does not diminish the role of the state in making a prostitute more vulnerable to that violence."[29] The court both acknowledged and rejected sex workers' agency. Prostitution is mostly not a choice; entering sex work is a product of exploitative circumstances. Yet the laws preclude the ability of sex workers to take precautionary steps to limit risk. In this way, sex workers are afforded the possibility of some agency – the agency to minimize risk – although the laws limit their ability to do so. This agency is shaped by the discourse of harm and harm reduction. While there are, then, internal tensions on the question of choice and agency, the court's reasoning nevertheless provides the discursive foundation for an entirely victimized and abjectified vision of prostitution.

The court then held that each of the laws violated the principles of fundamental justice. The bawdy-house and communication laws were found to be grossly disproportionate and the living-off-the-avails provision to be overly broad. The court's narrative was consistent: the objectives of the legislation pale in comparison to the way in which the laws increase the risk faced by prostitutes, particularly the most vulnerable street workers. Once again, legal reasoning was embedded in the harm and violence of prostitution.

On the bawdy-house laws, the court held that the objective was not to deter "prostitution per se" but to direct focus towards "the harm to the community in which such activities were carried on in a notorious and habitual manner."[30] While the court agreed that Parliament has the power to regulate against nuisance, the harms of the law were grossly disproportionate to the objective of combatting "neighbourhood disruption or disorder and to safeguard public health and safety." Nuisance was contrasted to high rates of homicide among sex workers, especially those who work on the street: "Parliament has the power to regulate against nuisances, but not at the cost of the health, safety and lives of prostitutes. A law that prevents street prostitutes from resorting to a safe haven such as Grandma's House while a suspected serial killer prowls the streets, is a law that has lost sight of its purpose."[31] The spectre of death is a recurring theme. Sex workers are at higher risk not only of violence but of murder, and the law makes it worse.

On the living-off-the-avails provision, the court held that although the object-ive of "target[ting] pimps and the parasitic, exploitative conduct in which they engage" was legitimate, the provision was overbroad: "The law punishes everyone who lives on the avails of prostitution without distinguishing between those who exploit prostitutes (for example, controlling and abusive pimps) and those who could increase the safety and security of prostitutes (for example, legitimate drivers, managers, or bodyguards)."[32] Once again, the problem was that the law prohibits sex workers from reducing the risk of harm.

Finally, on the communication provision, the court noted that the objective was not to deter prostitution per se, but in accordance with the *Prostitution Reference*, "to take prostitution 'off the streets and out of public view' in order to prevent the nuisances that street prostitution can cause." Like its reasoning in relation to the bawdy-house provision, the court held that the harm to sex workers was grossly disproportionate to this objective. And like the bawdy-house laws, the court returned to the violence of sex work and the murder of sex workers. The lower court had found that "the ability to screen clients was an 'essential tool' to avoiding violent or drunken clients" and that the communication provision impeded the ability of sex workers to do so. The Court of Appeal disagreed, suggesting that the importance of this "essential tool" was based only on anecdotal evidence and that prostitutes might, in any case, proceed even in the face of a perceived risk. The Supreme Court endorsed the lower court, agreeing with the dangers that the communication law presents to sex workers. While noting that the screening process might be imperfect, communication was nevertheless essential to reducing risk: "If screening could have prevented one woman from jumping into Robert Pick-ton's car, the severity of the harmful effects is established."[33] The court con-cluded that the harm to the "safety and lives of street prostitutes" was therefore grossly disproportionate to the objective of regulating the nuisance of street prostitution.

Once again, it was the spectre of violence and death that informed the court's decision in *Bedford*. Unlike in the *Prostitution Reference*, the abjection of seeing sex work was no longer the problem. Rather, the abjection was now constituted in and through the discourse of extreme violence and death. Abjection was the exploitative conditions of street prostitution and the ever-present risk of violence and death. Prostitution no longer needed to be cast out from the public view; prostitutes needed to be protected from its inherent excesses.

There is no doubt that sex workers face heightened risks of violence, and these criminal laws *do* make sex work less safe. My point is not to contest the dangers that sex workers routinely confront. My point is rather to observe the extent to which victimization has virtually occupied the field of the legal narrative. In the Supreme Court's narrative, sex work is always and only dangerous, violent, and victimizing. While allowing some liminal space for the idea that sex workers may "choose" to practise sex work, that space is all but foreclosed by the spectre of danger, exploitation, and ever-present violence. The legal narrative sits on the other side of the double-edged sword of abjection, of the helpless victim who must be saved. This abjection is also one that invokes disgust and that ultimately supports removing the sex worker from sex work. It is an abjected vision that foreshadowed the legislation to come.

There was nothing in the Supreme Court decision that suggested a more positive vision of sex work. The decision specifically rejected the idea that it supported a "right to a vocation."[34] Moreover, the final section on remedy gestured directly towards the possibility of the recriminalization of sex by the federal government, noting that Parliament is not "precluded from imposing limits on where and how prostitution may be conducted." Rather, the court stated that the criminal provisions and the issues that they raised were intertwined and that latitude in one area (such as hiring security) might allow regulation in another (regulating the nuisance of a bawdy house). The court concluded: "The regulation of prostitution is a complex and delicate matter. It will be for Parliament, should it choose to do so, to devise a new approach, reflecting different elements of the existing regime." Inviting Parliament to devise a new approach needs to be viewed within its power: it was an invitation to regulate criminally. Other modes of regulation, such as health, occupational safety, licensing and/or zoning simply would not fall within the jurisdiction of the federal government.[35]

Affective Governance in the Wake of the Supreme Court

In the aftermath of *Bedford*, the Conservative government took up the Supreme Court's invitation to reregulate sex work, introducing new, more restrictive criminal laws. The 2014 *Protection of Communities and Exploited Persons Act* (PCEPA) prohibits the purchase of sex services, advertising the sale of sexual services, receiving a material benefit from the purchasing offence, and communicating for the purposes of sexual services in public places that are or are next to school grounds, playgrounds, or daycare centres. The prohibition on the purchase of sexual services is based on the Nordic model, which asymmetrically addresses the demand for sex work by criminalizing clients rather than sex workers. This provision represents the first time that prostitution itself has been criminalized in Canada. The advertising provision is similarly asymmetrical, targeting those who advertise the sale of another person's sexual services but exempting a person who advertises the sale of their own sexual services. It, too, is an entirely new provision.

The material-benefit provision in the PCEPA effectively replaces the living-off-the-avails provision that was struck down by the Supreme Court in *Bedford*. Those who sell their own sexual services are exempted, provided that they benefit only from the sale of their own services. The provision further seeks to exempt legitimate family or business relationships, stating that it does not include those who receive a benefit in the context of legitimate living arrangements, a legal or moral obligation of support, goods and services offered to the general public, and goods and services offered informally for fair value. The federal government's fact sheet on the PCEPA provides the following examples of persons or organizations who would not be included in the material-benefit provisions: (a) children, spouses, roommates, (b) a person supporting a disabled parent, (c) accountants, landlords, pharmacists, and security companies, and (d) babysitting or protective services.[36] The material-benefit provision further stipulates that these exemptions do not apply if a person uses or threatens violence, abuses a position of trust, provides intoxicating substances to encourage the sale of sexual services, engages in procuring, or receives the benefit in the context of a commercial enterprise that offers sexual services for sale.

The new communication provision similarly replaces the communication provision struck down by the Supreme Court in *Bedford*. The provision narrows the public spaces within which communication for the purposes of the sale of sexual services takes place to areas where children are likely to be present, namely, schools, playgrounds, and daycare centres. Unlike the previous communication provision, which was about preventing street nuisances associated with sex work, this communication provision appears to be tailored to removing street prostitution from areas where children are present and potentially exposed.

The preamble to the PCEPA outlines the objectives of the new sex work offences, which go well beyond addressing the social nuisance of sex work. The act states that prostitution is a form of sexual exploitation that disproportionately impacts women and girls. It is intended to address "the exploitation that is inherent in prostitution and the risks of violence posed to those who engage in it" and "the social harm caused by the objectification of the human body and the commodification of sexual activity" by reducing the demand for prostitution. It aims to protect individuals and "communities from the harms associated with prostitution."[37]

The revised objectives of the sex-work laws are significant. First, these revised objectives may impact the constitutionality of the laws. In *Bedford,* the Supreme Court struck down the laws largely because the harm to sex workers was disproportionate to the social-nuisance objective. The court repeatedly emphasized that prostitution itself was legal and that the objective of the laws was not to deter or prevent it. With the new laws, the objective is of a different order: it is specifically intended to deter prostitution and prevent the exploitation of women and children that is deemed to be inherent in prostitution. While it remains unclear how the courts will balance these objectives with the harms in future constitutional challenges, it is likely that the objective will be considered weightier than simply preventing nuisance.[38]

Beyond the potential constitutionality of the new laws, the objectives demonstrate the ways in which the PCEPA embraces the double-edged sword of the abjection of prostitution. Following *Bedford*, the PCEPA adopts the language of harm and danger, purporting to reduce the risks to those involved in sex work. In fact, it goes beyond *Bedford* when it identifies sex work as inherently dangerous. When introducing the PCEPA, the federal government pledged $20 million over five years to help sex workers leave the trade. Sex workers are constituted in the language of exploitation and harm; they must be protected from sex work itself. Sex-worker agency and subjectivity are trumped by the abjection of harm. Accordingly, sex workers, when thoroughly victimized, are immune from prosecution under the purchasing-sexual-services and advertising provisions. However, they are not immune from the revised communication provisions. The language of harm here extends to harm to the community. At the same time as the law seeks to reduce demand for sex work, it also aims to remove the sight of prostitution from public areas where children might see it. The vision of abjection from the *Prostitution Reference*, that is, of the visibility of the prostitute that threatens the social order, to be removed from view from the *Prostitution Reference*, remains present. There are particularly strong echoes from Wilson J of "the harmful effects on those compelled to witness it, especially children."[39] The legislation sits squarely on the double-edged sword of the abjection of sex work and sex workers. Sex workers are victims who must be cast out of sex work. But sex work is simultaneously a blight from which society – represented by children – must be protected.

The new law has been criticized by scholars and activists as every bit as dangerous to sex workers as the laws struck down by the Supreme Court. Critics note that the sex-work laws will most negatively impact the most marginalized of sex workers.[40] The laws have, in turn, been challenged, and Ontario trial courts have held that the laws are unconstitutional, on grounds very similar to the *Bedford* decision.[41] In *R v Anwar*, the Ontario Court of Justice struck down the advertising ban in section 286.4 as violating section 2(b) of the Charter, and it struck down both the procuring provision of section 286.3 and the material-benefits provision of section 286.2 as violating section 7 of the Charter. In *R v NS*, the Ontario Superior Court similarly struck down the material benefits, procuring, and advertising provisions as violating section 7 of the Charter.[42] In both cases, the courts relied on expert evidence and the record from *Bedford*, highlighting the heightened risk of physical violence and the ways in which the law prohibits sex workers from taking precautions that would limit the risks of violence. In both cases, the courts' narratives replicated *Bedford* by depicting sex work as dangerous and sex workers as potential victims of violence. Also like *Bedford*, and unlike the PCEPA, there was a slight gesture towards the agency of sex workers: the law prevented them from taking the necessary precautions to reduce risk. It creates a small space from which sex-worker agency might emerge, yet it is an agency that remains deeply rooted in the abjection of harm.

Abjection and its deployment of disgust, in the exploitation of and violence towards sex workers and/or at the sheer sight of sex workers, continues to be central to the regulation of sex work. Even as harm reduction emerges as a dominant narrative in judicial discourse, the affective governance of sex work continues to rely on the abjection of sex workers, the denial of their subjectivity, and the imperative of casting them out from the social order. Challenging the continued criminalization of sex work through the discourse of harm may be strategically attractive; the laws *do* make sex work more dangerous. However, such challenges are embedded in abjection, and while they create some space for sex-worker agency, they simultaneously reinforce the affective terms through which the recognition of the full human subjectivity of sex workers is refused. While the judicial narrative has shifted, forty years of sex work and the Constitution have done little to displace the stickiness of abjection and disgust that continues to attach to the bodies of sex workers.

Recent efforts by sex workers, particularly the Canadian Alliance for Sex Work Law Reform, seek to address the problem head-on, arguing that sex-worker–specific criminal laws perpetuate the stigmatization of sex workers. Their law-reform proposal offers a comprehensive analysis of federal and provincial laws and a concrete set of recommendations predicated on the dignity of sex workers.[43] It is more difficult to translate these recommendations into the judicial discourse of constitutionality, yet that is precisely the task ahead for the constitutional challenge that has been brought by the alliance. The challenge is how to discursively frame the legal argument in a manner that highlights the harm caused by the criminal law to the autonomy and dignity of sex workers while being attentive to the ways in which disgust and abjection underlie stigma. The judicial approach to the legal regulation of sex and sexuality should be predicated on harm, but it must be harm disentangled from the disgust and abjection that continue to infuse the affective governance of sex work.

Notes

1 Elaine Craig, *Troubling Sex: Toward a Theory of Sexual Integrity* (Vancouver: UBC Press, 2011). Craig argues that it is possible to see a shift in the Supreme Court away from a morality-based approach towards one based more on sexual integrity; Alan Young, "The State Is Still in the Bedrooms of the Nation: The Control and Regulation of Sexuality in Canadian Criminal Law," *Canadian Journal of Human Sexuality* 17, 4 (2008): 203–20, sees a shift in sex laws other than sex work. Others have traced the alleged shift from morality to harm but are also less sanguine and more critical. Richard Jochelson, along with James Gacek and Kristen Kramer, have critically engaged with the claim, arguing that the harm-based approach post-*Labaye* has not eliminated the reliance on judicial subjectivity. See Richard Jochelson, "After Labaye," *Alberta Law Review* 46 (2009): 741–67; Richard Jochelson and Kristen Kramer, "Governing through Precaution to Protect Equality," *Canadian Journal of Sociology* 36 (2011): 283–312; Richard Jochelson and James Gacek, "Reconstitutions of Harm," *Alberta Law Review* 56 (2019): 991–1038; Richard Jochelson, James Gacek, and Lauren Menzie, "Sex, Sexuality, and the Law: 'Society's Proper Functioning' and Precautionary Governance of Sex Work," in *Criminal Law and Precrime: Studies in Canadian Punishment and Surveillance in Anticipation of Criminal Guilt* (New York: Routledge, 2019), 42–69.

2 Otto Penz and Birgit Sauer, *Governing Affects: Neoliberalism, Neo-bureaucracies, and Service Work* (New York: Routledge, 2019).

3 See "Affective Governance and the Sex Trade," special issue, *Journal of Political Power* 12, 3 (2019).

4 Eilís Ward, Isabel Crowhurst, and Birgit Sauer, editorial in "Affective Governance and the Sex Trade," 313–17.

5 Birgit Sauer, "Mobilizing Shame and Disgust: Abolitionist Affective Frames in Austrian and German Anti-sex-work Movements," in "Affective Governance and the Sex Trade," 318–38.

6 Eilís Ward, "'Killing Off' the (Unbearable) Sex Worker: Prostitution Law Reform in Ireland," in "Affective Governance and the Sex Trade," 358–73.

7 Julia Kristeva, *Powers of Horror: An Essay on Abjection* (New York: Columbia University Press, 1982), 4.

8 Sara Ahmed, *The Cultural Politics of Emotion* (Edinburgh: Edinburgh University Press, 2004), 86.

9 Imogen Tyler, "Against Abjection," *Feminist Theory* 10, 1 (2009): 77.

10 Judith Butler, *Bodies That Matter: On the Discursive Limits of Sex* (New York: Routledge, 1993), 16.

11 Ward, "'Killing Off' the (Unbearable) Sex Worker," 359.

12 Judith R. Walkowitz, *Prostitution and Victorian Society: Women, Class, and the State* (Cambridge: Cambridge University Press, 2011). The idea of the prostitute as threatening to the social order is an old trope, long deployed in the regulation of prostitution. Walkowitz, for example, explores how the "common prostitute" was regulated through the *Contagious Diseases Act* as a form of pollution that "threatened morally and physically to contaminate respectable society" (17).

13 Ward, "'Killing Off' the (Unbearable) Sex Worker," 368.

14 Caitlin Janzen, Susan Strega, Leslie Brown, Jeannie Morgan, and Jeannine Carriere, "'Nothing Short of a Horror Show': Triggering Abjection of Street Workers in Western Canadian Newspapers," *Hypatia* 28, 1 (2013): 142–62.

15 *Ibid*, 143.

16 *Ibid*, 145.

17 *Ibid*.

18 *Reference re ss 193 and 195.1(1)(c) of the criminal code (Man),* [1990], 1 SCR 1123 [*Prostitution Reference*]; *Canada (Attorney General) v Bedford,* [2013] 3 SCR 1101 [*Bedford*].
19 Dickson CJ held in the *Prostitution Reference* that although the liberty interest was engaged since both s 193 and s 195 could result in imprisonment, this interest was not engaged in a way that violated the principles of fundamental justice. He focused on whether the provision was void for vagueness and held that the words and phrases "prostitution," "keeps a bawdy-house," "communicate," and "attempts to communicate" were not so imprecise that their meaning could not be ascertained in advance. Dickson CJ also addressed the question of whether the principles of fundamental justice prevented Parliament from sending out conflicting messages about prostitution, by controlling it indirectly rather than directly criminalizing prostitution itself. Dickson CJ held that they did not: "The fact that the sale of sex for money is not a criminal act under Canadian law does not mean that Parliament must refrain from using the criminal law to express society's disapprobation of street solicitation." Lamer J went further, considering and rejecting whether the provisions infringed prostitutes' right to liberty (in not allowing them to exercise their chosen profession) or their right to security of the person (in not permitting them to exercise their profession to provide the basic necessities of life). Lamer J held that s 7 did not concern economic rights and did not extend to the right to exercise a chosen profession. There was no discussion of whether prostitution could be considered a profession.
20 *Prostitution Reference,* 1135.
21 *Ibid,* 1195.
22 Lamer J's focus on the harm of looking connects this case law to the Supreme Court's decisions on obscenity and indecency, which focus not on the harm to the women involved but rather on the harm to those who watch. For example, in *R v Mara and East,* [1997] 2 SCR 630, a case in which the court imported the Butler harms-based test to the law of indecency, the Supreme Court held that the harm of lap dancing was not the physical or other potential harms to women. Rather, it was the "attitudinal harm on those watching the performance" (34). Similarly, in *Little Sisters Book and Art Emporium v Canada (Minister of Justice),* [2000], 2 SCR 1120, which returned to the constitutionality of the obscenity provisions, Sopinka J stated, "Parliament's concern was with behavioral changes in the voyeur that are potentially harmful in ways or to an extent that the community is not prepared to tolerate" (60).
23 *Prostitution Reference,* 1208.
24 It is worth noting that this was how the case was framed by counsel for the applicants, and it was how the evidence was led. The trial court, the Court of Appeal, and, in turn, the Supreme Court accepted this discursive framing.
25 *Bedford,* 60.
26 *Ibid,* 64.
27 *Ibid,* 86.
28 *Ibid.*
29 *Ibid,* 89.
30 *Ibid,* 130.
31 *Ibid,* 136.
32 *Ibid,* 10.
33 *Ibid,* 158.
34 This reasoning is consistent with the longer jurisprudential history of s 7, where the court has been reluctant to include the choice of professions within the s 7 liberty interest, lest it open vast areas of economic policy to s 7 scrutiny. There is, in other words, nothing sexually exceptional about this particular conclusion.

35 Kent Roach, in "Joe's Justice: Substantive, Procedural and Remedial Equality," *Supreme Court Law Review,* 2nd ser, 104 (2022), suggests the need for a different kind of dialogue, one where it would be possible to suggest that a different level of government would be the more appropriate regulator. He observes that Joe Arvay "stressed that the provinces should regulate assisted dying and not the federal government through the criminal law power. I think he would have taken the same position with respect to regulating and licensing sex work. In both cases, provincial or municipal replies might have been more consistent with the Court's original decisions than Parliament's amendments to the Criminal Code."

36 This statement by the Department of Justice is not uncontroversial. Hamish Stewart has argued that these individuals may be prosecutable for material benefits because they are receiving the benefit "in the context of a commercial enterprise": "The Constitutionality of the New Sex Work Law," *Alberta Law Review* 54, 1 (2016): 69.

37 *Protection of Communities and Exploited Persons Act,* SC 2014, c 25 [PCEPA].

38 For a discussion of the constitutionality of the PCEPA, including the significance of the new objectives, see Stewart, "The Constitutionality of the New Sex Work Law."

39 *Prostitution Reference,* 1211.

40 Chris Bruckert, "*Protection of Communities and Exploited Persons Act:* Misogynistic Law in the Making," *Canadian Journal of Law and Society* 30, 1 (2015): 1–3.

41 See *R v Anwar,* [2020] OJ No 820, 2020 ONCJ 10, and *R v NS* 2021 ONSC 1628.

42 *R v NS,* 2021 ONSC 1628.

43 Canadian Alliance for Sex Work Law Reform, *Safety, Dignity, Equality: Recommendations for Sex Work Law Reform in Canada,* March 2017, http://sexworklawreform.com/wp-content/uploads/2017/05/CASWLR-Final-Report-1.6MB.pdf.

11

Carter Compliance
Litigating for Access to Medical Assistance in Dying in Canada

Eleni Nicolaides

IN ITS LANDMARK *Carter v Canada* (2015) ruling, the Supreme Court of Canada (SCC) reversed its precedent from *Rodriguez v British Columbia* (1993) to invalidate the absolute ban on medical assistance in dying (MAiD).[1] *Carter* led Canada to legalize MAiD through Bill C-14, but a restrictive reasonable-foreseeability criterion created conflict over its meaning and *Carter* or Charter compliance. By rejecting the Supreme Court's interpretation in *Carter,* C-14 was a rare Canadian example of coordinate constitutional interpretation and arguably the most significant challenge to the Supreme Court's interpretive monopoly in forty years under the *Charter of Rights and Freedoms.*[2]

Reasonable foreseeability was declared unconstitutional at trial in *Truchon v Attorney General of Canada* (2019).[3] The Liberal government decided to repeal the criterion through Bill C-7 without appealing *Truchon.* It added a mental-illness exclusion that again created conflict over its meaning and Charter compliance, which was ultimately given a two-year sunset clause.

C-7 offers an opportunity to examine the factors supporting *Carter* compliance. This chapter argues that public, expert, legislative, and judicial support for *Carter* reinforced the need for compliance in C-7. To do so, it first briefly summarizes *Rodriguez, Carter,* and C-14. It then turns to judicial decisions following *Carter* and Bill C-7 debates. It concludes with a discussion of the weaknesses in the federal government's litigation strategy and how this case lacked various supports for legislative noncompliance (e.g., judicial disagreement/error/overreach or strong parliamentary/public support).

Rodriguez

In 1992, Sue Rodriguez – in her forties with amyotrophic lateral sclerosis (ALS) – made an unsuccessful plea to the Standing Committee on Justice and Human Rights to lift the prohibition on MAiD.[4] In Rodriguez's Charter challenge, a five-to-four majority of the SCC upheld the prohibition. Under section 7 (the right to life, liberty, and security of the person), the majority stressed the sanctity of life and that the ban was not arbitrary because there was insufficient evidence on safeguards since blanket bans were a norm.[5] The four remaining justices would have invalidated the prohibition, giving three separate dissenting opinions that found violations of sections 7 and 15 (equality rights).[6]

Carter

In 2015, the SCC released its unanimous *Carter* ruling. This case resulted from the efforts of two women who sought MAiD, Kay Carter and Gloria Taylor, their families, a physician, and the British Columbia Civil Liberties Association (BCCLA).[7] The SCC found violations of the section 7 rights to life (by forcing those seeking MAiD to end their lives earlier than wanted, while still able), liberty (by preventing them from making medical decisions deeply entwined with their dignity, autonomy, and bodily integrity), and security of the person (by forcing them to endure intolerable suffering).[8]

The SCC narrowed the legislative objective to protecting vulnerable individuals from being induced into ending their lives during momentary weakness.[9] Examining section 7's principles of fundamental justice, the SCC found that the provisions were overbroad because they blocked those who are not vulnerable but rather competent and informed from MAiD.[10] The SCC found that the law was not minimally impairing under section 1 (the reasonable limits clause): the blanket ban was unjustified because the vulnerable could be protected from "abuse and error" through "properly designed and administered safeguards."[11] Evidence suggested practitioners could ensure that MAiD requests were voluntarily made – free from "coercion, undue influence, and ambivalence" – using existing procedures for assessing capacity and informed consent.[12] The SCC accepted the trial judge's finding that any vulnerability would be assessed on an individual basis, as in making medical and end-of-life decisions like withdrawing or refusing life-sustaining or life-saving treatment or palliative sedation.[13] The Supreme Court invalidated the Criminal Code ban[14] and suspended the declaration for twelve months. The SCC indicated that the ban was invalid insofar as it denies access to a competent, clearly consenting adult with a "grievous and irremediable medical condition (including an illness, disease or disability) that causes enduring suffering that is intolerable to the individual in the circumstances of his or her condition."[15]

This precedent reversal relied on changing facts,[16] including the addition of overbreadth as a principle of fundamental justice (see Hennigar, Chapter 9 in this volume).[17] Most medical ethicists now find no ethical distinction between MAiD and other end-of-life practices likely to result in death.[18] Permissive jurisdictions demonstrated effective safeguards[19] and the lack of a slippery slope.[20] Belgium, Colombia, Luxembourg, the Netherlands, Montana, Oregon, and Washington now allowed assisted death,[21] with more jurisdictions following suit. Quebec also introduced Bill 52, *An Act Respecting End-of-Life Care* in 2013 to allow MAiD.[22]

Bill C-14

In response to *Carter*, the federal Parliament tabled Bill C-14, *An Act to amend the Criminal Code and to make related amendments to other Acts (medical assistance in dying)* in April 2016.[23] Procedural safeguards included a written request before two independent witnesses, approval by two independent practitioners, and a ten-day waiting period.[24] MAiD access for mature minors, those with mental illnesses as their sole underlying conditions, and those seeking advance requests were to be studied further. Eligibility was given to adults with grievous and irremediable medical conditions, the capacity for informed consent, and access to Canadian public health services, through voluntary requests. The eligibility criteria in section 241.2(2) of the Criminal Code defined someone with a "grievous and irremediable" medical condition as having a "serious and incurable illness, disease or disability"; in an "advanced state of irreversible decline in capability"; and whose "natural death has become reasonably foreseeable." The last was not a clinical, MAiD, or primarily criminal term but a civil term that raised confusion.[25]

Many questioned the constitutionality of "reasonable foreseeability," including members of Parliament's Special Joint Committee, opposition parties, senators, interest groups such as the British Columbia Civil Liberties Association and Dying With Dignity, and legal experts such as the Barreau du Québec, the Canadian Bar Association, Joseph Arvay (lead counsel in *Carter*), Jocelyn Downie, and Peter Hogg.[26] They argued that the provision was more restrictive than the Supreme Court's parameters in *Carter* and violated the Charter by re-creating a blanket ban for those whose deaths were not reasonably foreseeable.

Then–justice minister Jody Wilson-Raybould eventually argued that the question was not whether the bill was compliant with *Carter* but with the Charter and that the courts "do not hold a monopoly on the protection and promotion of rights and freedoms."[27] By rejecting the judicially defined limit from *Carter* – that individual assessments of capacity and consent must be used instead of blanket exclusions that capture those who are not vulnerable – C-14 was a rare assertion of coordinate constitutional interpretation. It contrasted with the dominant legal position in Canada, which favours judges having the "final say" in constitutional interpretation.[28] A majority of the Senate voted in favour of removing reasonable foreseeability but later agreed to pass C-14 with reasonable foreseeability after the House of Commons rejected the amendment.

Post-*Carter* Cases: Interpreting *Carter* Eligibility

Lower-court decisions have supported *Carter* compliance in several ways. In *Canada (Attorney General) v EF*, a fifty-eight-year-old with a severe conversion disorder applied to the Alberta Court of Queen's Bench for MAiD after the suspended declaration lapsed but before C-14 passed.[29] Canada appealed the application, arguing that it could infer that those who are not terminal or have psychiatric conditions were excluded because the remedy in *Carter* only covers the case's factual circumstances.[30] The Court of Appeal of Alberta rejected these arguments, concluding *Carter* did not require the individual to be terminal or "near the end of life,"[31] and that those with psychiatric conditions are eligible if they are competent to consent.[32] In *IJ v Canada (Attorney General)*, Justice Perell from the Ontario Superior Court of Justice reiterated *EF*'s finding: *Carter* did not require the medical condition to be terminal or life-threatening.[33]

Post-C-14 Cases: Interpreting and Challenging Reasonable Foreseeability

In *AB v Canada (Attorney General)*, Justice Perell had to interpret "reasonable foreseeability" after C-14 passed. After physician disagreement about meeting reasonable foreseeability,[34] A.B., nearly eighty with osteoarthritis, applied for a declaration that the MAiD provider would not be criminally charged.[35] Justice Perell found that A.B. met the reasonable-foreseeability requirement.[36] He interpreted it as a person-specific medical question that does not require imminent death or a certain prognosis of lifespan.[37]

The BCCLA and Julia Lamb later adjourned their Charter challenge to reasonable foreseeability following evidence from Canada's expert witness that supported and advanced this interpretation. The expert, Dr. Li, noted that while reasonable foreseeability may have barred access when Lamb – who has spinal muscular atrophy – launched the challenge, *AB* and changes to clinical practice[38] pointed to her meeting the requirement by expressing *intent* to stop or refuse treatment or food and liquids.[39]

In September 2019, Justice Baudouin of the Quebec Superior Court ruled in *Truchon*, in which two applicants challenged the reasonable-foreseeability requirement and Quebec's end-of-life requirement under sections 7 and 15(1).[40] Jean Truchon, then fifty-one, had cerebral palsy, spinal stenosis, and spinal cord necrosis.[41] Nicole Gladu, then seventy-three, had polio and scoliosis as a child, later developing degenerative muscular post-polio syndrome, osteoporosis, and restrictive lung disease.[42] Physicians assessed both applicants as meeting the eligibility criteria aside from the impugned provisions,[43] which was perhaps also due to restrictive interpretation of the reasonable-foreseeability requirement in Quebec.[44]

Considering section 7, Justice Baudouin pointed to alternative plans by Truchon to refuse food and liquids and by Gladu to go to Switzerland.[45] She concluded that the impugned provision would force some to end their lives prematurely, thus infringing the right to life.[46] She agreed that the applicants had been blocked from making this fundamental decision concerning their physical integrity and were compelled to endure suffering, engaging the rights to liberty and security.[47] She rejected arguments that cited Gloria Taylor's circumstances in *Carter* to suggest that the SCC had restricted eligibility to those whose deaths are reasonably foreseeable.[48] She confirmed that "reasonable foreseeability" diverged from *Carter's* parameters, which do not require a temporal link to natural death but are intended to protect dignity and autonomy and alleviate suffering.[49]

Canada named three legislative objectives: (1) affirming the equal value of the lives of the elderly, ill, or disabled; (2) recognizing that suicide is a public health issue with wide-ranging impacts; and (3) protecting vulnerable persons from being induced into ending their lives.[50] Justice Baudouin narrowed the objective to the third.[51] She found that the provision was overbroad and grossly disproportionate relative to the objective of preventing informed, competent, invulnerable individuals such as Truchon and Gladu from accessing MAiD.[52] She found that the provision was not minimally impairing under section 1, because the evidence suggests Canada's assessment process is vigorous and has not led to overuse of MAiD.[53] She determined that the deleterious effects on the applicants' rights far outweigh any purported benefits of the law given the effectiveness of other safeguards.[54]

Under section 15 equality rights, Justice Baudouin found that there was a distinction made based on the enumerated ground of physical disability.[55] Truchon needed assistance to end his life because of his physical disability, but reasonable foreseeability made it criminal for anyone to assist him.[56] She concluded that Truchon had been deprived of the ability to make choices key to his life and death.[57] She found that the impugned provision was neither minimally impairing nor proportional in its effects under section 1 since it ignored decision-making autonomy and practitioners' ability to identify vulnerability.[58] Justice Baudouin applied the same principles to Quebec's statute.[59] Declaring the provisions invalid, she suspended the declarations for six months and granted the applicants constitutional exemptions.[60]

Audrey's Amendment

Audrey Parker, then fifty-seven with stage-four breast cancer that had spread to her brain, also called for changes to final consent. She died with medical assistance but earlier than she wished because she was concerned that the cancer's progression would prevent her from giving final consent required under C-14.[61] Parker's story was widely covered by the media. In February 2019, Dying With Dignity Canada started a campaign for Audrey's Amendment, which would allow a waiver of final consent, as adopted in C-7.[62]

Bill C-7

The federal Parliament's response to *Truchon* was Bill C-7, *An Act to amend the Criminal Code (medical assistance in dying)*, which was reintroduced in October 2020 by a new justice minister, David Lametti.[63] Lametti had voted against Bill C-14 as a parliamentary secretary on the belief it was unconstitutionally restrictive.[64] Bill C-7 repealed the ban on MAiD for those whose deaths are not reasonably foreseeable,[65] excluded those with only a mental illness as ineligible,[66] set out two different tracks of safeguards,[67] and waived final consent in certain circumstances. The final-consent waiver applies to those with reasonably foreseeable deaths who have been approved for MAiD but subsequently lose capacity in cases of advance-consent arrangements or failed self-administration.[68]

The safeguards for those whose natural deaths are reasonably foreseeable were loosened: C-7 removed the need for a second independent witness and ten-day waiting period (the latter could be waived under C-14 in certain circumstances) and waived final consent. Practitioners and patient advocates had recommended these changes because they contributed to suffering rather than acting as safeguards.[69] The safeguards for those whose deaths are not reasonably foreseeable are stricter: assessment by a second practitioner with expertise in the condition, and a ninety-day waiting period.[70] These applicants must be offered relevant consultations with mental health, disability, community, or palliative services.[71]

Significant opposition to repealing reasonable foreseeability came from most Conservative MPs,[72] disability groups,[73] some academics,[74] some legal experts (most in disability law),[75] some physicians,[76] religious groups,[77] and some senators.[78] Opponents criticized the attorney general of Canada for choosing not to appeal the *Truchon* ruling all the way to the SCC. They argued that Canada was obligated to defend the law passed by Parliament mere years earlier and that the opinion of one trial judge should not determine its constitutionality. Critics argued that the government should not make changes beyond what was required by *Truchon*, like loosening the procedural safeguards surrounding witnesses, the waiting period, and final consent.

Some opponents argued that removing reasonable foreseeability would make C-7 prone to a section 15 challenge because it would deny equal protection of the law to people with disabilities.[79] They also suggested that without better access to things such as palliative care, disability supports, housing, or income supports, and given the impacts of ableism and racism, those affected could not make a free choice about MAiD. Some raised the *Fraser* decision, in which a majority of the SCC held that different treatment could be discriminatory even if it is based on personal choice, to make this argument.[80] Others stressed international human rights obligations, citing the UN Special Rapporteur on the Rights of Persons with Disabilities.[81]

These arguments differed from the positions of people with disabilities who emphasized medical decision-making autonomy, such as Nicole Gladu and Julia Lamb (who challenged the reasonable-foreseeability requirement) or Senator Chantal Petitclerc (C-7's Senate sponsor).[82] The enhanced track of safeguards was included to address vulnerability while allowing access to those previously denied.[83] The minister for disability inclusion, Carla Qualtrough, also noted that better understanding of who accesses MAiD is important to the disability community,[84] and after a valuable Senate amendment to collect race-based data, the House added that it would collect data on Indigenous identity, disability, or other characteristics creating inequality.[85] Overseeing standards of practice in collaboration with vulnerable groups is a positive possibility.[86]

Others supported C-7 generally but believed that the mental illness exclusion was unconstitutional. This included rights and MAiD groups,[87] physicians,[88] academics,[89] legal experts,[90] and most senators.[91] The proposed blanket exclusion posed issues of overbreadth under section 7 and discrimination under section 15. Contrary to *Carter*, it imposed another blanket exclusion. Parliament's Special Joint Committee had suggested that those with mental illnesses be allowed access before C-14.[92] Both *EF* and *Truchon* held that *Carter* suggests that those with psychiatric conditions can be eligible for MAiD if they are competent to consent.[93] C-14 had no explicit mental-illness exclusion, and some had received MAiD in this context.[94]

Senators raised precedents such as *Starson v Swayze*, holding that people with mental illnesses are presumed to have the capacity to make medical decisions,[95] or *Ontario (Attorney General) v G*, recognizing the diversity of people with disabilities and the need to not discriminate based on prejudicial perceptions about mental illnesses.[96] The Canadian Psychiatric Association (CPA) noted the "inaccurate, stigmatizing, arbitrary and discriminatory" nature of the hard line drawn between physical and mental illnesses in C-7.[97] Psychiatrists such as Senator Stan Kutcher explained how physical and mental illnesses have high degrees of comorbidity, prognostic and diagnostic challenges, the potential for vulnerability, and can be grievous and irremediable after treatment.[98] Some psychiatrists disagreed,[99] though in part using evidence rejected in *Truchon* on suicide contagion and psychiatric MAiD practices.[100] CPA members remain divided, but consultations showed softening opinions post-C-14.[101]

The Senate passed an amendment to place an eighteen-month sunset clause on the mental illness exclusion to allow an expert panel to develop guidelines and safeguards.[102] The House accepted the amendment but extended it to twenty-four months.[103] The House rejected another Senate amendment that would have clarified that those with neurocognitive disorders would still have access to MAiD.[104] This relates to the problem that "mental illness" is not a clinical term, so the exclusion remains unclear. A majority 180 to 49 MPs voted in favour of the amended C-7,[105] reduced from the 213 to 106 majority before the accepted Senate amendments.[106] A Senate majority accepted the House's response, and C-7 received royal assent on March 17, 2021.[107]

Discussion and Conclusion

Why would Canada retreat from C-14's coordinate interpretation through C-7?

Litigation Strategy

Canada's litigation strategy unsuccessfully attempted to justify reasonable foreseeability in several ways. One was expanded legislative objectives that sought to balance section 7 rights and the protection of vulnerable individuals;[108] like in *Carter,* the legislative objectives were narrowed in *Truchon.* Canada argued that *Carter's* remedy only covered the factual circumstances of Gloria Taylor, terminally ill with ALS. When Canada sought an extension on the suspended declaration of invalidity from the SCC, however, Karakatsanis J noted that the Supreme Court had rejected in *Carter* that an individual needs to be terminal.[109] *EF, IJ,* and *Truchon* held that the SCC did not require the individual to be terminal or near death. Canada argued that C-14 complied with *Carter,* but C-14's backgrounder essentially conceded it did not, and *Truchon* reaffirmed this. Lametti noted the long-standing concerns about C-14's *Carter* and Charter compliance in C-7 debates, concerns he had personally raised before he was justice minister.[110]

If not *Carter*-compliant, Canada argued C-14 was Charter-compliant because reasonable foreseeability sought to protect the vulnerable and that the courts should consequently defer to the legislative reply as dialogue as in *O'Connor-Mills.*[111] A few legal experts and Minister Wilson-Raybould argued this during C-14 debates.[112] There were, however, conceptual ambiguities surrounding labelling C-14 a dialogue.[113] Dialogue theorist Peter Hogg noted that section 1 could not be used to narrow the entitled class of people provided by the Supreme Court's parameters but could be used for procedural safeguards.[114] Justice Baudouin concluded that *Carter* required vulnerability to be addressed through individual assessments rather than blanket exclusions, and the impugned provision was not saved under section 1.[115]

Truchon suggested that to justify reasonable foreseeability under section 1, Canada would need to present evidence that the assessment process and safeguards were insufficient without reasonable foreseeability. The SCC had deemed foreign jurisdictions without such restrictions safe in *Carter.*[116] While opponents argued Canada should defend the law passed mere years earlier, that would require the SCC to revisit issues it had decided mere years earlier too. An appeal would require Canada to continue arguing that providing MAiD to those whose deaths are not reasonably foreseeable or with mental illnesses is unsafe (undermining potential future parliamentary efforts) and/or to highlight deficiencies in Canada's existing MAiD regime. These were not politically appealing strategies for a government that had introduced the law.

Canada attempted to demonstrate that the assessment process and safeguards would be insufficient without reasonable foreseeability. However, in *Truchon,* Justice Baudouin rejected that the evidence presented concerning vulnerability,[117] suicide contagion,[118] and MAiD for psychiatric conditions was sufficient to relitigate findings from *Carter.*[119] She also criticized that most of the attorney general's experts lacked knowledge about Canadian MAiD practice or data, which she concluded do not demonstrate problems within the Canadian MAiD regime.[120]

The applicants' experts in *Truchon* provided supportive evidence on the Canadian MAiD process and data,[121] differentiated MAiD from suicide,[122] and concluded, like *Carter,* that the foreign data did not indicate abuse.[123] In 2019, MAiD recipients made up only 2 percent of deaths in Canada. Sixty-seven percent of MAiD recipients had cancer; 80 percent were aged sixty-five or older; 82 percent had received palliative care, while 90 percent who did not receive palliative care had access to MAiD; and 90 percent of people who required disability supports received them, with another 6 percent unknown.[124] Future data collection should eliminate gaps and work to capture support adequacy. An Ontario study concluded that MAiD decedents did not demonstrate social or economic vulnerability on various measures compared to all decedents; they were younger, with higher incomes, less likely to live in long-term or continuing care, more likely to be married, and more likely to have cancer.[125] C-7 allowed MAiD for those whose deaths are not reasonably foreseeable but with enhanced procedural safeguards justifiable under section 1 to address potential vulnerability. Evidence from other jurisdictions suggests that group vulnerability – including vulnerability based on disability, race, and poverty – does not correlate to a higher likelihood of requesting MAiD, something C-7's enhanced data collection will allow Canada to further analyze.[126]

C-7's opponents lament that the Charter protects the right to die but not enough supports to live. Section 7 of the Charter has not expanded to protect positive social and economic rights (see Hennigar, Chapter 9 in this volume).[127] Policy makers should, nevertheless, enhance health, disability, housing, and income supports alongside MAiD.[128] Discrimination in the broader medical system related to disability, race, or Indigenous identity must be remedied.[129]

But while opponents criticized *Truchon* as a single ruling by a trial judge that expanded MAiD beyond those near the end of life, the SCC did not intend for

MAiD to be restricted to near death in *Carter*. Justice Karakatsanis and rulings in *EF* and *IJ* noted this before C-14's passage. *AB* and the adjourned *Lamb* cases also attest that, through statutory interpretation and clinical guidelines on reasonable foreseeability, MAiD practice was not restricted to near death before *Truchon* and C-7. Nor were people with mental illness as their sole underlying condition excluded. Reasonable foreseeability prevented harmonization and certainty in MAiD practice.[130] These decisions (and legislative debates) suggest that the attorney general's interpretation was rejected over five years, not just in *Truchon*.

Canada could reasonably think it would lose on appeal, which is among the factors informing appeal strategy.[131] The party, parliamentary, and voter considerations (more on this below) behind an appeal strategy would also likely weigh in favour of C-7 rather than an appeal.[132] The Liberal government could also use the courts' legitimacy as a political resource to further justify C-7 following *Truchon*.[133] Had Canada appealed, it faced the prospect of continuing to fight Canadians such as Nicole Gladu in court.[134]

Supporting Noncompliance

C-14 also lacked several supports underlying previous instances of legislative noncompliance with Charter rulings. There was no dissenting SCC opinion in *Carter* that Parliament could assert, as in cases such as *Daviault*.[135] The outcome of legislative noncompliance with *Daviault*, which allowed an extreme intoxication ("automatism") defence for offences such as sexual assault under sections 7 and 11(d), went unsettled for decades.[136] Expert evidence to Parliament revealed that alcohol could not induce automatism. Automatism was also used (and misused) more frequently than expected.[137] The legislative reply that blocked the defence (section 33.1 of the Criminal Code) was only recently appealed to the SCC.[138] A shaky evidentiary basis, its use in subsequent cases, adoption of the dissenting opinion, and public outcry could have given the SCC pause to reconsider the defence, but these factors were not present for C-14. Further, the SCC ultimately invalidated s 33.1 in *R v Brown* and *R v Sullivan*. Minister Lametti then introduced, and Parliament quickly passed, Bill C-28, *An Act to amend the Criminal Code (self-induced extreme intoxication)*. Bill C-28 imposes criminal liability in cases of negligent self-induced extreme intoxication, in which the person departs "markedly from the standard of care expected of a reasonable person," complying with the legislative option suggested by the *voir dire* judge and echoed by Kasirer J in *R v Brown*.[139]

C-14 was primarily compared to legislative noncompliance with *O'Connor*, concerning the difficulty of accessing medical and counselling records of complainants in sexual assault cases under section 7,[140] later accepted in *Mills*.[141] The

SCC argued in *Mills* that Parliament could amend the common law to better protect women and children from sexual violence because it still provided a constitutionally acceptable procedure, notably that of the Supreme Court's four-justice minority.[142] Unlike C-14, legislative responses to *Daviault* and *O'Connor* revised common law rules using dissenting judicial opinions to better protect the rights of complainants relative to the rights of the accused, providing a check on courts that have treated complainants prejudicially.

The Supreme Court's support for dialogue also began to wane after *O'Connor-Mills*. When the SCC reviewed the legislative reply to *Morales,* a case concerning the right not to be denied reasonable bail without just cause,[143] it had to deal with Parliament reasserting the constitutional text against the judicial expansion of the right, a tactic unavailable to Parliament after *Carter*. In response to *Morales,* Parliament included the text of section 11(e) in section 515(10) of the Criminal Code on bail, while providing a list of scenarios that would meet just cause. A majority of the SCC in *Hall* severed the "any just cause" and "generality" parts of the provision, while upholding the language surrounding "maintaining confidence in the administration of justice," even though it allowed Parliament to basically achieve the public-interest objective for denying bail that *Morales* blocked.[144] Baker describes that as a result of backlash in legal circles to the Supreme Court upholding the legislative reply to *O'Connor* in *Mills,* the majority's reasoning tried to hide the modification of *Morales* while the minority rejected Parliament's noncompliance.[145]

A majority of the SCC then more hostilely rejected the legislative reply to *Sauvé,* the case in which the SCC found the absolute ban on prisoner voting rights under the *Canada Elections Act* unconstitutional. Though the 1993 *Sauvé* decision had suggested that a narrower ban on prisoner voting rights could be justified under section 1 – something legal experts largely dispelled about *Carter* – it found the narrower blanket restriction Parliament replied with (those serving sentences of two or more years) unconstitutional again in *Sauvé #2*.[146] The majority in the latter case was critical that the attorney general's "vague and symbolic objectives" would be achieved by disenfranchisement, especially given the range of offences under the narrower blanket ban.[147] In *Carter* and *Truchon,* the courts first narrowed the imprecise "social values" objectives[148] then found the blanket bans overbroad by capturing a range of people who were not vulnerable. The majority in *Sauvé #2* foreclosed any meaningful reply by Parliament by holding that dialogue between courts and legislatures "should not be debased to a rule of 'if at first you don't succeed, try, try, again,'"[149] a message that could have more directly applied to C-14.

We can also consider the more recent reply to *Bedford,* the case where the SCC unanimously invalidated the Criminal Code offences for common bawdy houses, living off the avails, and public communication for prostitution under section 7 because prostitution was itself legal. The legislative reply, Bill C-36, criminalized purchasing but not selling sex. C-36 may be challenged to the SCC following *R v Anwar* and *R v NS*.[150] Unlike *Carter, Bedford* did not answer whether Parliament could criminalize purchasing sex, so we do not know if the SCC would uphold the Nordic model's constitutionality. Yet C-36's continued restrictions on advertising and material benefits risk recreating violations identified under the old Criminal Code provisions under sections 7 and 1.[151] The Liberal government has not repealed the Conservative government's C-36 following a successful challenge at trial in *R v Anwar,* though this is politically less appealing on issues like sex work that lack majority public support.[152]

Parliament's support for C-14 was also tepid. The Liberal Party, then holding a majority of seats, supported C-14, and outside supporters included fourteen Conservative MPs and the Canadian Medical Association.[153] The latter supported reasonable foreseeability's removal by C-7.[154] The Liberal government, which held a minority in Parliament by *Truchon,* decided to repeal reasonable foreseeability through C-7, a position supported by Parliament's Special Joint Committee, the three opposition parties (NDP, Bloc, Green), and a majority of the Senate in C-14 debates. In comparison, legislative noncompliance with rulings such as *Daviault* and *O'Connor* received all-party support, while the opposition parties opposed the legislative avoidance of *Bedford*.[155]

The public may also play a role in determining the legitimacy of legislative noncompliance with Charter decisions.[156] The public generally has more confidence in the courts and the SCC than Parliament.[157] Looking at specific cases of noncompliance or avoidance, there was public opposition to decisions in *Daviault*[158] and *Sullivan,*[159] while a majority of respondents opposed the legalized buying or selling of sex.[160] Yet public-opinion polling demonstrates high percentages of support for MAiD, including *Carter* (86 percent),[161] removing the reasonable foreseeability provision (68–73 percent),[162] and advance requests (75–85 percent).[163] Some polling indicates that support for MAiD is similar across regions, health care practitioners, people with chronic physical or mental conditions or disabilities, political-party choice, or religious identities.[164] *Carter* compliance is consistent with the rarity of legislatures willing to stray from the Supreme Court's rulings[165] but also reflects the likelihood of losing on appeal, the lack of a dissenting opinion or judicial error/overreach, and weak parliamentary or public support for maintaining C-14's coordinate interpretation.

Future Issues
Looking to the future, the unclear reasonable-foreseeability criterion still differentiates between the two MAiD tracks.[166] Issues of access for those with

mental illnesses (unclearly defined and pending results of panel and parliamentary review), mature minors, or through broader advance requests remain areas for policy contestation and potential litigation. The Special Joint Committee recommended access for competent mature minors after three years.[167] The House rejected a Senate amendment to C-7 that would have allowed broader advance requests,[168] even though they are widely supported by Canadians.

With C-7, there were incentives for *Carter* compliance in the Supreme Court's unanimous ruling, which were reinforced by public, expert, parliamentary, and lower-court support. Possible future decisions in the follow-up to *Anwar* or *NS* may offer opportunities to better understand the factors shaping the Supreme Court's treatment of legislative noncompliance or avoidance. Given the long journey to *Carter*, it is unsurprising that Canadians, equipped with Charter rights and supportive judicial decisions, would challenge denials of MAiD access through C-14's reasonable foreseeability or C-7's initial mental-illness exclusion.

Notes

The author would like to thank Kate Puddister and Matt Hennigar for their valuable feedback on earlier drafts.

1 *Carter v Canada (Attorney General)*, [2015] 1 SCR 331 [*Carter*]; *Rodriguez v British Columbia (Attorney General)*, [1993] 3 SCR 519 [*Rodriguez*].
2 Eleni Nicolaides and Matthew Hennigar, "*Carter* Conflicts: The Supreme Court of Canada's Impact on Medical Assistance in Dying Policy," in *Policy Change, Courts, and the Canadian Constitution*, ed. Emmett Macfarlane (Toronto: University of Toronto Press, 2018), 313–35.
3 *Truchon c Procureur général du Canada*, [2019] QCCS 3792 [*Truchon*].
4 "'Who Owns My Life?' Asks ALS Patient Sue Rodriguez," CBC Digital Archives, original broadcast, *Prime Time News*, November 24, 1992, http://www.cbc.ca/archives/entry/who-owns-my-life.
5 *Rodriguez*, paras 584–608.
6 *Ibid*, paras 549–631.
7 *Carter*, paras 23–25.
8 *Ibid*, paras 57–69.
9 *Ibid*, paras 74–78.
10 *Ibid*, para 86.
11 *Ibid*, para 105.
12 *Ibid*, para 106.
13 *Ibid*, paras 115–16; see *Carter v Canada (Attorney General)*, [2012] BCSC 866.
14 S 241: "Every one who ... (b) aids or abets a person to commit suicide, whether suicide ensues or not, is guilty of an indictable offence and liable to imprisonment for a term not exceeding fourteen years." S 14: "No person is entitled to have death inflicted on them, and such consent does not affect the criminal responsibility of any person who inflicted death on the person who gave consent."
15 *Carter*, para 147.
16 *Canada (Attorney General) v Bedford*, [2013] 3 SCR 1101 [*Bedford*].
17 *Carter*, para 46.

18 *Ibid*, para 23.
19 *Ibid*, para 25.
20 *Ibid*, para 107.
21 *Ibid*, para 8.
22 Quebec National Assembly, *Bill 52: An act respecting end-of-life care* (Quebec: Quebec Official Publisher, 2013).
23 Bill C-14, 1st Sess, 42nd Parl, 2016, https://laws-lois.justice.gc.ca/eng/annualstatutes/2016_3/fulltext.html.
24 *Ibid*, s 241.1.
25 Jocelyn Downie and Kate Scallion, "Foreseeably Unclear: The Meaning of the 'Reasonably Foreseeable' Criterion for Access to Medical Assistance in Dying in Canada," *Dalhousie Law Journal* 41, 1 (2018): 29–30.
26 See Nicolaides and Hennigar, "*Carter* Conflicts"; Parliament of Canada, *Medical Assistance in Dying: A Patient-Centred Approach – Report of the Special Joint Committee on Physician-Assisted Dying* (Ottawa: The Committee, 2016); House of Commons, "Vote No. 76," 42nd Parl, 1st Sess, No 62 (May 31, 2016), http://www.parl.gc.ca/HouseChamberBusiness/ChamberVoteDetail.aspx?Language=E&Mode=1&Parl=42&Ses=1&FltrParl=42&FltrSes=1&Vote=76; *Debates of the Senate*, 42nd Parl, 1st Sess, No 45 (June 8, 2016), http://www.parl.gc.ca/Content/Sen/Chamber/421/Debates/pdf/045db_2016-06-08-e.pdf; BCCLA, "This Bill Does Not Respect the *Carter* Decision and Must Be Amended," May 5, 2016, http://www.parl.gc.ca/Content/HOC/Committee/421/JUST/Brief/BR8279666/br-external/BritishColumbiaCivilLibertiesAssociation-e.pdf; Dying With Dignity Canada, "Brief on Bill C-14," May 2, 2016, http://www.parl.gc.ca/Content/HOC/Committee/421/JUST/Brief/BR8300568/br-external/DyingWithDignityCanada-e.pdf; House of Commons, Standing Committee on Justice and Human Rights (SCJHR), "Evidence," May 2, 2016, http://www.parl.gc.ca/HousePublications/Publication.aspx?Language=e&Mode=1&Parl=42&Ses=1&DocId=8225950; Canadian Bar Association, "Bill C-14," May 10, 2016, https://sencanada.ca/Content/Sen/Committee/421/LCJC/briefs/LCJC_May10_2016_CdnBarAssc_e.pdf; SCJHR, "Evidence," May 5, 2016, http://www.parl.gc.ca/HousePublications/Publication.aspx?Language=e&Mode=1&Parl=42&Ses=1&DocId=8243908; SCJHR, "Evidence," May 4, 2016, https://www.ourcommons.ca/DocumentViewer/en/42-1/JUST/meeting-13/evidence; Senate, Standing Committee on Legal and Constitutional Affairs (SCLCA), "Evidence," June 6, 2016, http://www.parl.gc.ca/Content/SEN/Committee/421/lcjc/52666-e.htm?Language=E&Parl=42&Ses=1&comm_id=11.
27 Government of Canada, "Legislative Background: Medical Assistance in Dying (Bill C-14) – Addendum," 2016, http://www.justice.gc.ca/eng/rp-pr/other-autre/addend/index.html.
28 Nicolaides and Hennigar, "*Carter* Conflicts"; Dennis Baker, *Not Quite Supreme: The Courts and Coordinate Constitutional Interpretation* (Montreal/Kingston: McGill-Queen's University Press, 2010).
29 *Canada (Attorney General) v EF*, [2016] ABCA 155, para 7.
30 *Ibid*, paras 27–30 and 59.
31 *Ibid*, paras 32–33.
32 *Ibid*, paras 47–59.
33 *IJ v Canada (Attorney General)*, [2016] ONSC 3380, paras 16–20.
34 *AB v Canada (Attorney General)*, [2017] ONSC 3759, paras 32–37.
35 *Ibid*, para 2.
36 *Ibid*, paras 65–70.
37 *Ibid*, para 79.

38 Canadian Association of MAiD Assessors and Providers (CAMAP), "The Clinical Interpretation of 'Reasonably Foreseeable,'" 2017, https://camapcanada.ca/wp-content/uploads/2019/01/cpg1-1.pdf.

39 *Lamb v Canada (Attorney General)*, [2018] BCCA 266, Vancouver Registry S165851; Arvay Finlay, LLP, Re: *Lamb and BCCLA v AGC*, SCBC Action No S-165851, Vancouver Registry, September 6, 2019; Jocelyn Downie, "A Watershed Month for Medical Assistance in Dying," *Policy Options*, September 20, 2019, https://policyoptions.irpp.org/magazines/september-2019/a-watershed-month-for-medical-assistance-in-dying/; Thomas McMorrow, Ellen Wiebe, Ruchi Liyanage, Sabrina Tremblay-Huet, and Michaela Kelly, "Interpreting Eligibility under the Medical Assistance in Dying Law: The Experiences of Physicians and Nurse Practitioners," *McGill Journal of Law and Health* 14, 1 (2020): 51–108.

40 *Truchon*, para 5.

41 *Ibid*, paras 35–46.

42 *Ibid*, paras 51–57.

43 *Ibid*, paras 63–70.

44 McMorrow et al., "Interpreting Eligibility."

45 *Truchon*, paras 518–20.

46 *Ibid*, paras 521–22.

47 *Ibid*, paras 533–34.

48 *Ibid*, para 480.

49 *Ibid*, paras 497–501.

50 *Ibid*, para 551.

51 *Ibid*, para 555.

52 *Ibid*, paras 573–85.

53 *Ibid*, paras 620–24.

54 *Ibid*, para 631.

55 *Ibid*, para 654.

56 *Ibid*, paras 659–60.

57 *Ibid*, para 681.

58 *Ibid*, paras 688–90.

59 *Ibid*, paras 705–33.

60 *Ibid*, paras 763–70.

61 Audrey J. Parker, "Dear Facebook Friends," November 1, 2018, https://www.facebook.com/msaudreyparker/posts/10155758516927517.

62 Dying With Dignity Canada, "Audrey Parker's Last Message to Canadians," February 6, 2019, https://www.youtube.com/watch?v=XwRRKq29tsw; Dying With Dignity Canada, "New Campaign Calls for Audrey's Amendment," February 6, 2019, https://www.dyingwithdignity.ca/audrey_amendment.

63 Bill C-7, *An Act to amend the Criminal Code (medical assistance in dying)*, 1st Sess, 43rd Parl, 2020, https://parl.ca/DocumentViewer/en/43-1/bill/C-7/first-reading.

64 Joan Bryden, "David Lametti's Appointment as Justice Minister Raises Hope for Less Restrictive Assisted-Dying Law," *Globe and Mail*, January 16, 2019, https://www.theglobeandmail.com/canada/article-david-lamettis-appointment-as-justice-minister-raises-hope-for-less/.

65 Bill C-7, ss 241.2(3).

66 *Ibid*, ss 241.2(2.1).

67 *Ibid*, ss 241.2(3–3.1).

68 *Ibid*, ss 241.2(3.2).

69 See Green (CAMAP), SCLCA, "Evidence," November 23, 2020, https://sencanada.ca/en/Content/Sen/Committee/432/LCJC/02EV-55071-E; Minister Hajdu, SCLCA, "Evidence," November 25, 2020, https://sencanada.ca/en/Content/Sen/Committee/432/LCJC/04EV-55074-E.

70 Bill C-7, ss 241.2(3).

71 *Ibid*, ss 241.2(3.1)(g).

72 Brian Platt, "Conservatives Protest New Assisted Dying Bill, Say Justice Minister Should Have Appealed Court Ruling," *National Post*, November 3, 2020, https://nationalpost.com/news/politics/conservatives-protest-new-assisted-dying-bill-argue-justice-minister-should-have-appealed-court-ruling.

73 For example, Council of Canadians with Disabilities, "Disability Rights-Organizations' Public Statement on the Urgent Need to Rethink Bill C-7, the Proposed Amendment to Canada's Medical Aid in Dying Legislation," 2020, http://www.ccdenligne.ca/en/humanrights/endoflife/Statement-Bill-C7. The statement includes eighty-three organizations and individuals. See also Inclusion Canada, "Campaign to Stop Bill C-7," 2020, https://inclusioncanada.ca/campaign-to-stop-bill-c-7/.

74 For example, Frazee, SCJHR, "Evidence," November 10, 2020, https://www.ourcommons.ca/DocumentViewer/en/43-2/JUST/meeting-6/evidence; Chochinov, SCJHR, "Evidence," November 12, 2020, https://www.ourcommons.ca/DocumentViewer/en/43-2/JUST/meeting-7/evidence; Lemmens, SCLCA, "Evidence," November 24, 2020, https://sencanada.ca/en/Content/Sen/Committee/432/LCJC/03EV-55073-E.

75 For example, Ross (Christian Legal Fellowship), SCLCA, November 25, 2020; Rouleau (Constitutional Lawyer), Jacobs, Beaulac, and Grant, SCLCA, November 27, 2020, https://sencanada.ca/en/Content/Sen/Committee/432/LCJC/06EV-55076-E.

76 MAiD to MAD, "Physicians Together with Vulnerable Canadians," https://maid2mad.ca/. For example, Coelho, SCJHR, "Evidence," November 3, 2020, https://www.ourcommons.ca/DocumentViewer/en/43-2/JUST/meeting-4/evidence; Herx, SCJHR, "Evidence," November 5, 2020, https://www.ourcommons.ca/DocumentViewer/en/43-2/JUST/meeting-5/evidence. See examples of contrasting testimony by MAiD practitioners on vulnerability and capacity assessment: Daws, SCJHR, November 3; Green (CAMAP), SCJHR, November 5; Campbell, Holland, SCLCA, February 2, 2021, https://sencanada.ca/en/Content/Sen/Committee/432/LCJC/11ev-55129-e.

77 Canadian Conference of Catholic Bishops, "We Can and Must Do *Much* Better: Religious Leaders in Canada Oppose Bill C-7," 2020, https://www.cccb.ca/wp-content/uploads/2020/10/MAID_Religious-Leaders-in-Canada-oppose-Bill-C-7_EN_FINAL.pdf, including signatures of over fifty religious leaders.

78 For example, Senators Ataullahjan, Batters, MacDonald, Martin, Miville-Dechene, and Plett, *Debates of the Senate*, 43rd Parl, 2nd Sess, No 20 (December 14, 2020), https://sencanada.ca/en/content/sen/chamber/432/debates/020db_2020-12-14-e#35.

79 Inclusion Canada, "An Amendment to Ensure the Rights of Persons with Disabilities: Bill C-7," brief submitted to SCLCA, Pre-study of Bill-C7, https://sencanada.ca/content/sen/committee/432/LCJC/Briefs/InclusionCanada_b.pdf.

80 For example, Grant, SCLCA, November 27; Senator Pate, *Debates of the Senate*, 43rd Parl, 2nd Sess, No 21 (December 15, 2020), https://sencanada.ca/en/content/sen/chamber/432/debates/021db_2020-12-15-e#28; *Fraser v Canada (Attorney General)*, [2020] SCC 28.

81 "As Bill C-7 Reaches Senate, UN Watchdog Raises Concerns about MAiD for Persons with Disabilities," CBC Radio, February 2, 2021, https://www.cbc.ca/radio/asithappens/as-it-happens-monday-edition-1.5896324/as-bill-c-7-reaches-senate-un-watchdog-raises-concerns-about-maid-for-persons-with-disabilities-1.5897749.

82 Joan Bryden, "MAID Litigant Says Disability Doesn't Make Her Vulnerable to Pressure to End Her Life," CTV News, December 16, 2020, https://www.ctvnews.ca/canada/maid-litigant-says-disability-doesn-t-make-her-vulnerable-to-pressure-to-end-her-life-1.5233205; Julia Lamb, "Written Statement of Julia Lamb," November 26, 2020, https://bccla.org/wp-content/uploads/2020/12/2020-11-25-Julia-Lamb-Written-Statement-Bill-C-7_final.pdf; *Debates of the Senate*, 43rd Parl, 2nd Sess, No 20 (December 14, 2020), https://sencanada.ca/en/content/sen/chamber/432/debates/020db_2020-12-14-e#35; also see Sylvain Le May, SCLCA, "Evidence," February 3, 2021, https://sencanada.ca/en/Content/Sen/Committee/432/LCJC/12ev-55130-e.

83 Lametti, SCLCA, "Evidence," February 1, 2021, https://sencanada.ca/en/Content/Sen/Committee/432/LCJC/10ev-55128-e.

84 SCLCA, "Evidence," November 26, 2020, https://sencanada.ca/en/Content/Sen/Committee/432/LCJC/05EV-55075-E.

85 Senator Jaffer, *Debates of the Senate*, 43rd Parl, 2nd Sess, No 27 (February 11, 2021), https://sencanada.ca/en/content/sen/chamber/432/debates/027db_2021-02-11-e?language=e#42; *House of Commons Debates*, 43rd Parl, 2nd Sess, No 064 (February 23, 2021), https://www.ourcommons.ca/DocumentViewer/en/43-2/house/sitting-64/hansard.

86 See Mégie, SCLCA, February 3.

87 For example, British Columbia Civil Liberties Association, "BCCLA Reacts: New MAID Legislation Is a Mixed Bag for Patients' Rights and Compassionate Care," March 4, 2020, https://bccla.org/news/2020/03/bccla-reacts-new-maid-legislation-a-mixed-bag-for-patients-rights-and-compassionate-care/; Dying With Dignity Canada, "Our Position on the New Assisted Dying Legislation," March 16, 2020, https://www.dyingwithdignity.ca/c7_position; L'Espérance (Quebec Association for the Right to Die with Dignity), SCJHR, November 3.

88 For example, Association des médicins psychiatres du Québec, "Access to Medical Assistance in Dying for People with Mental Disorders: Discussion Paper," November 2020, https://ampq.org/wp-content/uploads/2020/12/mpqdocreflexionammenfinal.pdf; Gupta, SCJHR, November 5; Naud, SCJHR, November 12; Dembo, SCLCA, November 24; Smith, SCLCA, February 2. The Canadian Medical Association was concerned that excluding mental illness from being considered an illness, disease, or disability was potentially stigmatizing and suggested further review: Collins, SCJHR, November 5.

89 For example, Downar (Professor, Palliative Care), Downie (Professor, Health Law), SCLCA, November 24; Jocelyn Downie, "An Indefensible Amendment to Medical Assistance in Dying Legislation: The Government's Plan to Exclude Mental Illness from MAiD Is a Mistake – Clinical Standards and Social Supports Would Better Help Address Its Concerns," *Policy Options*, July 23, 2020, https://policyoptions.irpp.org/magazines/july-2020/an-indefensible-amendment-to-medical-assistance-in-dying-legislation/; Halifax Group, "MAiD Legislation at a Crossroads: Persons with Mental Disorders as Their Sole Underlying Medical Condition," Institute for Research on Public Policy, January 30, 2020, https://irpp.org/research-studies/maid-legislation-at-a-crossroads-persons-with-mental-disorders-as-their-sole-underlying-medical-condition/; Kirby (Professor, Bioethics/Medicine), SCLCA, November 27.

90 For example, Leroux, SCLCA, November 25; Ménard (Barreau du Québec), SCJHR, November 5; Roberge (Canadian Bar Association), SCJHR, November 12; Adams, SCLCA, February 2; MacKay, Chalifoux, SCLCA, February 1. Leroux and Ménard argued *Truchon*.

91 The majority of the Senate (fifty-seven to twenty-one) supported the sunset clause on exclusion: Senate, "Vote Details," February 9, 2021, https://sencanada.ca/en/in-the-chamber/votes/details/554255.

92 Parliament of Canada, *Medical Assistance in Dying.*

93 For *Truchon,* see para 421.

94 Joan Bryden, "Psychiatrists Dispute Exclusion of Mental Illness in Assisted Dying Bill," *National Observer,* November 23, 2020, https://www.nationalobserver.com/2020/11/22/news/exclusion-mental-illness-assisted-dying-bill-psychiatrists.

95 *Starson v Swayze,* [2003] 1 SCR 722; see Senator Simons, *Debates of the Senate,* December 15.

96 *Ontario (Attorney General) v G,* [2020] SCC 38; see Senator Carignan, *Debates of the Senate,* December 14.

97 Canadian Psychiatric Association (CPA), "Brief to the Senate of Canada Standing Committee on Legal and Constitutional Affairs," November 23, 2020, https://www.cpa-apc.org/wp-content/uploads/Brief-LCJC-23-Nov-2020-FIN.pdf.

98 Dembo, Gupta, Kirby, the Halifax Group, cited at notes 88–89 above; Senator Kutcher, *Debates on the Senate,* December 15; Stewart, Chaimowitz, SCLCA, February 3.

99 For example, Gaind, Kim, SCLCA, November 27; Sinyor, SCLCA, February 3.

100 *Truchon,* paras 374–83, 400–7, and 415.

101 CPA, *Medical Assistance in Dying: Results of Member Consultation,* 2020, https://www.cpa-apc.org/wp-content/uploads/2020-CPA-MAiD-Consultation-Report-EN.pdf.

102 Senate, "Vote Details," February 9.

103 *House of Common Debates,* February 23.

104 *Ibid;* Dalphond, *Debates of the Senate,* 43rd Parl, 2nd Sess, No 25 (February 9, 2021), https://sencanada.ca/en/content/sen/chamber/432/debates/025db_2021-02-09-e?language=e.

105 House of Commons, "Vote No. 72," 43rd Parl, 2nd Sess, No 71 (March 11, 2021), https://www.ourcommons.ca/members/en/votes/43/2/72?view=party. There were 144 Liberal yeas, 3 Liberal nays; 118 Conservative nays; 32 Bloc Québécois yeas; 24 NDP nays; 3 Independent yeas, 2 Independent Nays; 1 Green yea, 2 Green nays.

106 Fifteen Conservatives previously voted yea, all twenty NDP votes were previously yea, and all three Green votes were previously yea: House of Commons, "Vote No. 39," 43rd Parl, 2nd Sess, No 47 (December 10, 2020), https://www.ourcommons.ca/members/en/votes/43/2/39?view=party.

107 Senate, "Vote Details," March 17, 2021, https://sencanada.ca/en/in-the-chamber/votes/details/555864.

108 *Truchon,* paras 551–59.

109 See Arvay, SCJHR, May 5, 2016, 845–50.

110 SCJHR, November 3.

111 *Truchon,* paras 502–10.

112 Pothier, SCJHR, May 4; McMorrow and Chipeur, SCLCA, June 6; Canadian Association for Community Living, "Medical Assistance in Dying: A *Private Request,* a *Public Act* – Proposed Amendments to Bill C-14," brief submitted to SCJHR, May 2016, https://www.ourcommons.ca/Content/Committee/421/JUST/Brief/BR8235098/br-external/CanadianAssociationforCommunityLiving-e.pdf; Government of Canada, "Legislative Background."

113 Nicolaides and Hennigar, "*Carter* Conflicts"; Emmett Macfarlane, "Dialogue, Remedies, and Positive Rights: *Carter v Canada* as a Microcosm for Past and Future Issues under the *Charter of Rights and Freedoms,*" *Ottawa Law Review* 49, 1 (2018): 107–29.

114 SCLCA, June 6.

115 *Truchon,* paras 502–624.

116 Without temporal restrictions in the Netherlands, 92 percent of MAiD deaths still occur in the last six months of life expectancy: *ibid,* para 370.

117 *Ibid,* paras 274–310.

118 *Ibid,* paras 330–31 and 374–82.

119 *Ibid,* paras 400–7, 415; paras 251–52, 379–80, 463.

120 *Ibid,* paras 375–77 and footnote 398.

121 *Ibid,* paras 154–99.

122 *Ibid,* paras 351–74.

123 *Ibid,* paras 448–58.

124 For example, Health Canada, *First Annual Report on Medical Assistance in Dying in Canada, 2019,* July 2020, https://www.canada.ca/en/health-canada/services/medical -assistance-dying-annual-report-2019.html. For four interim reports, see Government of Canada, "Medical Assistance in Dying," 2020, https://www.canada.ca/en/health-canada/ services/medical-assistance-dying.html. Also see Wales (Palliative Care Physician), SCLCA, February 3.

125 James Downar, Robert A. Fowler, Roxanne Halko, Larkin Davenport Huyer, Andrea D. Hill, and Jennifer L. Gibson, "Early Experience with Medical Assistance in Dying in Ontario, Canada: A Cohort Study," *Canadian Medical Association Journal,* February 24, 2020.

126 See, for example, Margaret P. Battin, Agnes van der Heide, Linda Ganzini, Gerrit van de Wal, and Bregje D. Onwuteaka-Philipsen, "Legal Physician-Assisted Dying in Oregon and the Netherlands: Evidence Concerning the Impact on Patients in 'Vulnerable' Groups," *Journal of Medical Ethics* 33, 10 (2007): 591–97; Luai Al Rabadi, Michael LeBlanc, Taylor Bucy, Lee M. Ellis, Dawn L. Hersman, Frank L. Meyskens, Lynne Taylor, and Charles D. Blanke, "Trends in Medical Aid in Dying in Oregon and Washington," *JAMA Network Open* 2, 8 (2019): https://doi.org/10.1001/jamanetworkopen.2019.8648.

127 For example, *Gosselin v Quebec (Attorney General),* [2002] 4 SCR 429; *Tanudjaja v Canada (Attorney General),* [2014] ONCA 852.

128 See Dosani, SCLCA, February 1.

129 See, for example, on Indigenous care, Wieman (Indigenous Physicians Association of Canada), Nowgesic (Canadian Indigenous Nurses Association), Lafontaine (Aboriginal Health Program), SCLCA, November 26.

130 Downie, "A Watershed."

131 Matthew A. Hennigar, "Players and the Process: *Charter* Litigation and the Federal Government," *Windsor Yearbook of Access to Justice* 21 (2002): 107–9; Matthew A. Hennigar, "Why Does the Federal Government Appeal to the Supreme Court of Canada in Charter of Rights Cases? A Strategic Explanation," *Law and Society Review* 41, 1 (2007): 241–46.

132 See Matthew A. Hennigar, "Conceptualizing Attorney General Conduct in Charter Litigation: From Independent to Central Agency," *Canadian Public Administration* 51, 2 (2009): 193–215.

133 On court decisions as political resources, see, for example, Peter H. Russell, "Canadian Constraints on Judicialization from Without," *International Political Science Review* 15, 2 (1994): 165–75.

134 Lametti, SCJHR, November 3.

135 *R v Daviault,* [1994] 3 SCR 63.

136 *Ibid.*

137 SCJHR, "Evidence," June 13, 1995, https://www.ourcommons.ca/Content/Archives/ Committee/351/jula/evidence/161_95-06-13/jula161_blk-e.html; Janet Hiebert, *Charter Conflicts: What Is Parliament's Role?* (Montreal/Kingston: McGill-Queen's University Press, 2002), 100–1.

138 *R v Sullivan,* [2020] ONCA 333; Dennis Baker and Rainer Knopff, "Daviault Dialogue: The Strange Journey of Canada's Intoxication Defence," *Review of Constitutional Studies* 19, 1 (2014): 35–58.

139   *R v Brown*, [2022] SCC 18, paras 11–14; *R v Sullivan*, [2022] SCC 19; Bill C-28, *An Act to amend the Criminal Code (self-induced extreme intoxication)*, 1st Sess, 44th Parl, 2022, https://www.parl.ca/DocumentViewer/en/44-1/bill/C-28/royal-assent.

140   *R v O'Connor*, [1995] 4 SCR 411; see Hiebert, *Charter Conflicts*, 92–109.

141   *R v Mills*, [1999] 3 SCR 668.

142   *Ibid*, paras 59–60; see Baker, *Not Quite Supreme*, 18–19.

143   *R v Morales*, 3 SCR 711; see Baker, *Not Quite Supreme*.

144   *R v Hall*, [2002] 3 SCR 309, paras 33–45.

145   Baker, *Not Quite Supreme*, 35.

146   *Sauvé v Canada (Attorney General)*, [1993] 2 SCR 438; *Sauvé v Canada (Chief Electoral Officer)*, [2002] 3 SCR 68 [*Sauvé #2*]; see Christopher P. Manfredi, "The Day the Dialogue Died: A Comment on *Sauve v Canada*," *Osgoode Hall Law Journal* 45, 1 (2007): 105–23.

147   *Sauvé #2*, paras 21–22.

148   *Truchon*, para 555.

149   *Sauvé #2*, para 17.

150   *Bedford*; *R v Anwar*, [2020] ONCJ 103; Amanda Taccone, "London, Ont. Couple Who Challenged Canada's Prostitution Laws Continuing Fight," CTV News, March 31, 2021, https://london.ctvnews.ca/london-ont-couple-who-challenged-canada-s-prostitution-laws-continuing-fight-1.5369979; *R v NS*, [2021] ONSC 1628.

151   Bill 36, *An Act to amend the Criminal Code in response to the Supreme Court of Canada decision in Attorney General of Canada v Bedford and to make consequential amendments to other Acts*, 2nd Sess, 41st Parl, 2014.

152   Alex Boutilier and Tonda MacCharles, "Secret Poll Shows Canadians Deeply Divided on Prostitution Approach," *Toronto Star*, July 16, 2014, https://www.thestar.com/news/canada/2014/07/16/secret_poll_shows_canadians_deeply_divided_on_prostitution_approach.html.

153   Nicolaides and Hennigar, "*Carter* Conflicts," 325.

154   Collins (CMA), SCJHR, November 5.

155   Hiebert, *Charter Conflicts*, 93, 104, 112; House of Commons, "Vote No. 249," 41st Parl, 2nd Sess, No 123 (October 6, 2014), https://www.ourcommons.ca/Members/en/votes/41/2/249?view=party.

156   Baker, *Not Quite Supreme*, 150–52.

157   Angus Reid, "Canadians Have a More Favourable View of Their Supreme Court Than Americans Have of Their Own," August 16, 2015, http://angusreid.org/supreme-court/.

158   See Baker and Knopff, "Daviault Dialogue," 40.

159   In response to ONCA ruling: Jill Andrew, "Thank You to Everyone Who Signed My Petition," Facebook, June 6, 2020, https://www.facebook.com/JillAndrewTO/posts/2618566368384479.

160   Boutilier and MacCharles, "Secret Poll."

161   Ipsos, "Large Majority (86%) of Canadians Support (50% Strongly/36% Somewhat) Supreme Court of Canada Decision about Medical Assistance in Dying," February 6, 2020, https://www.ipsos.com/sites/default/files/ct/news/documents/2020-02/attitudes_toward_maid-release-2020-02-06-v1.pdf.

162   *Ibid*; Department of Justice, "What We Heard Report," 2020, online questionnaire, Table 5, https://www.justice.gc.ca/eng/cj-jp/ad-am/wwh-cqnae/toc-tdm.html; Joan Bryden, "Poll Finds Strong Support for Expanding Access to Medical Assistance in Dying," CityNews, February 25, 2021, https://toronto.citynews.ca/2021/02/25/medical-assistance-in-dying-poll/.

163 Department of Justice, "What We Heard Report," online questionnaire, Tables 8–9; Ipsos, "Large Majority."

164 Bryden, "Poll Finds"; Ipsos, "Large Majority."

165 Emmett Macfarlane, "Dialogue or Compliance? Measuring Legislatures' Policy Responses to Court Rulings on Rights," *International Political Science Review* 34, 1 (2013): 39–56.

166 Jocelyn Downie, "Will Parliament Take Steps to Clarify Medical Assistance in Dying Law?," *Policy Options*, June 9, 2020, https://policyoptions.irpp.org/magazines/june-2020/ will-parliament-take-steps-to-clarify-medical-assistance-in-dying-law/.

167 Parliament of Canada, *Medical Assistance in Dying*, 21.

168 *House of Commons Debates*, February 23. The majority of the Senate had approved Senator Wallin's amendment: *Debates of the Senate*, 43rd Parl, 2nd Sess, No 26 (February 10, 2021), https://sencanada.ca/en/content/sen/chamber/432/debates/026db_2021-02-10-e.

12

The Charter and the RCMP

Kent Roach

MUCH HAS BEEN written about the effects of the Charter on the criminal justice system. Legal rights and remedies that Pierre Trudeau was prepared to water down or even abandon to gain provincial consent to patriation have become the main staple of Charter litigation over the last forty years. This chapter critically examines the impact of the Charter on the RCMP. It takes an institutional legal-process approach that compares judicial to legislative and executive regulation of the police. This expands dialogic understandings of judicial review from the usual focus on court decisions and legislative responses.

In my view, the independent courts have an important role in protecting the rights of minorities and the unpopular, including those suspected or accused of a crime.[1] Nevertheless, I also take a realistic approach to the Charter's actual impact on the operation of the criminal justice system. On the twenty-fifth anniversary of the Charter, I concluded that the Charter had played a minimal role in determining Canada's rates of imprisonment, pretrial detention, or over-representation of Indigenous people in its justice system.[2] In this chapter, I argue that the Charter has not fundamentally changed the RCMP even though the RCMP needs to change.

The RCMP started as a paramilitary institution used to colonialize Canada's west and north. In 1956, the Supreme Court refused to judicially review a disciplinary decision because the RCMP, like the army, was entitled to impose its own form of discipline on "men sharing a special life."[3] Former Supreme Court justice Michel Bastarache has recently commented that the twenty-six weeks of basic training RCMP recruits undergo at Depot Division in Regina has changed little in the last century. It is still "intended to break a cadet down and rebuild her in the RCMP mode" and create "an esprit de corps based on paramilitary training. Unfortunately, the esprit de corps does not seem to extend to women."[4] His observations are remarkably similar to those made before the enactment of the Charter by the McDonald Commission in justifying the transfer of the RCMP's intelligence mandate to a civilian agency.[5] After examining 2,304 successful sexual harassment claims by women against the RCMP, Justice Bastarache concluded that "change cannot come from within the RCMP."[6] Whether or not that was its intended purpose, the Charter has failed to reform the RCMP. I argue that more active legislative and executive regulation, including restructuring of the RCMP, is urgently required to address the RCMP's culture and its exercise of police powers.[7]

The Charter and the Division of Powers Compared

The RCMP provides contract policing in eight provinces and three territories. It thus serves as the local police in much of Canada. The RCMP spends just under $2 billion on contract policing, employing over 18,500 people.[8] The provinces and territories cannot examine the administration and management of the RCMP, even when it provides contract policing.[9] Provinces also cannot hear complaints and impose discipline against RCMP officers.[10] The provinces cannot even hear a human rights complaint by Indigenous hunters that they were subject to arbitrary arrest by the RCMP.[11] The provinces, however, have jurisdiction over the administration of justice under section 92(14) of the *Constitution Act, 1867,* for good reason. For example, Saskatchewan created a Public Complaints Commission for the police that, by law, has First Nations and Métis members in the wake of the Saskatoon police's use of "starlight tours" that resulted in at least one Indigenous man freezing to death. That commission, however, cannot hear complaints against the over one thousand RCMP officers in over 110 detachments who provide day-to-day contract policing in Saskatchewan. As the late Peter Hogg observed, the division-of-powers jurisprudence amounts to "a substantial limitation of provincial power over the RCMP."[12]

The division of powers is less democratic than the Charter, which allows legislative limitations and overrides.[13] The main way around judicial decisions limiting provincial regulation of the RCMP is for the Supreme Court to change its mind or for provinces, municipalities, or First Nations to opt-out of contract policing by the RCMP. Surrey, British Columbia, is creating its own police service to replace the RCMP, and several First Nations on the Prairies are considering doing the same. If more communities exit contract policing to gain more local control over policing, it will have more to do with the division of powers than the Charter.

From Writs to Assistance to General Warrants

Before the Charter, Canadian courts embraced a crime-control system that was reluctant to exclude drugs and guns even if the police acted improperly in obtaining them.[14] RCMP officers had writs of assistance or roving search warrants under drugs and customs laws that had been specifically prohibited in the Fourth Amendment of the US Constitution. Influenced by American jurisprudence, the Supreme Court embraced warrant requirements under the Charter.[15] The federal government repealed writs of assistance in 1985. In 1987 cases, the federal government did not defend their constitutionality under the Charter. At the same time, the Supreme Court was willing to admit as evidence marijuana seized in reliance on the writs under the section 24(2) exclusionary rule that had been designed to avoid the more absolute American exclusionary rule.[16]

The impact of the warrant requirement on the RCMP or other police in Canada should not be overestimated. The court has made exceptions at borders. It also allows warrantless-consent and exigent-circumstances searches. Most warrants are granted by lower judicial officials who rarely deny warrants. The available evidence suggests they make a significant number of mistakes.[17] At the same time, courts will generally admit evidence obtained in good faith with a warrant.

When the Supreme Court ruled that warrantless seizures of blood, DNA, or bodily impressions or entries into homes to make arrests violated section 8 of the Charter,[18] Parliament quickly responded with new warrant schemes. For example, after the court ruled in 1990 that warrantless video surveillance of a hotel room where gambling was taking place violated section 8, Parliament responded with a broad general warrant provision authorizing all invasions of reasonable expectation of privacy that did not invade bodily integrity. As in the writ-of-assistance cases, the court nevertheless accepted the videotapes as evidence despite noting that police had asked Toronto hotels to alert them about "anything unusual as to Orientals attending hotels."[19]

Justice Bertha Wilson was the only judge who would have excluded the unconstitutionally obtained videotapes. She suggested that the Toronto police could not justify the warrantless videotaping by relying on its "discriminatory hiring practice" that prevented it from using Asian undercover officers. As will be seen, the court has only recently become more concerned about the dangers of systemic discrimination in policing. The courts, as opposed to the bodies that govern the police, however, would never question whether the police should devote resources to investigating gambling.

In its exclusionary decisions, the court has considered all drug crimes to be serious. It was Parliament and not the court under the Charter that decriminalized marijuana.[20] The Charter has not led to wholesale decriminalization of sex work even though, in *Bedford*, the court has accepted that police enforcement of laws against solicitation and brothels causes harm to sex workers and exposes them to predators.[21] Today, cities such as Vancouver are calling for decriminalization of the possession of all drugs as a means to take a public-health approach to the opioid epidemic. Increased judicial regulation of policing under the Charter is no substitute for legislative determinations about whether policing causes more harm than good.

The Limits of Judicial Regulation of Street Checks and Racial Profiling

In *R v Mann* (2004), the court used the Charter to extend police powers to authorize the stop of an Indigenous man in Winnipeg on reasonable suspicion but without reasonable and probable grounds to make an arrest under the

Criminal Code. The court reasoned that the stop was justified because it was not an arbitrary detention contrary to section 9 of the Charter. It also indicated that an initial frisk search by the police was justified because it was reasonable and required for officer safety.[22] Such judicial expansions of police powers have been heavily criticized. Parliament, not the courts, should expand police powers. Judicially created stop and frisk powers have disproportionate effects on Indigenous, racialized, and otherwise disadvantaged individuals.[23] In these cases, the due process provisions of the Charter have been used by the courts to expand and legitimate increased crime control activities by the police.[24]

Equality rights have not curbed overpolicing of racialized groups that are overrepresented in the criminal justice system but underrepresented among those in power in that system. A Black judge who dared to take notice that police have been known to overreact when dealing with Black youth while acquitting a Black fifteen-year-old who faced three charges for assaulting police officers had her comments challenged as biased all the way to the Supreme Court.[25] Although the majority in this 1997 case sustained the trial judge's acquittal, three of the five judges in the majority warned that the trial judge's remarks were "unfortunate," "troubling," and "very close to the line," while three judges in dissent held the trial judge's comments were over the line.[26]

A leading 2009 case ignored whether there had been racial profiling when three police officers approached a young Black man in Toronto. The court concluded that it need not consider whether the man had been racially profiled because he had not argued racial profiling in court. The failure of the accused to make such an argument may have been the result of the hostility of the courts at that time to allegations of racial profiling. In that case, the court found that the police had violated the accused's Charter rights but restructured its section 24(2) jurisprudence and admitted the drugs and gun the police discovered.[27] The courts will only review proactive stops when police hunches (perhaps based on racist stereotypes) that a person may have a gun or drugs turn out to be correct.

In *R v Le* (2019), the Supreme Court accepted that courts should consider the effect of race in determining whether the police engaged in an arbitrary detention contrary to the Charter, but also found no racial profiling.[28] At the same time, it split three to two over whether guns and drugs should be excluded after the police had entered a backyard in community housing without consent or a warrant and started questioning the Asian accused and four Black young men. The courts under the Charter generally send out ambiguous, complex, and conflicting signals to the police.[29]

In contrast to courts, legislatures can send out clearer messages to the police about what they can and cannot do. They can impose requirements that the police collect race-based data.[30] They can impose time limits and recording requirements on interrogations. Independent police-complaint bodies can examine cases where the police may have abused their power but did not discover incriminating evidence. The Civilian Review and Complaints Commission for the RCMP started a strategic investigation into RCMP street checks in April 2018 that was completed in June 2021.

The commission found that the RCMP had too restrictively defined street checks to encounters that resulted in an electronic record of information being made. It also found that RCMP policies failed to provide for informed consent by telling people they would not be arrested or detained if they refused to answer a Mountie's questions. The legal requirements of waiver of Charter rights are easier for a court to pronounce than for the executive to implement.

The commission also concluded that it was unable to determine "the incidence of racialized versus non-racialized street checks" and that the RCMP should consider better ways to record data about the race of those subject to street checks.[31] These recommendations by the small executive watchdog commission that has coast-to-coast-to-coast responsibilities and fifty-two full-time staff to hear complaints about twenty thousand Mounties have a greater potential to change policing policies than individual Charter decisions. Executive watchdog review remains important even in the age of the Charter in part because it can examine cases and complaints in cases that do not result in prosecutions. At the same time, the RCMP has discretion in whether and how to implement the commission's recommendations. The RCMP commissioner's response to the report demonstrated some resistance to requiring provincial divisions of the RCMP to implement different provincial restrictions on street checks.[32] The RCMP remains a federal institution even when it offers contract policing in the provinces and territories.

The Limits of Judicial Regulation of Strip Searches

In *R v Golden* (2001), the Supreme Court ruled five to four that the right against unreasonable search and seizure would be violated if police conducted a strip search without reasonable and probable grounds that they would discover evidence or a weapon.[33] A July 2020 report by the Civilian Review and Complaints Commission for the RCMP found that nineteen years after the *Golden* decision, the RCMP did not have adequate policies, training, documentation, or supervision of strip searches. Prisoners were still routinely strip-searched. The Iqaluit Detachment was singled out for documenting searches in only 3 percent of its files. Even so, in 158 of 162 documented cases, the detainees had been strip searched and even videotaped in the process. The officer in charge did not know the court's definition of a strip search.[34] Decisions such as *Golden* are not self-executing. They can leave people with an exaggerated sense of the restraints actually placed on the police.

The RCMP is not alone in not taking the many necessary steps to comply with *Golden*. In 2018, an Ontario police executive watchdog found widespread noncompliance, including over eighty reported decisions finding strip searches in violation of *Golden*. These cases, of course, do not account for unreasonable strip searches that did not find evidence or result in prosecutions. A civil liberties lawyer who was strip-searched after being arrested in connection with a protest and who was not prosecuted sued the police. The Supreme Court affirmed a five-thousand-dollar award of Charter damages, an amount that would not cover litigation expenses.[35] The experience of the police "breaking the Golden rule" is an important reminder that the judicial supervision of police conduct is episodic and often ineffective.[36]

The majority in *Golden* tried to encourage Parliament to regulate strip searches with a detailed code of conduct as is done in the United Kingdom. Parliament did not do this. It left the courts as de facto regulators of search practices. Police, in turn, have complained of receiving inadequate training and updates about Charter decisions. The police generally do not even receive systemic feedback about Charter issues arising from their own cases.[37]

The Limits of Judicial Regulation of Mr. Big Stings

In the 1990s, the RCMP developed a means to circumvent having to tell suspects that they had a right to a lawyer by devising elaborate and expensive "Mr. Big" stings to encourage suspects to confess crimes to an undercover officer posing as a criminal. Suspects were required to confess to continuing to enjoy the lucrative benefits that the RCMP supplied them as part of a fake criminal gang. Because the suspect did not know that the gang or its leader, Mr. Big, were in fact Mounties, neither the right to counsel nor the common law requirement that confessions be voluntary applied. In 2008, the RCMP's website proudly indicated it had used this technique in 350 cases. Today, there is no such information on the RCMP website.[38]

The RCMP pursued Mr. Big stings with a single-mindedness similar to the "tunnel vision" associated with wrongful convictions. As Kate Puddister and Troy Riddell have found, Parliament, the responsible federal minister of public safety, and police-complaints bodies took little interest in regulating such stings. This left the courts as de facto regulators. Between 1987 and 2012, the courts only excluded evidence in 13 of 153 reported Mr. Big cases.[39] Even when courts find the police have violated rights, they may be reluctant to exclude evidence that may be critical to the prosecution of a serious crime.[40]

In 2014, the Supreme Court of Canada responded to growing criticism of Mr. Big stings and created a presumption that confessions obtained from them were inadmissible.[41] The presumption was, however, rebuttable. The court has been split in subsequent cases, with majorities sometimes finding enough corroboration[42] and in other cases not sufficient corroboration to admit a suspect's confession made to a Mr. Big.[43] One problem, however, is that not all interactions between the accused and undercover officers are recorded. It is thus possible that the officers may deliberately or inadvertently give suspects information that may give false confessions a ring of truth.[44] Mr. Big stings appear from the extensive jurisprudence to have continued unabated even though they may still encourage unethical police conduct and false confessions. Parliament has not attempted to regulate Mr. Big stings, and the federal minister of public safety has not issued a public ministerial directive abolishing, regulating, or rationing them or even reporting how many are conducted.

The courts have responded to RCMP misconduct in some stings. The Supreme Court stayed counselling murder charges against a battered woman who had tried to hire an undercover Mountie to kill her husband. The court stressed that "on the record before us," the RCMP was "much quicker to intervene to protect Mr. Ryan than they had been to respond to her request for help in dealing with his reign of terror over her."[45] The RCMP complaints and review commission subsequently found that the RCMP had not violated any policies and acted properly.[46] In another case, the BC courts stayed proceedings on terrorism charges after the RCMP had used two hundred officers and $1 million to pressure a couple with addictions and mental health issues to agree to plant a fake bomb.[47]

The UK approach provides a counterpoint to Canada's reliance on judicial regulation. Undercover policing in the United Kingdom has been regulated by legislation since 2000.[48] It is subject to dedicated review by an executive watchdog, the Investigatory Powers Commission Office. Both the Home Office and the Inspectorate of the Constabulary have provided training and certification requirements. They stress the need for necessity and proportionality in stings and the need for care when dealing with vulnerable targets. To be sure, undercover policing in the United Kingdom has not been without controversy. Nevertheless, the UK experience demonstrates that indirect and ex-post judicial regulation in determining the admissibility of the fruits of undercover operations is not the only or likely the best form of regulation of police conduct.

The Limits of Judicial Regulation of Interrogations

In the Charter's early years, the Supreme Court enthusiastically required the police to inform those detained or arrested that they had a right to consult a lawyer. It interpreted the detention trigger for right-to-counsel warnings more broadly than the American courts had under *Miranda v Arizona*.[49] The Canadian court told police that they must hold off eliciting evidence from those arrested or detained until they had a reasonable opportunity to contact a lawyer. In 1990, the court gave police thirty days to amend their standard cautions so that detainees were told about legal aid if they could not afford a lawyer and the 1-800 duty counsel system, where all could seek free legal advice.[50] The court backed these new rules up with almost automatic exclusion of statements taken from the accused in violation of the Charter.

At the same time, the Supreme Court has never imposed requirements that interrogations must be videotaped even though such an approach is cost-effective, can screen out unwarranted allegations against the police, and can help detect false confessions where the police reveal "hold back" information only known to the real perpetrator. Parliament has failed to place time limits on interrogations or to provide protections for those who, because of mental disability or addictions, may be at risk of providing false confessions.

After its early activism, the Supreme Court has in the twenty-first century allowed prolonged interrogations that ignore repeated demands from detainees that they do not want to talk to the police. So long as the detainee has had a reasonable opportunity to contact counsel, most prolonged interrogations will be "Charter-proof."[51] In 2010, the Supreme Court ruled contrary to the US courts that lawyers did not have a right to be present during interrogations and that the police could continue to question a detainee and use deception even in the face of repeated statements that the detainee did not wish to talk.[52] The Charter has not prevented skilled police detectives from conducting successful and sophisticated interrogations that can use deceit and empathy and take many hours to obtain a confession. In contrast, police officers who are subject to criminal investigations after they have caused death or serious injury almost always effectively exercise their right to silence.

The Limits of Judicial and Legislative Regulation of Dynamic "No-Knock" Entries

Judicial regulation of the police is subject to trends in the Supreme Court. Although not as dramatic as changes in the US Supreme Court, the Canadian Supreme Court has become, over time, less willing to impose more restraints on the police. In 2005, the court allowed the police to ask detainees on the roadside about drinking and to ask them to perform sobriety tests even though Parliament had not authorized these forms of investigation.[53] Regardless of the judicial limits of regulation of the police, the intensity of the judicial regulation can depend on even subtle changes in the court's composition, past experience, and inclinations.

In 2010, a majority of the court upheld a no-knock dynamic entry by masked officers with a battering ram and drawn guns, stressing that the court should not engage in "Monday morning quarterbacking." Three judges dissented on the basis that the occupants of the house had neither criminal records nor a history of violence.[54] Even though Parliament has regulated house entries through warrants in response to another Charter decision, it still allows police to enter houses without a warrant or without an announcement if the goal is to stop the imminent destruction of evidence.[55] Parliament may be reluctant to be seen as "antipolice," especially on issues that may involve officer safety. In the absence of parliamentary action and national regulations, local police boards and police services themselves must play a regulatory role.

In 2021, then Ottawa police chief Peter Sloly prohibited the use of dynamic entries for his police if the only justification was the preservation of evidence. Arguably, this policy should have originated with the police service board of elected municipal council members and provincial appointees who govern the Ottawa police. The board, however, did not take the lead. It also subsequently seemed to take a hands-off approach during the "Freedom Convoy" occupation of Ottawa in February 2022.

Chief Sloly's policy was a positive step that resulted in a police service imposing more robust limits on itself than the courts were prepared to impose. Regulating police conduct is, however, a risky business, especially for those who, unlike judges, do not have guaranteed tenure. Chief Sloly received criticism from the police union for risking officer safety. He also received criticism from activists for continuing to allow no-knock entries. The criticism from both sides demonstrates how polarized opinion can make police reform very difficult.[56] Unfortunately, the result is often that the police are left to regulate themselves. Even then, progressive police leaders such as Chief Sloly (who resigned during the Ottawa occupation) are often not supported, especially by police unions. In addition, police boards and responsible ministers often defer to the police. This results in a governance gap that the courts alone cannot fill.[57] Canada has followed the American practice of relying on courts to regulate police conduct. As has become only too evident after the police murder of George Floyd, judicial regulation has not substantially improved American police practices.[58]

The Limits of Judicial Regulation of Police Use of Force

A CBC database recorded 152 cases in which the RCMP was involved in fatal encounters from 2000 to mid-2020, including 38 Indigenous deceased.[59] In 51 of the fatal encounters, the deceased had a firearm or a replica firearm; in 25 cases, the deceased had a knife or other sharp-edged instrument. In many other cases, there was no weapon at all. Some deaths in custody were related to drug toxicity, with police use of tasers and pepper spray also being contributing factors. The RCMP reported that 99.9 percent of all its interactions with the public do not involve the use of force, but even this resulted in Mounties drawing their guns 3,315 times in 2020 and shooting 19 people, 14 of them fatally.[60]

Section 7 of the Charter was used in 1993 to strike down a Criminal Code provision that allowed police to shoot any "fleeing felon." Nevertheless, the police officer in that case was acquitted of criminal negligence for causing bodily harm when he shot a suspected purse snatcher who was Black. The judge also refused to apply the Charter to prevent the officer from using a peremptory challenge to keep at least one Black person off the jury.[61] The Criminal Code was then amended to require police officers to believe on reasonable grounds that deadly force is necessary to protect someone from "imminent or future death or grievous bodily harm."[62] Even after this change, however, the police are still often not prosecuted or, if prosecuted, are often acquitted in shooting cases, frequently on the basis that there is at least a reasonable doubt that they acted in reasonable self-defence. Such conclusions can in part be related to a few oft-quoted lines in a 2010 Supreme Court decision stating that police "actions should not be judged against a standard of perfection" because officers "engage in dangerous and demanding work" and respond to "exigent circumstances."[63] The court's influential comments were made in the course of a decision where an Indigenous person received a mandatory minimum sentence for drunk driving as a remedy because a Mountie had punched him in the face and broken his ribs during the arrest and then failed to provide medical treatment when the man stated "I can't breathe" while in custody. The Indigenous man's statement had echoes of the George Floyd case. So too does the case of a sixty-seven-year-old residential school survivor, Paulsey Alphonse, who died in RCMP custody after what a pathologist concluded was a "boot stomp" that broke his ribs.[64] A Charter decision affirming sentence reductions as a Charter remedy has had the effect of frequently excusing unnecessary and disproportionate police use of force.

During the Charter era, there has been a trend in almost all provinces to independent investigations of police when they are involved in deaths or serious injuries. In most cases, these investigations end in a decision to not charge police criminally, often on the basis that the police were responding reasonably and used no more force than necessary. Such investigations and, when warranted, prosecutions affirm that the rule of law applies to police officers. At the same time, however, criminal investigations and prosecutions are blunt and often ineffective instruments to change police behaviour to prevent harm.

It appears that criminal charges have not been laid in any of the thirty-eight cases of fatal RCMP encounters with Indigenous people. For example, after an investigation by a Quebec independent office, the New Brunswick attorney general decided not to charge an RCMP officer in the killing of Rodney Levi, a forty-eight-year-old member of the Metepenagiag First Nation, in June 2020. The investigation stressed that Levi had knives in his hand and a taser did not work. The prosecutor also cited the Supreme Court's statement discussed above that police actions should not be judged by a standard of perfection. Deadly use of police force continues to be legally accepted in dealing with people who point knives while in a mental-health crisis.[65] Between 2007 and 2017, Canadian police fatally shot 260 civilians. During the same period, only 47 people were fatally shot by the police in Australia.[66] Australia, of course, does not have a constitutional bill of rights. Nevertheless, it does a much better job than Canada of de-escalation and avoidance of the use of deadly force by the police.

The Charter makes the criminal investigation of police officers more difficult. Police generally have access through their unions to expert legal advice, and officers often assert their right to silence. In 2013, however, the Supreme Court ruled against a long-standing practice in Ontario of both subject and witness officers consulting with counsel before preparing their notes about an incident. The court held that allowing such consultation would erode the public confidence promoted by the independent investigation of police-involved deaths and serious injuries. Three judges dissented and stressed that officers may need legal advice.[67] Police officers are much better positioned to exercise their Charter right to silence than others. They also have experience and legal expertise if they decide to testify in their defence.

The Problematics of Criminal Punishment of the Police

Accountability for police misconduct is often caught in the Goldilocks trap of being too little or too much. The dominant concern until quite recently has been that criminal sentences for crimes committed by police are too lenient. For example, the Supreme Court held in 1987 that an RCMP officer convicted of a disciplinary offence under the *RCMP Act* for assault could not claim protection against double jeopardy when he was subsequently charged with criminal assault in relation to the same actions against a person in his custody. Justice Wilson concluded that the officer "cannot complain, as a member of a special group of individuals subject to private internal discipline, that he ought not to account to society for his wrongdoing."[68] The officer in question only had to pay a $300 fine for his disciplinary offence and a $250 fine for his criminal assault. He continued to serve on the RCMP.[69]

On the other hand, the application of harsher penalties through mandatory minimum sentences may be too severe depending on the circumstances of the police misconduct.[70] In October 1999, RCMP Constable Michael Ferguson arrested twenty-six-year-old Darren Varley in the early morning for public intoxication. Ferguson punched Varley in the jaw while making the arrest. He then claimed that Varley had grabbed for his service weapon while he was being placed into a holding cell. Ferguson shot Varley in the stomach. According to the testimony of two witnesses, about three seconds later, Ferguson shot Varley in the head, killing him.

Ferguson was charged with murder, but two juries were unable to reach a verdict. A third trial took four months. After thirteen hours of deliberation, the jury convicted Ferguson of the lesser offence of manslaughter. Four days after the verdict, one of the jurors wrote a letter to the judge stating that she had been pressured into convicting. Ferguson unsuccessfully raised the juror's second thoughts on appeal.[71]

At sentencing, the trial judge held that imposition of the mandatory minimum sentence of four years' imprisonment would violate Ferguson's Charter right against cruel and unusual punishment. The trial judge was influenced by the harsh solitary confinement that Ferguson, as an ex-police officer, would face in jail in order to ensure his own safety.[72] He also interpreted the compromise manslaughter verdict as meaning the jury must have concluded that Ferguson never intended to kill Varley and that the "second shot was something which had been instilled in Mr. Ferguson through all of his firearms training."[73] Police training is often cited as a justifying or mitigating factor when the police are prosecuted. This does not, however, address the critical issue of whether the training places sufficient emphasis on de-escalation. The Charter has yet to be applied to police use of force and training policies to ensure respect for proportionality.

The prosecutor successfully appealed Ferguson's conditional sentence. The Supreme Court held that the trial judge had erred in minimizing the blameworthiness of Ferguson's actions, especially given the interval between the two shots. Ferguson was then sentenced to the mandatory minimum of four years' imprisonment. He only served two months in jail before being granted parole because the time he had already served under the conditional sentence during the appeal process counted towards his parole eligibility. The Varley family was understandably upset. Ferguson was so depressed and suicidal that he was excused from testifying at a 2011 fatal-inquiry hearing.[74] Criminal prosecutions are blunt instruments to respond to police violence. The available evidence suggests that criminal charges against the police have higher acquittal rates than other offences. Even when there are convictions, most cases do not result in imprisonment.[75]

The fatal-inquiry hearing found that several complaints had been made about Constable Ferguson's anger-management issues before Varley's death, but "they were not dealt with in an effective or timely way." The RCMP found that Ferguson's comment to a female colleague – "You're lucky you're a woman or I would deck you" – was not harassment because of a lack of intent.[76] The inquiry found twelve years after Varley's death that there were no policies or requirements that RCMP officers disarm in holding cells.[77] Even at the time of his 2004 conviction, the prosecutor had sensibly observed that "good change would be that there be a very clear policy for RCMP officers when you're arresting a prisoner to secure your weapon in a vault or something like that – for the benefit of the prisoner and the police officer."[78] The RCMP must change many of its policies but will not be forced to do so by the courts.

Relying on the courts to regulate police misconduct has limits. Effective executive and legislative control are also necessary. The 2013 *Enhancing RCMP Accountability Act* facilitated independent criminal investigation against RCMP misconduct but also produced a civilian complaint and review commission that is underpowered and under-resourced.[79] Although the vast majority of the over 3,500 complaints made annually against the RCMP are made directly to the commission, the RCMP still investigates complaints against itself. The commission only reviews a small percentage of complaints. The commission has done important work on systemic reviews including strip searches and street checks, but has a small annual budget of about $13 million. It is required to prioritize the review of individual complaints over systemic reviews. It can only make recommendations. It cannot release a report until the RCMP crafts its response, often causing extensive delays.[80] Executive watchdog scrutiny is critical to effective review of the police. Such watchdogs are the only hope for reviewing the vast majority of police actions, which do not result in prosecutions and Charter litigation. They also complicate our understanding of the separation of powers under the Charter.

The Charter and Police Unionization

In 1999, the Supreme Court upheld the exclusion of the RCMP from public-sector unionization as not violating freedom of association or equality rights under the Charter. The majority of the court stressed that the RCMP could still form and elect a representative association even if it did not have all the powers of a public-sector union. It also rejected the argument that the police officers' equality rights were violated given their distinct role. Two judges in dissent, however, held that the government's traditional concern, first articulated in an Order-in-Council enacted near the end of the First World War, that allowing the RCMP to unionize would provide it with divided loyalties when policing labour disputes, was improper and irrational.[81]

In 2015, the court reversed course. It held that the denial of collective-bargaining rights violated freedom of association and could not be justified as a reasonable limit on such rights. The court distinguished its 1999 case as not taking the same "generous and purposive"[82] approach it has taken to other Charter rights. The internal representation of RCMP officers was not independent enough from management, who determined their budget and generally prohibited the officers from making public statements.

The court stressed that the RCMP was Canada's only nonunionized police service. It was optimistic, perhaps overly optimistic, about the effects of unionization on the RCMP. It based this conclusion on one 1980 academic study that concluded that "the evidence suggests that respecting associational rights has the potential to ensure, rather than undermine, a positive working relationship and therefore enhance labour stability."[83] The court noted "while the RCMP's mandate differs from that of other police forces, there is no evidence that providing the RCMP a labour relations scheme similar to that enjoyed by other police forces would prevent it from fulfilling its mandate."[84] The court suspended its declaration of invalidity, giving Parliament twelve months "to enact any labour relations model it considers appropriate to the RCMP workforce, within the constitutional limits imposed by the guarantee enshrined in 2(d) and s.1 of the Charter."[85]

In early 2016, the government introduced a bill that allowed unionization but prohibited collective bargaining over law-enforcement techniques, transfers, appraisals, probation, discharges or demotions, conduct (including harassment), and uniforms. At the insistence of two senators who were former Mounties, the bill was amended to remove most of these restrictions. Senator Campbell argued that "the Commissioner is wrong. The idea that he can rule people's lives from Ottawa is wrong and has been for at least the last 40 years."[86] Senator White argued, "Exemptions concern me around law enforcement techniques, particularly when we talk about tactical units."[87] The Charter was only mentioned a few times in the Senate's debates and more as a rhetorical flourish than a serious argument that the initial limits that the government placed on the scope of collective bargaining could not be justified under section 1 of the Charter.[88] This episode complicates criticism that dialogue is dead or that the Charter causes policy distortions.

Commissioner Paulson of the RCMP argued in vain for management rights. He stated: "I wouldn't know where to start bargaining on law enforcement techniques." This drew a response from Senator Colin Kenny: "Why don't you start on having two people in a car after 10 o'clock at night?" After the killings of four Mounties in Mayerthorpe and three in Moncton, some believed the new RCMP union should be able to negotiate about the arms available to the

Mounties. Commissioner Paulson argued that the question was complex – "Should we be strapping carbines on when we go into domestics? Should we have carbines on when we do foot patrols?" – and should be left to management.[89]

The RCMP review commission subsequently found that seven Mounties, some armed with carbines, had informed Debbie Baptiste that her twenty-two-year-old Cree son, Colten Boushie, had been killed.[90] The union criticized the review commission's findings of discrimination when it found that one of the Mounties had asked Baptiste whether she had been drinking. The union argued that its members "felt and demonstrated compassion and respect" to the family during the twenty minutes spent searching the Baptiste house and informing them of Colten's death.[91]

The RCMP's first collective agreement, signed in 2021, raises the maximum salaries of almost 12,000 Mounties who are constables from $86,110 to $106,576. It also provides pay increases retroactive to April 2017. This was defended as necessary catch-up to other police services.[92] The collective agreement does not attempt to govern policy matters such as law-enforcement techniques, arms, harassment, transfers, demotions, and dismissals. Future bargaining (the current agreement expires in March 2023) has the potential to establish policing policies on matters such as law enforcement techniques and discipline that should be established by Parliament, the minister of public safety, the commissioner, or through a community- or province-wide police board for the RCMP detachment or division.[93]

A union has the potential to improve working conditions, including mental health care and transfers that move Mounties around the country in a manner that is difficult on their families and may prevent them from developing relationships with those they police. Nevertheless, police unions have generally resisted increased accountability and the development of broader approaches to community safety. Unionization will make the reform of Canada's largest and struggling police service considerably more difficult. RCMP unionization will increase the costs of policing, perhaps leading more municipalities, First Nations, and even provinces to opt-out of RCMP contract policing. Unionization through one Charter case may have a much greater impact on the RCMP than thousands of other Charter decisions that attempt to regulate police conduct.

Conclusion

Although much Charter litigation is directed towards the RCMP and other police services, its effectiveness in changing police conduct is open to doubt. In general, courts only review police misconduct in cases where incriminating evidence has been obtained. They decide whether Charter rights have been violated and whether evidence should be excluded under section 24(2) of the Charter in nuanced, lengthy judgments that weigh all the circumstances of the case. Although this may achieve justice in the individual cases, it often fails to send clear signals to the police.

In relying on the courts under the Charter to regulate police conduct, Canada has followed a path similar to the United States, one that has not remedied the fundamental problem of systemic discrimination in policing. The RCMP frequently interacts with Indigenous people who are overrepresented among those imprisoned and victimized by crime. The Charter has not remedied these deeply troubling issues of systemic and colonial discrimination, as illustrated by the shooting death of Rodney Levi and the treatment of Debbie Baptiste discussed in this chapter. The Charter has restrained some of the worst excesses of police powers, but it also allowed the police to gain new powers, including stop-and-search powers on the basis of reasonable suspicion.

The Charter decision that may turn out to have the greatest effect on the RCMP is the 2015 decision allowing RCMP officers to unionize. The scope of collective bargaining was significantly expanded by amendments made in the Senate. These amendments were motivated less by concerns with Charter compliance and more by concerns that RCMP officers should be able to bargain over issues such as transfers, harassment, and the equipment and law-enforcement techniques they can use.

By examining the effects of the Charter on the RCMP, this chapter seeks to inject a sense of realism into our debates about the Charter. The Charter has changed policing but to an extent that should not be exaggerated especially given the alternative routes not taken of more intense legislative and executive regulation of the police.

The Charter has become a shining national symbol while the RCMP is now a tarnished one.[94] But the RCMP's wounds have largely been self-inflicted and not caused by the Charter. In the end, the RCMP is an institution that requires fundamental reform that will not come from the courts or the Charter.

Notes

I thank Kate Puddister and an anonymous reviewer for helpful comments on an earlier draft.

1 Suspects and accused persons are often disadvantaged and unpopular and thus require protection from the independent courts. Kent Roach, *The Supreme Court on Trial: Judicial Activism or Democratic Dialogue*, rev. ed. (Toronto: Irwin Law, 2016), 205–7, 354–71.

2 Kent Roach, "A Charter Reality Check," *Supreme Court Law Review*, 2nd ser, 40 (2008): 717. For similar conclusions with respect to the systemic discrimination against other racialized groups, see Sealy-Harrington, Chapter 13 in this volume.

3 *The Queen and Archer v White*, [1956] SCR 154, 160.

4   Hon. Michel Bastarache, *Broken Dreams, Broken Lives: The Devasting Impact of Sexual Harassment on Women in the RCMP* (Ottawa: Merlo Davidson, 2021), iv, 66.
5   Commission of Inquiry Concerning Certain Activities of the RCMP, *Freedom and Security under the Law* (Ottawa: Supply and Services, 1981), vol. 2, ch. 2.
6   Bastarache, *Broken Dreams, Broken Lives,* 105.
7   For additional arguments about the need for reform with respect to both the RCMP's contract and federal policing mandates, see Kent Roach, *Canadian Policing: Why and How It Must Change* (Toronto: Delve, 2022), ch. 9.
8   Hon. Marco Mendicino, *Royal Canadian Mounted Police 2022–2023 Departmental Plan* (Ottawa: Ministry of Public Safety, 2022), 29. This is compared to just over $1 billion and just under 5,000 people devoted to federal policing, which includes organized crime, national security, and protective services. *Ibid,* 11.
9   *AG Quebec v Keable,* [1979] 1 SCR 218.
10 *AG Alberta v Putnam,* [1981] 2 SCR 267.
11 *Scowby v Glendinning,* [1986] 2 SCR 226.
12 Peter Hogg, *Constitutional Law of Canada,* 5th ed (Toronto: Thomson, 2008), 19.5(c).
13 Roach, *The Supreme Court on Trial,* 44–57.
14 *Poitras v The Queen,* [1974] SCR 649; *R v Wray,* [1971] SCR 272.
15 *Hunter v Southam,* [1984] 2 SCR 145.
16 *R v Hamill,* [1987] 1 SCR 301; *R v Sieben,* [1987] 1 SCR 295.
17 Casey Hill, Leslie Pringle, and Scott Hutchison, "Search Warrants: Protection or Illusion," *Criminal Reports,* 5th ser, 28 (2000): 89, finding 61 percent of randomly selected warrants in Ontario would be invalid under the Charter. Anne Krahn, Sarah Innes, Stacy Cawley, and Bettina Schaible, "Reaching for Excellence: Evaluating Manitoba's Process for Issuing Judicial Authorizations," *Manitoba Law Journal* 40, 1 (2017): 41, finding 20 percent of 100 randomly selected warrants in Manitoba would be invalid under the Charter.
18 *R v Stillman,* [1997] 1 SCR 607; *R v Feeney,* [1997] 2 SCR 13.
19 *R v Wong,* [1990] 3 SCR 36, 69.
20 *R v Malmo-Levine,* [2003] 3 SCR 571.
21 *Canada (Attorney General) v Bedford,* 2013 SCC 72.
22 *R v Mann,* [2004] 3 SCR 59.
23 James Stribopoulos, "In Search of Dialogue," *Queen's Law Journal* 31 (2005): 1; Benjamin Berger, "Race and Erasure in *R. v. Mann,*" *Criminal Reports,* 6th ser, 21 (2004): 58; David Tanovich, "The Colourless World of *Mann,*" *Criminal Reports,* 6th ser, 21 (2004): 47.
24 Richard Ericson, *The Constitution of Legal Inequality* (Ottawa: Carlton University Press, 1983).
25 *R v RDS,* [1997] 3 SCR 484.
26 *Ibid,* paras 145, 148, 152.
27 *R v Grant,* 2009 SCC 32.
28 *R v Le,* 2019 SCC 34.
29 When deciding not to exclude evidence under s 24(2), the court has recognized that police officers sometimes cannot realistically be expected to keep up with its complex Charter jurisprudence. *R v Cole,* 2012 SCC 53; *R v Aucoin,* 2012 SCC 66; *R v Vu,* 2013 SCC 60; *R v Omar,* 2019 SCC 32.
30 *Anti-Racism Act,* SO 2017, c 15; *Police and Criminal Evidence Act* (UK), 1984, c 60.
31 Civilian Review and Complaints Commission for the RCMP, *Review of the RCMP's Policies and Procedures Regarding Street Checks Report,* February 2021, 37.
32 RCMP, "Commissioner's Response to the CRCC's Review of the RCMP's Policies and Procedures Regarding Street Checks," April 29, 2021, https://www.crcc-ccetp.gc.ca/en/

commissioners-response-street-check. In response to Recommendation 7, Commissioner Lucki states: "[A]ny policies created by a division still need to be consistent with the national policy. It is incumbent on all RCMP business lines and divisions to ensure its members are aware of and comply with new or modified national policy, as well as any divisional supplements that may apply."

33 *R v Golden,* [2001] 3 SCR 679. I represented Aboriginal Legal Services of Toronto, which intervened to argue that the strip search was unconstitutional.

34 Civilian Review and Complaints Commission for the RCMP, *Review of the RCMP's Policies and Procedures Regarding Strip Searches,* July 2020, 29–30, 38.

35 *Ward v Vancouver,* [2010] 2 SCR 28. I represented the BC Civil Liberties, which intervened in this case in support of the damage award.

36 M.L. Friedland, "Reflections on Criminal Justice Reform in Canada," *Criminal Law Quarterly* 64, 274 (2017): 280–83.

37 Troy Riddell and Dennis Baker, "The Charter Beat: The Impact of Rights Decisions on Canadian Policing," in *Policy Change, Courts and the Canadian Constitution,* ed. Emmett Macfarlane (Toronto: University of Toronto Press, 2018), 176–80.

38 Kouri Keenan and Joan Brockman, *Mr. Big: Exposing Undercover Investigations in Canada* (Halifax: Fernwood Press, 2010), 23.

39 Kate Puddister and Troy Riddell, "The RCMP's 'Mr. Big' Sting Operation: A Case Study in Police Independence, Accountability and Oversight," *Canadian Public Administration* 55 (2012): 385.

40 For an account of this phenomena in the context of the Toronto 18 terrorism prosecutions, see Kent Roach, "The Dangers of Charter-Proofing the Toronto 18 Terrorism Prosecutions," *Manitoba Law Journal* 44, 1 (2021): 321, 346–48.

41 *R v Hart,* 2014 SCC 52, excluding statements. But see *R v Mack,* 2014 SCC 58, including statements obtained from a Mr. Big sting.

42 *R v Laruo,* 2019 SCC 25.

43 *R v Bradshaw,* 2017 SCC 35, [2017] 1 SCR 865. For cases where courts of appeal have admitted the fruits of Mr. Big stings since *Hart,* see *R v Moir,* 2020 BCCA 116; *R v Baranec,* 2020 BCCA 156; *R v Randle,* 2016 BCCA 125; *R v Johnston,* 2016 BCCA 3; *R v Yakimchuk,* 2017 ABCA 101; *R v Keene,* 2020 ONCA 635; *Subramaniam c R,* 2019 QCCA 1744; *R v Wingert,* 2020 ABCA 304; *R v Allgood,* 2015 SKCA 88; *R v Wruck,* 2020 ABCA 270; *R v Niemi,* 2017 ONCA 720; *Lebeuf c R,* 2016 QCCA 1882. See also Adelina Iftene and Vanessa Kinnear, "Mr Big and the New Common Law Confession Rule: Five Years in Review," *Manitoba Law Journal* 43, 3 (2020): 295; Christopher Lutes, "Hart Failure: Assessing the Mr. Big Confessions Framework Five Years Later," *Manitoba Law Journal* 43, 4 (2020): 209.

44 Brandon Garrett, "The Substance of False Confessions," *Stanford Law Review* 62 (2010): 1051.

45 *R v Ryan,* 2013 SCC 3, 35.

46 Ian McPhail, QC, *Public Interest Investigation,* Commission for Public Complaints against the RCMP, Ottawa, July 2013. For criticism, see Lori Chambers and Nadia Verrelli, "A Missed Opportunity: The Public Investigation into the Conduct of the RCMP in Matters Involving Nicole (Ryan) Doucet," *Canadian Journal of Law and Society* 32 (2017): 117.

47 *R v Nuttall,* 2018 BCCA 479.

48 *Regulation of Investigative Powers Act,* (UK), 2000, c 23.

49 *Miranda v Arizona,* 384 US 436 (1966).

50 *R v Brydges,* [1990] 1 SCR 190.

51 *R v Singh,* [2007] 3 SCR 405.

52 *R v Sinclair,* [2010] 2 SCR 310.

53 *R v Orbanski,* [2005] 2 SCR 3.

54 *R v Cornell,* [2010] 2 SCR 142.

55 *Criminal Code of Canada,* ss 529.3(2) and 529.3(3).

56 "Chief Sloly's Partial Ban on Dynamic Entries Raises Concerns for Both Activists and Officers," *Ottawa Citizen,* March 29, 2021.

57 For arguments that the police, including the RCMP, have been undergoverned by responsible ministers and other political authorities who should take more responsibility for the policies that govern police operations, see Roach, *Canadian Policing,* 185–89.

58 Craig Bradley, *The Failure of the Criminal Procedure Revolution* (Philadelphia: University of Pennsylvania Press, 1993); William Stuntz, *The Collapse of the American Criminal Justice System* (Cambridge, MA: Harvard University Press, 2012).

59 Inayat Singh, "2020 Already a Particularly Deadly Year for People Killed in Police Encounters, CBC Research Shows," CBC News, July 23, 2020, https://newsinteractives. cbc.ca/fatalpoliceencounters/.

60 RCMP, "2020 Police Interventions Report," https://www.rcmp-grc.gc.ca/transparenc/ police-info-policieres/intervention/2020/index-eng.htm.

61 *R v Lines,* [1993] OJ No 3284 (Ont Ct (Gen Div)); David Tanovich, "The Charter of Whiteness: Twenty-Five Years of Maintaining Racial Injustice in the Canadian Criminal Justice System," *Supreme Court Law Review* 40 (2008): 655.

62 *Criminal Code,* RSC 1985 c C-34, s 25(4).

63 *R v Nasogaluak,* 2010 SCC 6, para 35. This statement from the court was relied on to justify not charging an RCMP officer in the death of Rodney Levi. It was also used to justify not laying charges against the municipal police officer who shot an Indigenous woman, Chantel Moore, four times and killed her in June 2020 when she answered her door to a police safety check late at night while apparently possessing a steak knife. New Brunswick, Office of the Attorney General, *Review of the Report from the Bureau des Enquêtes Independents du Quebec (BEI) of Its Investigation following the Death of Chantel Moore and Legal Opinion,* June 7, 2021, 19, https://www2.gnb.ca/content/dam/gnb/Departments/ag-pg/PDF/review-report-bei.pdf. For arguments about the need to change police use of force policies to stress de-escalation and even retreat when officers are confronted with knives and examples of better policies in Australia, see Roach, *Canadian Policing,* 178–79.

64 Sherene Razack, *Dying from Improvement: Inquests and Inquiries into Indigenous Deaths in Custody* (Toronto: University of Toronto Press, 2015), 85.

65 New Brunswick, Office of the Attorney General, *Review of the Report from the Bureau des Enquêtes Independents du Quebec (BEI) of Its Investigation following the Death of Rodney Levi and Legal Opinion,* January 26, 2021, 11, https://www2.gnb.ca/content/dam/gnb/ Departments/ag-pg/PDF/Review-Report-Bureau-Enquetes-Independantes-Quebec.pdf.

66 Richard Farmer and Claire Evans, *Do Police Need Guns? Policing and Firearms, Past, Present and Future* (Singapore: Springer, 2021), 89, 96–97.

67 *Wood v Schaeffer,* 2013 SCC 71.

68 *R v Wigglesworth,* [1987] 2 SCR 541.

69 David Vienneau, "Police Have Right to Punish Officers Supreme Court Rules," *Toronto Star,* November 20, 1987.

70 For an account of the fallout, including two prison sentences and a suicide by the police, from the tasering death of Robert Dziekanski, see Curt Petrovich, *Blamed and Broken: The Mounties and the Death of Robert Dziekanski* (Toronto: Dundurn, 2019).

71 *R v Ferguson,* 2006 ABCA 36.

72 "'Jail Is Not a Safe Place for Me,' Says Cop Who Killed Prisoner," *Calgary Herald,* January 6, 2005.

73 *R v Ferguson,* 2004 ABQB 928, 3.

74 "Creek Family Fights to Keep Ex-Mountie in Jail," *Calgary Herald,* December 7, 2006.

75 Kate Puddister and Danielle McNabb, "When the Police Break the Law: The Investigation, Prosecution and Sentencing of Ontario Police Officers," *Canadian Journal of Law and Society* 36, 3 (2021): 394–96, Tables 3 and 4.

76 Report to the Minister of Justice and Attorney General, Public Fatality Inquiry, March 25, 2011, 17–19, https://open.alberta.ca/dataset/c07d0ea9-08cd-43c2-a32b-252e01f7cef2/resource/f7a30f50-3dca-4493-b6cb-f695a180ca7c/download/01236-report-to-minister-into-death-of-darren-john-varley.pdf.

77 "RCMP Acting on Fatality Report, Darren Varley Killed in 1999," *Calgary Herald,* April 27, 2011.

78 "Mountie Convicted in Jail Shooting," *Peterborough Examiner,* October 2, 2004.

79 SC 2013, c18.

80 See *British Columbia Civil Liberties Association v Canada (Royal Mounted Police),* 2021 FC 1475, finding excessive delay and imposing a maximum six-month time for the RCMP to respond to report absent exceptional circumstances.

81 *Delisle v Canada (Deputy Attorney General),* [1999] 2 SCR 989.

82 *Mounted Police Association of Ontario v Canada (Attorney General),* 2015 SCC 1, [2015] 1 SCR 3, 30, 127.

83 *Ibid,* 147.

84 *Ibid,* 153.

85 *Ibid,* 156.

86 Senate Committee on National Security and Defence, *Evidence,* 42nd Parl, 1st Sess, No 4 (June 6, 2017).

87 *Ibid.*

88 Conservative Senator Carignan did oppose the bargaining exclusions as a violation of the Charter because "about the only things left to negotiate were salary and some leave," and this infringed the scope of bargaining more than other similar laws. *Debates of the Senate,* 42nd Parl, 1st Sess, No 307 (June 20, 2016).

89 *Ibid.*

90 Kent Roach, "Report into RCMP's Treatment of Grieving Indigenous Families Left Out Key Systemic Problems," *Policy Options,* April 6, 2021, https://policyoptions.irpp.org/magazines/april-2021/report-into-rcmps-treatment-of-grieving-indigenous-family-left-out-key-facts-and-evidence-systemic-problems/.

91 National Police Federation, *Key Facts and Evidence Overlooked in CCRC Report,* March 21, 2021, https://npf-fpn.com/news-item/march-21-2021-crcc-report-overlooks-key-facts-and-evidence-in-rcmp-investigation-of-colten-boushies-death/.

92 Catharine Tunney, "Mounties to See Their Salaries Soar as First Collective Agreement Is Ratified," CBC News, August 17, 2021. See also Treasury Board of Canada Secretariat, *RCMP Regular Members and Reservists (RM): Agreement between the Treasury Board and the National Police Federation,* signed August 6, 2021, expiry March 31, 2023, https://www.tbs-sct.gc.ca/agreements-conventions/view-visualiser-eng.aspx?id=28.

93 One example of governance reform is the creation of the Yukon Police Council, chaired by Yukon's deputy minister of justice with a minimum of three of seven members from Yukon First Nations. The council provides advice on RCMP policing priorities and the needs and values of communities, including First Nations. Yukon Police Council, *Terms of Reference,* revised May 8, 2020, https://yukon.ca/sites/yukon.ca/files/jus-yukon-police-council-terms-reference-may-8-2020.pdf.

94 On the Charter as a national symbol, see McDougall, Chapter 5 in this volume.

13

The Charter of Whites
Systemic Racism and Critical Race Equality in Canada

Joshua Sealy-Harrington

> *Systemic discrimination ... is discrimination that results from the simple operation of established procedures ... none of which is necessarily designed to promote discrimination.*
> — BRIAN DICKSON, CHIEF JUSTICE OF CANADA, JUNE 25, 1987[1]

> *I've been struggling with the definition of systemic racism ... We put in policies and procedures to make sure we don't have systemic racism.*
> — BRENDA LUCKI, COMMISSIONER OF THE ROYAL CANADIAN MOUNTED POLICE, JUNE 10, 2020[2]

> *I'd invite you: what is the definition of systemic racism? There is no definition. It's tossed around.*
> — ERIN O'TOOLE, LEADER OF THE CONSERVATIVE PARTY OF CANADA, AUGUST 30, 2020[3]

> *We still can't get our leaders to talk about what systemic racism means. We still can't get them, after they take a knee, to stand up and actually do something. That means y'all don't want to do nothing anyway.*
> — CELINA CAESAR-CHAVANNES, FORMER LIBERAL MEMBER OF PARLIAMENT, FEBRUARY 9, 2021[4]

SYSTEMIC RACISM AND colourblindness are intimately linked (though, because of the ableist connotation of colour*blindness,* I will call the latter race evasiveness, unless I am directly quoting another scholar).[5] The former – systemic racism – refers to how intergenerational legacies and ongoing practices of oppression and dispossession translate into contemporary societal inequality.[6] The latter – race evasiveness – refers to the belief that those legacies and practices should not be accounted for in our contemporary legal, political, and economic thought.[7] Put plainly, systemic racism is an effect and race evasiveness is a cause. To be clear, reasonable people can disagree over how race should be accounted for in policy. But it is inconceivable to think that, without some such accounting, legacies and practices of racial subordination will simply expire. The staggering racial inequalities that persist in Canada – indeed, globally – are no accident. And their end – if ever – will be no accident, either.

Recently, a peer reviewer mildly questioned my discussion of race evasiveness – a concept more often discussed in America – when critiquing Canadian equality law. I was sympathetic to that peer reviewer's perspective: America does, indeed, have a particularly active jurisprudential[8] and scholarly[9] discourse on race evasiveness in constitutional equality law. Yet, when I think of race evasiveness and constitutional law, I have Canada especially in mind. Indeed, the less active conversation on race evasiveness in Canadian law is not proof of *less* evasion but *more* – an evasion *of the evasion itself.* To be sure, Canada has more progressive equality-law standards than America. In general terms, American equality law is formal (that is, concerned with *similar* treatment), whereas Canadian equality law is substantive (that is, concerned with *subordinating* treatment).[10] But, as the Supreme Court of Canada has consistently recognized – from its very first equality decision (*Andrews*) to its most recent (*Fraser*) – equality is about impact.[11] And on impact, Canadian equality law before the Supreme Court of Canada has been largely elusive in terms of promoting, or even broaching, racial equality. It is in this sense that I argue we have a "Charter of whites."

I will be blunt: were "race" not listed as a protected ground under the Charter, it is not apparent to me that there would have been much difference in the Supreme Court's first four decades of equality jurisprudence – at least, not for Indigenous and Black people, who are the focus of my analysis here.[12] The protected grounds enumerated in the Charter are "race, national or ethnic origin, colour, religion, sex, age or mental or physical disability." Yet the Supreme Court has barely considered racial discrimination claims. Race is, thus, *first listed* yet *last enforced* – a constitutional token to a promise of racial equality left not only with little success but with little attempt.

This chapter's thesis is straightforward: that systemic racial-justice advocacy under section 15 of the Charter is doctrinally viable and, thus, should be contemplated in the toolkit of social-change strategies in Canada.[13] There is plenty of social science literature on the character and pervasiveness of racial inequality in Canada – and this chapter does not comprehensively summarize that. Instead, this chapter – with reference to critical race scholarship and the court's first and latest equality decision under the Charter – explains how a consistent thread across all three authorities is an expansive vision of "critical race equality" that makes systemic and positive advocacy viable under Canadian constitutional law.

This chapter contains two parts. The first part discusses the theory of critical race equality, in particular, six principles I identify as animating a critical race perspective on equality rights. Those principles can be understood as criteria for evaluating the extent to which a theory of equality aligns with critical race theory and, in turn, bears certain capacities for promoting substantive racial justice. The second part discusses the practice of critical race equality by tracing a genealogy of critical race principles over the first thirty-five years of constitutional equality at the Supreme Court of Canada. I conclude by calling for a coalition of scholars, lawyers, and organizers to incorporate systemic and positive litigation in their social change toolkits with a view to translating our Charter of whites into a Charter for all.

The Theory of Critical Race Equality

This chapter argues that critical race theory principles are reflected in – and, indeed, have always been reflected in – Canada's constitutional text and jurisprudence. Making this argument, though, first requires identifying what those critical race theory principles are.

In his groundbreaking article "A Critique of Our Constitution Is Color-Blind," critical race theorist Neil Gotanda conducts a detailed examination of race evasiveness in American constitutional law.[14] His critique, of course, is framed in relation to the US Constitution. But the principles he notes as *absent* from American constitutional doctrine are *present* in Canadian constitutional doctrine. Those principles – that is, critical race equality principles – outline a vision of equality that is (1) ambitious, (2) contextual, (3) ideological, (4) comparative, (5) systemic, and (6) positive.

On principle one – ambition – Gotanda critiques the Supreme Court of the United States for adopting "a vision of race as unconnected to the historical reality of Black oppression," thereby limiting "the range of remedies available for redress."[15] This warrants elaboration. Simply put, how one conceptualizes *race* informs how they conceptualize *racism* and, in turn, how they conceptualize *antiracism* (that is, the pursuit of racial equality). Accordingly, where racial equality is at issue, a series of cascading political questions – which either expand or contract the ambition such equality entails – are engaged. With this in mind, Gotanda critiques ahistorical conceptions of race that limit racism to "individual prejudice" and, thus, construct "an ideological limitation on the remedies for racism."[16] Correspondingly, Gotanda advocates for an understanding of race situated within a historical frame, thereby responding to race's "institutional and structural dimensions beyond formal racial classification."[17] For example, Gotanda references economic aid as a remedy for structural racial subordination, which is only legible within a historical frame of racial capitalism.[18] And, more broadly, Gotanda points out how the "complex phenomenon called race" is intertwined with "particular manifestations of racial subordination – substandard housing, education, employment, and income for large portions of the Black community."[19] These are ambitious issues of social policy, there is no doubt. But they are issues, nonetheless, inseverable from enduring legacies of racial oppression. To neglect these issues, then, would be to neglect racial equality itself.

On principle two – context – Gotanda critiques American courts for their "simplistic" analysis.[20] He explains how a "deeper analysis" of "racial practice" demonstrates that structures of racial subordination are "highly contextualized, with powerful, deeply embedded social and political meanings."[21] Without first acknowledging these meanings, manifest forms of racial inequality have been overlooked by America's highest court[22] and even progressive scholars.[23] And all of this is complicated by how race itself – as a social rather than biological fact – cannot be assessed with precision.[24] Indeed, to hold out race as "objective and apolitical" is to disguise and discount the ways in which racial taxonomies institutionalize racial subordination.[25] In sum, when analyzing racial equality, the contextual nature of both equality and race necessitates a flexible analytical framework.[26]

On principle three – ideology – the opening line to Gotanda's article is illustrative: he "examines the ideological content of the metaphor 'Our Constitution is color-blind.'"[27] Specifically, Gotanda argues "that the United States Supreme Court's use of color blind constitutionalism a collection of legal themes functioning as a racial ideology – fosters white racial domination" by legitimizing, and thus maintaining, "the social, economic, and political advantages that whites hold over other Americans."[28] Given this, Gotanda stresses how "the real social conditions underlying a ... constitutional dispute" must be accounted for, including with reference to "social science analyses."[29] Some may call this activist judicial ideology (for a discussion on judicial activism, see Macfarlane, Chapter 2 in this volume). But, as Gotanda observes, there is already a "subliminal ideology" concealed "between the lines of the Court's articulated rationales and policies."[30] In other words, critical race equality is not *uniquely* ideological but rather *distinctly* so: the "color-blind constitutionalists live in an ideological world where racial subordination is ubiquitous yet disregarded" – a politics that "simply do[es] not reflect historical or present reality."[31] As such, where "activism" is understood to mean judicial reasoning that is overridden by ideology,[32] and given long-standing and demonstrated patterns of systemic racial inequality, it is those who evade race – not those who acknowledge it – who are more fairly characterized as activist.

On principle four – comparison – Gotanda is pointed: "one cannot declare two things to be equal or unequal without first comparing them."[33] While trite, this observation poses a fundamental challenge to America's race-evasive constitutional posture. Indeed, Gotanda explains how failing to recognize race in policy effectively forecloses racial equality: "that nonrecognition is self-contradictory. Nonrecognition fosters the systematic denial of racial subordination ... thereby allowing such subordination to continue."[34] At its height, race evasiveness can "suppress the existence of race from a narrative in which race was the center of the incident" – not simply a failure to promote equality, but a commitment to maintaining inequality.[35]

On principle five – systems – Gotanda remarks "at the outset" that his article "assumes the existence of American racial subordination."[36] Why? Because of "the systemic nature of subordination in American society."[37] In this respect, Gotanda draws on other leading critical race scholars – including Kimberlé Crenshaw[38] and Patricia Williams[39] – who have persuasively described their incredulity at the staggering racial inequality that conservative jurists attempt to explain *without* reference to an overarching system that perpetuates that inequality.[40] In Crenshaw's words, only such an incomplete analysis could sanction the oxymorons reflected in how "one can now have all-Black desegregated schools, all-white equal opportunity employers and nondiscriminatory housing with no Blacks present."[41] Further, Gotanda recognizes certain corollaries of conceptualizing inequality through a systemic lens, namely, (1) that intent cannot be required for inequality;[42] (2) that racial discrimination need not exhaust every member of a subordinated group to be recognized as such;[43] and (3) that causal chains between state policy and systemic inequality can be diffuse, particularly intergenerationally[44] – all of which reflect the powerful metaphor of race as a "miner's canary," aptly described by critical race scholars Lani Guinier and Gerald Torres:

> We maintain that one can identify race affirmatively in order to mobilize both a critique of the connection between race and power and to identify a base of support for changing the status quo. Focusing attention on the distress of the miner's canary does not mean that one must locate the pathology within the canary itself; one can still locate the problem in the atmosphere of the mine. Using race as the miner's canary allows us to depathologize conceptions of race, poverty, and powerlessness.[45]

Lastly, on principle six – positivity – Gotanda challenges the "public-private distinction" and its "extraordinarily slippery character."[46] Specifically, he explains how race-evasive interpretation "is part of a broader vision in which legal relations are seen as located either in a public sphere of government action or in a private sphere of individual freedom."[47] And this public-private dichotomization is the logical basis for resisting equality's positive character, that is, *public* intervention is opposed because it improperly infiltrates *private* spaces: "[D]esignation of an activity as public or private is a normative process. The familiarity of the public-private distinction obscures the contingent and political character of the initial designation, and subsequent challenges to the subordinating effects of such a 'neutral' distinction are then criticized as 'political.'"[48] Relatedly, Gotanda critiques American courts for adopting a "theory of racial social change" predicated on "'never' considering race."[49] By corollary, then, he advances a theory of race consciousness – that is, of not only *recognizing* but *disrupting* "ensconced interests – usually white."[50]

The Practice of Critical Race Equality

With six principles emanating from the theory of critical race equality summarized above – that is, ambition, context, ideology, comparison, systems, and positivity – I now turn to the practice of critical race equality in Canada.

I explore critical race practice in four subparts: (1) outlining our Charter of whites, which rarely considers (let alone remedies) racial inequality; (2) looking to the past (*Andrews*), where these six critical principles supportive of critical race equality were first judicially affirmed; (3) looking to the present (*Fraser*), where those principles were recently reaffirmed; and (4) looking to the future, where those principles should be strategically incorporated into social-change toolkits. Twenty-five years following the enactment of the Charter, David Tanovich critiqued the lack of "race talk" in criminal punishment.[51] And now, in this text written on the fortieth anniversary of the Charter, I am transposing that critique to equality rights under section 15.

The Charter of Whites

The Supreme Court's racial-equality jurisprudence under section 15 is limited.[52] For example, the court has never explicitly discussed anti-Black racism under section 15 of the Charter.[53] In *Fraser*, Justice Abella writes that "in the pursuit of equality, inequality can be reduced one case at a time."[54] With respect to anti-Black racism, one wonders whether *one case* will ever come.

The court has occasionally – but still infrequently – considered discrimination implicating Indigenous people under section 15. But the scope of those interventions has been minimal. For example, in *Kapp*, a majority of the court held that the government's decision to grant an ameliorative twenty-four-hour exclusive fishing licence to three Indigenous bands was not discriminatory, despite claims of discrimination by "mainly non-aboriginal" commercial fishers who were not granted the same exclusive licence.[55] (In other words, *Kapp* was not principally a claim of anti-Indigenous racism but rather one largely of "reverse racism" against mostly non-Indigenous claimants.)[56] In *R v Kokopenace*, the majority in a single paragraph[57] dispensed with the equality implications of Canada's systemically racist jury system.[58] According to the majority, the Indigenous accused in that case failed to "articulate a disadvantage" when his jury had 0 percent on-reserve representation, despite as much as 32 percent of the adult population in his district living on reserve (a questionable jury "of his peers").[59] And in *Ewert,* the court unanimously held that the state's risk-assessment tools for inmates are not discriminatory because, while they *risked* inaccuracy when applied to Indigenous inmates, no such inaccuracy was *proven* at first instance.[60]

This is what we are left with: almost thirty-five years of Supreme Court equality jurisprudence under the Charter; zero section 15 judgments explicitly centring Black people;[61] sparse progressive section 15 analysis concerning Indigenous people,[62] especially about actually repairing – or even just gesturing at repairs of – Canada's despicable colonial legacy.[63]

And, to be clear, there is ubiquitous systemic inequality confronting both communities. Black people in Canada have lower incomes, less education, higher unemployment, and suffer the highest rate of hate crimes.[64] They are also more likely to be arrested, charged, overcharged, struck, shot, or killed by police.[65] Indeed, from 2013 to 2017, a Black person in Toronto was nearly twenty times more likely than a white person to be fatally shot by police.[66] Black people are also dramatically overincarcerated.[67] Likewise, Indigenous people suffer ongoing cultural genocide; lack food security, clean water, and safe and accessible housing; have a crisis of overrepresentation in the child welfare and criminal punishment systems; and face various barriers in accessing equitable public health,[68] all of which was recently combined with the horrifying discovery of thousands of children's bodies in unmarked graves at Canada's residential schools, where the Canadian government and Catholic Church violently assimilated Indigenous children through rape, confinement, medical experimentation, and death.[69] There is, accordingly, an unquestionable *need* for greater systemic protection and support for Black and Indigenous lives in Canada. But what about a *right* to it?[70]

The Past: *Andrews* (1989)

The Supreme Court's first equality decision was *Andrews v Law Society of British Columbia.*[71] Despite dissenting in part, Justice McIntyre's opinion is the majority statement on section 15 of the Charter (because Justice Lamer signed onto Justice McIntyre's opinion,[72] Justices Wilson and L'Heureux-Dubé, along with Chief Justice Dickson, agreed with Justice McIntryre's section 15 analysis,[73] and Justice La Forest was "in substantial agreement" with that analysis as well).[74]

At first glance, the facts of *Andrews* do not scream "critical race theory." Indeed, the case involved a "British subject" who "had taken law degrees at Oxford" and "had fulfilled all the requirements for admission to the practice of law in British Columbia, except that of Canadian citizenship"[75] – no archetype of racial oppression.[76] But the legal principles outlined in the case nevertheless reflect core critical race equality insights.

First, the court's description of equality was ambitious. The goal: "a society in which all are secure in the knowledge that they are recognized at law as human beings equally deserving of concern, respect and consideration."[77] To achieve this lofty goal, the court indicated that equality must be given its "full effect" through "a generous rather than a legalistic" interpretation.[78] The precise generosity the court envisaged, of course, could not be detailed in one decision. But that generosity, at a minimum, included "a large remedial component" and an understanding that the Constitution demanded not only equality in the "formulation" of the law but also its "application."[79]

Second, the court's description of equality was contextual. This is implicit in how the court discussed equality itself: "a protean word" that "lacks precise definition" and that is "an elusive concept."[80] But it was also reflected in how the court discussed equality analysis: "the test cannot be accepted as a fixed rule or formula."[81]

Third, the court's description of equality was ideological. In other words, it did not shy away from the ways in which "equality" is value-laden. Rather, the court acknowledged and grappled with equality's "moral and ethical" dimensions.[82] In particular, the court recognized how equality is a "political symbol"[83] demanding interdisciplinary insight – a concept that is "at once a psychology, an ethic, a theory of social relations, and a vision of the good society."[84]

Fourth, the court described equality as comparative. Critically, however, the relevant comparison is not simply formal legislative distinctions. Rather, substantive equality analysis requires "comparison with the condition of others in the social and political setting in which the question arises."[85] Consequently, the comparisons under section 15 are not "mechanical," nor do they amount to a "categorization game" under applicable legislation.[86]

Fifth, the court described equality's systemic character. Despite acknowledging equality's contextual – and, thus, imprecise – nature, the court found "little difficulty ... in isolating an acceptable definition" with respect to equality's systemic attributes.[87] Indeed, it did not hesitate to include "adverse effect discrimination"[88] or "systemic discrimination"[89] within the scope of section 15's constitutional protection (and, seemingly, equated the two).[90] Most importantly, in defining systemic discrimination, the court adopted Justice Abella's definition from her historic report on employment equity: "If the barrier is affecting certain groups in a disproportionately negative way, it is a signal that the practices that lead to this adverse impact may be discriminatory."[91] With this definition in mind, the court emphasized disparate effects: "it is in essence the impact of the discriminatory act or provision upon the person affected which is decisive";[92] "it is the result ... which is significant";[93] and "the main consideration must be the impact of the law on the individual or the group concerned."[94] These can be read as judicial restatements of the miner's canary metaphor in critical race theory. Indeed, the court's choice of anchoring equality analysis in "enumerated and analogous grounds" can itself be understood as an analytical framework predicated on – to extend the metaphor – a flock of canaries, who "signal" suspect decision making by the state.

Various theoretical corollaries of equality's systemic character are, as they were by Gotanda, affirmed by the court in *Andrews*. Specifically, the court rejected – as requirements of discrimination – intent (that is, the government's motivation being the creation of inequality),[95] exhaustion (that is, the government's action impacting every group member of the subordinated class),[96] and causation (that is, the government's action being the sole or even primary source for the resulting inequality).[97]

Moreover, an additional consequence of equality's systemic character is that the government cannot insulate its activity from the charge of discrimination simply by rearticulating its conduct in neutral-sounding terms – for example, by justifying inequality as mere "qualifications required for entitlements to benefits."[98] Indeed, all such analysis of "limiting factors" on the scope of constitutional equality must be considered under section 1 of the Charter.[99] In the court's words, "any consideration of factors which could justify the discrimination," such as "the reasonableness of the enactment"[100] or its "proportionality,"[101] are left to section 1. And, as the court explained, sections 15 and 1 are "important to keep analytically distinct" because they carry distinct burdens of proof: claimants demonstrate inequality, governments justify it.[102]

Finally, a sixth equality principle affirmed in *Andrews* is its positive character (meaning, the ways in which it places not only limits on government action but also obligations). Like equality's systemic character, its positive nature is a crucial aspect of its scope and significance that is too often overlooked. At times, the court identified equality's positive character explicitly: for example, section 15 is "a compendious expression of a *positive* right to equality in both the substance and the administration of the law."[103] But elsewhere, this positive character is implicit. Simply put, when "the essence of true equality" is "the accommodation of differences"[104] and when "there is no greater inequality than the equal treatment of unequals,"[105] positive obligations are an unavoidable consequence of governing a pluralistic society. Indeed, the court specifically framed many of the "differences" it had in mind along racial lines (albeit in the whitewashed language of "many forms of discrimination" resulting from "contact ... with the indigenous population" and "immigration bringing those of neither French nor British background" to Canada).[106]

In brief, the Canadian government regulates a racially stratified society. And that racial stratification demands racial recognition and redress. The government cannot simply pass laws of general application and satisfy a substantive definition of equality. To the contrary, differences warrant "accommodation,"[107] and inequality warrants "differentiation."[108] This invariably positive obligation – to *accommodate*, to *differentiate* – has been doctrinally uncontroversial from the beginning of Canada's constitutional equality discourse. And absent such positive intervention, unconstitutional inequality necessarily follows.[109]

To be clear, equality's positive character does not amount to "a general guarantee of equality" in all circumstances.[110] But this caveat should not be overstated. As discussed, equality does involve "comparison with the condition of others in the social and political setting in which the question arises."[111] Therefore, section 15 was never intended to eradicate all social hierarchies, nor was it meant to disregard those hierarchies altogether. Rather, it was meant to account for social hierarchies in its evaluation and redress of substantive inequality. True, section 15 is "concerned with the application of the law."[112] But that application is indivisible from the society in which it occurs. In the court's words: "[I]t is the result ... which is significant."[113] And that result is the product of interaction between Canadian law and society. Positive obligations are not radical overreach but, instead, a constitutional duty inextricable from Canada's substantive equality commitments as they were first defined by its apex court.

The Present: *Fraser* (2020)

Just over three decades later, the Supreme Court in *Fraser* reaffirmed the critical race principles it first affirmed in *Andrews* – this time in a single majority judgment written by Justice Abella, representing six of the nine justices who participated in the ultimate decision.

The facts in *Fraser*, like those in *Andrews*, are not emblematic of critical race theory. Specifically, *Fraser* concerned the gendered adverse impact of the pension scheme for the Royal Canadian Mounted Police,[114] an institution recognized both past and present as a primary vehicle for white supremacist social control and violence in Canada.[115] Yet the principles animating the majority's reasoning in *Fraser* nevertheless track the critical race principles outlined in Gotanda's article and affirmed in *Andrews*.

On ambition, the court reiterates that section 15 reflects "a profound commitment to promote equality,"[116] a commitment that is "ambitious but not utopian."[117]

On context, the court reaffirms "the impossibility of rigid categorizations"[118] in equality analysis and, in particular, rejects "rigid rules"[119] or a "rigid template"[120] in its equality framework – all of which leaves courts with the flexibility needed to appreciate "the full context of the claimant group's situation."[121]

On ideology, the court echoes *Andrews* in terms of the normative dimension to substantive equality analysis.[122] Indeed, between *Andrews* and *Fraser*, the court's interdisciplinarity has only grown to include "barriers," "exclusion," and "environments," implicating considerations that are "legal,"[123] "economic,"[124] "social,"[125] "political,"[126] "physical,"[127] "cultural,"[128] "psychological,"[129] "historical,"[130] and "sociological."[131]

On equality's comparative character, the court confirms the "role of comparison" in section 15 analysis.[132] To be sure, the court rejects "formalistic comparison."[133] But this simply repeats the court's rejection of mechanical categorization games in *Andrews*.[134]

On equality's systemic character, the court confirms that equality concerns the law's "actual impact."[135] Indeed, the court's confidence in *Fraser* as to section 15's systemic scope is arguably even greater than in *Andrews*. In *Andrews*, the court had "little difficulty" recognizing section 15's systemic capacity.[136] And, even more forcefully, the court had "no doubt" in *Fraser* about recognizing "that adverse impact discrimination 'violate[s] the norm of substantive equality.'"[137]

The core idea of systemic discrimination transcending *Andrews* and *Fraser* distills to how disproportionate harm "signal[s]" discrimination[138] (again, an analogy with critical race theory's miner's canary). The court in *Fraser* consequently brought renewed focus to the impact of law – that is, "the importance of looking 'at the results of a system.'"[139] In turn, the court in *Fraser* reaffirmed the same corollaries of equality's systemic character as those outlined in *Andrews*: namely, that discrimination does not require intent,[140] exhaustion,[141] or causation.[142]

Lastly, the court in *Fraser* reaffirms equality's positive character. To be fair, the majority rejects that its finding generates a "freestanding positive obligation" to "secure specific societal results such as the total and definitive eradication" of social hierarchy.[143] But there is ample space between an idyllic post-oppression society and inadequate attention to persisting racial hierarchy. And the majority's reasons fall comfortably within that space. The majority recognizes that the "*absence* of accommodation" can be discriminatory[144] – a corollary of which, of course, is that substantive equality, at times, demands accommodation's presence, a positive obligation. Indeed, the majority provides that "[l]aws which distribute benefits or burdens without accounting for [physical, economic, and social] differences ... are the *prime targets*" of systemic discrimination claims.[145] Further, by dismissing the dissenting concerns about legislative chilling effects relating to incremental efforts at reform,[146] the majority, likewise, outlines a vision of substantive equality that is capacious enough to not only forbid government conduct but, at times, *obligate* it. On this final point, Justice Abella pivotally observes that discrimination is "frequently a product of continuing to do things 'the way they have always been done.'"[147] This describes, unquestionably, a positive obligation on states to disrupt long-standing discriminatory inertias.

The Future: Strategic Implementation of Critical Race Equality

In her *Fraser* majority reasons, Justice Abella wrote one passage that is of particular importance to systemic racial advocacy. She holds that "[a]ddressing adverse impact discrimination can be among the 'most powerful legal measures available to disadvantaged groups in society to assert their claims to justice' ... Not only is such discrimination 'much more prevalent than the cruder brand of openly direct discrimination,' it often poses a greater threat to the equality aspirations of disadvantaged groups."[148] This passage should be interpreted as a signal of a viable judicial appetite for incorporating litigation in our systemic racial justice strategies. Our failure to see, and remedy, systemic discrimination is no mere oversight; rather, it is, in the court's perspective, a failure to use the *most powerful* legal response to the *most prevalent* contemporary form of discrimination. As leading critical race scholar Patricia Williams explains:

> So-called formal equal opportunity has done a lot but misses the heart of the problem: it put the vampire back in its coffin, but it was no silver stake. The rules may be colorblind, but people are not. The question remains, therefore, whether the law can truly exist apart from the color-conscious society in which it exists, as a skeleton devoid of flesh; or whether law is the embodiment of society, the reflection of a particular citizenry's arranged complexity of relations.[149]

Our Charter of whites has been such a skeleton devoid of flesh. For many years, we have had a substantive equality framework capable of demanding structural change in Canadian society. We must now put that framework to use at strategic sites of grave systemic disparity while being mindful of its limitations, including how the Crown – as a common defendant – will have asymmetric tactical advantages (for example, the ability to aggressively settle disputes verging towards systemically progressive precedents).[150]

Equality challenges pertaining to the structural conditions of Black and Indigenous people may strike some as outlandish, but they should not. Fundamentally, the condition of Black and Indigenous people is inextricable from legacies of oppression and dispossession. And as critical race scholar Ian Haney-López observes, calling such persisting legacies "racist" is no overstatement but rather "aims to evoke a sense of moral repugnance and social duty by vivifying the fundamental injustice of entrenched racial inequalities."[151]

There is, simply put, *nothing* outlandish in calling the status quo systemically racist when it clearly is by the court's own definition. Rather, what *is* outlandish is that, despite a constitutional commitment to substantive racial equality, many disparities for Black and Indigenous people are not only persisting but getting worse. Indigenous women are Canada's fastest-growing prison population.[152] And last year was the deadliest in the preceding four years for police shootings, with 48 percent of racially identified victims being Indigenous and 19 percent being Black.[153] To acknowledge these "persistent systemic disadvantages"[154] in a constitutional analysis of equality is not "activist"; just the opposite, it is ignoring these stark disparities that would reflect "the most unneutral"[155] of reasoning.

The law's capacity to remedy such inequities is, as Williams notes, fundamentally an ideological issue: "Whether something is inside or outside the marketplace of rights has always been a way of valuing it."[156] Indeed: "In the law, rights are islands of empowerment. To be un-righted is to be disempowered, and the line between rights and no-rights is most often the line between dominators and oppressed. Rights contain images of power, and manipulating those images, either visually or linguistically, is central in the making and maintenance of rights."[157] But the law's ideological character should not stop us from advancing systemic discrimination claims at strategic sites of inequality. The court acknowledged – in both *Andrews*[158] and *Fraser*[159] – how equality is innately political. And so, while the court's equality legacy has been bookended by British lawyers (*Andrews*) and women RCMP officers (*Fraser*), its extension elsewhere – for example, to criminal punishment (*Sharma* and *Turtle*) – requires, at the very least, lawyers who are willing to make a case to the court.[160]

That said, where and how should such cases be advanced? Two key passages from *Fraser* provide some guidance. First, Justice Abella held that "[i]f there are clear and consistent statistical disparities in how a law affects a claimant's group, I see no reason for requiring the claimant to bear the additional burden of explaining *why* the law has such an effect."[161] Criminal punishment and inequitable access to public housing, health care, and education all have such "clear and consistent statistical disparities" with respect to race. We are, therefore, living in the midst of pervasive and unaddressed racial discrimination – racial inequality that has, for too long, circumvented critical judicial examination.[162] I believe that this is, in large part, a consequence of our failure to interrogate the law's "relentlessly individualizing" instincts[163] – that is, "how the rhetoric of increased privatization, in response to racial issues, functions as the rationalizing agent of public unaccountability, and, ultimately, irresponsibility."[164]

Second, Justice Abella was unequivocal with her findings in *Fraser*: the association between gender and fewer or less stable working hours was "clear."[165] She had "no doubt" that the RCMP's denial of full pension benefits to job-sharing employees perpetuated sexist prejudice, despite the fact that, as Justices Brown and Rowe observed, job sharing was "designed to be ameliorative" and was voluntarily chosen by the participants.[166] Such firm findings should, absent a racist double standard, translate into successful racial justice advocacy, where the statistics are even greater, where amelioration is not credibly contemplated, where choice is even more superficial, and where subordination is only more severe – even fatal. While "[p]ension design choices have ... 'far reaching normative, political and tangible economic implications for women,'" the same is true with respect to the design of our criminal punishment system and public housing, health, and education for Indigenous and Black people in Canada.[167] To extend section 15 to these systems is not "utopian" but rather integral to the "ambitious" project of remedying substantive inequality.[168] This project, of course, cannot – and should not – rest solely with courts, but the courts, nonetheless, can play a positive role.

I conclude with Williams's call for progressive equality rights, nearly as old as the Charter – and set in America – yet just as urgent today for advocacy in Canada: "For blacks, then, the battle is not deconstructing rights, in a world of no rights; nor of constructing statements of need, in a world of abundantly apparent need. Rather the goal is to find a political mechanism that can confront the *denial* of need."[169] Critical race theory scholarship, *Andrews,* and *Fraser* all coalesce around a crucial idea: that litigation is – unavoidably – one such political mechanism for confronting that denial of need.

I do not think that we should rely solely, or even primarily, on the courts. On one hand, founding critical race scholar Derrick Bell argues that "abstract legal rights, such as equality, could do little more than bring about the cessation of one form of discriminatory conduct that soon appeared in a more subtle though no less discriminatory form."[170] On the other hand, leading movement-law scholars argue that legal strategies may be "an aspect of rather than a totality of a struggle" for social change.[171] They note, astutely in my view, that "the work of rights, like the work of any law, is not simply about what it does on paper, but what it does in practice, and how people deploy it with ongoing contests over the shape of the world."[172] As the opening quotes to this chapter illustrate, Canada's ongoing contest over systemic racism is rife with political apathy. The Charter is, thus, a nontrivial interlocutory mechanism. Specifically, it enables racial justice advocates to influence the dialogue between various actors – courts, legislatures, and the broader public – upholding white supremacy. With this in mind, I urge coalitions of scholars, lawyers, and organizers to recognize the viability of our Charter, too long a Charter of whites, as one of many tools for challenging unconstitutional state neglect and advancing systemic racial justice.

Notes

The author would like to thank Jonnette Watson Hamilton, Jennifer Koshan, Archana George, and Kate Puddister for helpful comments on earlier drafts of this chapter.

1   *Canadian National Railway Co v Canada (Canadian Human Rights Commission)*, [1987] 1 SCR 1114, 1139 [*Canadian National Railway Co*].

2   Amanda Connolly, "RCMP Head Says She's 'Struggling' with Definition of Systemic Racism for Force," Global News, June 10, 2020, https://globalnews.ca/news/7049595/brenda-lucki-rcmp-systemic-racism/.

3   Andrew Russell, "Erin O'Toole Won't Say Whether He Believes There Is Systemic Racism in Canada," Global News, August 30, 2020, https://globalnews.ca/news/7304475/erin-otoole-systemic-racism-canada/.

4   "Can You Hear Me Now? With Celina Caesar-Chavannes," *The Bad + Bitchy Podcast*, February 9, 2021, 47:33, http://tun.in/tk6v2u.

5   I use "colourblindness" in my introductory remarks because it is a well-known term in the context of a particular conversation about constitutional equality law, namely, whether courts should be neutral to or accommodating of racial difference in their assessment of discrimination claims (see notes 8 and 9 below). However, given the ableist connotations in criticisms of colourblindness *phrased as such* – that is, criticisms that associate "blindness" with negative traits, for example, ignorance – I otherwise refer to the term as "race evasiveness" (unless I am directly quoting from another scholar, in which case I maintain their use of "colourblindness"). For criticism of using the term "colourblindness" and, relatedly, preferring the phrase "colourevasiveness," see Subini Ancy Annamma, Darrell D. Jackson, and Deb Morrison, "Conceptualizing Color-Evasiveness: Using Dis/ability Critical Race Theory to Expand a Color-Blind Racial Ideology in Education and Society," *Race, Ethnicity and Education* 20, 2 (2017): 147. And for broader discussion of how disability metaphors invoking blindness can carry ambivalent connotations insofar as blindness can *also* be associated with positive traits, for example, impartiality, see Naomi Schor, "Blindness as Metaphor," *Differences* 11, 2 (1999): 84; Doron Dorfman, "The Blind Justice Paradox: Judges with Visual Impairments and the Disability Metaphor," *Cambridge Journal of International and Comparative Law* 5, 2 (2016): 275 and 277; Joshua Sealy-Harrington, "Embodying Equality: Stigma, Safety, and Clément Gascon's Disability Justice Legacy," *Supreme Court Law Review* 103 (2d) 197 (2021): 235–37.

6   My definition of "systemic racism" warrants brief elaboration. The Supreme Court first defined systemic discrimination as "discrimination that results from the simple operation of established procedures ... none of which is necessarily designed to promote discrimination." See *Canadian National Railway Co*, 1139. However, implicit in this definition is why discrimination would follow "from the simple operation of established procedures." And that *why* is the legacies of racial subordination I make explicit in my definition of systemic racism. See, generally, Khiara M. Bridges, *Critical Race Theory: A Primer* (New York: Foundation Press, 2019), 147–53; Jamelle Bouie, "What 'Structural Racism' Really Means," *New York Times*, November 9, 2021, https://www.nytimes.com/2021/11/09/opinion/structural-racism.html.

7   Annamma, Jackson, and Morrison, in "Conceptualizing Color-Evasiveness," define colour evasiveness as "the racial ideology of denying the significance of race" (154).

8   See, e.g., *Plessy v Ferguson,* 163 US 537, 559 (1896) (Harlan J, dissenting) [*Plessy*]; *Minnick v California Department of Corrections,* 452 US 105, 128 (1981) (Stewart J, dissenting); *City of Richmond v JA Croson Co,* 488 US 469, 521 (1989) (Scalia J, concurring); *Metro Broadcasting v FCC,* 110 S Ct 2997, 3028 (1991) (O'Connor J, dissenting) (citing *Arizona Governing Comm v Norris,* 463 US 1073, 1083 (1983)).

9 See, for example, Cheryl I. Harris, "The Story of *Plessy v. Ferguson:* The Death and Resurrection of Racial Formalism," in *Constitutional Law Stories,* ed. Michael Dorf (New York: Foundation Press, 2004), 187–230; Lani Guinier and Gerald Torres, *The Miner's Canary: Enlisting Race, Resisting Power, Transforming Democracy* (Cambridge, MA: Harvard University Press, 2002), 32–66; Kimberlé Williams Crenshaw, "Color Blindness, History and the Law," in *The House That Race Built,* ed. Wahneema Lubiano (New York: Vintage Books, 1998), 280–88; Jody David Armour, *Negrophobia and Reasonable Racism: The Hidden Costs of Being Black in America* (New York: New York University Press, 1997), 115–53; Charles R. Lawrence III, "The Id, the Ego, and Equal Protection: Reckoning with Unconscious Racism," *Stanford Law Review* 39, 2 (1987): 317.

10 See, for example, Jonnette Watson Hamilton and Jennifer Koshan, "Adverse Impact: The Supreme Court's Approach to Adverse Effects Discrimination under Section 15 of the Charter," *Review of Constitutional Studies* 19, 2 (2015): 194–95.

11 *Andrews v Law Society of British Columbia,* [1989] 1 SCR 143, 56 DLR (4th) 1 [*Andrews*]; *Fraser v Canada,* 2020 SCC 28 [*Fraser*]. By "most recent," I mean most recent as of the time of this chapter's initial drafting. Since then, the court has released two equality decisions: *Ontario (Attorney General) v G,* 2020 SCC 28 [*G*], and *R v CP,* 2021 SCC 19 [*CP*]. However, neither *G* nor *CP* purports to overturn *Fraser* (see *G,* paras 40–44, 47, 51, 69; *CP,* paras 56–57, 111, 141, 153, 167). Accordingly, this chapter is largely undisturbed by those reasons.

12 I acknowledge that the nature of indigeneity as a racial category is contested (see, for example, Sebastien Grammond, "Disentangling Race and Indigenous Status: The Role of Ethnicity," *Queen's Law Journal* 33, 2 (2008): 487). However, racial logics are nonetheless present in the context of Indigenous subordination. For example, Dr. Kim TallBear observed in a recent guest lecture in my "Race, Racism and the Law" course at the University of Ottawa how notions of "Red" people extend racial logics to Indigenous communities (see, generally, Bethany R. Berger, "Red: Racism and the American Indian," *UCLA Law Review* 56, 3 (2009): 591). Moreover, race, ethnicity, and indigeneity are all concepts that, depending on context, can do useful analytical work in disentangling our processes of identity, identification, and subordination (regarding race and ethnicity, see Ian F. Haney Lopez, "Retaining Race: LatCrit Theory and Mexican American Identity in *Hernandez v. Texas,*" *Harvard Latino Law Review* 2 (1997): 279). Lastly, irrespective of the ways in which racial ideas and Indigenous subordination intersect, the critical race scholarship I draw on promotes a progressive interpretation of systemic discrimination under s 15. For this reason, I apply that critical race lens to systemic discrimination against Black and Indigenous people in this chapter. However, I acknowledge that litigation relating to Indigenous people can be supplemented through alternative constitutional analyses, including those relating to treaty rights and ss 25 and 35 of the Charter. See, for example, Sonia Lawrence and Debra Parkes, "*R v Turtle:* Substantive Equality Touches Down in Treaty 5 Territory," *Criminal Reports,* 7th ser, 66 (2020): 439.

13 Many other provisions of the Charter can, of course, promote systemic racial justice. But this chapter considers s 15 alone – in part because of the extent to which the court has been particularly silent on matters of substantive racial equality under that provision.

14 Neil Gotanda, "A Critique of Our Constitution Is Color-Blind," *Stanford Law Review* 44, 1 (1991): 1.

15 *Ibid,* 37.

16 *Ibid,* 43, 44n175.

17 *Ibid,* 44.

18 *Ibid.* By "racial capitalism," I mean the ways in which capitalism inherently deploys logics of difference to rationalize disparities. See Robin D.G. Kelley, "What Did Cedric

Robinson Mean by Racial Capitalism?," *Boston Review,* January 12, 2017, http://bostonreview. net/race/robin-d-g-kelley-what-did-cedric-robinson-mean-racial-capitalism.

19 Gotanda, "A Critique," 45. See also 63.

20 *Ibid,* 5.

21 *Ibid,* 6.

22 *Ibid,* 38, citing *Plessy.*

23 *Ibid,* 9–10, citing Herbert Wechsler, "Toward Neutral Principles of Constitutional Law," *Harvard Law Review* 73 (1959): 1.

24 Gotanda, "A Critique," 28. See, generally, Haney Lopez, "Retaining Race."

25 Gotanda, "A Critique," 34.

26 On the necessary imprecision of constitutional equality analysis, see, generally, Joshua Sealy-Harrington, "The Alchemy of Equality Rights," *Constitutional Forum* 30, 2 (2021): 53. On the necessary imprecision of race, see, generally, Ian F. Haney Lopez, "The Social Construction of Race: Some Observations on Illusion, Fabrication, and Choice," *Harvard Civil Rights–Civil Liberties Law Review* 29, 1 (1994): 1.

27 Gotanda, "A Critique," 2.

28 *Ibid,* 2–3. See also 18.

29 *Ibid,* 7, 51.

30 *Ibid,* 23.

31 *Ibid,* 46, 47n184.

32 See Macfarlane, Chapter 2 in this volume, 48.

33 *Ibid,* 21n87, citing Peter Westen, "The Meaning of Equality in Law, Science, Math, and Morals: A Reply," *Michigan Law Review* 82 (1983): 608.

34 *Ibid,* 16.

35 *Ibid,* 20.

36 *Ibid,* 3.

37 *Ibid,* 63.

38 *Ibid,* 45n178, citing Kimberlé Williams Crenshaw, "Forward: Toward a Race-Conscious Pedagogy in Legal Education" *National Black Law Journal* 11 (1989): 1, 3.

39 *Ibid,* 3n4, citing Patricia Williams, "The Obliging Shell: An Informal Essay on Formal Equal Opportunity," *Michigan Law Review* 87 (1989): 2129–30.

40 In Canada, Sonia Lawrence likewise starts from the perspective of undeniable racial subordination: "I start this paper with the proposition that we live in a society that is deeply shaped by racism and the colonial project." See Sonia Lawrence, "'The Admittedly Unattainable Ideal': Adverse Impact and Race under Section 15," in Law Society of Upper Canada, *Special Lectures 2017: Canada at 150 – The Charter and the Constitution* (Toronto: Irwin Law, 2017), 547.

41 Gotanda, "A Critique," 45n178.

42 *Ibid,* 15n69.

43 See, for example, *ibid,* 40, where he notes that "racial categories describe *relations* of oppression and unequal power" (emphasis added) such that "[i]t is unnecessary ... to have individual Negroes demonstrate that they have been victims" (citing *Bakke v Regent of University of California,* 438 US 265 (1977), 400 (Marshall J, dissenting).

44 See, for example, Gotanda, "A Critique," 45, where he describes "particular manifestations of racial subordination" such as "substandard housing, education, employment, and income for large portions of the Black community" not as "isolated phenomena" but rather as "aspects of the broader, more complex phenomenon called race."

45 Guinier and Torres, *Miner's Canary,* 57.

46 Gotanda, "A Critique," 5 (emphasis deleted), 15.

47 *Ibid,* 7.

48 *Ibid*, 13.

49 *Ibid*.

50 *Ibid*, 13. On the absence of race consciousness undergirding Canada's policy failure in counteracting racial inequality, see, generally, Keith Banting and Debra Thompson, "The Puzzling Persistence of Racial Inequality in Canada," *Canadian Journal of Political Science* 1 (2021).

51 David Tanovich, "The Charter of Whiteness: Twenty-Five Years of Maintaining Racial Injustice in the Canadian Criminal Justice System," *Supreme Court Law Review*, 2nd ser, 40 (2008): 657.

52 See Lawrence and Parkes, "*R v Turtle*," 430; Lawrence, "Adverse Impact," 548.

53 On my review, there are no Supreme Court judgments explicitly addressing anti-Black racism under s 15 of the Charter. Many thanks to Power Law students Jennifer Rogers, Léa Desjardins, and Chris Casimiro for their research assistance on this particular issue. That said, the court has addressed "anti-Black racism" under other Charter provisions – for example, concerning jury impartiality under s 11(d) (see, for example, *R v Spence*, 2005 SCC 71, paras 31–32) and concerning "disproportionate" policing of "racial minorities" under s 9 (see, e.g., *R v Le*, 2019 SCC 34, para 90; *R v CP*, 2021 SCC 19, paras 88–89).

54 *Fraser*, para 136.

55 *R v Kapp*, 2008 SCC 41, para 3.

56 In addition, Sonia Lawrence argues that *Kapp* was not even properly considered under s 15 in any event. See Sonia Lawrence, "*R v Kapp*," *Canadian Journal of Women and Law* 30, 2 (2018): 274.

57 2015 SCC 28, 128.

58 See, for example, Cynthia Petersen, "Institutionalized Racism: The Need for Reform of the Criminal Jury Selection Process," *McGill Law Journal* 38 (1993): 147; Ebyan Abdigir, Kvesche Bijons-Ebacher, Palak Mangat, Robert Cribb, and Jim Rankin, "How a Broken Jury List Makes Ontario Justice Whiter, Richer and Less Like Your Community," *Toronto Star*, February 16, 2018, https://www.thestar.com/news/investigations/2018/02/16/how-a-broken-jury-list-makes-ontario-justice-whiter-richer-and-less-like-your-community.html.

59 *R v Kokopenace*, 2015 SCC 28, paras 17, 28.

60 *Ewert v Canada*, 2018 SCC 30, paras 79, 91.

61 See note 53, above.

62 Other examples of jurisprudence considering s 15 of the Charter in the context of Indigenous people include *Corbiere*, [1999] 2 SCR 203; *Lovelace v Ontario*, [2000] 1 SCR 950; *Ermineskin Indian Band v Canada*, 2009 SCC 9; *Alberta v Cunningham*, 2011 SCC 37; *Kahkewistahaw First Nation v Taypotat*, 2015 SCC 30; *R v Barton*, 2019 SCC 33.

63 On what that repair could actually entail, see, generally, Yellowhead Institute, "Land Back: A Yellowhead Institute Red Paper," October 2019, https://redpaper.yellowheadinstitute.org/wp-content/uploads/2019/10/red-paper-report-final.pdf; Yellowhead Institute, "Cash Back: A Yellowhead Institute Red Paper," May 2021, https://cashback.yellowheadinstitute.org/wp-content/uploads/2021/05/Cash-Back-A-Yellowhead-Institute-Red-Paper.pdf.

64 See, for example, Graham Slaughter, "Five Charts That Show What Systemic Racism Looks Like in Canada," CTV News, June 4, 2020, https://www.ctvnews.ca/canada/five-charts-that-show-what-systemic-racism-looks-like-in-canada-1.4970352.

65 See, for example, Ontario Human Rights Commission, "A Disparate Impact: Second Interim Report on the Inquiry into Racial Profiling and Racial Discrimination of Black Persons by the Toronto Police Service," August 2020, 2.

66 See, for example, *ibid*, 8.

67 See, for example, Anthony Morgan, "Black Canadians and the Justice System," *Policy Options*, May 8, 2018, https://policyoptions.irpp.org/magazines/may-2018/black-canadians-justice-system/.

68 See, for example, Ontario Human Rights Commission, *To Dream Together: Indigenous People and Human Rights Dialogue Report*, September 2018, 37–43.

69 See, for example, Cindy Blackstock and Pamela Palmater, "Canada's Government Needs to Face Up to Its Role in Indigenous Children's Deaths," *The Guardian*, July 8, 2021, https://www.theguardian.com/commentisfree/2021/jul/08/canada-indigenous-children-deaths-residential-schools.

70 As Patricia Williams explains, the "rights/needs" dichotomy is one of many through which jurisprudence "purport[s] to make life simpler in the face of life's complication." See Patricia Williams, *The Alchemy of Race and Rights* (Cambridge, MA: Harvard University Press, 1991), 8.

71 *Andrews v Law Society of British Columbia*, [1989] 1 SCR 143 [*Andrews*].

72 *Ibid*, 158.

73 *Ibid*, 151.

74 *Ibid*, 193.

75 *Ibid*, 159.

76 That said, citizenship is, of course, a historical and contemporary marker of racial hierarchy. See, generally, Harsha Walia, *Border and Rule: Global Migration, Capitalism, and the Rise of Racist Nationalism* (Chicago: Haymarket Books, 2021).

77 *Andrews*, 171.

78 *Ibid*, 169, 171.

79 *Ibid*, 171.

80 *Ibid*, 164; "a protean word," citing John H. Schaar, "Equality of Opportunity and Beyond," in *Nomos IX: Equality*, ed. J. Roland Pennock and John W. Chapman (New York: Atherton Press, 1967), 228.

81 *Ibid*, 168. Indeed, as I have argued, a "clear legal test for equality is impossible." See Sealy-Harrington, "The Alchemy of Equality Rights," 53.

82 *Andrews*, 171, citing *Reference re an Act to Amend the Education Act* (1986), 53 OR (2d), 554 [*Re Education*].

83 *Andrews*, 164, citing Schaar, "Equality of Opportunity."

84 *Ibid*, 171, citing *Re Education*.

85 *Ibid*, 164. To be clear, substantive equality is not explicitly named in *Andrews* (indeed, it was not invoked by the court until its 1998 decision in *Eldridge* (see Lawrence, "Adverse Impact," 194n16). But its meaning – that is, prohibiting "subordinating treatment" of "already suffering" groups (*ibid*, 193–94) – is reflected in the court's reasons in *Andrews*.

86 *Andrews*, 168, citing *Mahe v Alta (Government)* (1987), 54 Alta LR (2d), 244.

87 *Andrews*, 173.

88 *Ibid*.

89 *Ibid*, 174.

90 I say the court equated "adverse effect" and "systemic" discrimination because it provides similar definitions for them. Specifically, it defines adverse effect discrimination as "where an employer ... adopts a rule or standard ... which has a discriminatory effect upon a prohibited ground on one employee or group of employees in that it imposes, because of some special characteristic of the employee or group, obligations, penalties, or restrictive conditions not imposed on other members of the work force" (*Andrews*, 173, citing *Ontario Human Rights Commission v Simpson-Sears*, [1985] 2 SCR, 551 [*Simpson-Sears*]). Similarly, it defines systemic discrimination as "practices or attitudes that have, whether by design or impact, the effect of limiting an individual's or a group's right to

the opportunities generally available because of attributed rather than actual character-istics" (*Andrews*, 174, citing *Canadian National Railway Co*, 1138–39, citing Canada, Royal Commission on Equality in Employment, *Report of the Commission on Equality in Employment* (Ottawa: Supply and Services Canada, 1984), 2). Lastly, the court passively references both definitions as reflecting a consistent idea about discrimination: "There are many other statements which have aimed at a short definition of the term discrimination. In general, they are in accord with the statements referred to above" (*Andrews*, 174).

91 *Andrews*, 174.

92 *Ibid*, 173.

93 *Ibid*, citing *Simpson-Sears*, 547.

94 *Ibid*, 165.

95 *Ibid*, 173.

96 *Ibid*, 167.

97 *Ibid*, 170, citing *Bliss v Attorney General of Canada*, [1979] 1 SCR, 190 [*Bliss*].

98 *Andrews*, 170, citing *Bliss*, 192.

99 *Andrews*, 177–78.

100 *Ibid*, 182.

101 *Ibid*, 178, contrasting Canadian law with law under the *European Convention on Human Rights*, described in *Belgian Linguistic Case (No 2)* (1968), 1 EHRR, 284.

102 *Andrews*, 178.

103 *Ibid*, 171, citing *Re Education* (emphasis added).

104 *Andrews*, 169.

105 *Ibid*, 164, citing *Dennis v United States*, 339 US 162 (1950), 184.

106 *Andrews*, 172.

107 *Ibid*, 169.

108 *Ibid*, 165, citing *R v Big M Drug Mart Ltd*, [1985] 1 SCR 295, 347.

109 *Andrews*, 167–68, discussing the court's decision in *Bliss*.

110 *Andrews*, 163–64.

111 *Ibid*, 164.

112 *Ibid*.

113 *Ibid*, 173, citing *Simpson-Sears*.

114 *Fraser*, para 3. For elaboration on the Charter and the RCMP, see Roach, Chapter 12 in this volume.

115 See, for example, Brandi Morin, "As the RCMP Deny Systemic Racism, Here's the Real History," *Toronto Star*, June 11, 2020, https://www.thestar.com/opinion/contributors/2020/06/11/rcmp-deputy-commissioners-words-on-racism-fly-in-face-of-150-years-of-history-and-pain-for-indigenous-peoples.html; Robyn Maynard, "Police Abolition/Black Revolt," *Canadian Journal of Cultural Studies* 41 (2020): 70–78; M. Gouldhawke, "A Condensed History of Canada's Colonial Cops," *The New Inquiry*, March 10, 2020, https://thenewinquiry.com/a-condensed-history-of-canadas-colonial-cops/.

116 *Fraser*, para 27.

117 *Ibid*, para 136.

118 *Ibid*, para 82.

119 *Ibid*, para 76.

120 *Ibid*.

121 *Ibid*, paras 42 and 57, citing *Withler v Canada (Attorney General)*, 2011 SCC 12, para 43.

122 *Fraser*, para 113, citing Elizabeth Shilton, "Gender Risk and Employment Pension Plans in Canada," *Canadian Labour and Employment Law Journal* 17 (2013): 140, citing Bernd Marin, "Gender Equality, Neutrality, Specificity and Sensitivity – and the Ambivalence of Benevolent Welfare Paternalism," in *Women's Work and Pensions: What Is Good, What*

Is Best? – Designing Gender-Sensitive Arrangements, ed. Bernd Marin and Eszter Zólyomi (Farnham, UK: Ashgate, 2010), 210.

123 *Fraser,* para 1.
124 *Ibid,* paras 1, 34, 76, and 88 (citing *Quebec (Attorney General) v A,* 2013 SCC 5, para 342 [*Quebec v A*]).
125 *Fraser,* paras 1, 34, 57, 76, and 88 (citing *Quebec v A,* para 342).
126 *Fraser,* paras 1 and 76.
127 *Ibid,* paras 34, 57, and 76.
128 *Ibid,* para 57.
129 *Ibid,* para 76.
130 *Ibid,* para 48, citing *Withler,* para 64.
131 *Fraser,* 48.
132 *Ibid,* citing *Withler,* para 62.
133 *Fraser,* para 93.
134 *Andrews,* 168, citing *Mahe,* 244.
135 *Fraser,* para 42, citing *Withler,* para 43.
136 *Andrews,* 173–74.
137 *Fraser,* para 47, citing *Withler,* para 2.
138 *Andrews,* 174, citing *CN Railway,* 1138–39, citing Royal Commission on Equality in Employment, *Report,* 2; *Fraser,* para 39, citing *CN Railway,* 1138–39, citing Royal Commission on Equality in Employment, *Report,* 2.
139 *Fraser,* para 39.
140 *Ibid,* para 69.
141 *Ibid,* para 72.
142 *Ibid,* paras 70–71 and 132–33.
143 *Ibid,* para 132.
144 *Ibid,* para 54 (emphasis in original).
145 *Ibid,* para 34 (emphasis added).
146 *Ibid,* paras 132–33.
147 *Ibid,* para 31.
148 *Ibid,* para 35 (citations omitted).
149 Patricia Williams, *The Alchemy of Race and Rights* (Cambridge, MA: Harvard University Press, 1991), 120.
150 Lawrence and Parkes, "*R v Turtle,*" 444.
151 Ian Haney-Lopez, "Post-racial Racism: Racial Stratification and Mass Incarceration in the Age of Obama," *California Law Review* 98, 3 (2010): 1071–72.
152 Geraldine Malone, "Why Indigenous Women Are Canada's Fastest Growing Prison Population," VICE, February 2, 2016, https://www.vice.com/en/article/5gj8vb/why -indigenous-women-are-canadas-fastest-growing-prison-population.
153 Kelly Geraldine Malone, Meredith Omstead, and Liam Casey, "Police Shootings in 2020: The Effect on Officers and Those They Are Sworn to Protect," CBC News, December 21, 2020, https://www.cbc.ca/news/canada/manitoba/police-shootings-2020-yer-review -1.5849788.
154 *Fraser,* para 42.
155 Charles L. Black Jr., "The Lawfulness of the Segregation Decisions," *Yale Law Journal* 69, 3 (1960): 421, 427.
156 Sealy-Harrington, "The Alchemy of Equality Rights," 227.
157 *Ibid,* 233–34.
158 *Andrews,* 164, citing Schaar, "Equality of Opportunity," 228.

159 *Fraser,* para 113, citing Shilton, "Gender Risk and Employment Pension Plans," 140, cit-
     ing Marin, "Gender Equality, Neutrality, Specificity and Sensitivity," 210.
160 *R v Sharma,* 2020 ONCA 478, para 67; *R v Turtle,* 2020 ONCJ 429, para 105.
161 *Fraser,* para 63.
162 *Ibid,* para 92, citing Diana Majury, "Women Are Themselves to Blame: Choice as a Jus-
     tification for Unequal Treatment," in *Making Equality Rights Real: Securing Substantive
     Equality under the Charter,* ed. Fay Faraday, Margaret Denike, and M. Kate Stephenson
     (Toronto: Irwin Law, 2006), 219.
163 Lawrence and Parkes, "*R v Turtle,*" 444.
164 Sealy-Harrington, "The Alchemy of Equality Rights," 47. Margot Young put this aptly in
     her oral remarks on a recent *Fraser* panel hosted at the UBC Peter A. Allard School of
     Law: "[T]his neoliberal idea of the self-biographizing individual who deserves to suffer."
     See "*Fraser v Canada*: 20/20 Vision on Equality?" (paper presented at Centre for Femi-
     nist Legal Studies, Peter A. Allard School of Law, October 30, 2020), 1:03:57, https://ubc.
     zoom.us/rec/play/aV2hcz8czxDVGoG8szx6vjF_MwaHZlXCZ4UypKncxVunXgo6K7
     GJJTTM_56ow_CKyGBz3WUwhKIRCOsy.NPggAPapXrC9ceXl?continueMode=true.
165 *Fraser,* para 106.
166 *Ibid,* para 108, 146, 197.
167 *Ibid,* para 113.
168 *Ibid,* para 136.
169 Sealy-Harrington, "The Alchemy of Equality Rights," 152.
170 Derrick Bell, "Racial Realism," *Connecticut Law Review* 24, 2 (1992): 373.
171 Amna A. Akbar, Sameer M. Ashar, and Jocelyn Simonson, "Movement Law," *Stanford
     Law Review* 73 (2021): 855.
172 *Ibid.*

14

Canada's Sex Problem
Section 15 and Women's Rights

Kerri A. Froc

IN 1949, SIMONE de Beauvoir asked the question, "What is a woman?" She is often quoted for stating, in reply, "One is not born, but rather becomes, a woman."¹ Yet it would be incorrect to assume that what she meant by this is that womanhood is entirely socially constructed. What she meant, rather, is that the conception of what "woman is" is overdetermined by patriarchal enforcement of the sexual hierarchy, which, by necessity, casts woman as Other. An accurate interpretation of what she meant, and the complexity of the interaction of sex and "gendering" in the construction of identity, lies at the centre of the current "sex problem" Canada faces in its jurisprudence under section 15 of the *Canadian Charter of Rights and Freedoms*.²

De Beauvoir argued that "the division of the sexes is a biological fact, not a moment in human history," yet "biological and social sciences no longer believe there are immutably determined entities that define given characteristics like those of the woman."³ We have come to recognize that gender is socially constituted, either in whole or in part – one is recognized as being of a particular gender, at least in part, by engaging in gendered practices, namely, those that society normatively considers "makes a woman a woman" or "a man a man" (like having children or being a breadwinner, respectively). However, "sex" (e.g., anatomy, chromosomes) is related to gendered practices in that males or females disproportionately engage in them. Judith Butler, one of the most famous theorists for suggesting that, in fact, gender – and *also* sex – is socially constituted, notes that not "all gendered possibilities are open" and there are "limits ... predicated on binary structures" of hegemonic cultural discourse; accordingly, gender is not "a set of free floating attributes."⁴ Consequently, individuals "perform" gender by either conforming to or resisting normative sex roles ascribed to them that are institutionally shaped (including by law). The push-pull of women undertaking the majority of caregiving is an example of such a gendering practice, arising due to socialization, economic structures that devalue "women's work" as a "labour of love" (and not economic reward), wage discrimination, cultural tropes associating mothering with hands-on care, legal incentives (such as income splitting in the *Income Tax Act*),⁵ and so forth.

According to Carol Smart, law itself "is gendered" because it "insists on a specific version of gender differentiation ... [It is] a process of producing fixed gender identities ... and at the same time [they are] naturalized."[6] Building on Smart's work, Joanne Conaghan reiterates that it would be a mistake to regard law as being a mere reflection of social gendering: it has "disciplinary effects on actual social relations by normatively re-inscribing certain patterns of sexed and gendered behaviour ... [L]aw is a gendering practice, that is, it acts ... to constrain and enable particular conceptions of gendered identity, behaviour, and selfhood."[7] Conaghan focuses on law's insistence on a rigid sex binary as its primary contribution to gendering constitutional rights.[8]

These gendering effects are not benign. In the process of calcifying masculinity and femininity into a binary set of stable, inherent traits, (constitutional) law also hierarchically orders them with hegemonically masculine traits at the apex. By now, the binaries mapping onto the sex binary are so well known as to be almost apocryphal: subject-object, public-private, strength-weakness, dependence-independence, mind-body, reason-emotion,[9] justice-care,[10] nature-civilization, abstract-concrete, active-passive, and so on.

What this chapter attempts to answer is not "What is a woman?" but "What does the Supreme Court of Canada conceive a woman to be?" Or, perhaps, "What does it see as the 'sex' element of sex discrimination?" These are questions to which the court has only begun meaningfully to attend, though there are hopeful gestures towards a more complex understanding of sex/gender(ing) in cases such as *Fraser v Canada*.[11] Its past attempts have conceptualized sex as being rooted almost entirely in inherent biological characteristics, with the result that courts have seldom recognized women's legal subordination as section 15 sex-equality violations. Only in 2018 did a female claimant finally win a Supreme Court of Canada Charter sex-discrimination case.

Concerning Charter sex-discrimination cases in the lower courts, even though the "patriation generation" anticipated that "women" would be the ones to make section 15 sex-discrimination claims almost exclusively, men initially made more of such claims overall, and more successful ones at that. In aggregate, men's claims were/are primarily to challenge laws that actually or are perceived as protecting women as a (biological) sex class. Women's claims primarily challenged laws adversely affecting them as a result of their gendered conduct, which may or may not have been considered by courts as sufficiently linked to their biological sex. Given the biologically based understanding of sex discrimination fostered by the Supreme Court, it is unsurprising, therefore, that, cumulatively, women's sex-discrimination claims to date have not been significantly more successful than men's. My data analysis indicates that women's success rate for sex-discrimination cases at all levels of court is 28 percent versus men's success rate of 26 percent.[12]

In a post-Charter legal landscape, seldom do contemporary laws explicitly make distinctions based on biological sex; instead, they make "neutral" distinctions that map onto gendered practices such as occupational segregation, caregiving and part-time work, or sexual assault. The underlying conceptual frame is that what men and women "do" is entirely separable from "who they are," contrary to our growing social understanding of the interrelationship between the two. Only the latter is a basis for constitutional protection because the moral wrong of discrimination is "impos[ing] a disadvantage on a person by reason of a characteristic that is outside the person's control."[13]

US legal theorist Kathrine Franke observed nearly three decades ago, in relation to American sexual equality jurisprudence, "biology is both a wrong and dangerous place to ground antidiscrimination law because it fails to account for the manner in which every sexual biological fact is meaningful only within a gendered frame of reference."[14] Similar to Franke, I maintain that the problem with Canadian Charter sex-equality jurisprudence is the "disaggregation" of sex and gender. However, it is not simply that the law is focusing on the wrong element from this dyad (sex rather than gender). The converse, a failure to recognize sex in favour of gender(ing) may lead us back down the road of *Bliss,* where, under the *Canadian Bill of Rights,* the Supreme Court of Canada refused to recognize pregnancy discrimination in unemployment insurance eligibility as sex discrimination against women, maintaining that the law was simply making distinctions between pregnant and nonpregnant people.[15] As I will argue, a complete sex-equality analysis requires accounting for both sex and gendered behaviour holistically.

Accordingly, my thesis is that for Canada to move closer to achieving sex equality, section 15 doctrine must recognize as sex discrimination any state-imposed inequality arising from a person's biological sex, the manner in which they practise gender (either by transgressing gender norms or performing devalued, feminized activities), or both in combination.

In what follows, I will provide an overview of the Supreme Court's treatment of sex/gender as well as its notable Charter sex-discrimination cases that demonstrate these aforementioned tendencies. I provide a brief quantitative analysis of sex-discrimination cases at all levels of court from 1986 to the present showing a remarkably meagre win-loss ratio for women. Women's lack of success is a function of the courts' conceptualization of sex discrimination – as tightly linked to one's innate status as biologically male or female. Lastly, I argue that courts analyzing sex discrimination under section 15 should look to the law's contribution to and enforcement of normative gender roles and sexual hierarchy ("gendering") as its representative case. They should discard their past approach to laws that make sex-based distinctions: that they are either discriminatory because biology is *irrelevant* in the circumstances or not discriminatory because they *merely reflect* natural, biological difference.[16] This revised approach does more than affirm the bromide that courts abandon formalism in their equality analysis but in fact calls them to fundamentally re-examine the nature of inequality and how they recognize the state's contribution to it. I argue that *Fraser* represents a break from the latter as the court's dominant frame for sex discrimination and may play a helpful role in grounding a new sex-equality doctrine.

(The Supreme Court of) Canada's Sex Problem

In sex-discrimination cases (both under the Charter and in human rights legislation), the Supreme Court has tended to use "sex" and "gender" inter-changeably to refer to inherent characteristics differentiating men and women.[17] Even though it has not formally recognized a distinction, its jurisprudence implicitly sets gendered behavioural practices as distinct and separable from biological sex. It has been most responsive to sex-discrimination claims when the claims centre biology (e.g., discrimination that would not have occurred "but for" the status of being biologically male/female). Even then, such claims are deemed to involve discrimination only where the legislative distinctions are "irrational" or arbitrary.[18] According to this framework for sex discrimination, what is illicit is misattribution (thinking something is a sex-based characteristic when it is not, a.k.a. sex-based stereotyping) and/or visiting adverse conse-quences on someone based on biological sex, that is, an inherent characteristic they have little or no ability to control or change, where sex is irrelevant to the logic underlying the law. At its most basic level, it must be a status claim, not a behavioural or "gendered" one.

This construction of sex inequality has the effect of both exaggerating and underplaying human agency in the perpetuation of rigid, traditional sex roles and sexual hierarchy. It underplays human agency by implying that laws are capable of reflecting sexual difference in a mechanical fashion, rather than being complicit in constructing that difference. Laws do not spring forth from bio-logical difference fully formed – they require human intervention and creative choices as to what to make of sexual difference and, in doing so, engage in "making" sexual difference.

As well, this deployment of biological difference obscures the court's choices in identifying certain social and legal practices as natural reflections of biological sex versus cultural artifacts. Some early cases explaining women's exclusion from professions and politics as a function of their biological capacity baldly illustrate the courts' complicity in forging a connection: "The natural and proper timidity and delicacy which belongs to the female sex evidently unfits it for many of the occupations of civil life."[19] In the Canadian context, the Supreme

Court agreed in *Bliss* that any inequality between the sexes in the area of unemployment-insurance benefits was a result of "nature" and not legislation.[20]

The containment of sex discrimination within a biological frame also exaggerates human agency by attributing everything that a court is unwilling to connect to biological sex as a product of individual preferences or choice. For instance, in the 1986 Illinois District Court case *EEOC v Sears,* Judge John Nordberg ruled that the underrepresentation of women in high-commission sales positions was not due to disparate treatment but women's preferences: "Sears has proven ... that men and women tend to have different interests and aspirations regarding work, and that these differences explain in large part the lower percentage of women in commission sales jobs ... especially in the particular divisions with the lowest proportion of women selling on commission."[21] This was despite the "unmistakably masculine" profile of the "Big Ticket Salesman" provided in the manual telling managers what type of person to hire for a commission sales position, as well as the "temperament scale" on which prospective applicants were scored, with an emphasis on whether the applicant had a low-pitched voice, had been a member of a football team, or had partaken in hunting, wrestling, or boxing.[22]

In the Supreme Court of Canada's first case on section 15, *Law Society British Columbia v Andrews,* Justice McIntyre stated that equality was inherently comparative and deemed his approach to the discrimination analysis as the "enumerated or analogous grounds approach." This meant that "[d]istinctions based on personal characteristics attributed to an individual solely on the basis of association with a group will rarely escape the charge of discrimination, while those based on an individual's merits and capacities will rarely be so classed."[23] McIntyre J's majority dicta on section 15 required courts to consider whether a claimant had been denied equality based on an "irrelevant" characteristic,[24] which could (and has) produced American-style analytic equivalence that flattens difference among those who claim under a ground. In *R v Kapp*, the court maintained that *Andrews* provided "a template which subsequent decisions have enriched but never abandoned."[25]

Equality law's emphasis on immutability reinforces the legitimacy of grounding sex discrimination in biological status. In *Andrews,* Justice La Forest insisted (contrary to Justice Wilson's approach based on "discrete and insular minorities") that analogous grounds in section 15 needed to be characteristics "typically not within the control of the individual and, in this sense, [are] immutable."[26] Obviously, the inclusion of grounds such as religion posed some difficulties for this theory of equality. Rather than confronting this challenge, however, the Supreme Court instead incorporated the legal fiction of "constructive immutability" into the test of whether grounds were "analogous" to those enumerated.[27] It is only when a claimant is incapable of conforming to a standard either entirely or because change would come only with great personal difficulty that equality provides relief. The discriminatory treatment is then based on status, on "who they are." As Robert Leckey says, placing such an emphasis on immutability (and, accordingly, on status), "bespeaks a majoritarian presumption that 'they' (minorities) would choose to be like 'us' (the majority) if they could only help themselves." It is therefore an approach based on formalism, that is, on "anti-classification" rather than group-disadvantaging "anti-subordination."[28]

The court's acceptance of equality as inherently comparative and grounds-based produced in Canada different riptides and undercurrents as to whether formalism was to be favoured over a group-disadvantaging, antisubordination approach. In *R v Turpin*, Wilson J identified group disadvantage as forming part of the considerations under the section 15 discrimination analysis. She referred to the need to consider legislative distinctions in their "larger social, political and legal context" and whether recognizing them as discriminatory would "advance the purposes of s. 15 in remedying or preventing discrimination against groups suffering social, political and legal disadvantage in our society."[29] Less than a year after this decision, however, Justice McLachlin, in dissent in *R v Hess*, forcefully challenged *Turpin*'s implication that claimants should be required to demonstrate disadvantage or that they be part of a "discrete and insular minority." She would have struck down Criminal Code section 146, which prohibited sexual exploitation of young girls by men. Wilson J did not insist on a contrary reading of her dicta in *Turpin* but stated she meant only that a distinction ought not to be considered discrimination automatically, because a court determining whether a distinction constitutes discrimination must also consider the larger "context."[30]

When she considered section 15 in *Hess*, Wilson J appeared to struggle with how to apply the earlier *Andrews* framework, particularly the close affiliation between grounds and discrimination mediated by as-yet-to-be developed contextual factors. She wished to evade the "rigid formalism" of a narrow application of the *Andrews* "grounds-based" approach, which could lead to a declaration that section 146(1) discriminated simply because it did not apply to women.[31] She resolved her quandary by focusing on the penetrative nature of the sexual act that composed the offence, ruling that criminal offences that "as a matter of biological fact can only be committed by one sex" do not violate section 15.[32] By constructing this element as the "core" of the offence, she was able to characterize sex between a woman and young males as a different matter entirely; whether this different act should be criminalized was "a policy matter best left to the legislature."[33] The lack of protection for underage males was also of no consequence in relation to the constitutionality of *this* provision, given that the legislature had decided that penetrative sex between males "should be dealt with separately" in another code section.[34] In echoes of *Bliss*, the fault lies in nature, not the law.

Weatherall carried on this theme of biological difference.[35] Male prisoners claimed that cross-gender frisk searches violated their section 15(1) rights, as female prisoners were not subject to them. Like *Hess*, the court's ruling is determined by biological difference, slightly augmented by consideration of social power relations. It noted: "Biologically, a frisk search or surveillance of a man's chest area conducted by a female guard does not implicate the same concerns as the same practice by a male guard in relation to a female inmate. Moreover, women generally occupy a disadvantaged position in society in relation to men ... [T]he effect of cross-gender searching is different and more threatening for women than for men."[36] The court could have easily made the same finding based on social meaning and behaviour alone – given women's sexualization and the social meaning of nonconsensual touching of women's breasts (and not men's chests), this was not an issue purely (or even primarily) about biological difference between secondary sex characteristics. Thus, the focus on biology was a distinct choice.

Symes v Canada was the Supreme Court's first opportunity to hear a sex-discrimination case advanced by a female litigant.[37] It upheld the nondeductibility of childcare from business income under the *Income Tax Act (ITA)* as a matter of statutory and constitutional interpretation.[38] Beth Symes maintained that the expenses for her nanny were critical to her ability to work the irregular hours required as a litigator and that either the *ITA's* business expense provisions required interpretation in accordance with Charter values to include childcare expenses or, alternatively, that they violated section 15(1).

The Federal Court of Appeal, foreshadowing the dissent in *Fraser*, questioned the propriety of using the Charter to challenge "socioeconomic legislation" and indicated that Symes's claim "risks trivializing the Charter."[39] The majority Supreme Court decision by Justice Iacobucci was more nuanced. Of note is that the court refused to consider having children as a purely individual "consumption choice," at least in relation to the statutory interpretation of "business expenses" under the *Income Tax Act's* section 18(1)(a). Characterizing the decision as a "choice" would be to ignore that "[p]regnancy and childbirth decisions are associated with a host of competing ethical, legal, religious, and socioeconomic influences."[40] So while the court rejected the notion that pregnancy and childbirth are purely "personal decisions," the court still conceptualized bearing children as a constructively immutable element of identity – it cannot be changed without great personal cost.

However, the contextual treatment of pregnancy and child-bearing contrasts with the description of working and caregiving in the majority's reasons under Charter section 15(1). Iacobucci J refers to the "discrete and insular minority" passage from *Andrews,* which he states is part of the contextual discrimination analysis.[41] This reference is curious in a case about sex discrimination and women, who experience subordination but are not a "minority," discrete, insular, or otherwise. Rather than simply being gratuitous, this reference is an organizing principle for the majority's determination of the impugned provision's constitutional compliance, highlighting a status, classification-based approach.

In deciding that there was no violation of section 15(1), the majority acknowledged the abundance of evidence that women disproportionately bear the "social costs" of childcare, but there was no evidence that they bear the economic costs. That the claimant paid all of the childcare in the case before the court was simply the result of a "family decision."[42] Iacobucci J indicated that the social costs, "although very real, exist outside of the Act."[43]

The court ignored the imperatives driving women's caregiving responsibilities through a confluence of systems – social (the sexual division of labour), economic (sex disparity in wages and occupational segregation), and legal (for example, a taxation system that rewards households following a stereotypical male breadwinner–female homemaker model and disincentivizes female employment).[44] All of these conspire together to structure responsibility for childcare in many two-income families – the question is often, "Does the female spouse earn enough to make the payment of childcare worthwhile?" The focus is very much on whether the woman's wage "pays for" the care, and by how much. Instead, the "gendering work" in the decision is done by abstract "social" forces and, more centrally, by the figure of Symes herself. Rebecca Johnson remarks that, in the case, "systemic blindness" causes the court to use the "rhetoric of choice ... to obscure the workings of power ... [It] uses power and participates in the construction of gender."[45]

Perhaps even more significant for my purposes is a nearly incomprehensible passage that comes later in the majority decision, where it muses about how a sex-discrimination case *could* have been successfully brought. Iacobucci J attempts to distinguish *Brooks* (pregnancy) and *Janzen* (sexual harassment), maintaining that in these two cases, only women could be subjected to the negative treatment at issue.[46] By contrast, men could also have caregiving expenses and be blocked from deducting them as business expenses by the *ITA*. However,

If a group or subgroup of women could prove the adverse effect required, the proof would come in a comparison with the relevant body of men. Accordingly, although individual men might be negatively affected by an impugned provision, those men would not belong to a group or sub-group of men able to prove the required adverse effect. In other words, only women could make the adverse effects claim, and this is entirely consistent with statements such as that found in *Brooks*, supra, to the effect that "only women have the capacity to become pregnant" (at p. 1242).[47]

The complexity and incoherence of this passage (which may obliquely refer to a potential claim by single mothers) is likely the result of the justices trying to "square the circle" between centring inherent biological characteristics in sex discrimination and still wanting to appear sensitive to the undeniable reality of deeply gendered social practices, such as childcare.

The next case, *Native Women's Association of Canada v Canada* (*NWAC*) shows the gendered "but for" logic underlying the conventional approach to sex discrimination.[48] The Native Women's Association of Canada unsuccessfully challenged the federal government's decision to exclude it from constitutional consultations surrounding the Charlottetown Accord and to fund only the participation of four national Indigenous groups, which, the NWAC alleged, were male-dominated. The claim asserted a violation of sex equality under sections 15 and 28 as well as freedom of expression.

The Supreme Court insisted that the NWAC's section 15 claim hinged exclusively on whether it could prove the groups were "male-dominated" and that the NWAC was more representative of women.[49] The evidentiary burden on the NWAC was to show a biological difference from the funded organizations in terms of the number of female bodies it could count within its organization and also to show that it differed in terms of an essentialized viewpoint of Indigenous women that it possessed but that the funded groups did not. In addition to its insistence on the NWAC establishing linkages between sex and political positions (rather than recognizing their ability to speak in their own voice as constitutive of their identity as Indigenous women), the court's decision, I argue, naturalized the association between hegemonic masculinity, voice, and leadership.[50]

In the two cases where men won their sex-discrimination cases, biology again triumphed, to the extent that the court equated biological distinctions with gendered, social disadvantage. In the first, *Benner v Canada (Secretary of State),*[51] the court perhaps can be forgiven for centring the sex-discrimination analysis on biological sex difference. It correctly found that requiring a security check of citizenship applicants who were children born abroad of Canadian mothers prior to 1977 (but not of those born abroad of Canadian fathers before the same date) constituted sex discrimination under section 15(1). The court explicitly made this finding because the law restricted citizenship "on the basis of something so *intimately connected to and so completely beyond the control of an applicant*" as the sex of a parent.[52] This biologically based discrimination allowed "the judges [to] 'see' the discriminatory nature of the entire scheme," which means "the rest of the legal analysis follow[ed] easily."[53]

No such forgiveness should be forthcoming for *Trociuk v British Columbia (Attorney General)*.[54] Trociuk claimed British Columbia's *Vital Statistics Act* violated section 15(1) by permitting mothers to mark fathers as "unacknowledged" on the birth registration, thereby allowing the mother alone to select the children's surname. His claim was based primarily on the biological distinction between "parents," as his experience fathering the children in question was limited. Trociuk and Reni Ernst had lived together for less than two years prior to the triplets' birth, and Ernst had separated from Trociuk when she became pregnant.

One needs to go back to the affidavits on the court record to uncover the abusive nature of Trociuk's behaviour towards Ernst, as it does not appear in the Supreme Court's narrative. Trociuk had seen the children only intermittently despite being granted regular access.[55] However, he brought numerous frivolous court applications (for example, seeking an order that Ernst's car be safety inspected), and he picketed Ernst's apartment complex.[56] Ernst details Trociuk's harassment of her over his not being acknowledged as the father on the birth certificate, his insistence that the children bear his surname, and her assessment that he was "primarily interested in control."[57] The court at one of the hearings also commented on his "obsessive nature."[58]

Unlike the aforementioned cases, *Trociuk* was decided under a different equality framework, one that modified the "grounds-based" approach. After *Andrews*, the Supreme Court of Canada split into three "camps" that each interpreted its dicta differently, and each approach received expression in the 1995 "trilogy" of equality cases: *Miron v Trudel*, *Egan v Canada*, and *Thibaudeau v Canada*.[59] The first camp, led by McLachlin J (as she then was) adopted a fairly conventional interpretation of *Andrews*, in which a distinction on a ground ordinarily constituted discrimination unless there was something in the circumstances that would cause judicial recognition of a violation to trivialize the equality guarantee. The second, a much narrower approach led by Justice Gonthier, would have rejected any claim of discrimination under section 15 where the distinction was "relevant to the legislative goal or the functional values underlying the impugned law." Lastly, an approach conceived by Justice L'Heureux-Dubé rejected grounds in favour of a group-disadvantage approach that ascertained whether the claimant group's human dignity had been violated, considering the vulnerability of the group and the seriousness of the law's impact.

The court revised the section 15 framework in 1999, in an attempt to integrate the aforementioned approaches. *Law v Canada* instituted a new requirement: to show discrimination, it was necessary for a section 15 claimant to demonstrate a violation of her human dignity.[60] Shifting the focus from grounds to "human dignity," Iacobucci J for the court provided a number of contextual factors to help guide the analysis. However, the factor the court said was "central" – "pre-existing disadvantage, stereotyping, prejudice, or vulnerability" – was only ever acknowledged in a perfunctory, "box-checking" fashion in subsequent cases. It never did work to inject a critical dose of reality into understandings of how oppression is experienced, into the "ineffable" question of whether and how a law violates "human dignity."[61] Instead, the factor upon which most cases turned was that of "correspondence ... between the ground ... and the actual need, capacity, or circumstances of the claimant."[62] As interpreted, the correspondence factor essentially reproduced the Gonthier "relevance" approach (despite its explicit rejection in the trilogy). It often permitted courts to indulge their own preconceived ideas about whether groups reasonably "deserved" negative treatment based on their difference, rather than conducting power-sensitive analyses of whether the impugned laws reinforced social hierarchy.

As *Trociuk* shows, the *Law* framework (which, ultimately, was replaced) also exacerbated the underlying tendency of the court to privilege an exclusively biological understanding of sex. It reduced the question of sex discrimination to whether the law was appropriately "sex blind" and, if not, whether it "merely" reflected natural difference (and thus "corresponded" to the claimants' needs or circumstances). Justice Deschamps, for the court, characterized the legislation allowing mothers to mark the father as "unacknowledged" and to select a child's surname as an "arbitrary exclusion of a father's particulars."[63] The fact that the father was not from a disadvantaged group was irrelevant in "logic and law."[64] She noted abstractly that "[p]arents have a significant interest in meaningfully participating in the lives of their children" and that including one's particulars on a birth registration as well as contributing to the determination of a child's surname are "significant mode[s] of participation in the life of a child."[65] Being excluded from a birth registration, she found, would send the signal that the legislature devalued fathers' relationships with children relative to that of mothers; she also found that grouping unjustifiably "unacknowledged" fathers together with those justifiably excluded, such as "rapists and perpetrators of incest," was "pejorative."[66] There could be a process to allow the latter to remain off birth certificates, without "exposing other fathers to the risk of arbitrary exclusion." Thus, the legislation violated section 15.

The case demonstrates the problem with a focus on biological status in section 15 rather than gendered relations of power and interactions among groups.

Distinctions based on biological sex are found to be "arbitrary" and discriminatory, without an analysis of how these distinctions operate in practice to counteract underlying disparities of power, particularly in relationships where biological fathers use their status to control and abuse mothers.[67]

Fraser's Difference

The majority decision in *Fraser v Canada* is a significant departure from these cases (see also Sealy-Harrington, Chapter 13 in this volume). It is the first successful sex-based adverse-effects claim under Charter section 15 and the second successful sex-discrimination case with women claimants (the first being *Alliance,* in 2018).[68] Joanne Fraser and her fellow appellants were among the small number of RCMP officers across Canada who took advantage of the force's "job-sharing" program, which permitted full-time members (mainly women with childcare responsibilities) to reduce their hours temporarily. However, unlike full-time members who were suspended, otherwise on leave without pay, or gradually reducing their hours in accordance with the pre-retirement transition leave policy, job sharers were not permitted to use their own money to buy back pension contributions that otherwise would have been made if they had maintained full-time hours. These members claimed that the lack of buy-back in the job-sharing program discriminated against them based on sex; the RCMP said that they were simply treated as other part-time employees.

Given so little jurisprudence on adverse effects in the section 15 context, Abella J took the opportunity to streamline and clarify how courts should identify adverse-effects discrimination (so that it qualifies as a "distinction" per the first leg of the section 15 test). She determined there was no onus on the claimants to engage in a "but for" analysis to show that any adverse effects proven by the evidence adversely affected a group *because* of sex. This potentially short-circuits the argument that succeeded in the *EEOC v Sears* case (that there are no adverse effects because claimants cannot refute that women self-select for less advantageous treatment because of their individual proclivities).

In outlining the new causation approach, the justice cited with approval Lisa Philipps and Margot Young's work dismantling the separation between inherent identity status and behaviour, recognizing that "individual traits, behaviours, choices or situations ... in social reality ... may be tightly linked to one group or another."[69] While members of the Supreme Court recognized this over twenty years ago in relation to sexual orientation,[70] the court continued to stumble over this divide when it came to gendered behaviour (as in *Symes*). All that is required, wrote Abella J, is evidence of the group's "full context," showing that "membership in the claimant group is associated with certain characteristics that have disadvantaged members of that group." While one can quibble with her phrasing of "characteristics" rather than (gendered) practices or behaviour, she quickly added that characteristics are both what people do and their bodily features.[71]

Additionally, Abella J reiterated that it is unnecessary for all members of the group to be adversely affected in the same way for a distinction based on adverse effects to be proven. She included both distinctions based on sex-based characteristics *and* gendered practices as examples of adverse effects that are non-inclusive of the entire group. She named past human rights decisions of the court in *Brooks* (recognizing that pregnancy discrimination is sex discrimination despite the fact that not all women become pregnant nor are they all pregnant at the same time) and *Janzen* (recognizing sexual harassment as sex discrimination) as the guiding cases.[72]

Justice Abella's "resurrecting" *Janzen* from the constitutional hinterlands is especially meaningful.[73] There, Dickson CJ tacitly acknowledged that the discriminatory harm of such behaviour concerns its stabilization and normalization of sexual hierarchy rather than being exclusively about distinctions based on "irrelevant" personal characteristics (as might be suggested in McIntyre J's interpretation of section 15 in *Andrews,* released three months before *Janzen*).[74] Despite the fact that men are occasionally sexually harassed, "'[s]exual harassment is a complex issue involving men and women, their perceptions and behaviour, and the social norms of the society' [citing Arjun P. Aggarwal] ... Aggarwal argues that sexual harassment is used in a sexist society to (at pp. 5–6): 'underscore women's difference from, and by implication, inferiority with respect to the dominant male group' and to 'remind women of their inferior ascribed status.'"[75] Abella J cited *Janzen* for its consideration of social relations in ascertaining a disproportionate impact, which means it does not precisely map onto biology. Men can also be harassed, especially if they exhibit feminine traits,[76] but sexual harassment has a particular gendered import in that it communicates women's (lack of) value.

Abella J's innovation in relation to comparison also results in an adverse-effects discrimination analysis focused more on the gendering effect of the law rather than arbitrary, sex-based treatment of individuals.[77] Comparing Fraser and colleagues first to other full-time members, she discounts the claimants' decision to job share as based on individual "choice" and natural inclination. This is both because "the fact that a person could avoid discrimination by modifying his or her behaviour does not negate the discriminatory effect" and that what may appear "natural" may be "social"; the "chosen" may, in fact, be "coerced."[78] Further, the justice also broadens the lens to compare women to men in the workplace, implying that working part-time or job sharing is *gendered* behaviour based both on who works part-time (women) and the reasons they do so (mainly childcare, given that women have "borne the overwhelming share of childcare responsibilities").[79]

The broader lens employed by Abella J continues in the second stage of the analysis, demonstrating that the law "has the effect of reinforcing, perpetuating or exacerbating disadvantage."[80] She points to the gendered nature of pension plans, historically "designed for middle and upper-income full-time employees with longer service, typically male."[81] The result is the "feminization of poverty." While the justice does not go much further than noting the economic consequences of the scheme, a logical correlative is the reinforcement of women's sex role as one of dependency, either on individual men or on the masculine state. Consequently, the claimants proved that the program perpetuated their disadvantage and therefore was discriminatory.

Conclusion

At the time of writing, Canada was still in the throes of the third wave of the COVID-19 pandemic. The toll that the pandemic took on women in particular put the frailty of judicial understandings of sex inequality into stark relief. More women than men in their prime working years (thirty to fifty-nine) have been diagnosed with COVID-19, which is likely reflective of their representation in the caring professions.[82] Furthermore, their male partners committed more – and more serious – domestic violence against them during stay-at-home orders.[83] They suffered more job losses from the pandemic, likely because of their over-representation in precarious employment and the service sector and because they left employment or had to reduce hours of paid employment due to children being at home.[84] It demonstrates more vividly than perhaps anything else the emptiness of the pre-*Fraser* approach to sex equality.

Justice Abella retired from the Supreme Court in 2021, and the sharply worded dissent by Justices Brown and Rowe in *Fraser* shows that there is a realistic possibility that the case represents not so much the turning of the page on a regressive sex-equality doctrine but a momentary reprieve. They ask the question, as if it bespeaks the obvious (no): "At one level, this appeal presents the simple question: is tying pension benefits to hours worked discriminatory?"[85] In their view, Abella J's approach penalizes the government because it "does not do enough" to remedy women's historical disadvantage, a matter that is inherently one of policy. Their approach is one that seeks to reinstate the division between sex and gendered behaviour. Much in the manner of *Symes*, they imply that job sharing may, instead, be explained by individual proclivities, even if they concede some link between sex and caregiving responsibilities:

[The majority's] analysis is unsound, since it assumes that correlation between the number of women who have taken advantage of the job-sharing program and evidence of disproportionate childcare responsibilities falling upon women is the function of *causation* ... [O]ne can readily assume that there are *many* factors involved, some of which will give rise to causation while others will simply be the result of coincidence (that is, caused by independent factors).[86]

In their view, the distinction is due to hours worked, comparing job-sharers to other part-timers and also to all those (whether full time or part time) who take a full leave without pay rather than job sharing. To them, the focus ought not to be on the gendered reinforcement of women's economic dependency and what this communicates regarding the value of their work. The dissenters search "in vain" for the moral wrong of arbitrary or unfair treatment and explicitly object to the "transformative" nature of Abella J's decision.[87] For her part, Justice Côté disaggregates sex and gender even further, denying any link between sex and parenting responsibilities.[88] She does so on the basis that "caregiving, unlike pregnancy, is not, *by definition,* associated with sex."[89] It is difficult to think of any judicial dicta that more directly confines sex to biological status.

Of course, one majority decision is not a "magic pill" that can solve Canada's sex problem. The problems are deeply seated and fundamentally concern how the law conceptualizes and naturalizes sex difference, how legal interpreters conceive of the moral wrong of inequality under the Charter, and perhaps most fundamentally, how we value women and what they have accomplished under disciplinary, gendered constraints primarily not of their making. Constitutional law making in the time of COVID may have at least one upside, namely, that it may provide some insight to members of the court that the "sex problem" evident in the jurisprudence is not women's problem. It is theirs.

Notes

1 Simone de Beauvoir, *The Second Sex*, trans. Constance Borde and Sheila Mallovany-Chevalier (New York: Vintage Books, 2011), 25, 330. Originally published in 1949 by Éditions Gallimard, Paris.
2 I use "gendering" here rather than "gender" to account for the fact that gender is less a static status than it is a process by which one's identity becomes associated with a particular gender as a result of the complex interaction of biological identifiers, one's own practices, culture, and social and legal practices, among others. *Canadian Charter of Rights and Freedoms,* Part I of the *Constitution Act, 1982,* being Schedule B to the *Canada Act 1982* (UK), 1982, c 11 [*Charter*].
3 De Beauvoir, *The Second Sex*, 25.
4 Judith Butler, *Gender Trouble: Feminism and the Subversion of Identity* (New York: Routledge, 1990), 12, 34.
5 See, for example, Kathleen Lahey, *Women and Employment: Removing Fiscal Barriers to Women's Labour Market Participation* (Ottawa: Status of Women Canada, 2005).
6 Carol Smart, "The Woman of Legal Discourse," *Social and Legal Studies* 1, 1 (1992): 36.

7 Joanne Conaghan, *Law and Gender* (Oxford: Oxford University Press, 2013), 104, citing Dorothy Chunn and Danielle Lacombe, eds., *Law as a Gendering Practice* (Toronto: Oxford University Press, 2000).

8 Gretchen Ritter, *The Constitution as Social Design: Gender and Civil Membership in the American Constitutional Order* (Palo Alto, CA: Stanford University Press, 2006).

9 Regarding its presence in legal culture, see Conaghan, *Law and Gender,* 95–97.

10 Carol Gilligan, *A Different Voice: Psychological Theory and Women's Development* (Cambridge, MA: Harvard University Press, 1982).

11 *Fraser v Canada (Attorney General),* 2020 SCC 28 [*Fraser*].

12 See Kerri Anne Froc, "Sex Discrimination Cases in Canada," https://doi.org/10.25545/2MZXoP, UNB, V1, Schedule "A": men's ratio of successful versus unsuccessful cases is twenty to fifty-six; women's ratio is twenty-eight to seventy-two. List last updated in April 2021. Thanks to my research assistants, Dominque Goguen and Nick Piccinin, who helped with compiling and updating this data.

13 Peter Hogg, *Constitutional Law in Canada* (Toronto: Thomson Reuters, online version updated to 2021), 55.8(b).

14 Katherine M. Franke, "Central Mistake of Sex Discrimination Law: The Disaggregation of Sex from Gender," *University of Pennsylvania Law Review* 144, 1 (1995): 99. Franke's insights helped provoke my findings of similar phenomena in the Canadian context.

15 *Bliss v Attorney General of Canada,* [1979] 1 SCR 183, 191 [*Bliss*].

16 Or perhaps, less commonly, the enforcement of the same treatment where biological difference is relevant.

17 See *Janzen v Platy Enterprises Ltd,* [1989] 1 SCR 1252; *Brooks v Canada Safeway Ltd,* [1989] 1 SCR 1219; *Symes v Canada,* [1993] 4 SCR 695 [*Symes*]; *Weatherall v Canada (Attorney General),* [1993] 2 SCR 872, *Gould v Yukon Order of Pioneers,* [1996] 1 SCR 571; *Benner v Canada (Secretary of State),* [1997] 1 SCR 358; *Newfoundland (Treasury Board) v NAPE,* 2004 SCC 66; *Centrale des syndicats du Québec v Quebec (Attorney General),* 2018 SCC 18 [*Centrale*]; *Quebec (Attorney General) v Alliance du personnel professionnel et technique de la santé et des services sociaux,* 2018 SCC 17 [*Alliance*]. The elision between sex and gender is also apparent in a number of other cases that do not concern sex discrimination.

18 One can see such ideas undergirding cases, from Justice McIntyre's reference to "irrelevant characteristics" in *Andrews* to Justice Abella's reference to "arbitrary" discrimination in *Kahkewistahaw First Nation v Taypotat,* 2015 SCC 30, before she entirely abandoned this notion in *Fraser*.

19 *Bradwell v The State,* 83 US 130 (1872), 141 per Bradley J (there, concerning whether the Fourteenth Amendment had been violated by the State of Illinois refusing to license Myra Bradwell to practise law).

20 *Bliss.*

21 *EEOC v Sears, Roebuck & Co,* 628 F Supp 1264 (ND Ill 1986), 1305.

22 Ruth Milkman, *On Gender, Labor, and Inequality* (Urbana: University of Illinois Press, 2016), 146–47.

23 *Law Society British Columbia v Andrews,* [1989] 1 SCR 143, 174–75, 179–80 [*Andrews*].

24 *Ibid,* 165. Colleen Sheppard, *Inclusive Equality: The Relational Dimensions of Systemic Discrimination in Canada* (Montreal/Kingston: McGill-Queen's University Press, 2010), 41–42.

25 *R v Kapp,* 2008 SCC 41, para 14 [*Kapp*].

26 *Andrews,* para 67.

27 *Corbiere v Canada (Minister of Indian and Northern Affairs),* [1999] 2 SCR 203.

28 Robert Leckey, "Chosen Discrimination," *Supreme Court Law Review* 18 (2002): 452, para 11.
29 *R v Turpin*, [1989] 1 SCR 1296, para 47.
30 *R v Hess; R v Nguyen*, [1990] 2 SCR 906, para 37 (per Wilson J) and paras 77–79 (per McLachlin J) [*Hess*].
31 *Ibid*, para 41.
32 *Ibid*, para 47.
33 *Ibid*, para 43.
34 *Ibid*, paras 43, 44.
35 *Weatherall.*
36 *Ibid*, para 6.
37 *Symes.*
38 *Income Tax Act*, RSC 1985 (5th Supp), c I-5.
39 *Symes*, para 24.
40 *Ibid*, para 78.
41 *Ibid*, para 116.
42 *Ibid*, paras 90, 132.
43 *Ibid*, para 135.
44 Christa Freiler, Felicite Stairs, and Brigitte Kitchen, with Judy Cerny, *Mothers as Earners, Mothers as Carers: Responsibility for Children, Social Policy and the Tax System* (Ottawa: Status of Women Canada, 2001), 29–31.
45 Rebecca Johnson, *Taxing Choices* (Vancouver: UBC Press, 2002), 1.
46 He selects a portion of *Janzen* referencing the fact that the heterosexual male sexual harasser in the specific case harassed only women. However, the Supreme Court in *Janzen* noted that men may also be harassed.
47 *Symes*, paras 148, 149.
48 *Native Women's Association of Canada v Canada (NWAC)*, [1994] 3 SCR 627.
49 Numerical representation is important but does not tell the whole story, considering the marginalization of women's participation within the larger Indigenous organizations: Joyce Green, "Constitutionalizing the Patriarchy: Aboriginal Women and Self-Government," *Constitutional Forum* 4, 4 (1993): 114; Kerri A. Froc, "Multidimensionality and the Matrix: Identifying Charter Violations in Cases of Complex Subordination," *Canadian Journal of Law and Society* 25, 1 (2010): 37.
50 Froc, "Multidimensionality and the Matrix," 45.
51 *Benner v Canada (Secretary of State)*, [1997] 1 SCR 358.
52 *Ibid*, para 85 (emphasis added).
53 Denise Réaume, "Discrimination and Dignity," *Louisiana Law Review* 63 (2003): 659n49.
54 *Trociuk v British Columbia (Attorney General)*, [2003] 1 SCR 835 [*Trociuk*].
55 *Ibid*, Darrell Trociuk's affidavit, 61–62, 86.
56 *Ibid*, 97, 88.
57 *Ibid*, Reni Ernst's affidavit, 167.
58 *Ibid.*
59 *Miron v Trudel*, [1995] 2 SCR 418; *Egan v Canada*, [1995] 2 SCR 513; *Thibaudeau v Canada*, [1995] 2 SCR 627.
60 *Law v Canada (Minister of Employment and Immigration)*, [1999] 1 SCR 497.
61 Later jurisprudence, beginning with *Kapp*, did away with the requirement to demonstrate a violation of human dignity. Instead, claimants were to focus on proving a law-perpetuated disadvantage through prejudice or stereotype. Abella J again was forced to "clarify" the *Kapp* framework in a later case, *Quebec (Attorney General) v A*, 2013 SCC 5, [2013] 1 SCR 61, para 330; she stated that the s 15 analysis could not be limited to the

perpetuation of prejudice or stereotype as this would impose an "ineffable" burden on claimants. To the extent that the correspondence factor required claimants to show that governments had no benign intent, the word "ineffable" accurately describes the burden on claimants throughout the 2000s.

62 *Ibid*, para 88.
63 *Trociuk*, para 1.
64 *Ibid*, para 20.
65 *Ibid*, paras 16 and 17.
66 *Ibid*, para 23.
67 Evan Stark discusses the phenomenon of "child abuse as tangential spouse abuse," which can take the form of "lengthy legal battles in which men who have shown little prior interest in their children's welfare demand custody or liberal visitation to continue their control": *Coercive Control: How Men Entrap Women in Their Personal Life* (New York: Oxford University Press, 2007), 251.
68 *Alliance* and its companion case, *Centrale*, are cases in which Abella J also wrote for the majority on s 15. They concerned pay-equity rights for women and contain traces of the same innovations that become more overtly expressed in *Fraser* (and thus, to avoid repetition, I focus my attention on the latter).
69 *Fraser*, para 34, citing Lisa Philipps and Margot Young, "Sex, Tax and the *Charter*: A Review of *Thibaudeau v. Canada*," *Review of Constitutional Studies* 2, 2 (1995): 258.
70 *Egan v Canada*, [1995] 2 SCR 513, 601, pr Cory J (in joint dissenting reasons written by him and Iacobucci J, with McLachlin J's concurrence) [*Egan*].
71 *Fraser*, para 57, citing *Ontario Human Rights Commission v Simpsons-Sears Ltd*, [1985] 2 SCR 536; *British Columbia (Public Service Employee Relations Commission) v BCGSEU*, [1999] 3 SCR 3.
72 *Brooks; Janzen.*
73 *Martin v Nova Scotia (Workers' Compensation Board)*, 2003 SCC 54, marks the last time the court cited *Janzen* in a Charter decision. Before *Fraser*, *Brooks* had never been cited in a Supreme Court of Canada Charter decision.
74 *Andrews.*
75 *Egan*, paras 49, 57.
76 Deborah Zalesne, "When Men Harass Men: Is It Sexual Harassment?," *Temple Political and Civil Rights Law Review* 7 (1998): 395, 397.
77 Abella J states specifically that there is no need for a claimant to prove that a distinction is arbitrary.
78 *Fraser*, para 89, citing Margot Young, "Blissed Out: Section 15 at Twenty," in *Diminishing Returns: Inequality and the Canadian Charter of Rights and Freedoms*, ed. Sheila McIntyre and Sanda Rodgers (Markham, ON: LexisNexis, 2006): 45, 55–56.
79 *Ibid*, para 98.
80 *Ibid*, para 76.
81 *Ibid*, para 108, quoting Royal Commission on the Status of Pensions in Ontario, *Report of the Royal Commission on the Status of Pensions in Ontario* (Toronto: The Commission, 1980).
82 Government of Canada, "COVID-19 Daily Epidemiology Update," updated May 9, 2021, https://health-infobase.canada.ca/covid-19/epidemiological-summary-covid-19-cases.html; Canadian Women's Foundation, "The Facts: Women and Pandemics," accessed May 9, 2021, https://canadianwomen.org/the-facts/women-and-pandemics/.
83 CBC News, "Violent Deaths of Women in Canada Increased in 2020, Study Finds," March 18, 2021, https://www.cbc.ca/news/canada/femicide-canada-1.5953953; A.L. Trudell and E. Whitmore, *Pandemic Meets Pandemic: Understanding the Impacts of*

Covid-19 on Gender-Based Violence Services and Survivors in Canada (Ottawa/London, ON: Anova/Ending Violence Association of Canada, 2020), http://www.anovafuture. org/wp-content/uploads/2020/08/Full-Report.pdf.

84 Zoe Rosenbaum, Liz Betsis, and Behnoush Amery, *Women in Recessions: What Makes COVID-19 Different?*, Labour Market Information Council, LMI Insight Report no. 39, March 2021, https://lmic-cimt.ca/publications-all/lmi-insight-report-no-39/#toc-7.

85 *Fraser,* para 140.

86 *Ibid,* para 180.

87 *Ibid,* paras 198–99.

88 *Ibid,* para 231.

89 *Ibid,* para 242.

15

Quebec and the "Sign Law" Thirty Years after
Ford and *Devine*
Ford Construit Solide

James B. Kelly

IN *MISCONCEIVING CANADA*, Kenneth McRoberts argues that the Trudeau conception of Canada as a multicultural, bilingual country with two official languages has been at odds with the political project undertaken by successive Quebec governments since the Quiet Revolution.[1] According to this argument, Trudeau downplayed that his answer to Canada's national question – official bilingualism, multiculturalism, and a national *Charter of Rights and Freedoms* – was incompatible with how Quebec governments had answered *la question nationale*. The two national questions competed during the megaconstitutional politics that began in the 1960s. Patriation would constitutionalize this disagreement and, in return, see the Trudeau government secure "substantial provincial consent" without the consent of Quebec.[2] According to Guy Laforest, "[t]he refusal of any Quebec government, whatever its political stripe, to sign the Constitution Act, 1982, is a manifestation of what André Laurendeau and Léon Dion termed the hurt dignity of the Quebec people."[3]

This chapter focuses on two landmark rulings, *Ford* and *Devine*, in which the Supreme Court of Canada invalidated provisions of Bill 101 that prohibited the use of languages other than French on public signs and commercial names.[4] These invalidations have been used as evidence for judicial policy impact and the strategic advantage that a constitutional instrument such as the *Charter of Rights and Freedoms* wields over a statutory mechanism such as Bill 101.[5] In this chapter, evidence for the centralization thesis and judicial impact is considered forty years after the patriation of the Constitution in 1982 and more than thirty years after the invalidation of the "sign law" provisions in *Ford* and *Devine*.

I do more than focus on the invalidation of provisions of the *Charter of the French Language* (hereafter *CFL*). This chapter considers judicial policy impact and how successive Quebec governments responded to the judicialization of la question nationale in the Charter era. Judicial impact is explored by asking the following questions. First, did the court's decisions change the *visage linguistique* of Quebec?[6] This question is particularly important. When the sign law was invalidated in 1988, it was considered an affront to the francization of commerce in Quebec that began during the Quiet Revolution. Second, is judicial invalidation enough to change policy direction? Finally, how are judicial decisions implemented, and what is the role of commercial actors in the implementation of *Ford* and *Devine*?

Why ask these questions? For one, enough time has passed to assess whether *Ford* and *Devine* were massive defeats for the Quebec government.[7] Advocates of the centralization thesis, as I labelled it in 2001,[8] overlooked that the sign-law provisions stood on many legs and *required* commercial interests to include languages other than French on public signs.[9] This chapter argues that Bills 178 and 86, as well as the supporting regulations introduced after 1988, are *Ford construit solide* (Built *Ford* Tough), preserving, with some exceptions, the French-only approach to commercial expression in Quebec. How can this be? This puzzle is explained by the Charter of Rights as a negative rights instrument, what *Ford* and *Devine* prohibit (French-only signs), what is permitted (languages other than French on public signs), but what is not required by commercial interests (to include languages other than French on public signs). Analyzed outside of the Meech Lake saga, perhaps *Ford* and *Devine* are not the decisions they were thought to be during the constitutional battles of the 1980s and 1990s.

Two Questions, Two Answers, and Two Charters

The history of Canada and Quebec since patriation centres on how to reconcile la question nationale with the judicialization of politics. The early years of the Mulroney era appeared to have squared the circle with the Meech Lake Accord, the "Quebec Round" of constitutional politics,[10] which had the specific goal of ending Quebec's opposition to the constitutional settlement reached in 1982.[11] According to Guy Laforest, the recognition of Quebec as a distinct society was designed to broaden the reasonable limits clause (section 1) of the *Charter of Rights and Freedoms* and to soften judicial interpretation involving the *CFL*.[12] What would be reasonable in Quebec under section 1 of the Charter would require an asymmetrical application of the *Charter of Rights and Freedoms* to reconcile this instrument with the constitutional recognition of Quebec as a distinct society within the Canadian federation. For Liberal premier Robert Bourassa, the Meech Lake Accord was an attempt to reverse the loss of jurisdictional sovereignty that the *Charter of Rights and Freedoms* presented to the *CFL* and the policy of interculturalism. The invalidation of the sign-law provisions of Bill 101 in *Ford* and *Devine*, which occurred during the three-year ratification period for the Meech Lake Accord, reinforced for Quebec the need for the distinct society clause and a provincial role in the appointment of Supreme Court of Canada justices.

Alain-G. Gagnon and Alex Schwartz argue that deficiencies in the federal structure and the Supreme Court of Canada undermine "the ability of the

Canadian federation to respond to the circumstances of national pluralism and further contribute to the alienation of Quebecers."[13] It is understandable when such a conclusion is reached, given the importance of the 1982 constitutional settlement, the judicialization of politics associated with it, and the invalidation of significant Quebec statutes by the Supreme Court of Canada. The invalidation of the sign-law provisions during the Meech Lake ratification period, the reaction to Quebec's use of the notwithstanding clause in response to *Ford* and *Devine*, and how this episode clouded the distinct society clause and section 33[14] did alienate Quebec within the federation, and they laid the groundwork for the 1995 referendum. How Quebec responded to the judicialization of the *CFL* and how the sign law was implemented casts doubt on the conclusions reached by Gagnon and Schwartz as well as other Québécois academics.[15] Similar to Frédéric Bérard, my conclusion about the judicialization of politics challenges the myth of centralization and a loss of policy autonomy for Quebec.[16]

Bill 101 and the Sign-Law Provisions

The *CFL* declared under section 1 that "French is the official language of Quebec" and applies this to all provincial responsibilities. The regulation of commercial expression on signs, posters, and advertising is collectively referred to as the "sign-law" provisions of Bill 101. Section 58 required that "public signs and posters and commercial advertising shall be solely in the official language," though it did provide the Office de la langue française with the discretion to allow bilingual signs or the sole use of languages other than French.[17] In addition, section 69 required that "[s]ubject to section 68, only the French version of a firm name may be used in Quebec."[18] Individuals or firms violating these provisions of Bill 101 were subject to fines under sections 205 and 206 that significantly increased with each additional infraction.

Several individuals found in violation of Bill 101 launched constitutional challenges against the bill in February 1984. Sections 58 and 69 were challenged as a violation of freedom of expression protected under section 2(b) of the *Canadian Charter of Rights and Freedoms* and section 3 of the Quebec *Charter of Human Rights and Freedoms*. Successful lower court judgments were appealed to the Supreme Court of Canada by the attorney general of Quebec.[19] On December 15, 1988, the *Ford* and *Devine* decisions were handed down by the Supreme Court of Canada. In *Ford,* sections 58 and 69 were invalidated as a violation of freedom of expression because of the close relationship between language, expression, and identity: "Language is so intimately related to the form and content of expression that there cannot be true freedom of expression by means of language if one is prohibited from using the language of one's choice."[20] Further, the court reasoned that language is "as the preamble of the

Charter of the French Language itself indicates, a means by which a people may express its cultural identity."[21]

In *Devine,* the court argued that the section 2(b) violation was noteworthy because it compelled the use of French on public signs and firm names and prohibited other languages: "That freedom is infringed not only by a prohibition of the use of one's language of choice but also by a legal requirement compelling one to use a particular language."[22] Commenting on Quebec's position that commercial expression should not be protected by section 2(b)[23] and, thus, that the challenged provisions of Bill 101 were nonjusticiable, the court rejected the argument because "there is no sound basis on which commercial expression can be excluded from the protection of s. 2(b) of the Charter."[24] The court reasoned in *Ford* that the protection under the Canadian and Quebec Charters "includes the freedom to express oneself in the language of one's choice."[25] Finally, "[a]lthough the expression in this case has a commercial element, it should be noted that the focus here is on choice of language and on a law which prohibits the use of a language."[26] According to Richard Moon, "section 2(b) was violated by both the prohibition on other languages and the compulsion to use French."[27]

While the court was supportive of the policy rationale of Bill 101 – to promote and maintain the visage linguistique of Quebec – it did not consider that the section 2(b) violation constituted a reasonable limitation under section 1 of the Charter. In its section 1 analysis, the court took issue with compelling the exclusive use of French: "Thus, whereas requiring the predominant display of the French language, even its marked predominance, would be proportional to the goal of promoting and maintaining a French 'visage linguistique' in Quebec and therefore justified under the Québec Charter and the Canadian Charter, requiring the exclusive use of French has not been so justified."[28] Indeed, the court did not accept that mandatory use of French was essential to the maintenance and promotion of the French language in Quebec, whereas the marked predominance of French, alongside other languages, would advance this objective and be consistent with the demographic reality of Quebec: "Such measures would ensure that the 'visage linguistique' reflected the demography of Quebec: the predominant language is French ... But exclusivity for the French language has not survived the scrutiny of a proportionality test and does not reflect the reality of Quebec society."[29]

The Supreme Court of Canada was authoritative, clear, and prescriptive in its judgment regarding the constitutionality of sections 58 and 69 of the *CFL;* authoritative in that it released its judgments in the name of "the Court," signalling that the *Ford* and *Devine* decisions must be adhered to and that there was no room for interpretive discretion; clear in that it outlined, without ambiguity, that the mandatory use of French and the prohibition of languages other than

French were a violation of freedom of expression protected by both the Canadian and Quebec Charters. And, finally, it was prescriptive, as the court outlined an approach to public signs and commercial expression that must be adhered to. Indeed, the standard of "marked predominance" was the policy standard established by the court to ensure the constitutionality of the sign-law provisions.

Charter of the French Language, 1988 (Bill 178)

The Bourassa government introduced two legislative responses to *Ford* and *Devine*: Bill 178, which, for a five-year period, overrode the court's decisions by invoking section 33 of the Charter, the notwithstanding clause; and Bill 86, which replaced Bill 178 when the notwithstanding clause expired in 1993. Assented to on December 22, 1988, Bill 178 amended section 58 to create the inside-outside rule for public signs, posters, and advertising. Section 68 was amended to reiterate that only the French version of a firm's name could be used in Quebec.[30] Section 58, the outside rule, established that "public signs and posters and commercial advertising, outside or intended for the public outside, shall be solely in French."[31] Bill 178, therefore, disregarded the court's ruling in *Ford* that the exclusive use of French was inconsistent with section 2(b) of the *Canadian Charter of Rights and Freedoms*, as well as freedom of expression protected in the Quebec *Charter of Human Rights and Freedoms*. Section 58.1, the inside rule, provided that "inside establishments, public signs and posters and commercial advertising shall be in French" but allowed for the use of languages in addition to French "provided they are intended only for the public inside the establishment and that French is marked predominant."[32] The inside-outside rule compelled the exclusive use of French on public signs, posters, and advertisements but did allow for limited use of languages in addition to French, so long as the signs were located inside and French was "marked predominant."

Recognizing that Bill 178 was at odds with the court's rulings, the Bourassa government invoked section 33 of the Charter. In justifying the use of the legislative override, Premier Bourassa argued that he alone possessed the moral authority to invoke section 33: "I repeat that I am the only head of government in North America who has the moral justification to act in this manner because I am the only leader of a people that is very much a minority on this continent. Who can best and better defend, protect and promote French culture than the Prime Minister of Quebec?"[33] During the December news conference defending the notwithstanding clause, Bourassa "suggested that invoking the notwithstanding clause was necessary because Meech Lake had not been ratified."[34] For Patrick Monahan, this statement was used by the critics of the Meech Lake Accord to argue that "the hidden agenda underlying the accord was the denial of the rights of the anglophone minority."[35] Outside Quebec, Bourassa's use of the notwithstanding clause was considered a decisive event that ultimately derailed the recognition of Quebec as a distinct society in the Meech Lake Accord.[36]

Why, then, did the Bourassa government amend the sign-law provisions in light of *Ford* and *Devine* and not reinvoke the notwithstanding clause when its use expired in 1993? Perhaps the Bourassa government's response in 1988 was simply a sign of the constitutional times, another example of what André Laurendeau and Léon Dion referred to as the "hurt dignity" of the Quebec people.[37] As Jamie Cameron noted, "Many years after the Meech Lake and Charlottetown Accords failed, it is difficult to convey the intensity, drama, and tensions of these moments in Canada's history."[38] In this raw political moment, the National Assembly protected the continued application of a statute of utmost importance to Quebec through section 33. Peter Russell questioned whether the use of the notwithstanding clause was necessary, as Bill 178 "might well have met the rule set down by the Supreme Court in the signs case that a law requiring predominantly (but not exclusively) French signs was a reasonable limit on freedom of expression."[39] I agree with Russell's assessment of Bill 178 but suggest that it would not have survived the political context,[40] which is why the Bourassa government ultimately invoked the notwithstanding clause. The irony is that its successor, Bill 86, is less consistent with the *Ford* and *Devine* decisions and, as I will argue, departs markedly from the constitutional standards established in 1988.

Why, then, did the Bourassa government appear to comply with *Ford* and *Devine* in 1993? One explanation is that five years after the invalidation of the sign-law provisions and three years after the demise of the Meech Lake Accord, political tensions had cooled, and Quebec recognized that it could achieve its objectives within the parameters of the *Ford* and *Devine* decisions. For instance, Robert Sharpe and Kent Roach argue in the context of *Ford* that "[w]hile the decision struck down the existing law, the Court's section 1 analysis gave Québec considerable latitude to pursue a vigorous language policy favouring the use of French."[41] There is much merit in this analysis. There is a more fundamental reason why, perhaps, the Bourassa government introduced Bill 86 – it recognized the paradox of the sign-law decisions and the implementation challenges that *Ford* and *Devine* faced. Unless commercial interests changed their public signs and firm names to include languages other than French consistent with the *Ford* standard that French be given "marked predominance," the sign-law provisions would function largely in their preinvalidation form. This argument will be revisited once the *Charter of the French Language*, 1993, is considered, and the actual impact on the public face of commercial expression in Quebec is assessed thirty years after *Ford* and *Devine*.

Charter of the French Language, 1993 (Bill 86)

Shortly before the five-year time limit on the notwithstanding clause expired in December 1993, the Bourassa government introduced its second legislative response to *Ford* and *Devine*. Bill 86 was introduced by Claude Ryan, the minister responsible for the *CFL*, on May 6, 1993, and it was assented to on June 18, 1993. Because the Bourassa government decided against reinvoking the notwithstanding clause, Bill 86 has been considered in legislative compliance with the court's earlier ruling that languages other than French be permitted on public signs, provided that French is given "marked predominance."[42]

A comparison of the 1988 and 1993 amendments and regulatory changes to the *CFL* in light of *Ford* and *Devine* is presented in Table 15.1. There were a number of changes in 1993 that complied with the court's rulings permitting the use of languages other than French on public signs, commercial expression, and firm names. For instance, the outside-inside rule of Bill 178 was repealed, and a new version of section 58 was implemented with the passage of Bill 86. The outside rule prohibiting the use of languages other than French on public signs and commercial expression was inconsistent with the *Ford* and *Devine* decisions but was legally permitted by the use of the notwithstanding clause between 1988 and 1993. The 1993 iteration of section 58 aligned with the court's decisions, as it clearly stated that commercial expression and public signs "must" be in French but "may" be permitted in other languages, provided that French is "marked predominant." As well, "only" the French version of a firm's name had been permitted under section 68 of the 1988 *CFL* (Bill 178), subject to certain exceptions within sections 58 and 68. If there were any doubts as to section 68's constitutionality and the exceptions to the French-only rule for firm names, they, too, were protected by the use of the notwithstanding clause in Bill 178. Finally, the Quebec government introduced a series of regulations in support of Bill 86, the most notable being a clear approach to the standard of "marked predominant," which roughly required that French be at least twice the size of any other language on a public sign, commercial expression, or firm name.[43]

Despite these instances of full legislative incorporation of the court's approach to commercial expression in the context of the sign-law provisions of Bill 101, Bill 86 and the *Regulation respecting the language of commerce and business, Charter of the French language,* do allow for legislative deviation from *Ford* and *Devine*. Section 58 contains a qualifying provision (in *italics*) that allows the Quebec government to decide "by regulation, the places, cases, conditions or circumstances where public signs and posters must be in French only," although it can allow for English-only signs or bilingual signs where French is not given "marked predominance." The point is this – the qualifying paragraph provides the discretion *whether* to comply (or not) with the Supreme Court of Canada's

Table 15.1

Charter of the French Language, 1993 (Bill 86) and supporting regulations

CFL section	Supporting regulations
58. Public signs and posters and commercial advertising must be in French. They may also be both in French and in another language provided that French is marked predominant. *However, the Government may determine, by regulation, the places, cases, conditions or circumstances where public signs and posters and commercial advertising must be in French only, where French need not be predominant or where such signs, posters and advertising may be in another language only.*	**Regulation defining the scope of the expression "marked predominate" for the purposes of the Charter of the French Language** 1. In signs and posters of the civil administration, public signs and posters and posted commercial advertising that are both in French and in another language, French is markedly predominant where the text in French has a much greater visual impact than the text in the other language. In assessing the visual impact, a family name, a place name, a trademark or other terms in a language other than French are not considered where their presence is specifically allowed under an exception provided for in the Charter of the French language (chapter C-11) or its regulations. 2. Where texts both in French and in another language appear on the same sign or poster, the text in French is deemed to have a much greater visual impact if the following conditions are met: (1) the space allotted to the text in French is at least twice as large as the space allotted to the text in the other language; (2) the characters used in the text in French are at least twice as large as those used in the text in the other language; and (3) the other characteristics of the sign or poster do not have the effect of reducing the visual impact of the text in French. 3. Where texts both in French and in another language appear on separate signs or posters of the same size, the text in French is deemed to have a much greater visual impact if the following conditions are met: (1) the signs and posters bearing the text in French are at least twice as numerous as those bearing the text in the other language; (2) the characters used in the text in French are at least as large as those used in the text in the other language; and (3) the other characteristics of the signs or posters do not have the effect of reducing the visual impact of the text in French.

4. Where texts both in French and in another language appear on separate signs or posters of a different size, the text in French is deemed to have a much greater visual impact if the following conditions are met:

   (1) the signs and posters bearing the text in French are at least as numerous as those bearing the text in the other language;

   (2) the signs or posters bearing the text in French are at least twice as large as those bearing the text in the other language;

   (3) the characters used in the text in French are at least twice as large as those used in the text in the other language; and

   (4) the other characteristics of the signs or posters do not have the effect of reducing the visual impact of the text in French.

68. A firm name may be accompanied with a version in a language other than French provided that, when it is used, the French version appears at least as prominently.

However, in public signs and posters and commercial advertising, the use of a version of a firm name in a language other than French is permitted to the extent that the other language may be used in such posters or in such advertising pursuant to section 58 and the regulations enacted under that section.

In addition, in texts or documents drafted only in a language other than French, a firm name may appear in the other language only.

Regulation respecting the language of commerce and business, Charter of the French language

15. A firm's commercial advertising, displayed on billboards, on signs or posters or on any other medium having an area of 16 m² or more and visible from any public highway within the meaning of section 4 of the Highway Safety Code (chapter C-24.2), must be exclusively in French unless the advertising is displayed on the very premises of an establishment of the firm.

16. A firm's commercial advertising on or in any public means of transportation and on or in the accesses thereto, including bus shelters, must be exclusively in French.

1988 decisions, which invalidated the "sign-law" provisions of Bill 101. More importantly, while section 68 appears to comply with the court, as it does allow for the use of bilingual firm names, it, too, contains a qualifying paragraph (in *italics*) that allows Quebec to derogate from this in accordance with section 58 "and the regulations enacted under that section."[44] As a result, the qualifying paragraph in section 58 that allows for a French-only approach to public signs is extended to firm names as well.

This legislative disagreement crystalizes in the regulations enacted in support of the 1993 iteration of section 58.[45] Division III of the regulation is titled "Public Signs and Posters and Commercial Advertising" and specifies the conditions when French must be used exclusively and not simply given "marked predominance." For instance, section 15 specifies "a firm's commercial advertising, displayed on billboards, on signs or posters or on any other medium having an area of 16 m² or more and visible from any public highway within the meaning of section 4 of the Highway Safety Code ... must be exclusively in French unless the advertising is displayed on the very premises of an established firm."[46] Similarly, public signs and commercial advertising on public transportation and bus shelters must be exclusively in French.[47]

These legislative and regulatory changes cannot be interpreted as straight compliance that resulted from the Bourassa government's decision not to reintroduce the notwithstanding clause in 1993. Nor can they be viewed as a clear legislative disagreement, which reinvoking the notwithstanding clause for an additional five years would surely have communicated. The statutory and regulatory changes work at cross-purposes, complying with and departing from the *Ford* and *Devine* decisions at the same time. Even a committed dialogue theorist would struggle to consider Bill 86 as dialogue in action, as the message is easy to discern – Quebec will decide under what conditions languages other than French are permitted on public signs, commercial advertising, and firm names.

Contemporary Challenges to the *Charter of the French Language*, 1993

Section 58 of the *Charter of the French Language*, 1993, was challenged in 1999 when an antique store owned by Simpson and Hoffman in the Eastern Townships displayed a bilingual firm name, "La Lionne et le Morse – The Lyon and the Walrus," giving the French and English equal weight.[48] Clearly in violation of section 58 of the *CFL* and accompanying regulations, as French was not "marked predominant," Simpson and Hoffman were fined five hundred dollars under section 205 of the *CFL*.[49] Initially successful at the Court of Quebec, the finding of unconstitutionality was reversed at the Superior Court. Upon appeal, the Quebec Court of Appeal upheld the constitutionality of section 58, arguing that the appellants had failed to demonstrate that the restrictions on languages other than French were no longer necessary in 1999.[50] An application for leave to appeal was filed with the Supreme Court of Canada (December 2, 2001), and the court dismissed the leave to appeal without reasons on October 11, 2002.[51] The Supreme Court of Canada, as well as the Quebec Court of Appeal, reached the correct decision, as Simpson and Wallace were clearly in violation of section 58. More importantly, section 58 is consistent with the constitutional standard established by the court in *Ford* requiring French to be given "marked predominance" on bilingual signs, which did not occur in the context of the signage for the Lyon and the Walrus.

The constitutionality of section 58, as well as sections 51 and 52, were once again considered by the Quebec Court of Appeal in 2017 when eleven anglophone businesses in the Montreal area were charged with various breaches of the sign-law provisions. Several businesses were found to be in breach of section 58 and the regulation defining "marked predominance" for the French language, as their signs were exclusively in English or, when French was present, it was not given "marked predominance." Others were found in violation of section 51, as merchandise was packaged exclusively in English. Finally, a number of businesses were found in violation of section 52, as their company websites were exclusively in English without any French content.[52]

In the 2017 challenge to Bill 86 (*Charter of the French Language*, 1993), the appellants argued that the Court of Appeal should revisit the *Ford* and *Devine* precedents, as the French language was no longer in jeopardy and the factual basis of 1988 decisions could no longer justify infringements on freedom of expression.[53] In response, the Court of Appeal argued that the appellants had not demonstrated that the status of the French language had materially changed; therefore, the Court of Appeal could not revisit the *Ford* and *Devine* precedents.[54] Finally, although the Court of Appeal acknowledged that the *Ford* and *Devine* decisions did not consider the issue of commercial advertising and the internet, this form of expression must be used in a manner that conforms with the *Charter of the French Language*.[55] In this respect, the judgment was less about the constitutionality of Bill 86 and the 1993 version of section 58 and largely about whether the Court of Appeal could revisit a precedent established by the Supreme Court of Canada, which it declined to do.

Starting in 2010, the Office québécois de la langue française began to interpret the *Regulation respecting the language of commerce and business, Charter of the French language*, to require firms with trademarks in English or established outside of Quebec to have a sufficient French presence in firm names and other forms of commercial expression. In 2015, the Quebec Court of Appeal ruled on this matter, as the actions of the Office de la langue française were challenged by several large multinational corporations that argued that their English-only names were permitted under Bill 101 and the exceptions provided under section 25 of the regulations for trademarked names.[56] In a unanimous ruling, the Quebec Court of Appeal determined that the companies had functioned within the exceptions provided by section 25 of the regulations and that the Office de la langue française's interpretation of the regulation after 2010 was not appropriate.[57] In response, the Couillard government amended the regulation in 2016 by adding sections 25.1 to 25.5 to require "a sufficient presence of French" on English trademarked names, or firms established outside of Quebec that used English-only names on their displays or other forms of commercial expression.[58] To facilitate this modification to section 58's application, a transitional period of three years was provided for companies to comply with this regulatory change.[59]

The legislative and regulatory changes introduced in response to *Ford* and *Devine* have, therefore, yet to face a serious or direct constitutional challenge. Lower court proceedings after 1993 involved weak cases where commercial signage was in clear violation of Bill 101,[60] or the interpretations of the regulatory requirements by the Office québécoise de la langue française were inconsistent with past practices and a clear reading of section 58 and the supporting regulations.[61] While the Supreme Court of Canada no longer permits the prohibition of languages other than French on commercial signs, the amendments to Bill 101 and the supporting regulations carve out exceptions to this rule, providing the Quebec government with the ability to prohibit languages other than French on public signs and other forms of commercial expression, albeit in a narrow set of circumstances. Perhaps the Quebec government considers these narrow exceptions as a more precisely tailored infringement that would survive the court's proportionality analysis under section 1 of the Charter. This is not an unreasonable assumption to make. Even when a senior court ruled against a public actor and its interpretation of Bill 101, as the Quebec Court of Appeal did in the *Best Buy* decision, the Quebec government has simply amended the regulations supporting the *Charter of the French Language* to require corporations to include "a sufficient presence of French" on their trademarked names and public signage.

Quebec's Visage Linguistique in the Twenty-First Century

It has been more than thirty years since the *Ford* and *Devine* decisions were decided at the end of the twentieth century. Enough time has passed to assess the policy impact of the Supreme Court of Canada's invalidation of the French-only provisions of commercial expression in the *CFL*. How has the public face of commercial expression changed in Quebec in this thirty-year period? In 1997 and 2017, the Office québécois de la langue française released studies that evaluated compliance with the sign-law provisions of Bill 101 on the Island of Montreal.[62] It has not conducted studies off the Island of Montreal, which is natural, given the concentration of anglophones on the Island of Montreal and the greater possibility of bilingual signs in this part of Quebec. As the Office québécois de la langue française is mandated to monitor compliance with the *CFL*, these studies are particularly relevant in understanding the impact of *Ford* and *Devine* on the Island of Montreal, particularly in its downtown commercial district and in the "West Island," where the anglophone population is largely concentrated.

The 1997 report surveyed over seven thousand businesses on the Island of Montreal over three years (1995, 1996, 1997) and reviewed a total of sixty-two thousand commercial messages.[63] For comparative purposes, Montreal is divided into two sectors, East and West, and Boulevard Saint-Laurent is the line of demarcation. Although it no longer holds, Boulevard Saint-Laurent is the traditional dividing line between francophone and anglophone Montreal. For greater clarity, the 1997 survey subdivided Montreal into four sectors: Centre, West, East, and North. The sectors correspond roughly to downtown Montreal (Centre); the "East End," which has the highest concentration of francophones (East); the "West Island," which has the highest concentration of anglophones (West); and the North, which shares a border with all the other sectors. Sherbrooke Street is the dividing line between the Centre, West, and North zones; Avenue Papineau is the dividing line for the East sector; and Avenue Atwater is roughly the dividing line between the West and Centre sectors. Finally, the CN Rail Lines are the demarcation between the North and West sectors.

On the Island of Montreal, the 1997 report found that nearly 98 percent of store signage contained French, and nearly 50 percent had an English presence in 1997.[64] The highest presence of French was in the East sector (99.3), and the highest presence of English was in the West zone (60.5). Further, nearly 46 percent of stores on the Island of Montreal had French-only signs in 1997, with the highest rates in the East (63.4), North (45.7), and Centre (40.1) zones and the lowest in the West (35.1).[65] In contrast, less than 1 percent of commercial enterprises had English-only signs in 1997.[66] In terms of the language used on billboards, the 1997 study found that nearly 85 percent were unilingual French, with a sector variance between the East (91.3) and West (79.2) and zone differences as follows: East (91.9), North (85.1), Centre (80.8), and West (78.5).[67] It can be concluded that within four years of Bill 86's passage and the 1993 iteration of section 58 of the *CFL* and the supporting regulations, the public face of commercial expression in Montreal remained overwhelmingly French. For instance, there were a significant number of French-only signs, despite the constitutional ability of firms to have languages other than French on public signs after 1993 with the expiration of the notwithstanding clause.

Twenty years later, the public face of commercial expression in Quebec has remained incredibly stable, and in some respects, there is a higher percentage of French-only public signs and forms of commercial expression on the Island of Montreal. The 2017 study contains a distinction that was not present in 1997 – signs with only French words and French signs that have words of an indeterminate nature (a surname, homonym, or word that cannot be assimilated to another language). Both are classified as "French-only" signs by the Office québécois de la langue française, though it does present data for both versions of "French-only" signs and forms of commercial expression. Based on a survey of 3,612 businesses on the Island of Montreal between February and May 2017, the Office québécois de la langue française estimated that 30.5 percent of company names were exclusively in French. When words of an indeterminate nature are added, this figure increases to 77.2 percent.[68] For the four zones on the Island of Montreal, the East zone remains the highest for storefronts with French-only signs (84.4), followed by Centre (80.5), North (78.9), and West (69.1).[69] Finally, among all commercial messages on the Island of Montreal (company names and other forms of commercial messaging), 65 percent were found to be written exclusively in French, with only 7.8 percent of commercial messaging in a bilingual format (French and English). Although the Office québécois de la langue française does not release data for the remaining regions of Quebec, one can conclude that the rate of French-only signs and forms of commercial expression is even higher off the Island of Montreal, or at least as high as the East sector, whose linguistic profile is 86 percent francophone, which is similar to Quebec outside of Montreal.

Conclusion: Built *Ford* Tough

In an analysis of the judicialization of language policy, Eugénie Brouillet argues, "Ces décisions judiciaire ont ainsi limité la capacité de légiférer du Québec afin d'assurer l'épanouissement de la langue française dans un environnement linguistique singulièrement difficile."[70] None of the evidence – be it legislative responses in which Quebec carved out exceptions to the *Ford* and *Devine* principles or the actions of commercial interests that have largely retained their French-only signs – supports such a position. The public face of commercial expression in Quebec remains overwhelmingly French, and public signs remain largely French-only more than thirty years after the *Ford* and *Devine* decisions. This is true on the Island of Montreal and even more so for Quebec outside of Montreal. And, if Bill 96 (*An Act respecting French, the official and common language of Québec*) is passed in its current version, the Legault government will intensify this trend of legislating around the *Ford* and *Devine* decisions.[71] Similar to Bill 21 (*An Act respecting the laicity of the State*), Bill 96 pre-emptively invokes the notwithstanding clauses of the Canadian and Quebec Charters to deny courts the ability to remedy any potential constitutional infringement.

How to explain this puzzle of judicial victories without policy impact? What have students of the judicialization of politics failed to consider when assessing judicial policy impact? To have a policy impact, a judicial decision must be implemented. There are public and private actions that inform an implementation chain: the responsible legislature that introduces amendments to legislation, and private actors responding to the new legislative framework. Whether to include languages other than French on public signs remains a policy choice for commercial businesses in Quebec. This chapter reinforces the enduring point made by Alan Cairns in his seminal article on the Judicial Committee of the Privy Council that we should not read too much into how a judicial decision, or judicial body, can change the fundamental character of Canadian federalism.[72] In the context of the sign law and section 58, the legislative responses are "Built *Ford* Tough" because of the complexity of commercial francization, the instruments used to achieve it, the role played by commercial actors as agents of implementation, and the commitment of successive governments to preserve Quebec's visage linguistique in the face of judicial invalidation.

Notes

This chapter is drawn from the following work in progress: James B. Kelly, "Confronting the Court: Legislative Disagreements in the Charter Era," under contract for UBC Press.

1 Kenneth McRoberts, *Misconceiving Canada: The Struggle for National Unity* (Don Mills, ON: Oxford University Press, 1997), 137–39.
2 Guy Laforest and Rosalie Readman, "More Distress Than Enchantment: The Constitutional Negotiations of November 1981 as Seen from Quebec," in *Patriation and Its Consequences: Constitution Making in Canada,* ed. Lois Harder and Steve Patten (Vancouver: UBC Press, 2016), 173–76.
3 Guy Laforest, *Trudeau and the End of a Canadian Dream* (Montreal/Kingston: McGill-Queen's University Press, 1995), 100.
4 *Ford v Quebec (Attorney General),* 2 SCR 712 (1988) [*Ford*]; *Devine v Quebec (Attorney General),* 2 SCR 790 (1988) [*Devine*].
5 Eugénie Brouillet, *La négation de la nation: L'identité culturelle Québécoise et le fédéralisme canadien* (Montreal: Septentrion, 2006), 324; Henri Brun, *Les institutions démocratiques du Québec et Canada* (Montreal: Wilson and Lafleur, 2013), 119.
6 The expression *visage linguistique* translates to "public face" and is used in Quebec in the context of public signs and commercial expression.
7 Jose Woerhling, "Convergences et divergences entre fédéralisme et protection des droits et libertés: L'exemple des États-Unies et du Canada," *McGill Law Journal* 46 (2000): 49–51.

8   James B. Kelly, "Reconciling Rights and Federalism during Review of the Charter of Rights and Freedoms: The Supreme Court of Canada and the Centralization Thesis, 1982 to 1999," *Canadian Journal of Political Science* 34, 2 (2001): 321–55.

9   Frédéric Bérard, *Charte canadienne et droits linguistiques: Pour en finir avec les mythes* (Montreal: Les Presses de l'Université de Montréal, 2016).

10   Peter H. Russell, *Constitutional Odyssey: Can Canadians Become a Sovereign People?* (Toronto: University of Toronto Press, 1993), 135–36.

11   Richard Simeon, "Meech Lake and Shifting Conceptions of Canadian Federalism," *Canadian Public Policy* 14 (1988): S8–S9.

12   José Woehrling, "La reconnaissance du Québec comme société distincte et la dualité linguistique du Canada: Conséquences juridiques et constitutionnelles," *Canadian Public Policy* 14 (1988): S51–S52.

13   Alain-G. Gagnon and Alex Schwartz, "Canadian Federalism since Patriation: Advancing a Federalism of Empowerment," in *Patriation and Its Consequences: Constitution Making in Canada,* ed. Lois Harder and Steve Patten (Vancouver: UBC Press, 2015), 261.

14   Peter H. Russell, "Canadian Constraints on Judicialization from Without," *International Political Science Review* 15, 2 (1994): 167.

15   James B. Kelly and Michael Murphy, "Shaping the Constitutional Dialogue on Federalism: Canada's Supreme Court as Meta-political Actor," *Publius: The Journal of Federalism* 35, 2 (2005): 214–43.

16   Bérard, *Charte canadienne et droits linguistiques.*

17   *Charter of the French Language,* RSQ 1977, c C-11. The name was changed to Office québécois de la langue française in 2003.

18   *Ibid,* s 69.

19   *Ford,* 722.

20   *Ibid,* 748–49.

21   *Ibid.*

22   *Devine,* 813.

23   *Ford,* 754.

24   *Ibid,* 767.

25   *Ibid,* 752.

26   *Ibid,* 767.

27   Richard Moon, *The Constitutional Protection of Freedom of Expression* (Toronto: University of Toronto Press, 2000), 186.

28   *Ford,* 779–80.

29   *Ibid.*

30   *Charter of the French Language,* RSQ 1988, c C-11.

31   *Ibid,* s 58.

32   *Ibid,* s. 58.1.

33   National Assembly of Quebec, *Journal des débats,* 33rd Leg, 2nd Sess, Vol 30, No 83 (December 20, 1988), 4425 (Robert Bourassa).

34   Patrick Monahan, *Meech Lake: The Inside Story* (Toronto: University of Toronto Press, 1991), 161.

35   *Ibid.*

36   L. Ian MacDonald, *From Bourassa to Bourassa: Wilderness to Restoration,* 2nd ed. (Montreal/Kingston: McGill-Queen's University Press, 2002), 295–96; Troy Q. Riddell and F.L. Morton, "Reasonable Limitations, Distinct Society and the Canada Clause: Interpretive Clauses and the Competition for Constitutional Advantage," *Canadian Journal of Political Science* 31, 3 (1998): 467, 485–89.

37 Laforest, *Trudeau and the End of a Canadian Dream*, 100.
38 Jamie Cameron, "To the Rescue: Antonio Lamer and the Section 2(b) Cases from Quebec," in *The Scared Fire: The Legacy of Antonio Lamer*, ed. Adam Dodek and Daniel Jutras (Toronto: LexisNexis Canada, 2009), 245.
39 Russell, *Constitutional Odyssey?*, 145–46.
40 Monahan, *Meech Lake*, 159–62.
41 Robert J. Sharpe and Kent Roach, *Brian Dickson: A Judge's Journey* (Toronto: University of Toronto Press, 2003), 434.
42 Garth Stevenson, *Community Besieged: The Anglophone Minority and the Politics of Quebec* (Montreal/Kingston: McGill-Queen's University Press, 1999), 214–16.
43 *Regulation Defining the Scope of the Expression "Markedly Predominant" for the Purposes of the Charter of the French Language*, RRQ, c C-11, r 11, 1993.
44 *Charter of the French Language*, RSQ, 1993, c C-11, r 9.
45 *Regulation Respecting the Language of Commerce and Business*, RRQ, 1993, c C-11, r 9.
46 *Ibid*, s 15.
47 *Ibid*, s 16.
48 *Entreprises WFH Ltée c Québec (Procureure Générale)*, 2001 QCCA 17598, para 6 [*Entreprises WFH Ltée*].
49 *Ibid*, para 4.
50 *Ibid*, para 61.
51 Supreme Court of Canada, *Bulletin of Proceedings*, October 11, 2002, https://decisions. scc-csc.ca/scc-csc/bulletins/en/item/314/index.do.
52 *156158 Canada Inc v Attorney General of Québec*, 2017 QCCA 2055, para 6 [*156158 Canada Inc*].
53 *Ibid*, para 12.
54 *Ibid*, para 95.
55 *Ibid*, para 115.
56 The multinational corporations that challenged the Office de la langue française's interpretation of s 58 of Bill 101 and s 25 of the regulation are Best Buy, Costco Wholesale, Gap Canada, Old Navy Canada, Guess Canada, Toys "R" Us Canada, and Curves International.
57 *Quebec (Attorney General) v Best Buy Stores Ltd*, 2015 QCCA 747, para 33 [*Best Buy*].
58 *Regulation Respecting the Language of Commerce and Business*, RRQ, 1993, c C-11, r 9, ss 25.1–25.5.
59 *Regulation to amend the Regulation respecting the language of commerce and business*, (2016) GOQ, 6–7.
60 *Entreprises WFH Ltée; 156158 Canada Inc.*
61 *Best Buy.*
62 Secrétariat à la politique linguistique, *L'évolution de la situation de l'affichage à Montréal de 1995 à 1997* (Montreal: Office québécois de la langue française, 1997); Éric Desautels, *Langue de l'affichage public des entreprises de l'île de Montréal: De février à mai 2017* (Montreal: Office québécois de la langue française, 2018). The Office québécois de la langue française released a similar report in 2012 that considered the language of commercial display on the Island of Montreal in 2010.
63 Secrétariat à la politique linguistique, *L'évolution de la situation*. The yearly breakdown of businesses and messages reviewed is as follows: 1995 (3,000 business and 26,000 messages); 1996 (2,000 and 17,000); 1997 (2,000 and 19,000).
64 *Ibid*, 5.
65 *Ibid*. See Table 3, "Percentage of Businesses with Unilingual French Signage, Island of Montreal, 1995, 1996, and 1997."

66 *Ibid*. See Table 4, "Percentage of Businesses with Unilingual English Signage, Island of Montreal, 1995, 1996, and 1997."

67 *Ibid*. See Table 9, "Percentage of Unilingual French Messages by Sector and by Zone, Island of Montreal, 1995, 1996, and 1997."

68 Desautels, *Langue de l'affichage public,* 17. The Office québécois de la langue française makes a distinction between signs with only French words and those with French and words of an indeterminate nature. Both are classified as "French-only" signs by the Office québécois de la langue française.

69 *Ibid,* 18.

70 "These judicial decisions have thus limited Quebec's ability to legislate to ensure the development of the French language in an environment of singular linguistic difficulty." Translated in Eugénie Brouillet, "Le fédéralisme Canadien d'hier à aujourd'hui: Quelle reconnaissance de la nation québécoise?," *Iura Vasconiae* (2010): 420.

71 Bill 96 was introduced by the Legault government on May 13, 2021. It represents the most comprehensive amendment of the *Charter of the French Language* since its passage in 1977. It was unanimously supported by all parties in the National Assembly (121 to 0). As of August 13, 2021, Bill 96 is before the Committee on Culture and Education, which began to scrutinize it on September 21, 2021.

72 Alan C. Cairns, "The Judicial Committee and Its Critics," *Canadian Journal of Political Science* 4, 3 (1971): 320–21.

16

Language Rights and the Charter
Forging the Next Forty Years

Stéphanie Chouinard

LANGUAGE RIGHTS ARE part of the national fabric of this country. Unlike some of the other provisions found in the *Canadian Charter of Rights and Freedoms*, they have a long history, some predating Confederation itself. Indeed, one can trace as far back as 1774, to the *Québec Act,* the first iteration of language rights in the British colonies.[1] The *Québec Act* recognized, for the French majority living on the territory of Quebec, among other things, the courts' right to proceed in French. These provisions, as well as the right to use French and English in Parliament and the Quebec National Assembly, were enshrined in section 133 of the *British North America Act,* thus recognizing a special status for French and English at the federal level and in Quebec (and, subsequently, Manitoba, in 1870).[2] Some of these rights, however, were quickly undermined, and in some cases abolished, in the years following Confederation.[3] Legislative and judicial bilingualism were reinforced in 1969 with the *Official Languages Acts* at the federal level and in New Brunswick (hereafter *OLA* and *OLANB*),[4] along with a recognition of the "equality of status and equal rights and privileges" for French and English.[5]

In light of this history, sections 16–23 of the Charter appear as a sort of patchwork, comprising the reaffirmation of the 1867 language protections, the elevation of key elements of the *OLA* and *OLANB* to constitutional status, and the addition of new rights in the domain of minority-language education. Thus, it was unclear in 1982 how much impact the Charter's language rights would have on the language regime compared to the historically restrictive regime that had been in place since 1867.

Moreover, Charter language rights were also politically salient in the early 1980s, when the separatist movement in Quebec was top of mind during the national-unity crisis and linguistic concerns stretched beyond the borders of that province. It is no coincidence that none of the language provisions of the Charter are subject to the notwithstanding clause. Jean Chrétien, then minister of justice, saw the necessity of putting language rights into the hands of judges:

> The courts will decide and it would be out of the political arena, where the matter is sometimes dealt with by some people who do not comprehend or do not want to comprehend.

> I think we are rendering a great service to Canadians by taking some of these problems away from the political debate and allowing the matters to be debated, argued, coolly before the courts with precedents and so on.
>
> It will serve the population, in my judgement very well.[6]

This political context adds a layer of complexity to the Supreme Court of Canada's interpretation of the newly entrenched language rights. The justices were quite cognizant of this. According to Robert Sharpe and Kent Roach: "The language debate is a familiar and distinctive theme in Canadian law and politics with profound significance for Canadian national unity. It has proved most difficult to resolve and was one of the Supreme Court of Canada's constitutional preoccupations [starting in 1982]."[7] As the Charter triggered a series of disputes between official-language minorities and their governments, finding a balance between protecting national unity and giving life to these sections of the Charter was and will be a challenge for the SCC.

While there has been a consistent flow of language-rights cases presented to the court since 1982, recent and upcoming cases indicate that several issues remain to be addressed, such as the extension of minority-language education rights beyond the scope of the letter of section 23, or the use of section 1 to limit language rights. Moreover, despite renewed protections for official languages since 1982, the French language continues to lose ground in Canada, triggering concerns for its vitality in the future. Meanwhile, the Canadian language regime was expanded further in 2019 with the adoption of the *Indigenous Languages Act*.[8] As the implementation of this legislation has been slow to progress, its substantive impact and the kind of jurisprudence it may foster have yet to be seen.

After presenting an overview of the important jurisprudential elements of the past forty years, I will attempt to shed light on some of the ways I foresee the scope of the Charter's language rights being tested in the future. Challenges such as the extension of language-education rights beyond what is explicitly mentioned in the Charter, supplementary protections for the French language, and the expansion of the *Indigenous Languages Act* and its convergence with official-language rights will be explored. I will show that the Charter and the jurisprudence that has flowed from it have had an important impact on Canada's language regime since 1982 but that this regime may be insufficient to respond to official-language communities' demands in future years.

Testing Charter Language Rights at the SCC: From Conservative Beginnings to Liberal Interpretations

1982–90: Prudent Beginnings

The first Charter language-rights case heard by the Supreme Court of Canada was, unsurprisingly, in the domain of education, as section 23 was the novel element of this part of the Charter. In *Quebec Protestant School Boards,* the court invalidated some of the *Charter of the French Language*'s (*CFL*) criteria for admission to public English-language schools, which were overly restrictive in comparison to the text of section 23.[9] According to the court, the drafters' intention was clearly to "remedy the perceived defects of [provincial minority-language] regimes by uniform corrective measures."[10] The constitutional invalidation of the *CFL*'s pertinent sections opened the door so that any anglophone educated in an English school in Canada, and not just in Quebec, could enroll their children in minority English-language schools in the province.

However, the justices' generous interpretation of section 23 was not repeated in 1986, when they were asked, in a trilogy of cases (*Macdonald, Bilodeau,* and *Société des Acadiens*), to clarify the scope of section 19(2) of the Charter (as well as section 133 of the *Constitution Act, 1867* and section 23 of the *Manitoba Act,* which were all deemed to be of the same nature and scope).[11] Justice Beetz, for the majority, explained that

> [u]nlike language rights which are based on political compromise, legal rights tend to be seminal in nature because they are rooted in principle ... This essential difference between the two types of rights dictates a distinct judicial approach with respect to each ... [I]n my opinion, the courts should approach [language rights] with more restraint than they would in construing legal rights.[12]

From this understanding of Charter language rights flowed three decisions in which the right to use English or French "by any person in, or in any pleading in or process issuing from, any court"[13] of Canada, New Brunswick, or Manitoba did not mean the right to be *understood* in that language. This interpretation elicited some criticism from the legal community. According to Denise Réaume, the court's "policy of restraint was inconsistent with the robust and generous interpretation that had already been accorded to language rights in other areas."[14] Meanwhile, Pierre Foucher highlights the court's refusal to account for the different contexts and the drafters' intent in 1982 in its interpretation of section 19, which in his view was erroneous.[15]

In 1988, two more Charter language-rights cases, *Ford* and *Devine*, were heard by the court (see Kelly, Chapter 15 in this volume).[16] These cases are peculiar in that section 2 rights (pertaining to freedom of expression) and section 15 rights (equality), rather than sections 16 to 23, were mobilized. Once again, the constitutional validity of sections of Quebec's *CFL* was challenged, this time with respect to the linguistic restrictions imposed on commercial signage and corporate names. The court interpreted language choice as being an intrinsic part of freedom of expression while also highlighting real concern for the protection of the French language in Quebec. It offered a compromise solution (the predominant use of French, with the possibility of adding any other language), which was eventually implemented by the province – but not before invoking the controversial notwithstanding clause, generating outrage throughout the country.[17]

In sum, the first decade following the adoption of the Charter saw mitigated success for official-language minorities trying to harness the newly entrenched linguistic protections.

1990–2003: Gradual and Not-So-Gradual Reinterpretations

The 1990 *Mahe* case was a landmark decision for minority-language instruction, as the court stated for the first time that section 23 could, where the number of potential pupils warranted it, entitle a community not only to homogeneous schools but also to the "management and control" of those schools through a publicly funded school board.[18] The justices asserted that the intent of section 23 was "to remedy past injustices and ensure that they are not repeated in the future," recalling historical violations with respect to access to minority-language education, particularly outside Quebec. This approach to management and control of minority-language instruction was consolidated three years later in *Reference re Public Schools Act (Man)*.[19]

Then, in 2000, the *Arsenault-Cameron* decision recognized the role of minority-language school boards as the proper spokespeople for the community, whose opinions must be respected so long as they didn't interfere with "the content and qualitative standards of educational programs"[20] of the province. Second, it found that minority communities, in order to be treated "equally" to the majority, must sometimes be treated differently, thus affirming the principle of substantive equality between the two linguistic communities. In 2003, the court went further and held, in *Doucet-Boudreau*, that the education minister's responsibilities must be fulfilled in a timely manner, considering the "urgent context of ongoing cultural erosion" faced by official-language minorities.[21]

In 1999, *Beaulac* overturned the court's 1986 interpretation of language rights in the domain of the judiciary.[22] According to Justice Bastarache, the 1986 decisions were an anomaly in the jurisprudence. On consulting Parliament's

Hansard, he concluded that the court had erred in its understanding of the legislator's intent. In 1978, during debates on amendments to the Criminal Code, the minister of justice had stated that

> [t]he right to be heard in a criminal proceeding by a judge or a judge and jury who speak the accused's own official language, even if it is the minority official language in a given province, surely is a right that is a bare minimum in terms of serving *the interests of both justice and Canadian unity*. It is essentially a question of fairness that is involved.[23]

Bastarache J continues in the next paragraph, stating that "the existence of a political compromise is without consequence with regard to the scope of language rights," disavowing Beetz J's interpretation.[24] He concludes that courts should ensure respect for "the absolute right to a trial in the official language of one's choice, providing the application is timely."[25]

This second period therefore saw the Supreme Court move towards a more generous interpretation of education rights and make an about-face in the domain of judiciary rights.

2004–10: Quebec and New Brunswick's Language Regimes and a New Test Case

Starting in 2005, the Supreme Court of Canada still faced several section 23 cases, but for the first time in twenty years, they took the form of judicial review of the *CFL* requested by Quebecers. In *Solski*, the court determined that the section of the *CFL* requiring the "major part" of a child's academic career to have taken place in English in order to grant them access to English-language public schools was valid, so long as this assessment was performed qualitatively as well as quantitatively.[26] What is striking about this case is that the court also recognized for the first time the need to apply section 23 asymmetrically between the two linguistic minorities. As the court explained,

> The application of s. 23 is contextual. It must take into account the very real differences between the situations of the minority language community in Quebec and the minority language communities of the territories and the other provinces. The latitude given to the provincial government in drafting legislation regarding education must be broad enough to ensure the protection of the French language while satisfying the purposes of s. 23.[27]

The *Gosselin* decision, rendered on the same day as *Solski*, also challenged the *CFL*, but from the perspective of the majority in Quebec, who claimed that the impossibility for francophone children to attend public English-language schools in Quebec was discriminatory. The court rejected this argument.[28] The *Nguyen* decision, rendered in 2009, was a sequel to *Solski* and *Gosselin* and followed the Quebec government's decision to further restrict access to public English-language education through "bridging schools."[29] While the court recognized that the use of such schools was a legitimate concern for Quebec and did not represent a "genuine" educational pathway,[30] it nevertheless struck down the sections of the *CFL* deemed to be overly restrictive.

The other cases heard by the court in this decade brought forward questions in novel areas of language rights and clarified the New Brunswick language regime. In *Charlebois,* Justice Charron for the majority found that the *OLANB* – and, incidentally, section 18(2) of the Charter – did not mandate municipalities to provide documentation in both official languages.[31] Meanwhile, in *Société des Acadiens et Acadiennes du Nouveau-Brunswick,* it was found that the RCMP, while acting as the New Brunswick provincial police force, was bound to the provincial language regime (which is more generous than the federal regime), pursuant to section 20(2) of the Charter.[32] Therefore, the RCMP was mandated to serve the population in both official languages everywhere in the province.

Finally, the *DesRochers* case called into question Part IV of the *OLA* (and section 20(1) of the Charter) regarding access to services.[33] The court affirmed that a minority-language community is entitled to a service that may be different than the service offered to the majority as per the principle of substantive equality but that this principle did not guarantee an equality of results, as the provisions of the *OLA* "do not entail requirement that government services achieve a minimum level of quality or actually meet the needs of each official language community. Services may be of equal quality in both languages but inadequate or even of poor quality."[34]

2011–20: Testing New Limits

The 2010 decade saw official-language minorities push the limits with respect to the scope of Charter rights, with mitigated results.

In *Conseil scolaire francophone de la Colombie-Britannique,* in 2013, the question at stake was whether one could file evidence in French before a provincial court in British Columbia.[35] The majority decision stated that the English language remains the only language accepted to date thanks to British legislation dating back to 1731, as the province has never adopted legislation to replace this law. The court explained that "while it is true that the *Charter* reflects the importance of language rights, it also reflects the importance of respect for the constitutional powers of the provinces."[36]

In 2015, the Supreme Court heard three language-rights cases.[37] In *Rose-des-Vents*, the court had to decide whether British Columbia met its minority-language instruction obligations in Vancouver, where there was only one French-language elementary school, whose facilities were considered inadequate, in the west end of the city.[38] The court set out the elements of a test for "true equivalency" of minority-language education, which compares "quality of instruction and facilities" as well as contextual and financial assessments of minority and majority schools,[39] therefore clarifying the scope of section 23. In *Conseil scolaire francophone du Yukon #23*, the court found that a French-language school board could not unilaterally broaden the admission of students to its school beyond the scope of the rights-bearers outlined in section 23, and that only the province or territory could decide to delegate to the school board this responsibility.[40]

In 2018, in *Mazraani*, the court reinforced section 19 rights regarding the right to use one's official language of choice in court.[41] According to this decision, it is the lawyers' but also the judges' duty to inform any party appearing before the court, including witnesses, of their right to an interpreter to express themselves in the language of their choice.[42] Failure to do so should result in a new hearing.

Finally, in 2020, the court further refined the test of true equivalency between majority- and minority-language education set out in *Rose-des-Vents* in *Conseil scolaire francophone de Colombie-Britannique*.[43] Moreover, Chief Justice Wagner refused to give credence to the province's two main arguments. The first claim was that the quality of education should vary based on the number of pupils attending a school (the fewer the children, the lesser the acceptable quality of education). The court answered that the "substantive equivalence" test should be applied using the same measures "regardless of the size of the school or program in question."[44] The second claim was that a province could curtail its section 23 obligations by invoking section 1 of the Charter for reasons of cost. The court answered that section 23 already had an "internal limit" in the form of the "where-numbers-warrant" requirement found at 23(3), which includes "cost and pedagogical needs, related to the number of students who might benefit from the right in question." Therefore, "[f]or an infringement of s. 23 to be justified under s. 1, it must not ... be supported by considerations that have already been taken into account at the numbers warrant stage."[45] The court thus closed a potentially devastating loophole for provincial governments to turn away from their constitutional responsibilities.

In sum, this last decade presented some advances in the domain of education while maintaining the status quo in other areas.

The Future of Language Rights: Opportunities and Obstacles

With this overview of important changes enacted to the language regime through Charter jurisprudence in mind, I now turn to the future. How can we expect the Charter's language rights to evolve in the next decades? This is, of course, impossible to predict with certainty, if only because we do not know what cases will be presented to the Supreme Court or how the political context will change. However, I proceed on the assumption that the text of the Charter will remain unamended.[46] The last time the idea of modifying the Constitution was broached, the federal government quickly and unceremoniously closed the door.[47] I do not foresee there will be much appetite for such discussions in future years. Therefore, the following discussion is based on the existing framework of Charter language rights.

Official-Language Equality and Furthering French-Language Protections

As discussed above, language rights in Canada predate the Charter, and some rights entrenched in the Charter echo former legislation, such as sections of the *OLA,* notably the equality of both official languages. In 2019, the *OLA* turned fifty, and this anniversary was accompanied by renewed pressure for a revision of the act,[48] which hasn't been thoroughly updated since 1988. These demands largely came from official-language minority communities, who have greatly benefitted from the *OLA,*[49] but calls for a reinforced *OLA* have also recently been heard from Quebec, where French as a language of use both at home and in the workplace is in a slow but constant decline.[50] As of 2016, Canada has reached the symbolic point where the proportion of the population who has a language other than French or English as a mother tongue has surpassed those who have French as a mother tongue (22.3 percent versus 21.4 percent, respectively).[51] Indeed, even as the total number of French speakers in Canada has risen, the proportion of Canadians who have French as a mother tongue or first official language spoken has continued to fall in recent decades. This trend has endured since the adoption of the Charter.[52]

In February 2021, then–official languages minister Mélanie Joly presented a reform plan for the *OLA* where further protections for French are central, particularly in Quebec.[53] On her telling, these reforms aim to stop the decline of French in the country. For example, Joly proposed that all businesses under federal jurisdiction of over fifty employees in Quebec have French as the mandated language of work. This has triggered pushback from the anglo-Quebecer community, according to whom both "official-language communities should have [the] same rights."[54] Voices coming from English-speaking Quebec remind us that Charter rights regarding the equality of status of both official languages, found in section 16, could indeed be used to challenge the minister's *OLA* reform plans, if she were to stray too far from this equality. This potential situation is an excellent example of the "constitutional displacement" of the *OLA*,[55] where the entrenchment of various sections of the act into the Charter has made future significant revisions of the *OLA* more difficult. In other words, if the official languages minister wishes to reinforce protections for one official language but not the other, she may have to face a constitutional challenge during which her government will have to justify the entrenchment of an asymmetry between the two official languages in the *OLA*, possibly under the principle of substantive equality.

That being said, a few other aspects of the *OLA* reform plan could have an indirect impact on Charter rights where the two overlap, such as the promise to strengthen bilingualism in the federal public service, which could have an impact on section 20 rights, and the proposal to extend the powers of the official languages commissioner, notably so as to make their recommendations enforceable. These new powers, if used appropriately by the commissioner, could support Parliament's aim to "advance the equality of status or use of French and English" within the federal governmental apparatus.[56]

However, if French continues to decline at the same pace as it has in the past forty years,[57] we could foresee both political strife towards the Charter and an increasingly forceful reconsideration of official bilingualism on behalf of Canadians in the future[58] – possibly to the benefit of "heritage" languages.[59] The tensions inherent in "multiculturalism within a bilingual framework" have already been highlighted in the literature, both from the standpoint of the failure of this regime to adequately account for francophone minority communities outside Quebec and their claims for recognition[60] and from the standpoint of the erasure of heritage languages in this framework.[61] As demographics continue to change, the relevance of the institution of official bilingualism may become more forcefully questioned.[62] The *OLA* reform plan's promise to tackle the issue of the lack of opportunities to learn French for members of the linguistic majority could mitigate French's loss of momentum, but it is impossible to know at this point whether the federal government's proposed changes[63] (and investments, notably in the training of more French-as-second-language teachers) will be sufficient in this respect.

Minority-Language Education: Striving for "Institutional Completeness"

One way to prevent the decline of official-language minority communities is through the reinforcement of minority-language schooling. It is now a widely accepted fact that the language spoken (and learned) at school is one of the most important factors in intergenerational language transmission, coming only second to familial linguistic habits (i.e., the language most spoken at home).[64] As we have seen, this is also something legislators and judges have understood, considering the section 23 rights entrenched and subsequently expanded by the Supreme Court. Such cases will likely continue to trickle up to the court in the years to come, if only because provincial governments continue to be recalcitrant in the implementation and allocation of proper funding for minority schools and because, as of the 2021 Census, changes to the questions pertaining to official languages will make the enumeration of section 23 rights-bearers more precise than ever before.[65] This new data should give some clarity to communities and governments embattled over the question of whether "numbers warrant" minority-language instruction facilities in certain areas.

However, the Charter only explicitly protects education from primary to secondary school – that is, kindergarten to Grade 12 (or secondaire 5 in Quebec). Meanwhile, the Canadian workforce in Canada is changing. First, more women work outside the home today than in 1982. In the past thirty-five years, women's share of the workforce has increased by over 25 percent; they represent nearly half of the labour force, compared to 37.6 percent in 1976.[66] As a consequence of both parents working outside the home, more families rely on daycare today than forty years ago. Second, the qualifications expected in the labour market have also changed in the last forty years, with employers expecting a higher degree of education from their employees. This means more Canadians today attend postsecondary institutions than they did when the Charter was adopted. In 1981, the proportion of the population aged fifteen and over in Canada with a postsecondary degree or diploma (either from a trade school, college, or university) was 37 percent.[67] Today, this proportion has almost doubled, to 65 percent.[68] These trends, which are showing no signs of slowing down, have led minority-language communities (and especially francophones outside Quebec, as anglo-Quebecers are comparatively well-served in this domain with three universities and a dozen colleges of their own) to ask their provinces to create – or, in some instances, to protect – French-language postsecondary institutions. For example, in the case of Ontario, this has meant public mobilization for the creation of the Université de l'Ontario français,[69] whereas in Alberta, a legal battle is shaping up to ensure funding for Campus St-Jean.[70]

In other words, societal changes are stretching the needs of official-language minorities beyond the scope of section 23, in the direction of both prekindergarten (early childhood) and postsecondary education. To use sociological terminology, the goal of these minorities is the attainment of "institutional completeness" in the domain of education, where members of these communities would be guaranteed the full spectrum of education in their language, no matter what pathway to the labour market they choose.[71] Whereas daycare spaces have begun to be addressed in the existing jurisprudence, access to, and proper funding of, postsecondary education will likely soon be tested in court in Alberta, unless an out-of-court settlement between the provincial government and the Association canadienne-française de l'Alberta (ACFA) is reached.

The Charter argument in a case such as this should be the following: if the province has the constitutional responsibility to provide its official-language minority with K-12 instruction in its own language, it will need trained personnel in that language to deliver the curriculum and manage the schools and school boards. This would mean constitutional protection for postsecondary programs in at least a few key domains (of course, education, but also the sciences, social sciences, psychology, and administration, for example). If the courts were to recognize this argument, which will soon be tested in the ACFA case discussed above and will likely make its way to the Supreme Court, it could open the door to a brand new generation of section 23 litigation. If the past forty years are any indication, several different provinces would be subsequently challenged in court, just as they have been since 1982.

Indigenous Language Protections: Charter Convergence?

Another domain where jurisprudential change seems inevitable pertains to Indigenous languages. As Canada comes to terms with its colonial legacy, the oppression (to the point of widespread endangerment and, in some cases, extinction)[72] of Indigenous languages compared to the treatment and protections afforded to French and English, at least since the 1960s, has become a symbol of "white settler colonialism."[73] It is a thorn in the side of recent governments as they have promised to make strides towards reconciliation – an issue that became particularly prominent in the aftermath of the Truth and Reconciliation Commission, which addressed head-on the cultural and linguistic dispossession experienced by Indigenous children in residential schools.[74]

In 2019, the federal government adopted with much fanfare the *Indigenous Languages Act*.[75] This legislation does not recognize Indigenous languages as official languages but rather aims to "support the efforts of Indigenous peoples to reclaim, revitalize, maintain and strengthen Indigenous languages," in partnership with Indigenous communities and in respect of community traditions.[76] While being listed as one of the codevelopers of this bill, the Inuit Tapiriit Kanatami, a national Inuit organization, has distanced itself from the final text of the act, stating that it did not go far enough in its support of Indigenous languages – particularly in the domain of government services and education. According to Inuit Tapiriit Kanatami, "For [Inuit] languages to remain strong, Inuit language schools and learning institutions need to be established ... Effective education requires new pedagogies that reflect our values, culture and languages. For our language to remain strong the Inuit language must be the primary language of instruction in our schools."[77] While this claim for stronger education rights for Indigenous languages is not answered in the first iteration of the *Indigenous Languages Act,* it could be addressed in future amendments. However, this step may not be necessary, as the answer to these claims may already be found in the Constitution. According to Gabriel Poliquin, a de facto protection for Indigenous languages may already exist in section 35 of the *Constitution Act, 1982,* which recognizes "existing aboriginal and treaty rights of the aboriginal peoples of Canada."[78] Considering the nature of Aboriginal rights as defined in the Supreme Court jurisprudence (that is, in *Sparrow* and *Van der Peet*),[79] to be recognized as an Aboriginal right, "an activity must be an element of a practice, custom or tradition integral to the distinctive culture of the aboriginal group claiming the right."[80] The use of a distinct language clearly represents an important "cultural practice." Moreover, the court has already recognized the role of education in protecting one's language and culture in existing language-rights jurisprudence, starting with *Mahe* in 1990. Therefore, the argument could be made that section 35 should include similar kinds of rights as those enshrined in section 23 seeking remedial action for Indigenous languages in the form of protection and public funding for primary and secondary education in those languages, "where the number of children ... warrants."[81] If such a claim were brought forward in the future, we could foresee a form of convergence between official-language and Indigenous-language education rights emerge, which would most likely have the benefit of aligning with the broad aims stated in the *Indigenous Languages Act.*

Another potentially useful section of the Charter with respect to Indigenous languages, which has not yet been tapped, is section 22, by far one of the least talked about elements of Charter language rights. It states that "[n]othing in sections 16 to 20 abrogates or derogates from any legal or customary right or privilege acquired or enjoyed either before or after the coming into force of this Charter with respect to any language that is not English or French." Already in 1982, it had been suggested that Indigenous peoples in Canada were the groups most likely to have claims to "customary language rights,"[82] and the *Sparrow* and *Van der Peet* cases have since validated this intuition through section 35. Such claims would also likely be bolstered by section 25 of the Charter pertaining to general Aboriginal rights. This could open the door to further protections for these languages and could mean, for example, that some of them could eventually become official languages in Canada.

Conclusion

This chapter offers both a retrospective and a prospective outlook on the evolution of Charter language-rights jurisprudence in Canada, taking stock of the strides made in Supreme Court of Canada jurisprudence since 1982 but also trying to imagine where those sections of the Charter will take Canadians next. We have seen that language rights are more obviously anchored in Canada's history than most other sections of the Charter but that these historical legal underpinnings, at one time more restrictive in nature, have gradually been reinterpreted in light of the contemporary context, reinforced by the legislators' newly professed intentions in their regard. We have also seen that while official-language minority communities' claims in court have generally benefitted from a liberal and generous interpretation of Charter rights, at least since 1990, they have also faced some limits with respect to the scope the judges are willing to read into those rights.

That being said – and with full recognition that trying to predict future developments is, at best, a perilous exercise – I have attempted to determine a few ways in which Charter language rights could still evolve and even be widened in scope. Section 23 is promising in this respect, both for official-language minorities as they seek "institutional completeness" in the domain of education and for Indigenous peoples seeking federal support for instruction in their own language and for whom section 23 jurisprudence, coupled with the Aboriginal rights highlighted in section 35, offers some promise. Whether this legal hypothesis will effectively be tested before the courts in the future remains to be seen.

In conclusion, if the text of Charter language rights remains untouched and the political context remains the same, one can hardly imagine as many twists and turns in the jurisprudence in the next decades as there have been since 1982. Several of the broad principles of interpretation of language rights, such as substantive equality and the remedial nature of those rights, seem to have now garnered consensus among the legal community. It would take nothing shy of a tectonic shift in the Canadian polity (i.e., a successful secession referendum in Quebec) to overthrow forty years of jurisprudence in the matter. But as some language rights have now been asserted without doubt, the jurisprudence has also shown an inability to meet official-language minorities' expectations in certain domains where they seek recognition. As previously determined by Emmanuelle Richez, these minorities may "have exhausted the potential of [Pierre Elliott] Trudeau's constitutional language regime and must now move beyond it if they want to ensure their future well-being."[83] This is certainly true, for example, in the provinces west of Manitoba, where francophones lost a historic battle in the 2015 *Caron* case.[84] For minority communities, this would mean relying less on constitutional challenges and more on political stealth to chart a new course in the domain of language rights. However, as legislators manifest a desire to push the boundaries of the language regime beyond its present scope, particularly with respect to furthering protections for the French language, the scope of Charter language rights could hinder, rather than bolster, such initiatives. Nevertheless, what is certain to remain true about Charter language rights for the next forty years is their special place in Canada's identity and their historical weight. If not handled with care, the explosive potential of these rights could trigger a very real political crisis. For that reason alone, one could assume that any new development in the domain of language rights in the future will be made cautiously, whether this evolution comes in the form of legislation or jurisprudence.

Notes

1 *Quebec Act,* 1774 (UK) 14 Geo III, c 83.
2 *British North America Act,* 1867 (UK), 30–31 Vict, c 3.
3 One may refer, for example, to the adoption in 1890 of the *Official Language Act* in Manitoba, an act found to be unconstitutional by the Supreme Court (in *Re Manitoba Language Rights,* [1985] 1 SCR 721), which nevertheless abolished French as a language of use in the province's legislative assembly, in provincial laws and courts, for ninety-five years. It also abolished Catholic and French-language education, provided in the *Manitoba Act.* New Brunswick, Nova Scotia, Ontario, and the North-West Territories all adopted similar legislation to curtail French-language education. For an overview of Canada's language-rights history, see Marcel Martel and Martin Pâquet, *Langue et politique au Canada et au Québec: Une synthèse historique* (Montreal: Boréal, 2010).
4 *Official Languages Act,* RSC 1985, c 31 (4th Supp); *Official Languages Act,* SNB 2002, c O-0.5.
5 *Official Languages Act,* s 2.
6 Cited in James B. Kelly, *Governing with the Charter: Legislative and Judicial Activism and Framers' Intent* (Vancouver: UBC Press, 2005), 94.
7 Robert J. Sharpe and Kent Roach, *Brian Dickson: A Judge's Journey* (Toronto: University of Toronto Press, 2003), 412.
8 *Indigenous Languages Act,* SC 2019, c 23.
9 *AG (Que) v Quebec Protestant School Boards,* [1984] 2 SCR 66.
10 *Ibid,* 79.
11 *MacDonald v City of Montreal,* [1986] 1 SCR 460; *Bilodeau v AG (Man),* [1986] 1 SCR 449; *Société des Acadiens v Association of Parents,* [1986] 1 SCR 549.
12 *Ibid,* paras 63–65.
13 *Canadian Charter of Rights and Freedoms,* Part I of the *Constitution Act, 1982* (UK), 1982, c 11, s 19(2) [*Charter*].
14 Denise G. Réaume, "The Demise of the Political Compromise Doctrine: Have Official Language Use Rights Been Revived?," *McGill Law Journal* 47 (2002): 598.
15 Pierre Foucher, "L'interprétation des droits linguistiques constitutionnels par la Cour suprême du Canada," *Ottawa Law Review* 19 (1987): 390.
16 *Ford v Quebec (Attorney General),* [1988] 2 SCR 712; *Devine v Quebec (Attorney General),* [1988] 2 SCR 790.
17 For a discussion of freedom of expression and language rights in Canadian courts, see Stéphanie Chouinard and Emmanuelle Richez, "The Tension between Freedom of Expression and Languages Rights in Canada: The *Ford* and *Devine* Legacy after Thirty Years," in *Dilemmas of Free Expression,* ed. Emmett Macfarlane (Toronto: University of Toronto Press, 2021), 203–21.
18 *Mahe v Alberta,* [1990] 1 SCR 342.
19 *Reference re Public Schools Act (Man), s 79(3), (4), and (7),* [1993] 1 SCR 839.

20 *Arsenault-Cameron v Prince Edward Island*, [2000] 1 SCR 3, para 53.
21 *Doucet-Boudreau v Nova Scotia (Minister of Education)*, [2003] 3 SCR 3, para 40.
22 *R v Beaulac*, [1999] 1 SCR 768.
23 *Ibid*, para 23 (emphasis in original).
24 *Ibid*, para 24.
25 *Ibid*, para 31.
26 *Solski (Tutor of) v Quebec (Attorney General)*, [2005] 1 SCR 201, para 27.
27 *Ibid*, para 34.
28 *Gosselin (Tutor of) v Quebec (Attorney General)*, [2005] 1 SCR 238.
29 *R v Nguyen*, [2009] 1 SCR 826 [*Nguyen*]. For a broader discussion of this phenomenon and the policy impact of these three court decisions, see James B. Kelly, "The Charter of the French Language and the Supreme Court of Canada: Assessing Whether Constitutional Design Can Influence Policy Outcomes," in *Policy Change, Courts, and the Canadian Constitution*, ed. Emmett Macfarlane (Toronto: University of Toronto Press, 2018), 250–68.
30 *Nguyen*, para 36.
31 *Charlebois v Saint John (City)*, [2005] 3 SCR 563.
32 *Société des Acadiens et Acadiennes du Nouveau-Brunswick Inc v Canada*, [2008] 1 SCR 383.
33 *DesRochers v Canada (Industry)*, [2009] 1 SCR 194.
34 *Ibid*, para 55.
35 *Conseil scolaire francophone de la Colombie-Britannique v British Columbia*, 2013 SCC 42, [2013] 2 SCR 774.
36 *Ibid*, para 56.
37 The third case heard in 2015 was *Caron v Alberta*, 2015 SCC 56, [2015] 3 SCR 511 [*Caron*]. While this case is fundamental for the language regime, denying any "promised right" to French speakers in today's Saskatchewan or Alberta upon the annexation of Rupert's Land to Canada in 1870, the court's decision relies on historical documentation and legislation and not on Charter provisions. For this reason, it will not be discussed here.
38 *Association de parents de l'école Rose-des-Vents v British Columbia (Education)*, [2015] 2 SCR 139.
39 *Ibid*, para 38–41. The test drafted in *Rose-des-Vents* determined that the province had not fulfilled its constitutional obligations because the overall experience offered in École Rose-des-Vents was not equivalent to majority institutions in the same area.
40 *Conseil scolaire francophone du Yukon, School District #23 v Yukon (AG)*, [2015] 2 SCR 282.
41 *Mazraani v Industrial Alliance Insurance and Financial Services Inc*, 2018 SCC 50.
42 *Ibid*, para 35.
43 *Conseil scolaire francophone de la Colombie-Britannique v British Columbia*, 2020 SCC 13.
44 *Ibid*, para 107.
45 *Ibid*, para 150.
46 On the reasons behind Canada's constitutional stasis, see Emmett Macfarlane, ed., *Constitutional Amendment in Canada* (Toronto: University of Toronto Press, 2016).
47 This took place in 2017, when the Government of Quebec introduced its new intergovernmental relations policy: Government of Quebec, *Quebecers: Our Way of Being Canadian* (Quebec: Secrétariat aux relations intergouvernementales, 2017). Prime Minister Justin Trudeau dismissed the idea of constitutional talks mere hours after the document was published.

48 Benjamin Vachet, "Loi sur les langues officielles: Les francophones s'impatientent," *ONfr+*, August 4, 2020, https://onfr.tfo.org/loi-sur-les-langues-officielles-les-francophones -simpatientent/.

49 Emmanuelle Richez, "Francophone Minority Communities: The Last Constitutional Standard-Bearers of Trudeau's Language Regime," *International Journal of Canadian Studies* 45–46 (2012): 35–53.

50 La Presse canadienne, "Deux études de l'OQLF confirment le déclin du français au Québec," *Radio-Canada*, March 29, 2021, https://ici.radio-canada.ca/nouvelle/1780961/ declin-francais-quebec-etudes-oqlf.

51 Statistics Canada, "Proportion of Mother Tongue Responses for Various Regions in Canada, 2016 Census," August 31, 2017, https://www12.statcan.gc.ca/census-recensement/ 2016/dp-pd/dv-vd/lang/index-eng.cfm.

52 Statistics Canada, "Figure 1: Proportion of the Population with French as Mother Tongue, Language Spoken Most Often at Home or First Official Language Spoken, or with the Ability to Conduct a Conversation in French, Canada, 1981 to 2011," *Census in Brief: French and the Francophonie in Canada,* July 2018, https://www12.statcan.gc.ca/ census-recensement/2011/as-sa/98-314-x/2011003/fig/fig3_1-1-eng.cfm.

53 Minister of Official Languages, *English and French: Towards a Substantive Equality of Official Languages in Canada* (Ottawa: Her Majesty the Queen in Right of Canada, 2021), https://www.canada.ca/en/canadian-heritage/corporate/publications/general -publications/equality-official-languages.html.

54 Marlene Jennings, "Opinion: Canada's Official Language Communities Should Have Same Rights," *Montreal Gazette,* April 1, 2021, https://montrealgazette.com/opinion/ opinion-canadas-official-language-minorities-should-have-same-rights.

55 Andrew McDougall, "Reflection on the Official Languages Act at 50: Was the Advent of the Charter So Great After All?," *International Journal of Canadian Studies* 59 (2021): 78–98.

56 *Charter,* s 16(3).

57 According to Statistics Canada, French was the mother tongue of 25.7 percent of all Canadians in 1981, compared to 21.4 percent in 2016. Statistics Canada, "Figure 1"; Statistics Canada, "Census in Brief: English, French and Official Language Minorities in Canada," August 31, 2017, https://www12.statcan.gc.ca/census-recensement/2016/as -sa/98-200-x/2016011/98-200-x2016011-eng.cfm.

58 On this topic, recent surveys seem to suggest that support for official languages and the role of French in Canada are generally holding steadfast but that those convictions are weaker today than they were two decades ago. For more information, see Andrew Parkin, *Official Bilingualism at 50: Are We Taking Full Advantage of Canada's Linguistic Duality?,* Confederation of Tomorrow: 2019 Survey of Canadians, Mowat Research 192 (Toronto: Mowat Centre, 2019), https://www. environicsinstitute.org/docs/default-source/project-documents/confederation-of -tomorrow-2019-survey---report-1/official-bilingualism-at-50---final-report.pdf? sfvrsn=644cc186_0.

59 Heritage languages are broadly defined as mother tongues learned and spoken at home but whose maintenance is not supported by one's social or political context. Nonofficial languages spoken by immigrant communities in Canada – such as Ukrainian, Hindi, or Mandarin – are considered heritage languages.

60 Rémi Léger, "Justice and Official Languages in Canada" (PhD diss., Queen's University, 2012).

61 Eve Haque, *Multiculturalism within a Bilingual Framework: Language, Race, and Belonging in Canada* (Toronto: University of Toronto Press, 2012).

62 The specific challenge of the recognition and inclusion of Indigenous languages within this framework will be addressed later in this chapter.

63 Minister of Official Languages, *English and French*, 14.

64 Rodrigue Landry and Réal Allard, "L'exogamie et le maintien de deux langues et de deux cultures: Le rôle de la francité familioscolaire," *Revue des sciences de l'éducation* 23, 3 (1997): 570.

65 Statistics Canada, *Minority Language Educational Rights: Technical Report on Changes for the 2021 Census,* July 2020, https://www12.statcan.gc.ca/census-recensement/2021/ref/98-20-0002/982000022020003-eng.cfm.

66 Statistics Canada, 2021, "Labour Force Characteristics by Sex and Detailed Age Group, Annual," Table 14-10-0327-01, April 2022, https://www150.statcan.gc.ca/t1/tbl1/en/tv.action?pid=1410032701.

67 Statistics Canada, 1998, "1996 Census: Education, Mobility, and Migration," The Daily, April 14, 1998, https://www150.statcan.gc.ca/n1/daily-quotidien/980414/dq980414-eng.htm.

68 Statistics Canada, "Education in Canada: Key Results from the 2016 Census," The Daily, November 29, 2017, online: https://www150.statcan.gc.ca/n1/daily-quotidien/171129/dq171129a-eng.htm.

69 Catherine Lévesque, "L'Université de l'Ontario français verra le jour," *La Presse,* January 20, 2020, https://www.lapresse.ca/actualites/education/2020-01-22/l-universite-de-l-ontario-francais-verra-le-jour.

70 Audrey Neveu, "Campus St-Jean: L'Alberta dépense 1,5 M$ pour se défendre contre l'ACFA," Radio-Canada, February 2, 2021, https://ici.radio-canada.ca/nouvelle/1767836/poursuite-acfa-campus-saint-jean-gouvernement-frais-avocats.

71 For a broader discussion on the notion of institutional completeness, see Raymond Breton, "Institutional Completeness of Ethnic Communities and the Personal Relations of Immigrants," *American Journal of Sociology* 70, 2 (1964): 193–205; Raymond Breton, "L'intégration des francophones hors Québec dans des communautés de langue française," *Revue de l'Université d'Ottawa* 55, 2 (1985): 357–76. As is recognized by the official language minister in her *OLA* reform plan, "institutional completeness in areas of activity such as education, health, immigration, culture and justice contribute directly to the vitality of communities."

72 Hugo Choquette, in "The Constitutional Status of Aboriginal Languages in Canada" (PhD diss., Queen's University, 2016), discusses at length the vitality of Indigenous languages in Canada today. As he explains, "of the fifty or so languages remaining today, only three (Cree, Ojibway, and Inuktitut) can be considered relatively safe if current trends continue" (2). All others are endangered or on the verge of disappearing.

73 Eve Haque and Donna Patrick, "Indigenous Languages and the Racial Hierarchisation of Language Policy in Canada," *Journal of Multilingual and Multicultural Development* 36, 1 (2015): 27–41.

74 Truth and Reconciliation Commission of Canada, *Honouring the Truth, Reconciling for the Future: Summary of the Final Report,* 2015, https://ehprnh2mwo3.exactdn.com/wp-content/uploads/2021/01/Executive_Summary_English_Web.pdf.

75 *Indigenous Languages Act.*

76 *Ibid,* s 5(b).

77 Inuit Tapiriit Kanatami, "Inuit Leaders Push for Strong Measures That Support the Revitalization, Maintenance and Protection of Inuktitut," press release, 2019, https://www.itk.ca/iyil/.

78 Gabriel Poliquin, "La protection d'une vitalité fragile: Les droits linguistiques autochtones en vertu de l'article 35," *McGill Law Journal* 58, 3 (2013): 573–605.

79   *R v Sparrow*, [1990] 1 SCR 1075; *R v Van der Peet*, [1996] 2 SCR 507 [*Van der Peet*].
80   *Van der Peet*, para 46.
81   As stated in the Charter, parts 3(a) and (b) of s 23.
82   Walter S. Tarnopolsky, "The Equality Rights," in *The Canadian Charter of Rights and Freedoms: Commentary*, ed. Walter S. Tarnopolsky and Gérard-A. Beaudoin (Toronto: Carswell, 1982), 441.
83   Richez, "Francophone Minority Communities," 36.
84   *Caron.*

17

The Provincial Courts of Appeal and Section 24(2) of the Charter

Lori Hausegger, Danielle McNabb, and Troy Riddell

AT ONE A.M., in a sparsely populated part of Windsor, Ontario, Omar Muhammed Omar and an acquaintance were stopped by the police on the lookout for an individual who had robbed a nearby Mac's convenience store a week earlier. The officers shone a light on the pair, and it was apparent that Omar was not the suspect; however, the officers still asked the pair to come towards them and show identification. As one of the constables asked Omar and his acquaintance questions about what they were doing and where they lived, he directed the two men to remove their hands from their pockets. When Omar removed his right hand from his pocket, the constable saw the barrel of a gun. He yelled "gun" and tackled Omar. Once the loaded handgun was secured, Omar was arrested and told of his right to counsel. During a subsequent search at the police station, a clear bag of cocaine was found on Omar.[1]

The trial judge found that Omar's section 9 rights against arbitrary deten-tion had been breached, but balanced the factors developed by the Supreme Court of Canada in *R v Grant* (2009) to decide that the evidence should not be excluded under section 24(2) of the Charter.[2] However, the Ontario Court of Appeal voted to overturn the trial judge's section 24(2) decision. Justice Sharpe argued that the trial judge had committed "reversible error" by not recognizing that the police conduct amounted to an objectively serious Charter breach, particularly as it paralleled the arbitrary detention clearly identified by the Supreme Court in *Grant*. While Justice Sharpe recognized the societal problems associated with guns and drugs, he argued that judges must consider the long-term repute of the administration of justice in apply-ing section 24(2).

Justice Brown, in dissent, reviewed arbitrary-detention decisions to demon-strate the nuances and contradictions in the jurisprudence, which made the trial judge's conclusions about the nature of the police conduct "at street level" reasonable and subject to deference. Brown J also cautioned that the majority's analysis risked reintroducing rigidity into the section 24(2) framework – some-thing the Supreme Court had repudiated in *Grant* when it moved away from its previous section 24(2) test.[3] He concluded that when thinking about the repute of the justice system, judges should understand that "it is fundamental to our social order that Canadian citizens can walk their public streets and exercise their Charter liberty rights without finding themselves at the wrong end of an illegal handgun."[4]

As we reflect on forty years under the *Charter of Rights and Freedoms*, reasonable observers can differ over the degree to which Charter decisions have influenced social policy in Canada, but it is undeniable that the legal rules surrounding police investigations have changed dramatically (see also Roach, Chapter 12 in this volume). Regardless of whether you have more affinity with Justice Sharpe's or Justice Brown's judgment, their written opinions make it clear that when police (or other state officials) have been found to violate Charter rules, and when judges must decide whether to exclude evidence under section 24(2), the stakes are high for the accused and the larger community. And, as demonstrated by quantitative research on section 24(2) decisions in trial courts,[5] there are many accused and many communities directly affected by such decisions.

More research has emerged on section 24(2) since the Supreme Court of Canada changed the test in *Grant* in 2009. However, this research generally overlooks the provincial courts of appeal. This is unfortunate because, given the paucity of section 24(2) decisions by the Supreme Court, it is the provincial courts of appeal that provide the most appellate feedback and guidance on this important question of Charter law.

Our research begins to fill this gap by studying section 24(2) decisions by provincial courts of appeal in British Columbia, Saskatchewan, Ontario, and Nova Scotia, pre- and post-*Grant*. What effect did an important Charter decision such as *Grant* have on the rate of exclusion of evidence? And do different jurisdictions exclude evidence at different rates? Given the impact of the exclusion decision on not only individual lives but also police behaviour and communities, it matters if the provincial court of appeal in Saskatchewan is deciding cases significantly differently from the provincial court of appeal in Ontario.

After exploring patterns across time and jurisdiction, we undertake a quantitative model to better understand influences on the exclusion decision. We find that the *Grant* test did make a difference in appellate court decision making. However, other factors also play a role in these courts' exclusion decisions. Particularly intriguing is the regional variation in section 24(2) outcomes. Our results, coupled with research highlighting provincial variation in section 24(2) outcomes at the trial level, suggest that the fragmentation and influence of localized norms within the criminal justice system shape the remedial application of section 24(2). We conclude by suggesting that to fully understand the impact of the Charter, more research should be conducted as to the causes and effects of provincial and local differences among courts and other criminal justice actors such as the police, Crowns, and defence counsel.

The Place of Provincial Courts of Appeal in the Judicial Hierarchy

Scholars often describe courts of appeal acting as "agents" for their "principal," the Supreme Court (and, by extension, trial courts acting as agents for their principal, courts of appeal). The main motivator cited for compliance is the threat of reversal, something all judges are assumed to care deeply about (for workload, reputation, or other purposes).[6] However, scholars also suggest that appellate courts lack enough carrots and sticks to make these relationships work perfectly.[7] In the United States, a multitude of studies suggest that courts of appeal judges are typically responsive to Supreme Court doctrine but find opportunities to "shirk" to follow their own policy preferences.[8]

In our own study of judges on Canadian Courts of Appeal, "avoiding reversal by the Supreme Court of Canada" was ranked very low as a motivator for decision outcomes.[9] And while judges as a whole spoke of being constrained by precedent, some judges we interviewed suggested that courts of appeal might at times deliberately stray from precedent in an effort to encourage the Supreme Court to change its doctrine and to give the Supreme Court "some guidance." Others suggested Supreme Court decisions are often "quite general in nature, which [leaves] room for appellate courts to fill in important details."[10] All of this suggests that provincial courts of appeal can play an important role in the Charter's impact through the cases they decide – even in those "routine" cases.

Earlier studies in Canada have found that provincial courts of appeal are much more likely to affirm lower court decisions particularly in criminal cases (although the Crown as an appellant generally fares better than the accused).[11] Studies suggest intermediate courts may give some deference to the lower courts.[12] In our survey of provincial courts of appeal justices, deference to the original court scored relatively high in its importance to decision outcomes. The Supreme Court has also increasingly emphasized deference to trial courts; "standards of review," according to one provincial court of appeal justice, are considered to be the "shackles that bind."[13] Perhaps relatedly, the vast majority of justices we interviewed (at least those who had sat on a lower court) argued that experience as a trial court judge was important to being a justice on a court of appeal and made them "less hasty to support appeals challenging trial court actions."[14]

All of this suggests some interesting possibilities for section 24(2) cases and the interpretation of the *Grant* test by appellate courts. Given the room for interpretation by lower courts that exists – particularly for recently created tests – and the infrequency of appeals from provincial courts of appeal to the Supreme Court, the decision to exclude evidence may function differently in different regions of the country. Of course, trial courts and courts of appeal may also differ in their interpretation and deference to the Supreme Court's doctrine in the area. With competing pressures on courts within the hierarchy, examining exclusion decisions, reversal rates, and influences on judicial decisions provides an interesting picture of the impact of courts on the Charter rights of Canadians.

The Background to Section 24(2)

There was debate during the drafting of the Charter on avoiding a US-style automatic exclusionary rule while not duplicating the pre-Charter era where (reliable) evidence was generally allowed at trial regardless of illegal state conduct.[15] The resulting compromise was entrenched in section 24(2) of the Charter, which provides that for evidence "obtained in a manner that infringed or denied any rights or freedoms guaranteed by this Charter, the evidence shall be excluded if it is established that, having regard to all circumstances, the admission of it in the proceedings would bring the administration of justice into disrepute."

The Collins/Stillman Framework

The court developed a framework for applying section 24(2) in *Collins* (1987) that was further elaborated upon in *Stillman* (1997). The Collins/Stillman test required judges to look at three broad sets of factors in determining whether to exclude evidence. The first factor focused on the *fairness of the trial* and was meant to protect against self-incrimination. Here, the court distinguished between evidence that was conscripted (or derived from unconstitutional actions by state officials) and evidence that was not conscripted. The second element of the test analyzed the *seriousness of the constitutional breach by police or other state officials*. The final part of the Collins/Stillman test required judges to consider the *effect of excluding evidence on the repute of the administration of justice*. Here, judges were to consider the seriousness of the offence and the importance of the evidence in the case.

The *Grant* Framework

The Collins/Stillman framework generated considerable criticism, including from notable criminal law professors such as Don Stuart, Steven Penney, and David Paciocco. In a somewhat unusual move, in *R v Grant* (2009), the court directly acknowledged the key problem that these scholars identified – that Collins/Stillman had undermined considerations of "all the circumstances" by largely reducing the exclusion decision to a binary one, dependent on whether the evidence was conscripted or not.[16] Moreover, treating both statements by the accused and bodily evidence as conscripted was conceptually problematic as, unlike statements, collecting bodily evidence may impact privacy and autonomy but does not engage questions about self-incrimination and the right to silence.[17] According to the court, this led to an "apparent incongruity," whereby innocuous breaches in impaired driving cases led to the exclusion of breath samples, while more serious breaches in other kinds of cases, such as drug seizures, did not result in exclusion.[18] Focusing on whether nonbodily physical evidence would have been discovered or not (thereby making the evidence conscripted) was "overly speculative" and sometimes led to "anomalous" results.[19]

To address these problems, the court in *Grant* proposed a more flexible framework that revolved around three major considerations: (1) the *seriousness of the Charter infringing state conduct*, (2) *the impact of the breach on the Charter-protected interests of the accused*, and (3) *society's interest in the adjudication of the case on its merits*. The second and third prongs of the *Grant* test depart in notable ways from Collins/Stillman. Under *Grant*, the risk that the collection of breath or bodily samples would bring the administration of justice into disrepute is now linked to the degree to which the collection of such evidence impacts privacy, dignity, and autonomy rather than being almost automatically excluded. The court specifically highlighted the collection of breath samples as generally being a less intrusive way of collecting reliable evidence.[20] Further, unlike in Collins/Stillman, under *Grant*, situations in which statements are obtained in a manner that violates the Charter increase the chances of exclusion but are not determinative.

Finally, the third prong of the *Grant* test acknowledges that "society generally expects that a criminal allegation will be adjudicated on its merits."[21] As such, the reliability of the evidence is an "important consideration." However, the court noted that truth seeking was only one factor in the section 24(2) analysis and that it would not be appropriate to return to the pre-Charter era, where reliable evidence was almost automatically admitted into trial. The significance of the evidence to the Crown's case can also be a consideration in the third prong.[22]

The court in *Grant* indicated that the trial judge's section 24(2) decision "may not command deference where an appellate court reaches a different conclusion on the breach itself," but the factual findings of the trial judge "must be respected."[23] In subsequent decisions, the court noted that if a trial judge has considered the *Grant* factors and made a reasonable finding, then the decision is "owed considerable deference on appellate review."[24]

Impact of the Section 24(2) *Grant* Framework on Lower Court Decisions

This revised section 24(2) test in *Grant* attracted considerable attention from law professors who analyzed the possible impact of the changed approach to section 24(2) decisions. David Paciocco expressed concern that the *Grant* test would afford trial judges "complete discretion" because of its "fickle" underlying principles.[25] Still, when writing with Lee Stuesser, he predicted that the *Grant* test would "change things dramatically" for breath samples in favour of greater inclusion.[26] Don Stuart, Tim Quigley, and Jonathan Dawe and Heather McArthur concurred that *Grant* would likely lead to much less exclusion in breathalyzer and bodily sample cases.[27]

Other predictions revolved around the nature of police conduct. David Porter and Brent Kettles proposed that *Grant* (read in light of *Morelli* and *Harrison*) would lead to *more* exclusion in cases involving warrant issues or misleading police testimony regarding searches, but Dawe and McArthur suggested that exclusion would now be narrowly reserved for cases involving the most "invasive searches or egregious police misconduct."[28] Similarly, Jordan Hauschildt argued that the Supreme Court's presumption of "good faith" on the part of police would lead to much lower levels of exclusion under *Grant*.[29] Overall, the majority opinion among Canadian legal academics was that *Grant* would lead to higher rates of admitted evidence.[30]

Empirical research on the exclusionary rule following *Grant* found higher levels of exclusion than the researchers anticipated.[31] Steven Penney and Moin Yahya's dataset from 2013 to 2018 found an overall exclusion rate of 70 percent. This was lower than the 75 percent rate they discovered in a sample of 2007 cases, but the difference was not statistically significant.[32]

Interestingly, several of these studies found variation in the exclusionary rates between trial and appellate courts. Specifically, there appeared to be lower rates of exclusion among appeal courts than trial courts. For example, for the years 2014–17, Benjamin Johnson, Richard Jochelson, and Victoria Weir found a 56 percent exclusion rate at the appellate level (total of forty-one *Grant* tests) compared to 74 percent at the provincial trial-court level and 62 percent at the superior trial level.[33]

Similarly, several studies identified salient differences in the implementation of the *Grant* framework across jurisdictions. Examining cases decided between 2014 and 2017, for instance, Johnson and colleagues found the provincial court in British Columbia had an exclusion rate of 89 percent, compared to 72 percent in Ontario and 67 percent in Nova Scotia.[34] They discovered regional differences at the appellate level as well, but with Ontario deciding nearly half of the forty-one cases in their dataset, regional analysis was difficult.

The studies noted above by the likes of Asselin, Madden, and Johnson and colleagues also analyzed patterns of exclusion for other variables such as the nature of the evidence at issue (with breath samples and bodily samples still excluded at fairly high rates). However, only Penney and Yahya considered the characteristics of the judge. They found that while the party of appointment and the judge's gender did not have a significant effect on the decision to exclude evidence, a judge's professional background did. Former defence lawyers were significantly more likely to exclude evidence than their colleagues.[35]

Although each of these studies contributes to our understanding of section 24(2) in the post-*Grant* context, they tend to focus more on trial-level courts.[36] When appellate-level courts are included, the number of cases tends to be small; there is no comparison between the pre-*Grant* and post-*Grant* eras; and individual judge characteristics are not considered.

This chapter aims to start filling this gap by analyzing section 24(2) decisions made pre- and post-*Grant* by provincial courts of appeal in four provinces: British Columbia, Saskatchewan, Ontario, and Nova Scotia. After examining patterns in the decisions to exclude evidence across time and province, we explore the factors that might be influencing those decisions. We begin by laying out our expectations for that analysis.

Expectations

What factors influence an appellate court justice's decision to exclude evidence? Our expectation is that various aspects of a justice's background and identity (such as policy preferences, professional background, and gender) will impact their decision making, as will elements of the case before them (such as the type of evidence at issue and the jurisdiction in which it is being heard). Most importantly, however, we expect judicial decisions to vary pre- and post-*Grant*.

Policy Preferences

One consistent finding from research in the United States is that the policy preferences of justices on courts of appeal can have some influence on their decision making,[37] but not as strong an influence as is found at the US Supreme Court.[38] In Canada, there has been less work done on policy preferences at the court of appeal level. However, studies of the Ontario Court of Appeal have found that policy preferences can affect judicial decisions – at least in some issue areas.[39]

Based on this prior research, we expect that liberal justices will be more likely to exclude evidence compared to other justices.[40] We do not expect this factor to have as strong an influence as in the United States but do want to control for its potential impact.

Findings from some of the US literature also lead us to anticipate that the influence of policy preferences may be affected by the collective decision making of judicial panels on provincial courts of appeal.[41] Considering that the vast majority of appeal-court decisions are unanimous, we anticipate that some judges may not vote based on their genuine political leanings but rather make decisions based on compromise.[42]

Professional Background

There has been less study of the impact that professional background might have on a justice's vote in criminal cases. In the United States, Frank Cross found that former assistant district attorneys were more likely to vote conservatively in criminal cases but found no effect for US attorneys or other practice types in the criminal area.[43] Others, such as Sisk et al., have found different voting patterns among defence attorneys in some criminal-issue areas (see also Frank et al.).[44] Our previous attempts to measure the impact of being a Crown or defence attorney on judicial decisions met with mixed results. For example, justices with previous defence experience were significantly more likely to vote for the rights claimant in criminal Charter cases coming before the Ontario Court of Appeal than justices with other professional backgrounds, but a justice having Crown experience had no impact in the same criminal cases.[45] This is consistent with what Penney and Yahya found in their study of trial-court decision makers in section 24(2) cases.[46]

Thus, we expect that justices with defence experience will be more likely to exclude evidence, compared to other justices; justices with Crown experience will be less likely to exclude evidence than other justices.[47] However, a number of justices had both Crown and defence experience. We don't have clear expectations as to what having both kinds of experience would do to a justice's propensity to exclude evidence, but we do want to investigate the potential effect and control for its impact.[48]

Gender

Previous studies have consistently found gender to have an influence on judicial decision making – but only in certain issue areas such as sex discrimination.[49] When looking at criminal cases, studies have found very mixed results – both in the United States and Canada.[50]

In light of this somewhat contradictory literature, we include gender in our investigation but do not have strong expectations for its impact.[51] Since the provincial courts of appeal hear cases as a panel, our analysis also considers the effect of gender on the collective decision making of judges.[52]

Case Context Factors: Evidence, Jurisdiction, and Grant

As we recounted earlier, in anticipating the application of the exclusionary test following *Grant*, several legal scholars predicted that particular types of evidence would be more susceptible to exclusion than others. Most notably, it was predicted that breathalyzer and bodily samples would be excluded less frequently in the wake of *Grant*. Given the predictions that evidence type matters, we investigate the impact of several types in our analysis of exclusionary decisions over time.[53] Finally, we include measures of the factors of most interest to us: Did the case occur before or after *Grant*, and in what jurisdiction? We expect evidence will be less likely to be excluded post-*Grant*. We expect this to hold true across jurisdictions but include measures to see if exclusion rates differ significantly from province to province.

Models

We use a multivariate model to determine what factors influence a justice's decision to exclude evidence at the provincial courts of appeal. Since the dependent variable is dichotomous, we estimate a logit model. Specifically, we analyze 1,032 decisions by justices on whether to exclude evidence in 344 cases[54] – both pre-*Grant* (1998–2008) and post-*Grant* (2011–20).[55] Our data includes decisions of justices hearing cases in British Columbia, Saskatchewan, Ontario, and Nova Scotia in those time periods.[56]

To capture all section 24(2) cases in a jurisdiction, case transcripts were compiled using both WestlawNext Canada and CanLII.[57] For a case to be included in our study, the case had to explicitly engage in a section 24(2) analysis. This includes two possible scenarios: rulings where the court engages in a fresh section 24(2) analysis, or cases in which the court reviews and explicitly comments on the trial judge's section 24(2) analysis. Following the methodology of past empirical studies, cases in which the panel of justices do not find a Charter violation were excluded from the logit analysis.[58]

Our dependent variable is dichotomous: a vote to exclude evidence or not. Our independent variables of interest include types of evidence, the jurisdiction of the court, and a measure of time (pre- or post-*Grant*). We also have a number of independent variables relating to judicial identity and background, including a justice's ideology, past professional experience, and gender. Because courts of appeal hear cases in panels of three (or five) justices and previous studies have found the effect of panel interactions on justices, we also include variables measuring if a male judge is sitting with a woman colleague and variables measuring whether a justice is siting with a colleague of an opposing ideology. Finally, we follow the findings of previous studies and include a variety of variables to control for their impact: seriousness of the offence(s), Crown as appellant, and previous trial court experience of the justice.

Results

General Patterns

Looking at all the cases coded for our jurisdictions of interest, pre-*Grant*, the courts of appeal excluded evidence 33.1 percent of the time. Post-*Grant*, that number dropped slightly to 30.8 percent. Table 17.1 shows the results for

Table 17.1

Exclusion of evidence by jurisdiction, pre- and post-*Grant*

Province	Pre-*Grant* exclusion rate (%)	Post-*Grant* exclusion rate (%)	Change following *Grant*
British Columbia	29.5 (13)	25.0 (10)	−4.5
Saskatchewan	53.3 (8)	42.4 (14)	−10.9
Ontario	32.2 (29)	28.3 (43)	−3.9
Nova Scotia	25.0 (2)	55.6 (5)	+30.6
Total	**33.1 (52)**	**30.8 (72)**	**−2.3**

exclusion rates by each provincial court of appeal, pre- and post-*Grant*. What is immediately obvious is that there is substantial regional variation in rates. A quick look at Table 17.1 suggests that *Grant* had some effect in British Columbia and Ontario but a more substantial effect in Saskatchewan, with Nova Scotia a drastic outlier. One qualification for Nova Scotia, of course, is the limited number of cases involved. More importantly, however, when we investigated these cases, we discovered that Nova Scotia's appellate court was bimodal in its decision making: it either did not see a rights violation at all (although some cases had dissents on this) or it excluded the evidence.

Grant also led to speculation about how courts would react to different types of evidence using the new framework. Table 17.2 suggests that commentator predictions were correct to a limited extent for bodily fluids (which includes breathalyzer results), as this type of evidence was excluded less often after *Grant*. However, a bigger effect can be seen with statements to the police that had a significant 34 percentage point decline in cases decided after *Grant*.

Table 17.2

Exclusion of evidence by type of evidence, pre- and post-*Grant*

Evidence type	Pre-*Grant* exclusion rate (%)	Post-*Grant* exclusion rate (%)	Change following *Grant*
Weapons	35.7 (5)	37.0 (20)	+1.3
Bodily fluids	26.3 (5)	23.1 (6)	−3.2
Drugs	30.4 (21)	40.7 (44)	+10.3
Statements	56.5 (13)	22.2 (6)	−34.3
Other	28.3 (15)	23.4 (18)	−4.9

Influences on the Exclusion Decision

Tables 17.3 and 17.4 (see appendix) report the results of our logit analysis and the influence of variables on a justice's decision to exclude evidence over the entire time period. Table 17.3 summarizes the results for the main factors we are interested in. A "yes" in the first column means that that factor demonstrated a significant effect on the exclusion decision.

Case Factors

We saw in Table 17.1 that most of the courts of appeal in our study excluded evidence at different rates pre- and post-*Grant*. Table 17.3 indicates those differences were significant – justices were 7.2 percentage points less likely to vote

Table 17.3

Summary of results, individual justices vote to exclude evidence

Variable	Significant?	Change in percentage points
Serious offence	–	–
Weapons	Yes	9.5
Bodily fluids	–	–
Drugs	Yes	8.5
Statements	Yes	11.7
Other evidence	–	–
BC	Yes	−9.3
SK	Yes	19.0
NS	Yes	18.1
Post-*Grant*	Yes	−7.2
J. gender	–	–
J. conservative	–	–
J. liberal	–	–
DefCrown	Yes	26.8
Defence experience	–	–
Crown experience	–	–
Crown appealed	Yes	16.7
Trial experience	Yes	9.1
Man with woman	–	–
Lib with cons	–	–
Cons with lib	Yes	24.1

to exclude evidence post-*Grant,* even after controlling for the effect of other influences. This finding suggests the Supreme Court's directions in *Grant* had an impact at the court of appeal level.

The other pattern found in Table 17.1 – differences across regions of the country – also shows up when controlling for other influences. Tables 17.3 and 17.4 demonstrate that provincial courts of appeal in British Columbia, Saskatchewan, and Nova Scotia all decide section 24(2) cases significantly differently from the court of appeal in Ontario in our time period. A court of appeal justice in British Columbia is 9.3 percentage points less likely to exclude evidence than an appellate justice in Ontario. And a court of appeal justice in Saskatchewan is 19 percentage points more likely to exclude evidence than a justice in Ontario. These jurisdictional differences are large and significant. They also have important implications that will need to be explored more.

We see different results for the effect of evidence on the decision to exclude – depending on the type. Despite differences in the rate of exclusion pre- and post-*Grant* (Table 17.2), our category of bodily fluids (which includes breathalyzers) did not have a significant impact on the decision to exclude over the entire time period. However, weapons, drugs, and statements by the accused to police were all more likely to inspire a vote to exclude than other types of evidence. Indeed, when statements to the police were at issue, justices were 11.7 percentage points more likely to vote to exclude. Thus, although Table 17.2 demonstrates that statements are less likely to be excluded post-*Grant,* they are still treated significantly differently than other types of evidence.

Justice Identity and Background

When exploring possible influences on a justice's decision, previous studies suggest the need to consider various aspects of a justice's identity and background. Table 17.3 demonstrates these factors have some impact on decisions but certainly not as clear or as strong as what has been found at the Supreme Court. A justice's ideology and gender did not show up as significant influences on their decision to exclude evidence. Interestingly, however, a justice sitting on a panel with someone from an opposing ideology may be influenced by that justice's presence. Conservative justices were 24 percentage points more likely to exclude evidence when sitting with one of their liberal colleagues. This influence, however, did not extend both ways. Liberal justices do not appear to be influenced by their conservative colleagues.

In contrast to the other judicial characteristics, one of the strongest effects in our model appears to be the effect of professional background – but not just any background. A justice being a Crown or defence attorney in the past did not significantly affect their decision making on section 24(2). But if a justice had been *both* a Crown and a defence attorney before reaching the bench, they were significantly more likely to vote to exclude evidence. In fact, these justices were 26.8 percentage points more likely to vote to exclude.

Controlling for Other Possible Influences

An earlier study suggested that a justice having previous experience as a trial court judge could have an impact on decisions. Given that, we included a variable accounting for that experience, which did, in fact, have a significant impact on the decision to exclude. Justices who sat on a trial court in the past were 9 percentage points more likely to exclude evidence. In addition, since the literature suggests the Crown tends to have more success and influence in court than the accused, we included a control for the presence of the Crown as the appellant in the case. This appears to affect a justice's decision.[59]

Discussion and Conclusion

As a lens into judicial decision making in the Charter era, our results support research that suggests that the influence of extralegal factors is more constrained at the court of appeal level. We found no differences in the decision to exclude evidence between justices based on gender and only limited differences based on political ideology (conservative justices were significantly more likely to support exclusion of evidence when sitting with a liberal colleague) and on professional background (justices with both Crown and defence experience were significantly more likely to exclude evidence).

The lack of evidence for strong extralegal influences points towards the importance of law and institutional structures in shaping decisions at the court of appeal level. The Supreme Court's call for appellate courts to be deferential to "reasonable" section 24(2) analyses at the trial level seems to have been heeded. In its 2015 *Cullen* case, the Saskatchewan Court of Appeal, for example, called a trial judge's decision to exclude a breath test a "close call" but supported the lower court's rationale.[60] Overall, courts of appeal upheld trial court decisions 68.8 percent of the time post-*Grant*.

Moreover, *Grant* was expected to be a change in "jurisprudential regimes"[61] that legal commentators believed would lower rates of exclusion overall – and we found a modest, but statistically significant, reduction in the exclusion of evidence following *Grant*. Underneath the modest net change, Table 17.2 reveals changes in the rates of exclusion for particular types of evidence following *Grant*. In particular, evidence considered to be "conscripted" under the Collins/Stillman test – statements, breath, and bodily substances – are excluded less frequently. The 2013 *MacMillan* case is an example of this phenomenon. The Ontario Court of Appeal ruled that, among other errors applying the *Grant* framework,

the trial judge mischaracterized the police conduct and placed too much emphasis (in an overly speculative manner) on whether the accused would have
provided a breath sample if her section 10(b) rights had not been violated.[62]

One cannot say whether the breath sample excluded in the Saskatchewan
Court of Appeal in *Cullen* would have been admitted by the Ontario Court of
Appeal in light of *MacMillan,* but the statistically significant differences between
provinces in the rate of exclusion are another manifestation of the human and
cultural factors at play in section 24(2) decision making. Other researchers have
found the same interprovincial variation at the trial-court level.[63] Although the
Supreme Court may try to create national standards for police investigations
around such Charter rights as the right to counsel, search and seizure, or arbitrary detention, it appears that the odds of getting a remedy for police violations
of constitutional standards depends on the province in which one lives.

Of course, there may also be intraprovincial variation in the rate of trial-level
Charter claims (owing to the culture of the defence bar and local policing practices), findings of police breaches of the Charter, and exclusion when breaches
have been found.[64] We do see some attempts by provincial courts of appeal to
shape the application of section 24(2), particularly in response to different applications at the trial level. The Ontario Court of Appeal in *Jennings* noted that two
diverging lines of cases had developed in Ontario on how to treat the Supreme
Court's comments about breathalyzer evidence in *Grant.*[65] The Ontario Court
of Appeal acknowledged that the breathalyzer comment in *Grant* was dicta but
stipulated that it was "no mere throwaway line." The trial judge, according to the
court, had fallen into error in treating any police breach of section 254(3) of the
Criminal Code as favouring exclusion under the first *Grant* factor.

The degree to which such pronouncements influence trial court decisions
remains to be investigated further. Studies from the United States highlight
noncompliance among trial courts and the need for "highly specific directions"
from appellate courts in published decisions to aid compliance.[66] How provincial
court of appeal decisions are interpreted and applied by other actors besides
judges within the criminal justice system, such as police, Crowns, and defence
counsel is also in need of further research.

Those fascinating questions are beyond the scope of our chapter. However,
our findings – that there are statistically significant differences in the rate of
exclusion between these courts of appeal – are another indicator of the real-life
application of Canada's national rights document. In a policy area marked by
historically strong influences of local autonomy (owing to institutional arrangements and cultures),[67] application of the Charter may either respond to, or be

distorted by (depending on one's normative perspectives), localized legal and policy preferences.

Appendix

Table 17.4

Logit analysis of expected influences on judicial votes to exclude evidence

Variable	B	SE	Sig.**
Constant	−1.314	0.325	
Serious offence	−0.318	0.222	0.151
Weapons	0.406	0.209	**0.053**
Bodily fluids	−0.251	0.304	0.204
Drugs	0.377	0.195	**0.053**
Statements	0.494	0.245	**0.022**
Other evidence	−0.184	0.195	0.343
BC	−0.448	0.179	**0.012**
SK	0.787	0.250	**0.002**
NS	0.744	0.377	**0.049**
Post-*Grant*	0.317	0.155	**0.021**
J. gender	0.204	0.187	0.137
J. conservative	−0.243	0.278	0.191
J. liberal	−0.101	0.200	0.616
DefCrown	1.102	0.400	**0.006**
Defence experience	0.054	0.275	0.422
Crown experience	0.283	0.263	0.281
Crown appealed	0.701	0.190	**0.000**
Trial experience	0.421	0.207	**0.042**
Man with woman	0.156	0.178	0.191
Lib with cons	0.607	0.389	0.119
Cons with lib	0.990	0.421	**0.010**

**Level of statistical significance: coefficients significant at the .05 level or better are shown in bold. One-tailed tests for variables in the expected direction.

N = 1032

Log likelihood = −622.85

Chi square of the model = 100.03 (21 df; sig. = 0.000)

Notes

We thank Mariel Alper and Ross Burkhart for their guidance on the quantitative portions of this chapter. And we thank Vanessa Arman, Brendan Dell, Brenna Friesen, Megan Maher, David Said, Alana White, Lily White, and Marc Zanoni for their help collecting the data used here.

1　*R v Omar,* 2018 ONCA 975 [*Omar*].
2　*R v Grant,* [2009] SCC 32 [*Grant*].
3　The earlier test was developed in *R v Collins,* [1987] 1 SCR 265; *R v Stillman,* [1997] 1 SCR 607.
4　*Omar,* para 137.
5　See, for example, Richard Jochelson, Debao Huang, and Melanie Murchison, "Empiricizing Exclusionary Remedies: A Cross Canada Study of Exclusion under S.24(2) of the Charter, Five Years after *Grant*," *Criminal Law Quarterly* 63 (2016): 206; Steven Penney and Moin Yahya, "Section 24(2) in the Trial Courts: An Empirical Analysis of the Legal and Non-legal Determinants of Excluding Unconstitutionally Obtained Evidence in Canada," *Osgoode Hall Law Journal* 58 (2021): 509.
6　Kirk Randozzo, "Strategic Anticipation and the Hierarchy of Justice in U.S. District Courts," *American Politics Research* 36 (2008): 669; Lawrence Baum, *The Puzzle of Judicial Behavior* (Ann Arbor: University of Michigan Press, 1997).
7　See, for example, Donald Songer, Jeffrey Segal, and Charles Cameron, "The Hierarchy of Justice: Testing a Principal-Agent Model of Supreme Court–Circuit Court Interaction," *American Journal of Political Science* 38 (1994): 673.
8　See, for example, Songer, Segal, and Cameron, "The Hierarchy of Justice"; Susan Haire and Donald Songer, "Appellate Court Supervision in the Federal Judiciary: A Hierarchical Perspective," *Law and Society Review* 37 (2003): 143.
9　Lori Hausegger and Troy Riddell, "Judges on Judging in Canadian Appellate Courts: The Role of Legal and Extra-Legal Factors on Decision-Making," *Ottawa Law Review* 52 (2021): 1.
10　*Ibid,* 19.
11　Ian Greene, Carl Baar, Peter McCormick, George Szablowski, and Martin Thomas, *Final Appeal: Decision Making in Canadian Courts of Appeal* (Toronto: James Lorimer, 1998), 176; Lori Hausegger, Matthew Hennigar, and Troy Riddell, *Canadian Courts: Law, Politics and Process* (Toronto: Oxford University Press, 2015).
12　See, for example, Peter McCormick, *Canada's Courts: A Social Scientist's Ground-Breaking Account of the Canadian Judicial System* (Toronto: James Lorimer, 1994).
13　Hausegger and Riddell, "Judges on Judging," 18.
14　*Ibid,* 21.
15　David M. Paciocco, "Section 24: Lottery or Law – The Appreciable Limits of Purposive Reasoning," *Criminal Law Quarterly* 58 (2011): 17–18.
16　*Grant,* para 102.
17　*Ibid,* para 105.
18　*Ibid,* para 106.
19　*Ibid,* para 120.
20　*Ibid,* para 111.
21　*Ibid,* para 79.
22　*Ibid,* para 84.
23　*Ibid,* para 129.
24　See *R v Côté,* [2011] 3 SCR 215.
25　Paciocco, "Section 24," 60.

26 David Paciocco and Lee Stuesser, *The Law of Evidence* (Toronto: Iriwin Law, 2008), 38.
27 Don Stuart, "Welcome Flexibility and Better Criteria from the Supreme Court of Canada for Exclusion of Evidence Obtained in Violation of the Canadian Charter of Rights and Freedoms," *Southwestern Journal of International Law* 16, 2 (2010): 313; Tim Quigley, "Was It Worth the Wait? The Supreme Court's New Approaches to Detention and Exclusion of Evidence," *Criminal Reports,* 6th ser, 66 (2009): 94; Jonathan Dawe and Heather McArthur, "Charter Detention and the Exclusion of Evidence after *Grant, Harrison* and *Suberu,*" *Criminal Law Quarterly* 56, 4 (2010): 422.
28 David Porter and Brent Kettles, "The Significance of Police Misconduct in the Analysis of S. 8 Charter Breaches and the Exclusion of Evidence under S. 24 in *R. v. Grant, R. v. Harrison* and *R. v. Morelli,*" *Criminal Law Quarterly* 58, 3–4 (2012): 530; Dawe and McArthur, "Charter Detention," 422.
29 Jordan Hauschildt, "Blind Faith: The Supreme Court of Canada, S. 24 and the Presumption of Good Faith Police Conduct," *Criminal Law Quarterly* 56, 4 (2010): 469.
30 Patrick McGuinty, "Section 24(2) of the Charter: Exploring the Role of Police Conduct in the Grant Analysis," *Manitoba Law Journal* 41, 4 (2018): 279.
31 *Ibid;* Mike Madden, "Marshalling the Data: An Empirical Analysis of Canada's Section 24(2) Case Law in the Wake of *R. v. Grant,*" *Canadian Criminal Law Review* 15 (2011): 229; Jochelson, Huang, and Murchison, "Empiricizing Exclusionary Remedies"; Ariane Asselin, "The Exclusionary Rule in Canada: Trends and Future Directions" (master's thesis, Queen's University, 2013), https://qspace.library.queensu.ca/bitstream/handle/1974/8244/Asselin_Ariane_J_201308_LLM.pdf;jsessionid=15CD8F090A62EA83497D4BA5CFF67403?sequence=1.
32 Penney and Yahya, "Section 24(2) in the Trial Courts," 533.
33 Benjamin Johnson, Richard Jochelson, and Victoria Weir, "Exclusion of Evidence under Section 24(2) of the Charter Post-*Grant* In the Years 2014–2017: A Comprehensive Analysis of 600 Cases," *Criminal Law Quarterly* 67 (2019): Tables 15–16. These differences are likely less dramatic when considering unreported trial decisions. Based on an analysis of appealed reported and unreported trial decisions, Penney and Yahya note that the rate of trial exclusion would likely be lower overall by approximately 10 percent because reported trial decisions are more likely to feature the exclusion of evidence: Penney and Yahya, "Section 24(2) in the Trial Courts," 535.
34 Johnson, Jochelson, and Weir, "Exclusion of Evidence," Table 15.
35 Penney and Yahya, "Section 24(2) in the Trial Courts," 538.
36 For an exception, see Justin Milne, "Exclusion of Evidence Trends Post *Grant:* Are Appeal Courts Deferring to Trial Judges?," *Canadian Criminal Law Review* 19 (2015): 373. Milne reviews how often appellate courts deferred to trial courts using a sample of sixty appellate decisions from 2011 to 2015 (post-*Grant*) and thirty-eight appellate decisions from 2001 to 2005 (pre-*Grant*).
37 Songer, Segal, and Cameron, "The Hierarchy of Justice"; Daniel Pinello, "Linking Party to Judicial Ideology in American Courts: A Meta-analysis," *Justice System Journal* 20 (1999): 219; Frank Cross, *Decision Making in the US Court of Appeals* (Palo Alto, CA: Stanford University Press, 2007).
38 Christopher Zorn and Jennifer Barnes Bowie, "Ideological Influences on Decision Making in the Federal Judicial Hierarchy: An Empirical Assessment," *Journal of Politics* 72 (2010): 1212.
39 James Stribopoulos and Moin Yahya, "Does a Judge's Party of Appointment or Gender Matter to Case Outcomes? An Empirical Analysis of the Court of Appeal for Ontario," *Osgoode Hall Law Journal* 45 (2007): 315; Lori Hausegger, Matthew Hennigar, and

Troy Riddell, "Does Patronage Matter? Connecting Influences on Judicial Appointments with Judicial Decision Making," *Canadian Journal of Political Science* 46 (2013): 665.

40 To test this expectation, we use a measure of the individual justice's ideology (1 = Liberal, 0 = Neutral, −1 = Conservative). We determined the ideology of justices using a totality-of-the-evidence approach. We examined past political donations, newspaper accounts of justices at the time of their appointment, and any other publicly available data (such as running for office, organizing a campaign, or fundraising) that ties a justice to a party and ideology. We prefer to use a measure like this – that firmly connects a justice to a particular party and ideology – rather than using the party of the appointing prime minister as a proxy, because of the smaller role ideology has played in judicial appointments in Canada. Indeed, some court of appeal justices were appointed to the s 96 trial court by one party and elevated to their current court by the opposing party.

41 Cass Sunstein, David Schkade, and Lisa Michelle Ellman, "Ideological Voting on Federal Courts of Appeals: A Preliminary Investigation," *Virginia Law Review* 90 (2004): 301; Sean Farhang and Gregory Wawro, "Institutional Dynamics on US Court of Appeals: Minority Representation under Panel Decision Making," *Journal of Law, Economics and Organization* 20 (2004): 299.

42 To test for this, we include in our quantitative model a dichotomous variable measuring if a liberal justice is sitting on a panel with someone who is conservative and a variable measuring if a conservative justice is sitting on a panel with someone who is liberal.

43 *Decision Making in the US Court of Appeals.*

44 Gregory C. Sisk, Michael Heise, and Andrew P. Morriss, "Charting the Influences on the Judicial Mind: An Empirical Study of Judicial Reasoning," *New York University Law Review* 73, 5 (1998): 1377; James Frank, Francis T. Cullen, and John B. Cullen, "Sources of Judicial Attitudes toward Criminal Sanctioning," *American Journal of Criminal Justice* 11 (1987): 151.

45 Hausegger, Hennigar, and Riddell, "Does Patronage Matter?"

46 Penney and Yahya, "Section 24(2) in the Trial Courts."

47 To test these expectations, we measured the professional background of justices using a number of different variables. To measure past Crown experience, we used a dichotomous variable (1 = some past experience, 0 = otherwise). We also use a dichotomous variable to measure past experience as a defence lawyer (1 = some past experience, 0 = otherwise).

48 To capture these effects, we included another dichotomous variable (DefCrown 1 = doing both during career, 0 = otherwise). To determine the past occupations of judges, we looked to publicly available resources such as biographies, press releases at time of appointment, and alumni and obituary write-ups.

49 Christina Boyd, Lee Epstein, and Andrew Martin, "Untangling the Causal Effects of Sex on Judging," *American Journal of Political Science* 54 (2010): 389; Jennifer Peresie, "Female Judges Matter: Gender and Collegial Decision Making in the Federal Appellate Courts," *Yale Law Journal* 114 (2005): 1759; Farhang and Wawro, "Institutional Dynamics."

50 For example, Cross, *Decision Making in the US Court of Appeals,* found that women voted more liberally in criminal cases. A study by Tajuana Massie, Susan Johnson, and Sara Margaret Green Massie found they voted more conservatively: see "The Impact of Gender and Race in the Decisions of Judges on the United States Courts of Appeal" (paper presented at the annual meeting of the Midwest Political Science Association, Chicago, April, 2002). And Donald Songer, Sue Davis, and Susan Haire found no

significant differences: "A Reappraisal of Diversification in the Federal Courts: Gender Effects in the Courts of Appeals," *Journal of Politics* 56 (1994): 425. Our own work on the Ontario Court of Appeal found that gender did have an effect but only in criminal, non-Charter cases, with women justices being significantly more likely to vote for the accused than their male colleagues: Hausegger, Hennigar, and Riddell, "Does Patronage Matter?"

51 We measure the gender of individual judges through a dichotomous variable (where 1 = woman, 0 = man).

52 We explore this possible panel effect using a dichotomous variable measuring whether a man is on a panel with a woman.

53 To test this expectation, we include five dichotomous variables that capture the type(s) of evidence in question in a case: weapons, breathalyzer/bodily fluids, drugs, statements by the accused to the police, and "other" kinds of evidence.

54 We had a team of student coders who were each assigned a particular court of appeal's cases. We hosted regular team meetings to review coding questions and examples to address any issues of intercoder reliability. We also spot-checked the coders' work to help ensure accuracy. After creating all the case-specific variables, we "flipped" the data, making a justice's vote to exclude the evidence the dependent variable. Thus, each row of our database represents a different justice's vote. All of the cases included in our database were decided by a panel of three justices, meaning each case has three rows in the database.

55 To analyze the post-*Grant* context, we start at 2011 rather than 2010 to allow for a maturation of the case law following the ruling.

56 Since past studies of trial courts have identified significant regional variations in how s 24(2) is applied, we chose provinces from the West Coast, mid-Prairies, Ontario, and Atlantic Canada to allow us to tap into differences across the country.

57 Each of these databases store many – but not all – court decisions across all levels of Canadian courts. They each have slightly different offerings, so using both allowed us to maximize the amount of available data on s 24(2). There is little transparency on the criteria required for cases to be reported on Westlaw and CanLII, which raises questions about how generalizable reported cases are for drawing conclusions and if more "novel" cases may be overrepresented. By using both databases, we believe some of these concerns are ameliorated.

58 See Madden, "Marshalling the Data"; Penney and Yahya, "Section 24(2) in the Trial Courts."

59 This variable is included as a control. We suspect the result – that exclusion is more likely if the Crown appeals – is an artifact of the fact that accused appeal much more frequently than the Crown, and lose those appeals with the evidence remaining included.

60 *R v Cullen*, 2015 SKCA 142.

61 Herbert M. Kritzer and Mark J. Richards, "Jurisprudential Regimes and Supreme Court Decision-Making: The Lemon Regime and Establishment Clause Cases," *Law and Society Review* 37 (2003): 827.

62 *R v MacMillan (T.)*, 2013 ONCA 161.

63 Benjamin Johnson, Richard Jochelson, and Victoria Weir, "Exclusion of Evidence under Section 24(2)," 56; Penney and Yahya, "Section 24(2) in the Trial Courts."

64 Personal communication with trial court judge; Troy Riddell and Dennis Baker, "The Charter Beat: The Impact of Rights Decisions on Canadian Policing," in *Policy Change, Courts and the Canadian Constitution*, ed. Emmett Macfarlane (Toronto: University of Toronto Press, 2018), 176–80.

65 *R v Jennings*, 2018 ONCA 260.

66 Christina Boyd, "The Hierarchical Influence of Courts of Appeals on District Courts," *Journal of Legal Studies* 44 (2015): 134; Jonathan Remy Nash and Rafael Pardo, "Rethinking the Principal-Agent Theory of Judging," *Iowa Law Review* 99 (2013): 331.

67 Kate Puddister, "How the Canadian Sentencing System Impacts Policy Reform: An Examination of the Harper Era," *Law and Policy* 43 (2021): 1; Karim Ismaili, "Contextualizing the Criminal Justice Policy-Making Process," *Criminal Justice Policy Review* 17 (2006): 255.

Part 3
Reconciliation

18

Canadians' Homeland Has Changed since Patriation Brought the Constitution Home

Peter H. Russell

I REMEMBER SO vividly bicycling to work in 1980 and being confronted at the bottom of Davenport Road in Toronto by a huge billboard showing a flock of Canada geese bringing the Constitution home to Canada. I loathed that kind of simplistic baby talk in what seemed to be Canada's never-ending engagement in constitutional politics. But at that time, I did not understand how much more there was to object to about that billboard than just its simplistic rhetoric. It assumed a national home far different from the homeland we settlers are now learning to share with the peoples whose homelands for centuries have been in what we call Canada, long before our forebears arrived.

We are also beginning to appreciate that in this land we call Canada there is more than one Constitution. The peoples who had lived here for centuries before the arrival of Europeans were ordered societies with established rules on governance that performed the function of what Europeans refer to as constitutions. Settler colonialism at its peak worked hard and with considerable success at destroying the constitutionalism practised by Indigenous peoples. However, Indigenous and non-Indigenous scholars have been recovering knowledge of how presettler constitutional systems worked.[1] Today's challenge is to work out how Indigenous constitutional traditions can be adapted to Indigenous peoples' self-government and their relationship with Canadian governments.

Two Decolonization Projects

Looking back, we can now see that patriation was the intersection of two decolonization efforts. For one, it ended the last vestiges of Canada's formal colonial subordination to the United Kingdom. For the other, it marked the beginning of the decolonization of Indigenous peoples within Canada. Indigenous leaders recognized the collision of these two decolonizing efforts by conducting an international campaign to stop Britain from breaking its treaties with Indigenous nations in order to complete Canada's decolonization.

In the first case, Canada did not have to fight for the end of its colonial status. For half a century, the United Kingdom had wanted to enjoy Canada as an independent ally rather than as a legally subordinate colony. The final decolonizing act was delayed only because of the difficulty Canadians were experiencing in deciding what combination of governments or peoples should have custody of Canada's constitution and, in that sense, be Canada's constitutional sovereign. In the second case, Indigenous peoples had to fight like hell, politically, to get on settler Canada's constitutional agenda. The patriation document, the *Constitution Act, 1982*, contains the first small indications of undoing settler colonialism in Canada.

Part II of that act bears the title "Rights of the Aboriginal Peoples of Canada" and would seem to be its most promising component for Aboriginal peoples whose homelands are in part or wholly within Canada's borders. Section 35(1) of Part II states that the "existing aboriginal and treaty rights of the aboriginal peoples of Canada are hereby recognized and affirmed."[2] The trouble with that wording is the word "existing" – a weasel word if ever there was one. It had been inserted there at the insistence of two western premiers, Manitoba's Stirling Lyon and Alberta's Peter Lougheed. They assumed it would minimize the force of Part II and would freeze the status quo with respect to the rights Aboriginal peoples were actually enjoying under Canadian law at that time, and not lead to an expansion of those rights. It was one reason why the only Indigenous organization that indicated its support for the patriation package of reforms to the Constitution of Canada was the Métis Association of Alberta. A second subsection defines "aboriginal peoples of Canada" as including "the Indian, Inuit and Métis peoples of Canada."[3] The representatives of most Aboriginal peoples were too apprehensive of what interpretation "existing aboriginal rights" might be given to support it.

Aboriginal and treaty rights were afforded some protection in the *Canadian Charter of Rights and Freedoms* from the Charter itself. Section 25 of the Charter provides that the Charter "shall not be construed so as to abrogate or derogate from any aboriginal, treaty or other rights and freedoms that pertain to the aboriginal peoples of Canada including ..." Section 25 then refers to any rights or freedoms recognized by the Royal Proclamation of 1763 and any rights and freedoms that may be acquired through "land claims agreements."[4] The concern behind this provision was that most of the rights and freedoms in the Charter are the rights of individuals and might collide with the collective rights of Aboriginal peoples. For instance, George III's commitment in his 1763 Proclamation to forbid settlement in such parts of his kingdom that had not been ceded to him or purchased by him and that were in Indian nations' or tribes "possession" might be challenged by a person of settler ancestry as a violation of the Charter right to equality under the law. Section 25 would rule out such a challenge. Similarly, it would rule out a Charter challenge by a non-Indigenous individual to harvesting rights secured to an Indigenous people under a modern land claims settlement.

It is difficult to see how section 25 of the Charter can be considered a first step, even a baby step, towards decolonizing relations with Indigenous peoples.

It is true that in his proclamation, King George commits to purchasing land from Indians "at some public Meeting or Assembly of the said Indians," and that may seem to honour, very vaguely, the nation-to-nation treaty-making agreements through which the King acquired land for settlers. But that promise is preceded by a statement that the King's purpose is "to reserve" for the Indian nations and tribes "under our Sovereignty, Protection and Dominion" the lands of North America not yet ceded to him or purchased by him. Indian nations are considered in this proclamation to be living on a huge reservation owned and operated by the British Crown. There is no mention of having just lost a war with those nations nor of making peace with twenty-four of them at Niagara in 1764 through Indigenous protocols. As for the rights and freedoms included in land claims settlements, they are the price Canada was willing to pay to entice First Nations to enter agreements aimed at extinguishing Aboriginal title.

The third reference to Indigenous peoples in the *Constitution Act, 1982* is in section 37(1), which calls for a First Ministers' constitutional conference at which "matters that directly affect the aboriginal peoples of Canada" will be on the agenda and to which the prime minister shall invite representatives of those peoples to participate.[5] The conference was to take place within a year of the coming into force of the *Constitution Act, 1982*. There is no sign here of any awareness that Aboriginal peoples have their own constitutional traditions that are much older than Canada or that before the period of heavy-handed settler colonization, alliances were the appropriate means of regulating relations between independent Amerindian nations and European powers. But at least section 37(1) recognized that there was work to be done in establishing just relations with Indigenous peoples.

The Interaction of Courts and Politics along the Path to Decolonization

Over the four decades since patriation, much work has been done to move relations along the path of decolonization – some of it in the courts, especially the Supreme Court of Canada, and some by more direct forms of political action. A pattern has emerged in which, when the limits of what it seems possible for Indigenous peoples to achieve in one arena are reached, the action shifts to the other arena.

In the 1980s, it looked at first like political negotiations would be most effective in moving the yardstick forward. The constitutional conference called for by section 37(1) took place in March 1983 and resulted in the first postpatriation amendment to the Constitution.[6] The amendment is the one and only made up to now under the "general procedure" of the new amending formula: resolutions of the two houses of the federal Parliament plus resolutions of at least two-thirds of the provinces that have at least 50 percent of the population. Quebec sent an observer but did not officially participate in the conference. This was because the government of Quebec had not accepted an amending process that failed to secure Quebec's control over its powers.

The agenda of the conference dealt exclusively with matters affecting Aboriginal peoples. It was agreed that two clarifications would be added to section 35. One states that rights gained through land claims agreements have the status of treaty rights, the other that section 35 rights "are guaranteed equally to male and female persons."[7] These were helpful but did not address the principal concern of Aboriginal peoples – recognition of Indigenous peoples' right to govern themselves. The 1983 amendment also rewrote Part IV of the *Constitution Act, 1982* on constitutional conferences. Now it provided that amendments to any of the three provisions in the Constitution that refer to Indigenous peoples – section 91(24) of the *Constitution Act, 1867,* section 25 of the Charter, and section 35 of the *Constitution Act, 1982* – can only be made following a constitutional conference of federal and provincial First Ministers in which the prime minister invites representatives of Aboriginal peoples to participate. It also called for such a conference within three years and another within five years.[8]

This commitment to more conferences was honoured; three were held in 1984, 1985, and 1987. These conferences exposed the limits of what could be achieved, at that time and right up to today, in advancing decolonization through intergovernmental negotiations. The topic at all three was the request of Aboriginal representatives to have the Constitution specify that "existing aboriginal and treaty rights" in section 35 includes Aboriginal peoples' "inherent right to self-government." Large segments of these conferences were televised, and polls showed a large majority of the Canadian population favoured Aboriginal peoples enjoying self-government. But the people and the politicians got hung up on the notion of an "inherent right."[9] They wanted the Constitution to spell out exactly what powers that would entail, whereas, for the Aboriginal participants, the "inherent right" was the responsibility their Creator had bestowed on them for looking after their people and the land of which they are a part, a responsibility that could not be carved up on the negotiating table with settler governments. In essence, it was a clash of two very different cultures of constitutionalism that made this grand kind of constitutional settlement impossible.

A month after the last failed effort to accommodate Indigenous peoples, the First Ministers were back at the constitutional conference table at Meech Lake to address Quebec's concerns. This time, there were no Indigenous issues on the table, and no Indigenous leaders were invited to attend. The focus was entirely on Quebec's discontents with patriation – or to use Prime Minister Mulroney's corny phrase, "on getting Quebec back into our constitutional family."[10] However, as the three-year deadline for securing the provincial legislatures' consent approached in June 1989, it was Elijah Harper – the only Indigenous member of Manitoba's Legislative Assembly, holding up a feather to signal his objection to proceeding before the 3,500 people, mostly Aboriginal, had spoken – who killed the Meech Lake Accord. An important protocol of Indigenous constitutionalism prevailed over settler constitutionalism.[11]

The Supreme Court of Canada then moved in with two decisions in 1990 that moved us a tad further along the path to decolonization. In *R v Sparrow*, the court rendered its first decision on the meaning of "existing Aboriginal and treaty rights" in section 35 of the *Constitution Act, 1982*.[12] In a unanimous decision, the court viewed the inclusion of that section in the patriation package as "the culmination of a long and difficult struggle in both the political forum and the courts for constitutional recognition of aboriginal rights."[13] So it rejected the "empty box" assessment of section 35 and found that even if Sparrow and the Musqueam people's right to fish for salmon had been regulated by settler governments, such regulation could no longer apply if it was being applied to a right that was "an integral part of their distinctive culture."[14]

That apparently good news was qualified by a "but," a huge "but" – the Canadian government could regulate this "recognized" and "confirmed" Aboriginal right if its regulation was enacted for a valid legislative objective and interfered no more than necessary. With some very creative jurisprudence, the Supreme Court created a reasonable limits clause for Aboriginal and treaty rights similar to the one that in section 1 of the Charter qualifies all Charter rights. The reason for this lies in the Supreme Court's assertion that "from the outset" (of the struggle to recognize Aboriginal rights) there was "never any doubt that sovereignty and legislative power, and indeed the underlying title, to such lands vested in the Crown."[15]

When you add up the score in *Sparrow*, it turns out that Canada's highest court recognizes settler government sovereignty over Indigenous peoples and also recognizes the right of Aboriginal peoples to carry on activities that have long been integral to their culture – unless a settler government acting within the powers assigned to it in Canada's constitution finds it necessary to restrict such an activity. To this, Aboriginal peoples could scarcely shout "free at last!"

R v Sioui, another Supreme Court decision made at the same time as *Sparrow*, was more promising.[16] It dealt with the interpretation of treaties with Aboriginal peoples. In earlier decisions, the Supreme Court of Canada, like its US counterpart, recognized the injustice of sticking strictly to the letter of the written texts, given the duplicitous manner in which the treaties had been written and used. In resolving contested issues about the meaning of treaties, the court in *Sioui* said the aim was to use various historical records that would make it possible "to choose from among the various possible interpretations of common intention the one which best reconciles the interests of both parties at the time the treaty was signed." This holding was a progressive move towards recognizing a constitutional process that, historically for both Indigenous peoples and settler governments, has been a legitimate way of regulating relations, and it opened up a path to the politics of treaty renovation.

Political Action in the 1990s Results in Progress towards Decolonization

In the summer of the same year that the Supreme Court rendered these decisions, the Mohawks of Kanesatake near the town of Oka and Kahnawake across the Mercier bridge south of Montreal took direct action to resist further encroachment on their lands – this time by the Town of Oka's decision to add nine holes to the town's golf course on a Mohawk burial ground.[17] The Mohawks were quickly joined by Indigenous peoples from across the country. The Indigenous barricades blocking a provincial highway and the Mercier Bridge, and the warriors' standoff with the Canadian army, the RCMP, and provincial police attracted worldwide attention. The dénouement of the Oka Affair did not lead to a settlement of the Mohawks' unresolved land issues or recognition of their sovereignty, but it did convince Canada's prime minister, Brian Mulroney, and his Cabinet that Canada needed a full inquiry into relations with Indigenous peoples – past, present, and future.

Canada's Royal Commission on Aboriginal Peoples (RCAP) was an international first. Canada was the first settler country in the world to have a commission of inquiry composed of Indigenous and non-Indigenous leaders conducting a thorough investigation of all aspects of the relationship between Indigenous peoples and newcomers to their territory. Its seven commissioners were selected by the recently retired chief justice of the Supreme Court of Canada, Brian Dickson. Four of the seven people he chose were Indigenous: George Erasmus, National Chief of the Assembly of First Nations and cochair of RCAP; Paul Chartrand, a leading Métis scholar in the Department of Native Studies at the University of Manitoba; Mary Sellett, the Labrador member of the Inuit Committee on National Issues; and Viola Robinson, president of the Non-Status and Métis Association of Nova Scotia. The non-Indigenous commissioners were cochair René Dussault, a justice of the Quebec Court of Appeal; Alan Blakeney, a former premier of Saskatchewan; and Bertha Wilson, a justice of the Supreme Court of Canada.

Before the RCAP completed its work, there was one change in its membership: Peter Meekison, a political science professor at the University of Alberta, replaced Alan Blakeney. Blakeney resigned from the commission because he held fast to the position that the distribution of powers in the Canadian constitution exhaustively distributed all governmental powers in Canada to the federal and provincial governments, so that the powers of any Indigenous government had to be delegated by either the federal government or a provincial government. Fairly early in the commissioners' deliberations, it became clear that Blakeney's position was incompatible with the other members' respect for Indigenous peoples' inherent right to self-government. Peter Meekison, like the other commissioners, believed that Aboriginal peoples had an inherent right to self-government.

From 1990 to 1996, the RCAP was the centre of action for resolving differences with Aboriginal peoples. It interacted with Canada's last round of megaconstitutional politics, which culminated in the referendum defeat of the Charlottetown Accord in October 1992. At one point, the commissioners met with First Ministers to discuss their vision of Indigenous peoples as partners in Confederation (the title of the RCAP's first publication). The referendum defeat of the Charlottetown Accord, a potpourri of proposed constitutional changes designed to address every source of constitutional discontent in the country, including those of First Nations, Inuit peoples, and the Métis, demonstrated that one big fix of Canada's constitutional concerns was not viable.

The RCAP was a landmark along the path to decolonization. It established one fundamental point that up to this point had been a barrier to any significant progress towards a decolonized relationship with Indigenous peoples – it abandoned acceptance of the claim of Canada's settler governments that they had sovereignty over Indigenous peoples – this was the point on which Alan Blakeney broke with the RCAP. Whatever the inherent right to self-government means, it is incompatible with a belief in the inherent justice of regarding Indigenous peoples as subordinate to settler peoples. This fundamental point is expressed in the title of the executive summary of the RCAP's five-volume final report: *People to People, Nation to Nation.*[18]

The RCAP reported to a government different from the one that created it. The Chrétien Liberal government did not disown the RCAP, but its response to its findings and recommendations was somewhat tepid. By putting forward hundreds of recommendations, the commissioners did not help themselves. None of the big, flashy items for structuring a new relationship, such as a new Royal Proclamation, an Aboriginal Treaties Implementation Act, an Aboriginal Lands and Treaties Tribunal, got done. Still, the RCAP's insistence on people-to-people and nation-to-nation relationships illuminated the way ahead in the decolonization project that began with patriation.

I had one personal experience of how progress towards decolonization would continue to stumble over claims to sovereignty. In 1999, I accepted the invitation of Jane Stewart, minister of Aboriginal affairs and northern development in the Chrétien government, to be Canada's "envoy" to the Dehcho Dene Nations in

Northwest Territories. With rising petroleum prices sparking oil and gas companies' interest in a Mackenzie Valley pipeline, the federal government was anxious to resume land and self-government negotiations with the Dehcho Dene Nations, whose homeland ("Deh Cho" means "big river" – i.e., the Mackenzie) a pipeline would have to traverse. The Dene's insistence that I be officially recognized as "Canada's envoy," rather than a negotiator or facilitator, indicated their determination to assert their sovereignty. My mission was to see if Canada and the Dehcho Dene Nations shared enough common ground to make a return to the negotiating table worthwhile.

My mission was successful, up to a point. After over a year of back-and-forth discussions, the Dehcho Dene Nations, through two grand assemblies, and Canada through its Cabinet, agreed to twenty-one common-ground principles, one of which was that both sides accept the Constitution of Canada. But I had to report that the parties did not agree on two points: one was that the Dene's cost of participating in land and self-government negotiations (hiring lawyers and staff, flying delegations to meetings, and so on) should be deducted from whatever cash payment results from a settlement. The Dehcho Dene Nations held that since it was Canada that wanted access to their territory, Canada should pay for all the negotiating costs. The second point on which the parties did not agree was sovereignty. When my minister, Jane Stewart, saw this, she asked me how it squared with acceptance of Canada's constitution. I pointed out that nowhere in the Constitution of Canada is there a statement that the United Kingdom or Canada claims sovereignty over any Indigenous people. With that clarification, Jane was able to get Canada to negotiate with the Dehcho Dene Nations.

Negotiations did proceed and within a year produced an interim agreement in 2001, which requires Dene consent for any new resource project on their lands and waters.[19] Agreement on a full comprehensive settlement of all land and governance issues has not yet been reached. But the Dehcho Dene Nations story shows how progress can be made in a consensual sharing of the country without formally recognizing the ideologically freighted claims of sovereignty. Minh Do's chapter in this volume on partnerships and comanagement backs up this observation (Chapter 21).

Back to the Courts

After the RCAP, the pace of litigating Indigenous issues picked up. Delgamuukw and other Hereditary Chiefs of the Gitksan and Wet'suwet'en people decided to seek recognition of their ownership of and jurisdiction over their homeland – fifty-eight thousand square kilometres of the British Columbia interior – in the courts. The *Delgamuukw* case reached the Supreme Court of Canada in 1997.

The court's decision was akin to climbing a mountain of loose stone – one foot forward and one backwards. For the first time, the court interpreted "existing aboriginal rights" in section 35 of the *Constitution Act, 1982* as not just carrying on a traditional activity but as Aboriginal peoples' ownership of their homeland and their freedom to do nontraditional things such as mining on their lands. But Aboriginal title, in the justices' view, was subject to legitimate encroachments by the settler state. The court also ruled that courts must give independent weight to oral history submitted by Aboriginal rights claimants. Chief Justice Lamer, who wrote the main opinion, reasoned that failure to do so would defeat the very purpose of Aboriginal rights, which is to reconcile "prior occupation of North America by distinctive aboriginal societies with the assertion of Crown sovereignty over Canadian territory."[20]

That last quote shows that the Supreme Court was still tied firmly in the straightjacket of British imperial and Canadian settler sovereignty over Indigenous peoples. In this respect, Canada's highest court was in line with the highest courts of other English-settler countries, namely, Australia, New Zealand, and the United States, all of which "have always held back from questioning the legitimacy of the full sovereign power of the settler state *over* the Aboriginal peoples."[21] This fundamental limit on the progress Indigenous peoples can make along the path to decolonization continues up to the present day. Indigenous peoples can use settler courts more as a shield than a sword – to defend gains they have made but not to overcome colonization.

Some of the gains Aboriginal peoples have made are gains previously made in the courts. This was most evident in the Supreme Court of Canada's 2014 decision in *Tsilhqot'in v British Columbia*.[22] The Tŝilhqot'in Nation's homeland is a mountainous area in central British Columbia. In 1983, British Columbia granted a licence to cut trees in the Tŝilhqot'in territory without their consent. The Xeni Gwet'in, one of the six bands that make up the Tŝihqot'in Nation, resisted this encroachment by barricading a bridge. BC's Court of Appeal had overturned the trial judge's decision that favoured the Tŝilqot'in on the grounds that common law Aboriginal title applies only to the specific sites where Indigenous peoples resided at the time Britain asserted its sovereignty over all of their homelands. If the BC Appeal Court's decision was upheld, the Tŝilhqot'in and all other Aboriginal peoples would be denied ownership of the land and waters that had sustained them for centuries.

In a unanimous decision, the Supreme Court reversed the BC Court of Appeal. The BC appellate judges had misinterpreted the court's decision in *Delgamuukw*. The court made it clear that it had never regarded Aboriginal title as applying only to the bits of land on which Aboriginal peoples had their settlements. Continuous use of land and efforts to exclude others from using it are the crucial tests for recognizing Aboriginal title. That was the test used by Justice Vickers, the trial judge, who spent five years taking extensive evidence. Vickers found that the Tŝilhqot'in were entitled to a declaration of Aboriginal title to most of the land claimed and a small additional area. In effect, for the first time, a land claim had been settled judicially rather than through negotiations.

Chief Justice Beverly McLachlin, the only member of the court that had rendered the *Delgamuukw* decision, wrote the judgment. But it is significant that her opinion was concurred in by the seven other judges participating in the case, including five appointed by the Harper government. It is difficult to resist suspecting that the Harper government hoped that its Supreme Court appointees would pare back the Supreme Court's jurisprudence on Aboriginal rights. If so, it is fortunate that his appointees let him down.

The Supreme Court not only declined to diminish the meaning of "existing aboriginal rights," but its decision in *Tsilhqot'in* strengthened the protection of them against infringements authorized by settler governments. In *Delgamuukw,* the court's test for a reasonable infringement of Aboriginal rights was breathtaking in its casualness – just about any government-supported resource project would meet the test. In *Tsilhqot'in,* the court ruled that justification for an infringement requires compelling and substantial reasons from both an Aboriginal and the general public's perspective. Moreover, the court viewed Aboriginal peoples on land they are recognized as owning as having "the right to proactively use and manage the land." In these contexts, the role of non-Indigenous governments that is consonant with their fiduciary duty and the "honour of the Crown" is not to lean on an Indigenous people to accommodate projects proposed by outside commercial interests but to work with the Indigenous owners to increase the benefits they can derive from the land and the well-being of the land.

Though all of the above is surely a gain for Indigenous peoples, these gains have been made within a legal system that continues to assume that the Crown (i.e., settler governments) has sovereignty over Indigenous peoples. Further significant progress towards decolonization will be made by Indigenous peoples themselves through national and international political activities.

Indigenous Peoples Advance Decolonization through International and National Initiatives

Indigenous internationalism is a logical response to colonization, which was, after all, a global affair. It began in the 1970s when revolutionary new modes of communication and transportation enabled Indigenous peoples embedded in different states to contact and meet one another.[23] One of the first Indigenous international events was the founding meeting of the Arctic Peoples Conference in Copenhagen in 1973. The United Nations was a tough forum to crack because the nation-states that make up the UN membership, including recently decolonized Third World countries, were uneasy about peoples or nations whose existence within their borders may challenge their own legitimacy. Nonetheless, by 1982, representatives of Indigenous peoples from various parts of the world, including Canada, were able to form the Working Group on Indigenous Peoples, which met annually in Geneva under the auspices of the UN's Human Rights Commission. The working group's main project was to draft a *Declaration of the Rights of Indigenous People* (*UNDRIP*), a project that it completed in 1993. It took another fourteen years for the UN General Assembly to adopt the declaration.

Canada was not among the 144 UN member states who voted for adoption of the declaration in 2007. In 2010, the Harper government agreed to support it as "an aspirational" document. In 2016, Carolyn Bennett, Justin Trudeau's minister of Crown-Indigenous relations, stated that Canada accepted *UNDRIP* without qualifications. Since then, steps have been taken to give *UNDRIP* legal force in Canada. In 2019, British Columbia enacted *The Rights of the Indigenous Peoples Act,* whose primary purpose is "to affirm the application of the Declaration of the Rights of Indigenous Peoples to the laws of British Columbia."[24] In December 2020, the federal minister of justice tabled similar legislation in the House of Commons.[25] Section 5 of Bill C-15 states that "Canada must, in consultation with Indigenous peoples, take all measures necessary to ensure that the laws of Canada are consistent with the Declaration."

It is difficult to assess the value of these efforts to give effect to the UN declaration in Canadian law. A "fact sheet" issued by the Coalition for the Human Rights of Indigenous Peoples points out that, "[i]n fact, the Declaration already has legal effect in Canada. Canadian courts have established that declarations and other sources of international human rights are relevant and persuasive sources for the interpretation of human rights in Canada's Constitution."[26] Both the BC act and the federal bill propose action plans to be made in collaboration with Indigenous peoples to implement the governments' commitments. I would suggest that these action plans investigate whether governments continue to treat lands that are not privately owned or occupied by public buildings as Crown lands. This would be a good test of how prepared settler governments are to recognize the homelands of Indigenous peoples.

Sovereignty is dealt with in the UN declaration only in an indirect way.[27] The first subsection of the declaration's final article, Article 46, states:

Nothing in this Declaration may be interpreted as implying for any State, people, group or person any right to engage in any activity or to perform any act contrary to the Charter of the United Nations or construed as authorizing or encouraging any action which would dismember or impair, totally or in part, the territorial integrity or political unity of sovereign and independent states.

Cutting through all the gobbledygook legalese, I think what this section does is rule out the declaration being used to legitimize an Indigenous group's plan to separate entirely from Canada or from any other UN member state. To the best of my knowledge, no Indigenous people in Canada has separatist aspirations. Still, it must be acknowledged that Article 46 qualifies Indigenous peoples' right to self-determination, enshrined in Article 3.

We have to look to a court action and a parliamentary event for a clear request from Indigenous peoples in Canada to settler governments to abandon their claim to sovereignty over Indigenous peoples and their homelands. Both have to do with residential schools, the most damaging policy resulting from European assumptions about the inferior worth of Indigenous peoples. A component of the 2007 Indian Residential School Settlement, the largest class-action in Canadian history, was the establishment of the Truth and Reconciliation Commission (TRC). The following year, the Parliament of Canada, with representatives of Indigenous peoples in attendance in full traditional regalia and the country watching on television, issued an apology for Canada's residential school program and endorsed the TRC. A request to settler governments to repudiate claims to sovereignty over Indigenous peoples and their homelands was made in the Ninety-Four Calls to Action in the TRC's final report in 2015.

The forty-fifth call is to the Government of Canada, "on behalf of all Canadians" and in collaboration with Aboriginal peoples, to develop and issue a Royal Proclamation of Reconciliation, the first item of which would "[r]epudiate concepts used to justify European sovereignty over Indigenous lands and peoples such as the *Doctrine of Discovery* and *terra nullius*." The forty-sixth call is addressed to the parties to the Indian Residential Schools Settlement and requests that they develop and sign a Covenant of Reconciliation that would include "[r]epudiation of concepts used to justify European sovereignty over Indigenous lands and peoples, such as the Doctrine of Discovery and *terra nullius*, and the reformation of laws, governance structures, and policies within their respective institutions that continue to rely on such concepts."

The Royal Proclamation has not yet been developed nor has the Covenant of Reconciliation. I suspect that one reason for this is the reluctance of the federal government and other non-Indigenous parties to the Residential

Schools Settlement to repudiate their claim to sovereignty over Indigenous peoples. Government lawyers are probably advising caution on this point, and the Trudeau government is wary of the political danger of being accused of giving Indigenous peoples a veto over resource projects on Indigenous lands. The flip side of having mutual vetoes is sharing. When two people marry or enter into an enduring relationship, they agree to share decision making on important issues such as having children and where to live. In effect, such an agreement does mean that each party has a veto, but that would be a very negative way of characterizing the marriage or relationship.

Conclusion

So where does that leave Canada and Indigenous peoples on the path to decolonization? Certainly, further along that path than in 1982. Jeremy Patzer and Kiera Ladner's contribution to this volume characterizes the progress made to date as "normalizing" but not "transformative" (Chapter 19). But I doubt that progress ever will be transformative in terms of how most Canadians think about Canada. A permanent legacy of colonialism may be a sense that governments responsible to the non-Indigenous majority are in charge of our country.

I believe that further progress towards decolonization will depend on Indigenous peoples asserting their sovereignty over their lands and people while using Canadian courts to protect gains they have made in Canadian law. This means that the powers of governance in Canada, the sovereign nation-state, will increasingly be shared three ways between independent federal, provincial, and Indigenous governments.

The homeland has changed significantly since Canadians brought their Constitution home in 1982. It is now clearly a homeland we all share with Indigenous peoples, and the Constitution includes Aboriginal constitutions as well as settler constructs. The land acknowledgments that are made today at the beginning of public events in Canada demonstrate the change that has taken place in our homeland. Of course, these land acknowledgments tend to be ritualistic, but so was singing "God Save the Queen." Who would have thought in 1982 that Canadians would come so far in sharing a homeland with Indigenous peoples? This is surely a new normal.

The only other consequence of patriation in 1982 that rivals reconciliation in importance is the expanded role that the Charter of Rights gave the courts in deciding issues of rights, a consequence that, to a limited extent, overlaps patriation's second decolonization project.

Notes

1 See Val Napolean, *Thinking about Indigenous Legal Orders* (Ottawa: National Centre for First Nations Governance, 2007); John Borrows, *Canada's Indigenous Constitution* (Toronto: University of Toronto Press, 2010); Heidi Bohaker, *Doodem and Council Fire: Anishinaabe Governance through Alliance* (Toronto: University of Toronto Press, 2020).

2 Canadian governments at this time used a small, lower-case "a" in referring to Aboriginal peoples, in the same way that racial categories such as "white" or "black" were written in the lower case. Later on, after the Royal Commission on Aboriginal Peoples, settler governments changed to the upper-case "A," treating "Aboriginal" as a political category. Throughout this chapter, I will write both "Aboriginal" and "Indigenous" in the upper case.

3 *Constitution Act, 1982*, being Schedule B to the *Canada Act 1982* (UK), 1982, c 11, s 35(2).

4 *Canadian Charter of Rights and Freedoms*, Part I of *ibid*, s 25(b).

5 *Constitution Act, 1982*, s 35.1.

6 *Constitution Amendment Proclamation, 1983*, SI/84-102.

7 *Constitution Act, 1982*, ss 35(3), 35(4).

8 *Ibid*, s 37.1

9 See Peter H. Russell, *Constitutional Odyssey: Can Canadians Become a Sovereign People?* (Toronto: University of Toronto Press, 2004).

10 As quoted in Mary Janigan, "Canada's New Deal," *Maclean's*, June 15, 1987, https://archive.macleans.ca/article/1987/6/15/canadas-new-deal.

11 Russell, *Constitutional Odyssey*, 151.

12 *R v Sparrow*, [1980] 1 SCR 1075.

13 *Ibid*.

14 *Ibid*.

15 *Ibid*.

16 *R v Sioui*, [1990] 1 SCR 1025.

17 See Geoffrey York and Loreen Pindera, *People of the Pines: The Warriors and the Legacy of Oka* (Toronto: Little Brown, 1991).

18 Royal Commission on Aboriginal Peoples, *People to People, Nation to Nation: Highlights from the Report of the Royal Commission on Aboriginal Peoples* (Ottawa: Minister of Supply and Services, 1996).

19 This agreement, some subsequent agreements, and the statement of common-ground principles can all be accessed online: "The Deh Cho First Nation Interim Measures Agreement," www.rcaanc-cirnac.gc.ca/eng/1100100032114/.

20 *Delgamuukw v British Columbia*, [1997] 3 SCR 1010, para 81.

21 Peter H. Russell, "High Courts and Rights of Aboriginal Peoples: The Limits of Judicial Independence," *Saskatchewan Law Review* 61, 2 (1998): 275.

22 *Tsilhqot'in v British Columbia*, 2014 SCC 44.

23 See Peter H. Russell, "The Global Dimensions of Aboriginal Politics," in *Education for Australia's International Future*, ed. Rodney Sullivan (Townsville: James Cook University, 1998), 104–11.

24 *The Rights of the Indigenous Peoples Act*, SBC 2019, s 2(a).

25 Bill C-15, *An Act respecting the United Nations Declaration on the Rights of Indigenous Peoples*, 2nd Sess, 43rd Parl, 2020.

26 Coalition for the Human Rights of Indigenous Peoples, *Myths and Misrepresentations: Implementing the UN Declaration on the Rights of Indigenous Peoples*, 2, https://www.afn.ca/wp-content/uploads/2020/11/UNDRIP_Implementation_ENG.pdf.

27 The declaration is included as an appendix to the BC act and federal Bill C-15.

19

Indigenous Rights and the *Constitution Act, 1982*
Forty Years On and Still Fishing for Rights

Jeremy Patzer and Kiera Ladner

FORTY YEARS AGO, Indigenous peoples took to the streets, the courts, offices of influence in Canada and the United Kingdom, and international institutions to have their voices heard at the constitutional table. While many contemporary Canadians might view a modern constitution with a *Charter of Rights and Freedoms* as an unmitigated good, the reality for Indigenous leaders in the era of patriation was much more complex. To be sure, from an Indigenous-rights perspective, a constitution that recognizes rights specific to Indigenous peoples sounds, at first blush, like a positive development. But would it hold as much promise as hoped? Or would the recognition flowing from it be insufficient, perhaps even amounting to further domestication of Indigenous self-determination? The idea of a Charter, on the other hand – the modern quintessence of philosophical liberalism's simultaneously individualizing and universalizing worldview – could more clearly be viewed as a potential source of danger to Indigenous peoples who had long fought for the recognition and preservation of distinct group rights.

Constitutionally, the Indigenous search for disruption and transformation was focused on the assimilationist underpinnings of Pierre Trudeau's liberalism, which, despite celebrating diversity and rights, sought to deny Indigenous rights and nationhood and assimilate Indigenous peoples into an ethnically plural, culturally inclusive, and bilingual society with a new sense of constitutionally derived nationalism. It sought to forge a national identity as a rights-holding, egalitarian, and multicultural nation with two founding peoples – a singular, bilingual nation that would accommodate the "other."[1] Many Indigenous leaders viewed the Charter in the same way that they had viewed Trudeau's 1969 White Paper on Indian policy, which sought to eliminate treaty rights, the *Indian Act*, and reserves as part of a larger project to assimilate Indigenous peoples as undifferentiated individuals into the Canada Trudeau was attempting to create. This is why they got involved. They did so to protect Indigenous rights from the assimilationist, "equality-through-sameness" liberal tradition that permeates the *Charter of Rights and Freedoms* and to seek constitutional recognition and protection of their rights, their nations, and their lands. Indigenous leadership saw an opportunity to create transformative and meaningful change through the constitutional recognition and affirmation of Aboriginal and treaty rights in section 35 of the *Constitution Act, 1982*[2] and through the insertion of section 25 so that Charter rights could not be used as justification to abrogate or derogate from the distinct rights of Indigenous peoples.[3] This is why they fought for protection of their rights in every venue possible – be it in the streets or before the Judicial Committee of the Privy Council, where, in 1981, the Treaty 6 leadership attempted to halt the patriation of the Constitution. In the end, this is also why many Indigenous leaders walked away – as they deemed the protection afforded by section 25 as lacking the requisite strength and the affirmation of Indigenous rights provided by section 35 as insufficient.

Forty years on, Indigenous peoples are still in the streets, the courts, offices of influence, and international institutions demanding the recognition and protection of their rights, their nations, and their lands. Contemporary history has continued to be defined by these constitutional ruptures, as is evidenced by the protests that occurred across Canada in January and February 2020 in support of a traditional Wetsuwet'en leadership recognized by the Supreme Court of Canada since 1997[4] and by the turmoil that surrounded the exercising of Mi'kmaw fishing rights recognized by the Supreme Court since 1999.[5] Instead, while section 35 of the *Constitution Act, 1982* has brought change for Indigenous peoples – notably the constitutional protection of treaty rights and inherent Aboriginal rights – the interplay of law and politics in the ensuing years has reduced the contemporary history of Indigenous rights in Canada to something more managed than transformed and more obscurative of fundamental questions concerning Indigenous sovereignties and constitutional orders.

Our contention is that a complete vision of the transformative promise of the *Constitution Act, 1982* requires acknowledgment of Indigenous peoples' sovereignty and their own legal and constitutional orders and that this acknowledgment was meant to be embedded within those sections of the Constitution – sections 35 and 25 – vigorously fought for by Indigenous leaders. With section 35 recognizing and affirming Aboriginal and treaty rights, constitutional standing and protection were provided to that which was protected by treaty or maintained as an inherent Aboriginal right – including fishing rights and sovereignty, as no Indigenous nation surrendered its sovereignty or its right to self-determination in a treaty.[6] But neither the courts nor Canadian governments have heeded the transformative and decolonizing constitutional visions of Indigenous peoples. None have shown a willingness to truly recognize Indigenous sovereignty or to reconcile themselves with concurrent (embedded) legal and constitutional orders. Instead, they have insisted on maintaining the status quo whereby Indigenous rights are managed and normalized by the state so as to reify Crown sovereignty and obfuscate Indigenous sovereignties. This chapter explores the legal and political contours of this recent history – flowing mainly from the courts' interpretation of section 35 – while paying close attention to the contrast between what Indigenous nations have sought and demanded, on the one hand, and what politics and the courts have given them, on the other hand. With particular emphasis on the struggles of the Mi'kmaq, we will see that – despite the Supreme Court's characterization of section 35 as "a promise to the aboriginal peoples of Canada"[7] – Indigenous peoples still find themselves endlessly fishing for rights.

Sowing the Seeds of Change

It should be noted that while it can be considered a "game changer" of sorts, the patriation of the *Constitution Act, 1982* was neither the first nor the sole legal event to bring about a modern shift in Indigenous rights in the Canadian legal-political landscape. The seeds of an initial source of change – sometimes termed "the modern principles of treaty interpretation" – were planted as early as the 1960s. The development of this new approach put in place, through a number of precedent-setting decisions, interpretive principles meant to offer a kinder, more generous approach to treaty disputes. It was a departure from what had been common since the late nineteenth century, when the Judicial Committee of the Privy Council ruled that the Crown's faithfulness to treaty promises would not be an issue justiciable in the courts, blithely stating that "their Lordships have had no difficulty in coming to the conclusion that, under the treaties, the Indians obtained no right to their annuities, whether original or augmented, beyond a promise and an agreement, which was nothing more than a personal obligation by its governor."[8]

By contrast, in the 1964 decision for *R v White and Bob*, Justice Norris of the British Columbia Court of Appeal insists that the word "treaty" should not become a casuistic "word of art" but rather that "the word of the white man" should simply continue to carry the sanctity it did at the time the engagements were made.[9] In the 1981 case of *R v Taylor and Williams*, the unanimous decision of the Ontario Court of Appeal asserts that, in approaching the terms of a treaty, "the honour of the Crown is always involved and no appearance of 'sharp dealing' should be sanctioned."[10] The judgment asserted that "if there is any ambiguity in the words or phrases used, not only should the words be interpreted as against the framers or drafters of such treaties, but such language should not be interpreted or construed to the prejudice of the Indians if another construction is reasonably possible."[11] Finally, the decision adds that "if there is evidence by conduct or otherwise as to how the parties understood the terms of the treaty, then such understanding and practice is of assistance in giving content to the term or terms."[12]

In 1983, the Supreme Court of Canada underscored and reinforced the newly developing principles of treaty interpretation in *Nowegijick v The Queen*, with Justice Dickson writing in the court's decision that both "treaties and statutes relating to Indians should be liberally construed and doubtful expressions resolved in favour of the Indians."[13] Two years later, Dickson delivered the judgment of the court for *Simon v The Queen*.[14] The *Simon* decision cautions that, "[g]iven the serious and far-reaching consequences of a finding that a treaty right has been extinguished, it seems appropriate to demand strict proof of the fact of extinguishment in each case where the issue arises."[15] Lastly, pertinent to landmark cases discussed in this chapter, and drawing on the *Simon* case, the judgment of the court in the 1990 case of *R v Sioui* maintained that "there is no reason why an agreement concerning something other than a territory, such as an agreement about political or social rights, cannot be a treaty within the meaning of s. 88 of the *Indian Act*."[16]

While the development of the modern principles of treaty interpretation manifests, as Chief Justice Dickson describes it in the *Simon* case, "a growing sensitivity to native rights in Canada,"[17] it is, of course, a doctrinal canon whose pertinence is largely reserved for matters negotiated and disputed *within treaties*, and for Indigenous nations with whom the Crown elected to sign treaties. A second major jurisprudential development, begun just prior to the passage of the *Constitution Act, 1982*, would offer the promise of change for those Indigenous peoples with whom the Crown failed to negotiate any treaties.

The landmark case of *Calder v British Columbia (Attorney General)* did not concern a discrete right to hunt or fish but rather concerned the Nisga'a people's claim to an unextinguished and exclusive title over their traditional territory in northwestern British Columbia.[18] Tribal councillors brought suit against the province seeking "a declaration that the aboriginal title, otherwise known as the Indian title, of the Plaintiffs to their ancient tribal territory hereinbefore described, has never before been lawfully extinguished."[19] The essence of the Nisga'a claim, therefore, was that their title to their traditional lands simply existed, and continued to exist, because it had not been lawfully taken away. Three Supreme Court justices found for the Nisga'a, and three against, with the seventh justice electing to dismiss their appeal on technical, procedural grounds. What was monumental about the *Calder* decision, however, was that the six out of seven justices who chose to hear the case on its merits agreed that the common law recognizes an *inherent* Aboriginal title, sourced simply in the prior occupation of Indigenous peoples, and that is not dependent on treaties, statutes, or royal proclamations for its recognition. This decision came down just a few years after the federal government, under the leadership of Pierre Trudeau, had introduced and retracted the highly controversial White Paper. The *Calder* decision was enough of a game changer that, seven months later, the federal government announced a new land claims negotiation policy for Indigenous peoples seeking recognition of their title to unceded traditional territory (see also Major and Stirbys, Chapter 20 in this volume). The newly developed Indian Claims Commission, in one of its early publications, even spoke of Prime Minister Pierre Trudeau's subsequent pivot on the issue of title:

> The decision not to pursue the issue further through the courts seems to have been chiefly a result of a change of attitude by the Government. The Prime Minister, speaking to a delegation from the Union of British Columbia Indian Chiefs immediately after the Supreme Court decision, told them that the judgment had led him to modify his views. He appeared to be impressed with the minority judgment and remarked, "Perhaps you have more legal rights than we thought you had when we did the White Paper."[20]

Trudeau's and Canada's political leadership were slowly being forced to come to terms with the stark realization that Indigenous peoples had more extensive rights than they likely had ever imagined and had ever been willing to concede, despite the negotiation of treaties and the persistence of Indigenous resistance from the onset of colonization. At the same time, Indigenous political leaders, activists, and thinkers continued to seek out new ways to protect Indigenous legal, political, and constitutional orders from further incursions by the state; to forge transformative forms of rights recognition; to embrace and facilitate cultural, economic, and political Indigenous resurgence; and to differentiate and protect inherent and treaty rights from the neoliberal rights talk and nationalism that dominated the political agenda – be it in the form of the White Paper, discourses of French and English binationalism, multiculturalism, or universalizing liberalist institutions such as the Charter.

Constitutional Visions

There was a strange multiplicity of constitutional visions among the Indigenous leadership in the era of patriation, cutting across multiple points of differentiation, including nation (i.e., Mohawk, Mi'kmaq, Nehiyaw), treaty vs nontreaty, or broader identity groupings (i.e., First Nations, Métis, and Inuit). There was, however, a consensus when it came to the need to protect Indigenous rights from the Charter given the incommensurability of Trudeau's universalizing, liberalist vision and Indigenous intellectual, political, and legal traditions. Indigenous leaders therefore attempted to mitigate the persistence of colonization by ensuring that Aboriginal and treaty rights were shielded from the purview and encroachment of Trudeau's brand of neoliberalism and constitutional nationalism, which came to dominate Canadian politics. But section 25 failed to be taken up as an "interpretive prism" – or shield, for that matter – in the way many had hoped.[21] In fact, section 25 has become virtually absent in Aboriginal law litigation given the Supreme Court's resistance to shielding Indigenous rights from the Charter – even section 15 on equality rights – and its insistence that it is nothing more than a commitment towards reconciling competing rights.[22]

Though there is little to write on the topic of section 25, both Canadian governments and the courts have consistently taken aim at section 35 in an attempt to give meaning to those rights and to define them in a manner cognizable to the state and consistent with its legal, political, and constitutional traditions. Indigenous leaders also sought to protect Indigenous rights – both rights flowing from treaty agreements and those inherent rights that extended from their own legal, political, and constitutional traditions – from continued legislative incursion and any potential future infringements. In essence, Indigenous leaders had developed an astute cynicism from past experience: generations of unsympathetic case law punctuated by a few promising decisions (whose full import could not yet be known), as well as the fickle vicissitudes of territorial, provincial, and federal politics. As Kiera Ladner and Michael McCrossan have argued, although Indigenous leaders walked away from the patriation process, they nevertheless succeeded in creating some semblance of a shield for Indigenous rights and encrypting their own constitutional, legal, and political orders within the Canadian constitution.[23] Similarly, James (Sakej) Youngblood Henderson, Marjorie Benson, and Isobel Findlay have argued that "the spirit of section 35(1), then, should be interpreted as 'recognizing and affirming' Aboriginal legal orders, laws and jurisdictions unfolded through Aboriginal and treaty rights."[24]

And yet, while rights can be created through political processes just as much as legal processes, the political process set in motion for section 35 failed. Namely, the *Constitution Act, 1982* specified that a constitutional conference would be held to iron out through negotiation a number of details, including what was meant by "the existing aboriginal and treaty rights of the aboriginal peoples of Canada."[25] In the end, none of the several conferences held between 1983 and 1987 resulted in a political consensus among the federal, provincial, territorial, and Indigenous leaders involved. Thus, after the beginnings of the modern principles of treaty interpretation, and the first major recognition of the inherence of (nontreaty-based) Aboriginal rights and title, what section 35 brought, at base, was the constitutionalization of the rights of Indigenous peoples, which could be either inherent rights sourced in prior occupation or rights based in treaties. This would be a more robust protection than that which had been afforded to Indigenous peoples previously, to be sure, but both the nature of these rights and the contours of their constitutional protection would be decided by the courts in the years that followed. In effect, the Supreme Court explicitly used its 1990 decision for the *Sparrow* case to explore "for the first time the scope of s. 35(1) of the Constitution Act, 1982" in order to "indicate its strength as a promise to the aboriginal peoples of Canada."[26]

Having an undefined and contested set of rights protected by the Constitution would ultimately give Canadian courts an outsized role in the legal politics of Indigenous rights in Canada. Similar to what Pierre Bourdieu has argued, courts and the broader juridical field in which they reside occupy a peculiar position in that they are not tools purely in the service of the powerful, nor do their jurisprudential deliberations enjoy absolute autonomy from the larger social and political context in which they operate.[27] This has created a particular dynamic for Indigenous rights within the Canadian context. On the one hand, similar to what we have seen thus far in modern legal history, courts can and will prod obstinate governments forward in their recognition of Indigenous rights. On the other hand, one can question the likelihood of finding a fundamental and transformative embrace of Indigenous claims – especially those rooted in fundamentally oppositional nationalities and sovereignties – when the very legitimacy of the courts as a site of arbitration of these disputes depends on the affirmation that ultimate and radical sovereignty resides in the Crown. The courts have thus continuously been asked to take up the charge of defining Indigenous rights despite their reluctance to provide transformative meaning to the concept, to question Canadian settler-colonialism and its logics, to ponder concurrent sovereignties, or to address Indigenous rights or treaties from the vantage of Indigenous constitutional, legal, and political orders. The courts have continued to be asked to take on this role despite their inability to see section 35 as a transformative moment in Canadian politics, one that recognized and affirmed Indigenous legal, political, and constitutional orders as unfolding within the Canadian constitution through Aboriginal and treaty rights – and as shielded by section 25.[28] The courts have taken on this charge with a limited and managerial approach to bringing change for Indigenous peoples, which they had begun through their pre-patriation Aboriginal and treaty-rights cases, suggesting that section 35 did not signify a new book, just a different chapter.[29] Thus, as scholars such as John Borrows and Kiera Ladner and Michael Orsini have argued, the courts have ignored the transformative vision and potential of section 35 and have instead insisted on maintaining Canada's path dependency, embracing an understanding of Indigenous rights antithetical to the living tree doctrine, which has defined the courts' relationship to the Constitution almost from the start.[30]

Fishing in Mi'kma'ki

Donald Marshall Jr. made multiple marks on Canadian legal history, including his fight for the recognition of the Mi'kmaw treaty right to engage in commercial fishing. In effect, the Mi'kmaq, who have never ceded their territories to a European power, have sought to affirm for years their own enduring constitutional order and autonomy through the continuation of a fishery to support their families and communities.[31] In August 1993, Marshall and a friend went fishing for eels in Pomquet Harbour, Nova Scotia. They caught 463 pounds of eel and sold them for $787.10. Marshall, arrested and prosecuted, mounted a defence based not on a claim of an inherent Aboriginal right but rather on a treaty right to engage in the commercial trade of products obtained through fishing. As the son of the former Kji-Saqmaw of the Santé Mawiómi (the traditional Mi'kmaw system of governance), Marshall had a solid understanding of the treaties and Mi'kmaw legal, political, and constitutional orders. Marshall understood that "the Mi'kmaq never accepted or delegated any degree of colonial jurisdiction over their fisheries, according to the treaty, the Mi'kmaq retained this jurisdiction."[32] But while Mi'kmaq had retained their fishing rights and the ability to regulate their fisheries (just as they always had done), the treaties did address other pertinent matters, including trade.

The treaties in question were not the "land cession" treaties characteristic of the Canadian west in the nineteenth century but rather treaties of peace and friendship signed between the British and Mi'kmaq in 1760 and 1761 – a period immediately following the Seven Years' War, when the two nations were seeking to normalize trade and establish peaceful relations. (The Mi'kmaq had previously had an alliance with the French.) Within the treaty in question is a trade clause, or "truckhouse clause," which states from the vantage of a Mi'kmaw signatory that "I do further engage that we will not traffic, barter or Exchange any Commodities in any manner but with such persons or the managers of such Truck houses as shall be appointed or Established by His Majesty's Governor at Lunenbourg or Elsewhere in Nova scotia or Accadia."[33] The courts below the Supreme Court were unwilling to recognize a continuing, positive right to trade sourced in a clause framed in negative terms – that is, in a commitment *not* to trade with anyone but British posts that had once been established for that purpose but no longer existed. The Supreme Court, on the other hand, was more conscientious of the principles of treaty interpretation that it and several provincial appellate courts had been developing in recent decades. The Supreme Court therefore recognized that even the terms of the treaty that were implied needed to be protected when they are necessary to give effect to the parties' common intent. The *Marshall* decision thus recognized a Mi'kmaw right to trade in goods obtained through their fishery.

Yet, while much of what we have seen in the modern principles of treaty interpretation emphasizes the call for liberal and generous interpretations of Indigenous peoples' treaty rights on the one hand, and constitutional protection of those rights, on the other hand, the fact of the matter is that there is much in the way of principles, rationalities, and mechanisms embedded within Aboriginal law that serve to manage, govern, and limit the rights and the opportunities of Indigenous peoples while diminishing Indigenous sovereignties and constitutional orders.

The jurisprudence on the infringement of rights and title is a prime example. In effect, with the same breath that the Supreme Court asserted in *R v Sparrow* that inherent Aboriginal rights – which are rights to discrete practices, such as hunting and fishing, which are *not* rooted in treaties, statute, or proclamation – were now protected by section 35 of the *Constitution Act, 1982* and could no longer be extinguished, the court affirmed that the Crown could infringe these constitutionally protected rights for compelling public purposes. Given the context of *Sparrow* as a simple subsistence-based fishing rights case, the decision uses the example of conservation of endangered fishing stocks as a primary hypothetical justification for infringement. Seven years later, in 1997, the Supreme Court imported the mechanism of infringement to treaty-rights jurisprudence with its decision for *R v Badger* and to Aboriginal title jurisprudence with *Delgamuukw v British Columbia*.[34] As a form of Indigenous right, however, claiming Aboriginal title over unceded traditional territories is something of an order of magnitude greater than a discrete, nonexclusive practice such as fishing. In effect, the Supreme Court's decision in *Delgamuukw* defined Aboriginal title as *sui generis* – a unique form of title – but kept to the common law tradition that title by its very nature suggests some form of exclusivity. With Aboriginal title defined as a form of constitutionally protected "exclusive use and occupation" of land with mineral rights and the capability of resource exploitation,[35] *Delgamuukw* raised the stakes of Aboriginal law across vast regions of Canada that were wholly unceded territory. Parallel with this, the *Delgamuukw* decision expanded the possible bases of infringement significantly:

[T]he range of legislative objectives that can justify the infringement of aboriginal title is fairly broad ... In my opinion, the development of agriculture, forestry, mining, and hydroelectric power, the general economic development of the interior of British Columbia, protection of the environment or endangered species, the building of infrastructure and the settlement of foreign populations to support those aims, are the kinds of objectives that are consistent with this purpose and, in principle, can justify the infringement of aboriginal title.[36]

As Jeremy Patzer has argued elsewhere, the judicial branch prizes the ability to manage the high stakes of Aboriginal law and, in the contemporary era, has de-emphasized some of the more rigid frameworks of legal obligation towards Indigenous peoples in favour of more flexible doctrines.[37] The concept of justified infringement serves this function against the spectre of unsettled claims for constitutionally protected rights and title, as does the Supreme Court's creation of a duty to consult Indigenous peoples (when the Crown is contemplating actions that could adversely affect rights or title) with no absolute obligation to arrive at an agreement.[38] To this end, the Supreme Court has also, at the cost of inconsistency and contradiction with decades of established doctrine, promulgated the power of infringement to the provinces and territories as well. After several years of pointed questions from legal scholars,[39] the court sought to bring clarity in *Tsilhqot'in Nation v British Columbia* by announcing its move away from the doctrine of interjurisdictional immunity – a doctrine that for generations had protected the federal government's exclusive head of power, enshrined in the *Constitution Act, 1867,* to legislate in regards to First Nations.[40] This raises the question of what it now means for Canada "to have a founding constitutional act that enumerates Indigenous peoples and their lands as the sole jurisdiction of the federal government, when the highest court has propagated the power to infringe Indigenous rights and title to all the provinces and territories as well."[41]

Even prior to the question of infringing established rights, there was also the fundamental question of *how* Indigenous rights are constituted, defined, or "recognized" by the courts. This became readily apparent in the jurisprudence for inherent Aboriginal rights when the majority opinion of the Supreme Court in the 1996 case of *R v Van der Peet* declared that "in order to be an aboriginal right an activity must be an element of a practice, custom or tradition integral to the distinctive culture of the aboriginal group claiming the right."[42] The decision goes on to specify that these integral practices, customs, and traditions must have continuity with practices that existed *prior to contact* with European society. This cultural rights approach to interpreting section 35 Aboriginal rights has been the subject of much critique since its invention. Brian Slattery has laid bare its arbitrary foundation in revealing that, in British law, "contact was a legally innocent event. It was only when the Crown acquired jurisdiction over a territory that the issue of the rights of the local inhabitants arose in British law."[43] Such a time threshold for defining what counts as an Aboriginal right also evinces a desire to limit the potentiality of Aboriginal rights to the quaint, small-scale, and subsistence-based.[44] As John Borrows has pointedly asked, "[W]hat would it be like for Canadians to have their fundamental rights defined by what was integral to European people's distinctive culture prior to their arrival in North America?"[45]

Relatedly, the courts, governments, and settler society in general have demonstrated their unease with certain types of Indigenous-rights claims – one of the most prominent examples being claims to rights that are commercial in nature. Commercial-rights claims were raised before the Supreme Court in the trilogy of cases that included the seminal *Van der Peet* decision. The claimants in *Van der Peet* and *NTC Smokehouse* found their claims to commercial rights dismissed outright based on the finding that their engagements in trade were incidental, and not integral, to their distinctive precontact cultures.[46] For the *Gladstone* case, however, the court was likely surprised to find that the Heiltsuk had engaged in the large-scale trade of a variety of goods during the precontact era and thus were able to overcome the jurisprudential and evidentiary slant of the cultural-rights approach. But while much of the Aboriginal rights case law does not restrict claimants to species-specific rights – in other words, one generally wins recognition of the right to hunt for food, not to hunt *moose* for food – the decision in *Gladstone* delivered by Chief Justice Lamer declares that the Heiltsuk demonstrated an Aboriginal right to sell, quite specifically, "herring spawn on kelp."[47]

To the extent that the commercial nature of their claims arouses discomfort – even hostility in some quarters – the *Gladstone* case from the West Coast (Aboriginal rights) and the *Marshall* case from the East Coast (treaty rights) both encountered casuistic, logically deduced principles that served to restrict the rights in question. In *Gladstone*, the majority opinion argued that, while the subsistence needs of any given First Nation are limited, the commercial sale of goods "has no such internal limitation" so long as the market is not sated. It therefore declares that the doctrine of priority first outlined in *Sparrow*, which states that Aboriginal rights holders should have priority over non-Indigenous interests in the fishery, must be "refined" in such a context.[48] The vague solution offered by Chief Justice Lamer quickly brought controversy for its thinly veiled political considerations:

> Although by no means making a definitive statement on this issue, I would suggest that with regards to the distribution of the fisheries resource after conservation goals have been met, objectives such as the pursuit of economic and regional fairness, and the recognition of the historical reliance upon, and participation in, the fishery by non-aboriginal groups, are the type of objectives which can (at least in the right circumstances) satisfy this standard. *In the right circumstances, such objectives are in the interest of all Canadians and, more importantly, the reconciliation of aboriginal societies with the rest of Canadian society may well depend on their successful attainment*.[49]

In effect, in response to this "regional fairness" aspect of the *Gladstone* decision, Kent McNeil has commented that if non-Aboriginal interests in the fishery "are in conflict with Aboriginal fishing rights today, then the historical reliance upon and participation in the fishery by those groups in the past was probably in violation of Aboriginal rights as well. Can reconciliation really be achieved by judicially-authorized perpetuation of past injustices rather than sitting down and working out mutually-acceptable solutions to these conflicts?"[50]

In the case of the Mi'kmaq, the Supreme Court used the above concepts and more to qualify their treaty right to catch and sell fish. In so doing, the court has confined and defined Mi'kmaw treaty rights in such a way that is both cognizable within Canada's neoliberal philosophical and legal traditions and more acceptable to Canadians, particularly those that took to the streets and to the waters in protest of Mi'kmaw fishing rights following the court's release of the *Marshall* decision. And yet the court did not even conceive of the Mi'kmaw treaty right on the same commercial scale as that of the Aboriginal right of the Heiltsuk. Rather, the *Marshall* decision fixates on one word –"necessaries" – in the historical record, written by the governor of Nova Scotia's secretary, in the minutes of a meeting between the governor and the *neighbouring* Maliseet and Passmaquody Nations. In essence, upon reading of the historical treaty request from other regional First Nations that the British establish a truckhouse "for the furnishing them with necessaries in Exchange for their Peltry," as the British functionary described it, the majority opinion determined that the Mi'kmaq, too, must have negotiated an ability to trade for only simple necessaries.

With a convenient rationale for limiting Mi'kmaw commercial fishing rights, the Supreme Court needed only to find a modern definition for the eighteenth-century concept of necessaries. Pulling a concept mentioned in a dissenting opinion in the BC Court of Appeal's decision for the *Van der Peet* case, the court determined for the *Marshall* case that the modern equivalent of necessaries is best described as a "moderate livelihood," which "includes such basics as 'food, clothing and housing, supplemented by a few amenities,' but not the accumulation of wealth. It addresses day-to-day needs."[51] Given its finding that the treaty right had this inherent limitation, Justice Binnie's judgment for the majority stated that commensurate catch limits could be set by federal regulation and enforced without constituting an infringement requiring the requisite burden of justification. Ultimately, the *Marshall* decision served to simultaneously obfuscate and supplement the treaty, given that the Crown's promises to the Mi'kmaq had never addressed any such limitations on Mi'kmaw fishing, nor the extension of British sovereignty to supplant that of the Mi'kmaq. For many Indigenous peoples, the settler colonial hostility to Indigenous rights to trade also represents a form of rank hypocrisy, given the centuries that European nations actively encouraged Indigenous nations to incorporate their traditional subsistence skills into trade relationships. In fact, treaty rights in early Canada were commonly recognized as capable of having a commercial component – the rights to hunting, fishing, and trapping under the Numbered Treaties in western Canada included.[52]

The controversial history of the *Marshall* decision played out on the evening news: the federal government felt entitled to accord the Mi'kmaq a severely impoverished number of lobster traps when compared to the non-Indigenous fishery, and, in the absence of agreement, the non-Indigenous communities around Burnt Church, New Brunswick, erupted in conflict and violence against Indigenous fishers and their property. Law enforcement and the Department of Fisheries and Oceans intervened as well, ultimately leaving some Mi'kmaw fishers dangerously capsized in the open waters of the Atlantic.

The West Nova Fishermen's Coalition, an intervenor representing non-Indigenous fishers in the first *Marshall* case, applied for a rehearing of the appeal in the hopes of swaying the Supreme Court further against the Mi'kmaq. The court took the opportunity to put out a second ruling in what became known as *Marshall No 2*, dismissing the motion and penning a *per curiam* judgment that defended the original decision.[53] In *Marshall No 2*, the court defensively outlines the narrow and limited nature of the treaty right recognized in the *Marshall* case. It also cites *Gladstone* in asserting that "the Minister's authority extends to other compelling and substantial public objectives which may include economic and regional fairness, and recognition of the historical reliance upon, and participation in, the fishery by non-aboriginal groups."[54] This is a striking insertion on the part of the Supreme Court because, in *Gladstone,* the court explicitly rejected the moderate livelihood principle due to the fact that the Heiltsuk had demonstrated a right to a larger commercial-scale herring spawn fishery. Therefore, in *Gladstone,* the court conjured the rationale for an adapted doctrine of priority precisely because it had felt that it could not make use of the moderate livelihood principle to limit Heiltsuk rights. This led the court to adopt the politicized principle of "economic and regional fairness" in order to limit Indigenous rights in the face of non-Indigenous hostility. Mi'kmaw fishers, even though the scope of their treaty right *was* reduced to a moderate livelihood, have had the "more political than legal" justification of economic and regional fairness foisted on them as well.[55]

The Mi'kmaq have therefore been accorded a treaty fishery, ostensibly rooted in Mi'kmaw practices and self-determination that have existed since time immemorial, which is now essentially Crown-regulated. The demonstrable aversion that both the courts and the Crown have to Indigenous control of

Indigenous institutions is a manifestation of their ongoing denial of Indigenous constitutional orders and Indigenous sovereignties. There is a parallel in this legal-political history to a criticism John Borrows aims at the *Tsilhqot'in* decision. Borrows laments the Supreme Court's decision to allow the provincial regulation of forests on Aboriginal title lands, for it is rooted in the Eurocentric notion that the absence of provincial regulation could lead to "legislative vacuums." For Borrows, this is just a symptom of "the Court's failure to recognize that Indigenous peoples have jurisdictional and governmental authority in relation to their lands," and that, on the contrary, "Indigenous law and legal authority would be revitalized and become even more effective if the Court had taken broader steps to recognize this power."[56]

Still Fishing for Rights

No matter the victories that have been achieved through judicial action, the fact is sections 25 and 35 have been left in the hands of the state to interpret, to manage, to normalize, and to limit those legal-constitutional orders that were unfolded through or encrypted in section 35 as Aboriginal and treaty rights. Though writing about the persistence of colonialism in education and "strategies for neutralizing the systemic nature of our oppression," Marie Battiste captures the magnitude of this problem so poignantly in suggesting that we must not conflate the disease with the cure.[57] Indigenous political and intellectual leaders have always understood this - after all, they walked away from the constitutional negotiations in 1981. The promise contained within section 35 and its constitutionalization of encrypted Indigenous rights has been questioned and contested right from the start, such that both courts and politicians have undermined this understanding of encrypted rights by means of limiting, managing, and normalizing these rights through obscurative judicial interpretive principles and the constant reification of a unitary Crown sovereignty. As Kiera Ladner and Michael Orsini have argued elsewhere, the actions of Canadian governments and courts have been consistent with the path dependency that has defined and confined Indigenous policy from the creation of Canada.[58] Despite the transformative vision and potential of sections 25 and 35, neither judge nor politician has strayed far from the past, largely marginalizing Indigenous visions of the Canadian constitutional order while always trying to confine and define Aboriginal and treaty rights so as to make them cognizable and acceptable for the settler state. In so doing, they have ignored the living tree doctrine and embraced an originalist approach to Aboriginal and treaty-rights jurisprudence, thereby developing "two distinct constitutional methods" for Indigenous and non-Indigenous peoples in Canada, producing an Aboriginal law that simultaneously "recognizes and denies Aboriginal rights."[59]

Attaining constitutional protection and recognition of Indigenous rights in the settler state's constitution has not proven to be an effective cure for Canada's treatment of Indigenous rights, its systemic oppression of Indigenous nations, or its dismissive treatment of Indigenous sovereignties and constitutional orders. The courts have simply not taken this step. Instead, they have continued to provide new ways to manage Indigenous rights and to make these rights more amenable to Canadians. As Kent McNeil argues in a comparative assessment of Indigenous rights in Australia and Canada,

> regardless of the strengths of legal arguments in favour of Indigenous peoples, there are limits to how far the courts in Australia and Canada are willing to go to correct the injustices caused by colonialism and dispossession. Despite what judges may say about maintaining legal principle, at the end of the day what really seems to determine the outcome in these kinds of cases is the extent to which Indigenous rights can be reconciled with the history of British settlement without disturbing the current political and economic power structure.[60]

Recognition and protection have not been transformative. For even when Indigenous peoples have won – and won big – the win has been mitigated by courts and governments intent on managing rights, reifying Crown sovereignty, and stifling legal and constitutional pluralism. Simply put, neither has been willing to – or has seen themselves as able to – apply the living tree doctrine or to disrupt Canada's path dependency by giving effect to the reality of coautonomous jurisdictions under section 35.

This is evident if we look to the Mi'kmaq. The *Marshall* decisions did not end the dispute over the fisheries, the meaning of the treaty, or the coexistence of multiple sovereignties. They did not allow Mi'kmaq to fish unchallenged, in accordance with Mi'kmaw laws (as set forth or interpreted today by either a band council or the Santé Mawiómi). Nor did the *Marshall* decisions eliminate government incursion into Mi'kmaw jurisdictions or end the state's insistence on managing, confining, defining, reconciling, and/or normalizing Mi'kmaw fishing rights. Nearly forty years after the patriation of Canada's constitution and the inclusion of sections 25 and 35 – in part, under the leadership of the Santé Mawiómi, their spokesperson Donald Marshall Sr, and their constitutional adviser James (Sakej) Youngblood Henderson[61] – and twenty-two years after the Supreme Court's *Marshall* decision, Mi'kmaq are still "fishing for a 'new' constitutional order."[62]

In September 2020, the community of Sipekne'katik (Indian Brook) launched its "self-regulated" moderate livelihood fishery outside of the limits of the commercial lobster season, in what had been used post-*Marshall* as the food-fishery season (wherein lobster could be provided to community members but not sold commercially). This was not the first time that Sipekne'katik had launched its own self-regulated fishery, as members of the community had gone fishing in defence of their rights immediately after *Marshall No 1*. Just as it had then, the dropping of a lobster trap outside of Canada's regulatory regime (but consistent with Mi'kmaw constitutional law and the rights protected by the treaties between the Mi'kmaq and the Crown) caused quite a stir. But this time, it was Sipekne'katik and not Burnt Church (Eskinuopitijk) that was the flashpoint.[63] This time, it was the non-Indigenous commercial fishers around the Mi'kmaw community of Sipekne'katik (in Middle West Pubnico and Saulnierville) who organized flotillas, threatened Mi'kmaq, vandalized property, and engaged in vigilantism – as people were beaten, lobster catches destroyed, traps vandalized, vehicles torched, and a lobster pound burned. Interestingly, this time, the Department of Fisheries and Oceans and law enforcement did not show up to stop Mi'kmaw fishers and impose Canadian law in their efforts to manage Indigenous rights assertions. Instead, they watched as non-Indigenous vigilantes attempted to manage the Indigenous fishery themselves.

This time, the government did not send in armed personnel to uphold its sovereignty or ask the Supreme Court to re-engage. Instead, Prime Minister Justin Trudeau upheld his father's constitution but did so in a manner that continues to manage Indigenous rights and obscure Indigenous constitutional orders, stating that the "government is accelerating the process of fully recognizing Indigenous fishers' rights to earn a moderate livelihood."[64] This time, the government is actively pursuing negotiations as to the meaning of "moderate livelihood" – negotiations that again seek to delimit Indigenous rights. For Canada, the question will be to either stay the course and continue to obfuscate Indigenous constitutional orders or move ahead with the nation-to-nation relationship that Justin Trudeau's Liberals campaigned on and find a way to come to terms with or reconcile the coautonomous jurisdictions that arise from concurrent constitutional orders. For the Mi'kmaq, the question remains the same as it did in 1981 when Mi'kmaw leaders walked away from the patriation process – to acquiesce and accept Crown sovereignty or to keep fishing (and fighting) for their treaty rights and their legal-constitutional orders.

Notes

The authors gratefully acknowledge the support of research assistants Dane Monkman, Hope Ace, and Nouran Hamzeh, as well as the support of the Canada Research Chairs Program.

1 Kenneth McRoberts, "Canada and the Multinational State," *Canadian Journal of Political Science* 34, 4 (2001): 683–713.

2   Section 35, recognizing the Indian, Inuit, and Métis peoples as Aboriginal peoples, states that "[t]he existing aboriginal and treaty rights of the aboriginal peoples of Canada are hereby recognized and affirmed": *Constitution Act, 1982,* being Schedule B to the *Canada Act 1982* (UK), 1982, c 11, s 35.

3   Section 25 of the Charter begins by stating that "[t]he guarantee in this Charter of certain rights and freedoms shall not be construed so as to abrogate or derogate from any aboriginal, treaty or other rights or freedoms that pertain to the aboriginal peoples of Canada": *Canadian Charter of Rights and Freedoms,* Part I of the *Constitution Act, 1982,* being Schedule B to the *Canada Act 1982* (UK), 1982, c 11, s 25.

4   *Delgamuukw v British Columbia,* [1997] 3 SCR 1010 [*Delgamuukw*].

5   *R v Marshall,* [1999] 3 SCR 456 [*Marshall No 1*].

6   Kiera Ladner, "Indigenous Constitutional Paradox: Both Monumental Achievement and Monumental Defeat," in *Patriation and Its Consequences: Constitution Making in Canada,* ed. Lois Harder and Steve Patten (Vancouver: UBC Press, 2015), 267–89; Kiera Ladner, "Treaty Federalism: An Indigenous Vision of Canadian Federalisms," in *New Trends in Canadian Federalism,* ed. Francois Rocher and Miriam Smith (Peterborough, ON: Broadview Press, 2003), 167–94.

7   *R v Sparrow,* [1990] 1 SCR 1075, 1083 [*Sparrow*].

8   *Attorney-General of Ontario v Attorney-General of Canada: Re Indian Claims,* [1897] AC 199, 213 (PC). At the time, the Judicial Committee of the Privy Council in the United Kingdom was Canada's highest court.

9   *R v White and Bob,* [1964] 50 DLR (2d) 613, 649 (BCCA), aff'd [1965] 52 DLR (2d) 481 (SCC) [*White and Bob*].

10 *R v Taylor and Williams,* [1981] 62 CCC (2d), 235, [1982] 34 OR (2d) 360 (ONCA) [*CCC*].

11 *Ibid,* 236.

12 *Ibid.* Justice MacKinnon even states that consideration should be given to the oral traditions of the tribe concerned.

13 *Nowegijick v The Queen,* [1983] 1 SCR 29, 36.

14 *Simon v The Queen,* [1985] 2 SCR 387 [*Simon*].

15 *Ibid,* 405–6.

16 *R v Sioui,* [1990] 1 SCR 1025, 1043. See also *Simon,* 410.

17 *Simon,* 399.

18 *Calder v British Columbia (Attorney General),* [1973] SCR 313.

19 *Ibid,* 345.

20 Indian Claims Commission, *Indian Claims in Canada: An Introductory Essay and Selected List of Library Holdings* (Ottawa: Research Resource Centre, Indian Claims Commission, 1975), 25.

21 William Pentney, "The Rights of the Aboriginal Peoples of Canada in the Constitution Act, 1982: Part 1 – The Interpretive Prism of Section 25," *UBC Law Review* 22 (1988): 57.

22 *R v Kapp,* [2008] 2 SCR 483.

23 Kiera Ladner and Michael McCrossan, "The Road Not Taken: Aboriginal Rights after the Re-imagining of the Canadian Constitutional Order," in *Contested Constitutionalism: Reflections on the Canadian Charter of Rights and Freedoms,* ed. James Kelly and Christopher Manfredi (Vancouver: UBC Press, 2009), 268.

24 James (Sakej) Youngblood Henderson, Marjorie Benson, and Isobel Findlay, *Aboriginal Tenure in the Constitution of Canada* (Scarborough, ON: Carswell, 2000).

25 *Constitution Act, 1982,* being Schedule B to the *Canada Act 1982* (UK), 1982, c 11, s 35.

26 *Sparrow,* 1082–83.

27 Pierre Bourdieu, "The Force of Law: Toward a Sociology of the Juridical Field," *Hastings Law Journal* 38, 5 (1987): 805–53.
28 Henderson, Benson, and Findlay "Aboriginal Tenure," 428; James (Sakej) Youngblood Henderson, "Empowering Treaty Federalism," *Saskatchewan Law Review* 58, 2 (1994): 241–329.
29 *Mitchell v MNR*, 2001 SCC 33, 1 SCR 911, 971.
30 John Borrows, "(Ab)Originalism and Canada's Constitution," *Supreme Court Law Review* 58, 2d (2012): 351–98; Kiera Ladner and Michael Orsini, "The Persistence of Paradigm Paralysis: The *First Nations Governance Act* as the Continuation of Colonial Policy," in *Canada: The State of the Federation 2003*, ed. Michael Murphy (Montreal/Kingston: McGill-Queen's University Press, 2005), 185–203.
31 Kiera Ladner, "Up the Creek: Fishing for a New Constitutional Order," *Canadian Journal of Political Science* 38, 4 (2005): 923–53.
32 *Ibid*, 926.
33 *Marshall No 1*, 468 (Binnie J's emphasis removed from quote).
34 *R v Badger*, [1996] 1 SCR 771; *Delgamuukw*, 1094.
35 *Ibid*, 1083, 1086.
36 *Ibid*, 1111.
37 Jeremy Patzer, "Indigenous Rights and the Legal Politics of Canadian Coloniality: What Is Happening to Free, Prior and Informed Consent in Canada?," *International Journal of Human Rights* 23, 1–2 (2019): 214–33.
38 *Haida Nation v British Columbia (Minister of Forests)*, 2004 SCC 73, [2004] 3 SCR 511.
39 See Kerry Wilkins, "*R. v. Morris*: A Shot in the Dark and Its Repercussions," *Indigenous Law Journal* 7, 1 (2008): 1–37; Kerry Wilkins, "Dancing in the Dark: Of Provinces and Section 35 Rights after 2010," *Supreme Court Law Review* 54 (2011): 529–62.
40 *Tsilhqot'in Nation v British Columbia*, 2014 SCC 44, [2014] 2 SCR 257
41 Patzer, "Indigenous Rights," 221. See also Nigel Bankes and Jennifer Koshan, "The Uncertain Status of the Doctrine of Interjurisdictional Immunity on Reserve Lands," *ABlawg: The University of Calgary Faculty of Law Blog*, October 28, 2014, https://ablawg.ca/2014/10/28/the-uncertain-status-of-the-doctrine-of-interjurisdictional-immunity-on-reserve-lands/.
42 *R v Van der Peet*, [1996] 2 SCR 507, 549.
43 Brian Slattery, "Making Sense of Aboriginal and Treaty Rights," *Canadian Bar Review* 79, 2 (2000): 217.
44 Ronald Niezen, "Culture and the Judiciary: The Meaning of the Culture Concept as a Source of Aboriginal Rights in Canada," *Canadian Journal of Law and Society* 18, 2 (2003): 1–26; Jeremy Patzer, "Even When We're Winning, Are We Losing? Métis Rights in Canadian Courts," in *Métis in Canada: History, Identity, Law and Politics*, ed. Christopher Adams, Greg Dahl, and Ian Peach (Edmonton: University of Alberta Press, 2013), 307–36.
45 John Borrows, "Frozen Rights in Canada: Constitutional Interpretation and the Trickster," *American Indian Law Review* 22, 1 (1997): 54.
46 *R v NTC Smokehouse Ltd*, [1996] 2 SCR 672.
47 *R v Gladstone*, [1996] 2 SCR 723, 747.
48 *Ibid*, 766.
49 *Ibid*, 775 (emphasis in original).
50 Kent McNeil, "How Can Infringements of the Constitutional Rights of Aboriginal Peoples Be Justified?," *Constitutional Forum* 8, 2 (1997): 36.
51 *Marshall No 1*, 502.

52 For an historical analysis of the Supreme Court's flawed justifications for eliminating treaty-based livelihood rights for western First Nations, see Frank Tough, "The Forgotten Constitution: The Natural Resources Transfer Agreements and Indian Livelihood Rights, ca. 1925–1933," *Alberta Law Review* 41, 4 (2004): 1025.

53 *R v Marshall,* [1999] 3 SCR 533.

54 *Ibid,* 562.

55 Kent McNeil, "How Can Infringements," 37. McNeil is actually citing Justice McLachlin's dissent in *R v Van der Peet* here, but it is McNeil in this case who is levelling that same critique at the erosion of constitutionally protected Aboriginal rights in the principles of the *Gladstone* decision.

56 John Borrows, "The Durability of Terra Nullius: *Tsilhqot'in Nation v. British Columbia,*" *UBC Law Review* 48, 3 (2015): 738, 739.

57 Marie Battiste, "Introduction: Unfolding the Lessons of Colonization," in *Reclaiming Indigenous Voice and Vision,* ed. Marie Battiste (Vancouver: UBC Press, 2000), xvii–xviii.

58 Ladner and Orsini, "Persistence of Paradigm Paralysis."

59 John Borrows, "Challenging Historical Frameworks: Aboriginal Rights, the Trickster, and Originalism," *Canadian Historical Review* 98, 1 (2017): 126.

60 Kent McNeil, "The Vulnerability of Indigenous Land Rights in Australia and Canada," *Osgoode Hall Law Journal* 42 (2004): 300.

61 "*Mi'kmaq Society v. Canada,*" Indigenous Law Centre, University of Saskatchewan, 2021, https://indigenouslaw.usask.ca/publications/mikmaq-society-v.-canada.php.

62 Ladner, "Up the Creek," 925.

63 Greg Mercer, "Two Decades after the Burnt Church Crisis, Disputes Flare Up over Indigenous Fishing Rights in Atlantic Canada," *Globe and Mail* (Halifax), September 27, 2020, https://www.theglobeandmail.com/canada/article-two-decades-after-the-burnt-church-crisis-disputes-continue-over/.

64 Michael Tutton, "Membertou First Nation to Become Latest to Join Mi'kmaq Livelihood Fishery in N.S.," *Canadian Press,* October 20, 2020.

20

Using the Master's Institutional Instruments to Dismantle the Master's Goal of Indigenous-Rights Certainty

Rebecca Major and Cynthia Stirbys

INITIAL RELATIONSHIPS BETWEEN the Crown and Indigenous Peoples were one of mutual respect between Nations.[1] Yet history shows that the Crown's overall record was about finding loopholes and ways not to uphold the sacred trust established early in the relationship. This lopsided power and control by the government characterized the relationship moving forward, creating an environment where Indigenous Peoples use government tools and instruments to regain their original and unique status in Canada. Indigenous Peoples were not initially invited into the constitutional negotiations regarding the patriation of the Constitution in the twentieth century, but once included, the government's aim was to control the narrative. If Indigenous rights were to be acknowledged, they would be defined under government terms. Once a process was established with the government safeguards in place to negotiate the definition of "Aboriginal" rights, the government lost control by not completing the process. By challenging the Crown through the courts using the patriated Constitution, Indigenous Peoples can gain control of government-desired certainty using the courts, with the caveat that this all exists under government-designed institutions.

Certainty is an explicit policy goal and part of the discourse of Indigenous rights in Canada – most recently illustrated in the 2019 federal election national debates when Andrew Scheer steered the conversation to certainty and pipelines when talking about Indigenous topics. In Indigenous policy, certainty is the use of consistent language in land and governance-claims policy. The Crown wants to control the number of Indigenous Peoples to whom they owe obligation with respect to fiduciary duty, by controlling who they address, whose interests are protected (the Crown's or Indigenous Peoples'), and who they negotiate with for land and resource development. Fiduciary duty is the guiding principle for Indigenous-Crown relations, according to the *Guerin* decision and elucidated by Senator Yvonne Boyer.[2] Certainty is embedded in the institutional relationship between the Crown and Indigenous Peoples in that it serves the government to control that definition. The following discussion explores how certainty is built on controlling all aspects of Indigenous Peoples' lives through legislation and how, in an attempt to maintain certainty, the Crown inadvertently opened a loophole that brought benefits to Indigenous Peoples by way of legislation that supports equity and human rights. Through legislative instruments, it was Indigenous Peoples themselves who steered the Crown back to upholding their fiduciary obligations to Indigenous Nations.

Institutionalized Relationships

Relationships were initially institutionalized between the Crown and Indigenous Peoples through agreements such as Peace and Friendship Treaties and Peace and Neutrality Treaties.[3] Nearing the end of this first recognized treaty era was the implementation of the Royal Proclamation of 1763, which further institutionalized the relationship through an authoritative statement from the Crown, which offered their protection to Indigenous Peoples. Later, in 1867, the territorial authority consolidated power under the *British North America Act* (*BNA Act*)[4] and with the passing of the *Statute of Westminster, 1931*.[5] The federal government desires unquestionable assurance (i.e., certainty) about the Indigenous Peoples with whom it has an obligatory fiduciary responsibility and because it wants certainty around specific control of lands and resources.[6]

In the institutionalization process of the Indigenous-Crown relationship, between 1850 and 1867, colonial administrators introduced legislation to determine who could be considered "Indian" to live on reserve.[7] In 1850, *An Act for the better protection of the land and property of the Indians in Lower Canada* was the first law to define who were Indigenous Peoples.[8] Initially, the definition took a broad interpretation that was sex-neutral and focused on "family, social and tribal or nation ties."[9] By 1869, under the *Gradual Enfranchisement Act*, the government took on the authority to determine who were "Indians" as individuals at the federal level of government.[10] This was how Eurocentric patriarchal norms were formally introduced into Indigenous familial customs and descent was assumed to come through male lineage. Importantly, these Christian-influenced versions of patriarchal ideas were not traditional power structures for Indigenous communities, as there was greater gender equality and Indigenous women were valued prior to contact. Consequently, the British Crown sought a means to "govern" through the *British North America Act, 1867*, eventually using the 1876 *Indian Act* as the mechanism. Not only did these methods structure the relationship, but they also positioned the government to control who participated in the relationship.

The British Crown's protectorate role was often reinterpreted through Canada's policies and legislation. The role became more about social and other means of control over Indigenous Peoples, especially as seen in interference in Indigenous Peoples' gender roles.[11] With the Indigenous Peoples' institutionalized relationship with the Canadian state through the Crown and historical arrangements, an irreversible constitutional/legal position was created. Former Federation of Saskatchewan Indians Chief Sol Sanderson explains that the *Royal Proclamation* is the "Bill of Rights" – meaning it is where Indigenous Peoples' rights as Nations were first recognized by the Crown, and it pointed to conditions where relationship conflicts would arise.[12] When revisiting this institutional relationship in the twentieth century in a policy piece known as the White Paper (a policy designed to terminate the special status of Indigenous Peoples in Canada), policy makers gave Indigenous Peoples an incentive to engage the Crown and organize in preparation for patriation discussions.[13]

Indigenous Efforts in Modern Constitutional Discussions

When Indigenous groups were left out of the constitutional discussion, losing their special constitutional status became one of their primary concerns.[14] Political action was the reaction of Indigenous leaders. In 1980, for example, the Union of BC Indian Chiefs (UBCIC) organized the "Constitution Express," a movement that involved loading two trains bound for Ottawa, following UBCIC President George Manuel's declaration of a "state of emergency" at the UBCIC assembly and a resulting position paper.[15] Madeline Knickerbocker and Sarah Nickel discuss how the Indigenous position in the process was marginalized to observer status in the constitutional talks, leading many Indigenous organizations to apply pressure on the federal government to have meaningful engagement.[16] The National Indian Brotherhood's response to marginalization in this process was to send a delegation to England; their constitutional position was stated to the UK Parliament on July 25, 1979.[17]

Other Indigenous lobby groups also engaged the government over the issue of constitutional involvement. The Native Council of Canada (NCC) was under the leadership of Harry Daniels, a Métis politician from Saskatchewan, when they applied pressure to include Indigenous Peoples in the patriation negotiations. In the preliminary stages of First Ministers' conferences, the NCC engaged the governments (federal and provincial) by submitting a brief in 1978.[18] In the brief, the NCC argued that they represented a historical national minority who required more substantial constitutional recognition for their role in bringing Manitoba into Confederation.[19] The NCC followed this argument with an official statement on nationalism.[20] It was very much organized around provincial entities at the time. A Saskatchewan delegation went to England to discuss the NCC's interest and involvement in constitutional discussions about patriation.[21]

This activism culminated in Indigenous engagement, and in recognizing Indigenous rights, the Canadian governments said "yes" and agreed to the inclusion of section 37 – the mechanism to define Indigenous rights – so long as they controlled the conversation that defined the rights Indigenous Peoples aimed to protect. This arrangement was accepted with conditions. In an official capacity, the National Indian Brotherhood (now called the Assembly of First Nations or AFN), the Native Council of Canada (now the Congress of Aboriginal Peoples or CAP), the Métis National Council (MNC; a breakaway group from the NCC), and the Inuit Tapirisat of Canada (renamed the Inuit Tapiriit Kana-tami or ITK in 2001)[22] were the four Indigenous organizations involved in the constitutional discussions.[23] The creation of sections 25 and 35 (Constitutional entrenchment of Indigenous Peoples and associated rights) and the section 37 inclusion illustrates how non-Indigenous governments created an avenue for Indigenous rights to be defined through negotiation, with the federal govern-ment and the provinces steering the conversation.

Certainty regarding Indigenous Peoples was deemed important because the governments were in the throes of developing a modern claims process. The Crown quickly learned that there were legally recognizable Indigenous rights in Canada. The language of certainty was an explicit policy goal in this new land claims policy, and attached to this thinking were conversations surround-ing Indigenous rights developed in the patriation talks. Through Part IV, section 37, of the *Constitution Act, 1982,* the Crown intended to establish certainty around "Aboriginal rights" through mandated First Ministers' conferences, a mechan-ism grounded in non-Indigenous institutions through which Canada maintained control.[24]

In addition to section 37, the government initiated the Special Committee on Indian Self-Government in 1982, which produced the *Penner Report.*[25] Both section 37 and the task force illustrate a desire for certainty regarding what rights and protections would mean moving forward. The task force was created in 1982 before the first section 37 First Ministers' conference, and it reported on proceedings in October 1983.[26] The hearings included Indigenous leaders and lobby organizations.[27] When it reported to the House of Commons, the com-mittee was explicit. The mandate was contextualized by section 91(24) of the *Constitution Act, 1867;* section 35 of the *Constitution Act, 1982;* economic restraints of government; and the upcoming First Ministers' conference.[28] The report discussed self-government and highlighted the need for a new relation-ship between Indigenous Peoples and the Crown.[29] As part of this reorganizing relationship, Indigenous Peoples would be recognized as self-governing.

According to Yale Belanger and David Newhouse, what made the *Penner Report* an essential part of Indigenous policy history in Canada is the acceptance and reinforcement of the argument advanced by the Federation of Saskatchewan Indians that Indigenous Nations were always self-governing.[30] This acknowledgment was coupled with the first time the government recognized its role in creating dependency through legislation.[31] Historically, the government blamed Indigenous Peoples for perceived shortcomings in advancement and socioeconomic conditions (see the 1966–67 *Hawthorn Report*, for example); by contrast, the *Penner Report* acknowledged the government's role in the disruption and colonial interference of Indigenous Peoples' lives.[32] In all, there were fifty-eight recommendations presented in the *Penner Report*, and it is through this report that a new narrative began with the creation of the Community-Based Self-Government policy in 1985. It is this policy that supported the creation of a new relationship between the Crown and Indigenous Peoples through self-government agreements.[33]

Although Indigenous Peoples (under the term "Aboriginal") and their associated rights were included through sections 25 and 35, the section 37 provision was added as a safeguard in 1983. For the Canadian state, it was a mechanism to define those protected rights and meant to bring clarity to protected rights under the newly patriated Constitution; however, the process was never completed.[34] The First Ministers' conferences took place between 1983 and 1987 and concluded with no resolution that satisfied the federal government and the provinces. This lack of resolve is significant because the Constitution leaves Indigenous rights to the courts to determine and define, and they have interpreted them broadly because of the Charter.[35] While trying to create certainty through section 37, the government never anticipated that the First Ministers' conferences would fail to complete the process. This definition was essential to the federal and provincial governments because it created certainty surrounding constitutionally protected rights.

Through the process of Indigenous-rights inclusion in the patriated *Constitution Act, 1982* the Crown demonstrated an ardent desire for certainty surrounding those rights through the inclusion of section 37. Further demonstrating the desire for certainty was the Crown's establishment of the parliamentary task force to seek definitions. The failure to agree on the definition and scope of rights has left the courts to define what has been coined "a box of rights" – provincial leaders referred to the box as empty while Indigenous leaders regarded it as full.[36] As Indigenous cases moved through the Canadian judicial system, sections 25 and 35 and the Charter resulted in expanded understandings of Indigenous rights rather than the narrowing of definitions.

Certainty in the Entrenchment of Rights

The patriation of the Constitution affected many facets of the Indigenous-Crown relationship, including the dynamics of Indigenous land claims. Until the 1970s, the federal government put little weight on Indigenous claims to land title. The

Calder decision made the government re-evaluate this position. Although the *Calder* decision was split, it brought to the forefront that Indigenous title to land existed and resulted in the creation of the Office of Native Claims in 1973.[37] As the first modern land claims office, the Office of Native Claims released the first policy statement by the Department of Indian Affairs and Northern Development (DIAND) under Jean Chrétien; the government's position was to resolve matters or achieve a sense of finality regarding Aboriginal title.[38] This finality was a means of creating certainty surrounding land use and occupancy moving forward, allowing the government to enter into land development without addressing the question of Indigenous title.[39]

Transactional understandings of the land existed in Canadian legislation, initially through the *Public Lands Grants Act,* 1903, which was amended several times before being brought under the *Federal Real Property Act,* 1992.[40] This understanding frames how and why the government desires certainty regarding Indigenous title to land. When certainty over who has rights and control is established, the government can work within transactional land understandings to develop income. This idea of certainty and its connection to defining con-stitutionally entrenched legal rights led the government to create controls as Indigenous Peoples became involved in the conversation. Little did the govern-ment realize that it was leaving itself open to Indigenous control should the First Ministers' conference fail to define constitutional protections.

Over time, Indigenous land claims policies underwent revisions and institu-tional reorganization, but always with certainty as the policy goal. The language of certainty is continued in agreements by using language as a policy goal in land and natural resource development. Even when the government updated policy by eliminating the extinguishment clause, the Comprehensive Claims Policy maintained the goal of certainty through policy frameworks.[41] The extin-guishment policy meant that an Indigenous collective negotiating with the Crown could relinquish all rights and title to their lands in exchange for a settlement agreement with the Crown. Following patriation in 1982, the federal government acknowledged in the Comprehensive Claims Policy that Indigenous groups found the extinguishment policy out of line with section 35's recognition and affirmation of Aboriginal rights.[42] Although policy changes happened, the federal government highlighted that certainty remained the policy's central objective.[43] The goal is grounded in an economic perspective, which explains why many Indigenous title cases pertaining to certainty involve resource development or infringements of protected Indigenous title through land use.

The year 2014 proved to be significant for comprehensive land claims. The federal government released an updated comprehensive land claims policy: *Renewing the Comprehensive Land Claims Policy: Towards a Framework for*

Addressing Section 35 Aboriginal Rights, and the Supreme Court of Canada decided *Tsilhqot'in Nation v British Columbia* (2014). Because of the Supreme Court decision, the federal government updated policy to no longer include the extinguishment clause, meaning that when an Indigenous group establishes their title and secures an agreement, they no longer need to relinquish title and rights to land. The government can no longer expect to have an absolute say and control of a territory. Further, the courts established that the federal and provincial governments must engage in meaningful consultation; section 35 of the *Constitution Act, 1982* contextualizes the discussion.[44] *Tsilhqot'in* highlights how the 1982 Constitution acts as a protection mechanism for Indigenous Peoples from federal and provincial legislative powers, imposing limits on them regarding Indigenous rights.[45] Where sections 25 and 35 of the *Constitution Act, 1982* were meant to be succinctly defined, lack of agreement in the First Ministers' conferences produced an opportunity for Charter protection of Indigenous rights.

Certainty in land and claims connects directly to certainty in Indigenous identity and membership. Government interference in Indigenous governance structures and cultural norms disrupted Indigenous societies and kinship identity. Canada used the *Indian Act* to destroy Indigenous organizing institutions and traditional governance systems. The most significant risk to Indian status and identity came by way of the federal and provincial governments' disregard for "the principle of consent in dealing with unceded Indian land and ... derogation from treaty rights."[46] The government interference in Indigenous governance structures and cultural norms happened through disruption to relationships with the land. The Crown, by way of the federal government, created certainty by legislating identity. The Crown could only acquire lands with the consent of the Indigenous Nations. Yet evidence shows that Canada's public officials (who are *not* the Crown) continuously sold off land for profit: consent was derived through "fraud, coercion, or misrepresentation – tactics which completely annulled the validity of such consent."[47] Indigenous societies and kinship identity were disrupted through the destruction of organizing institutions, evidenced in Canada's use of the *Indian Act* to infiltrate Indigenous Peoples' traditional governance systems.

Whenever new legislation or policies were introduced, Indigenous familial norms began to emulate Eurocentric inequality. For example, while Indigenous communities were more often matrilineal, women and children were included under the man's name under the new legislation.[48] The *Indian Act* guaranteed fewer rights for Indigenous women and their children with the advent of patriarchal norms. When an Indigenous woman married a non-Indigenous man, her Indian status was removed. This status removal prevented her children and future descendants from acquiring Indian status and any benefits derived from this status.[49] Concomitantly, Canada offered voluntary enfranchisement, "allowing an individual to not be considered an Indian and removed from their band," which would automatically remove Indigenous Peoples from their land and cultural norms.[50]

Moreover, if an Indian man decided to enfranchise, his wife and children were "automatically enfranchised along with their husband or father."[51] Enacting this new law also gave authority to Canada to enfranchise whole bands (i.e., Nations). Thus, kinship and community ties were no longer the basis for defining an "Indian"; in 1869, Indian status was built on the "predominance of men over women and children."[52] With the stroke of a pen, as they say, the Crown controlled identity and who got to access it through official legislation.

Many agree that the *Indian Act* is race-based legislation that is discriminatory to Indigenous Peoples as a whole. Had similar legislation been created for any other population, the perception would have been that it denied human rights under the *Canadian Human Rights Act*.[53] But despite the passing of the act in 1977 – and then, later, the *Canadian Charter of Rights and Freedoms*, guaranteed under the *Constitution Act, 1982* – Indigenous Peoples could not utilize the human rights process because, as "Indians," they fell under the *Indian Act*. The 1876 *Indian Act* is still used as an instrument to undermine Indigenous Peoples' rights. It was only after 2008 that First Nations Peoples registered under the *Indian Act* could use the *Canadian Human Rights Act*, and this change is the result of the Charter's emphasis on equity in section 15.[54] Section 15, importantly, makes all people equal under the law.

Many saw that so long as the *Indian Act* was still in place, it would continue to undermine and erode the rights of Indigenous Peoples. Despite the controversy, many Indigenous Peoples did not want to abolish it immediately. Harold Cardinal, a young Cree leader, explained the reasoning in 1969: "[N]o just society and no society with even pretensions to being just can long tolerate such a piece of legislation, but we would rather continue to live in bondage under the inequitable *Indian Act* than surrender our sacred rights."[55] The debate as to the relevance of the *Indian Act* continues in Indigenous communities and among Indigenous scholars. Suzanne Stewart at the University of Toronto has concluded that the federal government utilizes the *Indian Act* as a tool. This tool, described in military terms, is a process intended to "divide and conquer," and finds ways to create relational divisions within Indigenous communities.[56]

Following patriation of the *Constitution Act, 1982*, changes to identity under the *Indian Act* took place because Indigenous women challenged the government with a new tool – equality under the Charter. Three bills were introduced after 1985 to remove sex-based inequalities in the *Indian Act*: Bill C-31 (1985), Bill C-3 (2011), and Bill S-3 (2017). Bill C-31, an *Act to amend the Indian Act*, tabled in 1985, ensured "all enfranchisement provisions ... allow individuals, especially women who had lost status, to be reinstated as status Indians."[57] Bill C-31 was introduced to address the discriminatory provisions and "ensure compliance with the Canadian Charter of Rights and Freedoms."[58] After this amendment, an Indigenous woman was not automatically expected to join her husband's band when she married. As Indian women regained their status, this meant that they could also pass status on to their children. But there is a caveat. With the introduction of categories 6.1 and 6.2 (degrees of Indian status under the act, a similar idea to blood quantum without being actual blood quantum), categorizing status became a new mechanism to maintain control over who could access *Indian Act* identity.[59] As a means of correction, Bill C-3 was introduced in 2011. Bill C-3, *Gender Equity in Indian Registration Act*, was advanced by Sharon McIvor to address gender inequity.[60] As explained in *Knowing Your Rights as Indigenous Peoples*, Bill C-3 made changes to the registration provision, allowing a 6.2 parent to pass on their status; their grandchildren may also acquire status under certain conditions.[61] Although some gains were made with Bill C-3, inequities around accessing identity for legal recognition persisted.

Under the two Indigenous-led legislative changes (Bill C-31 and Bill C-3), Indigenous women challenged the goal of certainty of determining identity by using the Charter. Bill S-3 resulted from the *Descheneaux v Canada* decision in 2015, a case that argued that defining who is and isn't eligible for registration unjustifiably infringed section 15 of the Charter.[62] Legislative reform (as mentioned above for Bill S 3) is but one phase of a two-phase process. The minister of Indigenous-Crown relations also addressed other issues beyond removing the 1951 cut-off rule and its impacts on Indian registration. Band membership and First Nations citizenship, he said, must be seen through the lens of the Charter, the *UN Declaration on the Rights of Indigenous Peoples* in Canada, and the *Canadian Human Rights Act*.[63] The changes to registration in the *Indian Act* since patriation primarily lean on equality measures implemented through the Charter.

Looking back at every new bill tabled, the amendments only temporarily relieved gender inequities. However, it was through the *Descheneaux* decision that the Quebec Superior Court determined that "the registration provisions of the *Indian Act* ... continue[d] to unfairly discriminate against Indian women and their descendants and limit[ed] their ability to pass on Indian status, as compared to Indian men and their descendants."[64] In other words, says Stephen Nichols of Crown-Indigenous Relations and Northern Affairs Canada, the *Descheneaux* decision showed that sex-based discrimination had never actually been eliminated in the *Indian Act*; it had simply been pushed to subsequent generations.[65] It has finally been realized that the only way to remedy the inequities of the present is to go back to where they all started: the 1869 *Gradual*

Enfranchisement Act.[66] Following patriation of the *Constitution Act, 1982,* changes to identity under the *Indian Act* took place because Indigenous Peoples challenged the government with a new tool – equality under the Charter.

With the inclusion of Métis in the *Constitution Act, 1982,* Indigenous-identity assertions moved beyond gender. Under the *Indian Act,* the government limited who it was responsible for, not recognizing Indigenous Peoples beyond the *Indian Act* as a Crown responsibility. An illustration of this resistance to accepting responsibility for Indigenous groups is *R v Eskimo* in 1939. The province of Quebec proved through the law that Inuit were a federal responsibility under section 91(24) of the *British North American Act, 1867 (BNA Act).*

Similarly, under the context of section 91(24) of the *BNA Act,* responsibility for Métis and non-Status First Nations (First Nations not registered under the *Indian Act*) shifted to the federal government, despite their inclusion in section 35 of the *Constitution Act, 1982.*

Pushing back against the federal government's use of policy and legislation to control who it has relationships with and who it is responsible for, as per section 91(24) of the *BNA, 1867,* Harry Daniels, Leah Gardner, and Terry Joudrey launched the *Daniels* case in 1999. Supported by the Congress of Aboriginal Peoples, they sought three declarations: (1) that Métis and non-Status First Nations be defined by section 91(24) of the *BNA Act, 1867,* (2) that the Crown had both a responsibility and a fiduciary duty to Métis and non-Status First Nations, and (3) that Métis and non-Status First Nations Peoples had to be "consulted and negotiated with, in good faith, by the federal government on a collective basis through representatives of their choice, respecting all their rights, interests and needs as Aboriginal Peoples."[67]

Although Métis were already included in section 35 of the *Constitution Act, 1982,* the federal government never fulfilled its fiduciary duty towards Métis or non-Status First Nations Peoples by offering them similar rights and benefits as others under section 35. On April 14, 2016, the court ruled in the plaintiffs' favour: Métis and non-Status First Nations were granted section 91(24) rights and identity, upending the government's control of identity and access to section 35 and preconstitutional rights. Despite appeals by the government in the judicial process to maintain control over the certainty of identity, Indigenous aspirations successfully reduced the Crown's certainty surrounding Indigenous identity and, therefore, Indigenous rights-bearers.

Discussion

When discussing Indigenous rights, the issue of certainty arises time and time again. Certainty is essential for Indigenous and non-Indigenous parties for several reasons. Indigenous Peoples are interested in guarantees from the government when there are elevated levels of distrust because of a history of broken promises. At the same time, non-Indigenous parties (namely, colonial governments) want certainty so they can have exclusive power and authority when entering agreements with proponents. As colonial footprints grew on Turtle Island, Indigenous groups entered into agreements with governments in the form of treaties to protect a way of life. These treaties began as relationship agreements. The Peace and Friendship and Peace and Neutrality Treaties from the eighteenth century remain relevant today, as they were upheld through the Supreme Court of Canada in *Marshall* (1999).[68] In these historical relationship treaties, the Crown made promises of friendship and protection. Eventually, the treaties shifted to land agreements where representatives of the Crown (i.e., Canada) entered into agreements to secure title to land and power over lands.

Throughout this chapter, we examine the idea of certainty grounded in the colonial state's desire and how it impacts legislation relating to Indigenous Peoples. The Crown established certainty around identity to secure certainty around land; they finalized rights so they could have guarantees in transactional understandings of land. Despite resistance to including Indigenous voices in the constitutional discussions of the latter part of the twentieth century, Indigenous lobbying created a space to ensure Indigenous Peoples were not left behind. Agreeing to include Indigenous voices in patriation, colonial forces attempted to manage the situation by using section 37 to control Indigenous rights and identity. But because the negotiating parties could not agree, sections 25 and 35 remain intact and supported by other provisions in the Charter, which place a level of power in the hands of Indigenous Peoples.

The patriation of the Constitution and the newly scripted Charter provided new avenues for Indigenous Peoples to assert rights and effect change. Sections 25 and 35 of the *Constitution Act, 1982* were not the product of goodwill on behalf of the federal government. Initially, in constitutional discussions, Indigenous Peoples were not included; their inclusion came after lobbying and advocating for their involvement.[69] The lack of inclusion led to political organization by Indigenous Peoples and groups. As Douglas Sanderson from the University of Toronto argues, there will always be a legislative relationship between Indigenous Peoples and the federal government of Canada; otherwise, the assimilation process has succeeded.[70]

The Government of Canada has always interpreted Indigenous rights too narrowly, as evidenced through the well-known cases *Calder, Guerin, Sparrow, Delgamuukw,* and *Haida Nation;* each, in turn, supported the Tsilhqot'in appellants, who proved their long-term relationship to and occupancy of the land.[71] Through the *Tsilhqot'in* case, the Crown's control on certainty regarding Indigenous rights was weakened because, as John Borrows argues, "Aboriginal" title was to be construed in a much broader sense.[72] Borrows argues that the *Tsilhqot'in* case was a victory in so far as the Tsilhqot'in People proved Aboriginal title over their lands and territories, with which they can do as they please. They, like other Indigenous groups who claim title, now have an array of remedies to protect their interests. For example, "They can bring injunctions, claim damages, and secure orders for the Crown to engage if proper consultation and accommodation of Aboriginal title do not occur."[73] There are clearer remedies available to Indigenous groups because of the *Tsilhqot'in* case, including cancelling provincial projects if First Nations groups are not consulted (see Do, Chapter 21 in this volume).

The courts were left to interpret and define Indigenous rights and do so in the context of other rights now enshrined through the Charter. Although the courts assisted in shifting control of certainty towards Indigenous Peoples from the Canadian state, the courts themselves are problematic, as discussed in the work of Kiera Ladner, who explains that the courts are also a way to perpetuate colonialism.[74] Aligned with Ladner's argument, John Borrows states that even though the notion of *terra nullius* was challenged in the *Tsilhqot'in* case, Tŝilhqot'in title is "not presumed to exist in the same way as the Crown sovereignty and Crown underlying title are assumed to exist."[75] The issues of land and Aboriginal title will always closely align with status and identity because governments want to secure unquestionable sovereignty over the land – the fewer Indians with "distinct status," the greater access to land for the Crown. Historically, governments required consent from "Indians" before securing the land for settlement. While the consent process still holds today, so does the certainty goal, in requiring an answer to the question of "who" still has rights to the land.

To evaluate this shift in control of certainty surrounding Indigenous rights, let's look at how far the measuring stick has moved. For example, how does a government determine who it speaks with? When "Indigenous say" is paramount, then certainty has been repositioned. So long as the relationship exists within a colonial apparatus, and not on equal footing, the perpetual power imbalance remains. Through institutionalization, power structures were established; the rights of Indigenous Peoples were reinforced through these power structures, and Indigenous Peoples are using the system against itself to reposition power. Borrowing from Audre Lorde, we've adapted the title of her famous essay "The Master's Tools Will Never Dismantle the Master's House" not to suggest that Indigenous Peoples are slaves in the traditional colonial sense, but to suggest that dependency was historically derived and enforced through the Crown's instruments.[76] However, times are changing as Indigenous Peoples are using the Crown's judicial instruments to effect change.

Indigenous case law and policy change have been quite extensive since patriation of the Constitution. Patriation occurred when there was little understanding of Indigenous rights and governments assumed/presumed them to be quite limited. As case law evolved in the context of the Charter, expansion of the starting point for rights was seen in cases such as *Tsilhqot'in*. In this case, section 35 was examined in the context of provincial powers and how they are limited by section 35's existence.[77] What began as a limited view of land rights expanded at the beginning of the 1970s along with understandings of community rights and who gets a say in who a community is. The definition of "community" in *R v Powley*[78] is now used to negotiate community recognition and determine a community via case law. This *Powley* instrument creates a test for who the government must engage with, and that decision no longer rests exclusively with the Crown. When determinations are made by the community and must be respected by the Crown, a shift in power occurs, even if within the setting of colonial institutions. The fact that the First Ministers' conferences never defined Indigenous rights created an unforeseen opportunity and a new space for dialogue.

The space between the Crown and Indigenous Nations is the ethical space where Indigenous governance and Indigenous Peoples' self-determination as Nations is recognized.[79] Creating an ethical space is recognizing the imperative on the side of the Crown to consult. Sections 25 and 35 solidify the sacred trust that once was through the recognition of Aboriginal title and Indigenous Peoples' inherent rights. Ethical space is where the promise lies: it is time to polish the Covenant Chain, to recognize and re-establish the long-standing relationship between the Crown and Indigenous Nations, and to re-establish the trust. Also, ethical space is where the Crown/government comes back to acknowledge and respect Indigenous Peoples' original and unique status with the Crown. Indigenous Peoples can use certainty as a tool to guarantee their unique status and rights. In this way, we come back to the Royal Proclamation of 1763 (bypassing time and space – bringing us back full circle to the way it was meant to be – each Nation staying in their boat and keeping to their own business). It is more than aspirational because we, as Indigenous Peoples, have history on our side. Ethical space is not just about recognizing Indigenous Peoples' constitutional status but recognizing that the Crown's original agreements were made on a Nation-to-Nation basis.

Through sections 25 and 35 and the Charter, Indigenous Peoples are capturing a level of control over certainty despite governments' best efforts to control that conversation. The tools provided by the Charter (for all Canadians) are now tools that Indigenous Peoples can utilize to reclaim their authority over Indigenous lands and resources. The Crown anticipated limiting Indigenous rights during the First Ministers' conferences, but with the collapse of those discussions, a whole new set of legal arguments appeared to fill a box of rights through the courts – an unintended consequence, but one worth pursuing.

The master's house – the institutional setting and its structural control of certainty – is being dismantled through institutional instruments (the courts), by the very people the government sought to limit.

Notes

1 In this chapter, we capitalize "Peoples" and "Nation" when referring to Indigenous Peoples and Nations, to recognize that Indigenous Peoples carry unique status in Canada. We refer to the Crown as "they" rather than "it" because the relationship for Indigenous Peoples is with the head of state as a living and present being. The Crown represents a relationship; the federal government is a management institution.
2 Yvonne Boyer, "First Nations, Métis and Inuit Health Care: The Crown's Fiduciary Obligation," discussion paper, Series in Aboriginal Health No. 2, University of Saskatchewan, Native Law Centre, 2004, 5; *Guerin v The Queen,* [1984] 2 SCR 335 [*Guerin*].
3 Government of Canada, Indigenous and Northern Affairs Canada, Communications Branch, "Historic Treaties," Treaties and Agreements, July 30, 2020, https://www.rcaanc-cirnac.gc.ca/eng/1100100028574/1529354437231#chp3.
4 "The Substance of Great Britain's Obligations to the Indian Nations" (presented at the Fourth Russell Tribunal, Rotterdam, Netherlands, November, 1980).
5 Norman Hillmer, "Statute of Westminster, 1931," *Canadian Encyclopedia,* February 7, 2006, https://www.thecanadianencyclopedia.ca/en/article/statute-of-westminster.
6 Boyer, "First Nations, Métis and Inuit Health Care," 17.
7 Government of Canada, Indigenous and Northern Affairs Canada, *Background on Indian Registration,* November 28, 2018, section "Demographic Impacts of Past *Indian Act* Amendments," https://www.rcaanc-cirnac.gc.ca/eng/1540405608208/1568898474141#_Demographic_Impacts_of.
8 *Ibid.*
9 *Ibid.*
10 *Ibid.*
11 J.R. Miller, *Shingwauk's Vision: A History of Native Residential Schools* (Toronto: University of Toronto Press, 1996).
12 Sol Sanderson, "Occupying the Field: Part 4 of 4 Crown–Indian Nations Relations," AMNSIS YouTube Channel, February 20, 2021, 3:02, https://www.youtube.com/watch?v=bC2zGRGXgJw.
13 Indian Affairs and Northern Development, *Statement of the Government of Canada on Indian Policy 1969* (White Paper) (Ottawa: Indian Affairs and Northern Development, 1969).
14 Madeline Knickerbocker and Sarah Nickel, "Negotiating Sovereignty: Indigenous Perspectives on the Patriation of a Settler Colonial Constitution, 1975–83," *BC Studies* 190 (2016): 71.
15 *Ibid,* 75.
16 *Ibid,* 78.
17 UK, HL, *Parliamentary Debates,* "National Indian Brotherhood of Canada: Visit," vol 401 (July 25, 1979) (Earl Grey et al), https://hansard.parliament.uk/lords/1979-07-25/debates/ee0419bf-d7cc-4c24-85be-3b9be75b8fc1/NationalIndianBrotherhoodOfCanadaVisit.

18 The NCC represented Métis and non-Status First Nations Peoples and became the Congress of Aboriginal Peoples (CAP).

19 Douglas Sanders, "The Rights of the Aboriginal Peoples of Canada," *Canadian Bar Review* 16, 1 (1983): 425.

20 *Ibid.*

21 Frank Tomkins, discussion, Métis Nation–Saskatchewan Annual General Meeting, February 19, 2019, 15:21, https://www.youtube.com/watch?v=qLRSnOgNBVc&t=6s. The Saskatchewan delegation included Rod Bishop, Frank Tomkins, Jim Durocher, Jim Sinclair, and Wayne McKenzie.

22 Tapirisat means "brotherhood" in English. *Canadian Encyclopedia,* "Inuit Tapiriit Kanatami (ITK)," June 18, 2021, https://www.thecanadianencyclopedia.ca/en/article/inuit-tapiriit-kanatami-itk.

23 Noel Dyck and Tonio Sadik, "Indigenous Political Organization and Activism in Canada," *Canadian Encyclopedia,* June 6, 2011, https://www.thecanadianencyclopedia.ca/en/article/aboriginal-people-political-organization-and-activism.

24 S 37 addition.

25 Paul Tennant, Sally M. Weaver, Roger Gibbins, and J. Rick Ponting, "The Report of the House of Commons Special Committee on Indian Self-Government: Three Comments," *Canadian Public Policy/Analyse de Politiques* 10, 2 (1984): 212–13.

26 *Ibid,* 212–13.

27 Yale Deron Belanger, *Ways of Knowing: An Introduction to Native Studies in Canada,* 3rd ed. (Vancouver: Langara College, 2018), 304.

28 Canada, Parliament, *Minutes of the Proceedings of the Special Committee on Indian Self-Government,* 32nd Parl, 1st Sess, No 40 (October 12, 1983), https://primarydocuments.ca/40-indian-self-government-1982-83/.

29 House of Commons, Standing Committee on Indian Self-Government, *Minutes of Proceedings,* 32nd Parl, 1st Sess, No 40 (October 12 and 20, 1983), 14, http://caid.ca/PennerRep1983.pdf [*Penner Report*].

30 Yale D. Belanger and David R. Newhouse, "Emerging from the Shadows: The Pursuit of Aboriginal Self-Government to Promote Aboriginal Well-Being," *Canadian Journal of Native Studies* 24, 1 (2004): 154; *Penner Report,* 13.

31 S.I. Pobihushchy, "A Perspective on the Indian Nations in Canada," *Canadian Journal of Native Studies* 6, 1 (1986): 111, http://www3.brandonu.ca/cjns/6.1/pobihushchy.pdf; *Penner Report,* 13.

32 *Ibid,* 108; *Penner Report,* 13. The Hawthorn Report, officially *A Survey of the Contemporary Indians of Canada: Economic, Political, Educational Needs and Policies,* was a government study released in two volumes in 1966 and 1967. However, the report was shelved. The federal government released its White Paper in 1969.

33 Paul Tennant et al, "The Report of the House of Commons," 213. Government of Canada, Crown-Indigenous Relations and Northern Affairs Canada, *General Briefing Note on Canada's Self-Government and Comprehensive Land Claims Policies and the Status of Negotiations,* August 16, 2016, https://www.rcaanc-cirnac.gc.ca/eng/1373385502190/1542727338550.

34 *Constitutional Amendment Proclamation,* 1983, SI/84-102.

35 *R v Van der Peet,* [1996] 2 SCR 507, para 50.

36 Paul Tennant et al, "The Report of the House of Commons," 220.

37 Indian and Northern Affairs Canada, *Resolving Aboriginal Claims: A Practical Guide to Canadian Experiences* (Ottawa: Minister of Indian Affairs and Northern Development, 2003), https://www.aadnc-aandc.gc.ca/eng/1100100014174/1100100014179.

38 Indian Affairs and Northern Development, *Statement Made by the Honourable Jean Chrétien, Minister of Indian Affairs and Northern Development on Claims of Indian and Inuit People* (Ottawa: Indian and Northern Affairs, 1973); Indian Affairs and Northern Development, *Resolving Aboriginal Claims*, 4.
39 Indian Affairs and Northern Development, *Resolving Aboriginal Claims*, 3, 5.
40 Canada, *Guide to the Federal Real Property Act and Federal Real Property Regulation*, October 1996, https://www.canada.ca/en/treasury-board-secretariat/services/federal-real-property-management/guide-federal-real-property-act-regulation.html#PropertyAct.
41 Canada, Crown-Indigenous Relations and Northern Affairs Canada, *Renewing the Comprehensive Land Claims Policy: Towards a Framework for Addressing Section 35 Aboriginal Rights*, September 2014, 7, https://www.rcaanc-cirnac.gc.ca/DAM/DAM-CIRNAC-RCAANC/DAM-TAG/STAGING/texte-text/ldc_ccl_renewing_land_claims_policy_2014_1408643594856_eng.pdf.
42 *Ibid*, 6.
43 *Ibid*, 8.
44 *Tsilhqot'in Nation v British Columbia*, 2014 SCC 44, [2014] 2 SCR 256, paras 90, 139 [*Tsilhqot'in*].
45 *Ibid*, paras 118, 139, 142.
46 "The Substance of Great Britain's Obligations," 121.
47 *Ibid*, 83–85.
48 Government of Canada, *Background on Indian Registration*.
49 *Ibid.*
50 *Ibid.*
51 *Ibid.*
52 *Ibid.*
53 *Canadian Human Rights Act*, RSC 1985, c H-6, para 2, Canada, Justice Laws Website, July 12, 2019, https://laws-lois.justice.gc.ca/eng/acts/h-6/20190712/P1TT3xt3.html.
54 Canada, "Indigenous Peoples and Human Rights," https://www.canada.ca/en/canadian-heritage/services/rights-indigenous-peoples.html.
55 Royal Commission on Aboriginal Peoples, "The Indian Act, Vol. 1, Part 2," *Report of the Royal Commission on Aboriginal Peoples* (Ottawa: Government of Canada, 1996), 236.
56 As stated by Suzanne Stewart to Steve Paikin, "The Indian Act: What to Do with It?," *The Agenda with Steve Paikin*, May 30, 2019, https://www.youtube.com/watch?v=OC9fRBk7rZk&t=1264s.
57 Crown-Indigenous Relations and Northern Affairs Canada, *Background on Indian Registration*.
58 *Ibid.*
59 Cold Lake First Nations, "Bill S-3 An Act to Amend the Indian Act," *Knowing Your Rights as Indigenous Peoples*, YouTube, February 13, 2020, https://www.youtube.com/watch?v=hF7Qc-x4H1Y.
60 Crown-Indigenous Relations and Northern Affairs Canada, *Background on Indian Registration*.
61 Cold Lake First Nations, "Bill S-3."
62 Mandell Pinder LLP, "*Descheneaux v Canada*, 2015 QCCS 3555 – Case Summary," October 13, 2016, https://www.mandellpinder.com/descheneaux-v-canada-2015-qccs-3555-case-summary/.
63 Crown-Indigenous Relations and Northern Affairs Canada, *Background on Indian Registration*.
64 Mandell Pinder LLP, "*Descheneaux v Canada*."

65 Cold Lake First Nations, "Bill S-3."

66 *Ibid.*

67 *Daniels v Canada (Indian Affairs and Northern Development)*, 2016 SCC 12, [2016] 1 SCR 99, "Background" and para 2.

68 *R v Marshall*, [1999] 3 SCR 456.

69 Tomkins, discussion.

70 "The Indian Act: What to Do with It?"

71 *Calder v British Columbia (Attorney General)*, [1973] SCR 313; *Guerin; R v Sparrow*, [1990] 1 SCR 1075; *Delgamuukw v British Columbia*, [1997] 3 SCR 1010; *Haida Nation v British Columbia (Minister of Forests)*, [2004] 3 SCR 511.

72 John Borrows, *Law's Indigenous Ethics* (Toronto: University of Toronto Press, 2019), 97.

73 *Ibid*, 112.

74 Kiera Ladner, "Take 35: Reconciling Constitutional Orders," in *First Nations, First Thoughts: The Impact of Indigenous Thought in Canada*, ed. Annis May Timpson (Vancouver: UBC Press, 2010), 285.

75 Borrows, *Law's Indigenous Ethics*, 106.

76 Audre Lorde, "The Master's Tools Will Never Dismantle the Master's House," in *Sister Outsider: Essays and Speeches* (Berkeley, CA: Crossing Press, 1984), 110–14.

77 *Tsilhqot'in.*

78 *R v Powley*, [2003] 2 SCR 207, 2003 SCC 43.

79 Willie Ermine, "The Ethical Space of Engagement," *Indigenous Law Journal* 6, 1 (2007): 193–203.

21

Beyond Consultation
A Research Agenda to Investigate Partnerships and Comanagement in Land Governance

Minh Do

ALTHOUGH THE *CONSTITUTION Act, 1982* is celebrating its fortieth anniversary, the duty to consult has developed as an Aboriginal right protected under section 35 for only eighteen years. And yet this doctrine has advanced rapidly since it was first articulated as a legal obligation in the 2004 case *Haida Nation v British Columbia (Ministry of Forests)*. Initially, the duty arose in response to the dilemma of unrecognized Aboriginal rights being potentially threatened by ongoing Crown activity and regulation. Without legal protection, Crown activities could effectively "run roughshod" over claimed Aboriginal rights, thus stripping away the benefits of those rights before they are recognized by the state through treaty negotiations.[1] In the interim, before the scope of Aboriginal rights is delineated, Indigenous groups are entitled to constitutional protections in the form of consultation and, where appropriate, accommodation when a Crown action may adversely impact a claimed Aboriginal right.[2] Importantly, the scope of consultation and accommodation is highly contextual and should be proportionate to the strength of the claimed right and the significance of the potential adverse impacts.[3]

The duty to consult is a relatively new Aboriginal right but may already be perceived as an inadequate framework for upholding enduring engagement with Indigenous groups to protect Aboriginal rights. In contrast to the duty, more long-term governing arrangements that manage land and water resources are emerging. An example of these arrangements is Indigenous-Crown partnerships over strategic land-use planning. Land-use planning sets high-level direction over what can be done in a particular region and aims to balance sustainable resource stewardship with economic, environmental, social, and cultural objectives. These long-term agreements can uphold the Crown's consultation obligations and manage claimed resources in partnership with relevant Indigenous groups in the interim before treaties are finalized. The responsibilities between Indigenous nations and the Crown within some strategic land-use planning agreements can extend beyond the legal requirements of the duty. These partnerships are somewhat surprising given that the duty-to-consult jurisprudence carefully constrains the potential to dramatically challenge the Crown's decision-making authority or sovereignty, as evidenced by the Supreme

Court of Canada's insistence that Indigenous peoples do not exercise a veto over policy outcomes[4] and the Crown's control over structuring consultative processes.[5] The United Nations Declaration on the Rights of Indigenous Peoples (UNDRIP) details that Indigenous peoples have rights to equitable partnerships with settler states when their traditional territories may be affected by state action. Although UNDRIP has undoubtedly influenced Canadian governments' relationships with Indigenous peoples, many land-use planning agreements emerged before UNDRIP was recognized by the state in 2016. Why do these partnerships between Indigenous groups and Crown actors emerge?

This chapter proposes that policy theories that examine horizontal governance arrangements between state and nonstate actors are a useful starting point for explaining the patchwork of Indigenous-Crown partnerships in strategic land-use planning within the context of the developing duty-to-consult jurisprudence. Explaining why these arrangements emerge and their outputs can reveal whether the duty to consult creates incentives for the negotiation of long-term partnerships and whether these arrangements are a fruitful avenue to advance reconciliation and equitable governance agreements beyond project-specific consultation. Multilevel governance, policy networks, and collaborative governance present valuable frameworks to consider how Crown governance has changed in light of the duty's development. The intersection between the legal framework of the duty to consult and land-use plans demonstrates the importance of analyzing the legal effects of the duty on governance and Indigenous-Crown relations.

The chapter proceeds by first introducing the legal characteristics of the duty to consult as it has developed so far. Second, a brief description of strategic land-use plans and their relationship to the duty will be provided. The case of British Columbia will be used as it is the jurisdiction where most Indigenous nations within the province have not signed treaties with the Crown. Third, an explanation of multilevel governance, policy networks, and collaborative governance will be outlined. These theories will be explored to demonstrate their analytic utility to explain how and why Indigenous and Crown policy actors negotiate land-use planning agreements in the context of the duty to consult.

Legal Parameters of the Duty

The development of the duty to consult has been carefully investigated by many legal scholars.[6] The Supreme Court of Canada has reiterated that the duty emerges from the concept of the honour of the Crown, which is always at stake in dealings with Indigenous peoples.[7] The honour of the Crown imposes upon the Crown specific obligations towards Indigenous peoples. What constitutes honourable dealing between Indigenous peoples and the Crown is a significant analytical question.[8] The court has clearly stated that the honour of the Crown entails "concrete practices,"[9] and many scholars have evaluated the Crown's actions throughout consultation and accommodation to determine what constitutes honourable dealings from the judiciary's perspective.[10]

One notable aspect of honourable dealing is the Crown's determination of the scope of consultation and accommodation. Since the 2004 *Haida Nation* case, the duty has developed to consider different decision-making contexts in which it might be triggered. The duty is applied in both historical[11] and modern treaty[12] contexts. Crown actions that trigger the duty include strategic, higher-level decision making,[13] but not during the legislative process,[14] nor to address historical grievances.[15] Despite the Supreme Court's attempt to articulate the varying contexts that may trigger the duty, many outstanding questions remain. For instance, although the duty is not intended to address historical grievances, the reality of cumulative impacts from development in a region over time may require Crown decision makers to consider past and future impacts during consultation.[16] And yet, the Crown can unilaterally claim that certain cumulative impacts are beyond the scope of the Crown's immediate proposed action.[17] Due to the complexity of decision making, the Supreme Court's guidelines aim to provide flexibility as Crown and Indigenous policy actors negotiate both the terms of consultative participation and the substance of the rights at stake. In reality, the Crown can unilaterally dictate the scope of consultation, even as Indigenous nations face challenges with effectively participating in consultation across multiple projects over time.[18]

Honourable dealing is also expected when accommodation measures are negotiated. The lack of judicial guidance on the appropriate proportionality of proposed accommodation measures has generated concern that the duty to consult may focus too heavily on procedural safeguards and thus fails to act as a robust tool to advance equality and reconciliation.[19] Although the duty to consult is distinct from administrative-law principles,[20] this is a unique relationship worth investigating, particularly as administrative tribunals can be tasked with evaluating the adequacy of the Crown's consultation with affected Indigenous groups. Apart from assessing the judiciary's emphasis on procedural safeguards over substantive accommodation measures, the role of administrative decision makers and how they apply the duty to consult remains an interesting area of inquiry.[21]

In addition to evaluating the specific practices that make up the duty to consult, legal scholars have directed attention to how the duty advances the court's vision of section 35 within Canada's constitution. There is a concern that the duty continues a trajectory where Crown sovereignty is assumed over Indigenous peoples' traditional territories.[22] As such, the duty fails to recognize

Indigenous peoples' jurisdictional authority and imposes a legal framework that does not challenge the Crown's decision-making authority.[23] These observations are important to show how the duty contributes to the contested nature of Canada's constitutionalism. It is clear from the duty-to-consult jurisprudence that the court upholds the authority of Crown sovereignty and does not recognize Indigenous nations' inherent jurisdiction. Nevertheless, the court also clearly displays a preference for political negotiations to resolve competing claims between Indigenous groups and the Crown.[24] The duty to consult was also meant to provide flexibility for political negotiations to resolve conflict over jurisdictional control and regulation. Therefore, consultation and the negotiation of accommodation measures that fulfill the duty may prompt broader discussions about resource and land management between Indigenous groups and the Crown. It is thus possible that the duty to consult opens the possibility for lasting comanagement agreements.

The Duty to Consult and Strategic Land-Use Planning Arrangements

The duty is triggered when a specific Crown action may adversely affect Aboriginal rights or title. Because Crown action includes high-level decision making, land-use planning processes may also entail consultation and accommodation. Land-use planning is the process of "maximiz[ing] the potential of the environment for the use and enjoyment of the community as a whole, safeguard[ing] all users from unacceptable environmental hardship, and shar[ing] out the gains and losses to different users of land in an equitable manner."[25] The objective of land-use planning is to balance a wide range of human activities with the physical environment. Land-use plans can be tailored to address different settings, such as urban planning and resource management. Additionally, stakeholders can express priorities or objectives for specific areas.[26]

Many actors are involved in the land-use planning process, but the state has a privileged role in initiating these processes because of its legal status and resources. Within the Canadian context, all levels of government must coordinate with one another due to overlapping jurisdictional authorities and the powerful influence of higher levels of government. The federal and provincial governments create the policy direction within their jurisdictional competency in addition to the procedural and regulatory requirements for programs. Then municipal governments and their agencies operate within these constraints. Apart from the state, private actors, like developers, are instrumental in all stages of development. Private actors promote development and interact with regulatory agencies for project approval. They also secure financial resources and employ labour to carry out the project and manage it.[27] The public, such as various groups of organized interests, communicate to public officials their interests. Organizers of state-led planning processes may try to directly consult and include social groups to attain a variety of perspectives on the desirability of certain development projects over others.

The importance of land-use planning cannot be understated. Provincial public lands make up 94 percent of all land in British Columbia, and land-use plans currently cover over 90 percent of these provincial lands.[28] Moreover, land-use planning is all the more pertinent because the major industries in this province involve resource development, such as forestry, fishing, and mining.[29] Supporting these industries needs to be balanced with respecting Indigenous peoples' rights over their traditional territory. Since the Supreme Court has acknowledged the persistence of Aboriginal rights and title in British Columbia despite the fact that only 3 percent of lands are covered by treaty, former land-use planning arrangements that did not respect Indigenous peoples' unique constitutional status are no longer perceived as adequate or legitimate.

Interestingly, the early evolution of land-use planning in British Columbia was not directly impacted by the development of Aboriginal rights. However, after the duty to consult was articulated by the Supreme Court in 2004, the province shifted its policy trajectory, such as making commitments to pursue government-to-government land-use planning arrangements with certain Indigenous groups. In these instances, the duty's consultative framework appears to have paved the way for consensus-based partnerships or comanagement. In other cases, the province resisted its obligation to fulfill its duty to consult with Indigenous groups, leading to standoffs and political unrest by Indigenous groups demanding direct involvement in land-use planning. Therefore, consultation can also resemble tokenism or a distraction to attaining equitable relationships over land governance. The entrenchment of the duty has been met with different policy responses to land-use planning across different regions. This variation in land-use planning agreements deserves analytical attention since including Indigenous groups in these processes can fulfill consultation and accommodation obligations beyond project-specific impacts. Furthermore, these collaborative processes support the goal of reconciliation as envisaged by the judiciary. The importance of Indigenous groups' increasing involvement in land-use planning has been noted in the geography literature,[30] but few studies have systematically analyzed the relationship between the duty to consult and the negotiation of these agreements.[31] Policy theories that explain the emergence of horizontal partnerships between the state and nonstate actors may be most appropriate to understand how to identify the relationship between the duty-to-consult jurisprudence and the Crown's changing approach to land-use planning and governance.

Employing a Policy Lens: Multilevel Governance, Policy Networks, and Collaborative Governance

Scholars of public policy and public administration have analyzed patterns of governance that depart from hierarchical, state-centric models. The shift from thinking about "government" to "governance" reflects the reality that new actors, processes, and tools are required to govern the public. Under this framework, the state's primary role is to steer and coordinate new governing arrangements given pressures from the market economy, globalization, and localization.[32] These pressures are accompanied by demands for various actors to be included in decision making, as the state is no longer seen as the sole actor with the appropriate resources, expertise, or authority.[33] These demands are also salient in the context of settler states as the state's authority is directly challenged by Indigenous nations and their rights over traditional territories.

In the duty-to-consult jurisprudence, the Supreme Court qualifies the exercise of Crown sovereignty by clarifying that only honourable actions towards Indigenous peoples uphold the process of reconciliation that flows from section 35 rights.[34] Indeed, the creation of the duty is meant to provide procedural constraints to ensure the state acts legitimately when Crown actions may affect Aboriginal rights.[35] The duty also ensures that relevant Indigenous parties who have rights flowing from their prior occupancy on the land are formally included in decision-making processes. The court does not dispute the Crown's sovereign authority but acknowledges that Indigenous peoples' interests that flow from the exercise of their Aboriginal rights and title also need to be respected in decision making. The duty's objectives to include Indigenous rights holders in Crown decision-making processes are aligned with the changing trajectory of state governance, but there remains considerable variation in how the state can choose to incorporate Indigenous peoples in governance over specific policy areas, such as land-use planning. Policy theories that analyze horizonal-governing arrangements can identify how these arrangements arise and their policy consequences.

Multilevel Governance

Many policy frameworks have been produced to understand and analyze patterns of horizontal governance arrangements where the state relinquishes its top-down hierarchical control and plays a coordinative function between additional actors. Multilevel governance is an example of one such framework. Although there are various definitions of multilevel governance, the concept is distinguished by its focus on governing arrangements that involve "governments engag[ing] with a broad range of actors embedded in different territorial scales to pursue collaborative solutions to complex problems."[36] Therefore, multilevel governance is defined by specific actors, scales, and decision-making processes.[37] Arguably, the focus on scales and the decision-making relationship among actors is central to multilevel governance. Apart from horizontal-governing configurations, actors are occupying different scales of organization, such as at the subnational, national, and supranational levels. These scales may be redefined and contested[38] even as they are treated equally within the decision-making process.[39] Furthermore, actors in a multilevel governance system are participating in a negotiated order[40] rather than focusing on constitutional or legal frameworks,[41] and the various actors' participation has a tangible influence on policy outcomes.[42] The framework originated to investigate the expansion of supranational structures such as the European Union[43] and has developed to include the burgeoning role of local governments.[44] In the context of the European Union, multilevel governance is applied to explain new forms of political mobilization, policy-making processes, and state structures.[45] It has also been adopted in the Canadian context to describe and explain Indigenous peoples' changing relationship with the state and other policy actors.[46]

Land-use planning arrangements can fit the multilevel-governance criteria, particularly those where coordination between Indigenous and non-Indigenous governments is required in order for the governing arrangement to succeed. Resource-management plans between the federal, provincial, and Indigenous governments have been identified as instances of multilevel governance in the Canadian multilevel governance scholarship.[47] But this literature has not closely investigated the drivers of multilevel governance,[48] nor has it compared the policy consequences of multilevel governance with other types of governing arrangements. The literature appears to be ripe for more comparative analyses between multilevel governance and other forms of governance in specific policy areas rather than simply using it as a mere descriptor.[49]

Policy Networks

Another policy framework with analytic potential to explain Indigenous-Crown partnerships in land-use planning is policy networks. The definition of policy networks is broader than multilevel governance, as policy networks include decentralized but regularized and coordinated linkages among state and organized interests.[50] These structures constitute policy processes that exist alongside more formalized, hierarchical processes[51] and are now considered ubiquitous in policy making.[52] Unlike multilevel governance, there is no consideration of the geographical scale of the linkages between policy actors, and the relationship between actors can take on various forms. Depending on the resources, membership, and level of integration between the state and nonstate actors, networks can take on a variety of characteristics, for example, hierarchical, clientele pluralist, or corporatist.[53] This is another key difference from multilevel governance; relationships can be highly varied depending on the structure of the network and not necessarily grounded in cooperation and negotiation. The structural approach to policy networks is distinct from studies that conceive of policy networks as interpersonal interactions between actors.

In the public-policy scholarship, policy networks have arguably gained currency as a useful framework to explain policy change and outcomes. The structure of policy networks, rather than simply the actors that make up the network, may influence policy change and development. Theories such as neoinstitutionalism or policy learning are applied to explain how networks determine the rules and membership of policy making[54] and how the beliefs of certain policy communities adapt and compete with one another to influence policy outputs.[55] In contrast, explaining why policy networks emerge requires investigating the broader political and social context, such as macropolitical, -economic, and -social structures.[56] But perhaps most promising is to consider the dialectical relationship between the microlevel interactions of policy actors, the mesolevel structures of networks, and the macrocontextual forces and structures.[57] The Canadian literature on Indigenous-Crown land governance has thus far not engaged with the policy network concept, despite its potential to explain decision making about land governance that exists alongside the formal policy process and constitutional rules.

Collaborative Governance

Due to the broad definition of policy networks, multilevel governance's application in the Canadian public-policy scholarship may be understood as an example of a network with more specific characteristics.[58] Similarly, the term "collaborative governance" also describes a type of policy network where actors' relationships with one another are distinctly collaborative and driven by deliberation.[59] Collaborative governance can be considered a distinct area of study because these types of arrangements must entail an explicit and formalized process of including organized interests into multilateral and consensus-oriented decision making.[60] Moreover, this collaborative process is initiated by state agencies or institutions, participants must include nonstate actors, and these nonstate actors must be engaged in decision making throughout all stages rather than simply being consulted in certain ones.[61]

While multilevel governance emerged to address the development of supranational political structures, collaborative governance is connected to the deliberative democracy movement in the public administration literature.[62] In this movement, it is asserted that increased participation from nonstate actors, particularly citizens, will increase legitimacy, accountability, and transparency in the decision-making process. A major analytical contribution in the collaborative-governance literature is the clear distinction between the contextual conditions that influence collaborative arrangements and the drivers of collaboration that determine whether the arrangement will be successful.[63] Starting conditions may include asymmetries between actors' resources and histories of cooperation or conflict.[64] By contrast, the drivers of collaboration include leadership, incentives for participation among the relevant actors, interdependencies among participating actors, and high levels of uncertainty to tackle a policy problem.[65] The collaborative-governance literature also focuses attention on how the external environment of the collaborative group, the structure and process that guide the actions of the participating actors, and the resulting dynamics between participants all affect policy outcomes. This framework appears to be more developed for analytical comparisons than multilevel governance frameworks employed in the scholarship addressing Indigenous-Crown land-use planning policies. Collaborative governance also overlaps with the dialectic approach to policy networks, where both the agents within structures and the structures of the network itself can influence policy decisions and outcomes.

Connecting Law and Policy Frameworks
All three policy frameworks can be applied to investigate different Indigenous-Crown land-use planning arrangements. However, regardless of the framework employed, the specific legal relationship between Indigenous peoples and the state needs to be explicitly included. This legal context can influence the way in which these governance arrangements emerge, the structure of the governing arrangement, the dynamics between policy actors within the governing structure, and the resulting policy decisions and outcomes from the arrangement. The legal context may also change over time, as the duty-to-consult jurisprudence continues to unfold. Moreover, the recognition of the UN's Declaration on the Rights of Indigenous Peoples in Canada, which does not yet impact the Supreme Court's interpretation of Canadian constitutional law, may constrain state behaviour by changing norms and statutory mandates surrounding consent-based decision making.

Apart from the distinct legal relationships between Indigenous groups and the state, the effects of colonialism must be considered. For instance, the multilevel-governance framework is applied when state and nonstate actors govern together through negotiation, but relations between Indigenous peoples and governments in a settler-state context may have enduring hierarchical power relations. The disparity in power between the government and Indigenous groups is the result of the state's legacy and continuation of colonial practices.

Despite the emphasis on negotiation and collaboration in multilevel governance, those who seek to apply multilevel governance in Indigenous-Crown relations must consider how state laws and institutions structure the scope of Indigenous policy actors' leverage vis-à-vis the state.[66] Given this colonial context, the legal and constitutional responsibilities and relationships among various policy actors will continue to play a predominant role in decision-making processes, even structuring the terms of collaboration and negotiation. The prominence of Indigenous peoples' legal statuses means that formal constitutional rules will influence the interactions of actors, even though multilevel governance aims to focus on negotiated orders. The subsequent negotiation dynamics that are structured by constitutional rights may then result in varied policy outcomes and governing partnerships that could be critical to investigate.

Like multilevel governance, collaborative governance also directs attention to governance arrangements that are characterized by negotiation and consensus. There has been some uptake on applying collaborative governance to understand Indigenous-Crown land governance in Canada. In these studies, there is acknowledgment that the legal history of Indigenous peoples and the Crown influences both the starting conditions and drivers of collaboration, such as incentives for participation, leadership, and institutional design, which, in turn, affect policy decisions and outcomes.[67] However, these studies do not explain how the same legal framework, such as the duty to consult, may sometimes provide opportunities to negotiate collaborative land-use planning arrangements but at other times appears inconsequential to those negotiations. For example, the Nadleh Whut'en, a member of the Carrier Sekani First Nations (CSFN) in British Columbia, filed for judicial review to challenge the authorization of the Coastal GasLink pipeline in 2014. This lawsuit encouraged the province to renegotiate with the CSFN. Although the immediate objective was to reach an agreement on the status of the project, the Natural Resources Protocol that was subsequently signed had broader governance aims. The protocol committed the parties to establish a new shared decision-making process in matters relating to natural resources and create new processes for environmental and cultural stewardship.[68] This protocol would develop into new agreements, like the Collaboration Agreement in 2015, which further details the terms of collaborative decision making and explicitly "recognizes the existence of Carrier Sekani Aboriginal title and rights in the Territories."[69]

The CSFN leveraged a project-specific consultative process to demand collaboration in broader land-use planning. In contrast, the experience of the Haida Nation in British Columbia reveals that the duty to consult may not be useful to advance Indigenous control over land-use planning. The Haida Nation and the province signed two protocol agreements in 2001 after sustained political and economic pressure from logging boycotts and a legal challenge against the transfer of the largest tree farm licence on the island. In these agreements, the British Columbia government and the Haida Nation committed to cooperating in the creation of a strategic land-use plan that would be guided by an ecosystem-based management framework and a government-to-government process to resolve outstanding matters.[70] And yet the province reneged on its obligation to consult the Haida and uphold the land-use plan by authorizing logging in cultural cedar reserves.[71] This duplicity led to the Islands' Spirit Rising, which involved weeks of blockades to prevent logging. These protests successfully exerted political pressure to initiate negotiations to protect culturally and ecologically significant areas.[72] After three gruelling years of negotiations, governing agreements were finalized to detail the island's land-use planning and governance. This case depicts how the duty to consult may not always provide the conditions for successful land-use planning negotiations. This variation in land-planning outcomes is worth investigating further. Identifying the limits of the duty to produce policy change and the conditions under which change occurs may explain why the duty is sometimes heralded as a game changer for Indigenous peoples' participation in land planning and other times is considered an ineffective tool to produce sufficient change in Crown policy making.

The broader concept of policy networks may be able to account for some of the variation in different Indigenous-Crown governance arrangements and their relationship with consultation. A variety of policy networks can exist based on different levels of integration and the membership of networks. This conceptual flexibility can usefully capture the various Indigenous-Crown partnerships in strategic land-use planning that do not always resemble equal collaboration. Aboriginal rights or title holders have a prominent role to play in land-use planning, but other actors – such as industry, recreational users, and private landowners – may also partake in decision making. Depending on the region, different combinations of actors with varying levels of influence may make up the policy community; such a combination may be more significant to policy outcomes than the scale in which the actors reside, which is the analytical focus of multilevel governance.

Moreover, the dynamics and decision-making power of the actors in a policy network may be tied to contextual factors, including variation in the legal leverage between Indigenous groups. For instance, Indigenous nations may exercise different amounts of leverage in land-use planning depending on the strength of their rights claims. In the duty-to-consult jurisprudence, it is stated that Indigenous groups with strong rights claims will have more extensive opportunities to participate within consultation processes, such as negotiations for accommodation measures.[73] Therefore, groups with strong claims may be best positioned to use their leverage to pursue partnerships with the Crown under more equitable terms because these groups have a strong legal foundation for negotiating such an arrangement. In contrast, groups with more tenuous claims may still pursue land-use planning arrangements with the Crown, but the Crown may take on a more hierarchical role because of the perception of less legal risk. The fact that Indigenous groups have various and competing claims with one another is a reality of Aboriginal-rights recognition that may influence the power within these networks responsible for land-use planning.[74] As such, policy networks may be another potentially useful analytical tool to understand variation among different land-use planning arrangements.

A Promising Research Agenda: Looking beyond Consultation

The duty to consult's implementation affects the legal, political, and economic relationships between Indigenous peoples and the state. The Crown's obligation to consult and accommodate Indigenous peoples has had profound policy consequences, particularly in the areas of natural resource development and land-use planning. It is imperative to investigate whether the duty to consult can change the conditions to include Indigenous groups in a variety of land-use planning arrangements with the state beyond project-specific consultation. Analyzing the development of these various land-use planning agreements and the changing role of Indigenous nations in these plans is a way to clearly distinguish the effects of the duty to consult on broader policy processes and negotiations. Given this objective, employing public policy theories is a useful starting point as they provide a framework to understand how and why partnerships arise between the state and Indigenous actors. This chapter has shown that multilevel governance, policy networks, and collaborative governance are plausible frameworks to apply to cases where Indigenous peoples have been involved in the creation of land-use planning agreements. The cross-pollination of law and policy can simultaneously contribute to both fields: identifying the policy effects of legal obligations and rules provides empirical evidence to demonstrate whether the duty to consult is meeting its objective to advance reconciliation between the interests of Indigenous peoples and the state. Conversely, explicitly treating law and legal relationships as important conditions or variables that can influence the scope and nature of partnerships between policy actors can add significant explanatory value to existing policy frameworks.

Notes

1　*Haida Nation v British Columbia (Ministry of Forests),* [2004] 3 SCR 511, para 27, 2004 SCC 73 [*Haida Nation*].
2　*Ibid,* para 35.
3　*Ibid,* para 39.
4　*Ibid,* para 48.
5　*Ibid,* para 51.
6　See Sonia Lawrence and Patrick Macklem, "From Consultation to Reconciliation: Aboriginal Rights and the Crown's Duty to Consult," *Canadian Bar Review* 79 (2000): 252–79; Gordon Christie, "Developing Case Law: The Future of Consultation and Accommodation," *UBC Law Review* 39, 1 (2006): 139–84; Dwight Newman, *Revisiting the Duty to Consult Aboriginal Peoples* (Vancouver: UBC Press, 2014); Dwight Newman, "The Section 35 Duty to Consult," in *The Oxford Handbook of the Canadian Constitution,* ed. Peter Oliver, Patrick Macklem, and Nathalie Des Rosiers (Oxford: Oxford University Press, 2017), 349–65; Robert Hamilton and Joshua Nichols, "The Tin Ear of the Court: *Ktunaxa Nation* and the Foundation of the Duty to Consult," *Alberta Law Review* 56, 3 (2019): 729–60.
7　*Haida Nation,* para 16.
8　See Arthur Pape, "The Duty to Consult and Accommodation: A Judicial Innovation Intended to Promote Reconciliation," in *Aboriginal Law since Delgamuukw,* ed. Maria Morellato (Aurora, ON: Canada Law Book, 2009), 313–31; E. Ria Tzimas, "To What End the Dialogue?," *Supreme Court Law Review* 54 (2011): 493–527; Minh Do, "The Duty to Consult and Reconciliation: The Supreme Court's Idea of the Purpose and Practice of Consulting Indigenous Peoples," *International Journal of Canadian Studies* 58, 1 (2020): 73–91.
9　*Haida Nation,* para 16.
10　See Michael McCrossan, "Shifting Judicial Conceptions of 'Reconciliation': Geographic Commitments Underpinning Aboriginal Rights Decisions," *Windsor Yearbook of Access to Justice* 31, 2 (2013): 155–79; D'Arcy Vermette, "Dizzying Dialogue: Canadian Courts and the Continuing Justification of the Dispossession of Aboriginal Peoples," *Windsor Yearbook of Access to Justice* 29, 1 (2011): 55–72; Rachael Ariss, Clara MacCallum, and Diba Nazneen Somani, "Crown Policies on the Duty to Consult and Accommodate: Towards Reconciliation?," *McGill Journal of Sustainable Development Law* 13, 1 (2017): 1–54.
11　*Mikisew Cree First Nation v Canada (Minister of Canadian Heritage),* [2005] 3 SCR 388, 2005 SCC 69.
12　*Beckman v Little Salmon Carmacks First Nation,* [2010] 3 SCR 103, 2010 SCC 53.
13　*Rio Tinto Alcan Inc v Carrier Sekani Tribal Council,* [2010] 2 SCR 650, para 44, 2010 SCC 43 [*Rio Tinto Alcan Inc*].
14　*Mikisew Cree First Nation v Canada (Governor General in Council),* [2018] 2 SCR 765, 2018 SCC 40.
15　*Rio Tinto Alcan Inc,* para 45.
16　*Chippewas of the Thames First Nation v Enbridge Pipelines Inc,* [2017] 1 SCR 1099, para 42, 2017 SCC 41; Newman, "The Section 35 Duty to Consult," 359.
17　Minh Do, "Throughput Legitimacy and the Duty to Consult: The Limits of the Law to Produce Quality Interactions in British Columbia's EA Process," *Canadian Journal of Political Science* 53, 3 (2020): 588.
18　See Kaitlin Ritchie, "Issues Associated with the Implementation of the Duty to Consult and Accommodate Aboriginal Peoples: Threatening the Goals of Reconciliation and Meaningful Consultation," *UBC Law Review* 46, 2 (2013): 397–438.

19 See David Mullan, "The Supreme Court and the Duty to Consult Aboriginal Peoples: A Lifting of the Fog?," *Canadian Journal of Administrative Law and Practice* 24 (2011): 233–60; Veronica Potes, "The Duty to Accommodate Aboriginal Peoples Rights: Substantive Consultation?," *Journal of Environmental Law and Practice* 17, 1 (2006): 27–45; Janna Promislow, "Irreconcilable? The Duty to Consult and Administrative Decision Makers," *Constitutional Forum* 22, 1 (2013): 63–78; Hamilton and Nichols, "The Tin Ear of the Court."

20 Newman, "The Section 35 Duty to Consult," 364.

21 See Sari Graben, "Resourceful Impacts: Harm and Valuation of the Sacred," *University of Toronto Law Journal* 64, 1 (2014): 61–105; Sari Graben and Abbey Sinclair, "Tribunal Administration and the Duty to Consult: A Study of the National Energy Board," *University of Toronto Law Journal* 65, 4 (2015): 382–433.

22 *Haida Nation*, para 26.

23 Joshua Nichols and Robert Hamilton, "In Search of Honourable Crowns and Legitimate Constitutions: *Mikisew Cree First Nation v. Canada* and the Colonial Constitution," *University of Toronto Law Journal* 70 (2020): 341–75; McCrossan, "Shifting Judicial Conceptions of 'Reconciliation'"; Gordon Christie, "A Colonial Reading of Recent Jurisprudence: *Sparrow, Delgamuukw* and *Haida Nation*," *Windsor Yearbook of Access to Justice* 23, 1 (2005): 17–53. For a broader discussion on the merits of a legal order that contests constitutional foundations, see James Tully, *Strange Multiplicity: Constitutionalism in an Age of Diversity* (Cambridge: Cambridge University Press, 1995).

24 *Haida Nation*, para 20.

25 Hok Lin Leung, *Land Use Planning Made Plain* (Toronto: University of Toronto Press, 2003), 1.

26 West Coast Environmental Law Research Foundation, *West Coast Environmental Law's Guide to Forest Land Use Planning* (Vancouver: The Foundation, 1999), 1-1.

27 Leung, *Land Use Planning Made Plain*, 15.

28 British Columbia, "Land Use Planning for Provincial Public Land," https://www2.gov.bc.ca/gov/content/industry/crown-land-water/land-use-planning.

29 British Columbia, "Industry," https://www2.gov.bc.ca/gov/content/data/statistics/business-industry-trade/industry.

30 See Libby Porter and Janice Barry, *Planning for Co-existence? Recognizing Indigenous Rights through Land-Use Planning in Canada and Australia* (London: Routledge, 2016); Ryan Walker, Ted Jojola, and David Natcher, eds., *Reclaiming Indigenous Planning* (Montreal/Kingston: McGill-Queen's University Press, 2013).

31 The exception is Clara MacCallum Fraser and Leela Viswanathan, "The Crown Duty to Consult and Ontario Municipal-First Nations Relations: Lessons Learned from the Red Hill Valley Parkway Project," *Canadian Journal of Urban Research* 22, 1 (2013): 1–19.

32 See Jon Pierre, *Debating Governance: Authority, Steering, and Democracy* (Oxford: University of Oxford Press, 2000); Jon Pierre and B. Guy Peters, *Governance, Politics and the State* (Houndmills, UK: Macmillan Press, 2000); Lester M. Salamon, "The New Governance and the Tools of Public Action: An Introduction," in *The Tools of Government: A Guide to the New Governance*, ed. Lester M. Salamon (Oxford: Oxford University Press, 2002), 1–47; Stephen P. Osborne, ed., *The New Public Governance? Emerging Perspectives on the Theory and Practice of Public Governance* (London: Routledge, 2010); Jean Hartley, Eva Sørenson, and Jacob Torfing, "Collaborative Innovation: A Viable Alternative to Market Competition and Organizational Entrepreneurship," *Public Administration Review* 73, 6 (2013): 821–30.

33 Grace Skogstad, "Who Governs? Who Should Govern? Political Authority and Legitimacy in Canada in the Twenty-First Century," *Canadian Journal of Political Science* 36, 5 (2003): 955–73.

34 *Haida Nation*, para 32.

35 Ryan Beaton, "*De Facto* and *De Jure* Crown Sovereignty: Reconciliation and Legitimation at the Supreme Court of Canada," *Constitutional Forum* 27, 1 (2017–18): 25–33.

36 Chris Alcantara and Jen Nelles, "Indigenous People and the State in Settler Societies: Toward a More Robust Definition of Multilevel Governance," *Publius* 44, 1 (2014): 185.

37 *Ibid.*

38 Jennifer Silver, "Weighing in on Scale: Synthesizing Disciplinary Approaches to Scale in the Context of Building Interdisciplinary Resource Management," *Society and Natural Resources* 21, 10 (2008): 925.

39 Guy Peters and Jon Pierre, "Multi-level Governance and Democracy: A Faustian Bargain?," in *Multi-level Governance*, ed. Ian Bache and Matthew Flinders (Oxford: Oxford University Press, 2004), 7.

40 Alcantara and Nelles, "Toward a More Robust Definition of Multilevel Governance," 191.

41 Peters and Pierre, "Multi-level Governance and Democracy," 7.

42 Ian Bache, "Partnership as an EU Policy Instrument," *West European Politics* 33, 1 (2010): 58–74.

43 See Lisbet Hooghe and Marks Gary, *Multi-level Governance and European Integration* (Oxford: Oxford University Press, 2001); Markus Perkmann, "Policy Entrepreneurship and Multilevel Governance: A Comparative Study of European Cross-Border Regions," *Environment and Planning C: Government and Policy* 25, 6 (2007): 861–79; Ian Bache, "Europeanization and Multi-level Governance: EU Cohesion Policy and Preaccession Aid in Southeast Europe," *Southeast European and Black Sea Studies* 10, 1 (2010): 1–12.

44 See Steve Graham and Simon Marvin, *Splintering Urbanism: Networked Infrastructures, Technological Mobilities and the Urban Condition* (London: Routledge, 2001); Jefferey M. Sellers, "The Nation-State and Urban Governance: Toward Multilevel Analysis," *Urban Affairs Review* 37, 5 (2002): 611–41; Harvey Lazar and Christian Leuprecht, *Spheres of Governance: Comparative Studies of Cities in Multilevel Governance Systems* (Kingston/Montreal: McGill-Queen's University Press, 2007); Martin Horak and Robert Young, eds., *Sites of Governance: Multilevel Governance and Policy Making in Canada's Big Cities* (Montreal/Kingston: McGill-Queen's University Press, 2012); Carey Doberstein, "Metagovernance of Urban Governance Networks in Canada: In Pursuit of Legitimacy and Accountability," *Canadian Public Administration* 56, 4 (2013): 584–609.

45 Simona Piattoni, *The Theory of Multi-level Governance: Conceptual, Empirical, and Normative Challenges* (New York: Oxford University Press, 2010), 18.

46 See Martin Papillon, "Canadian Federalism and the Emerging Mosaic of Aboriginal Multilevel Governance," in *Canadian Federalism: Performance, Effectiveness and Legitimacy*, ed. Herman Bakvis and Grace Skogstad (Toronto: Oxford University Press, 2008), 291–313; Kiera Ladner, "Colonialism Isn't the Only Obstacle: Indigenous Peoples and Multilevel Government in Canada," in *Federalism, Feminism and Multilevel Governance*, ed. Marian Sawer Hausmann and Jill Vickers (London: Ashgate, 2010), 83–96; Martin Papillon, "Adapting Federalism: Indigenous Multilevel Governance in Canada and the United States," *Publius: The Journal of Federalism* 42, 2 (2012): 289–312; Alcantara and Nelles, "Toward a More Robust Definition of Multilevel Governance," 183–204; Martin Papillon and André Juneau, eds., *Canada: The State of the Federation 2013 – Aboriginal Multilevel Governance,* Institute of Intergovernmental Relations (Montreal/Kingston: McGill-Queen's University Press, 2015); and Christopher Alcantara and Michael Morden,

"Indigenous Multilevel Governance and Power Relations," *Theory, Politics, Governance* 7, 2 (2019): 250–64.

47 Alcantara and Nelles, "Toward a More Robust Definition of Multilevel Governance," 198.

48 Joel Krupa, Lindsay Galbraith, and Sarah Burch, "Participatory and Multi-level Governance: Applications to Aboriginal Renewable Energy Projects," *Local Environment* 20, 1 (2015): 86.

49 *Ibid*, 199.

50 Grace Skogstad, "Policy Networks and Policy Communities: Conceptualizing State-Societal Relationships in the Policy Process," in *The Comparative Turn in Canadian Political Science*, ed. Linda White Richard Simeon, Robert Vipond, and Jennifer Wallner (Toronto: University of Toronto Press, 2008), 207–8.

51 *Ibid*.

52 Grant Jordan and William Maloney, "Accounting for Sub-governments: Explaining the Persistence of Policy Communities," *Administration and Society* 29, 5 (1997): 579.

53 David Marsh and R.A.W. Rhodes, eds., *Policy Networks in British Government* (Oxford: Clarendon Press, 1992); William Coleman and Grace Skogstad, eds., *Policy Communities and Public Policy in Canada* (Toronto: Copp Clark Pitman, 1990); William Coleman, Grace Skogstad, and Michael Atkinson, "Paradigm Shifts and Policy Networks: Cumulative Change in Agriculture," *Journal of Public Policy* 16 (1997): 273–301.

54 David Marsh and Martin Smith, "Understanding Policy Networks: Towards a Dialectical Approach," *Political Studies* 48 (2000): 4–21.

55 Paul Sabatier and Hank Jenkins-Smith, eds., *Policy Change and Learning: An Advocacy Coalition Approach* (Boulder, CO: Westview Press, 1993).

56 Skogstad, "Policy Networks and Policy Communities," 212.

57 Colin Hay, "Globalization, Social Democracy, and the Persistence of Partisan Politics: A Commentary on Garrett," *Review of International Political Economy* 7, 1 (2002): 138–52.

58 Skogstad, "Policy Networks and Policy Communities," 217. However, the European multilevel-governance literature contends that there are key differences between multilevel governance and policy networks. See, for example, Piattoni, *The Theory of Multi-level Governance*, 30.

59 Peter DeLeon and Danielle M. Varda, "Toward a Theory of Collaborative Policy Networks: Identifying Structural Tendencies," *Policy Studies Journal* 37, 1 (2009): 59–74.

60 Chris Ansell and Alison Gash, "Collaborative Governance in Theory and Practice," *Journal of Public Administration Research and Theory* 18, 4 (2008): 547–48.

61 *Ibid*, 544–45.

62 See Archon Fung and Erik Wright, *Deepening Democracy: Institutional Innovations in Empowered Participatory Governance* (New York: Verso, 2001); Tina Nabatchi, "Addressing the Citizenship and Democratic Deficits: Exploring the Potential of Deliberative Democracy for Public Administration," *American Review of Public Administration* 40, 4 (2010): 376–99; Carmen Sirianni, *Investing in Democracy: Engaging Citizens in Collaborative Governance* (Washington: Brookings Institution Press, 2009).

63 Kirk Emerson, Tina Nabatchi, and Stephen Balogh, "An Integrative Framework for Collaborative Governance," *Journal of Public Administration Research and Theory* 22, 1 (2012): 9.

64 Ansell and Gash, "Collaborative Governance in Theory and Practice," 550–54; Steve Selin and Deborah Chavez, "Developing a Collaborative Model for Environmental Planning and Management," *Environmental Management* 19, 2 (1997): 191.

65 Emerson, Nabatchi, and Balogh, "An Integrative Framework for Collaborative Governance," 9–10; John Bryson, Barbara Crosby, and Melissa Middleton Stone, "The Design

and Implementation of Cross-Sector Collaborations: Propositions from the Literature," *Public Administration Review* 66, s1 (2006): 44–55.

66 Alcantara and Morden, "Indigenous Multilevel Governance and Power Relations," 253–54.

67 See William Nikolakis and Ngaio Hotte, "How Law Shapes Collaborative Forest Governance: A Focus on Indigenous Peoples in Canada and India," *Society and Natural Resources* 33, 1 (2020): 46–64; Sara Singleton, "Native People and Planning for Marine Protected Areas: How 'Stakeholder' Processes Fail to Address Conflicts in Complex, Real-World Environments," *Coastal Management* 37, 5 (2009): 421–40.

68 Carrier Sekani First Nations and Province of British Columbia, *Natural Resources Protocol*, March 31, 2014, s 6.

69 Province of British Columbia and Carrier Sekani Tribal Council, Collaboration Agreement, April 2, 2015, s 3.1, https://www2.gov.bc.ca/assets/gov/british-columbians -our-governments/indigenous-people/aboriginal-peoples-documents/cstc_-_collaboration_ agreement_-_signed_april_2015.pdf.

70 The Province of British Columbia and the Council of the Haida Nation, *Haida Gwaii Strategic Land Use Agreement*, September 13, 2007, 2, https://www2.gov.bc.ca/assets/ gov/farming-natural-resources-and-industry/natural-resource-use/land-water-use/ crown-land/land-use-plans-and-objectives/westcoast-region/haidagwaii-slua/haida_ gwaii_slupa.pdf.

71 Louise Takeda and Inge Røpke, "Power and Contestation in Collaborative Ecosystem-Based Management: The Case of Haida Gwaii," *Ecological Economics* 70, 2 (2010): 185.

72 Louise Takeda, *Islands' Spirit Rising: Reclaiming the Forests of Haida Gwaii* (Vancouver: UBC Press, 2005).

73 *Haida Nation*, para 43.

74 See also Peter Russell, "The Supreme Court and Federal-Provincial Relations: The Political Use of Legal Resources," *Canadian Public Policy* 11, 2 (1985): 161–70, for a discussion of how constitutional rights are resources during political bargaining between governments.

22

Indigenous Sovereignty, Canadian Constitutionalism, and *Citizens Plus*
The Unended Quest of Canada's Original Hedgefox

Samuel V. LaSelva

ALAN CAIRNS WAS invited twice by Queen's University to deliver the prestigious MacGregor Lecture at its Institute of Intergovernmental Relations. The result was the publication in 1992 of *Charter versus Federalism: The Dilemmas of Constitutional Reform* and in 2005 of *First Nations and the Canadian State: In Search of Coexistence.* The institute's director noted in the foreword to the first book that Cairns was a leading analyst of the Canadian federal system and his insightful comments and critiques in many books and articles had "shaped in no small measure the way in which Canadians view their constitution."[1] Cairns was enormously productive between 1987 and 2002; his work from that period included *Citizens Plus: Aboriginal Peoples and the Canadian State,* which resulted in the second invitation. The institute's director then noted that, in addition to his stature as one of Canada's pre-eminent constitutional scholars, his research on "citizens plus" had the potential to "better bridge the gaps between Aboriginal and non-Aboriginal Canadians" and merited "careful public deliberation in the period ahead."[2]

What remains uncertain, however, is how successful Cairns was in helping to bridge the gaps in a country deeply scarred by its colonialist past. Two reviews of *Citizens Plus* by prominent Indigenous scholars are especially noteworthy in this regard. In one, Cairns is commended for making "a cogent and compelling argument for integration as the middle road between assimilation and parallelism." The reviewer goes on to say that the "aboriginal political elite may deride his views as imperialistic. But in this case, they shouldn't be believed."[3] In the other review, *Citizens Plus* is described as a "book by another old white guy who doesn't know much about Indians" and who, from the deceptive "middle ground" of Canadian politics, "sings another verse of the assimilationist song." The reviewer concludes by telling Cairns, Tom Flanagan, and "the new assimilationist camp" to "stop talking, and get out of our way."[4] Cairns did not stop talking. He wrote many more articles and book chapters and engaged in a vigorous debate with Flanagan on the respective merits of *Citizens Plus,* Flanagan's book *First Nations? Second Thoughts,* and the *Report of the Royal Commission on Aboriginal Peoples (RCAP).* He also published, shortly before his death in 2018, "Aboriginal Research in Troubled Times," as a kind of farewell message to the next generation of Canadian constitutional scholars.

Cairns was unquestionably an engaged intellectual. But, as Peter Russell has noted in the Festschrift *Insiders and Outsiders: Alan Cairns and the Reshaping of Canadian Citizenship*, his contributions to public debates had the same form as his academic writings, and their impact came "from the strength of his intellectual analysis."[5] The Festschrift also contains Cairns's "My Academic Career." In it, he notes that his early research – especially his Oxford DPhil thesis on Africa, published as *Prelude to Imperialism: British Reactions to Central African Society, 1840–1890* – provided him with "a way of thinking" and a lasting concern for questions related to "the rise and fall of an imperial relationship, how the citizen-state relation can be made legitimate, and the clash of cultures."[6] Students of his constitutional ideas almost never discuss *Prelude to Imperialism*, yet its importance is difficult to exaggerate, given his statement in the Festschrift. In fact, *Citizens Plus* is in many respects a sequel to *Prelude to Imperialism*, linked by research that includes the *Hawthorn Report*, *Charter versus Federalism*, *Disruptions*, and other writings. Cairns was not likely to "stop talking," given his many-sided engagement with the issues canvassed in *Citizens Plus*. He also brought to the discussion of Canada's most difficult constitutional issue a distinctive "voice" and the theoretical orientation of the "hedgefox," which, he believed, provided greater insights into "a modernizing Aboriginality" than either Flanagan's Hayekian perspective or the parallelism of the *Report of the Royal Commission on Aboriginal Peoples*. But not even Canada's hedgefox saw or said everything, and what he did not explicitly say, especially with respect to the conundrum of sovereignty, ultimately reveals a significant gap in both Canadian and Indigenous constitutional theorizing. It is a gap that remains to be adequately filled by other members of the society of explorers, in their quest to make sense of the Canadian mosaic and the constitutional morality required to bridge the tragic divide.[7]

Prelude to Imperialism and After: "Whose Side Is the Past On?"

Cairns's doctoral research on Europe's encounter with Africa in the pre-imperial period carved out research themes and an intellectual orientation that prefigured many of his later projects on Canadian constitutional conflicts. His dissertation also had the distinction of publication under two different titles: in Great Britain, *Prelude to Imperialism*, in the United States, *The Clash of Cultures*. Cairns regarded both titles as expressive of the encouragement he had received "to think about big issues."[8] Imperialism and the clash of cultures are certainly big topics, and several of the chapters prefigure Cairns the engaged intellectual who is admired for *Charter versus Federalism* and sometimes condemned for

Citizens Plus. Those chapters have controversial titles such as "The Impossibility of Cultural Relativism" and "How Can Savages Be Civilized?" A mixed response to Cairns's many-sided orientation also appears in a review of *Prelude to Imperialism* published in 1966. Cairns is praised for having produced an "important book" that "lays bare ... the mind ... of many of those unofficial Victorians who went to Africa during the five decades after 1840." But there is a caveat. "It is to be regretted," the reviewer adds, "that Mr. Cairns ends his book with a number of paragraphs about the necessity of European imperialism for the development of African society."[9] That Cairns viewed his concluding paragraphs differently seems evident from what he wrote forty years later: "The last chapter of my thesis ... concluded with private chagrin that the anti-imperial views with which I arrived in Oxford had not survived my exposure to the anarchic conditions in Africa's interior."[10]

Cairns might have been wiser to stick to his initial negative appraisal of imperialism. Even so, his views are more cautious and nuanced than the reviewer seems to imply. The final assessment of imperialism as an historical event, he writes, will doubtless be somewhere between the "enthusiasm of those who rhapsodized over its birth, and the ... hostility of those who watch and hasten its demise."[11] Moreover, all the reviews concluded that it was "a most valuable book" based on exact scholarship; or that it contained many insights and "more detailed evidence than ... seen before" about the travellers, traders, and missionaries who interacted with traditional African societies in the period before state-sponsored imperialism.[12] One of Cairns's important insights relates to the missionaries who assumed that they had something the African wanted, knew what was best, and would be readily accepted. None of this was true, he remarks, because "it ignored the cultural determination of values [and] seriously underestimated the involvement of an individual in his culture."[13] The missionaries' position, he goes on to observe, "was the religious counterpart of an imperial mentality. It contained the germ of a theocracy in the same way that Rousseau's general will contained the germs of dictatorship."[14] Nevertheless, Cairns concludes the book by emphasizing that although the means were certainly "imperfect," the results remain, and "formerly technologically backward peoples who have experienced imperial rule" are more capable of meeting contemporary demands than those who have not.[15]

Like many of his later writings, Cairns's published dissertation is not easy to characterize or assess. The difficulty is exacerbated by the high quality of its scholarship and subtle analysis. Moreover, Cairns is usually described as a "Canadianist" and political scientist; yet in the Festschrift, he reflects on why, for almost a decade, he became "an Africanist" and immersed himself in literature usually read by anthropologists.[16] His answer outlines the family ties, personal relationships, and educational background that influenced his decision. Just as significant is his view of the academic enterprise. "The sequence of the University of Toronto and Oxford, particularly given the African focus of my thesis topic," he writes, "allowed me to escape the behavioural revolution in American political science."[17] Cairns did not simply escape something. He also immersed himself in a wide range of social science and philosophic subjects and orientations. He was an intellectual trespasser and repeatedly endorsed Albert Hirschman's views on crossing academic boundaries. In *Reconfigurations,* after citing Hirschman, he comments: "[W]e are compelled to trespass because the shifting reality outside our windows is disrespectful of the disciplinary categories and boundaries we employ."[18] Cairns also admired Isaiah Berlin's famous essay "The Hedgehog and the Fox," which describes the contrasting intellectual orientations between those who know many things (the fox), and those who know one big thing (the hedgehog). Applying the distinction to his own work, he concluded that he was neither entirely a fox nor entirely a hedgehog, but a "hedgefox."[19] When he wrote his doctoral dissertation and later works, Cairns was, if nothing else, a trespassing hedgefox who cannot be captured by rigid categorizations or simplistic assessments.

Such an image of Cairns is incomplete, however, unless it is combined with his lifelong admiration for Dean Inge's aphorism: "If you marry the spirit of your own generation you will be a widow in the next." The aphorism is quoted in the preface to *Prelude to Imperialism,* frames his 1977 presidential address to the Canadian Political Science Association on "The Government and Societies of Canadian Federalism," and is accorded a prominent place in his concluding reflections on "Aboriginal Research in Troubled Times." The aphorism, as Cairns appears to have understood it, is expressive of the viewpoint of the intellectual outsider and is a cautionary warning against simplistic adherence to the dominant viewpoint or "prejudices" of the age. There are many earlier articulations of it stretching back to Socrates' famous and fatal questioning of the dominant assumptions of his own age. Moreover, Cairns frequently combined Dean Inge's insight with Julien Benda's warning against intellectual partisanship and excessive particularism in *The Treason of the Intellectuals.* In fact, the last sentence of "Aboriginal Research in Troubled Times" sums up Cairns's message by simply quoting Benda. "Amid the cacophony of voices," he writes, "we must find a place for the scholar who, in the simple but elegant language of Julien Benda, is 'the man of study ... who, silently seated ... reads, instructs himself, writes, takes notes.'"[20] It may be only a slight exaggeration to say that Cairns's voice as a scholar and engaged intellectual begins with Dean Inge, ends by combining Dean Inge and Julien Benda, and always emphasizes the importance of the trespasser and the hedgefox.

Cairns had a voice; he also insisted that "one of the most difficult challenges ... is to bring an authentic, personal voice to the collective disciplinary task of research and writing."[21] His advice to graduate students was to avoid "the homogenizing pressures of the discipline," develop a personal voice, and in that way contribute "to our common enterprise."[22] What he never explicitly answered was whether a voice necessarily constitutes a fixed ideological position. Even so, it may be possible to gain insight into his likely answer by considering the uses he made of Dean Inge's aphorism in the works already noted. In *Prelude to Imperialism,* the aphorism serves as a warning to those who, because of the now prevalent opposition "to the policies of imperialism and racial hegemony," are inclined to take sides and selectively choose "material in favour of the non-white races."[23] Its second appearance comes in a very different context. It serves as the starting point of an elaborate cautionary message to the governments of Canadian federalism, warning them that their aggressive pursuit of conflicting interests may eventually lead to the fragmentation of Canada.[24] The last use frames his long-standing rejection of the 1969 White Paper on Indian Policy. "The believers in and advocates of assimilation," he writes, "were not immunized against the moral and intellectual climate of their era. Their beliefs and behavior confirm the accuracy of Dean Inge's statement."[25] Cairns's voice made him a distinctive member of the society of explorers, but, as the uses of Dean Inge's aphorism illustrate, it did not provide him with a rigid ideological position or a settled constitutional vision.

Reconfigurations, published three decades after *Prelude to Imperialism,* has as its subtitle "Canadian Citizenship and Constitutional Change." It comes closest to expressing what could, conceivably, be described as Cairns's constitutional vision. *Citizens Plus* is also important, but it represents only one part of Cairns's engagement with the larger "ongoing crisis of Canadian statehood" and the "potential constitutional paradigm shift" in Canadian federalism. Moreover, *Reconfigurations* contains an essay on Indigenous peoples in Canada that anticipates many of the themes of *Citizens Plus.* What makes *Reconfigurations* especially noteworthy is its introduction and concluding chapter, titled, respectively, "Whose Side Is the Past On?" and "Dream versus Reality in 'Our' Constitutional Future?" Cairns's answer to the question about the past is: on everyone's side and no one's side. This is because, in contemporary Canada, the constitutional past is the subject matter of heated controversy and redefinition by women, Indigenous peoples, ethnic communities outside the mainstream, and other minorities. In Canada, the slogan is increasingly "Every Group Its Own Historian." The introduction ends with three observations. First, a country and people are more than "a smorgasbord of particular items"; and the past – its successes and failures – is only one of the lenses required for constitutional self-understanding. Second, a "final meta-narrative ... is probably doomed to fail," yet Canadians "should not slacken in our efforts to see ourselves in the large." Third, Cairns states that his own objective is not to provide a grand theory but to reduce the "blooming, buzzing confusion" of the contemporary Canadian constitutional landscape.[26]

How successful *Reconfigurations* is in achieving this objective, readers can judge for themselves. What is important for understanding Cairns's constitutional voice, however, is his description of Canada and the conclusions set out in "Dream versus Reality in 'Our' Constitutional Future." His recurring image is Canada as a heterogeneous society and a people in flux, "whether our vantage point is Canada or Quebec or Aboriginal communities." Canadians, he writes, are "in the grip of competing nationalisms driven by pride, resentment, humiliation, and anger – emotions that can easily get out of control." The task that confronts Canada, he concludes, is to construct a constitutional order that (1) is sensitive to the demands of territorial minorities for some measure of self-rule; (2) protects dispersed minorities; (3) appreciates that no culture is an island; (4) accepts the reality of multiple identities; and (5) understands the creative but limited power of constitutional change. He regards these considerations as relevant to every reimagined Canada that "we can postulate." To accept them, he says, "is the beginning of constitutional common sense. To deny them is comparable to denying the force of the laws of gravity – and equally likely to produce unfortunate results."[27] In *Reconfigurations*, his constitutional voice is the antithesis of Panglossian and has Voltairean, even Hobbesian, dimensions. It reminds those who are working to transform their country that their conflicting dreams can become nightmares if they ignore Canadian pluralism.

Nation-to-Nation, Hayekian Orthodoxies and the Return of Grand Theory: "We Talk, You Listen"

That Cairns never forgot the research he undertook on "the clash of cultures" for *Prelude to Imperialism* is evident in his second MacGregor Lecture on *First Nations and the Canadian State*, but important traces of it can also be found in *Charter versus Federalism*. The constitutional changes precipitated by the Charter, he writes in his first MacGregor Lecture, should not be thought of like the addition of a detached garage that coexists alongside other buildings: "Rather, the appropriate perspective is that of the anthropologist observing a tribe whose traditional arrangements ... are irrevocably transformed ... by recently arrived Christian missionaries."[28] In his second MacGregor Lecture, his earlier research on Africa is omnipresent, as it is in *Citizens Plus*. One reason why Indigenous-state relations are so difficult in Canada, he writes, is because they are caught between "the Third World nationalism that toppled empires" and "Fourth World peoples," who cannot simply oust a colonizer of vastly superior numbers, must accept that there are other people living on the land now, and must find ways to live together. Even the Indigenous people of Haida Gwaii, Cairns observes, realized that they could not claim all the land or turn their island into an independent nation. The vital issue, then, is coexistence, accommodation, and reconciliation. Cairns notes that although his engagement in this quest is complex and incomplete, one of his key objectives is to expose the errors of "grand simplifiers," in whose camp he places both the 1969 White Paper and the 1996 *RCAP*.[29]

Cairns distinguishes grand theorists from grand simplifiers; regards the former, but not the latter, as justly celebrated members of the society of explorers; and informs readers that his preference is for theories of the middle range and the perspective of the hedgefox. Contemporary grand theorists are discussed in Quentin Skinner's well-known collection of essays on, among others, the postmodernist Michel Foucault, the philosopher of science Thomas Kuhn, the political theorist John Rawls, and the anthropologist Claude Lévi-Strauss. All of them recognize, paradoxically, the importance of the local or contingent while unashamedly returning, Skinner writes, "to the deliberate construction of those grand theories of human nature and conduct which Wright Mills and his generation had hoped to outlaw from any central place in the human sciences."[30] Cairns also cites Wright Mills, but his focus is Mills's discussion of intellectual craftsmanship, and Mills's emphasis on the importance in social science of a "voice" and not writing in "prose manufactured by a machine."[31] Cairns regarded as equally enlightening Robert K. Merton's discussion of "sociological theories of the middle range." These were theories that lie between "the minor but necessary working hypotheses that evolve ... during day-to-day research and the all-inclusive systematic effort to develop a unified theory that will explain all the observed uniformities."[32]

The "grand simplifiers," in Cairns's view, include not only the White Paper and the *RCAP* report, as already noted, but also, as will be suggested below, Flanagan's *First Nations? Second Thoughts*. The White Paper was withdrawn shortly after its publication with Trudeau acknowledging that he and his government had been "naïve in some of its statements" and had acted on "perhaps the prejudices of small 'l' liberals, and white men at that."[33] Flanagan has repeatedly reiterated his "libertarian" or "neoconservative" view of Indigenous rights, insisting in the 2019 third edition that *First Nations? Second Thoughts* continues to deserve a place in public discussion because "it is one of the few fundamental challenges to ... the 'aboriginal orthodoxy.'" Flanagan identifies the Aboriginal orthodoxy with the *RCAP* and sees it as exemplifying the eight propositions rejected in his book. To the proposition that First Nations have unique rights because they were here first, Flanagan replies: "[T]o differentiate the rights of earlier and later immigrants is a form of racism." To the proposition that First Nations can successfully exercise their inherent right to self-government on reserves, he writes: "Aboriginal government is fraught with difficulties stemming from small size, an overly ambitious agenda, and dependence on transfer payments. In practice, aboriginal government produces wasteful, destructive, familistic factionalism." Acceptance of the *RCAP* would turn Canada into a modern version of the Ottoman Empire and the "grave problems associated with the aboriginal octagon make it a stop sign for human progress." Flanagan acknowledges his partisanship and says that his views on "politics and society owe a great debt to Frederick Hayek, now widely recognized as one of the most influential thinkers of the late twentieth century."[34]

Whether Cairns regarded Hayek as more of a grand theorist than a grand simplifier, or the reverse, is difficult to determine. In the *Policy Options* debate, he describes Flanagan's book as having "Hayek in wings" and adds that it is beyond his competence to fully engage Hayek.[35] Nevertheless, Cairns cannot sidestep Hayek altogether, because Flanagan uses Hayekian ideas to suggest that the citizens-plus approach will have many of the same negative consequences as the nation-to-nation recommendation of the *RCAP* that Cairns rejects. Thus, although the exchange begins with Flanagan congratulating Cairns on his "demolition of today's conventional wisdom about aboriginal issues," and Cairns suggests (in another context) that "Flanagan's arguments are ... the most thoughtful ... critiques of aboriginal policy ... offered so far," their debate demonstrates, when examined closely, that they are as much opposed to each other as to the *RCAP*.[36] This is easiest shown in the case of Cairns's opposition to Flanagan, if it is recalled that he rejects as grand simplifiers both the White Paper and the *RCAP*. In *Policy Options*, Cairns discusses many difficult issues with Flanagan, but he also emphasizes that Flanagan's "counter-orthodoxy is not new. What you describe as your radical approach was the conventional approach ... from Confederation up to and including the 1969 White Paper."[37] Since Cairns rejects not only the *RCAP* but also the White Paper as simplistic, and since Flanagan's book is a detailed version of the White Paper position, then all three are, in his view, untenable grand simplifiers.

Flanagan's critique of Cairns and citizens plus is less easily presented, but its most important dimensions derive, arguably, from the implicit use he makes of Hayek.[38] Moreover, since Flanagan puts Hayek "in the wings," it falls on Cairns to draw him out. In reply to Flanagan's defence of uniform citizenship, Cairns begins by noting that the Hawthorn Report (in which he was a principal investigator) and the citizens-plus proposal are "a positive response to two facts: the priority of presence, and the fact that the majority had built a flourishing, wealthy society on the dispossession of Aboriginal, especially Indian peoples." He goes on to say: "[Y]our analysis is hostile to any 'plus' recognition – partly because ... you think it will backfire, and more generally, as an admirer of Hayek, you share his distrust of *dirigiste* [state-sponsored] pursuits of social justice." On Flanagan's view, as Cairns understands it, little should be done for Indigenous peoples beyond what is minimally unavoidable, even though the depressing legacy of colonialism leaves Canada with the unfortunate reality of Indigenous peoples whose separate identities have been reinforced and scarred by discrimination, and many of whom live in small communities scattered throughout the country. Cairns also challenges Flanagan's thesis about the *inherent* problems of Indigenous self-government. In his book and the *Policy Options* debate, Flanagan bases his rejection of Aboriginal rights, including citizens plus, on Hayekian grand theory. Cairns's final reply to Flanagan is that his simplistic Hayekian radicalism "is purchased at the very high price of losing touch with the reality it seeks to influence."[39]

The *RCAP*, in Cairns's estimation, made much the same mistake as Flanagan's book, at least with respect to theory. Reflecting on Canada's failures, he writes: "[O]ur past failures ... were caused by misguided theory, and the belief that successful policy could be devised without real discussion with Aboriginal peoples." He is equally convinced that the *RCAP* "lacks a workable political theory."[40] Several statements in other works help to explicate what Cairns meant. In his second MacGregor Lecture, as noted above, he distinguished grand theory and grand simplifications and put the *RCAP* in the latter category. In another work, he notes: "The Report's heavy emphasis on legal analysis and rights along with advocacy of a nation-to-nation relationship discouraged attention to, and sociological analysis of, the majority society as such."[41] Finally, in "Aboriginal Research in Troubled Times," he observes that (1) the accommodation of small Indigenous nations with majority non-Indigenous settler peoples is even harder than escaping from Third World colonial status; (2) both Indigenous and non-Indigenous scholars are living in an era of transition shrouded in ambiguity; (3) the *RCAP* downplayed crucial "social facts" and employed a "utopian strategy"; (4) therefore, the report failed to provide "quality independent advice, suggested by the phrase 'Telling It Like It Is!'"[42]

Just as important as "Telling It Like It Is!" – especially when dealing with contentious topics – is Vine Deloria's "We Talk, You Listen." Deloria was one of the twentieth century's most influential Native American voices; his core message was that Indigenous peoples, whose way of life had been suppressed for many centuries, needed to be heard because of the significance of what they had to say about the problems that plagued American society, from the environmental crisis to the crisis in race relations.[43] In Canada, Cole Harris concluded his sobering reflections on settler colonialism with identical advice to his fellow settlers: "After many years of telling Indigenous people what to do, it is necessary to listen to them."[44] Cairns understood the importance of listening; he emphasized that many misguided theories and policies had resulted from the unwillingness to listen. But simply to reverse the roles was equally misguided. Even in his doctoral research on Africa, the emphasis is on listening and speaking. "If an analogy may be permitted," he wrote, "while a marriage is perhaps best understood as a partnership, a separate study of husbands and wives does shed light on the marriage relationship."[45] The *RCAP* engaged in "we talk, you listen," but it left out vital information and crucial perspectives. In the intellectual exploration of the clash of cultures from *Prelude to Imperialism* to "Aboriginal Research in Troubled Times," one of Cairns's recurring themes is the importance, and difficulty, of all sides engaging in "we talk, you listen" while also "telling it like it is."

"Telling It Like It Is": Indigenous Sovereignty, Canadian Constitutionalism, and the Spectre of Hobbes

To the extent that "telling it like it is" implies a transcendent "objectivity," it is an untenable precept. All views are situated. Cairns, however, frequently associated the precept not with a rarefied objectivity but with the scholar's duty to expose what he called, in the 1989 Timlin Lecture, "Ritual, Taboo, and Bias in Constitutional Controversies in Canada." The lecture focused on two subjects: Canada without Quebec or the attempt by Quebec sovereigntists to limit participation in an independence referendum to "insiders," and the important but limited relevance of Indigenous self-government. He stressed the danger of intellectual monopolies based on exclusive appeals to the insider's perspective. He quoted Byran Schwartz's observation that an academic "may be so sincerely outraged by the injustices done to aboriginal groups that ... she loses the ability to rationally assess ... the past or proposals for the future." He also discussed Merton's seminal article on "insiders" and "outsiders" and used it to criticize the claim that outsiders were to be excluded because they lacked the relevant knowledge that insider status brings. In theology, the "insider" and "outsider" distinction often appears in discussions about God or religious faith: must one believe in order to understand, or is it necessary to understand in order to believe? Cairns was in the latter group, although he welcomed the insider's perspective. Cairns's main conclusion is that both insiders and outsiders must be heard, because of "their special strengths as agents of inquiry and understanding."[46]

There is an easily detected link from the Timlin Lecture and "Telling It Like It Is" to *Citizens Plus* and "Aboriginal Research in Troubled Times." There is also a connection with *Prelude to Imperialism,* the clash of cultures, and Dean Inge's aphorism. Just as significant for Cairns's larger constitutional vision is the connection with the 1977 essay on "The Other Crisis of Canadian Federalism," with *Charter versus Federalism,* and with the 1997 commentary on "Looking into the Abyss." The theme of "The Other Crisis" is that federalism is not the happy solution to the problems of Canadian diversity that Macdonald and Cartier had hoped for in 1867, nor is it the "two scorpions in a bottle" postulated by René Lévesque. Rather, it often comes closer to big governments acting like "eleven elephants in a maze" that produces "a lame duck constitution" and makes the future of Canada uncertain.[47] In *Charter versus Federalism,* he argues that the Charter enhances citizen rights but fails to solve the problems of federal diversity as envisaged by Pierre Trudeau. Since the 1960s and with the adoption of a Charter that recognizes many different group identities, Canadians have drifted "into a situation of ethnic and racial pluralism that makes the state's task of ... renewing the consensus of who we are" as challenging as managing the economy. The 1982 constitutional settlement, Cairns argues, is not "a stable resting-point," and Canadians cannot escape further transformative changes rooted in their "galloping ethnic and racial pluralism."[48]

"Looking into the Abyss" focuses explicitly on constitutional "taboos." Published shortly after the nearly successfully 1995 Quebec sovereignty referendum, it notes that Canadians outside of Quebec have overcome the taboo of publicly discussing Plan B, but "their governments ... [maintain] a taboo on discussing Plan C." As Cairns understands them, Plan A involves the renewal of federalism; Plan B is about establishing ground rules for the possible secession of Quebec; and Plan C would focus on Canada without Quebec. Cairns attempts to "tell it like it is," and what he says is far from Panaglossian. He insists that the optimistic scenarios of Quebec sovereignists were misplaced, because the possibility of significant violence could not be discounted and Canada would not have available to it a "velvet divorce" where the central authority simply "devolved to the two successor states." Such an outcome was not possible partly because Canada outside of Quebec was a pluralistic and fragmented federal system composed of competitive governments. There would also be difficult problems within Quebec, because the losing side would include "virtually all of Quebec's Anglophones, allophones, and aboriginal peoples, and the ethnic division would be wide, deep, and bitter." Finally, there would be disputes over territorial boundaries. Creating a Canada without Quebec, Cairns concludes, would be "a Herculean task" for Quebec, Indigenous peoples, and the rest of Canada – made even more difficult by a failure to "tell it like it is" about the pluralism of Quebec, Canada, and Indigenous peoples.[49]

Citizens Plus shifts the focus away from Quebec. It is a crucial part of Cairns's oeuvre, but it is far from self-evident how successful it is in finding "the middle ground" capable of "bridging the divide," or even what it reveals about his constitutional vision. The largest part of the book is concerned with exposing the limitations of the *RCAP*, followed by Cairns's own conceptualization of Indigenous rights. Equally important is Cairns's lengthy discussion of Indigenous peoples in Canada as victims of empire and subjects of misguided assimilationist policies. He notes, for example, that both Third and Fourth World anticolonialism were responses to similar indignities: the most basic was the ultimate indignity of being placed under the paternal authority of others, ostensibly for one's own good, coupled with sermonizing by European settlers on the ladder of civilization, the virtues of progress, and the inferiority of Indigenous cultures.[50] Moreover, Cairns did not just question the policy of John A. Macdonald and others "to do away with the tribal system and assimilate the Indian people in all respects with the inhabitants of the Dominion." He insisted that, although Indigenous self-government would inevitably be "partial, not total," it constituted "the most significant goal for Aboriginal peoples" partly because "nothing else can equal the enhancement of dignity it offers when its responsibilities are well handled," and because it could be a site for an "evolving Aboriginality" in a globalizing world.[51]

Citizens Plus has, then, three main objectives: to expose the limitations of the *RCAP*, to articulate the required "middle ground," and to identify attributes of a "modernizing Aboriginality." Cairns did not say the last word on these topics, but he did raise important and still unsettled questions. Thus he suggested that the *RCAP*'s constitutional vision, summarized as "parallelism" or "the nation-to-nation theory," was flawed because it failed to take adequate account "of three social facts – the large and growing urban [Indigenous] population, the one-third who declared an Aboriginal ancestry but did not have an Aboriginal identity, and the extent and significance of intermarriage."[52] Moreover, the report's view of side-by-side coexistence was unsatisfactory as a moral theory, he believed, because it took too little account of the positive emotional bonds required to hold Indigenous peoples and other Canadians together and appealed, instead, almost exclusively to guilt and atonement for the history and legacy of colonialism. "The Report's delicate juggling task," he surmises, "was to say, 'we are not you,' while hoping the majority would not respond, 'they are not us.'" Such a strategy "provides a weak answer to the need for empathy and mutual responsibility."[53] Finally, the report had too limited a conception of "modernizing Aboriginality," which requires ongoing and positive interactions between Indigenous peoples and other Canadians. Parallelism was unsatisfactory both as a constitutional vision and as a conception of modernized Aboriginality, because "Aboriginal Peoples are not the Canadian counterparts of Old Order Amish."[54]

The least developed aspect of *Citizens Plus* is the "middle ground" required to "bridge the divide." Thus, in *Policy Options,* Flanagan expresses skepticism about resurrecting the Hawthorn Report's concept of "citizens plus," partly because the "plus" was not spelled out in the initial report, and it is not spelled out thirty-five years later. Cairns's reply is to provide additional examples of the "plus" component from state funding for Indigenous organizations to the establishment of Nunavut, but he also says that the required policies will be worked out under conditions "when our ignorance is great."[55] Similarly, the MacGregor Lectures contain a new "Postscript: A Recipe for Living Together"; it was added at the request of readers to translate the "general argument" into "more specific recommendations." Cairns prefaces the postscript by saying that the "readers' suggestion was a tall order" and that his additional remarks will be "at the macro level." The additional remarks emphasize the need to protect Indigenous rights from the nation-building aspect of the Charter, the desirability and limitations of Indigenous self-government, and the failure of the Indigenous-rights provision in the *Constitution Act, 1982* to live up to its initial promise. Cairns concludes by suggesting that a viable "Recipe for Living Together" should blend what Charles Taylor says about patriotism in an essay on democracy with Taylor's comments on "deep diversity" in another essay.[56] This blending of patriotism (to Canada) and deep diversity (within Canada) is, of course, similar to what Cairns is himself attempting to do, although he uses different terminology.

Cairns rejected the nation-to-nation theory because he regarded it as too focused on living apart in ways that were incompatible with the lived reality of many Indigenous individuals and with the sociological facts that define and constrain the Fourth World nationalism of Indigenous communities in Canada. Is the problem, then, that Indigenous communities think of themselves as nations? If one rejects the nation-to-nation theory, must one then also reject the idea that Indigenous communities are nations? Flanagan certainly rejects both ideas.[57] Cairns's position is harder to determine beyond saying that he rejects the nation-to-nation theory. Moreover, Cairns focused so much attention on the nation-to-nation theory that he may have contributed to obscuring some of the other and even more challenging theoretical issues at stake. For the deepest challenges to "bridging the divide" come not from Indigenous communities as nations but from ideas about the incommensurability of cultures coupled with assertions of unconstrained national self-determination or sovereignty.

Consider, for example, one of the best-known Indigenous articulations of the incommensurability of cultures thesis, Mary Ellen Turpel's seminal article "Aboriginal Communities and the Canadian Charter: Interpretive

Monopolies, Cultural Differences." Section 25 of the Charter is about Indigenous peoples; it prohibits the Charter from being "construed so as to abrogate or derogate from any aboriginal, treaty, or other rights or freedoms." The purpose of Turpel's article is not to emphasize the importance of section 25 as a constraint on Pierre Trudeau's nation-building conception of the Charter and as a protection of Indigenous distinctiveness. Rather, she goes much further and postulates an incommensurability of cultures. Cultural differences, she writes, should be understood "as manifestations of differing human (collective) imaginations, of different ways of knowing"; they go beyond gaps in knowledge and are about "irreconcilable or irreducible elements of human relations." She also provides illustrations and conclusions. One illustration is that "some First Nations base their social interactions on the Four Directions ... roughly translated as *trust, kindness, sharing and strength*." In contrast, other Canadians are portrayed as immersed in a property-based Lockean "rights paradigm" that is "a highly individualistic and negative concept of social life." Given such differences in ways of life, she denies the (cultural) authority of Canadian courts to adjudicate disputes involving Indigenous values and "seriously questions whether differences can be or should be put before the court." Finally, "if irreconcilable conceptions of law exist ... what is to be done?" Her answer is that the optimal solution would be the "toleration of differences and the recognition of autonomous or incommensurable communities."[58]

For anyone familiar with the history and practice of colonialism, or with imperialist schemes based on simplistic assertions of universal values, it is difficult not to intuitively endorse Turpel's ideas – or some other version of relativism that, like Ruth Benedict's *Patterns of Culture*, celebrates "co-existing and equally valid patterns of life."[59] What is not self-evident, however, is that a commitment to "co-existing and equally valid patterns of life" follows from cultural relativism or cultural incommensurability. "From the fact that each people believes in the validity of its own values," wrote Morris Ginsberg, "it does not follow that it believes ... that differing value systems all deserve respect. It is far more likely that each will claim superior excellence for itself."[60] The relevance of this conclusion reaches beyond colonialism and imperialism. The Indigenous reviewer of *Citizens Plus*, who told Cairns to "get out of our way," also said: "[T]his country is screwed up anyway, and ... our people had nothing to do with creating the problem."[61] Such a statement seems some distance from Ruth Benedict's idea. Moreover, if moral relativism or cultural incommensurability is coupled with insider practices – by white settlers or Indigenous peoples, or both – of "we talk, you listen," the outcome becomes even more unpalatable.

In "Looking into the Abyss," as noted above, Cairns focused primarily on Quebec and drew attention to the frequently neglected, negative implications of Quebec's pursuit of sovereignty. Hobbes is not discussed, but his description is of a Canadian future torn by Hobbesian rivalries. The question he never answered is whether a one-sided pursuit of Indigenous cultural and political self-determination (or sovereignty) by hundreds of Indigenous nations within Canada would have equally unfortunate results.

Conclusion: The Canadian Mosaic and the Unended Quest

A reviewer of *Prelude to Imperialism* said of Cairns's first book, on Africa, what some readers of his later works, on Canada, may also think. "He is to be credited with insights too numerous to mention," yet "one occasionally loses track of the overall direction of the argument."[62] Such a judgment seems plausible enough. After all, Cairns wrote on big topics, trespassed on many academic disciplines, combined scholarly aloofness with public engagement, and thought of himself as a never-before-seen hedgefox. Even so, there is a sentence in "My Academic Career" that points to the overall direction of much of his work: "In looking back, it's striking how many of the subjects I wrote about were very clearly responses to the political and constitutional discontents of a troubled country."[63] What, then, makes Canada a troubled country? Cairns gave at least two answers. His first and best-known answer is that fundamental changes – beginning in the 1960s, in the international system and in Canada's domestic social, political, and ethnic landscape – produced significant challenges to the Confederation settlement of 1867 and eventually led to the adoption of the *Constitution Act, 1982*. Moreover, the changes of 1982 – including the Charter as "the citizen's constitution" of a robustly pluralistic Canada, provisions on Indigenous rights that rendered assimilation obsolete but left many questions about self-government unsettled, and a new amending formula that satisfied almost no one – produced a wrenching transformation that has not yet run its course. Canada, then, is a troubled country because it is in transition to an unknown future.[64] Cairns also had a second answer, which he never developed. In his first MacGregor Lecture, he said that, in 1867, "Canadians ... were a project for the future, not an inheritance from the past."[65]

If Cairns's two answers are combined, Canada becomes a country in transition and a "troubled" country from 1867 to the present. Such an understanding of Canada is by no means implausible. In *The Canadian Identity*, W.L. Morton attempted to describe the essential characteristics of Canada and included among them "the concept of a nationality made up of a mosaic of peoples and cultures." He goes on to call it "an unusual concept, which flew in the face of most human experience." There were periods of stability and periods of significant stress in Canadian history, but the mosaic idea "continued and clarified itself" as a reflection of the lived experience of the people who made up Canada. Morton concluded his analysis by emphasizing that "because it was so integral a part of Canadian life, obviously Canada stood or fell with the success or failure of the mosaic."[66]

Cairns did not focus significantly on Canada as a mosaic, in his first or second MacGregor Lectures. However, in *Citizens Plus*, he discussed Harold Cardinal, the celebrated Indigenous author of *The Unjust Society*. He noted similarities between Cardinal's ideas and citizens plus, including Cardinal's endorsement of "a Canadian cultural mosaic."[67] In fact, Cardinal stressed that Indigenous peoples wanted to be "colourful red tiles" in the mosaic, "taking our place where red is both needed and appreciated." However, Cardinal was, like Cairns, a complex thinker. He also insisted that "we are sovereign nations" and warned that if "Indian rights and dignity" were not adequately recognized, Indigenous peoples would "organize ... to destroy your society, which they feel is destroying our people."[68] What then is Cairns's reply to Cardinal on sovereignty based on his writings from *Prelude to Imperialism* to "Aboriginal Research in Troubled Times"? One reply must surely be to draw out more fully, and in a cautionary fashion, the negative Hobbesian implications for all Canadians, including Indigenous peoples, of "Looking into the Abyss." Cairns also has another reply, articulated in the concluding pages of *Citizens Plus*. It emphasizes the importance – indeed, the necessity – of strengthening the bond of mutual empathy between Indigenous peoples and non-Indigenous Canadians. It points, implicitly, not to Hobbes but to the Truth and Reconciliation Commission and other engagements directed at bridging Canada's most tragic and difficult divide.[69] That Cairns provided two such different, but complementary, responses to the unfinished 1982 constitutional agenda and its Indigenous-rights provisions is further evidence that he was a hedgefox committed to "telling it like it is."

Notes

I am grateful to Cole Harris, Emmett Macfarlane, and Stephen Newman for their very helpful comments on my essay.

1   Douglas Brown, Foreword to Alan C. Cairns, *Charter versus Federalism: The Dilemmas of Constitutional Reform* (Montreal/Kingston: McGill-Queen's University Press, 1992), vii.

2   Harvey Lazar, Foreword to Alan C. Cairns, *First Nations and the Canadian State: In Search of Coexistence* (Kingston: Queen's University, Institute of Intergovernmental Relations, 2005), ix.

3   Suzanne Methot, review of *Citizens Plus: Aboriginal Peoples and the Canadian State*, by Alan C. Cairns, *Quill and Quire* 66, 3 (2000): 56.

4   Taiaiake Alfred, "Of White Heroes and Old Men Talking," review of *Citizens Plus*, by Alan C. Cairns, *Windspear*, June 1, 2000, 4–6.

5 Peter H. Russell, "Citizenship in a Multinational Democracy," in *Insiders and Outsiders: Alan Cairns and the Reshaping of Canadian Citizenship,* ed. Gerald Kernerman and Philip Resnick (Vancouver: UBC Press, 2005), 273.

6 Alan C. Cairns, "My Academic Career," in Kernerman and Resnick, *Insiders and Outsiders,* 345; Alan C. Cairns, *Prelude to Imperialism: British Reactions to Central African Society, 1840–1890* (London: Routledge and Kegan Paul, 1965).

7 Cairns admired Polanyi's idea of "a society of [intellectual] explorers": Michael Polanyi, *The Tacit Dimension* (New York: Anchor Books, 1967), 82–83.

8 Cairns, "My Academic Career," 334.

9 A.C. Ross, review of *Prelude to Imperialism,* by Alan C. Cairns, *Africa* 36, 3 (1966): 329–30.

10 Cairns, "My Academic Career," 335.

11 Cairns, *Prelude to Imperialism,* 247.

12 Philip Mason, review of *Prelude to Imperialism,* by Alan C. Cairns, *Man* 3, 2 (1966): 412–13; Roger Anstey, review of *Prelude to Imperialism, Journal of African History* 8, 1 (1967): 167–68.

13 Cairns, *Prelude to Imperialism,* 163.

14 *Ibid,* 163–64.

15 *Ibid,* 249.

16 Cairns, "My Academic Career," 332.

17 *Ibid,* 336.

18 Alan C. Cairns, *Reconfigurations: Canadian Citizenship and Constitutional Change* (Toronto: McClelland and Stewart, 1995), 62.

19 *Ibid,* 10.

20 Alan C. Cairns, "Aboriginal Research in Troubled Times," in *Roots of Engagement: Essays in the History of Native-Newcomer Relations,* ed. Kerry M. Abel, Myra Rutherdale, and P. Whitney Lackenbauer (Toronto: University of Toronto Press, 2017), 426–27.

21 Alan C. Cairns, *Constitution, Government, and Society in Canada* (Toronto: McClelland and Stewart, 1988), 13.

22 Cairns, "My Academic Career," 345.

23 Cairns, *Prelude to Imperialism,* xiii.

24 Cairns, *Constitution, Government and Society in Canada,* 141.

25 Cairns, "Aboriginal Research in Troubled Times," 406.

26 Cairns, *Reconfigurations,* 20, 25, 29–30.

27 *Ibid,* 317, 346–48.

28 Cairns, *Charter versus Federalism,* 72.

29 Cairns, *First Nations and the Canadian State,* 4–6, 3.

30 Quentin Skinner, ed., *The Return of Grand Theory in the Human Sciences* (Cambridge: Cambridge University Press, 1985), 13, 12.

31 C. Wright Mills, *The Sociological Imagination* (New York: Oxford University Press, 1981), 211, 220–21.

32 Robert K. Merton, *Social Theory and Social Structure,* 3rd enlarged ed. (New York: Macmillan, 1968), 39; Cairns, *Reconfigurations,* 10.

33 Pierre Elliott Trudeau, *Conversation with Canadians* (Toronto: University of Toronto Press, 1972), 21.

34 Tom Flanagan, *First Nations? Second Thoughts,* 3rd ed. (Montreal/Kingston: McGill-Queen's University Press, 2019), viii, 6–8, 194.

35 "Flanagan and Cairns on Aboriginal Policy," *Policy Options,* September 2001, 49.

36 *Ibid,* 43; Cairns's comment is printed on the back cover of Flanagan's book.

37 *Ibid,* 47.

38 F.A. Hayek's most important work for the Flanagan-Cairns debate is *Law, Legislation and Liberty*, vol. 2, *The Mirage of Social Justice* (Chicago: University of Chicago Press, 1976), 62–100.

39 "Flanagan and Cairns on Aboriginal Policy," 48. See also H.B. Hawthorn, *A Survey of the Contemporary Indians of Canada*, vol. 1 (Ottawa: Indian Affairs Branch, 1966), 270–93, 303–5, 349, 391–401.

40 Cairns, *Citizens Plus*, 85, 145.

41 Alan C. Cairns, "Aboriginal Nationalism, Canadian Federalism, and Canadian Democracy," *Saskatchewan Law Review* 70 (2007): 99, 104–5.

42 Cairns, "Aboriginal Research in Troubled Times," 410, 414, 424–25.

43 Vine Deloria, *We Talk, You Listen* (Lincoln: University of Nebraska Press, 2007 [1970]), 181–97.

44 Cole Harris, *A Bounded Land: Reflections on Settler Colonialism in Canada* (Vancouver: UBC Press, 2020), 285.

45 Cairns, *Prelude to Imperialism*, xv.

46 Alan C. Cairns, *Disruptions: Constitutional Struggles from the Charter to Meech Lake* (Toronto: McClelland and Stewart, 1991), 214, 216, 221. See also Robert K. Merton, "Insiders and Outsiders: A Chapter in the Sociology of Knowledge," *American Journal of Sociology* 78, 1 (1972): 9–47.

47 Cairns, *Constitution, Government, and Society in Canada*, 183, 188.

48 Cairns, *Charter versus Federalism*, 124–25.

49 Cairns, "Looking into the Abyss: The Need for a Plan C," C.D. Howe Institute, *The Secession Papers* 96 (September 1997): 6, 11, 14–15, 19–20, 20, 26–27.

50 Cairns, *First Nations and the Canadian State*, 7.

51 Cairns, *Citizens Plus*, 17, 114.

52 Cairns, "Aboriginal Research in Troubled Times," 402.

53 Cairns, "Aboriginal Nationalism, Canadian Federalism, and Canadian Democracy," 121.

54 Cairns, *Citizens Plus*, 203.

55 "Flanagan and Cairns on Aboriginal Policy," 43, 49.

56 Cairns, *First Nations and the Canadian State*, 4, 43, 59.

57 Flanagan, *First Nations? Second Thoughts*, 67–88.

58 Mary Ellen Turpel, "Aboriginal Communities and the Canadian Charter: Interpretive Monopolies, Cultural Differences," *Canadian Human Rights Yearbook* 60 (1989–90): 4–5, 14–15, 17, 24, 29, 45.

59 Ruth Benedict, *Patterns of Culture* (London: Routledge and Kegan Paul, 1966), 3–4, 201.

60 Morris Ginsberg, "On the Diversity of Morals," *Journal of the Royal Anthropological Institute* 83, 2 (1953): 132; Steven Lukes, *Moral Relativism* (New York: Picador, 2008), 39.

61 Alfred, "Book Review: *Of White Heroes and Old Men Talking*," 6.

62 Anstey, review of *Prelude to Imperialism*, 168.

63 Cairns, "My Academic Career," 338–39.

64 Cairns, *Disruptions*, 17, 132–38, 260–63.

65 Cairns, *Charter versus Federalism*, 35.

66 W.L. Morton, *The Canadian Identity* (Toronto: University of Toronto Press, 1972), 147.

67 Cairns, *Citizens Plus*, 68.

68 Harold Cardinal, *The Unjust Society: The Tragedy of Canada's Indians* (Edmonton: M.G. Hurtig, 1969), 15, 35, 170.

69 Truth and Reconciliation Commission of Canada, *Final Report of the Truth and Reconciliation Commission of Canada*, vol. 1, *Summary* (Toronto: James Lorimer, 2015), 319–37.

Part 4
Constitutional Change

23

The Invisible Transformation of Canada's Constitutional Amendment Rules

Richard Albert

AFTER DECADES OF failed negotiations, Canada's First Ministers finally agreed in 1981 on a homegrown package of procedures to amend the Constitution.[1] These intricate rules are codified in Part V of the *Constitution Act, 1982,* quite possibly the longest set of amendment procedures in any constitution.[2] This prolixity was not unexpected. Part V was designed as a comprehensive road map for all constitutional changes; it even includes a procedure to amend Part V itself.[3]

Part V has never been amended. And yet the Part V of today is not the Part V of forty years ago at patriation. The rules of amendment codified in Part V have been altered in ways not reflected in their text, exposing a fascinating phenomenon: the invisible transformation of Canada's constitutional amendment rules.

Reading Part V therefore reveals something of an optical illusion. On one hand, its detailed procedures paint a portrait of order and finality; they present the text of Part V as the only site for locating the rules of amendment, and they make no reference to any external body of rules that may be relevant for amending the Canadian constitution. On the other hand, many of the postpatriation changes to the Constitution's amendment rules are nowhere to be found in Part V. These procedural and substantive changes to Part V exist outside the *Constitution Act, 1982* in judicial decisions, subconstitutional legislation, and political practices. The relocation of amendment rules from the text of the patriated Constitution of Canada to places beyond the codified constitution undermines the appearance of authority in Part V and generates an unsteady disjunction between constitutional text and constitutional reality.

In this chapter, I shine a light on the invisible transformation of Part V and explore the consequences of this phenomenon for the Constitution of Canada. I show that the unseen modification of Part V reveals the limits of codification, exposes the impossibility of a truly written constitution, exacerbates the difficulty of constitutional reform in Canada, and suggests that Canadian constitutionalism reflects both its inherited Commonwealth traditions and its more modern American influences.

The Amendment Rules in Part V

Virtually every constitution in the world codifies a procedure for its amendment.[4] The Canadian constitution proved an exception to this rule because it had no domestic amendment procedure when it was created in 1867. Amendment was possible, but only by the Parliament of the United Kingdom,[5] which had enacted the Constitution of Canada as a colonial statute. Patriation finally brought an end to this extraterritorial arrangement when decades of inter-governmental negotiations ultimately yielded the comprehensive set of home-grown and domestically deployable amendment procedures now codified in Part V.[6]

The Escalating Structure of Constitutional Amendment

Part V creates an escalating architecture of constitutional amendment.[7] Part V authorizes five procedures of constitutional amendment, each one different from the other in the quantum of federal and provincial consent required for its successful use. Not only does each of the five procedures differ in what it demands of political actors, but each differs also in what it may be used to amend. What results is a hierarchy of constitutional importance: each of the five amendment procedures rises in its degree of difficulty in parallel with the importance of the subject matter to which each procedure is assigned. This escalating structure of amendment creates a complex framework that incorporates both procedural and substantive restrictions on amendment.

One of these five amendment procedures in Canada applies exclusively to provincial constitutions. This provincial unilateral amendment procedure authorizes a provincial assembly to amend its own constitution in relation only to purely provincial subjects.[8] In terms of the degree of approval required, this procedure appears to be the easiest, as it requires the agreement of a unicameral legislature alone, since no provincial assembly in Canada has a second chamber.

The federal unilateral amendment procedure authorizes Parliament to amend the Constitution by ordinary legislation "in relation to the executive government of Canada or the Senate and House of Commons."[9] Either the House of Commons or the Senate may initiate an amendment under this procedure, and in either case, the other house must approve the proposed amendment – and then receive royal assent – in order for the amendment to become valid.[10] This procedure may be used only for amendments related to Parliament's internal constitution, including parliamentary privilege and legislative procedure.[11] By comparison to some of the more onerous procedures of amendment, this one is a limited delegation of power to Parliament because its use is "subject to sections 41 and 42,"[12] each reserved for more significant amendments and therefore more difficult to use since they require a higher degree of legislative approval.

The bilateral amendment procedure adds a layer of difficulty to the federal unilateral amendment procedure. It requires approval from the House of Commons and the Senate as well as from the legislative assemblies of the affected provinces.[13] The additional degree of difficulty comes from the requirement of provincial ratification. This procedure applies to amendments that entail a shared federal-provincial interest in respect of one province, of some provinces, but not of all provinces. An amendment using this procedure may be initiated by either house of Parliament or by any provincial legislative assembly.

The fourth option in Canada's escalating structure of amendment is the multilateral default amendment procedure.[14] Known as the 7/50 procedure, it requires the approval of the House of Commons and the Senate as well as the legislative assemblies of at least seven provinces whose aggregate population amounts to at least half of the total population.[15] It is the default procedure because it must be used for amendments involving any subject not otherwise assigned to one of the other four amendment procedures. Moreover, it applies exclusively to specific subjects, including proportional representation in the House of Commons, the powers and staffing of the Senate, the creation of new provinces, and certain matters involving the Supreme Court.[16] Either house of Parliament or any provincial assembly may initiate an amendment under this procedure, which is much harder to use than the bilateral amendment procedure.

The fifth and most difficult path to constitutional amendment under Part V is the unanimity procedure.[17] It requires the approval of the House of Commons and the Senate as well as each of the country's provincial legislative assemblies.[18] Part V specifies that this unanimity procedure must be used for amendments to a handful of constitutional rules: Canada's relation to the monarchy, the right to provincial representation in the House of Commons not less than a province's standing in the Senate, Canada's official languages beyond their provincial or regional use, the composition of the Supreme Court of Canada, and Part V itself.[19] An amendment using this procedure may be initiated by either house of Parliament or any provincial legislative assembly.

Failed Efforts to Amend the Amendment Rules
Since patriation, federal and provincial actors have successfully used these procedures a total of eleven times. They have been deployed for various kinds of reforms, including changing the name of a province, amending the law of elections, and reinforcing treaty rights. The most common path to amendment has been the bilateral procedure; it has been used successfully seven times.[20] The federal unilateral procedure has been used successfully three times;[21] the multilateral default procedure, once;[22] and the unanimity procedure, never.

Alongside these amendment successes, there have been massive amendment failures in Canada. The Meech Lake and Charlottetown Accords envisaged substantial reforms to the patriation package, the former largely in relation to

Quebec and the latter involving the vast landscape of Canada's constitutional arrangements. The country, in many ways, has yet to recover from these two failed attempts at large-scale constitutional reform. Proposed in 1987, the Meech Lake Accord sought principally to fulfill Quebec's conditions for approving the *Constitution Act, 1982,* including recognizing Quebec's distinctiveness, giving Quebec a larger role in immigration and in Supreme Court appointments, imposing limits on the federal spending power, and granting Quebec a veto.[23] The Charlottetown Accord proposed a major overhaul of the Canadian Constitution beyond those parts involving Quebec alone.[24] It proposed once again to recognize that Quebec is a "distinct society," yet it also sought to entrench a "Canada Clause" that would express Canadian values to guide judges in their interpretation of the Constitution. The Charlottetown Accord also sought more robustly to protect Aboriginal rights, to update the federal distribution of powers, to strengthen language rights, and to reform the Senate, the House of Commons, and the Supreme Court.

Importantly, the Meech Lake and Charlottetown Accords each proposed to amend the Constitution's amendment procedures. The Meech Lake Accord would have effectively removed the list of specifically assigned amendment subjects from the multilateral default procedure, making the procedure exclusively a default procedure for those matters not expressly assigned to an amendment procedure.[25] This proposed change would have given each province a veto over proposed amendments affecting a national interest of federal-provincial concern. The Meech Lake Accord proposed also to require First Ministers to gather at least once each year to discuss matters of national scope, including Senate reform and fisheries.[26] All of these proposals and others died with the failure of the Meech Lake Accord.

The Charlottetown Accord likewise proposed several amendments to Part V. One would have made it clear that amendments to the House of Commons and Senate require use of the unanimity procedure.[27] Another would have required the unanimity procedure for all amendments related to the Supreme Court, except its nomination and appointment processes, which would be amendable using the multilateral default procedure.[28] The Charlottetown Accord would have also revised the amendment procedure for creating new provinces and changing provincial boundaries.[29] In addition, the Charlottetown Accord would have compensated those provinces that chose to opt-out of certain amendments made using the multilateral default procedure.[30] And the last category of amendments to Part V would have required that "there should be Aboriginal consent to future constitutional amendments that directly refer to the Aboriginal peoples."[31]

None of those proposed amendments to Part V succeeded. And since then, there have been no further proposals to amend the rules of amendment in Part V, though political actors had an opportunity to revisit Part V in 1996. The *Constitution Act, 1982* instructed Canada's First Ministers to meet within fifteen years of its coming into force in an intergovernmental conference to review the Constitution's new amendment rules.[32] Canada's First Ministers did in fact meet, on June 20–21, 1996, to review Part V. But it is reported that the discussion on this subject "was of very short duration and there was no decision on how further discussion might be pursued on this matter."[33] At every turn, then, efforts to amend the procedures of Part V have failed, often dramatically.

The modern history of constitutional politics in Canada highlights a key rule in Part V: any amendment to Part V must be made using the unanimity procedure codified in Part V itself.[34]

Uncodified Alterations to Part V

Today, the text of Part V remains indistinguishable from the text adopted forty years ago at patriation. And yet the rules of constitutional amendment in Canada are not what they were then. They have been modified substantially by every major political institution acting jointly or on its own. Courts, legislatures, and executives have transformed Part V to such a degree that we might well say that the Constitution contains a new set of amendment procedures that remains hidden to those who look only to its text to ascertain the country's rules of constitutional change.

Law Making and Policy Making

There are laws and policies at the federal and provincial level – and in the territories – that have altered the operation of Part V.

Consider first federal law making. Political actors in Quebec have long called for veto power in constitutional amendments. The veto featured centrally as one of the amendments proposed in the failed Meech Lake Accord. The veto once again took centre stage a few years later, in 1995, when Quebec held its secession referendum. This time, the federal government offered a trade to voters in Quebec: vote against secession and, in return, you will get the veto you have always wanted.[35]

A slim majority of Quebec voters chose Canada, and the federal government had to hold up its end of the bargain. The veto power took the form of the *Regional Veto Law*, an act of Parliament adopted in 1996.[36] The law has changed how political actors may initiate an amendment using the multilateral default procedure. It does not give Quebec an exclusive veto over major amendments, but it does deliver on the promise made to the province. The law requires federal Cabinet ministers to secure the consent of a majority of provinces before proposing an amendment. That majority must include Quebec, Ontario, British

Columbia, and at least two of the Atlantic provinces and two of the Prairie provinces representing at least half of their respective regional populations.[37] The law, then, is not quite a formal veto. It operates instead as a functional veto shared by what the law defines as the different regions of Canada, including the group of Atlantic and Prairie provinces as separate regions alongside British Columbia, Ontario, and Quebec as individual regions for purposes of the law.[38] The *Regional Veto Law* gives each of these five regions its own power to veto any amendment proposed using the multilateral default procedure.

The *Regional Veto Law* effectively reverses the sequence of amendment activity contemplated by Part V. Ordinarily, the federal government would introduce an amendment proposal, both houses of Parliament would subsequently approve it, and only then would the provinces begin to deliberate and ultimately vote on the proposal. But under the *Regional Veto Law*, the federal government cannot introduce an amendment without the sponsoring Cabinet minister first securing the necessary provincial approvals from the various regions of Canada. The multilateral default amendment procedure has effectively been altered by an ordinary statute.

Separately, provinces and territories have passed laws of their own that alter the operation of Part V. Their laws have an effect similar to the *Regional Veto Law*: they insert additional steps in the amendment process. Moreover, they apply beyond the multilateral default amendment procedure to every amendment procedure requiring legislative approval to ratify an amendment. The additional step these laws insert into Part V is a referendum or plebiscite.

We can divide these referendum and plebiscite laws into three categories. First, some of these laws – in Alberta and British Columbia – require either a binding or advisory referendum on any amendment requiring provincial ratification.[39] Second, other laws – in New Brunswick, Saskatchewan, Yukon – authorize but do not require governments to hold binding referendums before the Legislative Assembly votes to ratify an amendment.[40] And still other laws – in Northwest Territories, Nunavut, Quebec, Prince Edward Island, and Newfoundland and Labrador – authorize but do not require an advisory referendum or plebiscite before a legislative ratification vote.[41] These provincial and territorial laws alter Part V without indicating these alterations in its text.

The federal government has likewise altered the operation of Part V in relation to the Senate, drawing on the nonpartisan advice of expert advisers, including Emmett Macfarlane, one of the editors of this volume, who recounts in his latest book the nonconfidential advice he offered.[42] The new Senate appointments process creates an advisory board responsible for recommending new senators to the prime minister.[43] This new process is not written down in law; it is an executive policy. After an initial "transitional process," the Government of Canada announced a "permanent phase of the independent Senate appointments process" that now offers all eligible Canadians the opportunity to apply for a senatorial appointment.[44] The stated purpose of this reform was to foster a "high standard of integrity, collaboration, and non-partisanship in the Senate."[45]

Just like the *Regional Veto Law,* the new process for Senate appointments has achieved what neither Meech nor Charlottetown could. Today, senators are selected under a new process that differs from how they have historically been chosen. The Senate has been reformed, but not by a constitutional amendment. Formal appointment continues to be made by the governor general, but the selection process itself has changed as a result of this new consultative process. The new process for Senate appointments may well be an improvement on the previous method of senator selection. But the key is that senator selection has changed in a material way. Although the prime minister retains the discretion to choose whom to nominate, his or her range of discretion is narrowed. The creation of the advisory body is a significant change that would have been appropriately passed as a constitutional amendment had it been possible to amend the Constitution without opening the door to collateral matters. Paradoxically, the choice not to formalize the new process in a law, and instead to promulgate it informally, has perhaps saved it from unconstitutionality. There can be no doubt that the new process is, in fact, new and that it changes the way senators are selected, for better or worse, but there is room to debate whether this informal change to senator selection has been achieved contrary to the requirements in Part V.

Interpretation and Convention
In addition to its invisible transformation by law making and policy making, Part V has been changed by judicial interpretations and arguably also by constitutional conventions.

Consider judicial interpretation.[46] In the *Secession Reference,* the court identified a series of principles that political actors must respect in passing any amendment to formalize the secession of a province from Canada: constitutionalism, democracy, federalism, the protection of minorities, and the rule of law (see Mathieu and Guénette, Chapter 24 in this volume).[47] The court acknowledged that these principles "are not explicitly made part of the Constitution by any written provision,"[48] neither in Part V's detailed enumeration of the various amendment procedures nor anywhere else in the codified portions of the Constitution. Yet, for the court, these are all nonnegotiable principles that together "dictate major elements of the architecture of the Constitution itself and are as such its lifeblood."[49] These central principles of the Constitution of Canada are not without bite. The court suggested that any single one of them could form the basis for refusing to recognize the validity of the negotiated outcome of a majority vote on a clear referendum question on secession.[50] The *Secession Reference* must therefore be understood as adding to Part V a specific restriction on any secession amendment.

The court went further in the *Supreme Court Act Reference*.[51] Here was the central question: Which amendment threshold applies to amendments to the Supreme Court of Canada? The court resolved that the multilateral default procedure must be used to amend any of the court's "essential features," which the court defined to entail "the Court's jurisdiction as the final general court of appeal for Canada, including in matters of constitutional interpretation, and its independence."[52] In reaching its conclusion, the court constitutionalized the *Supreme Court Act*, an ordinary act of Parliament that now possesses constitutional status insofar as certain amendments to it and to the court cannot be made without a constitutional amendment. This raises a tension with the text of Part V, which neither mentions the court's "essential features" nor gives any guidance about what that term must be defined to mean. The court created this concept and then declined to define it comprehensively and exhaustively, saying only that its essential features *include* certain items and keeping for itself the power in the future to identify what other items qualify as essential features.[53] This may be an even clearer example of judicial alteration of Part V than the *Secession Reference*.[54]

Part V has also been changed arguably by constitutional convention. The source of the constitutional convention in both cases is the ratification process used for the 1992 Charlottetown Accord. Political actors chose to put the accord to the people in a consultative referendum held in every province and territory.[55] Part V does not require a referendum for ratifying an amendment, nor does it even mention it as a possibility, let alone recognize its legal validity as part of the process of constitutional amendment. Yet political actors felt compelled to put the package to a referendum, given that the Meech Lake Accord, proposed immediately prior, had been closed to direct input from the people from start to finish.[56] The referendum failed to win popular approval.[57] The failure of the referendum ultimately put an end to the Charlottetown Accord even though Part V does not make a referendum a condition for the successful ratification of an amendment.

The first constitutional convention arising out of the choice to put the Charlottetown Accord to the people may be the use of a referendum for future large-scale constitutional amendments. The Charlottetown referendum may have set a precedent that political actors will feel obliged to follow, either out of obligation to follow past practice or out of self-preservation if they believe that Canadians have now come to expect to be consulted on major changes to the Constitution. The second constitutional convention possibly arising out of the Charlottetown referendum is that territories may now expect to be included as official actors in the ratification of an amendment to the Constitution of Canada. Territories participated as equal partners in the Charlottetown referendum, and the referendum laws they have since adopted – requiring territorial referendums before the Legislative Assembly votes to ratify an amendment to the Constitution of Canada, as discussed in the prior section – suggest they now expect to participate in major amendments. Neither of these, of course, appears in the text of Part V.

The Constitution Seen through Part V

There is so much more than meets the eye to Part V. We have seen that Canada's amendment rules are found both inside the text of Part V and outside its intricately codified rules. This creates a disjunction between constitutional text and political reality. But so what? Does this have any meaningful consequence for constitutional change in Canada, does it tell us anything about the nature of our Constitution, and does it reveal anything about Canadian constitutionalism?

Amendment Impossibility?

The invisible transformation of Canada's amendment rules has immediate implications for the difficulty of amending the Constitution.[58] The onerous escalating structure of amendment rules in Part V already makes the Constitution extraordinarily rigid. But amendment is now considerably more difficult, perhaps even virtually impossible, for any amendment coalition seeking to use the multilateral default procedure or the unanimity procedure. This is the direct result of the modification of Part V by law making, policy making, interpretation, and convention.[59]

The *Regional Veto Law* combines with the provincial and territorial laws to impose additional requirements for amending the Constitution. These requirements are significant. The *Regional Veto Law* frontloads the work of securing the consent of the regions to an amendment made using the multilateral default amendment procedure. Where that consent is withheld, no federal Cabinet minister may propose an amendment. And yet, even if consent is granted, there is no assurance that both houses of Parliament will approve the amendment proposal nor that the required number of legislative assemblies will ratify the amendment, assuming the proposal makes it out of Parliament.

This is where the *Regional Veto Law* intersects with the provincial and territorial laws on referendums and plebiscites. Where a province gives its consent to a federal Cabinet minister introducing an amendment, no law requires the Legislative Assembly to ratify it later on. There are several reasons. First, an amendment made using the multilateral default amendment procedure may take up to three years to ratify.[60] This passage of time may lead to the formation of a new government – with different priorities – in a province that had earlier consented to the initiation of the amendment when first approached by the federal Cabinet minister. Second, even if the same government remains in power, the political palatability of the amendment may diminish over time. And third, the provincial and territorial laws requiring or permitting referendums or plebiscites before a legislative assembly can vote to ratify an amendment to the Constitution of Canada inserts an unpredictable variable in the process. It is one thing for a government to hold a referendum but quite another to win it. Nothing is guaranteed in a referendum or plebiscite, and this adds a significant element of volatility to any amendment process that already erects multiple veto gates along the path to ratification.

The two possible Charlottetown-era constitutional conventions on large-scale constitutional amendment only add to the degree of amendment difficulty. The first is the use of a national referendum before legislative assemblies vote on an amendment to the Constitution of Canada. If political actors treat the Charlottetown precedent as a constitutional convention, it will present both a distinguishable and duplicative requirement for constitutional amendment. It will be duplicative where legislative assemblies are prohibited from voting on an amendment without the province first holding a referendum. This will apply only to some of the provinces and territories whose laws require a referendum before a vote in the Legislative Assembly. In these cases of duplication, we can assume that the province or territory will hold only one referendum, rather than two: one vote commanded by the Charlottetown precedent and a separate one required by its own laws. On the other hand, the Charlottetown precedent is distinguishable from the provincial and territorial laws because not all provinces and territories require a referendum before their legislative assemblies can vote on an amendment to the Constitution of Canada. In either case, passing a large-scale constitutional amendment will be even harder than Part V indicates.

The second Charlottetown-era constitutional convention concerns the role of territories. Part V makes no mention of territories among the body of institutions whose authorization is required to ratify an amendment to the Constitution of Canada. Yet each of Canada's territories participated as partners equal to the provinces in the Charlottetown referendum. If this Charlottetown precedent is treated as binding, it will exacerbate the existing amendment difficulty of Part V because it will add another set of legislative hurdles to ratify a major constitutional amendment.

The court's case law has also made it harder to amend the Constitution in relation to matters that are national in scope. For amendments to the court's "essential features," political actors will now have to pass through the multilateral default procedure. What is more, the meaning of what counts as the court's "essential features" is to be determined by the court itself. We can understand this move as an instance of self-entrenchment, surely understandable for any institution interested in its self-preservation. To borrow from the American tradition of constitutionalism, we might describe the *Supreme Court Act Reference* as Canada's "*Marbury* moment," a reference to the landmark US Supreme Court judgment in which the court declared itself supreme.[61] With respect to secession, political actors must not only meet the amendment threshold required by Part V (the court did not identify which amendment procedure must be used, by the way) but they must also respect the uncodified principles enumerated by the court as necessary constraints on any secession amendment. Each of these judicial interpretations inserts an additional hurdle to constitutional amendment beyond the already onerous requirements codified in Part V.

For its part, the new Senate appointments process has achieved what neither the Meech nor Charlottetown Accords could: it has changed the way senators are selected. The creation of the new appointments process reveals just how difficult it was to amend the Constitution on matters of national scope. The new appointments process could not have been approved by amendment in the present political context because approval would have required recourse to the multilateral default amendment procedure – and that is unworkable today. It is no wonder, then, that political actors elected to take a subconstitutional path to reform the Senate. Creating the new appointments process as an executive policy required no opposition approval nor any provincial input or consent. It was the product of a majority government with a clear goal in mind and a clear path to success that was possible without involving other partners in Confederation. This constitution-level change to a fundamental part of the Constitution was therefore achieved at a much lower political cost than ordinarily required to amend the Constitution, yet it is arguably the functional equivalent of a constitutional amendment without incurring the trouble one requires.

Traditions of Constitutionalism
The seeds for these irregular modifications of Part V were planted at patriation. It was unclear at the time how those seeds would grow because patriation opened several paths that Canada's constitution might take. The newly codified rules of amendment along with the new *Charter of Rights and Freedoms* pulled the country closer to an American model of constitutionalism. But the notwithstanding clause and the inclusion clause retained the Commonwealth model of

parliamentary supremacy and of unwritten constitutionalism, respectively.[62] Only time would reveal which path Canada would follow. Today, forty years later, the evolution of Part V reveals that Canada has taken a third path all its own, in some ways hewing more closely to its inherited Commonwealth traditions while in others embracing its more modern American influences.

The codification of Canada's rules of amendment in Part V followed the model of the US Constitution. Written in 1787, the US Constitution codifies its own elaborate rules of constitutional amendment in Article V,[63] though without nearly as much detail and creativity in amendment design as the Canadian constitution, no doubt because Canada's own rules were written with the benefit of centuries of learning from the United States and other constitutional states. The codification of Part V in Canada's patriated constitutional text invited an American-style judicial interpretation of these rules where there exist gaps or ambiguities in the written word. The court's judgments in the *Secession Reference*,[64] the *Supreme Court Act Reference*,[65] and the *Senate Reform Reference*[66] each changed the prevailing legal understanding of Part V without a corresponding alteration to its text. And, importantly, the court's amendment case law puts the court at the top of the constitutional pyramid of power, as the court now possesses the power to determine what may be amended using each amendment procedure and whether a proposed amendment is inconsistent with the Constitution.[67]

In contrast, the modern Canadian history of law making, policy making, and convention in connection with Part V reflect the UK model of constitutional change. Law making to circumvent the strictures of Part V – whether the *Regional Veto Law* or the provincial and territorial statutes on referendums and plebiscites – springs from a self-conscious political understanding of parliamentary supremacy. In its policy making to circumvent the strictures of Part V, namely, through the new Senate appointments process that bypasses Parliament, the executive accounts for the risk of parliamentary backlash to its innovative constitutional workaround. And the possibility in Canada of political practices maturing into constitutional conventions that defy the codified rules of change in Part V – for example, the Charlottetown precedent growing into a conventional obligation to hold a referendum for future major constitutional changes – has a peculiarly British lineage insofar as constitution-level texts must coexist often unsteadily with unwritten constitutional norms. The inclusion clause in the *Constitution Act, 1982* foretells this eventuality when it states quite clearly that the Constitution of Canada "includes" certain codified higher laws.[68] The word "includes" communicates that the list of higher laws is not an exhaustive enumeration. And this, in turn, suggests that the Constitution comprises not only other codified laws but moreover uncodified rules such as the unwritten constitutional principles highlighted in the preamble of the *Constitution Act, 1867,* which declares that Canada shall have "a Constitution similar in Principle to that of the United Kingdom."[69] These features are central to the British model of political constitutionalism.

Our Canadian norms of amendment constitutionalism therefore now blend elements of the distinctly American constitutional culture of codification and the corresponding judicial power of constitutional review with the peculiarly British tradition of unwritten constitutionalism and legislative supremacy. The Canadian model is a third way that we can describe as neither fully legal amendment constitutionalism nor fully political amendment constitutionalism. It is a distinct model of amendment constitutionalism that reveals both strengths and weaknesses in comparison with other models. Its main strength is the wide latitude it creates for innovation to respond to political imperatives in the face of a rigid constitution. And its main weakness is the lack of congruence between its codified rules of law and its larger contextual political reality.

Conclusion: The Inevitability of Unwrittenness

The late John Gardner once asked whether there can ever be a fully written constitution.[70] He concluded that written constitutions can, indeed, be entirely written: "Where there is a written constitution, there is no logical obstacle to the whole law of the constitution being written law."[71] Even where judges must interpret written constitutions to resolve inconsistencies, to fill gaps, and otherwise to make sense of the words in the text, we can define those constitutions as written because a judicial interpretation "cannot but become part of their meaning *qua* written."[72]

The Canadian model of amendment constitutionalism offers a different answer to the question. Yes, a significant portion of the amendment rules in the Constitution of Canada is written down in constitutional acts. And although many of the country's amendment rules also exist outside of constitutional acts, they are nonetheless written somewhere, for instance, in ordinary legislative statutes, executive policy documents, and judicial rulings. If the question, then, is whether much of the Canadian Constitution is written, the answer is yes.

But a sizeable part of amendment rules in the Canadian constitution remains unwritten. Must a referendum be held in any future major constitutional change? The answer is nowhere written down. Must a province hold an advisory referendum before voting to ratify a resolution to amend the Constitution of Canada? The codified portions of Canada's constitution offer no guidance to that question. What are the "essential features" of the Supreme Court of Canada that are amendable only with the multilateral default procedure? Again, Part V does not give us an answer. The answer will be revealed to us by the court itself when political actors seek to amend something material to the functions and powers of the court.[73] And must the territories be included in the community of ratifying actors for a future national constitutional amendment? The codified rules of Part V do not acknowledge any role for territories, but political practice may have changed those written rules in ways unseen to a plain reading of its text.

The invisible transformation of Part V reveals a profound truth about the nature of amendment constitutionalism in Canada. Amendment rules are by design codified in Part V of the *Constitution Act, 1982,* but the operation and evolution of those rules are in large part inevitably unwritten, consistent with Canada's tradition of self-consciously written and unwritten constitutionalism – a combination that raises both positive and problematic consequences for constitutional change in the country. These consequences are positive for constitutional politics because they invite creativity, innovation, and adaptation to the complex political realities of our multinational state. The consequences are problematic because they undermine the democratic rule-of-law values of predictability, transparency, and accountability that inspired the creation of written constitutions.[74] As we mark the fortieth anniversary of patriation, our task as scholars is neither to decry nor to celebrate that the codified portions of our Constitution do not reflect all the rules of amendment constitutionalism but instead to acknowledge that this is a fundamental feature of our Constitution.

Notes

1   For a brief account, see Peter W. Hogg, "Formal Amendment of the Constitution of Canada," *Law and Contemporary Problems* 55 (1992): 255–57.
2   See *Constitution Act, 1982,* being Schedule B to the *Canada Act 1982* (UK), 1982, c 11 [*Constitution Act, 1982*], Part V.
3   *Ibid,* s 41(e).
4   See Francesco Giovannoni, "Amendment Rules in Constitutions," *Public Choice* 115 (2003): 37.
5   There were a couple of exceptions, including ss 92(1) and 101 of the *Constitution Act, 1867* (UK), 30 and 31 Vict, c 3, reprinted in RSC 1985, Appendix II, No 5 [*Constitution Act, 1867*], which authorized amendment of provincial constitutions and of courts, respectively.
6   James Ross Hurley, *Amending Canada's Constitution: History, Processes, Problems and Prospects* (Ottawa: Minister of Supply and Services, 1996), 25–63.
7   See *Constitution Act, 1982,* ss 38–49.
8   *Ibid,* s 45.
9   *Ibid,* s 44.
10 *Ibid.*
11 See Ian Greene, "Constitutional Amendment in Canada and the United States," in *Constitutional Politics in Canada and the United States,* ed. Stephen L. Newman (Albany, NY: SUNY Press, 2004), 251.

12 See *Constitution Act, 1982,* ss 44.
13 *Ibid,* s 43. Senate approval may be bypassed where the Senate does not adopt an approval resolution within 180 days after the House of Commons has adopted its own and the House of Commons adopts it again. *Ibid,* s 47.
14 *Ibid,* s 38.
15 *Ibid.* Again, Senate approval may be bypassed. *Ibid,* s 47.
16 *Ibid,* s 42.
17 See *Constitution Act, 1982,* ss 41.
18 As with amendments using the bilateral amendment procedure or multilateral default procedure, the Senate may be bypassed. *Ibid,* s 47.
19 *Ibid.*
20 See *Constitution Amendment, 1998 (Newfoundland Act),* SI/98-25, (1998) C Gaz II; *Constitution Amendment, 2001 (Newfoundland and Labrador),* SI/2001-117, (2001) C Gaz II; *Constitution Amendment Proclamation, 1997 (Quebec),* SI/97-141; *Constitution Amendment Proclamation, 1993 (Prince Edward Island),* SI/94-50, (1994) C Gaz II, 2021; *Constitution Amendment Proclamation, 1993 (New Brunswick Act),* SI/93-54, (1993) C Gaz II, 1588; *Constitution Amendment Proclamation, 1987 (Newfoundland Act),* SI/88-11, (1988) C Gaz II, 887.
21 See *Fair Representation Act,* SC 2011, c 26; *Constitution Act, 1999 (Nunavut),* SC 1998, c 15; *Representation Act, 1985,* SC 1986, c 8, s 3.
22 See *Constitutional Amendment Proclamation, 1983,* SI/84-102, (1984) C Gaz II, 2984.
23 Meeting of the First Ministers on the Constitution, *The 1987 Constitutional Accord* (Ottawa: June 3, 1987) [*Meech Lake Accord*]; see also Peter W. Hogg, *Meech Lake Constitutional Accord Annotated* (Toronto: Carswell, 1988), 3–4 (annotating Meech Lake Accord).
24 Coordinating Committee, *Consensus Report of the Constitution: Final Text,* Doc CP22–41/1992 (Charlottetown August 1 = 28 1992) [*Charlottetown Accord*]
25 *Meech Lake Accord,* s 9.
26 *Ibid,* s 13.
27 *Charlottetown Accord,* art 57.
28 *Ibid.*
29 *Ibid,* art 58.
30 *Ibid,* art 59.
31 *Ibid,* art 60.
32 See *Constitution Act, 1982,* s 49.
33 See Canadian Intergovernmental Conference Secretariat, *First Ministers' Conferences: 1906–2004* (Ottawa: CICS, 2004), 103.
34 See *Constitution Act, 1982,* ss 41.
35 See Robert A. Young, "Jean Chrétien's Québec Legacy: Coasting Then Stickhandling Hard," *Review of Constitutional Studies* 9 (2004): 38–39.
36 *An Act respecting constitutional amendments,* SC 1996, c 1.
37 *Ibid,* s 1(1).
38 *Ibid.*
39 *Constitutional Referendum Act,* RSA 2000, c C-25, ss 2(1), 4; *Constitutional Amendment Approval Act,* RSBC 1996, c 67, s 1.
40 See *Referendum Act,* SNB 2011, c 23; *The Referendum and Plebiscite Act,* SS 1990–91, c R-8.01; *Public Government Act,* SY 1992, c-10.
41 See *Consolidation of Plebiscite Act,* RSNWT 1988, c P-8; *Elections and Plebiscites Act,* SNWT 2006, c 15; *La Loi sur la consultation populaire,* LRQ 2000, c C-64.1; *Plebiscites Act,* RSPEI 1988, c P-10; *Elections Act,* SNL 1992, c E-3.1.

42 Emmett Macfarlane, *Constitutional Pariah: Reference re Senate Reform and the Future of Parliament* (Vancouver: UBC Press, 2021), 100–6.

43 Government of Canada, "Government Announces Immediate Senate Reform," press release, December 3, 2015.

44 Government of Canada, "Minister of Democratic Institutions Announces Launch of the Permanent Phase of the Independent Senate Appointments Process," press release, July 7, 2016.

45 *Ibid.*

46 The Court's reference jurisdiction gives it immense power. See Carissima Mathen, *Courts without Cases: The Law and Politics of Advisory Opinions* (Oxford: Hart, 2019); Kate Puddister, *Seeking the Court's Advice: The Politics of the Canadian Reference Power* (Vancouver: UBC Press, 2019).

47 *Reference re Secession of Quebec,* [1998] 2 SCR 217, paras 55–82 [*Secession Reference*].

48 *Ibid,* para 51.

49 *Ibid.*

50 *Ibid,* para 88.

51 *Reference re Supreme Court Act, ss 5 and 6,* [2014] 1 SCR 433.

52 *Ibid,* paras 90–105.

53 *Ibid,* para 94.

54 See Emmett Macfarlane, "Judicial Amendment of the Constitution," *International Journal of Constitutional Law* 19 (2021): 1894.

55 *Referendum Act,* SC 1992, c 30.

56 See Mary Dawson, "From the Backroom to the Front Line: Making Constitutional History or Encounters with the Constitution: Patriation, Meech Lake, and Charlottetown," *McGill Law Journal* 57 (2012): 983.

57 Chief Electoral Officer of Canada, *The 1992 Federal Referendum – A Challenge Met: Report of the Chief Electoral Officer of Canada* (Ottawa: Elections Canada, 1994), Part 2, 58.

58 See Emmett Macfarlane, "The Future of Constitutional Change in Canada," in *The Canadian Constitution in Transition,* ed. Richard Albert, Vanessa MacDonnell, and Paul Daly (Toronto: University of Toronto Press, 2019), 67–72.

59 See Richard Albert, "The Difficulty of Constitutional Amendment in Canada," *Alberta Law Review* 53 (2015): 85.

60 See *Constitution Act, 1982,* s 39(2).

61 See *Marbury v Madison,* 5 US (1 Cranch) 137 (1803).

62 Section 33 of the *Constitution Act, 1982* codifies the notwithstanding clause. Section 52(2) codifies the inclusion clause. I discuss the inclusion clause in a subsequent paragraph.

63 *Constitution of the United States,* art V (1789).

64 *Secession Reference.*

65 *Ibid.*

66 *Reference re Senate Reform,* [2014] 1 SCR 704.

67 See Richard Albert, "The Theory and Doctrine of Unconstitutional Constitutional Amendment in Canada," *Queen's Law Journal* 41 (2015): 143.

68 The inclusion clause reads as follows: "(2) The Constitution of Canada includes (*a*) the Canada Act 1982, including this Act; (*b*) the Acts and orders referred to in the schedule; and (*c*) any amendment to any Act or order referred to in paragraph (*a*) or (*b*)."

69 *Constitution Act, 1867,* Preamble.

70 John Gardner, "Can There Be a Written Constitution?," in *Oxford Studies in Philosophy of Law,* vol. 1, ed. Leslie Green and Brian Leiter (Oxford: Oxford University Press, 2011), 162.

71 *Ibid.*
72 *Ibid,* 194.
73 See Emmett Macfarlane, "The Future of Canadian Constitutional Amendment," in *Constitutional Amendment in Canada,* ed. Emmett Macfarlane (Toronto: University of Toronto Press, 2016), 294–99.
74 See Richard Albert, *Constitutional Amendment: Making, Breaking, and Changing Constitutions* (Oxford: Oxford University Press, 2019), 268–71.

24

Still Not Cheering
Understanding Quebec's Perspective on 1982

Félix Mathieu and Dave Guénette

"And no one cheered." Keith Banting and Richard Simeon used this expression in 1983 to describe the perceived lack of enthusiasm resulting from the *Constitution Act, 1982*.[1] Four decades later, however, its legal consequences and the events that took place the year before it passed have penetrated social imaginaries in Canada. For some, this period is celebrated as the final milestone that led to a profound political refounding of *Canadianness*, which is now synonymous with multiculturalism, institutional bilingualism, and individual rights and equality.[2] But from the point of view of Quebec, the *Constitution Act, 1982* is not celebrated in the same way, at least not with the same excitement and not by the majority of its people or its political actors. Even though Quebec does not amount to a "monolithic bloc," one could say that a fair share of Quebecers, most notably those who are old enough to have vivid memories of the event, perceive the *Constitution Act, 1982* as nothing less than a seismic constitutional upheaval,[3] as the rejection of dualism – the sociopolitical myth conceiving Canada as a pact between two founding peoples, two distinct societies.[4]

That said, it is important to recall that what came with the patriation of the Constitution in 1982 was not a *tabula rasa*. The *Constitution Act, 1982* did not replace the *Constitution Act, 1867*, thus marking the beginning of a completely new constitutional order, detached from the past. In fact, it added yet another layer to the complex Canadian constitutional architecture. One could even argue that 1982 was in line with the famous metaphor picturing the Canadian Constitution as a living tree. Indeed, while patriation represents a major evolution, it did not alter the country's democratic institutions or the division of constitutional powers between the federal and provincial governments. The *Canadian Charter of Rights and Freedoms*, which the Constitution entrenched within the constitutional order, was not the first piece of legislation that aimed to protect individual rights in Canada,[5] and the amending formula may appear as the final logical step[6] in the Canadian march towards the country obtaining full sovereignty from the United Kingdom.[7]

That interpretation, in which patriation is presented as encapsulating the living-tree metaphor, shall be accepted by some. But it may be rejected by others. This simply showcases that more than one legitimate view on the impact of a major political and constitutional event can coexist in a pluralist society.

Over the past four decades, significant critical perspectives on 1982 have emerged from Quebec scholars and intellectuals.[8] Many of these criticisms are rooted in an "identity politics" perspective, from which one can easily fall into the trap of analyzing Canadian politics as a zero-sum game.[9] While this may lead to fascinating and thoughtful views on why Quebec was, indeed, "right" or "wrong" not to agree to patriation, we believe another, original perspective may be more convincing for all Canadians who believe in the core value of federalism.

In this chapter, we offer a federalist perspective on why it is fully legitimate for Quebec not to cheer when it comes to interpreting what happened in 1981–82. Our focus is more on the process of patriation than on its substance. Indeed, while the Charter is fairly popular in Quebec, the process by which it was enacted remains controversial in the province. Many Quebecers applaud the Charter for its content but not the process that led to it.

To interpret this phenomenon, we ground our argument with the rationale put forward by the Supreme Court of Canada in its 1998 *Reference re Secession of Quebec*. In its decision, the court identified a nonexhaustive list of the "underlying principles" animating the whole of the Constitution: federalism, democracy, constitutionalism and the rule of law, and respect for minorities.[10] In particular, the court stressed that these principles "infuse our Constitution and breathe life into it."[11] It went even further by stating that "it would be impossible to conceive of our constitutional structure without them."[12] Most importantly, the court added: "[O]bservance of and respect for these principles *is essential to the ongoing process of constitutional development and evolution of our Constitution as a 'living tree.'"*[13]

Following the court's normative rationale, we ask ourselves this: Was the whole dossier of the patriation of the Constitution conducted in accordance with Canada's underlying constitutional principles? Although providing an exhaustive answer to that question goes beyond the scope of this chapter, we focus on Quebec and its broad constitutional relationship with Canada. In doing so, we emphasize the principles of federalism, democracy, and constitutionalism and the rule of law. Because it does not inform our conclusions here in any significant way, and due to limited space, we do not discuss the principle of the protection of minorities.[14]

For Canadians who believe in the normative content of federalism, we offer a legitimate and sound argument for comprehending Quebec's repeated refusal to sign the *Constitution Act, 1982:* it represents a break from some of Canada's most fundamental underlying constitutional principles.

While it is important to recall that the *Reference re Secession of Quebec* was made public more than fifteen years after patriation, it in no way affects the validity of this argument. As the court wrote in the reference: "Behind the written word is an historical lineage stretching back through the ages, which aids in the consideration of the underlying constitutional principles. These principles inform and sustain the constitutional text: they are the vital unstated assumptions upon which the text is based."[15] Hence, these principles are said to have inspired the Constitution from the very beginning of the Canadian odyssey.[16] Therefore, they should have guided the reasoning and action of those who proceeded to patriation.

We propose an original analysis of the impact of the *Constitution Act, 1982* on Quebec's broad constitutional relationship with Canada. In so doing, we use the underlying constitutional principles the Supreme Court identified in *Reference re Secession of Quebec* as an analytical framework. Partly echoing the court's reasoning, our analysis follows a three-step operation, one for each underlying principle under study: (1) federalism, (2) democracy, and (3) constitutionalism and the rule of law.

Federalism

The first principle identified by the Supreme Court in *Reference re Secession of Quebec* is federalism. In nonambiguous terms, the court suggests that our "political and constitutional practice has adhered to an underlying principle of federalism."[17] This principle, which is said to be "inherent in the structure of our constitutional arrangements ... has from the beginning been the lodestar by which the courts have been guided."[18] However, from the point of view of Quebec, and following the court's interpretation, to what extent was the principle of federalism respected with regards to the patriation of the Constitution? To answer this question, we look at 1982's impact on the sociopolitical myth that influences our understanding of the country's path, and then we deal with its impact on the provinces' institutional capacity as self-governing bodies.

Canada as a "Pact" Between ...

The premises of any society's underlying sociopolitical myths should never be considered politically irrelevant.[19] In a neo-Durkheimian fashion, we contend that these premises represent the very symbolic foundation upon which *demoi* (a plurality of *demos*, "people") come to imagine themselves as salient, singular political communities.[20]

In Canada, at least three divergent "storylines" have emerged to make sense of the 1867 "confederal pact."[21] They may be understood as contrasting attempts to reconstruct the historical and sociopolitical origins of the country; hence, they explain and justify what shall be the legitimate provincial control over constitutional amendments.[22] It should be stressed, though, that none of these founding myths take into consideration Indigenous peoples as a formal "federal partner."[23]

In a nutshell, the first myth is that of a "pact between two founding peoples." Notoriously attributed to Henri Bourassa, this imagined – yet not imaginary – conception of Canada entails a specific political grammar punctuated by three interconnected concepts: dualism, biculturalism, and bilingualism. The Tremblay Commission in the 1950s embraced a similar discourse, while André Laurendeau and, later on, Guy Laforest can be seen as the intellectual successors of Bourassa's cherished myth. Following it, the legitimate "natural limits" within which the constitutional living tree can evolve are constrained by the principle of prior approval and explicit consent of both founding peoples or partners: Quebec, as the heir of the people of French descent in North America, on the one hand, and the anglophone-majority nation, as the heir of the people of British descent, on the other. While this sociopolitical myth has been time and again advanced by the Quebec government,[24] it has been empirically demonstrated that it is, indeed, the most popular myth of all among Quebecers for recasting Canada's origins.[25]

The second sociopolitical myth is that of a pact between four provinces or British colonies: those that were represented at the time of the Charlottetown and Quebec Conferences in the fall of 1864 – Ontario (Canada West), Quebec (Canada East), New Brunswick, and Nova Scotia. As a natural evolution of this social imaginary, every time a province was added to the Canadian federation, they entered *ipso facto* into the select club of legitimate partners within the political association. Whereas Henri Bourassa can be seen as the spiritual father of the first myth, Ontario premier and "Father of the Confederation" Oliver Mowat is closely associated with this second one. From it flows the idea that any legitimate process leading to a major amendment of the constitutional order ought to be accepted by all provinces.

Finally, the third sociopolitical myth looks back at 1867 and concludes that the *Constitution Act, 1867* is a simple, ordinary statute of the British Parliament. One can find the materialization of this vision in the Report of the Royal Commission on Dominion-Provincial Relations (the Rowell-Sirois Commission). From this perspective, until the formal patriation of the Canadian constitution, the only legitimate "natural limits" in which the constitutional tree could flourish were those indicated by the Parliament of Westminster. Hence, subject to the approval of London, there would be no legitimacy deficit were the federal government to proceed unilaterally to enhance a constitutional amendment.

In the end, the vision that won the day in 1981–82 can be understood as an imperfect compromise between the second and third sociopolitical myths. For one thing, Ottawa did not proceed unilaterally – although not for lack of try-ing.[26] Nevertheless, it did advance its agenda without obtaining Quebec's (explicit or implicit) consent, somehow falling short of Oliver Mowat's vision. In any case, it violated the normative foundation upon which the first sociopolitical myth rests, the one most cherished – even today – by Quebecers: Henri Bou-rassa's vision of a pact between two founding peoples.

From this perspective, one can understand Quebec's repeated refusal to "sign" the *Constitution Act, 1982*, because this critical moment indeed broke with Quebec's most valued sociopolitical myth. As a consequence, 1982 also confirmed the substitution of dualism with multiculturalism, and it denied Laurendeau's vision for the cultural or societal entrenchment of bilingualism (via biculturalism).

Reducing the Provinces' Institutional Capacity as Self-Governing Entities

With the advent of the *Constitution Act, 1867*, a proper federal institutional architecture replaced the unitarian regime that had been established in 1840, in the aftermath of the Rébellion des Patriotes. In accordance with the discus-sions that took place in Charlottetown and Quebec City in fall 1864, the modern Canadian federation attributed a set of autonomous jurisdictions to both orders of government, and it also provided for shared competencies to be implemented in coordination between the central and federated powers.[27] As such, the *Constitution Act, 1982* did not add or withdraw any specific jurisdiction for either order of government. However, it did impact provincial autonomy, but more indirectly.

In theory, following, for instance, the rationale of Pierre-Joseph Proudhon's *The Principle of Federation*,[28] when provinces in a federation act within the sphere of their own jurisdiction, they should enjoy full autonomy in defining the substance of their laws. This is what parliamentarians in the National Assembly of Quebec had in mind when they passed, in 1977, the *Charter of the French Language* (Bill 101). However, since the *Canadian Charter of Rights and Freedoms* "defines the Canadian people in non-federal terms,"[29] it contributed to levelling down the concrete autonomy of the provinces, particularly with regard to linguistic matters and education.[30] That is, the entrenchment and codification of given rights and freedoms within the constitutional order led to a certain judicialization of politics, whereas the judiciary – and ultimately the Supreme Court – has sole authority in interpreting the meaning of said rights and freedoms.[31] Hence, the courts have gained more power to invalidate (prov-incial) legislation in the interests of constitutional conformity. The horizon of policy choices available to provincial legislatures has consequently shrunk to meet *a posteriori* judicial review.[32] Moreover, Peter Hogg and Allison Bushell's conception of a "Charter dialogue between Courts and Legislatures" is misconceiving,[33] as, in practice, the phenomenon may be more accurately depicted as a monologue, "with judges doing most of the talking and legislatures most of the listening."[34]

In particular, section 23 of the Charter has forced the provinces (more specifically, Quebec) to adapt to "national" (or, more accurately, "pan-Canadian") standards in the field of education, even though this is an autonomous provincial jurisdiction. As Eugénie Brouillet writes:

> This provision gives a right of access to public or subsidized minority-language education in the province to children whose parents meet certain conditions. The terms of this right were formulated precisely to counter the corresponding provisions of the *Charter of the French Language* relating to the language of instruction in Quebec, provisions that were perfectly valid at the time of their adoption by the National Assembly in 1977.[35]

Alan C. Cairns shares a similar understanding:

> These sections [on minority-language educational rights] sacrifice the rights of provincial majorities to determine language policy in educational settings in order to further a particular vision of the pan-Canadian community. The holder of such minority rights can judge the behaviour of provincial governments through the national lens provided by the Charter.[36]

There is no doubt that the *Constitution Act, 1982* contributed to indirectly limiting provincial autonomy and thus sanctioned a federal deficit of respect for self-governance.[37] This is especially true when considering that before the enactment of the *Canadian Charter of Rights and Freedoms* in 1982, Quebec had already adopted its own *Charter of Human Rights and Freedoms* in 1975. It did so autonomously, before having the Canadian Charter imposed on it. This interpretation contributes to explaining Quebec's repeated refusal to sign the *Constitution Act, 1982*.

Democracy

In the *Reference re Secession of Quebec*, the Supreme Court outlined a second principle: democracy. According to the court, this "is a fundamental value in our constitutional law and political culture."[38] It added that the principle of democracy "has always informed the design of our constitutional structure, and continues to act as an essential interpretive consideration to this day."[39] In analyzing the impact of the *Constitution Act, 1982* vis-à-vis the democratic principle, we first address the issue of the legitimate majority in 1982 and then discuss the functioning of the federal democracy.

A Tale of ~~Two Legitimate Majorities~~ One Legitimate Majority

Democracy – as with several other concepts in the social sciences – may have many different meanings.[40] Nonetheless, taking the Supreme Court of Canada's conception of it seriously, one must at least take into consideration the intimate connection it stressed between democracy and autonomy. As written in the 1998 reference, "[D]emocracy is fundamentally connected to substantive goals, most importantly, the promotion of self-government."[41] Moreover, the court also stressed that the necessary connection between democracy and federalism "means, for example, that in Canada there may be different and equally legitimate majorities in different provinces and territories and at the federal level. No one majority is more or less 'legitimate' than the others as an expression of democratic opinion."[42] Therefore, through democracy, each "legitimate majority" shall exercise its right to self-government, which means willingly give itself its own set of rules (*auto-nomos*).

In representative democracies, having elected political leaders negotiating and reaching an agreement that will lead to a formal amendment of the Constitution can absolutely be considered legitimate.[43] Some could even argue that in plural societies this might be the best way to reach a compromise and harmonize power relations.[44] Otherwise put, *demoi* may exercise their *kratos* (i.e., their power) in various ways.

Even though the possibility of organizing a referendum for citizens to express their support or opposition was, indeed, on the table at the time of patriation,[45] this idea was not implemented. Rather, elected representatives of all provinces and the Canadian prime minister took matters into their own hands. However, one partner was excluded from the last negotiation that led to the constitutional amendment: Quebec. Indeed, during the night of November 4–5, 1981, which is remembered in Quebec as the "Night of the Long Knives," officials of the central government and all nine English-speaking provinces either negotiated the deal or were notified of its draft without expressly and conclusively reaching out to the Quebec delegation. Since this agreement led directly to the patriation of the Constitution, it seems reasonable to conclude that it forced a new set of rules on Quebec (certainly a Canadian province but, not least, a [nonsovereign] *demos* of its own) without that province accepting its terms or its reach.

For that reason, Premier René Lévesque stated on November 9, 1981, that "Quebec has been shamefully betrayed" by its federal partners.[46] From Quebec's point of view, the agreement resulted in the complete rejection of the myth of the two founding peoples, as well as the court's rationale of "different and equally legitimate majorities in different provinces and territories and at the federal level." It replaced those with a rather unitarian conception of the Canadian *demos* in which a given "legitimate majority" dominates other possible expressions of different yet equally legitimate majorities.

Federal Unitarian Democracy

Pierre Trudeau responded to René Lévesque's accusation of betrayal by arguing that, in fact, Quebec had accepted the new constitutional pact since he himself and seventy-three out of seventy-five of Quebec's MPs in Ottawa agreed to it.[47] If Canada were a unitary state, this line of reasoning would have been absolutely legitimate. However, because Canada is a federal state, this statement reflects a serious democratic deficit. Simply put, two competing "majorities" conflicted: the first one, represented by Pierre Trudeau, tried to prove its legitimacy with the fact that the Liberal Party of Canada "had been elected in 1980 with the largest number of votes ever gained by any party in any Quebec election, federal or provincial"; the other, represented by the equally popular politician René Lévesque, fuelled its own legitimacy by arguing that the Parti Québécois "had won two successive provincial elections in 1976 and 1980 with respectable majorities."[48]

Again, following the Supreme Court's argument that "in Canada there may be different and equally legitimate majorities," no one majority has more legitimacy than others. Hence, the actions of Quebec's MPs in Ottawa shouldn't have trumped the actions of parliamentarians in the National Assembly of Quebec. The latter having expressed their explicit rejection of this manoeuvre, patriation ought to be interpreted as a political *tour de force*, where one majority was revealed to bear more legitimacy than the other.

On November 25, 1981, in the correspondence between Lévesque and Trudeau in the aftermath of the agreement, Léveque formally forwarded his government's order, by which Quebec exercised its "right of veto" over patriation.[49] A week later, on December 1, 1981, the National Assembly of Quebec voted in a resolution setting out the conditions necessary for Quebec to sign the new constitutional act.[50] They included recognition of Quebec's distinctiveness in Canada. As explained by Donald Smiley, Ottawa's refusal to listen to Quebec's requests resulted, among other things, in the betrayal of the province's electorate and a perpetual legitimacy deficit in the Canadian constitutional order.[51] Indeed, from Quebec's perspective, the agreement was not the materialization of a federal democracy but rather the demonstration of a unitarian conception of it.

Constitutionalism and the Rule of Law

In *Reference re Secession of Quebec,* the Supreme Court then addressed a third underlying principle, that of constitutionalism and the rule of law, and distinguished between its two components. Among other things, for the court, "the rule of law vouchsafes to the citizens and residents of the country a stable, predictable and ordered society in which to conduct their affairs."[52] Constitutionalism "requires that all government action comply with the Constitution."[53] With regard to this third underlying principle, we focus on two reasons why Quebecers see patriation as a moment of rupture, as a break with the historical roots of the living tree.

The 1981 and 1982 References: Gang of Eight v Ottawa and Quebec v Ottawa

Prior to the events culminating in patriation in 1981–82, a commonly accepted assertion was that (unanimous) provincial consent was necessary for major constitutional amendments.[54] In that spirit, echoing attempts to reform the Constitution during the previous decades, the federal government convened its political partners for a federal-provincial conference in September 1980 to embark on a journey that would lead to the patriation of the Constitution. Reflecting on the fiasco that resulted from that conference – whether it was planned or not does not matter[55] – the federal government concluded that the failure to achieve anything had been due mostly to the process: "There were too many complex issues on the table and the level of consent required was too high"; the government decided that "unilateral federal action was necessary to break the logjam."[56]

Supported by two provinces (Ontario and New Brunswick), the federal government then decided to proceed unilaterally. Of course, this led to major opposition from the eight other provinces (the Gang of Eight). Was it even legal to proceed? Three provincial courts of appeal (Manitoba, Quebec, and Newfoundland) took up the issue, which eventually led the Supreme Court of Canada to clarify the legal stance for the unilateral patriation proposition.[57] In the *Re: Resolution to Amend the Constitution,* the court confirmed that the Parliament of Canada had the jurisdiction to proceed unilaterally but that a "substantial degree of provincial consent" was required by convention.[58] In what could be called the Gang of Eight v Ottawa, the provinces somehow won the day against the federal government, thus fuelling the sociopolitical myth associated with Oliver Mowat.

However, Prime Minister Trudeau then interpreted "substantial degree of provincial consent" to mean that unanimity was not required, nor was the consent of both "founding peoples," including, as a representative of French-descent people, Quebec – a sociopolitical myth it devoted a great deal of energy to rejecting.[59] Hence, following the Kitchen Accord and the Night of the Long Knives, when the federal government reached an agreement with all provincial leaders with the notable exception of Quebec, Trudeau's understanding of "substantial degree of provincial consent" was secured. The Rowell-Sirois sociopolitical myth had to be adjusted for this manoeuvre to be acceptable to most provinces – with the notable exception of Quebec. In the end, this eroded the normative foundation of Mowat's vision and overruled Bourassa's conception of a pact between two founding peoples.

The Constitution was patriated on April 17, 1982, with the proclamation of the *Constitution Act, 1982* by the Queen. But Quebec continued its battle against patriation, and the Supreme Court was again asked to intervene. This time, it was asked to answer specifically whether Quebec indeed had a conventional veto right in the patriation process. According to Dennis Baker, Quebec's case was strong. Indeed, the evidence "before the Court of pre-1982 constitutional change consisted of five 'positive precedents' of successful constitutional amendments agreed to by all provinces."[60] Baker adds: "More telling, in this respect, were the 'negative precedents' of unsuccessful constitutional amendments and constitutional conferences in 1951, 1960, 1964 and 1971, each of which failed because of the objections of one or more provinces."[61] Even more revealing for the conception of Canada as a pact between two founding peoples: on "two instances, the historical record was perfectly clear that all political actors were operating under the assumption that a constitutional amendment could not move forward without the agreement of Quebec."[62]

Summarizing Quebec's position, the Supreme Court wrote: "The reason advanced by the appellant for the existence of a conventional rule of a power of veto for Quebec is the principle of duality, this principle being however understood in a special sense."[63] Indeed, in its factum, the counsel for Quebec indicated that

> the word "duality" covers all the circumstances that have contributed to making Quebec a distinct society, since the foundation of Canada and long before, and the range of guarantees that were made to Quebec in 1867, as a province which the Task Force on Canadian Unity has described as "the stronghold of the French-Canadian people" and the "living heart of the French presence in North America."[64]

The court ended up rejecting the stance of Quebec in the reference. Consequently, it also rejected the possibility of a veto power for the province. Therefore, during the second act of this Canadian drama, Quebec v Ottawa, the federal government prevailed. To quote Baker again, "[I]t is hard to avoid the conclusion that the Court's opinion was torqued to arrive at a specific result: to avoid invalidating the freshly enacted *Constitution Act, 1982*."[65]

To Quebec, this course of action was contrary to the "federal spirit" and to its perspective on Canadian federalism, as it denied the normative force of the principle *quod omnes tangit ab omnibus tractari et approbari debet*, that is, "what affects all must be discussed and approved by all."[66] Otherwise put, by looking at the necessity of obtaining Quebec's approval before proceeding to a constitutional amendment – which did impact, *inter alia*, Quebec's legislative autonomy – the whole process was doomed to end in a serious federal deficit. Even if the process ended with compliance with the rules established by the Supreme Court – in other words, in line with the underlying principle of constitutionalism and the rule of law – Quebec's view remained that it was a break with Canada's constitutional roots.

Denying Quebec's Veto ... Only to Give It Back Again

Over the long haul, it has been Quebec's position that it has a veto right over any process that would lead to a major amendment of Canada's Constitution – especially if it alters its own autonomous powers. That veto is perfectly compatible with the principle of unanimity, that is, an extension of Oliver Mowat's sociopolitical myth. Indeed, before 1981, "the best argument for a Quebec veto appeared to be based on the premise that the agreement of every province was necessary to 'patriate' or significantly alter the Constitution."[67] As the government of Quebec reiterates in its most recent statement on constitutional policy:

> Over the course of the many rounds of constitutional negotiations on the procedure for amending the constitution in the years prior to patriation, several matters were recognized as requiring a consensus among the federative partners. For the Government of Québec, obtaining a veto over certain important matters meant that fundamental changes to the workings of the Federation could not be made without its consent. The right of veto was constantly stated by successive Québec governments.[68]

However, the Supreme Court decided to rule that only a substantial degree of provincial consent – and not unanimous consent – was required to patriate the Constitution. Moreover, it stated that said substantial degree of provincial consent ought not necessarily include Quebec, that is, La Belle Province did not have a veto power. Quebec's historical position was denied.[69] But the amending formula adopted in 1982, perhaps surprisingly, puts forward a procedure that would require the agreement of all ten provinces to change the Constitution in a similar way to what patriation did.[70] In other words, had the amending formula adopted in 1982 been in place prior to patriation, Quebec's consent to patriate the Constitution would have been required.

As Henri Brun, Guy Tremblay, and Eugénie Brouillet write: "Paradoxically, the 1982 constitutional reform thus protects Quebec in a way that simply was not respected when the Constitution was changed in 1982."[71] Put differently, the political authorities who brought about patriation did not see fit to subject themselves to the same rigour they imposed on their counterparts in the future. The three constitutionalists then qualify the situation as an "absurdity," since

> Quebec has no interest in making the 1982 *coup de force* unalterable. What it wants is the possibility to make amendments to the Constitution it refused in the first place. On the other hand, the federal government and English Canada, which are happy with the constitutional order they have imposed on Quebec, have no problem cementing it as it stands.[72]

In the end, we find it difficult not to share their position on this issue. In a nutshell, looking back at the patriation process, Quebec saw its traditional view on its veto power being denied, only for it to be granted afterwards, when it was too late to use it anyway. While we contend that this may not be formally a breach of the underlying principle of constitutionalism and the rule of law, Quebec sees it nonetheless as a breach of its spirit.

Conclusion

To depart from Keith Banting and Richard Simeon's pessimistic view of the 1982 patriation, it's worth asking: Why can't all Canadians who believe in federalism celebrate patriation? What's missing? While Quebecers are not alone in being unsatisfied with the contemporary constitutional order – for one thing, Indigenous peoples are still not considered or empowered as fully legitimate, distinct, and nonsubordinated partners in the Canadian political association – any attempt to answer this question should take seriously La Belle Province's admonitions. It is our understanding that implementing policies and actions to respond to the shortcomings identified in this chapter would contribute to the flourishing of a healthy federal spirit in Canada. Furthermore, by living up to the normative rationale of the underlying constitutional principles of federalism, democracy, and constitutionalism and the rule of law, Canada could authentically reconnect with the very roots of the constitutional living tree. While the "constitutional fruit" may not be ripe yet, we should not forget that it is never too late to plow the land. And as the saying goes – the ox is slow, but the earth is patient.

In the end, we stick with our initial statement: a legitimate and sound argument for comprehending Quebec's repeated refusal to sign the *Constitution Act, 1982* is that this episode represents a break from some of Canada's most fundamental underlying constitutional principles. In a more detailed fashion,

Quebec refused to "sign" the *Constitution Act, 1982* for the following reasons:

- It marked a rupture; indeed, it broke with Quebec's most valued sociopolitical myth (Henri Bourassa's vision) which laid out a road to amend the constitutional order with full legitimacy.
- It denied Quebec's (imagined) veto, only to give it back right after in the form of a unanimity requirement for some significant constitutional amendments.
- It contributed to limiting (indirectly) Quebec's institutional autonomy, notably as per the National Assembly of Quebec's desire to pass legislation to protect what makes it a *société distincte*.
- It violated the principle there shall coexist different yet equally "legitimate majorities in different provinces and territories and at the federal level."
- As a result of the above, it dishonoured the basic federal principle of *quod omnes tangit ab omnibus tractari et appropbari debet*, since a deal was reached between the Canadian partners without it having been discussed with and approved by Quebec.

Notes

1   Keith Banting and Richard Simeon, eds., *And No One Cheered: Federalism, Democracy and the Constitution Act* (Toronto: Taylor and Francis, 1983).
2   Alan C. Cairns, *Charter versus Federalism: The Dilemmas of Constitutional Reforms* (Montreal/Kingston: McGill-Queen's University Press, 1992); Simon Langlois, *Refondations nationales au Canada et au Québec* (Quebec: Septentrion, 2018); Noura Karazivan and Jean Leclair, eds., *Pierre Elliott Trudeau's Intellectual, Political and Constitutional Legacy/L'héritage intellectuel, politique et constitutionnel de Pierre Elliott Trudeau* (Montreal: LexisNexis, 2020).
3   See Guy Laforest, *Trudeau and the End of a Canadian Dream* (Montreal/Kingston: McGill-Queen's University Press, 1995); Réjean Pelletier, *Le Québec et le fédéralisme canadien: Un regard critique* (Quebec: Presses de l'Université Laval, 2008); Guy Laforest, *Interpreting Quebec's Exile within the Federation: Selected Political Essays* (Brussels: P.I.E. Peter Lang, 2015); Evelyne Brie and Félix Mathieu, *Un pays divisé: Identité, fédéralisme et régionalisme au Canada* (Quebec: Presses de l'Université Laval, 2021).
4   Stéphane Paquin, *L'invention d'un mythe: Le pacte entre deux peuples fondateurs* (Montreal: VLB éditeur, 1999).
5   *Canadian Bill of Rights,* SC 1960, c 44; *Canadian Human Rights Act,* RSC, 1985, c H-6. In Quebec, the *Charter of Human Rights and Freedoms,* CQLR, C-12, was adopted in 1975.
6   Although the amendment rules have "evolved" in an "invisible transformation" since 1982, as demonstrated by Richard Albert in Chapter 23 of this volume.
7   That being said, as discussed by Philippe Lagassé in Chapter 25 of this volume, there might be "cracks in the foundation" with regards to the Crown in the constitutional architecture of Canada. That has best been demonstrated in the case of the royal succession: *Motard v Attorney General of Canada,* 2019 QCCA 1826.
8   See Antoine Brousseau Desaulnier and Stéphane Savard, eds., *La pensée fédéraliste contemporaine au Québec: Perspectives historiques* (Quebec: Presses de l'Université du Québec, 2020).

9 See Daniel Weinstock, "Les 'identités' sont-elles dangereuses pour la démocratie?," in *Repères en mutation: Identité et citoyenneté dans le Québec contemporain,* ed. Jocelyn Maclure and Alain-G. Gagnon (Montreal: Québec Amérique, 2001), 227–50.

10 For a detailed discussion of the meaning of these four underlying constitutional principles, see Dave Guénette and Félix Mathieu, "Le *Renvoi relatif à la sécession du Québec,* 20 ans plus tard: Fédéralisme, démocratie, constitutionnalisme et protection des minorités," in *Ré-imaginer le Canada: Vers un État multinational?,* ed. Félix Mathieu and Dave Guénette (Quebec: Presses de l'Université Laval, 2019), 3.

11 *Reference re Secession of Quebec,* [1998] 2 SCR 217, para 50 [*Secession Reference*].

12 *Ibid,* para 51.

13 *Ibid,* para 52 (our emphasis).

14 That being said, it is important for us to reiterate that the principle of the protection of minorities is as important as the other underlying principles. In previous work, we studied it alongside the principles of federalism, democracy, and constitutionalism and the rule of law. See Mathieu and Guénette, *Ré-imaginer le Canada;* Dave Guénette and Félix Mathieu, "Le Canada face à ses principes constitutionnels sous-jacents en temps de crise: Regards sur la gestion de la COVID-19," *Les Cahiers de droit* 62 (2021): 495–537. In the specific case of this chapter, the principle of the protection of minorities cannot explain lack of enthusiasm for the *Constitution Act, 1982* in Quebec, as the province already had its own *Charter of Human Rights and Freedoms.*

15 *Secession Reference,* para 49.

16 See Peter H. Russell, *Canada's Odyssey: A Country Based on Incomplete Conquests* (Toronto: University of Toronto Press, 2017).

17 *Secession Reference,* para 55.

18 *Ibid,* para 56.

19 Gérard Bouchard, *Les nations savent-elles encore rêver? Les mythes nationaux à l'ère de la mondialisation* (Montreal: Boréal, 2019).

20 Benedict Anderson, *Imagined Communities: Reflections on the Origin and Spread of Nationalism* (London: Verso, 1983).

21 See Stéphane Paquin, *L'invention d'un mythe: Le pacte entre deux peuples fondateurs* (Montreal: VLB éditeur, 1998).

22 *Ibid,* 157.

23 See Christa Scholtz, "Part II and Part V: Aboriginal Peoples and Constitutional Amendment," in *Constitutional Amendment in Canada,* ed. Emmett Macfarlane (Toronto: University of Toronto Press, 2016), 85.

24 See Quebecers, *Our Way of Being Canadian: Policy on Québec Affirmation and Canadian Relations* (Quebec: Government of Quebec, 2017), 13–18.

25 Jocelyn Létourneau, *Je me souviens: Le passé du Québec dans la conscience de sa jeunesse* (Montreal: Fides, 2014).

26 See *Re: Resolution to Amend the Constitution,* [1981] 1 SCR 753.

27 See, in particular, ss 91 to 95 of the *Constitution Act, 1867;* see also Eugénie Brouillet, Alain-G. Gagnon, and Guy Laforest, eds., *The Quebec Conference of 1864: Understanding the Emergence of the Canadian Federation* (Montreal/Kingston: McGill-Queen's University Press, 2016).

28 Pierre-Joseph Proudhon, *The Principle of Federation* (Toronto: University of Toronto Press, 1979 [1863]).

29 Cairns, *Charter versus Federalism,* 85.

30 On this topic, see Stéphanie Chouinard, Chapter 16 in this volume. See also Dave Guénette and Félix Mathieu, "Minority Language School Boards and Personal Federalism in Canada – Recent and Ongoing Developments in Quebec," *Constitutional Forum* (2022): 19.

31 Eugénie Brouillet, *La négation de la nation: L'identité culturelle québécoise et le fédéralisme canadien* (Quebec: Septentrion, 2005), 330.

32 José Woehrling, "Le principe d'égalité, le système fédéral canadien et le caractère distinct du Québec," in *Québec-Communauté française de Belgique: Autonomie et spécificité dans le cadre d'un système fédéral,* ed. Pierre Patenaude (Montreal: Éditions Wilson and Lafleur, 1992), 141.

33 Peter Hogg and Allison Bushell, "Charter Dialogue between Courts and Legislatures," *Osgoode Hall Law Journal* 35, 1 (1997): 75.

34 F.L. Morton and Rainer Knopff, *The Charter Revolution and the Court Party* (Peterborough, ON: Broadview Press, 2000), 166; see also James B. Kelly, *Governing with the Charter: Legislative and Judicial Activism and Framers' Intent* (Vancouver: UBC Press, 2005).

35 Brouillet, *La négation de la nation,* 331 (translated by the authors).

36 Cairns, *Charter versus Federalism,* 85.

37 See Gerald Baier, Chapter 3 in this volume.

38 *Secession Reference,* para 61.

39 *Ibid,* para 62.

40 Francis Dupui-Déry, *Démocratie: Histoire politique d'un mot aux États-Unis et en France* (Montreal: Lux Éditeur, 2019).

41 *Secession Reference,* para 64.

42 *Ibid,* para 66.

43 As Martin Loughlin writes in "The Concept of Constituent Power" (*European Journal of Political Theory* 13, 2 (2014): 229), "From a relational perspective, constituent power vests in the people, but this does not mean that political authority is located in the people (qua the multitude) as adherents to the principle of popular sovereignty."

44 Arend Lijphart, *Democracy in Plural Societies: A Comparative Exploration* (New Haven, CT: Yale University Press, 1977).

45 Richard Albert, "Trudeau's Threat: The Referendum at Patriation," in *Pierre Elliott Trudeau's Intellectual, Political and Constitutional Legacy/L'héritage intellectuel, politique et constitutionnel de Pierre Elliott Trudeau,* ed. Noura Karazivan and Jean Leclair (Montreal: LexisNexis, 2020), 463–85.

46 "Discours du trône, Quebec, November 9, 1981," *La Société du patrimoine politique du Québec,* archivespolitiquesduquebec.com/discours/p-m-du-quebec/rene-levesque/discours-du-trone-quebec-9-novembre-1981/.

47 Allan Blakeney, "A Western Perspective on the Constitution," *Canadian Parliamentary Review* 14, 2 (1991): 8.

48 *Ibid.*

49 See James Ross Hurley, *Amending Canada's Constitution: History, Processes, Problems and Prospects* (Ottawa: Minister of Supply and Services Canada, 1996), 243.

50 Quebec, National Assembly, *Votes and Proceedings,* 32nd Leg, 3rd Sess, No 12 (December 1, 1981), 143.

51 Donald Smiley, "A Dangerous Deed: The Constitution Act, 1982," in *And No One Cheered: Federalism, Democracy and the Constitution Act,* ed. Keith Banting and Richard Simeon (Toronto: Taylor and Francis, 1983), 78.

52 *Secession Reference,* para 70.

53 *Ibid,* para 72.

54 See Paul Gérin-Lajoie, *Constitutional Amendment in Canada* (Toronto: University of Toronto Press, 1950); Hurley, *Amending Canada's Constitution,* 53; Mollie Dunsmuir and Brian O'Neal, *Quebec's Constitutional Veto: The Legal and Historical Context* (Ottawa: Library of Parliament, Research Branch, 1992).

55 See André Burelle, *Pierre Trudeau: L'intellectuel et le politique* (Montreal: Fidès, 2005), 296–97.

56 Hurley, *Amending Canada's Constitution,* 54.

57 House of Commons, Special Joint Committee of the Senate and the House of Commons on the Constitution of Canada, *Proposed Resolution for a Joint Address to Her Majesty the Queen respecting the Constitution of Canada* (1981).

58 See *Re: Resolution to Amend the Constitution,* [1981] 1 SCR 753.

59 See Dave Guénette and Félix Mathieu, "Le Québec face à la vision Trudeau: La question des nations minoritaires et de leur fragilité," *Supreme Court Law Review* 99 (2d) (2020): 213.

60 Dennis Baker, "The Origins and Implications of Canada's 'Constructive Unamendabilty': A Comment on Richard Albert's *Four Unconstitutional Constitutions and Their Democratic Foundations,*" *Cornell International Law Journal Online* 50 (2017): 31.

61 *Ibid.*

62 Indeed, "the successful 1964 amendment had the support of the other nine provinces as early as 1962, but Quebec stood alone in delaying it until it 'finally gave its consent' in 1964; in 1971, Prime Minister Pierre Trudeau thought he had achieved the agreement of all the provinces, but Quebec Premier Bourassa withdrew Quebec's consent a few weeks later, resulting in the abandonment of the Victoria Charter" (*ibid,* 31–32).

63 *Re: Objection by Quebec to a Resolution to amend the Constitution,* [1982] 2 SCR 793, 812.

64 *Ibid,* 813.

65 Baker, "The Origins and Implications," 32.

66 See Félix Mathieu and Alain-G. Gagnon, "L'esprit fédéral et les principales déclinaisons du fédéralisme," in *Cinquante déclinaisons de fédéralisme: Théorie, enjeux et études de cas,* ed. Félix Mathieu, Dave Guénette, and Alain-G. Gagnon (Quebec: Presses de l'Université du Québec, 2020), 35.

67 Dunsmuir and O'Neal, "Quebec's Constitutional Veto."

68 Quebecers, *Our Way of Being Canadian,* 51.

69 As René Lévesque wrote to Pierre Elliott Trudeau on November 25, 1981: "I wish to point out in this connection that the Government of Quebec has always maintained that the assent of Quebec was constitutionally required to any agreement that would allow patriation of the Constitution and establishment of the amending formula for the future": Hurley, *Amending Canada's Constitution,* 243.

70 See s 41 of Part V of the *Constitution Act, 1982.*

71 Henri Brun, Guy Tremblay, and Eugénie Brouillet, *Droit constitutionnel,* 6th ed. (Cowansville: Éditions Yvon Blais, 2014), 235 (our translation).

72 *Ibid,* 250 (our translation).

25

Cracks in the Foundation
The Crown and Canada's Constitutional Architecture

Philippe Lagassé

IN 1985, THE Law Reform Commission of Canada published a working paper titled *The Legal Status of the Federal Administration*.[1] The paper addressed the challenge of reconciling modern public law concepts and aspirations with the medieval idea of the monarch as the personification of the state and the Crown as the locus of sovereign authority. Given the recently patriated Canadian constitution and its *Charter of Rights and Freedoms,* this was a live issue. Yes, Canada was now fully independent and had entrenched constitutional rights and protections, but this contemporary, liberal regime had been placed over a feudal, colonial base. To borrow the Supreme Court's architectural analogy,[2] Canada had built a modern structure atop an antiquated stone foundation. The Law Reform Commission working paper, in effect, asked if this old foundation could still hold up the new building.

The past four decades have shown that the commission had legitimate concerns. On the one hand, the idea of the Crown as the state and source of sovereign authority has been resilient, notably with respect to Canada's evolving separation-of-powers doctrine. On the other hand, the monarchy has run into difficulties with the *Constitution Act, 1982,* both in terms of how the monarch interacts with the Charter and the amending procedure. Returning to our architectural analogy, this chapter argues that, while it is still supporting the new building, cracks have appeared in the old stone foundation. For now, these cracks can be ignored as we continue to admire our modern constitutional construction. Yet, at some point, these fissures could lead to structural problems.

This chapter begins with a brief overview of the Crown and Canada's constitutional order from Confederation to patriation. It then examines how the Crown has evolved alongside Canada's postpatriation separation-of-powers doctrine, focusing on the Supreme Court of Canada's ruling in *Mikisew Cree First Nation v Canada (Governor General in Council)*.[3] The chapter then considers how the meaning of "the Queen" was diluted to avoid a clash between monarchy and the Charter in *McAteer v Canada (Attorney General)*.[4] Next, the chapter considers how courts in Ontario and Quebec determined that a "principle of symmetry" exists between the Canadian and British Crowns and how the Quebec Court of Appeal excluded this rule from the office of the Queen and the unanimous amending formula in *Motard v Procureur général du Canada*.[5]

The chapter concludes with a discussion of how these rulings have left us with an unanswered constitutional puzzle regarding the Crown and the office of the Queen.

In presenting this analysis of the Crown and the Canadian constitution, I acknowledge a glaring omission: a detailed discussion of the relationship between the Crown and Indigenous peoples. Although this question is touched on briefly in this chapter, and at greater length in other chapters in this volume (see Patzer and Ladner, Chapter 19, and Major and Stirbys, Chapter 20), I acknowledge that any treatment of the nature of the Canadian Crown is incomplete without an in-depth analysis of the honour of the Crown and how Crown sovereignty must be reconciled with treaties established with Indigenous peoples. The following is a settler perspective on the Crown and the Canadian state, one that acknowledges my embryonic knowledge of Indigenous history, governance, law, and understandings of treaty relations.[6]

The Crown and the Canadian Constitution

Canada was confederated under the Crown of the United Kingdom of Great Britain and Ireland with the passage of the *British North America Act, 1867* by the Imperial Parliament at Westminster. Although Canada was a self-governing Dominion, with a constitution "similar in principle to that of the United Kingdom," the new nation was not an independent state. Sovereignty over and within Canada resided with the Imperial Crown, as personified by the sovereign of the United Kingdom. As the concept of the state in English law, the Imperial Crown and the sovereign of the United Kingdom thus served as Canada's legal personality.[7] Canada was an emanation of Her Majesty in right of the United Kingdom. In turn, this meant that Canada was ultimately subject to the British Queen-in-Council for imperial policy decisions, to the laws passed by the British Crown-in-Parliament, and to the Judicial Committee of the Privy Council for judicial appeals.[8]

This distribution of the Crown's sovereign authority was mirrored within Canada. Executive power was vested in the Queen, as represented by the governor general, who acted on the advice of the governor general-in-council federally, and by lieutenant-governors-in-council, provincially. A Parliament composed of the Queen, Senate, and House of Commons was vested with legislative power in areas of federal jurisdiction, while similarly composed legislatures were empowered in areas of provincial jurisdiction. Lastly, federal and provincial courts were established to provide justice in the Queen's name. At this stage in Canada's constitutional development, it must be stressed, the Crown remained that of the United Kingdom, as personified in both a legal and natural capacity by a single sovereign.[9]

Canada's movement towards national autonomy and eventual independence began after the First World War. This process started with a division of the Crown by constitutional convention. At the 1926 Imperial Conference, it was agreed that the sovereign would only act on the advice of Canadian ministers when exercising royal prerogatives for and within Canada. When war came again in 1939, this meant that the King declared war separately for the United Kingdom and Canada; hence, His Majesty in right of the United Kingdom was at war with Germany for seven days before His Majesty in right of Canada joined the fight.[10] Canada's legislative autonomy was also secured in the postwar period with the negotiation of the *Statute of Westminster 1931*. This act ended the invalidity of Canadian laws that ran counter to British statute, as well as the application of British laws to Canada by paramount force.[11] The formal sovereignty of the British Crown-in-Parliament over the Dominion remained, but the *Statute of Westminster 1931* provided that the British would only legislate for Canada on the request and consent of the Canadian Cabinet.

Given the legislative autonomy that the *Statute of Westminster 1931* granted, it was necessary to rely on constitutional convention to maintain common laws of royal succession. The preamble to the *Statute of Westminster 1931* held that, in order to maintain "a common allegiance to the Crown," the parliaments in the Dominions would need to assent to changes to the law of succession and the royal style and titles. This was included in the preamble to address the fact that British amendments to the law of succession and royal style and titles would no longer apply by paramount force to Dominions that had incorporated the statute into their own law. While the preamble did not have the force of law, it established a convention of mutual parliamentary assent to alterations affecting the monarchy. As fate would have it, this issue came to the fore during the abdication of King Edward VIII. In December 1936, the Canadian Cabinet requested and consented that the British Parliament's abdication act extend into Canadian law to ensure that the abdication and removal of any of the King's future heirs to the line of succession applied to Canada. Canada's Parliament then provided its assent to these legal changes in early 1937.[12]

In the decades that followed, Canada took further steps towards full autonomy, including establishing a unique Canadian citizenship and ending all appeals to the Judicial Committee of the Privy Council in the 1940s. The push to achieve full sovereign independence began in earnest two decades later in the late 1960s. As discussed in other chapters in this volume, the federal government aimed to include a *Charter of Rights and Freedoms* in a new Canadian constitutional framework, while the provinces sought to ensure that their interests were protected through a constitutional amending formula.

While the Crown was not at the forefront of the constitutional negotiations between the federal government and the provinces leading up to the patriation of the Constitution, it was certainly in the background. Protecting the offices of the Queen and the viceregal representatives under a stringent amendment process had been proposed early in the negotiations, as seen in the 1971 Victoria Charter. The urgency of protecting the monarchical status quo, however, took on greater importance after the federal government tabled Bill C-60, its proposed constitutional framework, before Parliament in 1978.[13]

Bill C-60 did not try to make Canada a republic, nor did it remove or alter the Crown as the concept of the state and source of sovereign authority. Instead, the bill aimed to formalize the governor general's standing as the primary manifestation of the Crown in Canada. Among other things, this involved vesting the governor general with the executive power and the power of command-in-chief of the armed forces and making that office the monarchical part of Parliament. The Queen, meanwhile, was to be more clearly Canadianized. Under the royal styles and titles enacted by the Canadian Parliament in 1952, the sovereign remained both British and Canadian as "Elizabeth the Second, by the Grace of God of the United Kingdom, Canada and Her other Realms and Territories Queen, Head of the Commonwealth, Defender of the Faith."[14] Section 30 of Bill C-60 would have altered the royal styles and titles such that "[t]he sovereign head of Canada is Her Majesty the Queen, who shall be styled the Queen of Canada and whose sovereignty as such shall pass to her heirs and successors in accordance with law." While Bill C-60 would have pushed the Queen to the margins of the Canadian constitutional order, it would have made the monarchical office plainly Canadian in name and law.

Monarchist opposition to the provision of Bill C-60, and the more fundamental focus on the amending formula and Charter, ensured that the changes it proposed to the offices of the Queen and governor general were abandoned. When the constitutional negotiations finally ended in late 1981, the Crown's status as the concept of the state and sovereign authority, along with the Queen's pre-eminent position in the formal 1867 constitutional framework, and the royal style and titles from 1952 were left untouched. Instead, the parties returned to the language of the 1971 Victoria Charter, placing the offices of the Queen, governor general, and lieutenant-governors under the unanimous amending procedure. Importantly, while this provision was meant to preserve and protect the monarchical status quo, it left open the question of what was included under these offices. Along with a minimalist schedule that omitted historical English and British acts of constitutional importance to Canada, such as the *Bill of Rights 1689* and the *Act of Settlement 1701*, the drafters of what would become the

Constitution Act, 1982 left it to the courts to divine the meaning and scope of these offices.

Thankfully, as Canadian politicians celebrated their constitutional agreement, the English Court of Appeal settled a fundamental question about the nature of the Crown in Canada leading up to patriation. In *Alberta Indians,* the court was asked to consider what obligations Her Majesty in right of the United Kingdom owed to First Nations treaty peoples in Canada. The court found that, owing to the divisibility of the Crown that had occurred after the 1926 Imperial Conference, these obligations now belonged to Her Majesty in right of Canada alone. As Lord Justice May observed: "In matters of law and government the Queen of the United Kingdom is entirely independent and distinct from the Queen of Canada."[15] While Bill C-60 had not passed, the sovereign head of Canada, and the legal personality of the Canadian state, had nonetheless become the Queen of Canada, separate and distinct from the Queen of the United Kingdom. With Canada on the cusp of becoming formally independent, this prevented the Crown, still identified as that of the "United Kingdom of Great Britain and Ireland" in the renamed *Constitution Act, 1867,* from becoming a still greater conceptual muddle than critics had long complained it already was. Or so it seemed.

The Crown and the Separation of Powers

The relationships between the branches of the state prior to patriation were best captured by the preambular clause of a constitution "similar in principle to that of the United Kingdom" in the *British North America Act, 1867.* This clause meant that, while there was a clear distinction made between the executive power, legislative power, and the judicature, constitutional convention bound the three together. Cabinet ministers were drawn from the houses of Parliament, the attorney general sat in Cabinet, and judges were appointed by the Crown on the advice of Cabinet. The three branches were legally separate and performed distinct functions, but they were nonetheless politically fused to varying degrees. Most importantly, though, prior to patriation, Canada remained under the sovereign authority of the British Crown-in-Parliament. The legislative supremacy of the Parliament at Westminster meant that one branch was formally dominant.

Patriation made the separation of powers more salient in two interrelated ways. First, it ended the legislative supremacy of the British Parliament and replaced it with the supremacy of the Constitution itself, as set out in section 52 of the *Constitution Act, 1982.* Coupled with the Charter, this enhanced the power of the judiciary as the interpreter of the Constitution as the supreme law.[16] Yet with this greater authority came a recognition that the judiciary would need to be mindful of the particular functions and responsibilities of the legislative and executive branches. Whether the judiciary has truly respected these boundaries is open to debate.[17] What matters here is that talk of a Canadian separation-of-powers doctrine became more prominent.

As the formal repository of sovereign authority, the Crown would seem to be in tension with a separation-of-powers doctrine. Certainly, in its original conception, the authority of the Crown would not have been understood as separable. The sovereign who governed with their council was the same as the sovereign who summoned and met their Parliament. Although judicial independence was long established in England, justice was still carried out in the name of that sovereign, as well. Yet, just as the Imperial Crown came to be divided in the twentieth century, the sovereign authority of the Crown in Canada came to be parsed according to the separation of powers. Indeed, in a manner analogous to divisibility between the realms,[18] the sovereign Canadian Crown was adapted to the separation of powers through the idea of distinct capacities. The Crown in its executive capacity, acting on the advice of council, was distinguished from the Crown in its legislative capacity, fulfilling its parliamentary functions and acting on the advice of the houses. To paraphrase Lord Justice May: in matters of law, the executive Crown-in-Council is entirely independent and distinct from the legislative Crown-in-Parliament.

This adaption of the Crown to the separation of powers is seen in the Supreme Court's judgment in *Mikisew Cree First Nation*. As part of this ruling, the court considered whether the duty to consult First Nations under the honour of the Crown applied to the Crown-in-Parliament. A majority of the court found that the duty to consult First Nations belonged to the Crown in its executive capacity alone. Under the separation of powers, moreover, the majority held that the courts should not review whether the honour of the Crown had been respected as part of the legislative process. Justice Brown offered the strongest defence of this finding. He argued that the duty to consult binds ministers of the Crown in their executive capacity, not in their capacity as parliamentarians: "While Cabinet ministers are members of the executive, they participate in this process – for example by presenting a government bill – not in an executive capacity, but in a legislative capacity."[19] Under the separation of powers, Brown noted, the constitutional duty to consult First Nations must be "understood as excluding the parliamentary (and, indeed judicial) functions of the Canadian state."[20] This reinforced that the honour of the Crown does not attach itself to the Crown's legislative capacity.

Brown's findings, moreover, reinforced why common legal definitions of the Crown led to a category mistake in this instance. In an effort to simplify the Crown and sustain this late medieval concept in modern constitutional theory,

British jurisprudence had concluded that "the Crown" referred to either the sovereign or the government/executive. Canadian courts and constitutional scholars followed suit.[21] While treating the Crown as analogous to the executive was useful in most instances, it glossed over how the Crown's authority operates in the other branches of the state. This is arguably what led to the conceptual error in the appellants' case: positing that the Crown acting in Parliament was the Crown as the executive. As Brown clarified, "The Crown represents a collection of powers and privileges, and the term 'Crown' is primarily *but not exclusively* used to denote two aspects of the Canadian state: the Monarch and the executive."[22] When the Crown is more correctly understood as a locus of sovereign authority generally, then, "no activity of the state is independent of the Crown."[23] The Crown that acts in the Parliament is not the executive but one part of the legislature as a separate branch of the state.

Mikisew stands as one of the few postpatriation Supreme Court judgments that recognize the Crown's role as the sovereign authority and concept of the state. In questioning whether the honour of the Crown should apply to the Crown-in-Parliament, the Mikisew Cree pushed the court to provide a coherent explanation of what the Crown is in Canada and how it operates under the separation of powers. The Mikisew Cree's challenge elicited clarity about the nature of the Crown in Canada after patriation in a manner similar to how the Indian Association of Alberta compelled the English Court of Appeal to outline the distinction between the Queen of Canada and the Queen of the United Kingdom leading up to patriation. In both cases, courts highlighted the monarchical foundation of sovereignty and the state in Canada while adapting it to contemporary constitutional realities, but at the cost of Indigenous peoples' understanding of their treaty relationship with the Queen.

The Crown and the Charter

The requirement that new citizens swear allegiance to the Queen was the subject of repeated litigation following patriation. At issue in these cases was whether the statutory requirement to swear allegiance to the Queen infringed on Charter rights to freedom of expression, freedom of religion, and equality. This question was first brought before the courts by civil rights lawyer Charles Roach. His challenges failed in both Ontario and federal courts. The substance of the dismissals was that one part of the Constitution, the Charter, could not be used to challenge another, the monarchy.[24] As well, the requirement to swear allegiance to the "symbolic keystone" of the Constitution was effectively "pledging an acceptance of the whole of our Constitution and national life," which includes the right to call for constitutional change, including the abolition of the monarchy.[25] Operating in the background of the Roach cases were two interpretations of the oath, one that emphasized the sovereign's centrality in the Canadian constitution, and another that stressed the Queen's symbolic status.

These two interpretations would come to the fore in the findings of two Ontario courts in another challenge to the citizenship oath, *McAteer v Canada (Attorney General)*. The appellants in *McAteer* challenged the citizenship oath to the Queen on effectively the same grounds as Roach. The requirement that new citizens swear "true allegiance to Her Majesty Queen Elizabeth the Second, Queen of Canada, Her Heirs and Successors" was challenged as an infringement of their Charter rights. In his judgment, Justice Morgan of the Superior Court of Ontario provided a comprehensive review of the historical roots and functions of the Crown in the Canadian constitution. He noted that the monarch is the repository of sovereignty and that the "Crown sits at the sovereign apex of the legal and political system."[26] He further observed that the Crown as the executive power is distinct from the Crown-in-Parliament, and it is further acknowledged that while the Crown's ministers now control almost all royal powers, the sovereign does retain certain personal and reserve powers. Morgan next stressed that the sovereign is an institution of the state, not merely a natural person, and that the sovereign is the embodiment of the Crown. This became particularly important when Morgan addressed the applicants' argument that they should not be forced to swear "personal fidelity" to the monarch.[27] According to Morgan, the oath should not be understood as a reference to the Queen as a person but "as an equality-protecting Canadian institution."[28]

Although he found that the oath did impinge on the appellants' freedom of expression, Morgan noted that "[i]t would seem, however, that the Applicants' problem is not so much that they take the oath seriously. Rather their problem is that they take it literally."[29] This distinction was then used to deny that new citizens are being asked to swear allegiance to a wealthy British woman: "Not only is the Canadian sovereign not foreign, as alleged by the Applicants in identifying the Queen's British origin, but the sovereign has come to represent the antithesis of status privilege."[30] Because the Crown is the Canadian state and locus of sovereign authority, "the oath to the Queen is in fact an oath to a domestic institution that represents egalitarian governance and the rule of law." Finally, in summing up this part of the ruling, Morgan reinforced his effort to bridge the medieval and the modern: "The normative clash that forms the essence of [the applicants'] position is premised on a misunderstanding born of literalism. Once the Queen is understood, in context, as an equality-protecting Canadian institution rather than as an aristocratic English overlord, any impairment of the Applicants' freedom of expression is minimal."[31] As a result, the infringement on the appellants' freedom of expression was justifiable under section 1 of the Charter.

The Ontario Court of Appeal upheld the dismissal of the appellants' claim while further denying that the oath involved an impingement of their freedom of expression. In her ruling, Justice Weiler noted that "[t]he Constitution Act, 1982 completed the 'Canadianization' of the Crown."[32] Further, "As Canada has evolved, the symbolic meaning of the Queen in the oath has evolved."[33] Citing the former chief justice of the Supreme Court, Bora Laskin, she held that "[h]er Majesty has no personal physical preserve in Canada ... [O]nly the legal connotation, the abstraction that Her Majesty or the Crown represents, need be considered for the purposes of Canadian federalism."[34] Ascribing a personal meaning to "Her Majesty" or "the Crown" "is [an] anachronism."[35] Accordingly, Weiler found: "The oath to the Queen of Canada is an oath to our form of government, as symbolized by the Queen as the apex of our Canadian parliamentary system of constitutional monarchy."[36] Going one step further than Morgan, Weiler effectively cast the medieval as wholly symbolic and the modern as the sole matter of interpretive importance:

> Although the Queen is a person, in swearing allegiance to the Queen of Canada, the would-be citizen is swearing allegiance to a symbol of our form of government in Canada. This fact is reinforced by the oath's reference to "the Queen of Canada," instead of "the Queen." It is not an oath to a foreign sovereign. Similarly, in today's context, the reference in the oath to the Queen of Canada's "heirs and successors" is a reference to the continuity of our form of government extending into the future.[37]

Having established that the Queen is a symbol for Canada's system of government, Weiler then dismissed the claim that swearing the oath is a form of compelled speech: "[T]he oath promotes the unwritten constitutional principles of the rule of law and democracy, as well as the values for which this country stands ... Rather than undermining freedom of expression, the oath amounts to an affirmation of the societal values and constitutional architecture of this country, which promote and protect expression."[38]

A cursory glance would suggest that the Ontario Superior Court and Court of Appeal adopted the same reading of the meaning of "the Queen" in the oath. Both rulings emphasized the symbolism of the Queen and argued against the appellants' literal reading. Yet the subtle differences between the judgments point to differing understandings of the monarchy's relevance in the Canadian constitution. These divergences, in turn, informed their opposing interpretations of the citizenship oath as a form of compelled speech. Morgan emphasized the continuing reality of the Crown's centrality in the Constitution, including the sovereign's role as the personification of the state, whereas Weiler implied that Canada has a Potemkin monarchy. The degree to which the Queen had constitutional meaning – the degree to which Canada was interpreted as meaningfully monarchical – determined whether swearing allegiance to the sovereign affects one's freedom of expression. The more monarchical the Constitution was understood to be, the more tangible the tension between the Crown and the Charter, as the Law Reform Commission had warned.

The Crown and the Amending Formula

The second series of postpatriation Charter challenges directed at the monarchy dealt with the law of royal succession. In *O'Donohue v Canada,* the appellant argued that the exclusion of Roman Catholics from the line of succession to the throne, as per the provisions of the *Act of Settlement 1701,* violated the Charter's equality rights.[39] As part of his ruling in this case, Justice Rouleau of the Ontario Superior Court found that one part of the Constitution could not be used to challenge another. Rouleau also emphasized the centrality of the monarchy to the Canadian Constitution, going so far as to give the *Act of Settlement 1701* constitutional status in Canada. He further found that there was a constitutional requirement for Canada to have the same law of royal succession as the United Kingdom, according to what he termed a "symmetry" and "principle of union" between the British and Canadian monarchs. As Rouleau found: "These rules of succession, and the requirement that they be the same as those of Great Britain, are necessary to the proper functioning of our constitutional monarchy and, therefore, the rules are not subject to *Charter* scrutiny."[40]

While *O'Donohue* established that the law of royal succession could not be challenged on Charter grounds, the ruling raised several questions regarding what would be required to change the law of succession for Canada. Rouleau's finding that the *Act of Settlement 1701* formed part of the Canadian constitution suggested that Canada had its own law of royal succession. Yet the "principle of symmetry" between the Canadian and British Crowns articulated by Rouleau implied that Canada and the United Kingdom must have the same monarch and, hence, identical rules for determining who sits on their respective thrones. Rouleau held that the constitutional convention found in the preamble to the *Statute of Westminster 1931,* wherein the Dominions would assent to alterations to the laws of royal succession by the British Parliament, ensured that the "principle of symmetry" would be respected. Any Canadian attempt to break this symmetry, furthermore, would engage the unanimous amending formula, since it would "bring about a fundamental change in the office of the Queen."[41] Canada, therefore, was found to have a law of royal succession as part of its Constitution, but constitutional convention demanded that these laws be identical to those of the United Kingdom, and any deviation from this convention would require the unanimous agreement of the Senate, House of Commons, and provincial legislatures.

This mix of constitutional law, convention, and the amending formula suggested that the rules pertaining to royal succession were complex and contestable. Indeed, Rouleau's alchemic approach highlighted questions left unsettled by patriation: Did Canada have its own laws of royal succession, or was the identity of the Queen of Canada still determined by British law? And regardless of whether the laws of royal succession were Canadian or British, would changes to them touch on the office of the Queen under paragraph 41(a) of the *Constitution Act, 1982*? The answers to these questions would be provided a decade later in *Motard*.

At the 2011 Commonwealth Heads of Government in Perth, Australia, the First Ministers of the Queen's realms agreed to a British proposal to liberalize the laws of royal succession, notably ending male-preference primogeniture. Each realm would bring about these changes according to its own relevant legal and/or constitutional procedures. In the United Kingdom, this would involve legislating changes to its laws of royal succession. New Zealand and Australia also enacted changes to their laws, including the *Bill of Rights 1689* and *Act of Settlement 1701*, which had been explicitly recognized as part of their law when they became independent states in the 1980s.[42]

Canada opted for a different approach. Relying on the preamble to the *Statute of Westminster 1931*, Parliament hastily passed a law, the *Succession to the Throne Act, 2013*, which assented to the expected changes in British law. The Canadian act rested on the premise that Canada had no law of succession of its own; instead, following the "principle of symmetry," the Canadian act relied on the principle that whoever is sovereign of the United Kingdom is the sovereign of Canada. When the United Kingdom altered its law of succession, Canada's only responsibility was to express its assent.

Two law professors from Université Laval subsequently challenged Canada's *Succession to the Throne Act, 2013* in *Motard*, with the Quebec government as an intervenor. They held that Canada's approach was deficient in light of how the *Statute of Westminster 1931* had been applied during the abdication of Edward VIII and that changes to the succession to the throne necessitated a unanimous amendment, on the grounds that the rules regarding who holds the office of the Queen form part of the office. The federal government and intervenors who supported the Canadian legislation offered an alternative reading of the abdication and subsequent precedents.[43] They further emphasized that the "principle of symmetry" was part of the Canadian constitution as per section 9 and the preamble to the *Constitution Act, 1867*. Assenting to a change in the British laws of royal succession, moreover, did not require a constitutional amendment.

Both the Quebec Superior Court and Court of Appeal ruled in favour of the federal government.[44] They found that the sole rule governing the identity of the Canadian sovereign was the principle of symmetry. The Canadian government's request and consent that the British abdication act extended to Canada in 1936 did not imply that Canada had its own law of succession, nor did it establish a Canadian law of succession.[45] More consequentially, the courts further found that the rules determining who holds the office of the Queen do not form part of the office. While the courts might have found that the principle of symmetry fell under the office of the Queen, they opted for the more categorical position that the office only deals with the Queen's constitutional powers and functions.[46]

As Marie-France Fortin has argued, the finding that the monarchical office does not include matters of royal succession is consistent with the late medieval doctrine of the King's two bodies.[47] The courts' interpretation that the monarchical office is concerned with functions and powers is also consistent with previous rulings regarding the office of the lieutenant-governor in Ontario. However, this finding is at odds with what the Supreme Court found with respect to senatorial and judicial offices in the *Senate* and *Supreme Court* references.[48] From a historical perspective, moreover, it is difficult to conclude that the provincial premiers and monarchists who fought to preserve Canada's ties to the British monarchy did not intend for the "office of the Queen" to shield that connection under the unanimous amending formula. Assuming that the principle of symmetry was taken as a given during the patriation negotiations, it would appear rather unlikely that these premiers and monarchists thought that the connection between the British and Canadian Crowns could be severed under the general amending formula or by the federal Parliament alone. Yet, since the Supreme Court refused to hear *Motard*, the lower courts' interpretation stands.

O'Donohue and *Motard* were manifestations of the tension between the antiquated and the modern in Canadian public law, although the Law Reform Commission did not understand that tension in these terms. In an effort to balance the monarchical status quo with the Charter, while avoiding the political challenges associated with the amending formula, the federal government and the courts have revived an imperial understanding of the Crown in Canada. The Crown found in the *Constitution Act, 1867* is not the separate and distinct Queen of Canada, as the English Court of Appeal found in *Alberta Indians,* but the Queen of the United Kingdom. In the words of Justice Rancourt, writing for the Quebec Court of Appeal in *Motard:* "La Reine dont il est question dans la *Loi constitutionnelle de 1867* ne peut donc être que celle du Royaume-Uni."[49] It was necessary for the court to arrive at this conclusion in order to connect the principle of symmetry to the preamble to the *Constitution Act, 1867*. Absent this reading of the preamble, which is narrow in terms of how it understands the Crown but expansive in terms of how it understands "similar in principle," there would be no constitutional hook for the symmetry.[50] As Luke Beck has argued in comparing the Canadian and Australian approach to the law of royal succession: "The rule of symmetry has a major flaw. The analysis in both *O'Donohue* and *Motard* starts from the proposition that the constitutional preamble leads to the conclusion that there is a constitutional demand that the Canadian monarch be shared in common with the British monarch. Neither case gives detailed reasons for this conclusion."[51] To make up for this lack of detailed reasons, the courts have offered a simple one: although patriation made Canada a fully sovereign and independent state with no remaining constitutional ties to the United Kingdom, laws set by the British Parliament still determine who holds the office of the Queen for Canada. This was an interpretation that was rejected fifty years before patriation by the Canadians who negotiated the *Statute of Westminster 1931* and helped craft the preamble to that very act. Having British law automatically apply to Canada in this way was considered incompatible with Canadian autonomy.[52] Nearly one hundred years later, and forty years after Canada's complete independence and sovereignty,[53] Canadian courts have effectively re-embraced an application of British laws of royal succession to Canada by paramount force, but this time through a constitutional principle rather than imperial parliamentary sovereignty.

Conclusion

Of all the constitutional issues and challenges facing Canada, the meaning and status of "the Crown" are near the bottom of the list, if not dead last. The monarchy is increasingly irrelevant in a modern, liberal, and increasingly progressive Canada.[54] And yet the Crown remains central to the formal Canadian constitution, to the exercise of political power, and to the concept of the state. While Canadians may not care about the monarchy, the Crown continues to underpin the legal entity known as Canada. A degree of conceptual clarity and consistency about the Crown is, therefore, a goal worth pursuing.

Unfortunately, clarity and consistency about the Crown have been in short order since patriation. While commentators have long noted that the Crown is "a convenient cover for ignorance,"[55] the *Constitution Act, 1982* has exacerbated this tendency. As this chapter has argued, the Law Reform Commission's concern that the medieval Crown was at odds with modern Canadian public law was well founded. When the separation of powers is at issue, the Crown has proved adaptable, reflecting its divisibility and distinct capacities. Faced with Charter challenges and the amending formula, however, the courts have had to twist and contort their interpretations of "the Queen" and her office to avoid unpalpable outcomes or compromises. This has led to contradictory, if not incoherent, rulings regarding the Queen.

These inconsistencies of convivence are worth reiterating. In 1981, the Indian Association of Alberta was told that the Queen of Canada was "entirely independent and distinct" from the Queen of the United Kingdom. Similarly, in 2016, the appellants in *McAteer* were informed that they were not being asked to swear allegiance to a foreign monarch. Yet, in 2019, the Quebec Court of Appeal found that the Queen named in the *Constitution Act, 1867* can only be the Queen of the United Kingdom. Although the cases dealt with three separate issues, litigants may wonder why she is the Queen of Canada when treaty rights and the citizenship oath are in question but the Queen of the United Kingdom when the laws of royal succession are at issue. Relying on a subtle equivocation, they would likely be told that Canada merely takes the sovereign of the United Kingdom as the Canadian monarch according to a constitutional principle of symmetry, not that the Queen of Canada is the Queen of the United Kingdom.[56] But the litigants would still be justified in asking how this symmetry aligns with an entirely independent and distinct Queen of Canada and the finding that the "Constitution Act, 1982 completed the 'Canadianization' of the Crown."[57] They might be forgiven for concluding that the Queen and the Crown are either Canadian or British depending on which is the most politically expedient answer.[58]

Canadian monarchists, by contrast, have been comforted by the Queen's conceptual slipperiness. The courts' varying interpretations of her meaning and office have protected the monarchy from Charter challenges and the amending formula.[59] Defenders of the constitutional status quo can be satisfied for the same reasons; the courts have not allowed the Crown to be used as a vehicle to reopen the Constitution. What critics see as conceptual inconsistency and fuzziness can be defended as sensible pragmatism.[60] Yet this pragmatism is accompanied by a risk: the very trouble that the pragmatic approach is meant to avoid could be brought about by it.

In accepting the federal government's argument that there is a principle of symmetry that identifies the Canadian sovereign as the sovereign of the United Kingdom, but that this "rule of recognition" does not fall under the office of the Queen, courts in Quebec have left us with a constitutional puzzle. The puzzle is twofold. First, the principle of symmetry leaves unanswered the question of how Canada would identify the Queen, the personification of the state and sovereign authority, if the United Kingdom became a republic. It might be posited that Canada would simply continue to take as its sovereign the person who was previously the monarch of the United Kingdom, as well as their heirs and successors according to what was previously British law. Alternatively, the case might be made that Canada could leave the office of the Queen empty, since the governor general could exercise all monarchical powers under the Letters Patent, 1947. Both these solutions, however, border on the incredulous. The simpler answer seems to be that Canada is betting that the United Kingdom will never abandon the monarchy. As wagers go, this may be a good one, but it remains a gamble.

In the event that Canada loses this bet and is forced to establish procedures related to who can hold the office of the Queen, the second aspect of this puzzle would emerge: What mechanism could be used to set these new rules? *Motard* suggests that it would not be the unanimous amending formula. This would imply that the general amending formula would apply. Yet, in light of how changes to the royal succession were addressed in 2013, the federal government would have a strong case in arguing that Parliament could unilaterally legislate or amend the Constitution under section 44 of the *Constitution Act, 1982* to establish these procedures. Interestingly, however, this interpretation would mean that Parliament currently has the authority to unilaterally alter the identity of the monarch in Canada. Monarchists who cheered the rulings in *Motard* might be less enthusiastic if they considered what this could mean under a government committed to republicanism. Similarly, provincial governments may be surprised by the loss of their veto over who holds the highest office of the Canadian state.

In refusing to grant *Motard* leave, the Supreme Court has opted to leave this puzzle unsolved. It might be argued that this is politically and constitutionally wise. Simply put, unless the United Kingdom becomes a republic, there is no need to deal with this issue and the questions it would raise about the Queen's office. In this case, however, the Supreme Court's silence arguably reflects a regrettable disinterest and deflection. The substance of the changes to the royal succession assented to by Parliament in the *Succession to the Throne Act, 2013* were uncontroversial, while the challenge brought by the Université Laval professor was seen as an effort to give Quebec a constitutional bargaining chip.[61] The next time this question arises, however, the debate is likely to be livelier, particularly if the aim is to cut Canada's ties with the House of Windsor or deal with an unexpected British constitutional development. If and/or when this occurs, the puzzles left by *Motard* will need to be solved. At that point, the Supreme Court will hopefully clarify what steps need to be taken to patch or replace the old stone foundation holding up Canada's modern constitutional construct.

Notes

1 Law Reform Commission of Canada, *The Legal Status of the Federal Administration*, Working Paper 40 (Ottawa: LRCC, 1985).

2 *Reference re Senate Reform*, [2014] 1 SCR 704 [*Reference re Senate Reform*].

3 *Mikisew Cree First Nation v Canada (Governor General in Council),* [2018] 2 SCR 765 [*Mikisew*].
4 *McAteer v Canada (Attorney General),* 2013 ONSC 5895; 2014 ONCA 578.
5 *Motard v Procureur général du Canada,* 2019 QCCA 1826 [*Motard*].
6 For an introduction to these issues, see Myra J. Tait and Kiera L. Ladner, eds., *Surviving Canada: Indigenous Peoples Celebrate 150 Years of Betrayal* (Winnipeg: ARP, 2017).
7 For a discussion of the relationship between the Crown and the English concept of the state, see Martin Loughlin, "The State, the Crown and the Law," in *The Nature of the Crown: A Legal and Political Analysis,* ed. Maurice Sunkin and Sebastian Payne (Oxford: Oxford University Press, 1999), 33–76; Janet McLean, *Searching for the State in British Legal Thought* (Cambridge: Cambridge University Press, 2012).
8 Maurice Ollivier, *Problems of Canadian Sovereignty from the British North America Act, 1867 to the Statute of Westminster, 1931* (Toronto: Canada Law Book Company, 1945).
9 For an overview of constitutional thinking at this time, see Peter Oliver, *The Constitution of Independence: The Development of Constitutional Theory in Australia, Canada, and New Zealand* (Oxford: Oxford University Press, 2005), chaps 2–3.
10 Norman Hillmer and Philippe Lagassé, "Parliament Will Decide: An Interplay of Politics and Principle," *International Journal* 71, 2 (2016): 328–37.
11 Anne Twomey, "Royal Succession, Abdication, and Regency in the Realms," *Review of Constitutional Studies* 22, 1 (2017): 33–53.
12 Philippe Lagassé, "Royal Succession and the Constitutional Politics of the Canadian Crown, 1936–2013," *The Round Table: The Commonwealth Journal of International Affairs* 107, 4 (2018): 451–62.
13 House of Commons, Bill C-60, *An Act to amend the Constitution of Canada,* 3rd Sess, 30th Parl, 1977–78.
14 *Royal Style and Titles Act* [1952], RSC 1985, c R-12.
15 *The Queen v The Secretary of State for Foreign and Commonwealth Affairs, ex parte: The Indian Association of Alberta* (1981) 4 CNLR 86 [*Alberta Indians*].
16 For an early appreciation of this evolving constitutional order, see Philip Resnick, "Montesquieu Revisited, or the Mixed Constitution and the Separation of Powers in Canada," *Canadian Journal of Political Science* 20, 1 (1987): 97–115.
17 Dennis Baker, *Not Quite Supreme: The Courts and Coordinate Constitutional Interpretation* (Montreal/Kingston: McGill-Queen's University Press, 2010).
18 Anne Twomey, "Responsible Government and the Divisibility of the Crown," *Public Law* (Winter 2008): 742–67.
19 *Mikisew,* para 113.
20 *Ibid,* para 128.
21 See, for example, *Clyde River (Hamlet) v Petroleum Geo-Services Inc,* [2017] 1 SCR 1069, para 28.
22 *Mikisew,* para 128 (emphasis in original).
23 *Ibid.*
24 *Roach v Canada (Minister of State for Multiculturalism and Citizenship),* 1994 CanLII 3453 (FCA), [1994] 2 FC 406.
25 *Ibid,* per MacGuigan JA.
26 *McAteer et al v Attorney General of Canada,* 2013 ONSC 5895, para 16.
27 *Ibid,* para 42.
28 *Ibid,* para 68.
29 *Ibid,* para 59.
30 *Ibid,* para 63.
31 *Ibid,* para 68.

32 *McAteer v Canada (Attorney General)*, 2014 ONCA 578, para 47 [*McAtteer*].
33 *Ibid*, para 48.
34 *Ibid*, para 52.
35 *Ibid*.
36 *Ibid*.
37 *Ibid*, para 54.
38 *Ibid*, para 74.
39 *O'Donohue v Canada*, 2003 CanLII 41404 (Ont SC).
40 *Ibid*, para 37.
41 *Ibid*, para 30.
42 Australia, *Imperial Acts Application Act 1986*, A1986-93; New Zealand, *Imperial Laws Application Act 1988*, 1988 No 112.
43 For contrasting views on these questions and precedents, see the contributions by Mark D. Walters, Serge Joyal, Anne Twomey, Julien Fournier, Patrick Taillon, Geneviève Motard, and André Binette in Michel Bédard and Philippe Lagassé, eds., *The Crown and Parliament* (Montreal: Éditions Yvon Blais, 2015).
44 *Motard*.
45 *Ibid*, paras 78–89.
46 *Ibid*, paras 90–92.
47 Marie-France Fortin, "The King's Two Bodies and the Canadian Office of the Queen," *Review of Constitutional Studies* 20, 2 (2020–21): 117–44.
48 *Reference re Senate Reform; Reference re Supreme Court Act, ss. 5 and 6*, [2014] 1 SCR 433.
49 *Motard*, para 46.
50 It has been argued that s 2 ("The Provisions of this Act referring to Her Majesty the Queen extend also to the Heirs and Successors of Her Majesty, Kings and Queens of the United Kingdom of Great Britain and Ireland") of the *British North America Act, 1867*, which was repealed in 1893, provides evidence for the existence of the principle of symmetry found in the preamble. Aside from the fact that this section was repealed, its existance suggests that it, not the preamble, would have provided the constitutional hook for the principle of symmetry. That this section existed in fact undermines the argument that the preamble was meant to express this principle. Put differently, s 2 did what the preamble is now held to be doing, suggesting that the drafters did not intend for the preamble to be read this way. In *Sue v Hill*, moreover, the Australian High Court denied that a similar provision in the Australian constitution still referred to the Queen of the United Kingdom owing to the divisibility of the Crown, as found by the English Court of Appeal in *Alberta Indians*. See *Sue v Hill*, [1999] HCA 30, paras 47–94.
51 Luke Beck, "The Role of Religion in the Law of Royal Succession in Canada and Australia," *Queen's Law Journal* 43, 1 (2018): 73.
52 Lagassé, "Royal Succession and the Constitutional Politics of the Canadian Crown."
53 *Reference re Secession of Quebec*, [1998] 2 SCR 217, para 46.
54 "Canadians to Ottawa: In Hiring Next GG, Cut Pay, Review Job Description, Take Final Decision Out of PM's Hands," Angus Reid Institute, February 18, 2021.
55 F.W. Maitland, *The Constitutional History of England* (Cambridge: Cambridge University Press, 1908), 418.
56 For an argument that the Queen of Canada is, in fact, still the Queen of the United Kingdom, see Andrew Heard, "The Crown in Canada: Is There a Canadian Monarchy?," in *The Canadian Kingdom: 150 Years of Constitutional Monarchy*, ed. D. Michael Jackson (Toronto: Dundurn, 2018), 113–32.
57 *McAteer*, 2014, para 47.

58 For a defence of this politically expedient approach to the Crown, see David E. Smith, Christopher McCreery, and Jonathan Shanks, *Canada's Deep Crown: Beyond Elizabeth II, the Crown's Continuing Canadian Complexion* (Toronto: University of Toronto Press, 2022).

59 John Fraser, D. Michael Jackson, Serge Joyal, and Michael Valpy, "The Supreme Court Reaffirms the Canadian Crown's Importance to Our Country's Sense of Order," *Globe and Mail,* June 26, 2020.

60 Warren J. Newman, "The Succession to the Throne in Canada," in *Royal Progress: Canada's Monarchy in an Age of Disruption,* ed. D. Michael Jackson (Toronto: Dundurn, 2020), 127–52.

61 Fraser et al, "The Supreme Court Reaffirms."

26

The Urban Gap

Ran Hirschl

CANADIAN CITIES ARE often described as "the outcasts of Canadian federalism"[1] and "the forgotten stepchildren of both federal politics and scholarship."[2] Lacking any direct constitutional powers, cities and municipalities in Canada exist only as bodies of delegated provincial authority, entirely dependent on provincial legislation for their power and sources of revenue. Given that 85 percent of Canada's population lives in cities, and that over 50 percent of the nation's population is concentrated in six metro areas, some of which are among the most diverse cities in the world, it would be something of an understatement to say that the constitutional nonstatus of cities in twenty-first-century Canada – purportedly one of the world's leading constitutional democracies – reflects serious constitutional datedness and creates a major democracy deficit, possibly in violation of some of the country's major constitutional pillars, as defined by the Supreme Court of Canada in the *Quebec Secession Reference*.[3]

The near-complete silence of the Canadian constitution concerning cities is arguably one of the most critical gaps in contemporary Canadian government. The combination of a mid-nineteenth-century spatial governance structure established by the *Constitution Act, 1867* (in which cities are fully subjugated by a binary federal-provincial constitutional matrix) and a rigid amending procedure established by the *Constitution Act, 1982* (which renders formal constitutional transformation in this area nearly impossible) has created a constitutional deadlock. Naturally, political power holders at both the federal and provincial levels, whether due to the high costs of constitutional change in this area or because they are gaining from the status quo, lack a strong incentive to voluntarily delegate constitutional power and authority to cities. The outcome is the systemic underrepresentation of cities qua order of government and of city dwellers as equal members of the Canadian polity.

The constitutional datedness and stagnation with respect to cities further suggest that what is neutrally termed "cooperative federalism" or "intergovernmental relations" is essentially a form of "bargaining in the shadow of law" where critical power imbalances among the negotiating parties dictate the actual terms of engagement. It also highlights a stark gap between Canada's commitment to the values of political representation, equality, multiculturalism, and diversity, protected through a set of key Charter provisions and landmark Supreme Court rulings, and the reality of an urban nation whose main cities are home to the vast majority of new immigrants and first-generation Canadians and feature extraordinary levels of what sociologists term "super diversity" (48 percent of Toronto's population and 41 percent of Vancouver's population are first-generation Canadians – the world's first and third most diverse cities, respectively).[4] While the *Constitution Act, 1982* may not be blamed for originating these systemic deficiencies, it has failed to address or even to acknowledge the urban challenge and in some key respects has further exacerbated it.

In this chapter, I examine three aspects of the urban gap in Canada's constitutional architecture: (1) the pertinent constitutional terrain and its demonstrable city-related deficiencies; (2) the jurisprudential front – how Canadian courts have interpreted the constitutional (non)status of cities; and (3) avenues for potential reform in this area beyond the direct constitutionalization of city status or transformative judicial interpretation, both of which have proven rather futile in bringing about the meaningful advancement of the constitutional standing of Canadian cities.

Mapping the Pertinent Constitutional Terrain

The Constitution Act, 1867 established the constitutional (and, by extension, political) landscape for the current relationship between federal and provincial governments and municipalities. In that mid-nineteenth-century document, cities are virtually nonexistent, with no residual authority of their own. Section 91 of the *Constitution Act, 1867* lists the main legislative areas reserved for the federal government, while section 92 sets out the legislative areas reserved for the provincial governments. There are two key provisions in section 92: section 92(8), which gives the provinces exclusive control over municipalities, and section 92(16), which gives the provinces authority over all matters of a local or private nature. Other provincial powers include jurisdiction over "hospitals, asylums, charities, and eleemosynary institutions" (s. 92(7)) as well as "shop, saloon, tavern and auctioneer licenses" (s. 92(9)). In this reckoning, "municipal institutions" – conceived some 155 years ago, when Toronto's population was fewer than 50,000 and what is now Vancouver was nothing more than a small sawmill station with a couple of hundred residents – are creatures of provincial governments, controlled exclusively by provincial authority.

Initially, most provinces (with the exceptions of Nova Scotia and Prince Edward Island) enacted pan-municipal legislation that provided municipalities with a general statutory framework. Each of these acts outlined the varying levels of political authority, autonomy, and fiscal capacity that each province gave to its municipalities. These general municipal acts were traditionally treated as "laundry-list" legislation, granting municipalities only those powers that the provinces explicitly spelled out. In other words, as creatures of statute, cities could only make laws to the extent that their enabling statutes permitted them to do so. With no concept of home rule in Canadian constitutional discourse, this approach is commonly seen as a legacy of the American Dillon's Rule.[5] The provinces continued to carry full responsibility for land-use planning and enjoy full autonomy to create their own framework legislation to structure their land planning systems.[6] The federal government could also affect land-use planning at the provincial and municipal levels through the financial support of targeted projects, such as urban development and infrastructure programs. Lacking even minimal legislative powers and funding sources, Canadian cities' autonomous voice in this constitutional matrix has been very limited.

Gradually trending away from the legacy of Dillon's Rule, most provinces have, over the past twenty-five years, introduced new or extensively reformed municipal frameworks that have expanded the autonomy and scope of municipal powers.[7] In general, provinces have extended city powers through the introduction of new statutes for cities (e.g., Saskatchewan's *Cities Act,* 2002); through the broad expansion of powers for all municipalities within the province (e.g., Alberta); and through the use of so-called charters tailored specifically to selected cities (e.g., Vancouver, Winnipeg, Montreal) or similarly enabling provincial legislation (e.g., *The City of Toronto Act,* 2006).[8] But while the provinces' reforms have responded to the need for more flexible governance structures in Canada's larger cities, they have done so without giving away any "final-word" authority.[9] In fact, few countries in the world have witnessed Canada's level of resistance by senior levels of government to loosening restraints and regulations on cities.[10]

The actual effect of the *City of Toronto Act,* to pick one prime example of supposed city empowerment, on city power has been modest, at best. In fact, by the end of 2006, many of the special privileges that had been carved out for Toronto, such as the authority to delegate decision-making power to smaller community councils, had also been afforded to other Ontario municipalities through ongoing reforms to the province's general municipal legislation.[11] Empirical measures of city autonomy across Canada further suggest that, while there is some variance among provinces in terms of city political status, very limited fiscal autonomy is awarded to any Canadian city. Toronto's situation in this regard is similar to that of far smaller cities such as Saskatoon (population 250,000, largest city in Saskatchewan) or Saint John (population under 100,000, largest city in New Brunswick).[12] Comparative studies of city fiscal autonomy suggest that, with the exception of London (United Kingdom), Toronto stands out as the world city most limited in its taxation powers.[13]

Several cities, notably Montreal, Winnipeg, and Vancouver, enjoy what is known as "charter city" status – essentially an agreement between a given city and its provincial government to grant that city enhanced control over its own affairs, including fiscal affairs. Such specifically tailored status differentiates that city from other municipalities in the same provincial jurisdiction and is aimed to provide it with flexibility in terms of reform, spending responsibilities, and access to revenue. Although such city charters have been used throughout Canada's history, and extensively in Quebec, the modern city charter has generally been used in response to the unique administrative responsibilities and challenges that face large Canadian cities.[14] However, the impact in practice, particularly with respect to revenue generation, has been considerably more modest.[15] What is more, as Andrew Sancton observes, such city charters are considered ordinary pieces of provincial legislation without special constitutional significance and are, therefore, not protected from provincial amendment or repeal, like all legislation relating to municipal powers in Canada.[16] It is generally agreed that, although there are no immediate negative effects to a large city by its designation as a charter city, a charter does not offer more than modest positive effects in the form of concrete powers of revenue generation. These benefits vary depending on the political culture of each province. For example, the Province of British Columbia has historically been hesitant to exercise direct authority over municipalities, while the Ontario government does not tend to show the same restraint.[17]

To help mitigate these variances, federal governments, driven by changing ideational preferences and strategic electoral considerations, have occasionally committed themselves to urban renewal through multilevel funding schemes, often focusing on infrastructure projects and social-inclusion initiatives, thus making big cities the obvious benefactors of such joint funding schemes. However, none of these programs involves even a rudimentary plan, let alone a fully developed one, for constitutional renewal that would transfer meaningful legislative, tax collection, or policy-making prerogatives to cities. Provincial governments, often with the tacit or explicit support of the federal government, continue to exclusively call the shots, constitutionally speaking. Meanwhile, recent data indicate that for every household tax dollar paid to Canada, Canadian cities collect ten cents (Ontario municipalities, including Toronto, collect only nine cents).[18]

Moreover, the same constitutional order creates dense electoral districts (ridings) in several major urban centres alongside sparsely populated ones in largely rural areas. The result is a blatant departure from the "one person, one vote" principle, to the detriment of voters in urban centres, particularly underrepresented minorities who congregate in cities. In the *Saskatchewan Reference* ruling (1991) – arguably one the most politically consequential decisions of the Supreme Court of Canada (SCC) in the last few decades – the Supreme Court of Canada considered the validity of Saskatchewan's *Representation Act, 1989,* which established provincial ridings with variances in population across constituencies, each riding containing a population within 25 percent of the provincial quotient (see Small, Chapter 8 in this volume).[19] While the court's decision in the *Saskatchewan Reference* has drawn considerable criticism (some scholars have referred to the ruling as one "of the most unfortunate episodes in Canada's legal history" or as "antiquated and highly problematic"),[20] it has been closely adhered to in lower court rulings concerning challenges, mostly based on the *Charter of Rights and Freedoms'* section 3 (democratic rights) and section 15(1) (equality rights), to the ±25 percent of the average rule in drawing electoral boundaries.[21]

The dilution of the urban vote in Canada following the *Saskatchewan Reference* decision has been significant. Even within Ontario, federal electoral districts vary in population from fewer than 60,000 (e.g., rural Kenora, in northwest Ontario) to over 100,000 (e.g., Toronto-Danforth, in the heart of Toronto) per riding. In some cases, the population rises to over 110,000 per riding, such as in Brampton, Markham, Richmond Hill, or Thornhill, neighborhoods that are home to extensive first-generation Canadian citizen populations. And these stark differences do not reflect the concentration of nonvoting, yet-to-naturalize immigrant populations in major urban centres, an issue that further exacerbates the relative underrepresentation of ridings in big cities.[22] The unfortunate outcome has been a chronic underrepresentation of major urban centres in key national decision-making forums.[23] As Michael Pal and Sujit Choudhry point out, it is rather ironic that a systemic constitutional underrepresentation of Canadian urban centres with large minority populations hinges, at least in part, on the *Saskatchewan Reference*'s rationale of community interest and minority protection as justifying large variances across electoral districts.[24] They further argue that minority groups in urban centres continue to suffer from vote dilution and that such underrepresentation runs counter to the "effective representation" standard and may, therefore, infringe section 3 even under the *Saskatchewan Reference.*[25]

The entrenched malapportionment of urban voters is further exacerbated by the spatial dimension of political preferences. As Jonathan Rodden has shown, in multidistrict, single-member first-past-the-post electoral systems (e.g., in the United States, United Kingdom, Canada, Australia, India, and elsewhere), urban centres tend to be underrepresented compared to rural areas, mainly because of the historical concentration of left-leaning voters in cities and the aggregative wide margin of progressive candidate wins in urban electoral districts compared to more moderate right-leaning candidate wins in rural districts.[26]

To add to the constitutional datedness and systemic city underrepresentation, the federal and provincial governments lack strong incentives to reshuffle the pertinent constitutional cards. Such a reshuffling would result in a major loss of their respective revenue and planning control; most importantly, it would not result in any immediate political gain for either of the major parties. Predictably, a pre-election commitment by Justin Trudeau and the Liberal Party in 2015 to revise the electoral system in order to veer closer to a fully democratic "one person, one vote" principle was abandoned by the Trudeau government in early 2017, citing "lack of consensus on the matter."

Material to the stalemate and contributing to the lack of political incentive to transform the constitutional status of cities is, of course, Canada's rigid constitutional amending formula adopted by the *Constitution Act, 1982*. In fact, comparative constitutional law scholars note that Canada's constitution is among the most difficult to change via formal constitutional amendment and is quite likely even harder to amend than the US Constitution – commonly considered one of the world's most difficult democratic constitutions to change by formal amendment (see Albert, Chapter 23 in this volume).[27] Consequently, the costs and risks associated with advancing a key constitutional amendment even under the so-called 7/50 rule institutionalized in section 38 of the *Constitution Act, 1982*, let alone under the unanimous-support rule enshrined in section 41, are simply way too high for any prudent political power holder to consistently commit to. In other words, a combination of a dated pre-urbanization constitutional order established by the *Constitution Act, 1867*, an amendment formula introduced by the *Constitution Act, 1982*, and the political power imbalance and incentive structure this combination creates render a formal constitutional transformation in the status of Canadian cities highly unlikely.

The Jurisprudential Angle: The 2018 Toronto City Council Slashing as an Illustrative Case

Ontario's capital city, Toronto, is Canada's largest metro area and the fourth-largest city in North America (after Mexico City, Los Angeles, and New York) and consistently ranked among the world's top financial centres.[28] Metropolitan Toronto's population has passed 7 million with a growth rate of approximately 18 percent over the last decade – nearly double that of Canada or Ontario. The City of Toronto itself, home to more than 3 million people, has far more people than five of Canada's provinces. Nonetheless, the city has none of the constitutional or self-government prerogatives that the provinces possess. It is estimated that every second immigrant to Canada settles in the Greater Toronto Area; consequently, over 48 percent of the city's population is foreign-born.[29] On a practical level, given its size and unique demographic composition, the city carries much of the day-to-day brunt and responsibility of sustaining viable multiculturalism in the public sphere.

And yet, exclusive provincial control over the city remains intact. It explicitly manifested itself in 2018, when newly elected Ontario premier Doug Ford (Progressive Conservative Party), a former city councillor and brother of the former Toronto mayor, Rob Ford, introduced legislation to reduce the number of city councillors at Toronto's City Hall from forty-seven to twenty-five.[30] Arguing that "big government" ought to be slashed – and citing chronic inefficiency in city council and the need to expedite municipal decision making concerning housing, infrastructure, and transit – Ford suggested that city electoral wards should be aligned with the twenty-five federal and twenty-five provincial electoral ridings. To that end, in August 2018, the Ontario government adopted Bill 5, the *Better Local Government Act, 2018*.[31] When a judge of the Ontario Superior Court of Justice issued a stern ruling that such a change amid a looming municipal election (October 2018) would violate the Charter's free-expression guarantee,[32] Premier Ford threatened to invoke the Charter's override clause, also called the "notwithstanding clause" (section 33). This clause, which had never been used before in Ontario, permits federal and provincial legislation to operate (for up to five years) notwithstanding its apparent violation of certain Charter rights.[33] It is worth noting that, of all possible policy areas and the many thousands of contested provincial and municipal decisions made since 1982 (the year the Charter was adopted), the first time the Province of Ontario threatened to invoke the notwithstanding clause, it did so to keep Canada's largest city in line.

As expected, the province appealed the single judge ruling by the Ontario Superior Court of Justice. A three-member panel of the Ontario Court of Appeal unanimously stayed the Ontario Superior Court's initial ruling on the matter.[34] The provincial government gave an undertaking that it would not invoke the override clause if a stay were granted, which did not affect the decision.[35] The court suggested that the judge "stretch[ed] both the wording and the purpose of s. 2(b) beyond the limits of that provision."[36] Noting that the Charter guaranteed the right to vote and to stand for office only with respect to federal and provincial elections, the court indicated that any disruption to the municipal election did not infringe voters' or candidates' democratic or free-expression rights.[37] Though only an interlocutory decision, it signalled that "the judgment under appeal was probably wrongly decided."[38] Following the decision, Premier Ford expressed his sense of vindication, while the city has continued to litigate the appeal on the merits.[39]

Eventually, a five-member panel of the Ontario Court of Appeal released its final ruling on the matter in September 2019. In a three-to-two decision, it dismissed the City of Toronto's claims, reaffirming the ultimate constitutional nonexistence of Canadian cities through their complete subjugation to provincial legislation. The majority opinion did not mince words in stating that the City of Toronto's position was unsubstantiated given that the Toronto City Council "is a creature of provincial legislation. Provincial legislation governs everything from its composition to the scope of its jurisdiction."[40] The majority opinion went on to determine that although the city's main argument is framed as a matter of protecting freedom of expression in the context of a municipal election,

> in reality the applicants' complaint concerns the timing of the legislature's decision to change the composition of City Council – a change that is undeniably within the legitimate authority of the legislature ... [A]dditional arguments raised by the City of Toronto and supporting interveners – drawing on unwritten constitutional principles and jurisdictional limits inherent in the division of powers – are similarly erroneous and unsupported by constitutional jurisprudence. In short, the Act [to change the structure of the city's highest elected body in the midst of an election] is constitutional, and the appeal must be allowed.[41]

Perhaps most importantly, in its address of Toronto's claim that unwritten constitutional principles may inform the framework established by section 92(8) of the *Constitution Act, 1867,* the majority opinion serves as a blatant "exhibit A"–like illustration of the nonstatus of Canadian cities:

> Courts have sometimes used unwritten constitutional principles to fill "gaps" in the Constitution ... No such gap exists here ... [T]his is not the case of constitutional framers having not addressed a social or technical development – like aeronautics or nuclear energy – because they simply could not have seen it coming. Municipal institutions, including municipal governing bodies, long pre-dated 1867 ... [T]he decision was made not to constitutionalize these institutions, but rather to put them under the jurisdiction of provincial legislatures.[42]

And to finish with a rhetorical exclamation mark, the court concluded that "there is no open question of constitutional interpretation here. Municipal institutions lack constitutional status."[43] The proper route to change that, the court stated, is via constitutional amendment, not judicial interpretation. As we have seen, however, the amendment route is, for all practical purposes, nonusable in this context.

The final chapter of the City of Toronto versus Ontario saga was written in October 2021. In a high-profile decision split five to four, the Supreme Court dismissed an appeal by the City of Toronto.[44] With respect to freedom of expression (i.e., whether section 2(b) of the Charter protects the expression of electoral participants from substantial mid-election changes), the majority held that because section 2(b) mostly imposes negative (or non-interference) obligations on the government, the relevant test (*Baier*) is whether the effect or purpose of a failure to provide a platform for expression amounts to effectively precluding the expression. In this case, expression was not effectively precluded because there was still time for all candidates to re-orient their campaigns. According to the dissenting opinion, changing the ward structure during a campaign destabilized the electoral process and undermined the ability of candidates to express and communicate with voters, thereby infringing upon freedom of expression. Moreover, the infringement is not justified under section 1 because the province has not given any reason as to why it decided to introduce the change in the middle of an election period.

With respect to the key question of whether municipal electors who are given a vote in a democratic election are entitled to effective representation as granted in section 3 of the Charter, the court held that section 3 makes clear that its protections only apply to federal and provincial elections. Even if these protections were to apply to municipal elections, the court held effective representation is mostly concerned with voter parity, which in this case is not violated merely because the wards have been made bigger.

On the question of the status of constitutional conventions – a possible avenue for change in city status given the reality of the rigid constitutional framework – the majority held that unwritten constitutional principles (e.g., democracy and the rule of law) may not be drawn upon to invalidate legislation, but merely to provide context and meaning to express constitutional protections. According to the dissenting opinion, by contrast, unwritten constitutional principles are of foundational importance, ought to have full legal force, and may be drawn upon to invalidate legislation even if the legislation complied with all express constitutional provisions. And so, in the end, the most high-profile case involving city status in twenty-first-century Canada revolved predominantly around freedom of expression Charter rights and had little to offer to advocates of enhanced city status, neither by way of the ruling's conceptual jurisprudential framework nor by its concrete outcome.

As reflected in both the Ontario Court of Appeal's dissenting opinion and in the Supreme Court's dissenting opinion, other constitutional jurisprudence has embraced a more "permissive yet restrictive" approach than that characterizing the relationship between Ontario and Toronto. In a long string of rulings stretching back to the late 1930s and continuing until the mid-1990s, Canadian courts have interpreted section 92(8) as giving broad powers to provincial legislatures to regulate and control "municipal institutions," including the power to restructure, amalgamate, or abolish municipalities.[45] However, since the 1990s, there has been some movement towards recognizing broader and more flexible city authority in both the legislative and judicial spheres. The 1994 Supreme Court ruling in *Shell Canada Products Ltd v Vancouver (City)* exhibited a shift from the old limited approach to municipal authority.[46] In that case, the Council of the City of Vancouver passed two resolutions that prevented the city from doing business with Shell Canada and declared Vancouver a "Shell-free" zone until Shell Canada stopped conducting business in apartheid South Africa.[47] Justice McLachlin (as she then was), in what has become an authoritative dissent, warned against "confining modern municipalities in the straitjackets of tradition" and asserted that "[i]f municipalities are to be able to respond to the needs and wishes of their citizens, they must be given broad jurisdiction to make local decisions reflecting local values."[48] Here, McLachlin rejected the majority's decision, which held that the resolution was *ultra vires* as it was not expressly or implicitly authorized by Vancouver's enabling statute and was unrelated to the purposes of the statute, having no identifiable benefit to the citizens of Vancouver.[49] McLachlin's approach has come to play an important role in establishing a more open-minded approach to judicial interpretation of municipal powers. Of course, this approach still bases a municipality's power exclusively on provincial legislation. However, a more generous interpretation of this legislation means that cities are able to wield a more robust set of powers. We may view this approach as a judge-made way of responding to the limited constitutional status of municipalities while maintaining provincial legislative supremacy. By 2000, the Supreme Court and several provincial courts had adopted McLachlin's broad and purposive approach to interpreting provincial enabling statutes for municipalities.[50]

Another move towards promoting municipal autonomy may be seen in the Supreme Court's 2001 ruling in *Spray-Tech v Hudson (Ville)*, one of Canada's leading cases on the limits of municipal autonomy.[51] Here, the court endorsed a collaborative tri-level regime for the regulation of pesticides.[52] Bylaws that regulate areas of shared jurisdiction are valid so long as they do not conflict with federal or provincial legislation. According to the court, the "mere existence of provincial (or federal) legislation in a given field ... [does not necessarily] oust municipal prerogatives to regulate the subject matter."[53] As the "environment" is not a subject of legislation under the *Constitution Act, 1867,* the matter is a subject of bi-jurisdictional responsibility.[54] Since the municipal regulations under scrutiny were stricter than both the federal and provincial ones, the court held that, despite the existence of federal and provincial legislation concerning pesticides, the City of Hudson's bylaw regulating the use of pesticides within its territory under the "general-welfare" provision of its enabling statute, the *Cities and Towns Act,* was valid. However, in his concurring opinion, Justice LeBel was clear in noting that no real terrain change in municipal government is to be assumed: "A tradition of strong local government has become an important part of the Canadian democratic experience. This level of government usually appears more attuned to the immediate needs and concerns of the citizens. Nevertheless, in the Canadian legal order, as stated on a number of occasions, municipalities remain creatures of provincial legislatures."[55]

Despite some modest jurisprudential moves towards recognizing enhanced municipal autonomy as an important policy objective, Canadian courts remain cautious to ensure that bylaws do not exceed the proper scope of municipal authority. The courts apply the federalism doctrines of federal paramountcy, "pith and substance," and "interjurisdictional immunity" to ensure that municipalities do not exceed the powers granted to them by their enacting statutes. In order to prevent municipalities from circumventing the limits of their delegated power, courts have often found municipal bylaws *ultra vires* on the grounds that their pith and substance encroaches on exclusive federal power.[56]

In summary, Canadian cities, among the most diverse in North America and the world, remain constitutionally powerless and are subject to a pre-megacity constitutional framework adopted in the mid-nineteenth century. Since the 1990s, there has been a modest move in both the jurisprudential and the provincial legislative arenas towards granting municipalities more power, all while maintaining provincial constitutional supremacy (and the corresponding federal constitutional silence) with respect to cities.

Avenues for Potential Reform?

The discussion thus far has explicated the systemic constitutional underrepresentation of Canadian cities created by the *Constitution Act, 1867* and maintained over the last 155 years and highlighted the rather slim prospects for altering that situation through formal constitutional change, given the rigid amending formula enshrined by the *Constitution Act, 1982.* As we have seen, the jurisprudential record has been (relatively) less hostile to cities, but it, too, has been bound by the formal confines of the Canadian constitution. Given that the two main avenues for transformation – constitutional amendment and innovative jurisprudence – have proven limited (at best) in bringing about transformation in city status, what other avenues may hold some promise in this area?

One possibility raised by scholars of local government in Canada is to rely on identifiable long-standing principles in Canadian constitutional practice to advance city power even if these principles are not formally entrenched.[57] Such principles include the much-discussed "living tree" interpretive doctrine, provincial constitutionalism as complementary to the federal Constitution, provincial human-rights codes that may be drawn on to enhance city status, or "manner and form" provisions (self-imposed procedural limitations on future legislation such as referendum or super-majority requirements) that provinces could legislate to assign some elevated status to an empowering municipal act or city charter.

Despite its modest impact on de facto city autonomy in either Canada or the United States, some advocates of city power continue to support the city charters idea. In its ideal type, as described recently by John Sewell, once the province and the city agree on the powers and other arrangements to be included in a city charter deal, provincial legislation is passed and ratified by the city by majority resolution, after which "the province and city would then jointly request of the federal government an amendment under section 43 of the Canadian Constitution, often called a 'single province' or 'bilateral' amendment."[58] At minimum, Sewell suggests, such an amendment would

> set out the requirement that any future changes to the City Charter would require the consent of the city. It might also outline the procedure by which other cities could achieve a City Charter. Finding the province and city in agreement, and assuming public support for the idea, the federal government would place the amendment before the House of Commons. If passed by a majority vote, the amendment would then go to the Senate for ratification.[59]

A closely related idea is to draw on the notion of subsidiarity in arguing for the devolution of power to cities. While the concept of subsidiarity is not entrenched in the Canadian constitutional order, and so its status as an operative principle in Canadian federalism remains unclear, the Supreme Court of Canada refers to it occasionally, notably in cases involving urban governance.[60] In its decision in *Spray-Tech* (2001) – discussed earlier in this chapter – the Supreme Court of Canada defined the principle of subsidiarity as "the proposition that law-making and implementation are often best achieved at a level of government that is not only effective, but also closest to the citizens affected and thus most responsive to their needs, to local distinctiveness, and to population diversity."[61] This definition of subsidiarity incorporates the rationales of effectiveness in governance, geographical proximity and democratic accountability, flexibility and responsiveness, and diversity. When combined with the ideals of democratic stakeholding or the all-affected principle (essentially, representation in policy-making processes ought to proportionally reflect those affected by these processes), with Canadian cities' uniquely diverse demographic composition, and possibly also with other pertinent concepts that seem at least worth considering in this context, such as the federal "duty to consult" with Indigenous communities before actions are taken that affect the interests of such communities, it does not require a major leap of imagination to envisage a subsidiarity-based argument for enhanced city power.

Another idea to consider here is a creative application of the notion of community standards – essentially entailing contextualized, locality-specific criteria for applying constitutional principles in certain contested areas. Per minimum, it may prove helpful in alleviating the one-rule-fits-all imposition of values, worldviews, and policy preferences on either side of the urban-rural divide. The community-standards doctrine was first introduced in the United States in the context of obscenity jurisprudence. In his opinion in *Miller v California* (1973), Chief Justice Burger captured the essence of its rationale in stating that "it is neither realistic nor constitutionally sound to read the First Amendment as requiring that the people of Maine or Mississippi accept public depiction of conduct found tolerable in Las Vegas, or New York." "People in different States vary in their tastes and attitudes," he continued, "and this diversity is not to be strangled by the absolutism of imposed uniformity."[62] A similar rationale has also guided, in various ways, constitutional jurisprudence in other common law countries, from the United Kingdom to Australia to Canada (e.g., *R v Butler*, 1992).[63] While not drawing an explicit comparison to the community-standards doctrine, David Barron has further suggested that deference to municipal constitutional interpretation may be informed by the similar principles of localism and geographic variation. Here, "a city should be entitled to assert its status as an independent, democratic polity that is capable of, and interested in, interpreting the state constitution or the Federal Constitution to enforce limits on central power."[64] In doing so, cities would provide a "special constitutional insight."[65] Overall, Barron argues, "[A] city's authority to engage in constitutional review would be expanded, but it would not be unlimited"; the city would be limited to its jurisdictional boundaries in questioning the enforcement of state law on constitutional grounds.[66]

Related to this line of thought are ideas concerning city-based political identity and solidarity as complementing the nation-state as the primary framework for collective identity. Such ideas have taken the form of Daniel Bell and Avner de Shalit's argument concerning some cities having their own defining ethos or values;[67] of Warren Magnusson's argument concerning the possibility of "seeing like a city" as an alternative to the hegemonic, statist "seeing like a state" notion;[68] or Loren King's intriguing argument that cities may well qualify as the main source of identification by their residents and as "imagined communities" characterized by dense spatial integration and considerable interdependence among their residents.[69] If cities do "inspire durable loyalty," King argues, then they could be viable candidates "for recognized membership as distinct parties to a federal union."[70]

Attempts to legally materialize such abstract notions of city-based collective identity have seldom taken root in Canada. One noteworthy exception, its limited practical implications notwithstanding, is the *Montréal Charter of Rights and Responsibilities (MCRR)*, which commits the city to work with its inhabitants to build a framework for citizens' rights and reciprocal responsibilities in the city. It promotes values such as a sustained struggle against poverty and discrimination and respect for justice and equity, and it commits to transparent management of municipal affairs based on citizen involvement and to building trust in democratic organizations. As the first of its kind on a city level, the charter has received much international attention, including recognition at the 2006 UN-Habitat World Forum III for its focus on inclusion, urban policies, and local democracy. In 2012, the *MCRR* was revised through public consultation in accordance with a provision of the charter that provides for periodic evaluation to make improvements. In this revision, new city commitments were added, further expanding the city's commitment to the values of democracy, environmental protection, and sustainable development.

Its groundbreaking vision notwithstanding, the concrete legal stature of the *MCRR* remains limited, being a mere municipal bylaw. The *MCRR* is binding on all Ville de Montréal elected officials, managers, and employees, including those working for boroughs or paramunicipal or city-controlled corporations. The commitments therein are also binding on any person or organization performing duties on behalf of the city. However, section 86.1 of the *MCRR* provides that the *MCRR* "may not serve as the basis for a judicial or jurisdictional remedy nor ... be cited in judicial or jurisdictional proceedings." Consequently, the only available recourse to ensure compliance with the *MCRR* is with the Ombudsman de Montréal. While the *MCRR* allows the ombudsman to intervene and investigate decisions that were voted on by City Council, the Executive Committee, or a borough council, the external *constitutional* capacity of the *MCRR* or of the Ombudsman de Montréal to enforce resolutions is narrow at best.

A different avenue of potential change is electoral reform. As we have seen, city underrepresentation in Canada is not merely the byproduct of a city's nonstatus in Canada's dated yet rigid constitutional framework; it also stems from a combination of demographic trends and deficiencies in Canada's federal electoral system leading to dilution of urban voters' voice. Post-1982 constitutional jurisprudence repeatedly emphasizes the centrality of democracy to Canada's identity and the significance of political rights protected by section 3 of the Charter, including the right to effective representation and the right to meaningful participation in the electoral process. Accordingly, the question of federal electoral reform, and what avenue of constitutional amendment it ought to follow, has been the subject of lively debate among politicians, media pundits, and scholars alike.[71]

Various proposals for electoral reform have been put forward over the past two decades, mainly at the provincial level. For the purposes of this discussion, an intriguing idea in the city context is an electoral system termed "rural-urban proportional representation" (RUP). In a RUP system, advanced by the think tank Fair Vote Canada, proportional representation exists across the map, but this representation is structured differently in urban areas than in rural areas.[72] Urban ridings have multiple seats per riding, with the number of seats proportionate to the riding's population. Rural ridings have only one member per riding. Because these rural, single-member ridings do not provide proportional representation, rural voters are additionally represented by "top-up" seats, allocated proportionally to top up the representation of rural, nonplurality voters. (Top-up or adjustment seats are common in northern European electoral systems, notably in Sweden, Denmark, and Iceland, as a means to address spatial underrepresentation, whether urban or rural.) Thus, RUP aims to respond directly to the political implications of urban agglomeration, distinguishing between the needs of cities and those of rural areas and attempting to accommodate the diversity of political perspectives in dense urban areas. Importantly, it does so without compromising the representation of rural voters.

Conclusion

The urban gap is one of the most burning challenges in contemporary Canadian government. At the fortieth anniversary of Canada's most recent constitutional overhaul, the time has come to reconsider the constitutional nonstatus of Canadian cities. Fresh thinking on Canada's urban gap by constitutional scholars, jurists, and policy makers is the call of the hour.

In the meantime, a Victorian constitutional framework adopted over 150 years ago, when less than 15 percent of Canada's population at the time resided in cities, continues to govern one of the most urbanized countries in the world.[73] A formal change in the constitutional status of cities is rendered near impossible due to a rigid amendment procedure enshrined in the *Constitution Act, 1982* and the strong disincentive it creates for federal or provincial political power holders to constitutionally emancipate cities. The urban gap is further deepened by the ever-intensifying pressure on Canadian cities – among the most diverse in the world – to deliver core public services, advance the constitutional values protected by the Charter, and carry the brunt of on-the-ground social integration and multicultural accommodation. As the prospects for formal constitutional enhancement of city status appear slim, and as Canadian courts have been, by and large, reluctant to generously interpret city powers absent a formal change in this area, the focus shifts to alternative avenues, ranging from city charters to electoral reform to bolstered cooperative federalism in the shadow of constitutionally entrenched power imbalances between cities, provinces, and the federal government.

Notes

Parts of this chapter draw on ideas I developed in Ran Hirschl, *City, State: Constitutionalism and the Megacity* (Oxford: Oxford University Press, 2020).

1 Luc Turgeon, "Cities within the Canadian Intergovernmental System," in *Contemporary Canadian Federalism*, ed. Alain-G. Gagnon (Toronto: University of Toronto Press, 2009), 367.

2 Loren King, "Cities, Subsidiarity, and Federalism," in *Federalism and Subsidiarity: NOMOS LV*, ed. James Fleming and Jacob Levy (New York: New York University Press, 2014), 295.

3 As is well known, in its decision in the 1998 *Quebec Secession Reference* case, the Supreme Court of Canada stated that the Canadian constitution is based on four equally significant underlying principles: (1) federalism, (2) democracy, (3) constitutionalism and the rule of law, and (4) the protection of minorities. None of these principles trumps any of the others. See *Reference re Secession of Quebec*, [1998] 2 SCR 217.

4 In 2019, approximately a quarter of a million newcomers to Canada, or 72 percent of the 341,000 immigrants to Canada during that year, settled in the country's largest cities. According to a 2022 Statistics Canada report, "Canada continues to urbanize as large urban centres benefit most from new arrivals to the country ... From 2016 to 2019, Canada welcomed a record high number of immigrants and more than 9 in 10 settled in census metropolitan areas." Statistics Canada, "Canada's Largest Urban Centres Continue to Grow and Spread," February 9, 2022, https://www150.statcan.gc.ca/n1/daily -quotidien/220209/dq220209b-eng.htm. In 2020, Canada admitted 401,000 permanent residents (a record high annual intake since 1913), the vast majority of whom settled in urban centres.

5 Formulated by jurist John Dillon in the 1860s, Dillon's Rule requires that every exercise of city power be traced back to a specific legislative grant of authority. The presumption is that cities do not have legislative authority unless it is granted explicitly to them through a concrete, identifiable piece of legislation. In other words, municipal corporations owe their origin to, and derive their powers and rights wholly from, the state legislature. See Ron Levi and Mariana Valverde, "Freedom of the City: Canadian Cities and the Quest for Governmental Status," *Osgoode Hall Law Journal* 44 (2006): 415–18.

6 The federal government controls land use for lands under its direct control, for example, national parks and waterways, areas of the national capital, and so on.

7 Joseph Garcea, "The Empowerment of Canadian Cities: Classic Canadian Compromise," *International Journal of Canadian Studies* 49 (2014): 86–89.

8 *City of Toronto Act, 2006*, SO 2006, c 11, Schedule A. The act came into effect on January 1, 2007.

9 Garcea, "The Empowerment of Canadian Cities," 87.

10 See Alison Smith and Zachary Spicer, "The Local Autonomy of Canada's Largest Cities," *Urban Affairs Review* 54 (2018): 932. See, generally, Alan Broadbent, *Urban Nation: Why We Need to Give Power Back to the Cities to Make Canada Strong* (Toronto: HarperCollins, 2008).

11 See David Siegel, "Ontario," in *Foundations of Governance: Municipal Government in Canada's Provinces*, ed. Andrew Sancton and Robert A. Young (Toronto: University of Toronto Press, 2017), 25–26; Andrew Sancton, "The False Panacea of City Charters? A Political Perspective on the Case of Toronto," *University of Calgary School of Public Policy Research Papers* 9, 3 (2016): https://journalhosting.ucalgary.ca/index.php/sppp/article/view/42564/30447; Harry Kitchen, "Is 'Charter-City Status' a Solution for Financing City Services in Canada – or Is That a Myth?," *University of Calgary School of Public Policy Research Papers* 9, 2 (2016): https://journalhosting.ucalgary.ca/index.php/sppp/article/view/42566/30448.

12 See Smith and Spicer, "The Local Autonomy of Canada's Largest Cities."

13 See, for example, Enid Slack, *International Comparison of Global City Financing: A Report to the London Finance Commission*, Toronto, Institute on Municipal Finance and Governance (IMFG), 2016; Enid Slack, "How Much Local Fiscal Autonomy Do Cities Have?," *IMFG Perspectives* 19 (2017): https://munkschool.utoronto.ca/imfg/uploads/432/imfgperspectives_no19_local_fiscal_autonomy_enidslack_july_25_2017.pdf.

14 Levi and Valverde, "Freedom of Canadian Cities," 447.

15 See Kitchen, "Is 'Charter-City Status' a Solution"; Michael Dewing and William Young, "Municipalities, the Constitution, and the Canadian Federal System," Background Paper 276E, Parliamentary Information and Research Service, 2006, 18.

16 According to Andrew Sancton, one of Canada's leading scholars of municipal law and local government, city charters are "nothing more" than "ordinary statutes" subject to provincial subjugation at any time. See Andrew Sancton, *Canadian Local Government: An Urban Perspective*, 2nd ed. (Oxford: Oxford University Press, 2015), 30.

17 Sancton, "The False Panacea of City Charters?"

18 See Sunil Johal, Kiran Alwani, Jordann Thirgood, and Peter Spiro, "Rethinking Municipal Finance for the New Economy," Mowat Centre 187, March 2019; Tomas Hachard, "It Takes Three: Making Space for Cities in Canadian Federalism," *IMFP Perspective Papers* 31 (2020): https://tspace.library.utoronto.ca/bitstream/1807/103012/3/IMFG_%20No.31%20Perspectives_Hachard_Nov2020.pdf.

19 *Reference re Provincial Electoral Boundaries (Saskatchewan)*, [1991] SCR 158.

20 See, for example, David Johnson, "Canadian Electoral Boundaries and the Courts: Practices, Principles and Problems," *McGill Law Journal* 39 (1994): 224–47; Mark Carter, "Reconsidering the Charter and Electoral Boundaries," *Dalhousie Law Journal* 22 (1999): 53–92; Brian Studniberg, "Politics Masquerading as Principles: Representation by Population in Canada," *Queen's Law Journal* 34 (2009): 611–68.

21 See, for example, *Reference re: Order in Council 215/93 Respecting the Electoral Divisions Statutes Amendment Act*, 1994 ABCA 342; *Charlottetown (City) v Prince Edward Island*, 142 DLR (4th) 343, 362 (PE SCTD 1996).

22 Michael Pal and Sujit Choudhry, "Is Every Ballot Equal? Visible-Minority Vote Dilution in Canada," *IRPP Choices* 13, 1 (2007): https://irpp.org/research-studies/choices-vol13-no1/.

23 *Ibid*, 6.

24 *Ibid*, 4.

25 Michael Pal and Sujit Choudhry, "Still Not Equal? Visible Minority Vote Dilution in Canada," *Canadian Political Science Review* 8 (2014): 85–101.

26 Jonathan Rodden, *Why Cities Lose: The Deep Roots of the Urban-Rural Divide* (London: Basic Books, 2019); Jowei Chen and Jonathan Rodden, "Unintentional Gerrymandering: Political Geography and Electoral Bias in Legislatures," *Quarterly Journal of Political Science* 8 (2013): 239–69.

27 See, for example, Richard Albert, "The Difficulty of Constitutional Amendment in Canada," *Alberta Law Review* 53 (2015): 85–113.

28 The City of Toronto itself is home to approximately 3.5 million people. The Greater Toronto Area (GTA) or the Greater Toronto and Hamilton Area (GTHA) are home to approximately 7.5 million people.

29 According to the Statistics Canada 2011 National Household Survey, as of 2011, 48.6 percent of the population of Toronto was foreign-born. A similar challenge is evident in Vancouver, Canada's third-largest city, where approximately 41 percent of the city's population are first-generation immigrants.

30 Section 128(1) of the *City of Toronto Act, 2006* gave the city the authority to enact a bylaw to divide or subdivide Toronto into wards or to dissolve existing wards. Accordingly, in 2016, the City of Toronto Council voted to increase the total number of wards from forty-four to forty-seven, following a thorough review of demographic trends and population projections to 2030.

31 *Better Local Government Act, 2018,* SO 2018, c 11.

32 *City of Toronto et al v Ontario (Attorney General),* 2018 ONSC 5151.

33 Such invocations are rare. Since 1982, there have only been a handful of significant instances where governments have either invoked or seriously attempted to invoke this clause. Even the changing of the guard in Ottawa following the 2006 federal election and the ensuing nine years of Conservative government have not changed that trend.

34 *Toronto (City) v Ontario (Attorney General),* 2018 ONCA 761 [*Toronto (City) v Ontario*].

35 *Ibid,* para 8.

36 *Ibid,* para 12.

37 *Ibid,* paras 13–19.

38 *Ibid,* para 20.

39 Nick Westoll and David Shum, "Ontario's Appeal Court Sides with Ford Government, Paves Way for 25-Ward Election," Global·News, September 19, 2018.

40 *Toronto (City) v Ontario,* para 1.

41 *Ibid,* paras 6–8.

42 *Ibid,* para 94.

43 *Ibid,* para 95.

44 *Toronto (City) v Ontario (Attorney General),* [2021] SCC 34 (decision released October 1, 2021).

45 *Ladore v Bennett* (1939) is often considered the first major ruling of that string: *Ladore v Bennett,* [1939] AC 468, [1939] 13 DLR 1, [1939] 12 WWR 566 (PC). For more recent illustrations, see, for example, *R v Sharma,* [1993] 1 SCR 650; *R v Greenbaum,* [1993] 1 SCR 674; *East York (Borough) v Ontario (Attorney General)* (1997), 34 OR (3d) 789 (Gen Div), aff'd (1997), 36 OR (3d) 733 (CA), leave to appeal to SCC refused [1997] SCCA 647.

46 *Shell Canada Products Ltd v Vancouver (City),* [1994] 1 SCR 231.

47 *Ibid,* para 237.

48 *Ibid,* para 245.

49 *Ibid,* para 280.

50 See, for example, *Nanaimo (City) v Rascal Trucking Ltd,* [2000] 1 SCR 342, paras 18–31; *United Taxi Drivers' Fellowship of Southern Alberta v Calgary (City),* [2004] 1 SCR 485; *Croplife Canada v Toronto (City),* [2005] OJ No 1896, 10 MPLR (4th) 1.

51 *114957 Canada Ltée (Spray-Tech, Société d'arrosage) v Hudson (Ville),* [2001] 2 SCR 241 [*Spray-Tech*].

52 *Ibid,* para 39.

53 *Ibid.*

54 *Ibid,* para 33.

55 *Ibid,* para 49.

56 See, for example, *Rogers Communications Inc v Chateautguay (Ville),* [2016] 1 SCR 467.

57 See, for example, Kristin R. Good, "The Fallacy of the 'Creatures of the Provinces' Doctrine: Recognizing and Protecting Municipalities' Constitutional Status," *IMFG Papers on Municipal Finance and Governance* 46 (2019): https://munkschool.utoronto.ca/imfg/research/doc/?doc_id=523.

58 John Sewell, "Toward City Charters in Canada," *Journal of Law and Social Policy* 34 (2021): 134.

59 *Ibid.*

60 See Eugénie Brouillet and Bruce Ryder, "Key Doctrines in Canadian Legal Federalism," in *The Oxford Handbook of the Canadian Constitution,* ed. Peter Oliver, Patrick Macklem, and Nathalie Des Rosiers (Oxford: Oxford University Press, 2017), 425.

61 *Spray-Tech,* para 3.

62 *Miller v California,* 413 US 15 (1973).

63 *R v Butler,* [1992] 1 SCR 452.

64 David J. Barron, "Why (and When) Cities Have a Stake in Enforcing the Constitution," *Yale Law Journal* 115 (2006): 2252.

65 *Ibid,* 2238.

66 *Ibid,* 2252.

67 Daniel A. Bell and Avner de-Shalit, *The Spirit of Cities: Why the Identity of a City Matters in a Global Age* (Princeton, NJ: Princeton University Press, 2011).

68 See, for example, Warren Magnusson, *Politics of Urbanism: Seeing Like a City* (London: Routledge, 2012).

69 King, "Cities, Subsidiarity, and Federalism."

70 *Ibid,* 316.

71 See, for example, Andrew Potter, Daniel Weinstock, and Peter Loewen, eds., *Should We Change How We Vote? Evaluating Canada's Electoral System* (Montreal/Kingston: McGill-Queen's University Press, 2017). On the constitutional dimensions of electoral reform, see Emmett Macfarlane, "Constitutional Constraints on Electoral Reform in Canada: Why Parliament Is (Mostly) Free to Implement a New Voting System," *Supreme Court Law Review* 76 (2016): 399–417.

72 Fair Vote Canada, "Rural-Urban Proportional: PR Tailored for Canada's Geography," https://www.fairvote.ca/rural-urban-proportional. The RUP system is partly based on the electoral system that Alberta and Manitoba used provincially early in the twentieth century. There, cities had proportional representation in multimember ridings with a single transferable voting system, while rural ridings were single-member. A deficiency with the old Alberta-Manitoba approach was that it left rural voters out of proportional representation. RUP fixes this problem by adding rural top-up seats.

73 Canada's population in the mid-1860s was estimated at 3 million, of which approximately 400,000 resided in cities. As of 2021, Canada's population is 38.5 million, of whom approximately 33 million live in cities.

Contributors

Richard Albert, William Stamps Farish Professor in Law, the University of Texas at Austin.

Gerald Baier, associate professor, Department of Political Science, University of British Columbia.

Stéphanie Chouinard, associate professor, Department of Political Science, Royal Military College of Canada, cross-appointed at Queen's University.

Brenda Cossman, professor, Faculty of Law, University of Toronto.

Erin Crandall, associate professor, Department of Politics, Acadia University.

Minh Do, assistant professor, Department of Political Science, University of Guelph.

Kerri A. Froc, associate professor, Faculty of Law, University of New Brunswick.

Dave Guénnette, postdoctoral fellow, Faculty of Law, McGill University.

Mark S. Harding, assistant professor, Department of Political Science, University of Guelph.

Lori Hausegger, associate professor, Department of Political Science, and director, Canadian Studies Program, Boise State University.

Matthew Hennigar, associate professor, Department of Political Science, Brock University.

Ran Hirschl, Professor of Government and Earl E. Sheffield Regents Professor of Law, University of Texas at Austin.

James B. Kelly, professor, Department of Political Science, Concordia University.

Kiera Ladner, professor, Department of Political Science, University of Manitoba.

Philippe Lagassé, associate professor and William and Jeanie Barton Chair in International Affairs, the Norman Paterson School of International Affairs, Carleton University.

Samuel V. LaSelva, professor, Department of Political Science, University of British Columbia.

Andrea Lawlor, associate professor, Department of Political Science, King's University College, Western University.

Emmett Macfarlane, associate professor, Department of Political Science, University of Waterloo.

Rebecca Major, assistant professor, Department of Political Science, University of Windsor.

Félix Mathieu, assistant professor, Department of Political Science, University of Winnipeg.

Andrew McDougall, assistant professor, Department of Political Science, University of Toronto.

Danielle McNabb, doctoral candidate, Department of Political Studies, Queen's University.

Eleni Nicolaides, PhD candidate, Department of Political Science, University of Guelph.

Jeremy Patzer, assistant professor, Department of Sociology and Criminology, University of Manitoba.

Kate Puddister, associate professor, Department of Political Science, University of Guelph.

Troy Riddell, associate professor, Department of Political Science, University of Guelph.

Kent Roach, professor and Prichard-Wilson Chair of Law and Public Policy, Faculty of Law, University of Toronto.

Peter H. Russell, professor emeritus, Department of Political Science, University of Toronto.

Joshua Sealy-Harrington, J.S.D. candidate, Columbia Law School, Columbia University, and assistant professor, Faculty of Law, Toronto Metropolitan University.

Tamara A. Small, professor, Department of Political Science, University of Guelph.

Dave Snow, associate professor, Department of Political Science, University of Guelph.

Cynthia Stirbys, assistant professor, School of Social Work, University of Windsor.

Mark Tushnet, William Nelson Cromwell Professor of Law, Emeritus, Harvard Law School, Harvard University.

Index